WORLD MOUNTAIN RANGES

SCOTLAND

by
Chris Townsend

2 POLICE SQUARE, MILNTHORPE, CUMBRIA LA7 7PY
www.cicerone.co.uk

ACKNOWLEDGEMENTS

This book has been over six years in the writing, during which time I have revisited many areas of the Scottish mountains (and visited some for the first time) and spent many hours in front of the computer screen. My family – Denise and Hazel Thorn – have been very patient as the book slowly progressed and deserve my deepest thanks for their tolerance and understanding. Jonathan Williams at Cicerone has also been very patient about the time it took for the book to be completed. I also owe much to companions on the hills, of whom there have been many over the years, especially Denise and Hazel, Cameron McNeish, John Manning, Mark Edgington, Kieran Baxter, Chris Ainsworth, Andy Hicks, Graham Huntington and Simon Willis.

Cairn Toul from Ben Macdui, Cairngorms ▶

ISBN-13: 978 1 85284 442 4

DEDICATION

To Denise, for her love and truly amazing patience.

ADVICE TO READERS

Readers are advised that, while every effort is made by our authors to ensure the accuracy of guidebooks as they go to print, changes can occur during the lifetime of an edition. Please check Updates on this book's page on the Cicerone website (www.cicerone.co.uk) before planning your trip. It is also advisable to check information on such things as transport, accommodation and shops locally. Even rights of way can be altered over time. We are always grateful for information about any discrepancies between a guidebook and the facts on the ground, sent by email to info@cicerone.co.uk or by post to Cicerone, 2 Police Square, Milnthorpe LA7 7PY.

WARNING

Mountaineering can be a dangerous activity carrying a risk of personal injury or death. It should be undertaken only by those with a full understanding of the risks and with the training and experience to evaluate them. While every care and effort has been taken in the preparation of this guide, the user should be aware that conditions can be highly variable and can change quickly, materially affecting the seriousness of a mountain walk. Therefore, except for any liability which cannot be excluded by law, neither Cicerone nor the author accept liability for damage of any nature (including damage to property, personal injury or death) arising directly or indirectly from the information in this book.

To call out the Mountain Rescue, ring 999 or the international emergency number 112: this will connect you via any available network. Once connected to the emergency operator, ask for the police.

Front cover: Ladhar Bheinn and Loch Hourn
Frontispiece: View over Loch Linnhe to Ben Nevis from Stob Coire a' Chearcaill

CONTENTS

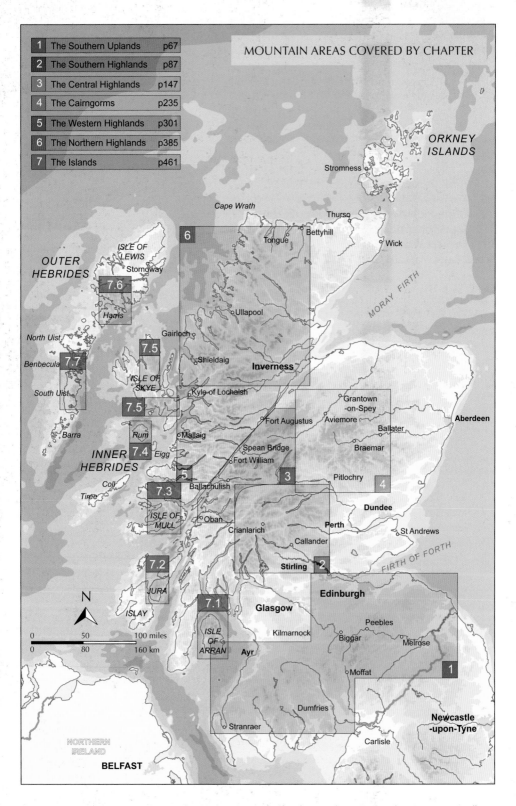

MOUNTAIN AREAS COVERED BY CHAPTER

ORKNEY
ISLANDS

Stromness

Cape Wrath

Thurso

Bettyhill
6   Tongue   Wick

OUTER
HEBRIDES
ISLE OF
LEWIS
Stornoway

7.6

Ullapool

MORAY FIRTH

Harris

North Uist

Gairloch

7.7
Benbecula

7.5

Shieldaig

Inverness

South Uist

ISLE OF
SKYE

Kyle of Lochalsh

Grantown
-on-Spey

Barra

7.5

Fort Augustus

Aviemore

Ballater

Aberdeen

Rum

Mallaig

Spean Bridge

Braemar

INNER
HEBRIDES

7.4 Eigg

Fort William

Coll

5

Ballachulish

Pitlochry

4

Tiree

7.3

ISLE OF
MULL

Oban

3

Dundee

Crianlarich

Perth

St Andrews

Callander

FIRTH OF FORTH

7.2

Stirling

2

JURA

Edinburgh

N

7.1

Glasgow

ISLAY

Peebles

Kilmarnock

Biggar

Melrose

0   50   100 miles
0   80   160 km

ISLE
OF
ARRAN

Ayr

Moffat

1

Dumfries

Newcastle
-upon-Tyne

NORTHERN
IRELAND

Stranraer

Carlisle

BELFAST

Looking up into Coire a' Chriochairean from Coire Ardair, Creag Meagaidh ▶

INTRODUCTION

The Scottish Highlands have a natural beauty unique of its kind.

W. H. Murray (1913–1996)

Scotland is a country of mountains, from the great heather-clad whalebacks separating it from England in the south to the rocky peaks abutting the Atlantic Ocean in the far northwest. A mere 441km from south to north and varying in width from 50 to 248km with a total area of 78,772km², Scotland is not a big country but it is largely made up of wild mountainous terrain. The mountains may not be high compared with those in other countries – only ten are above 1200m – but many are steep and dramatic and rise directly from sea level. There is a huge variety of scenery packed into this small country. Whether you like climbing steep rock cliffs, snow and ice mountaineering, walking long ridges, skiing over great plateaus, bagging summits, threading a way through the glens, camping beside remote lochans or wandering through old forests the Scottish mountains have something to offer.

Many areas of Scotland are often described as 'wilderness'. However in the sense of pristine land never affected by humans this only applies to any great extent to the 12 per cent of land that lies above 700m, the montane zone above the treeline. (In *Scotland's Beginnings* (NMSE, 2007) Michael A. Taylor and Andrew C. Kitchener say that only 15 per cent of montane habitats have been affected by human activities.) But a place can be wild without being untouched by humanity. I like the definition used in the National Trust for Scotland's excellent Wild Land Policy:

Wild land in Scotland is relatively remote and inaccessible, not noticeably affected by contemporary human activity, and offers high-quality opportunities to escape from the pressures of everyday living and to find physical and spiritual refreshment.

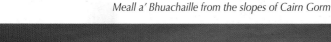

Meall a' Bhuachaille from the slopes of Cairn Gorm

◀ *On the rim of Stob Coire an t-Sneachda, Cairngorms*

Loch Hourn and Knoydart from Beinn Sgritheall

So there is much wild land in Scotland. And that is certainly what it feels like to anyone walking the hills. But too much of the Scottish mountain landscape has been damaged by a slow process of attrition over the decades that has reduced the feeling of wilderness and left the landscape looking worn and tattered. This process goes on, and indeed is accelerating in places, largely because of the industrialisation of the hills in the name of fighting climate change. All those who love the Scottish hills should ensure that they don't add to the damage and support those organisations that protect and restore the landscape.

Scotland divides into three main regions, each trending from southwest to northeast: the Southern Uplands, the Midland Valley or Central Lowlands and the Scottish Highlands, the last including the many islands lying off the west coast.

The Southern Uplands include the rolling moorland hills of the Borders and the more rugged mountains in Dumfries and Galloway to the west. The hills aren't high – none reach 900m and only seven rise above 750m. They aren't very rocky either and the relatively gentle terrain will appeal to the walker rather than the mountaineer or rock climber. Scotland's longest path and the only one that runs coast to coast, the 341km (213-mile)

Southern Upland Way, weaves through the forests and moors of the region.

The Southern Uplands dwindle away into the lowland belt where most of Scotland's population lives, with their last outlier actually in the city of Edinburgh, Scotland's capital, in the form of Arthur's Seat. The break in the hills is only brief, however, and from many places in the Lowlands hills can be seen rising to the north, first the Campsie Fells and Ochil Hills, the foothills of the Highlands, and beyond them the first Highland peaks. Mountains then dominate the landscape all the way to the north coast. Of these summits 510 rise above 3000 feet (914.4m), of which 283 are regarded as separate mountains. These are the famous Munros, named for the man who first listed them back in 1891. There are hundreds of lower hills too, all of them offering something to the mountain lover. This is the land of the golden eagle and the red deer, a land wild and challenging.

In the west great sea lochs, Scotland's fjords, bite into the mountains, twisting and turning their way inland below steep enclosing walls. The mountains here are rough and rocky, jumbled together in tightly packed groups that tower over narrow glens and dark, sombre lochs. The rugged terrain offers challenges to hillwalkers, especially in winter when snow blankets the tops, while the many cliffs offer routes of all difficulties for rock and ice climbers. There is water everywhere with burns tumbling down every hillside, bringing sound to the landscape even on those rare days when the wind is still. After heavy rain the hills are laced with a tracery of white water as temporary streams lash down the slopes. In the glens the burns rush and quiver over the rocks, gathering the water from the slopes above, and quickly turn into short, fierce rivers as they plunge to the sea. In places freshwater lochs and lochans fill the glens, often fringed with trees, remnants of the old Caledonian forest that once covered much of the lower slopes of the hills.

Heading east the hills become more massive and rounded, the glens broader and flatter. There is less rock and more heather, fewer pointed peaks and more undulating plateaus split by long, broad valleys that are home to major rivers such as the Tay, Dee and Spey. This landscape reaches its fulfilment in the Cairngorms, a land of huge, high-level sweeps of arctic tundra ringed by steep-sided corries and pine and birch-forested glens. When the snow falls this is ski touring country of the highest quality, with opportunities to glide for miles across the summits before swooping down gullies and bowls back to the glens.

The Highlands are split by the water-filled gash of the Gleann Mor (the Great Glen), stretching coast to coast from Fort William to Inverness. North and west of the Great Glen the mountains are even more rocky, rugged and tangled in the rough lands of Ardgour, Moidart and Knoydart. This is wild, remote country, hard of access but full of rewards for those who make the effort to get there.

Further north still the hills become more ordered, stretching out in long ridges between big wide glens – Shiel, Affric, Cannich, Strathfarrar. Here you can stride for hours high above the world, in the heart of the Highlands, with hills fading into the distance all around. Once Glen Carron is reached the Highlands change again. Now the mountains are isolated steep-sided rocky peaks and ridges, strange shapes soaring abruptly out of boggy moors dotted with shining lochans. Here the sense of wildness is even stronger and there is a primeval feel to the landscape. These crumbling rock giants are ancient. You can feel the age of the earth as you clamber over its bones. There are fewer hills here and as the north coast is approached the numbers dwindle even more and the distances between them grow.

From the west coast and many of the western summits islands can be seen, ripples of dark ragged peaks, mysterious and exciting, against the bright sea. The southernmost, Arran, lies in

Backpackers on a traverse of the Moidart hills

the Firth of Clyde, cut off from the other islands by the Mull of Kintyre. Arran is internally divided too; half Highland, half Lowland. Tucked into the northern Highland half the mountains are compact but steep and rocky, a surprising challenge in such a little space. Heading out to sea and northwards the Inner Hebrides line the coast from Islay to Skye. Four are of particular interest to the mountaineer – Jura (with its distinctive Paps), Mull, Rum and Skye, the latter holding perhaps the finest mountains in Scotland, the Cuillin, a curving jagged ridge of volcanic rock containing an amazing array of cliffs, pinnacles, towers, spires, arêtes and buttresses.

From Skye a long line of undulating land can be seen to the west. The Long Isle appears unbroken from here, but in fact consists of a chain of islands, the Outer Hebrides or Western Isles. Most are low, with fine machair beaches the main attraction, but Harris and South Uist have rocky hills, the last western outpost of the Highlands. To reach comparable hills further west you now have to cross the Atlantic.

ABOUT THIS BOOK

This book is a resource for the hillwalker, ski tourer and mountaineer. It is packed with information about the exciting prospects that exist in the Scottish mountains to help readers make the most of them. Intended as a guide to the best Scotland has to offer the outdoor enthusiast, it will give you all the information you need to plan a trip.

The following symbols are used throughout the text to indicate different mountain activities, as well as other local points of interest, such as lochs, waterfalls and visitor centres.

- 🚶 low-level/passes walks
- 🚶 long distance walks
- ⛰ summit walks
- 🧗 scrambles
- 🧗 rock climbs
- ❄ winter climbs
- ⛷ ski tours
- ℹ other local points of interest

The focus is on helping the reader to get the most out of a trip to one of Europe's wildest and most challenging landscapes.

The guide covers all the mountainous areas of Scotland from south to north, divided into seven regions (see overview map on page 10): the **Southern Uplands**, lying south of the Midland Valley; the Southern Highlands, the area north of the Midland Valley to Glen Orchy, Rannoch Moor, Loch Rannoch and Loch Tummel; the **Central Highlands**, the area north of the Southern Highlands bordered by the A9 road in the east and Loch Linnhe and the Great Glen in the north; the **Cairngorms**, the hills east of the A9; the Western Highlands, the area north and west of Loch Linnhe and the Great Glen as far as the Dingwall to Kyle of Lochalsh railway line; the **Northern Highlands**, all the hills north of the Dingwall to Kyle of Lochalsh railway; and finally the **islands** of Arran, Jura, Mull, Rum, Skye, Harris and South Uist. Some of these divisions are geographic – the Southern Uplands are clearly distinct from the other areas, the Great Glen is a major feature splitting the Highlands – but others are less precise and as much for convenience as topography. The Southern and Central Highlands could be said to be one area but for the sake of organisation and ease of reference it's better to treat them as two.

Each regional chapter covers individual glens important for mountain-goers, groups of hills that form coherent massifs and individual hills of significance. It begins with an introductory page pointing out particular highlights and a chapter contents list. (Each highlight is signified within the chapter by a ☆.) The chapter then starts in the west and south and heads east and north, following the lie of the land. In addition to an opening overview map, further maps throughout each chapter illustrate each section in turn (see Appendix E for a full index of maps and their scales).

There are suggestions for suitable bases for forays into the mountains and there is information about huts, hostels and campsites for walkers and climbers. A summary box at the end of each chapter gives information on access and accommodation plus recommended maps, guidebooks and other relevant literature. A selection of the finest walks, scrambles and ski tours is outlined in each chapter. However this is not a route guide and detailed descriptions are not provided. I have completed almost all of the routes mentioned myself, excepting the rock and ice climbs.

The introduction to the guide – this chapter – gives all practical advice and information needed

Looking along the Cam Loch to Suilven

before leaving home, alongside background to the mountains including natural history, geology, general history and the history of outdoor pursuits. The best areas for different pursuits are described and all the Munros – the 3000ft summits – and Corbetts – the 2500–3000ft summits – listed in the appendices.

The aim of the book is to inspire and entertain as well as inform; to show first-time visitors just what the Scottish mountains have to offer and provide a new perspective for those who have been here before. Visitors are throughout encouraged to tread softly in the Scottish mountains and to act in such a way that damage to this environment is minimised, ensuring that it survive into the future.

In my descriptions I have given my opinions as to the relative qualities of walks, glens, lochs, mountains and the landscape in general and highlighted those I think are the best the area has to offer. These are necessarily my personal opinions and not objective statements of fact; indeed, I hope readers will disagree with some of them. My aim is to encourage mountain-goers to think about what they see and experience, not to tell them how they should see and what they should experience. No hill is totally dull or completely uninteresting. So much depends on the context. Those interested in flowers might find a long slog up a steep hillside in spring a wonderful experience. Ski tourers might find swooping over gentle rolling hills exhilarating and exciting. Walkers plodding through peat bogs on those same hills on a grey rainy day might find them tedious. And a storm on any hill can make the ascent an adventure.

PRACTICALITIES

WHEN TO GO

There is no reason not to visit the Scottish mountains at any time of the year. Most facilities are open year round, although many campsites are closed during the winter and some visitor information centres are also closed during the winter. The main holiday season runs from mid-July to early September and this is when the mountains are at their busiest, so it is a good time to visit less well-known and less accessible areas. On public holidays and bank holidays the hills are at their most crowded, especially in the spring and summer, and banks, Post Offices and some other facilities may be closed.

PUBLIC HOLIDAYS

- New Year's Day
- 2 January
- Good Friday
- Early May Bank Holiday (first Monday in May)
- Spring Bank Holiday (last Monday in May)
- Summer Bank Holiday (first Monday in August)
- St Andrew's Day (30 November)
- Christmas Day
- Boxing Day

Note: when New Year's Day, 2 January, Christmas Day, Boxing Day or St Andrew's Day fall on Saturday or Sunday the holiday is moved to the following Monday or Tuesday.

The exact dates for each year can be found on the Scottish Government website: www.scotland.gov.uk/Publications/2005/01/bankholidays.

Because of Scotland's location, from 55–59° north, there are long hours of daylight in May, June and July and very short ones in November, December and January. The city of Glasgow in the Midland Valley has 17½hrs of daylight on 30 June and 7hrs 6mins of daylight on 31 December. The town of Wick in the far north has 18hrs 19mins of daylight on the longest day in June but only 6hrs 20mins of daylight on the shortest day in December. This makes the late spring and early summer the best time for long ventures in the hills. In late autumn and winter it's better to plan shorter trips and to keep a careful eye on the time.

Walking, both low and high-level, can be carried out year round, although between October and May hillwalkers will need an ice axe and crampons and the skill to use them if there is snow on the mountains. Rock climbing is possible year round, as long as the cliffs are not clad in ice and snow, but is a chilly activity in the winter. When snow and ice are present it's time for winter climbing and, if the snow is deep and widespread enough, ski touring. Good snow conditions are unpredictable and can occur anytime from October through to May. That said, February, March and April are the best months for snow and ice pursuits most years. Whenever there's enough snow for winter climbing or for skiing then there is a risk of avalanches. The Scottish Avalanche Information Service (see below) issues daily avalanche warnings between mid-December and mid-April. For further information on avalanches see *A Chance in a Million? – Scottish Avalanches* by Bob Barton and Blyth Wright (SMT, 2nd edition 2000).

WEATHER

The main feature of Scottish weather is that it's unpredictable. As the northerly part of an island lying in the Atlantic Ocean off the western edge of Europe Scotland has a maritime climate, which means wet and windy. Storms are likely at any time of year. However because of the Gulf Stream temperatures are higher than in other places at the same latitude. As a generalisation the weather is warmer and wetter in the west, cooler and drier in the east. This is because the prevailing weather comes from the southwest, bringing moisture picked up during its long passage over the Atlantic. In the Highlands there is measurable rainfall over 250 days a year, often in the form of drizzle or wet

Cloud sweeping in over the Cuillin Ridge

mist. The Western Highlands are the wettest area, with over 3000mm of rain per year (as high as 5500mm in Knoydart).

When the winds come from the northwest the air is colder and from October to May can bring snow rather than rain. Weather from the north and east is drier and even colder. When northeast winds blow in winter and spring, snow is likely and the heaviest falls are usually in the easternmost mountains, the Cairngorms, where snow falls on over a hundred days on the summits, although it often lies for less than half that.

Although the wind blows most often from the southwest the actual direction in the mountains depends on the topography. Wind is often funnelled through passes and down glens and can swirl around in corries. Wind speed increases with height so if it's windy in the glen it's likely to be extremely windy on the summits. The highest wind speed recorded in Britain was 278kph (173mph) at the weather station on the summit of Cairngorm on 20 March 1986. The strongest winds usually occur between October and May and winds of 160kph (100mph) and more occur on the mountains every year during this period. Wind speeds over 50kph (30mph), which are strong enough to make walking difficult, can occur at any time of the year. I've recorded wind speeds of 93kph (58mph) at 610m on the island of Harris in August.

On average there are less than 1100 hours of sunshine in the Highlands each year. In parts of the Lowlands there are over 1400 hours. The sunniest months of the year are May and June, when daylight hours are long. The dullest month is December. However, while there's a better chance of sunny days in May and June than in other months, good weather isn't guaranteed and there can be long periods of sunshine in other months. In general eastern Scotland is sunnier than the west whatever the time of year.

When the sun is shining temperatures can rise into the 20s Celsius but mostly temperatures in the 10–15° range can be expected in summer and 0–10° in the winter. Temperature usually drops by about 0.6°C for every 100m rise in altitude so summits are colder than glens. On Ben Nevis the annual mean temperature is -0.3°C. The increase in wind speed with altitude often means that summits feel even colder than the difference in temperature would suggest. January and February are usually the coldest months. The coldest nights occur when it's calm and clear and snow covers

19

WEATHER FORECASTS

An excellent book on Scottish weather is *So Foul and Fair a Day: A History of Scotland's Weather and Climate* by Alastair Dawson (Birlinn, 2009).

- **Scottish Avalanche Information Service** www.sais.co.uk
  email avalanche@dcs.gla.ac.uk for an email forecast
- **Met Office mountain area forecasts** www.metoffice.gov.uk/loutdoor/mountainsafety/
- **Metcheck Mountain** www.metcheck.com/V40/UK/HOBBIES/mountain.asp
- **Mountain Weather Information Service** www.mwis.org.uk
  MWIS gives forecasts for five different areas – the Northwest Highlands, West Highlands, Cairngorms National Park and Monadliath, Southeastern Highlands, Southern Uplands. The best forecast for the mountains. Highly recommended.
- **AccuWeather.com** www.accuweather.com/ukie/mountain-forecast.asp
- **BBC Radio Scotland**
  On 92–95FM, 810MW. Outdoor Conditions Forecast 1904 Monday–Friday (following the 1900 news bulletin), 0704 and 2204 Saturday and 0704 and 2004 Sunday
- **Cairngorm Automatic Weather Station** www.phy.hw.ac.uk/resrev/aws/weather.htm

the ground. At those times glens can be colder than the surrounding hills, as cold air sinks. Inland areas are usually colder than coastal ones. The lowest temperature recorded in Scotland is -27.2°C, at Braemar in the southern Cairngorms on 11 February 1895 and 10 January 1982 and also at Altnaharra in the Northern Highlands on 30 December 1995. The warmest months are July and August. The highest temperature ever recorded in Scotland was 32.9°C at Greycrook in the Borders on 9 August 2003.

Sometimes the daytime temperature may be cooler in the glens than high on the hills. This is known as an inversion and can give rise to wonderful conditions if you are high in the hills with the summits bathed in sunshine and the glens filled with grey clouds.

Because weather and snow conditions are unpredictable, having up-to-date information before any trip is wise. There are many sources for this, including the internet, radio, TV, newspapers and by phone. Forecasts are often posted in climbing shops, visitor centres, cafés and bars and car parks in mountain areas. Information is gathered from many weather stations including the automatic one on the summit of Cairn Gorm, in operation since 1977, whose readings can be seen on the internet. The Meteorological Office also has automatic weather stations on Aonach Mor and the Cairnwell Pass.

Climate change may change all of the above in time. In particular snowfall is becoming more erratic and less frequent in many years. Climate scientists predict less snow in the future, which will make winter climbing and ski touring even more activities to be grabbed when conditions are suitable and may finish downhill skiing, already marginal, completely.

GETTING THERE

Scotland is easily accessible by air, road and rail.

By air

Scotland's major airports are Glasgow, Prestwick, Edinburgh and Aberdeen. There are ten regional airports in the Highlands and Islands of which the most useful for mountaineers are Inverness and Stornoway.

British Airways flies from London Heathrow and Gatwick to Glasgow; Ryanair flies from many European airports (including London Stansted and Paris Beauvais-Tillé) to Prestwick; British Midland flies from London Heathrow to Glasgow, Edinburgh, Aberdeen and Inverness; Flybe flies from many British cities to Aberdeen, Edinburgh and Inverness; easyJet flies to Glasgow, Edinburgh, Aberdeen and Inverness from London and other English airports.

AIR INFORMATION

- **Highlands and Islands Airports**
  ☎ 01667 462445 www.hial.co.uk
- **British Airways** ☎ 0845 7222111
  www.british-airways.com
- **British Midland** ☎ 0870 6070555
  www.flybmi.com
- **Eastern Airways** ☎ 08703 669669
  www.easternairways.com
- **easyJet** ☎ 0870 6000000
  www.easyjet.com
- **Flybe** ☎ 0871 7002000
  www.flybe.com
- **Highland Airways** ☎ 0845 4502245
  www.highlandairways.co.uk
- **Loganair**
  ☎ 0871 7002000 www.loganair.co.uk
  ☎ 0870 3331250 www.ryanair.com

By rail

Taking the train is perhaps the most relaxing way to reach the Scottish mountains and gives splendid views of the landscape, especially from the West Highland Line from Glasgow to Fort William and then on to Mallaig. Many trips can begin directly from a railway station as there are many stations on the lines to Oban, Fort William, Mallaig, Inverness and Kyle of Lochalsh that give access to the hills. Direct train services from south of the border to Edinburgh and Inverness on the East Coast Main Line are run by East Coast trains; those to Edinburgh and Glasgow on the West Coast Main Line by Virgin Trains. ScotRail runs train services within Scotland. Sleeper services are available to Fort William and Inverness from many British cities, an excellent way to reach the hills as you can alight at intermediate stations early in the morning, refreshed after a night's sleep, and set out immediately.

TRAIN INFORMATION

- **National Rail Enquiries** ☎ 08457 484950
  www.nationalrail.co.uk
- **ScotRail** ☎ 08700 005151
  www.scotrail.co.uk
- **East Coast trains** ☎ 08457 225333
  www.eastcoast.co.uk
- **Virgin Railways** ☎ 0870 7891234
  www.virgintrains.co.uk

Carn Gorm from the southwest

By bus

Buses are an inexpensive way to travel around Scotland. National Express operates coaches from London and other cities to many places in Scotland, Scottish Citylink runs services between towns and Stagecoach (formerly Rapsons) runs many rural services in the Highlands. Up-to-date information on regional bus services is available from the excellent Traveline Scotland website and the UK Bus Timetable Website.

BUS INFORMATION

- **National Express** ☎ 08705 808080
  www.nationalexpress.com
- **Scottish Citylink** ☎ 08705 505050
  www.citylink.co.uk
- **Stagecoach** www.stagecoachbus.com
- **Traveline Scotland** ☎ 0871 2002233
  www.travelinescotland.com
- **UK Bus Timetable Website Directory**
  http://timetables.showbus.co.uk
- **Post bus information (Royal Mail)**
  www.postbus.royalmail.com

By car

Cars can be the cheapest form of transport for parties of two or more and are convenient when you have much gear to carry and when you want to move between different bases.

Where they are not so useful is for long backpacking trips, as getting back to the start by public transport can be difficult and time-consuming. The main roads into Scotland are the M74/A74, A68 and A1 and progress on these roads can be quite fast. Once you get into the hills roads rapidly become narrower and more winding and allowance should be made for this.

GETTING AROUND

Availability of public transport in the mountainous areas of Scotland varies. Many areas have good bus or train services, but some have minimal or no services. Public transport is particularly useful for long distance walks where you finish a long way from your starting point. Post buses often carry passengers and are a good way to access remote glens. Details

of these and other bus services can be obtained from Traveline Scotland (☎ 0871 2002233, www.travelinescotland.com) and the Royal Mail (☎ 08457 740740, www.postbus.royalmail.com).

Ferries to the islands are mostly run by Caledonian MacBrayne, a western Scotland and Hebridean institution. Flights are not very useful for internal travel, although Highland Airways fly from Inverness to Stornoway, and Loganair fly from Glasgow to Aberdeen and Inverness.

Cars give freedom of movement but driving on Scottish minor roads can be a shock to some people. There are often no road markings and many roads are single track with passing places. It's wise to allow plenty of time for journeys along such roads and to be prepared to stop for other traffic frequently.

FERRIES

- **Caledonian MacBrayne** ☎ 08705 65000
  www.calmac.co.uk
- **Corran Ferry** ☎ 01397 709000
  www.lochabertransport.org.uk/
  corranferry.html
- **Knoydart Ferry Service** ☎ 01687 462320
  www.knoydart-ferry.co.uk
- **Arnisdale Ferry Service** ☎ 01599 522247
  www.arnisdaleferryservice.com

ACCOMMODATION

Although finding accommodation without booking in larger towns is likely most of the year this isn't so in villages or during the peak holiday months of July and August. Places may be booked up at New Year and Easter too. Anywhere along the West Highland Way is likely to be booked well in advance from May to September inclusive. Accommodation information is available from Visit Scotland, the website of the Scottish Tourist Board (see box below).

Hotels, guest houses and B&Bs

Serviced accommodation in hotels, guest houses and bed and breakfast establishments can be found throughout Scotland's hill areas. Everything from basic one star B&Bs to luxurious (and expensive) five star hotels is available. In the larger towns

Over Phawhope bothy, Ettrick Water, Southern Upland Way

like Inverness, Fort William and Oban there is a large range of accommodation. There is also much accommodation to be found away from towns and villages. Most establishments welcome walkers and climbers, especially those along long distance paths, such as the West Highland Way and the Southern Upland Way, and in popular mountain areas. Some hotels, such as the Clachaig Inn in Glen Coe and the Sligachan Hotel on the Isle of Skye, have a long tradition of catering to walkers and climbers and are famous in the history of Scottish mountaineering.

Self-catering
Self-catering accommodation has the great advantage that you can come and go when you like. Everything from caravans to farmhouses and chalets is available in the Scottish mountains.

Club huts
Many mountaineering and climbing clubs have self-catering huts in the Scottish mountains available to club members and members of the Mountaineering Council of Scotland, which maintains a list of huts with contact details on its website.

Hostels and bunkhouses
Hostels provide good budget accommodation for individuals and groups. The Scottish Youth Hostels Association (SYHA) has more than 70 hostels, some of them basic ones in remote mountain areas such as Loch Ossian and Glen Affric. You don't have to be a member of the SYHA to stay at one of their hostels but it does cost less if you are. You can join in advance or at a hostel.

There are also over 120 independent hostels and bunkhouses in Scotland, many linked together in the Scottish Independent Hostels organisation. This isn't an organisation you can join to get a discount (like the SYHA) and all the hostels are privately run. Many of the hostels are in mountain areas and some, such as Achnashellach (Gerry's Hostel) in Strathcarron, have a place in the history of Scottish mountaineering. Scottish Independent Hostels (www.hostel-scotland.co.uk) publishes a free Blue Hostel Guide, available as a booklet or a download from the internet.

Bothies
Bothies are unlocked shelters away from roads that are available for use by anyone. There are many bothies in the Scottish hills, many maintained by the Mountain Bothies Association (MBA), an organisation any regular bothy user should support. The bothies system only works if people respect both the bothies and other users. The MBA has a Bothy Code (see below) that should be followed by all who stay in bothies.

Bothies can be crowded, closed or in disrepair. It's unwise to rely on a bothy for shelter and carrying a tent or bivouac gear is always a good idea. Bothies provide a roof over your head and sometimes a sleeping platform, chairs, tables and even a fireplace or wood stove. There are no other amenities and a sleeping bag, mat, stove and cooking equipment and food are required.

THE BOTHY CODE

Respect other users
• Please leave the bothy clean, tidy and with dry kindling for the next visitors.

Respect the bothy
• Guard against fire risk and don't cause vandalism or graffiti.
• Please take out all rubbish which you don't burn.
• Avoid burying rubbish: this pollutes the environment.
• Please don't leave perishable food: this encourages mice and rats.

Respect the surroundings
• Human waste must be buried carefully out of sight. Please use the spade provided.
• For health reasons never use the vicinity of the bothy as a toilet.
• Keep well away from the water supply.
• Conserve fuel. Never cut live wood.

Please note
• Bothies are available for short stays only. Permission should be obtained for longer visits.
• Unless the safety of the group requires the use of shelter in bad weather, bothies are not available for groups of 6 or more because of overcrowding and the lack of facilities such as toilets.
• For the same reasons groups are asked not to camp outside bothies.
• Groups wishing to use a bothy should seek permission from the estate.
• Finally, please ensure the fire is out and the door properly closed when you leave.
• Bothies are used at your own risk.

Campsites

There are plenty of official campsites in the Scottish mountains, ranging from the basic with little more in the way of facilities than a toilet and tap to the luxurious with individual pitches, showers, shops, games rooms and more. Visit Scotland, Scotland's national tourist organisation, publishes a regularly updated book called *Scotland: Where to Stay Caravan and Camping*. Scottishcamping.com publishes an annual touring map called *The Definitive Campsite Guide to the Highlands and Islands of Scotland* and has a directory of campsites on its website. The Camping and Caravanning Club has its own website and publishes a Big Sites Book for members with sites linked to Ordnance Survey map sheets.

ACCOMMODATION INFORMATION

• **Mountain Bothies Association**
  www.mountainbothies.org.uk
• **Mountaineering Council of Scotland (club huts)** ☎ 01738 493942
  www.mcofs.org.uk/find-a-hut.asp
• **Scottish Camping** ☎ 01224 860347
  www.scottishcamping.com
• **Scottish Independent Hostels**
  www.hostel-scotland.co.uk
• **Visit Scotland** ☎ 0845 2255121
  www.visitscotland.com
• **Scottish Youth Hostels** ☎ 01786 891400
  www.syha.org.uk
• **The Camping and Caravanning Club**
  ☎ 02476 694995
  www.campingandcaravanningclub.co.uk
• **UK Campsite** www.ukcampsite.co.uk

Wild Camping

There are ample opportunities for wild camping away from roads in the Scottish mountains and it is the best way to stay in the hills, a way to experience them 24hrs a day, soaking yourself deeper into the wilds. Long a de facto right and accepted in most areas, wild camping is now a legal right under the Land Reform (Scotland) Act 2003. Wild camping brings responsibilities with it and campers should always ensure they have as little impact on the environment as possible. All rubbish should be carried out, faeces buried well away from water and the ground left undisturbed. The Mountaineering

Wild Camping in the Glen Affric area

Council of Scotland (☎ 01738 493942) publishes useful advice, *Wild Camping: A Guide to Good Practice*, on its website: www.mcofs.org.uk/assets/pdfs/wildcamping.pdf.

MAPS AND GUIDEBOOKS

Maps

Scotland is blessed with excellent maps. Two Ordnance Survey series, the 1:50,000 Landranger and the 1:25,000 Explorer, cover the whole country. Harvey's 1:25,000 Superwalker maps and 1:40,000 British Mountain Maps cover many Scottish hill areas, are designed for walkers and climbers and are printed on waterproof paper.

Both OS and Harvey maps are available in digital form on CD-ROM or as downloads from several companies – Anquet, Fugawi, Garmin, ISYS, Memory-Map, Magellan, Quo and Tracklogs. With digital maps you can draw routes and then print out the relevant section of the map. You can also download routes in the form of waypoints to a GPS receiver. The Scottish Mountaineering Club (SMC) publishes GPS Data Sets for the routes in its guidebooks to the Munros and the Corbetts. Many GPS units now have mapping and Satmap's Active 10 GPS is specially designed for outdoor use and

MAP SOURCES

- **Anquet** ☎ 0845 2709020 www.anquet.co.uk
- **Fugawi** ☎ 01506 406277 www.fugawi.com
- **Garmin** ☎ 02380 524000 www.garmin.com
- **Harvey Maps** ☎ 01786 841202 www.harveymaps.co.uk
- **ISYS (Mapwise)** ☎ 0845 1665701 www.isysoutdoors.com
- **Magellan** ☎ 01529 733845 www.magellangps.com
- **Memory-Map** ☎ 0870 7409040 www.memory-map.co.uk
- **Satmap** ☎ 08458 730104 www.satmap.com
- **Quo** www.mapyx.com
- **Tracklogs** ☎ 01298 872537 www.tracklogs.co.uk
- **Ordnance Survey** ☎ 08456 050505 www.ordnancesurvey.co.uk
- **View Ranger** ☎ 01223 421355 www.viewranger.com

Checking the map in the Cairngorms on the approach to the Lairig Ghru from the Chalamain Gap

works with Ordnance Survey maps on memory cards. Memory-Map and Garmin make similar GPS units. OS mapping is also available for GPS-enabled mobile phones from companies like View Ranger.

Guidebooks, CD/DVDs, websites and magazines
There is a huge number of guidebooks to the Scottish mountains for walkers, climbers and skiers. The Access, Bases, Maps and Guides section at the ends of each chapter lists maps and guides recommended for the area covered and the Further Reading section in Appendix B (page 521) has a list of guides that cover the whole, or large parts of, the country, including guides on CD/DVDs, and websites. But do remember that although guides are useful you don't have to follow their routes and can explore the mountains with just a map and compass, finding your own way through passes, up ridges and across summits.

EQUIPMENT FOR HILLWALKERS

Scotland's maritime climate means that wet and windy weather is always likely and conditions can change very quickly. **Wind- and waterproof jackets and trousers** should always be worn or carried.

Those made from waterproof/breathable fabrics such as eVent, Gore-Tex or Paramo Directional are the most comfortable. **Warm clothing** is essential too. In summer a light fleece jacket is usually all that's required. In winter a second thicker fleece or an insulated jacket may be needed and should be carried just in case – it'll prove useful at rest stops anyway. Those who feel the cold will probably want to carry a warm hat and gloves year round. They are certainly needed between October and May, when spares are a good idea, especially with gloves which can easily get wet and cold.

Footwear with good grip is needed to deal with the rough and often wet terrain. When the hills aren't snow-covered this doesn't have to mean boots – trail shoes or even, in warm weather, trekking sandals are lighter weight and perfectly suitable. When there is snow and ice on the hills footwear should be suitable for use with crampons. For non-technical routes flexible crampons can be fitted to walking boots or even trail shoes. For any graded snow or ice climb stiffer footwear is needed. A walker's or general mountaineering ice axe is required for hillwalking and easy climbs on snowy hills; specialist climbing tools will be needed for harder climbs.

Map and compass will be used frequently and are best carried in a garment pocket or a map case for easy access. If they're in the pack it's tempting not to check them until you really are lost. A GPS receiver can be useful but isn't essential.

In case of benightment or an accident it's worth carrying some form of **shelter**. A light, compact and inexpensive plastic survival bag will do most of the year, but something more substantial is better for winter conditions. These bags don't let any moisture in or out, which means you'll get pretty damp from condensation if you spend any time in one. Bivi bags made from waterproof/breathable fabrics are more comfortable but also much more expensive and usually a bit heavier. One is worth having if you plan on spending the occasional night out and don't want to bother with a tent. Group shelters (bothy bags) are an alternative to survival and bivi bags, or you could carry both. A group shelter is a large wind- and waterproof nylon bag that a group pulls over their heads and then sits on the edge to hold down. Group shelters warm up amazingly quickly and are great for morale in cold stormy weather. They come in various sizes designed to hold from two to ten people and are recommended for winter conditions.

Small pieces of closed cell foam, called **sitmats**, are useful as insulated seats on cold or wet ground and can be used inside group shelters. They can be carried down the back of a rucksack, where they provide extra padding.

In winter a good **torch** or headlamp should be carried as daylight hours are short. Conversely from May to August a tiny light will do, as it probably won't be needed.

Dark glasses may not spring to mind as likely to be useful in Scotland, but on sunny days when snow lies on the hills they can be essential to prevent snow blindness. In those conditions sunscreen and a sunhat are useful too, as they are during summer heatwaves. In blizzards snow goggles protect the face and mean you can see at least a little.

In summer **midge repellent** can be essential for sanity and a midge hood can be useful, especially for campers. Tightly woven long clothing also keeps out midges.

A small **first aid kit** will help with minor injuries. Many people now carry **mobile phones** in case they need to call for help, but note that coverage in the hills is very patchy and phones often won't get a connection, especially in deep glens and corries. If you do carry one please only use it to call out the mountain rescue in a real emergency from which you can't extricate yourself.

Trekking poles are popular with many walkers and can take some of the weight off your leg joints, as well as being useful for balance when crossing streams and on rocky terrain. They are particularly useful when carrying heavy loads. Telescopic poles are best so you can adjust their length or collapse them and carry them on the rucksack when not needed, or when scrambling. Note, however, that trekking poles are not a substitute for an ice axe on steep snow-covered slopes.

Don't forget **food and drink**. In summer you can dip water out of streams and, except on high ridges, don't need to carry much. In winter a hot drink can be very welcome and an insulated flask is worth its weight in the rucksack.

For day walks your **rucksack** needn't be very big. One with a 20–30 litre capacity should do for summer, a 30–45 litre one for winter. If you'll be venturing onto snow-covered hills make sure there are straps for attaching an ice axe and crampons. Few rucksacks are waterproof (although some come with waterproof covers) so it's always wise to pack gear inside waterproof stuffsacks or a waterproof sack liner.

For backpacking a larger rucksack will be needed. For short trips of one or two nights and for those who travel very light a 40–50 litre pack may be big enough, but most people will find a pack of at least 55 litres necessary. For comfort the pack should be the right length for your back and should have a padded hipbelt that curves round your hips.

Backpackers will of course need a **tent**, a **sleeping bag** and **cooking gear**. For Scottish conditions tents should be capable of standing up to strong winds and have porches large enough to store wet gear and to cook in safety, which may be necessary in storms and when the midges are biting. Insect netting doors on the inner tent will keep the midges out and allow some ventilation. In summer a very light sleeping bag, rated to +5° or 0°C, will be adequate for all but the coldest sleepers. Between October and May night temperatures can drop below zero and a sleeping bag rated to -10°C or below is a good choice. A sleeping mat to provide insulation from ground cold and a degree of comfort is also needed in cold weather, and is useful year round. All types of stove fuel – alcohol (methylated spirits), butane/propane cartridges, paraffin and unleaded petrol or Coleman fuel – are available in most towns in the hills so any type of stove can be used. A windshield is an essential accessory.

Quotation from James Hutton at Knockan Crag in the Northern Highlands

THE MOUNTAINS

TOPOGRAPHY AND GEOLOGY

*'The scenery of the Highlands and Islands
is that of solid rock.'*
F. Fraser Darling and J. Morton Boyd,
The Highlands and Islands

The modern science of geology began in Scotland with James Hutton of Edinburgh (1726–1797), whose field observations led him to work out how rocks were formed and how ancient they must be at a time when the accepted view was that the earth was just 6000 years old (see Jack Repcheck's interesting book *The Man Who Found Time: James Hutton and the Discovery of the Earth's Antiquity* (Pocket Books, 2004) and the website www.james-hutton.org.uk). Scotland was a natural place for geology to develop as it has an amazing diversity of rocks and landscapes in such a small area.

Anyone walking or climbing in the Scottish hills will have intimate contact with geology. A basic understanding of how the hills were formed and why they look as they do heightens appreciation and is worth acquiring. In some places, such as the Cuillin Hills on the Isle of Skye, being able to identify different rocks could even be a safety factor. The fascinating geology of Scotland is complex and diverse and there is only space to touch very briefly on it here. However there are several good books on the subject worth reading by those who would like to learn more. For the layperson with no geological training (like myself) I particularly recommend *Land of Mountain and Flood: the Geology and Landforms of Scotland* by Alan McKirdy, John Gordon and Roger Crofts (Birlinn, 2007), and *Scotland's Beginnings: Scotland Through Time* by Michael A. Taylor and Andrew C. Kitchener (NMSE, 2007). Ronald Turnbull's *Granite and Grit: A Walker's Guide to the Geology of the British Mountains* (Frances Lincoln, 2009) also covers Scotland well. The British Geological Survey provides useful geological information and maps on the back of Harvey's British Mountain Maps.

That Scotland divides into three distinct regions, the Southern Uplands, the Midland Valley or Central Lowlands and the Highlands, is due to the underlying geology. Two major fault lines, where earth movements have caused rocks to shift in relation to each other, run southwest to northeast across the country – the Southern Uplands Fault and the Highland Boundary Fault. The Midland Valley lies between the two. As you cross the faults the difference in the landscape is immediately apparent.

The Highlands are divided by two more major fault lines. The Great Glen fault is the most obvious, a coast to coast trench splitting the Northern and Western Highlands from the Central and Southern Highlands. Further north still the Moine Thrust differentiates the western edge of the mainland and the Hebrides from the rest of the Highlands. The Southern Uplands finish to the south at the Solway Fault, which runs roughly along the border with England.

The Scottish hills are the ancient remnants of the once huge Caledonian mountain range, which came into being 400–500 million years ago when two of the great plates that underlie the surface of the earth collided, forcing rocks together so they crumpled, buckled and rose up to form a mountain range that may have been as high as the Alps. Back then what is now Scotland lay south of the equator. Gradually this proto-Scotland, as part of much larger land masses, moved north. At times 'Scotland' was swampy, at others a desert. Great sedimentary deposits covered the land and were eroded away.

Then around 65 million years ago the Caledonian mountains, now heavily eroded, began to break up, roughly down the line of the chain. The gap between the divided range became the Atlantic Ocean, formed over millions of years and continuing to widen today. Geological studies show that the Scottish mountains were once part of the same range as the Appalachian Mountains of North America. As the mountains tore apart and the Atlantic formed, a line of huge volcanoes developed along the western edge of Scotland, the remnants of which are still visible today. The power of these eruptions forced the mountains up in the west and gave Scotland a west–east tilt still present today.

Today's mountain landscape consists mainly of a dissected plateau, eroded by rivers and rainfall over hundreds of millions of years. The pattern of the glens and stream courses was mostly set before the ice ages. However the details of the landscape were formed during and immediately after the last ice age, which began some 27,000 years ago and, after several retreats and re-advances, finished about 11,000 years ago, just yesterday in geological time. It was the Swiss geologist Louis Agassiz who first worked out that glaciers had carved out the landscape after a trip to Scotland in the 1840s, when he visited several places including Glen Roy (see Chapter 3), where he recognised that the Parallel Roads were the shores of an ancient lake.

The ice ground down the mountains, forming many of the features we admire today – steep-sided armchair-shaped hollows (known as corries), corrie lochans, jagged peaks, cliffs, hanging valleys, truncated spurs, narrow arêtes, U-shaped valleys (glacial troughs), loch filled trenches, polished slabs and moraines. The exact form these features take depends on the underlying geology and the degree of glaciation, which accounts for the difference between different regions. Since the ice age erosion has continued with rain, snow, ice and frost carving and shaping the landscape.

The rocks that make up Scotland come from many different geological periods and include the three major types: sedimentary, igneous and metamorphic.

Sedimentary rocks are made of tiny fragments, eroded from pre-existing rocks, which have been deposited by wind, water or glacier. The initially soft, loose sediments were turned to rock by compression as layer after layer built up. Clay, sand and gravel are the constituents of most sedimentary rock, forming shales and sandstones. The remains of living matter can form sediments too – coal is made of plants and limestone of sea shells, for example. Fossils are often found in sedimentary rock. Sedimentary rock usually occurs in layers, or strata, which may have been folded or contorted by earth movements since they were laid down. The Southern Uplands outside of the Galloway Hills are built mainly of folded greywacke (a coarse-grained sedimentary rock composed of quartz, feldspar and other rock fragments), shales and mudstones covered by glacial deposits. Water and ice have carved these rocks into smooth rounded hills lacking jagged peaks, cliffs or even rock outcrops. In the Highlands sedimentary rocks only occur in a few places, mainly west of the Moine Thrust on a coastal strip, running south from Cape Wrath to the Sound of Sleat, that separates the Isle of Skye from the mainland. This is Torridonian sandstone, which produces distinctive and dramatic stepped mountains such as Liathach, Beinn Eighe, Slioch, An Teallach, Suilven and Quinag. Inland from the Torridonian sandstone is a band of limestone, which gives rise to a cave system on the western slopes of Ben Mor Assynt and distinctive bright green vegetation around the crofting community of Elphin.

Igneous rocks ('fire rocks') are made from hot molten magma brought up from the depths of the earth, often by volcanoes. As the magma cools, either on the surface, in the form of lava, or under the surface, where it has been intruded into other rocks, it hardens and turns to stone. The distinction between rock formed on the surface and rock formed underground has practical significance as extrusive rock, which has cooled rapidly on the surface, is fine-grained and smooth while intrusive rock, which has cooled more slowly underground, is coarse-grained and rough. The Cuillin Hills of Skye are mostly made of dark gabbro, an intrusive rock, but in places paler basalt has been extruded into the gabbro. Gabbro is fantastic rock for scrambling and climbing because it is so rough and provides excellent grip even when wet. Basalt is much slicker, especially when wet, and it can be quite a shock to step from one to the other without realising it. Igneous rock scenery is typically rugged and steep with many cliffs. Granite, an igneous rock, forms the Galloway Hills, which is why they are more rocky and mountainous than the rest of the Southern Uplands. In the Highlands igneous rocks make up the Ben Nevis and Glen Coe area, the Cairngorms and the mountains on the islands of Arran, Mull, Skye and Harris. Igneous rocks make up 25–30 per cent of the Caledonian mountains.

The commonest rocks in the Highlands are **metamorphic**, formed from igneous and sedimentary rocks that have been changed by great pressure and extremely high temperatures in the earth. In the Outer Hebrides and the northwest Highlands very ancient metamorphic rock is found, known as Lewisian Gneiss, which was formed 2–3 billion years ago. The rocks that form most of the rest of the Highlands are much younger, only about 400 million years old, and are sedimentary rocks – schists from clay and psammites from

The Carn Mor Dearg Arête sweeping up to the summit of Carn Mor Dearg from Ben Nevis

sandstone – metamorphosed during the building of the Caledonian mountain range. These are known as the Highland Schists and are divided into two groups, the Moine Schists (found in the Northern, Western and Central Highlands and the northern Cairngorms) and the Dalradian Schists (found in the Central and Southern Highlands and the southern Cairngorms). Mountains built from metamorphic rocks are generally not as dramatic as those made from igneous rocks, but many are still fine peaks.

HIGHLAND GEOPARKS

The North West Highlands Geopark
In 2005 Scotland's first Geopark was opened in the Northwest Highlands. Geopark is a European designation, recognised by UNESCO, and was granted here because of the outstanding geology and landscape of the area, which is internationally important. The 2000km^2 park stretches from Achiltibuie near Ullapool to Cape Wrath and the north coast and follows the Moine Thrust. Significant mountains in the park include Ben Mor Coigach, Suilven, Ben More Assynt, Quinag, Arkle and Foinaven. Information, including details of geology trails, can be found at Scottish Natural Heritage's excellent Knockan Crag Nature Reserve Visitor Centre, 21km north of Ullapool.
www.northwest-highlands-geopark.org.uk, www.knockan-crag.co.uk

Lochaber Geopark
This geopark was designated in 2007. It stretches from Rannoch Moor in the south to Knoydart in the north and includes the volcanic rocks of Ben Nevis, Glen Coe and the Cuillin of Rum plus the Parallel Roads of Glen Roy, actually the shorelines of ancient ice-dammed lakes. This fascinating geological area also includes Scotland's highest mountain Ben Nevis, deepest freshwater loch – Loch Morar – and deepest pothole – Uamn nan Claig-Ionn ('cave of the skulls'), on the Appin Peninsula.
www.lochabergeopark.org.uk

GEOLOGY AND LANDSCAPE BOOKS

Geology and Landscapes of Scotland by Con Gillen (Terra, 2003)

Granite and Grit: A Walker's Guide to the Geology of British Mountains by Ronald Turnbull (Frances Lincoln, 2009)

The Highland Geology Trail by John L. Roberts (Luath, 2000)

Highland Landforms by Robert J. Price (Aberdeen University Press, 1991)

Hutton's Arse: 3 Billion Years of Extraordinary Geology in Scotland's Northern Highlands by Malcolm Rider (Rider-French Consulting, 2005)

Land of Mountain and Flood: The Geology and Landforms of Scotland by Alan McKirdy, John Gordon and Roger Crofts (Birlinn, 2007)

Landscapes Fashioned by Geology by Scottish Natural Heritage (SNH, 1994–2005, 14 booklets)

Hostile Habitats: Scotland's Mountain Environment: a Hillwalker's Guide to Wildlife and Landscape edited by Nick Kempe and Mark Wrightman (SMT, 2006)

Scotland's Beginnings: Scotland Through Time by Michael A. Taylor and Andrew C. Kitchener (NMSE, 2007)

The Waterfalls of Scotland by Louis Stott (Aberdeen University Press, 1987; out of print but well worth seeking out)

The Man Who Found Time: James Hutton and the Discovery of the Earth's Antiquity by Jack Repcheck (Pocket Books, 2004)

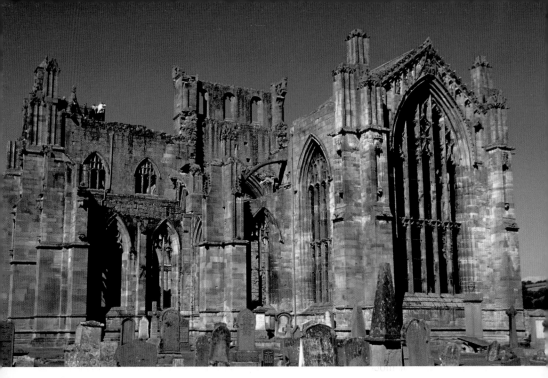

The ruins of Melrose Abbey on the Southern Upland Way

HISTORY, CULTURE AND
THE RISE OF MOUNTAINEERING

'I would love to be on the Buachaille,
thigh-deep in snow.'
Duncan MacIntyre,
the Glenorchy Bard (1724–1812)

Mountaineering for recreation is a Victorian invention. However, this doesn't mean that there was no appreciation or enjoyment of the mountains before modern mountaineering. As Ian Mitchell shows in his excellent and fascinating book *Scotland's Mountains Before the Mountaineers* (Luath, 1999) those who lived in the mountains had a deep understanding and knowledge of them and also explored and climbed them. They hunted deer and game birds, grazed their cattle in high pastures and took them over the hills to market. Some of them stole cattle and often had to hide themselves from their enemies. Travelling the mountains was part of their everyday life. The mountains were their home. There were visitors too. Map makers, scientists, road builders and others explored the mountains long before the mountaineers arrived. The first recorded ascent of Scotland's highest mountain, Ben Nevis, was made by the botanist James Robertson in 1771. By the end of the 18th century guided ascents of the mountain were available and tourism in Scotland was becoming popular. In the Southern Highlands Ben Lomond, much more easily accessible from the Lowlands than other hills, was being regularly walked by visitors as early as the 1770s.

However records of this period are sketchy and hard to find. By contrast, mountaineering from the 1880s, when the first mountaineering clubs were formed, has been well documented, giving the impression that no mountaineering had gone on beforehand. Yet, as Ian Mitchell says, the Gaelic names of the mountains, which are both descriptive and evocative, show that they were known to the inhabitants long before the first recreational mountaineers arrived.

Mountains are also important in Scottish culture, playing a major part in literature – such as Robert Louis Stevenson's *Kidnapped*, Sir Walter Scott's *Rob Roy* and other works (which were particularly influential in popularising the Highlands and creating the modern romantic view of Scotland) and the poetry of Sorley MacLean and Norman MacCaig – in music, from traditional airs to modern bands like Teenage Fanclub and Runrig, and in art, most famously with Sir Edwin Landseer, painter of one of the best-known and romantic Highland pictures, *Monarch of the Glen*.

As well as being the birthplace of the study of geology the Scottish landscape played other parts in the development of scientific knowledge. Perhaps the most curious of these were the experiments by Astronomer Royal Nevil Maskelyne to calculate the density of the earth by measuring the deviation of a plumbline from vertical caused by the attraction of a mountain, which took place on Schiehallion in the Southern Highlands in 1774. James Hutton, the founder of geology, travelled through the Highlands to Caithness in 1764 engaged on geological research and then visited Glen Tilt in the southern Cairngorms in 1785 in search of proof of his theory that granite intrusions were injected from below into older rocks in the form of molten magma. He found the evidence in the bed of the River Tilt close to Forest Lodge, high up the glen where it is squeezed between the steep walls of two Munros, Carn a'Chlamain and Braigh Coire Chruinn-bhalgain.

The development of modern mountaineering and hillwalking began around the middle of the 19th century when those with enough money to climb mountains for the sake of the experience, rather than for scientific or pecuniary reasons, formed clubs and started to organise and record their ascents. At the heart of this development were the Alps, and the Alpine Club (founded in 1857), and it was a few decades before the Scottish mountains were taken seriously by mountaineers – at first being regarded merely as a training ground for alpinism. The first regional Scottish outdoor clubs were formed in the 1850s, mostly for walking, but some dedicated themselves to climbing. There was no national club, however, until the influential Scottish Mountaineering Club (SMC) was founded in 1889.

By the time the mountaineers arrived both the Southern Uplands and the Highlands were calm and peaceful for the first time in many centuries. Scotland has been inhabited for at least 8500 years but the country itself only became unified around 700 years ago. Even then both the Southern Uplands and the Highlands were often violent and dangerous places with clans fighting among themselves and with the civil authorities. In the Southern Uplands the mid- and late 1600s were particularly bloody, a period known as the 'killing time' when Scots who supported the National Covenant, which called for them to have control over their religion rather than have it run by the English crown, began an armed struggle against the government. King Charles II's troops killed any Covenanters they could find, including those who simply wished to worship in their own way and were not involved in

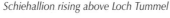

Schiehallion rising above Loch Tummel

violence. Walkers in the western Southern Uplands will come across many monuments to this grim period of history.

The Convenanters' struggle ended with the joint accession of William and Mary to the throne in 1689, the so-called Glorious Revolution. In the Highlands their rule led to more trouble, however. Many Highlanders – known as Jacobites (from Jacobus, the Latin for James) – wanted Mary's father James VII (James II of England and successor to his brother Charles II after the latter's death in 1685), who had fled to France when William landed with his troops, back on the throne and there began a 67 year period of intermittent insurrection. The most infamous event of the time was the Massacre of Glencoe in 1692 when government troops billeted with the MacDonalds in the glen turned on their hosts and massacred many of them, forcing others to flee into the winter night. The struggle to restore the Stuart dynasty to the British throne finally ended with the uprising of 1745 and the defeat of Charles Edward Stuart (Bonnie Prince Charlie), grandson of James VII, and his army at the Battle of Culloden the following year. Charles' travels through the Highlands and Islands while being hunted by troops before he was taken by ship to France have become part of the romantic story of Scotland, but it should never be forgotten that he and his followers wanted to reintroduce an absolute monarchy and that the aftermath of his rebellion was devastating, both for the people of the Highlands and for the land itself.

Following Culloden the Prince went on the run and travelled through the Highlands for 20 weeks, often at night, sleeping rough in the hills and walking hundreds of miles while being searched for by government troops. It is this arduous journey of survival and his eventual escape to France that has given the story of the Prince a romantic gloss, as it was undoubtedly difficult and dangerous, especially for someone used to the trappings and comfort of royalty.

After the '45 rising the government set out to ensure there would be no more Jacobite rebellions. Jacobite supporters were ruthlessly suppressed and many killed. Lairds were no longer allowed to raise armies from their clans and the wearing of tartan and the kilt and the use of the Gaelic language were banned.

At this time, in order to move troops efficiently and quickly the first proper roads were built, giving much better access to the Highlands. Between 1724 and 1736 General Wade had built 250 miles (400km) of roads; following Culloden, another 1000

Dun Telve broch in Gleann Beag in the Western Highlands

miles (1600km) were constructed over the next 50 years, many by General Caulfeild. Many of today's highways take the same line as these military roads, such as the A9 over the Pass of Drumochter between Tayside and Strathspey, but some of the old roads are now walkers' routes, such as the Corrieyairack Pass from Fort Augustus to Strathspey. Many of these roads fell into disrepair, however, and the Highlands were really opened up by the Scottish engineer Thomas Telford in the first half of the 19th century. From 1803 onwards he constructed over 935 miles (1500km) of roads and built the Caledonian Canal through the Great Glen, linking the west and east coasts.

The end of the Jacobite rebellion brought great changes to the Highlands as the military power of the clan chiefs was broken. Their wealth now lay in the clan lands they claimed as their own rather than in people. To make money many brought in sheep or sold their land to others as grazing in order to exploit the growing demand for wool south of the border. This had such an effect on the Highlands that it became known as the Coming of the Sheep. The population of the area was already quite high and many emigrated, either by choice or because they were forced out. Sheep farmers needed land rather than people and for 90 years from the 1780s onwards many people were driven from their homes in the notorious Clearances, leaving once-populated glens empty. Many moved to the coast or else emigrated to the US, Canada, Australia and other countries to find work or to escape the potato blight that caused starvation in the 1840s.

As the demand for wool declined in the mid-1800s many Highland estates changed from sheep to deer and the modern sporting estate was born. Over-grazing by high numbers of sheep and deer prevented the regeneration of shrubs and trees and led to the impoverished, damaged ecosystem that covers too much of the mountain areas today. The sporting estate is often presented as the historic use of the land and touted as the best way to keep the mountains in their natural state. Neither is true.

In the early 19th century some landlords rented small landholdings known as crofts to their tenants, who had no security of tenure and could be evicted without notice. As demand for land for sheep and deer grew many crofts were reduced in size but rents stayed the same. Some crofters were dispossessed and forced to share other crofts which were too small to support them. Continued maltreatment

eventually forced the crofters into revolt, leading to the so-called Battle of the Braes on the Isle of Skye in 1882, when crofters resisted the police sent to evict them. In the aftermath of this incident the government set up the Napier Commission, which resulted in the granting of security of tenure to crofters and the creation of the Crofters' Commission to manage crofting estates. There are now some 17,725 crofts in the Highlands and Islands. More recent changes in the law have allowed crofters to buy their crofts, either individually or as groups such as the Assynt Crofters' Trust.

At the same time as the crofters were battling for their rights the first recognisably modern mountaineers were starting to climb the hills and record their activities. Skye was popular with these first climbers, partly due to the rugged nature of the Cuillin range and also because access was easier than on much of the mainland. From the 1820s steamers made the islands and coastal towns like Fort William more accessible than inland areas, until the railways started to arrive from the middle of the century onwards. Travel by water was much easier and quicker than travel by horse-drawn coaches on rough roads. The railways initially kept Skye more accessible too. The first trains reached Inverness in 1855, then Strome on Loch Carron on the west coast, from where ferries ran to Skye, in 1870. Fort William, below Ben Nevis, wasn't accessible by train until 1894.

The nature of the mountains attracted the first climbers to Skye too. The most difficult summits, the only ones requiring rock climbing, are found in the Cuillin and these presented a suitable challenge for aspiring alpinists. Even before the alpinists arrived Sheriff Alexander Nicolson, who was from Skye, became arguably the first modern mountaineer (Mitchell says he 'straddled two worlds, that of the pioneer and that of the mountaineer'). He certainly climbed for the excitement and challenge and made many first ascents in the Cuillin from 1865 onwards, including the highest summit, Sgurr Alasdair, which was later named after him (Alexander is a translation of Alasdair), and Sgurr Dubh Mor. Nicolson also wrote about his climbs in magazines and newspapers, helping to popularise the mountains.

Nicolson climbed his last new route, his eponymous chimney on Sgurr nan Gillean, at the age of 52 in 1879. The next year the first of the truly modern mountaineers, SMC founder William Naismith, of the famous Naismith's Rule for calculating times on the hill, arrived on Skye and made the first ascent of the north top of Bidein Druim nan Ramh. A year later the Pilkington brothers, members of the Alpine Club and from the famous glass-making family, climbed the Inaccessible Pinnacle. The floodgates were open.

> Naismith's Rule: Allow 1hr for every 3 miles of distance and 30mins for every 1000ft of ascent, without stops (or 1hr for every 4.5km and 30mins for every 300m of ascent).

The Cuillin remained the centre of Scottish climbing for over a decade. Then in 1892 the first major climbs on the north face of Ben Nevis were achieved by John, Edward, Charles and Bertram Hopkinson, three brothers and a son from northern England. They climbed most of the way up Tower Ridge, then walked to the summit and descended the whole ridge the next day. Two days after that they climbed the Northeast Buttress. Oddly, despite the pioneering nature of these climbs, they went unreported until 1895, when a note appeared in the Alpine Club's *Alpine Journal*. Over the next few years climbers spread out, making the first rock and snow climbs everywhere from Lochnagar to Glen Coe to the Isle of Arran. Scottish winter climbing was and remains a popular and distinct activity.

Since the 1880s Scottish mountaineering history has been documented in the SMC *Journal*. The first issue appeared in 1891 and it has been published regularly ever since (annually since 1942), keeping an unbroken record of Scottish mountain activities. Selections from the journal are collected in *A Century of Scottish Mountaineering*, edited by W.D. Brooker (SMC, 1988), which includes writing by many of the leading names in Scottish climbing such as W.W. Naismith, Harold Raeburn, J.H.B. Bell, W.H. Murray, Jimmy Marshall, Robin Smith, Tom Weir and Tom Patey.

Mountaineering in Scotland doesn't only mean rock and ice climbing of course. Hillwalking is, and has been since the very early days, the most popular activity. Soon after the SMC was founded one of its leading members, Sir Hugh Munro, compiled the first tables of mountains over 3000 feet (914.4m), which were published in the September 1891 edition of the SMC *Journal*. According to Munro there were 283 separate mountains, soon to be known as

Munros, and 255 subsidiary Tops. Climbing all these summits was an obvious goal for mountaineers and Munro himself set out to do so; he had just three of the 538 left to climb when he died in 1919. The first Munroist, as those who complete the separate mountains are called, was the Rev A.E. Robertson, who climbed his final summit in September 1901, just ten years after the list first appeared (although there are some questions over whether he actually reached the summit of Ben Wyvis).

It was 1923 before all 538 summits were definitely climbed by one person, another clergyman, the Rev A.R. Burn, who was also the second person to complete the Munros. Since then over 4000 people have completed the Munros and Munro bagging, as it is known, is probably the single most popular activity in the Scottish mountains. Munro's tables have had four major revisions, some controversial, since 1891. The latest published revision (1997) contains 284 Munros and 227 tops. However the Munro Society is carrying out a survey of summits near to 3000 feet (914.4m) with modern GPS survey equipment. Of the summits surveyed so far one, Sgurr nan Ceannaichean, listed in the Tables as 915m since 1981, has been measured as 913.43m and is thus not a Munro, which neatly reduces the number of separate mountains to 283, as in Munro's original list. The other mountains listed as 915m in the Tables, Beinn Teallach and Ben Vane, have been measured as 914.6 and 915.76m and so remain Munros. The Ordnance Survey and the SMC have accepted these surveys as accurate so these are now the official heights. Other changes can be expected.

Munro's *Tables* are published by the SMC and contain a list of all recorded Munroists in chronological order. This list also appears on the SMC's website: www.smc.org.uk. By the end of 2008 4254 people had climbed the Munros. There is also an organisation for those who have completed the Munros. The Munro Society (www.themunrosociety.com) was set up as

a forum through which Munroists could pool their interest in and knowledge of the Scottish mountains. Many compleaters are minded to give something back to the hills to which they devoted so much time and effort and, in return, provided so many rewarding experiences. The Munro Society is providing a channel through which such goodwill may be put to practical use.

Munro's *Tables* also contain 'other tables of lower hills'. These are the 219 hills between 2500 and 3000 feet in height (762–914.4m; there are now 220 as they have been joined by former Munro Sgurr nan Ceannaichean), known as Corbetts after their compiler J. Rooke Corbett (who was the second person to complete the Munros and Tops in 1930), the 224 hills between 2000 and 2500 feet (609.6–762m), known as Grahams, after the late Fiona Graham who compiled a list of them in 1992, and the 89 hills over 2000 feet (609.6m) in the Scottish Lowlands, known as Donalds after compiler Percy Donald. Unlike the Munros, the Corbetts and Grahams have strict definitions – there must be a drop of 500 feet (152.4m) all round in the case of the first and 150m in the case of the second.

The introduction of metres here throws up an anomaly that many readers will have noted. How do these tables fit into a metric world? The Munro minimum of 914.4m is hardly a height anyone would choose to define a list of hills. The Corbetts cover hills between 762 and 914.4m, the Donalds hills over 610m in the lowlands and the Grahams hills between 610 and 761m. Logically, modern lists would cover hills between 500 and 750m, 750 and 1000m and over 1000m. Bagging hills is not a logical activity however and the Munros have a historical tradition and weight behind them that keeps them at the forefront of hillwalkers' aims: the magic number is still 3000 feet. And the reason for climbing the Munros and other hills is for satisfaction and pleasure, not logic.

Once the Munros had been climbed the next obvious challenge was to climb them in one continuous trip. This feat was first achieved in 1974 by Hamish Brown, who wrote one of the classic books of the Scottish hills about it, *Hamish's Mountain Walk: The First Traverse of all the Scottish Munros in One Journey* (first published in 1978 and republished by Sandstone Press in 2010). Since then at least 20 people have completed continuous rounds. Only two of these have been in winter, however, due to the severity of the season, the first by Martin Moran in 1984–1985, as described in his *The Munros in Winter* (David & Charles, 1986), and more recently the first continuous winter round on foot by Steve Perry in 2005–2006. Perry walked between all the hills and camped most of the time, while Moran was supported by his wife with a minivan and driven between each group of hills. Both walks were major achievements given

Steve Perry on the summit of Ben Hope at the finish of the first continuous winter round of the Munros

the severity of Scottish winter weather and short hours of daylight. Also a great achievement was Mike Cawthorne's winter walk over the 135 1000m summits in 1997–1998, which is memorably described in his excellent book, *Hell of a Journey* (Mercat Press, 2000).

Inevitably hill runners took up the challenge of achieving the fastest round. The current record was set by Stephen Pyke in 2010 – an astonishing 39 days and 12 hours. Pyke used a bicycle for road sections and a canoe to reach some of the hills. The fastest time solely on foot is 66 days and 7hrs, set in 1994 by Mike Cudahy.

Meanwhile walkers added other summits to the Munros. The most obvious are the Tops and this author was the first to climb all the Munros and Tops in one walk in 1996 (see *The Munros and Tops* (Mainstream, 2nd edition 2003)). The next year Andrew Allum completed the longest walk ever in the British hills, taking in the Munros, Tops, Corbetts, Grahams, Donalds and all the hills over 2000 feet (609.6m) high in England and Wales. Then there are those who repeat the Munros many times. Steve Fallon has done 14 rounds, which is even more amazing than it sounds as he completed a round every year for 11 years (www.stevenfallon.co.uk).

Books

A Cairngorm Chronicle by A.F. Whyte (Millrace, 2007)

A Century of Scottish Mountaineering: An Anthology from the Scottish Mountaineering Club Journal edited by W.D. Brooker (SMC, 1988)

A High and Lonely Place: The Sanctuary and Plight of the Cairngorms by Jim Crumley (Whittles, 2001)

A View from the Ridge by Dave Brown and Ian Mitchell (The Ernest Press, 1991)

Always a Little Further: A Classic Tale of Camping, Hiking and Climbing in Scotland in the Thirties by Alastair Borthwick (Diadem, 1983, out of print)

Among Mountains by Jim Crumley (Mainstream, 1993)

Bell's Scottish Climbs by J.H.B. Bell (Gollancz, 1988).

Burn on the Hill: The Story of the First 'Compleat Munroist' by Elizabeth Allan (Bidean Books, 1995)

Hamish's Mountain Walk: The First Traverse of all the Scottish Munros in One Journey by Hamish Brown (Sandstone Press, 2010)

Hell of a Journey: On Foot through the Scottish Highlands In Winter by Mike Cawthorne (Mercat Press, 2000)

Highways and Byways in the West Highlands by Seton Gordon (Birlinn, 1995, first published 1935)

Highways and Byways in the Central Highlands by Seton Gordon (Birlinn, 1995, first published 1935)

Legends of the Cairngorms by Affleck Gray (Mainstream, 1887)

Magic Mountains by Rennie McOwan (Mainstream, 1994)

Mountain Days and Bothy Nights by Dave Brown and Ian Mitchell (Luath, 1987)

Mountaineering in Scotland and Undiscovered Scotland by W.H. Murray (Baton Wicks, 1997)

On the Trail of Queen Victoria in the Highlands by Ian R. Mitchell (Luath, 2000)

On the Trail of Scotland's Myths and Legends by Stuart McHardy (Luath, 2005)

Scotland's Mountains before the Mountaineers by Ian R. Mitchell (Luath, 1999)

Scotland's Mountains by W.H. Murray (SMT, 1987)

Seton Gordon's Scotland by Seton Gordon (edited by Hamish Brown) (Whittles, 2005)

The First Fifty: Munro-Bagging without a Beard by Muriel Gray (Corgi, 1993)

The First Munroist: The Reverend A.E. Robertson: His Life, Munros and Photographs by Peter Drummond and Ian Mitchell (The Ernest Press, 1993)

The Heart of the Cairngorms by Jim Crumley (Colin Baxter, 1997)

The Heart of Skye by Jim Crumley (Colin Baxter, 1994)

The Last Hundred: Munros, Beards and a Dog by Hamish Brown (Mainstream, 1994)

The Life and Times of the Black Pig: A Biography of Ben Macdui by Ronald Turnbull (Millrace, 2007)

The Munroist's Companion: An Anthology compiled and edited by Robin N.Campbell (SMT, 1999)

The Munros and Tops: A Record-Setting Walk in the Scottish Highlands by Chris Townsend (Mainstream, 2nd edition 2003)

The Munros in Winter: 277 Summits in 83 Days by Martin Moran (David & Charles, 1986)

The Munro Phenomenon by Andrew Dempster (Mainstream, 1995)

The Weathermen of Ben Nevis 1883–1904 by Marjory Roy (The Royal Meteorological Society, 2004)

Walking the Watershed: The Border to Cape Wrath along Scotland's Great Divide by Dave Hewitt (TACit Press, 1994)

The Weekend Fix by Craig Weldon (Sandstone Press, 2009)

Wilderness Dreams: The Call of Scotland's Last Wild Places by Mike Cawthorne (In Pinn, 2007)

Organisations

Scottish Mountaineering Club www.smc.org.uk

The Munro Society www.themunrosociety.com

SCOTTISH MOUNTAIN NAMES

Sgurr nan Ceathreamhnan, A'Bhuidheanach Beag, Braigh Coire Chruinn-bhalgain, Carn na Saobhaidhe, Beinn Liath Mhor a'Ghiubhais Li. Seemingly incomprehensible and unpronounceable, many Scottish mountain names cause hillgoers as much if not more problems than their ascents. The names derive from four languages, primarily Gaelic, followed by Norse, found mainly in the Hebrides and Caithness and Sutherland, Scots, found in the Southern Uplands, and finally Brythonic (Brittonic) or Old Welsh, the language of the Celtic people who inhabited southern Scotland before the Scots arrived from Ireland, and the Angles from the south. Brythonic has only left a few hill names such as the Ochils. Confusingly the language of the Scots was Gaelic while Scots is descended, like English, from the Germanic languages of the tribes who invaded Britain from the 5th to 7th centuries AD. The word 'hill' itself is Germanic and appears quite often in Scotland. Mountain is a Middle English word, derived from the Old French *montaigne*, and arrived in Britain after the Norman Conquest of 1066.

Some names are combinations, as successive peoples adopted and adapted the names of their predecessors. In particular Gaelic and Norse became intermingled, sometimes to the extent that disentangling them is just about impossible. Scots took words from both Gaelic and Norse too.

By the time the first detailed maps were compiled by the Ordnance Survey in the mid -19th century Norse had long since ceased to be used and no one remembered the Norse derivation of names. Scots was a written language and presented no real problems to the map makers. Although Gaelic was also written in the Highlands place names were passed on by word of mouth

Footpath sign in Gaelic and English

and the map makers, most of whom did not speak Gaelic, wrote down what they thought they heard, inventing spellings without understanding what the words meant. This led to many names being corrupted, some so much so that it's not clear what the original Gaelic was or what the names mean. However we should be grateful that the map makers bothered to try and record the names at all: they could easily have been lost.

As you would expect hill names reflect the interests and observations of the local people who created them. Thus they describe the colours, shapes, sizes, positions and distinguishing features of the hills and the legends, people and wildlife and plants associated with them. For example Meall Bhuidhe means 'yellow hill', Beinn Mheadhoin means 'middle mountain', Garbh Bheinn means 'rough mountain' and An Socach means 'the pig's snout' (a reference to its shape). Unsurprisingly descriptive names like these occur in different places: there are at least 28 hills called Meall Bhuidhe, according to Peter Drummond's *Scottish Hill Names* (Scottish Mountaineering Trust, 2nd revised edition, 2007), which were named at a time when people had no knowledge of the names of hills outside their local area. Names referring to legends and people are more specific in usage and tend to only occur once, for example as Schiehallion, 'the Fairy Hill of the Caledonians', and Ben Challum, 'Malcolm's hill'.

Pronunciation of hill names is best learnt by hearing them spoken, for example on the CD-ROM guides to the Munros and Corbetts from the SMC and ISYS. A point worth noting is that the baffling 'bh' and 'mh' are pronounced as 'v'. Gaelic experts disagree on how some names are pronounced and you may hear several different versions.

And those names at the beginning of this section? They translate as 'peak of the quarters', 'the little yellow place', 'upland of the corrie of round blisters', 'cairn of the fox's den' and 'big grey hill of the colourful pine'.

MORE ABOUT MOUNTAIN NAMES

Scottish Hill Names: Their Origin and Meaning by Peter Drummond (2nd revised edition, SMT, 2007)

The east side of Loch Lomond, with Ben Lomond rising into the clouds

NATIONAL PARKS AND OTHER PROTECTED AREAS

Ironically for the country of John Muir, famed as the 'father of national parks' in the US, Scotland came late to the national parks idea, the first, **Loch Lomond and the Trossachs**, only being established in 2002. Lying in the southwest corner of the Highlands this park contains many fine mountains, including Ben Lomond, Ben Lui, Ben More and the Arrochar Alps, as well as several lochs and much attractive deciduous woodland. In total there are 21 Munros and 20 Corbetts in the park, which covers $1865km^2$.

Scotland's second national park, the **Cairngorms**, is over twice the size at $3800km^2$, and by far the largest national park in the United Kingdom (and there is a Scottish Government initiative to extend the southern boundary of the Park, making it even larger). The Cairngorms contains five of Scotland's six highest mountains – Ben Macdui, Braeriach, Cairn Toul, Sgor an Lochain Uaine and Cairn Gorm. There are 55 Munros and 19 Corbetts in the park. The largest area of high ground in Scotland is found in the Cairngorms, with 10 per cent of the park above 800m and 68 per cent over 400m high. Below the arctic tundra are found some of the last remnants of the Caledonian pine forest and three major river valleys, those of the Spey, Don and Dee.

As well as national parks Scotland has **National Scenic Areas** (NSAs), which are Scotland's only national landscape designation. NSAs, run by Scottish Natural Heritage, are 'those areas of land considered of national significance on the basis of their outstanding scenic interest which must be conserved as part of the country's natural heritage. They have been selected for their characteristic features of scenery, comprising a mixture of richly diverse landscapes including prominent landforms, coastline, sea and freshwater lochs, rivers, woodlands and moorlands'. There are currently 40 NSAs in Scotland, covering a total land area of $10,205km^2$ and a marine area of $3579km^2$. There is a good argument that the whole of the Highlands should be an NSA or equivalent and treated as a whole rather than in parts. This would prevent the nibbling away of the landscape at the edges and in the spaces between the NSAs. The Highlands form a complete natural whole: protecting only bits of this unity leads to a degradation of the entire area, protected and unprotected. It's like picking out the most beautiful parts of a painting and saying that it doesn't matter if the rest of the picture becomes stained, torn and tattered.

Unlike in many countries Scotland's national parks contain towns and roads as well as wild land and are not just dedicated to the preservation of the environment, although this is their prime aim. The parks don't own the land they manage either and they have to work in conjunction with those who do, a mix of private landowners, government agencies and conservation charities. The last two types of organisation own land that they manage for conservation both inside and outside the national parks. The biggest landowning body is the **National Trust for Scotland** (NTS), a conservation charity that has owned wild land since the 1930s. Of the many properties owned by the NTS those of interest to mountaineers are Kintail, Morvich and neighbouring West Affric, which include the ridge of the Five Sisters of Kintail, the Falls of Glomach and upper Glen Affric; Torridon, which includes Liathach and Beinn Alligin, two of the finest peaks in the Highlands; Mar Lodge, a vast sweep of the eastern Cairngorms including Ben Macdui, Ben Avon and Beinn a'Bhuird; Ben Lomond; Ben Lawers National Nature Reserve, which also includes Meall nan Tarmachan; the Grey Mare's Tail in the Southern Uplands, which includes Loch Skene and the Corbett White Coomb; Goatfell, the highest peak on the Isle of Arran; and finally incomparable Glencoe and Dalness, home to the Aonach Eagach, Bidean nam Bian and Buachaille Etive Mor.

Formed in 1983 to protect and conserve wild places and inspired by and named after the great Scots born campaigner for wilderness, the **John Muir Trust** (JMT) owns several mountain estates including Ben Nevis, the highest mountain in Scotland. Other properties are: Schiehallion in the Central Highlands; Li and Coire Dhorrcail in Knoydart, which includes Ladhar Bheinn, one of the finest mountains in the Western Highlands; the magnificent mountain of Quinag above Loch Assynt, three of whose summits are Corbetts; Sandwood Bay in the far northwest, which is wild and beautiful, although it doesn't contain any high mountains; and three contiguous estates on the Isle of Skye, Strathaird, Torrin and Sconser, which contain the Red Hills, the Munro Bla Bheinn and part of Loch Coruisk in the heart of the Cuillin. The JMT also works with other organisations and has assisted the Assynt Foundation in the purchase and

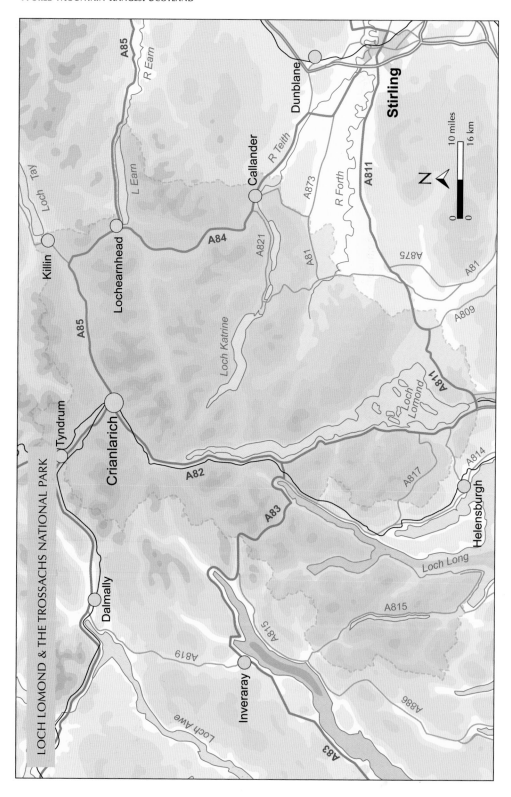

LOCH LOMOND & THE TROSSACHS NATIONAL PARK

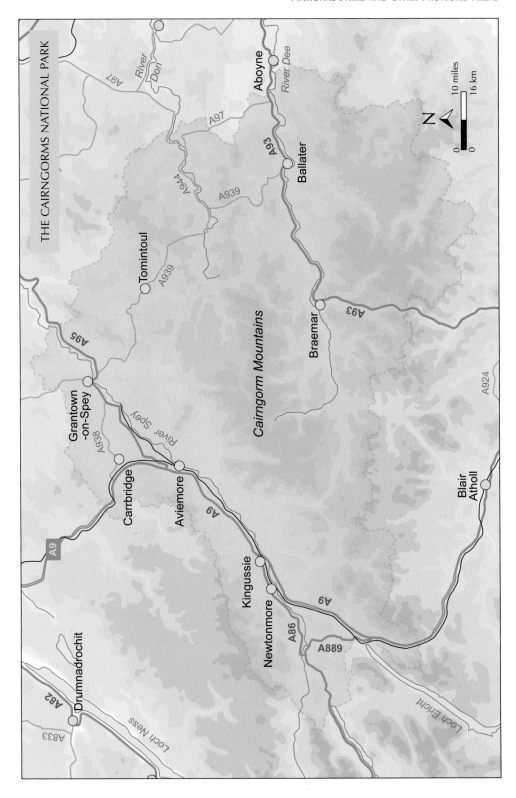

THE CAIRNGORMS NATIONAL PARK

Rum National Nature Reserve covers the whole of the island of Rum

running of the Assynt and Drumrunie estates in the northwest Highlands, which include the mountains Canisp, Cul Mor, Cul Beag and iconic Suilven.

The **Royal Society for the Protection of Birds** (RSPB) owns several estates in mountain areas, most of them quite small. However Abernethy Forest in the northeast Cairngorms is a huge area of Caledonian pine forest running right up to the lower edges of the mountains and containing beautiful Lochs Garten and Mallachie. The RSPB also owns the woodlands of Inversnaid, which rise steeply from the east shore of Loch Lomond.

NATIONAL PARKS AND PROTECTED AREAS:
CONTACT INFORMATION FOR REGULATORY BODIES

- **Forestry Commission Scotland**, Silvan House, 231 Corstorphine Road, Edinburgh, EH12 7AT
  ☎ 0845 3673787 email fcscotland@forestry.gsi.gov.uk www.forestry.gov.uk/scotland

- **John Muir Trust**, 41 Commercial Street, Edinburgh EH6 6JD
  ☎ 0131 5540114 email admin@jmt.org www.jmt.org

- **RSPB Scotland, Dunedin House**, 25 Ravelston Terrace, Edinburgh, EH4 3TP
  ☎ 0131 3116500 email rspb.scotland@rspb.org.uk www.rspb.org.uk/scotland

- **Scottish Natural Heritage**, Great Glen House, Leachkin Road, Inverness, IV3 8NW
  ☎ 01463 725000 email enquiries@snh.gov.uk www.snh.org.uk

- **The National Trust for Scotland**, Wemyss House, 28 Charlotte Square, Edinburgh, EH2 4ET
  ☎ 0131 2439300 email information@nts.org.uk www.nts.org.uk

- **Loch Lomond and the Trossachs National Park**, The Old Station, Balloch Road, Balloch, G83 8BF
  ☎ 01389 722600 email info@lochlomond-trossachs.org www.lochlomond-trossachs.org

- **Cairngorms National Park**, 14 The Square, Grantown-on-Spey, PH26 3HG
  ☎ 01479 873535 email enquiries@cairngorms.co.uk www.cairngorms.co.uk

Scottish Natural Heritage (SNH), the government body responsible for nature conservation, owns several national nature reserves of interest to mountaineers. Beinn Eighe, the first national nature reserve in Britain, contains several summits, including Beinn Eighe itself, and remnants of the Caledonian forest rising above Loch Maree. Creag Meagaidh contains the cliffs of Coire Ardair, a major winter climbing area, Creag Meagaidh itself, and a wonderful example of forest regeneration thanks to the simple expedient of reducing grazing pressure. The whole island of Rum, containing two Corbetts, is also owned by SNH. Ben Lui, one of the finest peaks in the Southern Highlands, and Ben Wyvis in the Northern Highlands are also SNH nature reserves.

Forestry Commission Scotland, the government body responsible for Scotland's woods, also owns much land in mountain areas such as the Glenmore Forest Park in the Cairngorms, which includes the Corbett Meall a'Bhuachaille, Glen Affric in the Northern Highlands, one of the most beautiful glens in Scotland, the Queen Elizabeth Forest Park on the east side of Loch Lomond and Galloway Forest Park in Southwest Scotland, which contains Glen Trool and the most rugged hills in the Southern Uplands. The Forestry Commission was once responsible for unappealing blanket conifer forests, planted and maintained with no thought for the landscape or the natural environment, but it's now more conservation minded and is working to restore the Caledonian forest that it once destroyed in some areas.

Despite all these government designations and private conservation estates much of Scotland's mountain landscape is still unprotected and threatened by various forms of industrialisation. Much more needs to be done to conserve what we have left. Wild land is an increasingly rare resource. We need wildness and nature for ourselves and for future generations and should be prepared to work hard to preserve it. Instead of myriad different designations (I haven't even mentioned those of the European Habitats and Birds Directives) that overlap in some places but leave others uncovered there needs to be a presumption of protection for the Highlands as a whole so the area can be treated as a unity rather than a collection of disparate places, some worthy of protection, some not.

PLANT AND ANIMAL LIFE

The Scottish mountains are a harsh northern environment, wet, cold and windswept. Yet they are home to a rich array of plant and animal life, much of it rare elsewhere. The highest summits have always been bare and stony, with minimal vegetation and few inhabitants. The increase in the severity of the weather with altitude makes a huge difference to the environment and the plants and wildlife that can survive there. Sheltered slopes can be richer in life than those exposed to storms regardless of height. As well as altitude and exposure to the weather the type of vegetation found is also dependent on how wet the ground is, well-drained soils having different plants to boggy areas.

However the lower hillsides and glens were once more richly vegetated than most are now and there was much woodland. Most of this ancient Caledonian forest, part of the boreal forest or taiga that rings the northern world, has disappeared over the last two thousand years, partly due to the climate becoming cooler and wetter, especially in the west, and partly due to felling. In many places the remnants of the old forest can be seen in the form of roots and stumps in bogs formed of the peat that replaced the forest. Over-grazing by sheep and deer has prevented regeneration in most areas and also reduced the variety of grasses, flowers and bushes found. In many treeless glens this once widespread richness can still be seen in the thin green strips of woodland lining gullies and ravines too steep for grazing animals and on inaccessible islands out in lochs, which are often densely forested.

Most of the so-called forests you see in Scotland are commercial plantations, often of non-native species such as Sitka Spruce, a tree of the Pacific Northwest of America first introduced into Scotland by the great Scottish plant hunter and wilderness explorer David Douglas in the 1820s and now the commonest tree in Scotland. The close spacing and uniform age of trees in plantations usually shades out all undergrowth, creating a somewhat unnatural ecosystem that is dark and gloomy to walk through, where walking is possible. These forests are normally planted in rectangular blocks that look artificial and are clear-felled when the timber is mature, leaving an ugly desolation. Happily many forest managers are now designing forests to look more natural and are planting other trees along the fringes and breaking up the solid outlines of plantations, which makes them aesthetically more attractive and better for wildlife. The Forestry Commission Scotland changed direction completely in the late 20th century, going from felling natural forest and replacing it with commercial plantations to felling the latter and encouraging the regeneration of the natural forest in many places. Rather than just producing timber the Forestry Commission is now meant 'to protect and expand Scotland's forests and woodlands and increase their value to society and the environment'. Poor forestry still mars too much of the Scottish hills but the situation is improving.

There are remnants of the old forest still clinging on in places, especially in the Cairngorms and Glen Affric. To walk among the huge Scots pines in a wood rich with the accumulated life of hundreds of undisturbed years is a wonderful experience. In many areas, such as the Creag Meagaidh and Beinn Eighe National Nature Reserves, regeneration is taking place thanks to reduced grazing pressures achieved by a lowering of deer and sheep numbers and sometimes by fencing to keep animals out. Trees may be planted in fenced areas too, particularly where there is no sign of regeneration, something Trees for Life, whose aim is the restoration of large areas of Caledonian forest, are doing in Glen Affric and other areas. However, although better than having no forest restoration at all, fencing restricts regeneration to the enclosed plots, leading to an artificial chequerboard appearance, and means the forest cannot spread naturally. Although it does allow some trees to grow, putting a forest in a cage is not the way to restore the whole environment to health. Where the forest is free there is nothing more inspiring than seeing young trees spreading out across a formerly bare hillside. A good place to see this is on the slopes of Meall a'Bhuachaille in the northern Cairngorms, from the path from Glenmore to Ryvoan Pass.

Down in the Southern Uplands, where natural woodland is much rarer than in the Highlands (the Borders Forest Trust says over 99 per cent has been lost), is a very interesting project, the Carrifran Wildwood. Carrifran is a dramatic valley running up into the hills from Moffatdale to the summit of White Coomb. The aim of the project is to re-establish a natural forest in Carrifran. Since 2000, when the project began, over 450,000 trees and shrubs have been planted (see www.carrifran.org.uk). In 2009 an interesting account of the project so far, *The Carrifran Wildwood Story*, by Myrtle & Philip Ashmole, was published by Borders Forest Trust.

Regenerating Scots pine forest on the slopes of Meall a'Bhuachaille in the Cairngorms

The Scottish hills were never blanketed with trees and those of us in favour of an increase in natural forest cover are not arguing for the disappearance of the hills under a dense forest. Studies show that forest cover has varied over time and that some areas may have never been wooded. There is no way to restore the forest to how it was in any particular period anyway (and how would you choose which period this would be?), but by reducing grazing pressure trees can return to areas where they will grow now, creating a more healthy and complete ecosystem and providing shelter and food for animals and birds. A fringe of trees ringing the mountains and a natural timberline where the trees slowly become smaller and less dense before disappearing altogether also makes for a more aesthetically pleasing mountain landscape. Regeneration projects and proposals should not be about blanket forestry but aimed at allowing the return of a natural forest adapted to the terrain and the environment that will be dense in some places and open in others, with many clearings and meadows.

The main trees of the old forest are Scots pine, oak and birch. Pines are dark and massive with flaky plated bark that glows dark red in sunshine. Birches are much more delicate and the leaves turn a brilliant yellow and orange in the autumn, a display to match any fall colours in the world. Oak trees were the chief forest tree in the southern and western Highlands, but now there are even fewer of these remaining than pines. Places they can be seen include the Trossachs, the Tay valley near Aberfeldy and the Pass of Killiecrankie. Aside from the three main trees the natural forest contains aspen, rowan, holly, alder, willow and other trees.

In the old pine forest thick mats of vegetation cover the ground below the trees, consisting mainly of blaeberry, whose finger-staining purple berries are a summer treat, cowberry, ling, bell heather and mosses. Juniper bushes are common in eastern forests and can grow as high as 15m. The same plants occur under birch but the less shaded ground also has various grasses and far more in the way of wild flowers such as violets, bluebells and wood anemones, found only in clearings in the pine forest.

Above the forest proper, dwarf trees and shrubs may occur – stunted, twisted Scots pine at first, and then, higher up the mountain, juniper and willow. This montane scrub is rare in Scotland but is returning in areas where grazing has been reduced. This gradual thinning out and fading away of the forest with altitude is far more aesthetically pleasing than the abruptness of a fenced forest edge and also ecologically richer and healthier. The natural height at which the forest ends varies with altitude and climate. It's much lower in the wetter west. In the drier Cairngorms stunted Scots pine grow as high as 650m.

Outside of the forest coarse grasses – matgrass, tufted hair grass, purple moor grass, sheep's fescue, deer-grass and more – make up much of the vegetation, along with patches of soggy sphagnum moss. In many glens there are large areas of bracken, whose delicate pale green fronds unfurl in the spring and then turn a rich golden brown in the autumn, having formed dense dark undergrowth in summer, which can make walking difficult. On drier slopes blaeberry and heather are common, the latter covering hillsides with the great swathes of shining purple for which Scotland is famous in summer. Many small flowers lurk among the grasses and the heather but most will only be seen by those looking for them. In wet boggy areas fluffy white bog cotton stands out (and is a warning to stay away: it grows in very soft, almost liquid ground) and you will also see the golden spikes of bog asphodel and the shrub-like, sweet-scented bog myrtle. Various orchids, looking rather exotic, grow in marshes too. Look close and the purple flower of the insectivorous common butterwort may be seen rising on a single thin stalk from a roseate of flat sticky leaves. On dry slopes the pretty little yellow tormentil is common and easy to spot while high in the hills mats of pink moss campion, lying close to the ground, can be found. Botanists will find much more. Anyone interested in wild flowers will find Michael Scott's field guide *Scottish Wild Flowers* (Collins, 2008) worth a place in the rucksack.

The only large wild **mammal** left in Scotland is the red deer, of which hundreds of thousands roam the hills. Red deer are magnificent creatures, especially the stags, with their massive antlers, which are shed and grow anew each year. Although red deer are naturally animals of the forest and the forest edge, in Scotland they have had to adapt to life on the open hill, which is where large herds may be seen. In the autumn breeding season, known as the rut, the rival stags can be heard roaring and bellowing, a wild and elemental sound that takes you far from civilisation when you hear it echoing round the glen as you lie under the stars. At other times the short sharp bark of a lookout hind signals that she is aware of your presence and is warning her grazing companions. Soon a stream of running deer is likely to be seen flowing across the hillside. In winter red deer have a thick greyish coat but in summer this changes to the thinner redder coat that gives them their name. Deer numbers were encouraged to expand following the creation of the big sporting estates in the mid- to late 19th century, to ensure there were plenty of them to hunt. The very high numbers of deer prevent forest regeneration, however, and need to be reduced across the Highlands. There are no natural predators remaining (wolves would have been the main one) except human beings.

Few other wild mammals live on the open hillside. Mountain hares are common in some areas, especially in the east. Their coats turn white in winter, which makes them easy to see when no snow is lying. Occasionally a red fox, bigger and greyer than lowland ones despite being the same species, may be seen loping across a hillside. Much more rarely a badger, normally a woodland creature, might be observed high in the hills. In all my years of wandering in the Scottish hills I've seen only one once, running around in bright sunshine at almost 700m on the slopes of Seana Bhraigh in the Northern Highlands.

In the forests the small roe deer and the larger, introduced, sika deer live, although neither is likely to be seen very often. Sika can interbreed with red deer and produce fertile offspring. An increasing number of mainland red deer are actually sika/red hybrids. The Scottish wildcat is even shyer, and also nocturnal, and so is hardly ever observed. It too is often a hybrid, due to interbreeding with domestic cats. Much more likely to be seen and heard are red squirrels, which are still common in conifer forests (75 per cent of British red squirrels are now found

Wild goats

in Scotland). American grey squirrels, which have replaced red squirrels in many areas, are found in deciduous woodland in central and southern Scotland. Smaller low ground mammals that may be seen include stoats, which turn white in winter, and rabbits. By water, fresh or salt, otters are found, a wonderful sight, while off the coast seals bask on rocky islets or bob up and down in the sea.

One formerly domesticated animal that has gone wild is the goat. Feral goats are found in several disparate places such as the Galloway Hills, the Isle of Rum, the shores of Loch Lomond and the slopes of Slioch. With their manic yellow eyes, shaggy coats and long curving horns goats certainly look wild when you encounter them suddenly in the mist. They live on steep rocky slopes where sheep and deer rarely venture and can be found from the forests to the summits.

In the Cairngorms you may be startled to come across a herd of reindeer high in the hills. These aren't wild animals, native reindeer having long ago died out, although they are allowed to roam free. They are owned by the Cairngorm Reindeer Centre, which you can visit in Glenmore in the northern Cairngorms (www.reindeer-company.co.uk).

Of the many mammals that once inhabited Scotland but which have died out, often due to hunting or persecution, some are being reintroduced. The first of these is the beaver, which became extinct in the 16th century. The Scottish Wildlife Trust and the Royal Zoological Society of Scotland released three beaver families in three locations in the Knapdale Forest on the Mull of Kintyre in May 2009.

Another much more emotive mammal now extinct in Scotland is the wolf. The last Scottish wolf is said to have been killed in 1743, although written evidence suggests strongly that wolves had been wiped out by 1680. Over three hundred years without wolves is too long. There is no reason other than fear and ignorance why wolves couldn't run wild again in the Scottish Highlands. It is wonderful to listen to the howling of a wolf pack below a bright moon. I have done so in the vast wildernesses of Canada. I would love to be able to do so at home in the Highlands. There are people working for the reintroduction of wolves. I support them: wolves are an essential part of the wild north, and by this I mean wolves running free and not contained in some fenced safari-type park, however large, as has been proposed.

Ptarmigan in winter plumage (main picture); Snow bunting (inset).

Scotland is home to three **reptiles** – adder, viviparous lizard and slow-worm – and three amphibians – common frog, common toad and palmate newt. Of these frogs are the most likely to be seen, especially in the spring when they congregate for mating and spawning in standing water of all sizes and at all altitudes. They can be very noisy at this time, emitting a low rumbling croak. I once heard dozens of frogs croaking from peaty pools at 800m in the Fannichs, a throbbing sound that could be heard clearly several hundred metres away. Of the reptiles, adders and lizards may very occasionally be seen basking in the sunshine on rocks or slithering down a bank or through the undergrowth. The clearest view of an adder I've ever had was when I came upon one curled up on a bothy doorstep. As I approached it slowly unwound itself and unhurriedly slithered off into the grass. Adders are poisonous of course but bites are extremely rare as these snakes are shy and only bite if handled or trodden on.

Birds are seen far more often than mammals, from small brown birds flitting through the heather (usually meadow pipits) to large birds of prey floating high above the mountaintops. Chief among the latter is the magnificent golden eagle, the bird that symbolises wild nature, and which is found in the roughest, remotest mountains. Above the forest and the lower hills and moors a more common raptor is the buzzard with its distinctive mewing cry. Buzzards are scavengers, filling the niche of vultures in other countries, and can often be seen perched close to roadsides waiting for a vehicle to knock down a rabbit. Although the effortless glide of eagles and buzzards, often covering half the sky with barely a wing flap, is impressive the bird that gives the best aerial displays is the raven, which can be seen twisting, turning and diving around cliffs and rocky ground from the coast to the summits.

Sitting on a summit eating lunch you might notice small black and white finch-like birds

MIDGES

Between mid May and mid September the Scottish hills are plagued by tiny biting flies called midges. These little monsters often appear in large swarms in calm, humid weather and can make life unbearable. Insect repellent is essential and head nets a good idea. Midges can't fly in more than a breeze so going high and choosing windy campsites is a good idea in summer. They can't fly very fast either so aren't a problem while you're moving. Midges also don't come out in bright sunshine, heavy rain or strong winds, but hazy sunshine, drizzle or gentle breezes provide just the humid conditions they like. There are several species of midges, of which the main one is the aptly named *Culicoides impunctatus*. Midges leave an itchy red spot where they have sucked your blood (squash one that has fed and it leaves a red smear). With some people this itch disappears in a few hours or even minutes, with others it may last for days. After-bite products can help.

fluttering about nearby in the hope of some crumbs from your sandwiches. These are snow buntings, which live year round on the highest peaks. Another high-level resident is the much bigger ptarmigan, a member of the grouse family. The mottled grey plumage makes ptarmigan hard to see when they crouch on the stones or scuttle across the ground. In winter they turn white, making them much more visible when there's no snow. Dotterel, a summer migrant, also live and nest on the high ground, especially the rolling plateaus of the eastern Highlands. These pretty, delicate-looking plovers, identifiable by the white stripe above the eye and the reddish-brown breast, sit tight on their eggs, often only flying up when you're practically standing on them. Dotterel are mostly silent but you'll often hear the plaintive lonely whistle of their much more common high country relative, the golden plover. Approach the young or nest of a golden plover and an adult will try and lure you away by running across the ground just ahead of you, sometimes trailing a wing as if it were broken.

On lower slopes and moorland hills red grouse can startle you by exploding noisily out of the heather almost at your feet. The red grouse is a game bird and in shooting areas the land is managed to try and maximise grouse numbers. On eastern hills you will often see a pattern of thick dark and light stripes, the paler ones being where the heather has been burnt – muirburn – to allow it to regenerate and maintain the moor, which would otherwise eventually be colonised by trees, and to provide fresh shoots for the grouse to eat. The result of burning is a mix of new and old heather patches on the moor.

Two much rarer grouse live in the forests, the black grouse and the huge turkey-like capercaillie. You'll be lucky to see these among the trees but if you do both are a fine sight. The woods are also home to the noisy and distinctive crested tit and the unusual Scottish crossbill, with its crossed mandible with which it twists seeds out of pine cones. Many other birds live in the forest. The best way to see them is to sit quietly on the edge of a clearing and watch and wait.

In the spring cuckoos arrive in the Highlands, calling loudly, often for much of the night as many campers know. They can sometimes be seen flying low and pursued by small birds, which either mistake them for hawks, due to their curved beaks, or recognise them as the parasites they are. Cuckoos lay their eggs in meadow pipits' nests.

One iconic bird that nests in trees but fishes in rivers and lochs is the osprey, once extinct in Scotland but now breeding in an increasing number of sites every year after first returning to Loch Garten in the Cairngorms in the 1950s. You can still see these fish hawks at the original nest site, an old dead pine heavily shored up to preserve it, at the RSPB's Loch Garten reserve. The ospreys returned by themselves. Two other magnificent birds of prey have been reintroduced to Scotland – the sea eagle, which is found on the west coast and around the Inner Hebrides, and the red kite, which is now found in many areas including Galloway in the southwest and the Black Isle north of Inverness in the Highlands.

Small lochans dot the Scottish Highlands and many are home to the wild and exciting black-throated and red-throated divers, large diving birds with long pointed beaks and an eerie wailing cry that conjures up untamed nature and which can raise the hairs on the back of your neck when it rises through the darkness of a mountain night. A less disturbing but still piercing cry is the thin whistle of the common sandpiper, a summer visitor found beside many streams and lochs and often seen scuttling along the shore and bobbing up and down on rocks. In rushing streams and the shallower rivers live dippers, small dumpy birds with white breasts that fly straight into the water and swim through it.

Along the coast and on lower lochans and rivers grey herons can be seen standing hunched over the water, watching silently for fish or frogs. Sometimes they can be seen flying lazily, their huge wings flapping slowly, looking almost pterodactyl-like with their long necks and beaks and long trailing legs. Various ducks, geese and swans may be seen on both inland and sea lochs. On the coast cormorants and shags, slightly primeval-looking dark birds that often hold their wings out wide, perch on rocks or fly lower over the water. Further away from land, and often seen from ferries en route to the islands, rafts of guillemots and razorbills float on the sea while fat puffins with their fantastically striped beaks flap their little wings furiously as they skim above the waves. Much more graceful and agile are the cream coloured gannets that stop suddenly in the air and then plunge, missile-like, straight down into the sea for fish.

There are many, many more birds to be seen. A good field guide is useful for identification. Of the many available a good one for Scotland is Valerie Thom's *Scottish Birds* (Collins, 2005).

If you are interested in wildlife I suggest carrying a small lightweight pair of binoculars. These will make watching birds and animals easier and lessen the temptation to get too close to them, which can cause stress and drive them away from essential food sources or their nests or young.

This only touches on the wonderful variety of life in the Scottish hills of course. There are adders and frogs, butterflies and beetles and many more interesting creatures. To identify these there are many good field guides. Two series I like and use regularly are the Mitchell Beazley Pocket Guides, which are light enough to carry in the pack, and the Collins Pocket Guides, which are a bit heavier but more detailed.

For those who wish to know more in general about the natural history of the Scottish hills *Hostile Habitats: Scotland's Mountain Environment: A Hillwalker's guide to Wildlife and Landscape* edited by Nick Kempe and Mark Wrightman (SMT, 2007)

is recommended as an introduction. Also good is F. Fraser Darling and Morton Boyd's classic *The Highlands and Islands* (Penguin, 1989), first published in 1964. The history and prospects for the forest are described in two excellent books: *People and Woods in Scotland: A History* edited by T.C. Smout (Edinburgh University Press, 2002) and John Fowler's *Landscapes and Lives: The Scottish Forest Through The Ages* (Canongate, 2003). There is also much fascinating material in *Flora Celtica: Plants and People in Scotland* by William Milliken and Sam Bridgewater (Birlinn, 2004). The books of Seton Gordon, one of the great Scottish naturalists of the 20th century, are worth seeking out too. A selection from them is available, called *Seton Gordon's Scotland*, edited by Hamish Brown (Whittles, 2005). Scottish Natural Heritage has a selection of interesting publications in their Naturally Scottish series, covering everything from Red Squirrels to Red Kites (www.snh.org.uk). The Scottish Wildlife Trust publishes a magazine, *Scottish Wildlife*, three times a year.

NATURAL HISTORY BOOKS

Days of the Golden Eagle by Seton Gordon (Whittles, 2002)

Flora Celtica: Plants and People in Scotland by William Milliken and Sam Bridgewater (Birlinn, 2004)

Hostile Habitats: Scotland's Mountain Environment: A Hillwalkers' Guide to Wildlife and Landscape edited by Nick Kempe and Mark Wrightman (SMT, 2006)

Landscapes and Lives: The Scottish Forest through the Ages by John Fowler (Canongate, 2003)

People and Woods in Scotland: A History edited by T.C. Smout (Edinburgh University Press, 2002)

Scottish Birds by Valerie Thom and Norman Arlott (Collins, 2005)

Scottish Wild Flowers by Michael Scott (Collins, 2005)

Seton Gordon's Scotland edited by Hamish Brown (Whittles, 2005)

The Highlands and Islands (New Naturalist Series) by F. Fraser Darling and Morton Boyd (Penguin, 1989)

Natural History Organisations

- **RSPB Scotland**, Dunedin House, 25 Ravelston Terrace, Edinburgh, EH4 3TP
  ☎ 0131 3116500 email rspb.scotland@rspb.org.uk www.rspb.org.uk

- **Scottish Natural Heritage**, Great Glen House, Leachkin Road, Inverness, IV3 8NW
  ☎ 01463 725000 email enquiries@snh.gov.uk www.snh.org.uk

- **Scottish Wildlife Trust**, Cramond House, 3 Kirk Cramond, Edinburgh, EH4 6NZ
  ☎ 0131 3127765 email enquiries@swt.org.uk www.swt.org.uk

- **Trees for Life**, The Park, Findhorn Bay, Forres, IV36 3TZ
  ☎ 01309 691292 email trees@findhorn.org www.treesforlife.org

- **Borders Forest Trust**, Monteviot Nurseries, Ancrum, Nr Jedburgh, Roxburghshire, TD8 6TU
  ☎ 01835 830750 email enquiries@bordersforesttrust.org www.borderforesttrust.org

The huge cairns of the Three Brethren on Minchmuir on the Southern Upland Way

MOUNTAIN ACTIVITIES

Peakbagging, Hillwalking and Scrambling

Scotland has some of the wildest and most chal-lenging walking country in Europe. The main mountain activity for walkers is peak bagging, as all bar a very few summits can be reached by rough walks or easy scrambles without any technical climbing. With 284 Munros (summits over 3000 feet, 914.4m), 219 Corbetts (summits between 2500 and 3000 feet, 762–914m) and 224 Grahams (summits between 2000 and 2500 feet, 609.6–762m) plus associated tops and lower hills there are plenty of peaks to climb.

Hillwalking takes place year round, but basic winter mountaineering skills are needed when there is snow on the hills. Scrambles on steep and exposed ridges such as the Aonach Eagach in Glencoe and Liathach in Torridon become serious technical undertakings in winter conditions.

Paths

Most paths in Scotland are not waymarked, although many have cairns, sometimes at intermit-tent intervals. Walkers and mountaineers need to be able to navigate with map and compass and/ or GPS. Navigation skills are not hard to learn and

mean you will have the freedom of the hills and be able to deal with poor visibility (not uncommon in the Scottish hills) and paths that are hard to follow or which fade away.

Long Distance Routes

Scotland has four officially designated Long Distance Routes, managed by Scottish Natural Heritage: the West Highland Way, the Southern Upland Way, the Great Glen Way and the Speyside Way. All the official routes are waymarked with a thistle sym-bol. There are many more 'unofficial' long distance routes, such as the Highland High Way from Drymen to Fort William (a high-level alternative to the West Highland Way), the Rob Roy Way (see 2:3), the Cape Wrath Trail (see 5:11 and 6:8), the Sutherland Trail (see 6:9) and the Skye Trail (see 7:5), and often these routes have their own guidebooks, details of which are given in the relevant chapters.

However you don't need someone else to design a long distance walk for you. It's much more challenging, exciting and fulfilling to plan your own and in Scotland this is quite feasible and the opportunities are many. I've crossed the Highlands from coast to coast by 13 different routes, walked from the English border to John O'Groats, from the southernmost to the northernmost Munro, from Fort William to Ullapool, and over all the Munros and

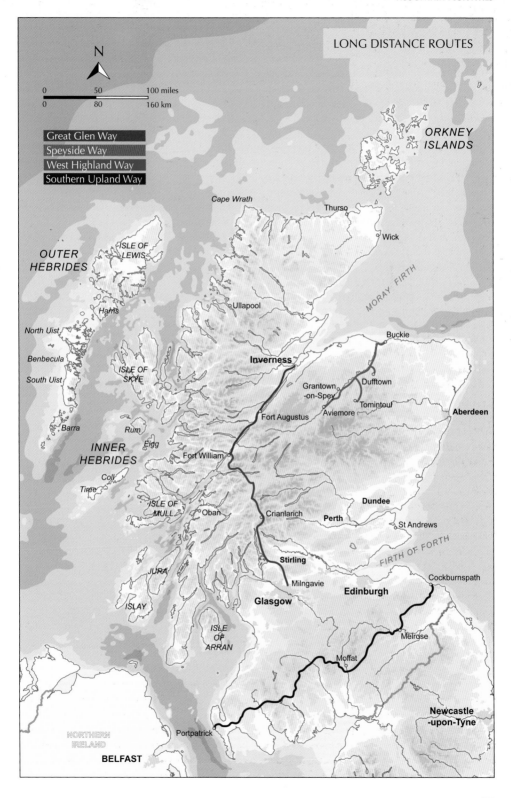

LONG DISTANCE ROUTES

N

| 0 | 50 | 100 miles |
| 0 | 80 | 160 km |

Great Glen Way
Speyside Way
West Highland Way
Southern Upland Way

ORKNEY
ISLANDS

Cape Wrath

Thurso

Wick

OUTER
HEBRIDES

ISLE OF
LEWIS

MORAY FIRTH

Harris

Ullapool

North Uist

Benbecula

ISLE OF
SKYE

Buckie

South Uist

Inverness

Grantown
-on-Spey

Dufftown

Tomintoul

Barra

Rum

Eigg

Fort Augustus

Aviemore

Aberdeen

INNER
HEBRIDES

Fort William

Coll

Tiree

ISLE OF
MULL

Oban

Crianlarich

Dundee

Perth

St Andrews

JURA

Stirling

FIRTH OF FORTH

Milngavie

Edinburgh

Cockburnspath

ISLAY

Glasgow

ISLE
OF
ARRAN

Melrose

Moffat

NORTHERN
IRELAND

Portpatrick

Newcastle
-upon-Tyne

BELFAST

53

Tops on one continuous walk, not to mention many shorter walks of a week or so. Link the coasts, two towns or a series of summits or plan a circular route (round the Cairngorms, round the coast of Skye) and off you go. Routes can follow glens or coastlines or go over the summits. One of the most unique and imaginative walks, first done by Dave Hewitt in 1987 and described in his book *Walking the Watershed* (TACit, 1994), was along the watershed of Scotland from Hobb's Flow on the border with England to Cape Wrath. *TGO* magazine organises a popular coast-to-coast walk in the Highlands called the TGO Challenge, for which entrants plan their own route. See www.tgochallenge.pwp.blueyonder. co.uk for more details.

The West Highland Way

Opened in 1980, the West Highland Way was Scotland's first official long distance walk. It's also the most popular with around 17,000 people walking the whole route each year and 50,000 people walking parts of it. The West Highland Way starts in the Lowlands at Milngavie near Glasgow, crosses the Highland Boundary Fault and runs through the Southern and Central Highlands to Fort William below Ben Nevis. En route the 152km (95-mile) path follows the east shore of Loch Lomond, runs through Glen Falloch and Strath Fillan below the Ben Lui and Beinn Dorain hill groups, crosses Rannoch Moor on the old Glencoe road below the Black Mount, passes by Buachaille Etive Mor and the mouth of Glencoe, climbs over the hills east of the Aonach Eagach via the Devil's Staircase and rounds the Mamores range via the Lairig Mor (Big Pass) before finishing in Glen Nevis. Despite the name it is mostly a low-level route, the highest point being the Devil's Staircase at 550m (General Wade's soldiers gave the pass its name when building a road here in the 1700s, as it was very arduous carrying building materials up the steep slopes).

The West Highland Way is never very far from roads and villages – Drymen, Crianlarich, Tyndrum, Bridge of Orchy, Kinlochleven – and there are also hotels and youth hostels outside the villages (Rowardennan, Inversnaid, Inveroran, Kingshouse) so walkers can stay in accommodation every night (or camp on official campsites), but wild camping is also possible and there are many splendid sites, especially if you venture a little off the route. You can even have your luggage transported by vehicle each day so you need carry only a light daypack. Some of the hotels along the route offer this service as well as Travel-Lite, who are independent of where you stay.

While the West Highland Way is an interesting and enjoyable walk, experienced and adventurous walkers may want to deviate from the official route and climb some of the fine hills to either side. Many walkers finish their trip by climbing Ben Nevis as well. Highlights of the route are the stretch along the side of Loch Lomond, on a rough path through fine deciduous woodland, and the track below the Black Mount across Rannoch Moor, where there is a real sense of wildness and remoteness, with steep rocky mountains towering above you.

Most people take 6–8 days to walk the whole way. Unsurprisingly the route is well signposted and easy to follow. Both Milngavie and Fort William can be reached by bus and train, with direct services from Glasgow. More details of the West Highland Way can be found in Chapter 2, section 2:4, and Chapter 3, section 3:4.

Information

www.west-highland-way.co.uk
www.travel-lite-uk.com

Guidebooks

The West Highland Way by Terry Marsh (Cicerone, 2009)
The West Highland Way: Official Guide edited by Bob Aitken and Roger Smith (Mercat, 8th edition, 2006)
The West Highland Way: Recreational Path Guide by Anthony Burton (Auram, 1996)
The West Highland Way by Jacquetta Megarry (Rucksack Readers, 2003)
West Highland Way by Charlie Loram (Trailblazer, 2006)
Not the West Highland Way by Ronald Turnbull (Cicerone 2010) – detours and ascents from the WHW staging posts

Maps

Harvey's West Highland Way.
The Footprint map of the West Highland Way

The Southern Upland Way

Scotland's first and only official coast to coast path runs 340km (212 miles) right through the Southern Uplands, from Portpatrick on the west coast to

Southern Upland Way waymark on Blake Muir with Innerleithen in the distance

Cockburnspath on the east. It is covered in detail in Chapter 1.

There are regular buses to Portpatrick from Stranraer, which can be reached by train, and from Cockburnspath to Edinburgh and Berwick-upon-Tweed.

Information
www.dumgal.gov.uk/southernuplandway
www.southernuplandway.com

Luggage Transfer
www.thewayforward.org

Guidebooks
The Southern Upland Way by Alan Castle (Cicerone, 2007)
The Southern Upland Way: Official Guide by Roger Smith (Mercat, 2005)
The Southern Upland Way: Recreational Path Guide by Anthony Burton (Auram, 1997)

The Great Glen Way
Opened in 2002, the Great Glen Way is Scotland's newest long distance path. It runs 117km (73 miles) along the length of the Great Glen fault line from Fort William northeast to Inverness, separating the Central and Western Highlands. More details will be found in 5:3.

Information
www.greatglenway.com
www.greatglenway.fsnet.co.uk

Guidebooks
The Great Glen Way: Two-way Trail Guide by Paddy Dillon (Cicerone, 2007)
Great Glen Way by Jacquetta Megarry and Sandra Bardwell (Rucksack Readers, 2005)
The Great Glen Way by Brian Smailes (Challenge, 2003)

Map
Harvey's Great Glen Way

The Speyside Way
The Speyside Way runs southwest from Buckie on the northeast coast of Scotland to Aviemore in the Cairngorms, along the valley of the River Spey, with spurs to Dufftown and Tomintoul. There are plans to extend the route further west, closer to the source of the Spey. The total current length,

including the side spurs, is 135km (84 miles) and the route takes around 5–7 days to walk. It's a low-level route and not completely in the hills, starting on the coastal plain and passing through farmland into wooded foothills and open moors before reaching the heights of the Cairngorms. It's a walk for those who like rivers and forests rather than high mountains. The walking is easy on good well-marked paths and there is plenty of accommodation along the way and plenty of potential distractions too, especially for those who appreciate malt whisky, as the way runs through the heart of whisky country and there are many opportunities for distillery visits. Aviemore is accessible by train and bus, while Buckie can be reached by bus from nearby Elgin, which is on the Inverness–Aberdeen rail line.

Information www.speysideway.org

Guidebooks
The Speyside Way by Alan Castle (Cicerone, 2010)
The Speyside Way by Jacquetta Megarry and Jim Strachan (Rucksack Readers, 2008)

Map Harvey's Speyside Way

Rock Climbing

Very few of Scotland's hills require even scrambling to reach the summits. However large cliffs abound in the mountains and there are thousands of rock climbs of every grade available on widely differing types of rock – granite, gabbro, gneiss, rhyolite, quartzite, schist, sandstone – and every sort of feature – huge slabs, narrow arêtes, steep gullies, overhanging crags, vertical walls and more. Some cliffs are easily accessible; some are remote and little visited.

From south to north major rock climbing regions on the mainland mountains include the Arrochar Alps, where there are many climbs on the mica schist of The Cobbler, a Corbett requiring a short scramble to reach the summit; Glen Coe, with a mass of classic and extreme climbs on the cliffs of the Buachaille Etive Mor, Bidean nam Bian and the Aonach Eagach; the northeast face of Garbh Bheinn in Ardgour; the tremendous north face of Ben Nevis, which is the largest cliff and has the longest routes in Britain; the cliffs of Coire Ardair,

Creag Meagaidh; the Cairngorms, especially the northeast corrie of Lochnagar, the eastern face of Beinn a'Bhuird, the Loch Avon basin with the great Shelter Stone Crag and the Northern Corries of Cairn Gorm; and Torridon, especially the Triple Buttress in Coire Mhic Fhearchair of Beinn Eighe. There is much climbing on the islands too, from the granite cliffs of Cir Mhor on Arran to the huge remote Sron Uladal on North Harris in the Outer Hebrides. The classic island for rock climbing is Skye, where there is a wealth of spectacular climbs on the most magnificent rock scenery in Scotland in the incomparable Cuillin.

Whether it's short steep hard routes or long mountaineering classics every type of rock climbing is to be found in the Scottish mountains. There are many opportunities for new routes too, and not just at the extreme end of the grades. You can climb on popular crags in the company of others or seek out remote cliffs where hardly anyone ever goes. Scottish climbing on mountain cliffs is traditional and adventurous in nature and the accepted ethics mean that bolts and pegs (except in winter) are not acceptable and that protection should be removed after use.

Guidebooks
Rock Climbing in Scotland by Kevin Howett (Francis Lincoln, 2004)
Scottish Rock Climbs by Andy Nesbit (SMC, 2005)
Scottish Rock: North and *Scottish Rock: South* by Gary Latter (Pesda Press, 2009 and 2008)

Winter Mountaineering

Under snow the Scottish mountains look and feel much bigger, grander and more exciting; the scars of summer vanish, paths and cairns are buried and hidden, and there is an alpine feel to the world. Although by the calendar winter lies between the winter solstice on 21 December and the spring equinox on 21 March, in the Scottish mountains winter conditions can occur any time between early October and late May and can last from a few days to several weeks. I've needed an ice axe in May on hills that were free of snow in January. Any ascent of a snow-covered hill is winter mountaineering and requires some snow skills and knowledge even if the climb is an easy plod through the snow. Basic ice axe techniques – self-belay and self-arrest – and crampon skills are needed, as is the ability to navigate in white-out conditions, plus an awareness and knowledge of avalanche danger. Short daylight hours, low temperatures, white-outs, strong winds and blizzards make the hills in winter much more serious than in summer. Although the temperatures aren't generally anything like as low as in higher mountain ranges the combination of damp air, strong winds and temperatures around zero makes for conditions in which staying warm and dry are more difficult than in colder, drier places. Good clothing suitable for Scottish winters is essential. In March and April daylight hours start to lengthen and the weather isn't usually quite as fierce as earlier in the season, so these can be the best months for winter mountaineering if there's any snow and ice.

SCRAMBLING AND CLIMBING GRADES

The grading of climbs is an imprecise process, and there can be much disagreement among mountaineers, but generally comparative grading gives an idea of the difficulty and seriousness of a route. Although usually listed separately scrambling and rock climbing grades merge into each other, with the hardest scrambles and easiest rock climbs overlapping. Under snow conditions scrambles should be graded as snow and ice climbs.

Scrambling Grades

- 1: Easy route finding, minimal hazards, little exposure, no technical difficulties, large holds
- 2: Short exposed sections, route finding skills needed, escape may be difficult in places
- 3: Some easy rock climbing, escape difficult, longer exposed sections. A rope is advisable except for experienced rock climbers
- 3S/4: Serious with much exposure, possibly short sections of lower grade rock climbing. For experienced climbers only

Rock Climbing Grades

- Moderate (M)
- Difficult (D)
- Very Difficult (VD or V Diff)
- Severe (S)
- Hard Severe (HS)
- Very Severe (VS)
- Hard Very Severe (HVS)
- Extremely Severe (E1 to E10)

Snow and Ice Climbing Grades

- I: snow gullies around 45° and easy ridges
- II: steep snow gullies and the easiest buttresses, possibly with short ice pitches and difficult cornice exits
- III: icy gullies, sustained buttresses with short technical sections
- IV: steep ice up to 60–70°, technically difficult mixed snow and rock routes
- V: steep ice up to 80°, mixed climbing with long technically difficult sections
- VI: vertical ice, very difficult and technical mixed terrain
- VII: long sections of vertical ice and/or very difficult and technical mixed climbing, possible overhanging sections
- VIII+: the hardest routes – long and extremely technical

Many summer hillwalks and scrambles become serious mountaineering expeditions in winter conditions, requiring good climbing skills and rope work. Frozen snow and ice can make even an easy summer walk a testing proposition. Some hills and ridges – for example Liathach, An Teallach and the Aonach Eagach (all Grade II climbs in winter) – have no easy ascent routes when under snow. And even seemingly gentle hills can have overhanging cornices that are invisible in blizzards (Beinn a'Chaorainn above Loch Laggan in the Central Highlands is notorious for this and several people have fallen through the cornices along the summit ridge into Coire na h-Uamha).

While many hillwalkers will find the easiest routes up snow-covered hills quite challenging enough, winter climbers seek out the steepest cliffs, gullies and ridges. There are winter climbs of all grades and types on the Scottish mountains, from traditional snow gullies via pure ice climbing up frozen waterfalls to steep buttresses where technically difficult mixed climbing on snow, ice and rock takes place. The main areas for winter climbing are the same as those for rock climbing, with pride of place and popularity going to Glen Coe, Lochnagar, Creag Meagaidh, the Northern Corries of Cairn Gorm and the North Face of Ben Nevis. The Cuillin Ridge in winter conditions is a major winter prize and a serious undertaking, but it's rarely in condition and never for very long.

Guidebooks

Scottish Winter Climbs: Scottish Mountaineering Club Climbers Guides by Andy Nisbet and Rab Anderson (SMC, 1996)

Scotland's Winter Mountains by Martin Moran (David & Charles, 1998)

Winter Climbs in Ben Nevis and Glen Coe by Mike Pescod (Cicerone, 2010)

Winter Climbs in the Cairngorms by Allen Fyffe (Cicerone, 2000)

Ski Touring and Ski Mountaineering

Despite the erratic snow pattern and marginal conditions there are five downhill ski resorts in the Highlands – Nevis Range just north of Fort William, the Glencoe Mountain Resort on Meall a'Bhuiridh in the Black Mount, Cairngorm Mountain on the northern slopes of the Cairngorms, Glen Shee in the southern Cairngorms and The Lecht on the eastern edge of the Cairngorms. Most of the year there is no snow and these resorts are just intrusive scars on the mountains, a tangle of bulldozed roads, the forlorn metal skeletons of the lifts and other detritus. When there is snow it's often blasted by the wind to an unpleasant hard, rutted, icy surface while storms frequently make skiing difficult or impossible. At times the snow can be soft and the weather kind and the skiing quite good, but overall I wouldn't recommend a Highlands resort for a downhill skiing holiday. If the lack of snow of the 1990s and 2000s continues the future of the resorts will be in doubt, unless they expand into areas other than skiing, as Aonach Mor is doing with mountain biking and summer gondola trips and Cairn Gorm with the year round funicular railway.

Although Scotland is a poor location for downhill ski resorts it can be a superb one for real skiing away from the tackiness and industrial desolation of the mountain despoiling mechanical junk. Long before ski lifts were thought of mountaineers were skiing in the Scottish hills. In 1892, just three years after the formation of the SMC one of its founders, W.W. Naismith, inspired by Nansen's account of the first crossing of Greenland, tried ski touring on the Campsie Fells just to the north of Glasgow. Naismith was impressed with the potential of skis and wrote in Vol II of the SMC *Journal* that 'skis might often be employed with advantage in winter ascents in Scotland'. (He also predicted, presciently, that skiing 'might eventually become popular' in the Alps.) Twelve years later, in Vol VIII of the *Journal* (1904) W.R. Rickmers wrote that 'skiing is to my mind the finest variety of mountaineering'.

In 1907 the Scottish Ski Club was founded with some tough membership requirements including 'five different tours of 15 miles each, ascending at least 3000 feet in all or three different tours of 25 miles each, ascending at least 4000 feet in all'. All the tours had to be in Scotland and 'the main object of the qualification is to encourage touring'. These touring qualifications were dropped in 1945. Five years later the first Scottish ski tow was in operation on Mount Blair in Glen Shee and skiing was going downhill, literally and figuratively. The degeneration of skiing into mass industrial tourism ruined a number of Scottish mountainsides, but compared to the Alps Scotland was relatively untouched.

On the summit of Ben Macdui on a ski tour across the Cairngorm Plateau

Thankfully plans for the despoliation of Braeriach, Beinn a'Bhuird, Ben Wyvis and other mountains by ski resorts never came about.

Meanwhile the real skiers were still out there, touring in the mountains, rather than partaking in 'glorified tobogganing', as lift-served downhill skiing was described by one Theo Nicholson in a letter objecting to ski tows written in 1947. In 1953 Norman Clark achieved the first ski tour of the four 4000ft summits in the Cairngorms (Braeriach, Cairn Toul, Ben Macdui and Cairn Gorm). Nine years later in April 1962 the great Cairngorms expert Adam Watson added the summits of Beinn a'Bhuird and Ben Avon to these four on an impressive 16hr trip covering 61km and 2650m of ascent, all done on long skinny skis and while carrying ice axe, sleeping bag, camera, binoculars and food consisting of six tins of fruit. The establishment of long distance mountain ski tours, such as the classic Alpine Haute Route from Chamonix to Zermatt, led some ski mountaineers to try and establish a Scottish Haute Route. A 100-mile (160km) route was worked out, starting at Corndavon Lodge in the eastern Cairngorms, finishing in Fort William and going over Ben Avon, Beinn a'Bhuird, Ben Macdui, Cairn Toul, The Fara, Ben Alder, Sgor Gaibhre, Beinn na Lap, Sgurr Choinnich Mor, Aonach Beag, Carn Mor Dearg and Ben Nevis. The first traverse of this serious and demanding route took place in the spring of 1978 when David Grieve and Mike Taylor took a week to complete it, using bothies for accommodation.

The most dangerous skiing, as the name suggests, is extreme skiing, which in Scotland usually means the descent of steep gullies that are graded snow climbs, such as Aladdin's Couloir in Coire an t-Sneachda in the Northern Cairngorms.

Most skiers will be content on much easier terrain and much shorter routes. The opportunities in Scotland are many. Perhaps the most reliable and best ski touring is in the Cairngorms, but I must admit to a bias here as I live in the region and have skied there every year for over 25 years. The Ben Lawers range, Creag Meagaidh and the Monadh Liath also offer excellent skiing. The further west you go the steeper and more serious the skiing becomes and the more likely you are to spend as much or more time using ice axe and crampons as skis.

Climate change may wipe out Scottish snow and end any form of skiing (and winter climbing) but this hasn't happened yet (and a shift of the Gulf Stream southwards, which could be a result, would mean colder, snowier winters) and there are still many good ski touring days every winter. Even when the downhill resorts have a shortage of snow there may be plenty on the tops or even down in the forests.

Types of ski touring

There are three basic types of ski touring: Alpine, Telemark and Nordic. The last two also fall into the category known as Free-Heel, to distinguish them from alpine skiing with its locked down heel in descent. All are suitable for the Scottish hills. Alpine and Telemark gear is designed for maximum control on steep slopes so it's best suited to big mountains and long descents. Nordic gear is lighter in weight and easier and less tiring to use on flat and undulating terrain but doesn't give as much control on steep downhills. I'd choose light Telemark or Nordic gear (the categories do overlap) for touring in the Cairngorms, Monadh Liath or other rolling hills but heavy Telemark or Alpine for steeper mountains where the skiing is mostly up or down. Whatever the type of equipment climbing skins are very useful for long or steep ascents. Ice axe and crampons may be needed on all but the most gentle tours and snow shovels should be carried in case of avalanche or benightment when they can be used to dig a snow shelter. Avalanche knowledge is essential for skiing in avalanche terrain. Transceivers are useful if someone is buried in an avalanche and should be carried but they aren't substitutes for avalanche awareness and careful route selection.

Guidebooks

Ski Mountaineering in Scotland edited by Donald Bennett and Bill Wallace (SMC, 1987)

Ski Touring in Scotland by Angela Oakley (Cicerone, 1991) (Out of print but well worth seeking out)

History

Skisters: The Story of Scottish Skiing by Myrtle Simpson (Landmark Press, 1982)

A Century of Scottish Mountaineering edited by W.D. Brooker, Chapter 8: On The Boards (SMC, 1988)

Avalanche debris on A'Mharconaich above Drumochter Pass

MORE ABOUT MOUNTAIN ACTIVITIES

Instructional Books
Hillwalking by Steve Long (Mountain Leader Training UK, 2003)
Mountaincraft and Leadership edited by Eric Langmuir (Sport Scotland, 1995)
The Backpacker's Handbook by Chris Townsend (Ragged Mountain Press, Third Edition 2005)
The Hillwalker's Guide to Mountaineering by Terry Adby and Stuart Johnston (Cicerone, 2003)
The Mountain Skills Training Handbook by Pete Hill and Stuart Johnston (David & Charles, 2000)

Organisation
The Mountaineering Council of Scotland ☎ 01738 493942 www.mcofs.org.uk.
The MCoS is the representative body for hillwalkers, climbers and ski tourers in Scotland and provides a range of services as well as campaigning on access and conservation issues.

Training
Glenmore Lodge National Outdoor Training Centre, Aviemore, PH22 1QU
☎ 01479 861256 email enquiries@glenmorelodge.org.uk www.glenmorelodge.org.uk.

RESPONSIBLE MOUNTAINEERING

Avalanches
Snow brings with it the risk of avalanches and every winter mountaineer or ski tourer should understand the danger. The Scottish Avalanche Information Service issues daily avalanche warnings between mid-December and mid-April and these should always be checked before venturing onto snow-covered hills. Plan your route based on the level of forecast risk.

Avalanche forecasting is not precise however and even if the forecast is for low or moderate risk care should be taken and personal observations made. Digging snow pits to check the snow for any weak layers and doing shear tests is always worthwhile. If in doubt stay off potential avalanche terrain.

Avalanches occur when a layer of snow isn't bonded adequately to the snow or the ground below. Soft snow lying on an icy layer is a classic avalanche scenario. Snow build-up on smooth steep terrain can also be dangerous. One notorious place for avalanches is the Great Slab in Coire Lochain in the Northern Cairngorms, a fairly smooth steep section of rock at the back of the corrie on which snow builds up but doesn't stick well. It avalanches every year, often several times.

The greatest period of risk is during and immediately after a heavy snowfall but that doesn't mean the snow is guaranteed to be safe at other times. In Scotland the greatest risk is from windslab avalanches, usually triggered by their victims, due to the normally windy weather, which redistributes snow on the lee side of slopes. Slopes in the range of 30–45° are where slab avalanches are most likely to occur. Convex slopes, where the snow is stretched, are more dangerous than concave ones, where the snow is compressed. Ridges are usually safe from avalanche danger, unless there is a double cornice, which can occur in unexpected places. Always stay well away from cornice edges, as the fracture line may be further back than expected if they collapse. Climbers should beware of cornice collapse from above when the snow is unstable. In case of avalanche it is advisable to carry a snow shovel and an avalanche transceiver (and practise with them).

Guidebook
A Chance in a Million? – Scottish Avalanches by Bob Barton and Blyth Wright (SMT, 2nd edition 2000)

Information
Scottish Avalanche Information Service
www.sais.gov.uk

Mountain Rescue
Scotland is served by a network of well-trained volunteer mountain rescue teams. If necessary they are backed up by the RAF Mountain Rescue with helicopters. There is no charge for rescue but donations to the teams are always welcome. To call out

the mountain rescue dial 999 and ask for mountain rescue. Anyone calling out a rescue team should provide them with as much information as possible including names and numbers of victims, precise location, nature of injuries and weather conditions.

If in need of assistance the recognised international distress signal is six blasts on a whistle or flashes of a light, followed by a minute's pause and then repeated.

Website
Scottish Mountain Rescue Committee
www.mrc-scotland.org.uk

Access

Scotland's access rights are some of the best in the world and mean that you don't need to worry about whether you are trespassing or need permission to be on a hill. In few other countries is there a right of access to virtually all land, regardless of owner. As far as the mountains are concerned there has always been a de facto right of access in most areas. Since the Land Reform (Scotland) Act 2003 was passed this has become a statutory right that includes the right to camp wild as well as to walk and climb. Many people worked for many years to achieve these rights and walkers and mountaineers should give thanks that they did so.

The right of access involves responsibilities both for those taking access and for landowners and managers. These responsibilities can be summed up as respect for the environment (don't wreck it!), respect for other people and taking care of yourself. All this is covered in the *Scottish*

Scottish Rights of Way Society signpost

Outdoor Access Code, issued in book form, and on the web, by Scottish Natural Heritage (2005). Despite what has been written elsewhere these responsibilities are not onerous or complex but are mostly a matter of commonsense, politeness and respect. The key to remember with access is that it is a right that applies to everyone unless they misbehave. Landowners have responsibilities too, the main one being not to hinder access. Unless there is a very good reason (such as dangerous agricultural or forestry work) land managers have no right to restrict access and when they need to do so it should be for a specific area and for as short a time as possible. Signs or notices stating that access isn't allowed or trying to deter access by implying danger from firearms – 'high powered rifles in use' – or animals (I've even seen a sign reading 'Danger, Stags') are against the spirit of the access rights and can be ignored.

Stalking

Deer stalking has been used by a minority of estates as a reason to try and keep people off the hills for several months of the year (and more in some places). The right of access means that estates cannot do this (they never had a legal right to do it previously). The stag stalking season runs from 1 July to 20 October, although on most estates stalking doesn't begin until mid August. Stalking doesn't usually take place on Sundays. Avoiding stalking where possible helps maintain good relations between walkers and mountaineers and landowners. Estates should offer alternative routes and only request people to stay out of specific corries rather than to keep off a hill range altogether. Some estates put up notices at access points to provide this information. An increasing number are members of the Hillphones scheme, organised by the Mountaineering Council of Scotland and Scottish Natural Heritage, where you can ring to hear a recorded message telling you where stalking is taking place. Phone numbers and information on the estates involved are available on the Hillphones website and in an annual booklet.

Information
Scottish Outdoor Access Code
www.outdooraccess-scotland.com
Hillphones www.hillphones.info

Footpath Trust sign

ENVIRONMENTAL ETHICS

Although the Scottish hills are wild and beautiful they are under pressure from various sources, including commercial forestry, mass industrial tourism (ski resorts, funicular railways, gondolas, car parks, visitor centres), bulldozed roads, 4WD tracks, over-grazing, wind farms, hydroelectric schemes, electricity pylons and other developments. Over the years these have gradually reduced the wildness of too much of the Highlands. I hope that all who love the Scottish hills would like to give something back and I urge everyone to support the organisations working to conserve and restore the hills such as the John Muir Trust, the National Trust for Scotland, the Scottish Wild Land Group and the Mountaineering Council of Scotland. Scotland's wild land is unique and precious and is worth fighting for.

Although the real threats to the beauty and wildness of the hills come from industry rather than mountaineers we do have an impact. Minimising this needn't be difficult or tedious and is well worth doing. Without care popular paths can easily become eroded scars and oft-used campsites shabby and worn.

Leave no Litter
The basic principle is to leave nothing. All litter should be taken home and it can help if you carry a plastic bag to put other people's rubbish in too. Litter includes orange peel and other organic matter as well as paper and plastic.

Paths
Hill paths are a mixture of purpose-made walkers' paths, old stalkers' and shepherds' paths, sheep tracks that walkers have turned into footpaths and paths that exist because walkers have followed each other, usually up and down the quickest, most direct routes. Well-located and well-constructed paths can withstand countless pairs of feet. However many paths are not well designed or built and are easily damaged.

The ideal path is only wide enough for one person, as that has the least physical and visual impact on the land. To ensure narrow paths stay like this walkers should go in single file. Walk side by side and you break down the edges, widening the trail, damaging vegetation and leading to erosion and unsightly scars.

Multiple trails through bogs and soft ground mar too many places. Often the cause is a desire to keep your feet dry. The original line of the path slowly sinks under the pressure of boots and, sometimes, mountain bike tyres and water begins to collect in hollows, forming puddles and muddy sections. To avoid the expanding bogs people walk round the edges, widening the path and allowing the water to spread. Over time the trail becomes a wide muddy morass with many bypass trails curving out to the sides as walkers try to keep their feet dry. To avoid this think of the path rather than your feet and stick to the main line even if it does mean muddy boots and possibly damp feet. Where the old path is impossible to find in the deep churned up mud try not to spread out at the sides but stay on the already damaged ground. If you really want to keep your feet dry wear gaiters or waterproof socks rather than tiptoeing round the edge of boggy paths. Alternatively, splash through the first puddle and get your feet wet. After that it doesn't matter.

Zigzags or switchbacks are often found on stalkers' paths and paths that have been realigned. They are easier to ascend and less likely to break down due to erosion than paths that go straight up. A zigzagging path can be a joy to climb and is much easier on the knees in descent than a steep one. However too often people choose a direct line and cut the corners of zigzags. This damages the vegetation, which results in the soil breaking down and ruts appearing, down which water runs, soon turning the shortcut into a wide scar. On some paths it can be hard to follow the original line, as so many shortcuts have been made. As well as not using shortcuts you can block them off with rocks or stones to discourage others from using them so that the land has a chance to heal.

Path maintenance and construction is costly – many agencies have little money for this – and takes a long time. Where path repairs are being undertaken following the requests of the work party can prevent further damage being done. And when repairs have been done please stick with the new path so that damaged areas can recover. New paths can stand out and may initially appear worse than the scars they replace but in time they should weather and blend into the hillside.

Cross Country

Leaving paths behind can be exciting and adventurous. It also brings you into closer contact with the land, no longer held at arms length by that strip of brown earth or grey stone. However the potential for damage is greater too. The main thing to avoid is creating a new path. A group should spread out and not walk in single file, as this could leave the beginnings of a path. Quite a few paths developed because someone took a particular route and others then followed the faint trail they made. Don't build cairns either, as these just about guarantee that others will follow. In fact new cairns in a pathless area could be dismantled and the stones scattered (on a non-vegetated area to avoid damage) so they won't attract others.

Wild Camping

Regularly used sites in the hills are all too often very obvious due to rings of stones on the ground, patches of bare dirt or flattened vegetation and litter sticking out from under rocks. Often there is network of paths too, leading to the nearest water, back to the main path and off into areas used for toilets.

When using a site like this the aim should be not to spread the damage and, if possible, to reduce it. Not using these sites may seem a good idea but if all that means is that you camp close by it could spread the damage, which would be even worse. If possible well-used sites should be tidied up and any litter removed. Rings of stones, often used to hold down tent pegs – usually unnecessarily – can be broken up and the stones returned to the nearest pile of rocks or put in the nearest stream. Rings of stones pockmark vegetation and destroy the wild feel of a place. Over the years I have spent hours dismantling such rings.

Much wild camping takes place on little or never before used sites. With these the idea should be to leave no sign of your camp. Firstly, this means camping on durable ground that won't be easily marked. Dry ground or at least well-drained ground is best for this as soft ground is easily marked. Grass is ideal. Such sites are more comfortable too. If your site does start to flood move rather than dig drainage ditches.

A good site is found not made. If you need to clear vegetation or rocks to turn somewhere into a campsite it's better to go elsewhere.

When walking round a site or going to fetch water stick to hard ground if possible and try not to create the beginnings of paths. If you carry a large water container you can collect all you need in one go so you don't tramp back and forth to the nearest stream or pool, possibly damaging the bank and

Wild camping in the Beinn Dearg hills, Northern Highlands

making a path that others may follow. In stormy weather this makes camping more comfortable too as you can stay in your tent.

Unless there's no choice don't camp right next to water, however; especially, avoid small upland lakes as you might disturb animals and birds that live there and depend on this habitat.

Wild sites should ideally only be used for one night, especially high up, where the ground is more vulnerable to damage. If you want to stay in an area longer move your camp, unless it's on a really durable surface such as bare ground. Staying in the same place for several nights can damage the vegetation under your tent and round the site, leaving a scar and a string of little paths radiating in all directions.

Before leaving a site check nothing has been left behind, including any scraps of litter, and fluff up any flattened vegetation. It should look as if no one has camped there.

Camp Fires and Stoves

Campfires are traditional, romantic and potentially very damaging. First there is a general fire risk in dry conditions, especially in areas with much peat or in woodland. Then there is a shortage of fuel in many wild areas and what dead wood there is should be left for the animals, birds and insects that need it. If there's enough wood for a fire collect it from a wide area rather than stripping one place bare. And never ever break branches off living trees. Standing dead trees should be left alone too. Birds nest in them and they can add to the scenic attractions of an area.

Unless carefully built and sited fires leave scars too, blackening rocks and leaving patches of bare burnt earth in meadows. The only places it's really acceptable to have campfires is in bothies with proper fireplaces and below the high tide mark if there is plenty of washed up wood. Instead of a fire rely on a stove for cooking and clothing and a sleeping bag for warmth.

Low profile stoves can scorch vegetation however so it's best to find a flat rock to stand them on or else carry a thin sheet of aluminium foil to put under the stove. If the midges and the rain let you cook outside your tent porch look for a kitchen site that will stand being used regularly. Bare ground or rock is ideal. Soft vegetation is easily damaged.

Alterations to kitchen areas should be unnecessary. If you want a seat sit on a rock or your foam pad. Try and keep the kitchen area clean as spilt food and litter attract scavenging birds, like crows and gulls, which may then prey on local species. If you do drop or spill anything it's best to pick it up straight away. It's easy to forget otherwise. (This applies to lunch and snack stops too. There is evidence, for example, that the crow and gull population in some parts of the Cairngorms has increased in part because of food scraps left by walkers.) Food scraps include food that has burnt onto your pan. Scrape this off and into a plastic bag and take it home for disposal. Wash dishes and pans away from water too and dump the wastewater into vegetation rather than streams or pools.

Sanitation

Too often at a wild campsite or a good lunch spot one of the first things you notice are ugly strands of soiled pink toilet paper creeping out from under a nearby rock. It's even worse if this is in the middle of the site or next to the stream you are planning on drinking from. As well as unsightly it's potentially unhealthy. There is still clean water in the Scottish hills. If we want it to stay this way then sensible toilet practices are essential. What this means is burying faeces and toilet paper or, preferably, carrying the latter out in a sealed plastic bag (loo paper can be burnt but only if there's absolutely no chance of starting a fire.) Toilet sites should be situated at least 30m from running water if possible (difficult in some wet areas). They should also be well away from paths and anywhere people might camp or stop for lunch. Carry a small trowel to dig a hole. In winter an ice axe can be used – but there's no point in just burying excrement in snow that will melt in the spring, so you'll need to find some bare ground or somewhere where the snow cover is thin. Campers can use a tent peg as a digging tool. Following burial, replace the excavated earth to fully cover the site.

Plant and Animal Life

The fauna and flora are part of the beauty and attractions of the hills. Care should be taken to minimise disturbance to them. Never pick flowers, many of which are protected by law, but also tread carefully and try to avoid crushing them. High in the hills ground-nesting birds such as dotterel, golden plover and ptarmigan are easily disturbed. Many walkers will be familiar with ptarmigan trailing apparently broken wings as they try and lure you away from their eggs or young. If birds or animals seem agitated by your presence move away or detour round them. In winter try not to disturb herds of deer. Survival in harsh weather is difficult enough without having to expend energy running away from humans.

INFORMATION AT A GLANCE

Formalities Any visitor from outside the United Kingdom needs a valid passport. Visitors from outside the EU may also require visas. Visa requirements can change rapidly.

Health precautions No essential inoculations are required for foreign visitors.

International dialling code The code for calling Scotland from abroad is 00 44.

Languages English is standard. Gaelic is spoken in some areas, especially in the western Highlands and on the Islands. Scots may be heard in many places too.

Mountain Bothies Mountain Bothies Association www.mountainbothies.org.uk. Contact the Mountaineering Council of Scotland (see below) for details of mountaineering clubs and club huts.

National Mountaineering Organisation
The Mountaineering Council of Scotland ☎ 01738 493942 www.mcofs.org.uk

Walking The Rambler's Association Scotland ☎ 01577 861222 www.ramblers.org.uk/scotland

National Tourist Office Visit Scotland ☎ 0845 2255121 www.visitscotland.com

CHAPTER 1: THE SOUTHERN UPLANDS

The Galloway, Carsphairn, Lowther, Tweedsmuir, Moorfoot and Lammermuir Hills and the Southern Upland Way

THE SOUTHERN UPLANDS: CHAPTER SUMMARY

Location
From the border to the Midland Valley

☆ Highlights

⬤ LOW-LEVEL/PASSES WALK
- Glen Trool (1:2)

⬤ SUMMIT WALK
- The Merrick (1:2)
- White Coomb (1:5)

⬤ OTHER HIGHLIGHTS
- Sanquhar (1:3)

Contents

◄ View along Loch Skeen to Lochcraig Head, Tweedsmuir Hills

The chain suspension bridge over the river Tweed in Melrose, Southern Upland Way ▶

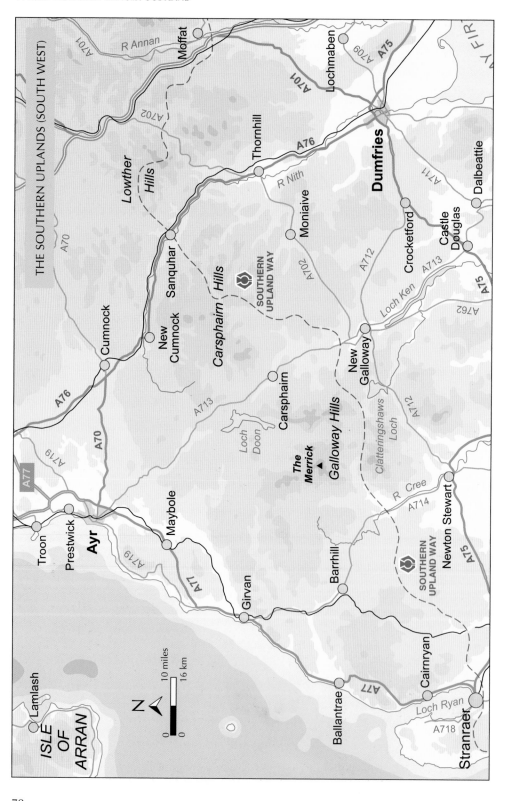

THE SOUTHERN UPLANDS (SOUTH WEST)

R Annan
Moffat
A701
A702
Lochmaben
A709
A75
A701
Lowther Hills
Thornhill
A76
R Nith
Dumfries
A711
Dalbeattie
Moniaive
Crocketford
Castle Douglas
A712
A75
Sanquhar
Carsphairn Hills
SOUTHERN UPLAND WAY
A702
A713
A762
Cumnock
New Cumnock
A76
A713
Carsphairn
Loch Ken
New Galloway
Galloway Hills
A712
A70
Loch Doon
Clatteringshaws Loch
A719
A77
A70
Maybole
The Merrick ▲
R Cree
A714
Newton Stewart
A75
Troon
Prestwick
Ayr
A719
A77
Girvan
Barrhill
SOUTHERN UPLAND WAY
Lamlash
N
10 miles
16 km
0
0
ISLE OF ARRAN
Ballantrae
A77
Cairnryan
Loch Ryan
A718
Stranraer

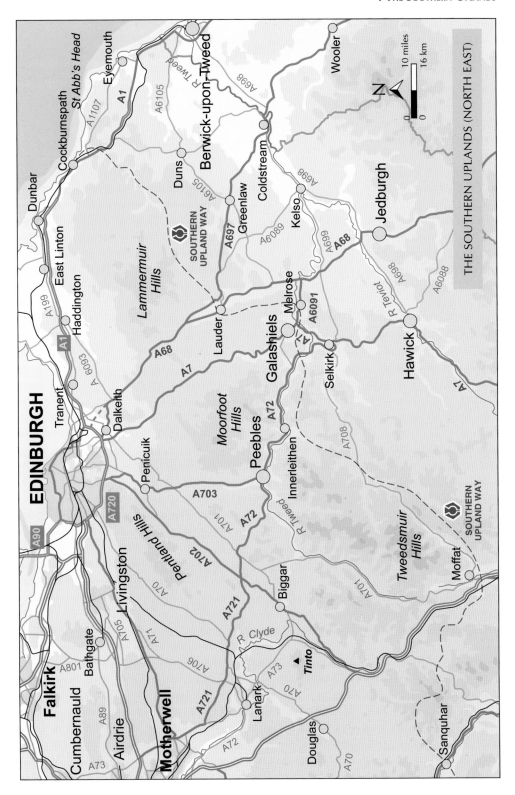

THE SOUTHERN UPLANDS (NORTH EAST)

INTRODUCTION

*There was no plan of campaign in my head, only just to go on and on
in this blessed, honest-smelling hill country.*
John Buchan, *The Thirty-Nine Steps*

Scotland's southernmost hills roll right across the country from west to east, separating Scotland from England. Their southern boundary is the Solway Fault, running northeast from the Solway Firth to near Berwick-upon-Tweed, which marks the line where Scotland and England collided and joined together around 420 million years ago as the Iapetus Ocean separating them closed and the Caledonian mountains were built. The border with England is never far from the Solway Fault. Their northern boundary is the eponymous Southern Upland Fault, again running northeast, some 190km from just north of Stranraer to just south of Dunbar. Between these two geological fault lines lie 10,000km² of mainly rounded, rolling hills (these apt adjectives recur constantly in descriptions of this area). The underlying rocks

are sedimentary, mainly greywacke, a rather dull dark grey sandstone. These rocks were folded and deformed during the upheavals that built the Caledonian mountains, when they were scraped off the floor of the Iapetus Ocean and forced upwards and northwards as England and Scotland came together. Intrusions of granite into these rocks formed the Galloway and Cheviot Hills. The heat of these intrusions changed the greywacke, turning it into hornfels, a much harder metamorphic rock. In the Tweedsmuir Hills the highest summits are made of grit and quartzite, tougher more erosion-resistant rocks than greywacke.

Mostly the Southern Uplands are smooth, rounded, gently sloping hills covered with grass or heather (and conifer plantations in many areas). The lines of hills and the valleys between them – often

Wild camp by Loch Enoch, Galloway Hills

known here as dales, not glens, revealing a Norse rather than Gaelic influence – mainly follow the southwest to northeast trend of the faults bordering them. The hills we see today were carved by glaciers during the last ice age and have since been eroded by water to form a dissected plateau with summits of similar height, generally 450–600m although some rise to over 800m. In Galloway the granite and hornfels give rise to a much more rugged landscape with crags, rocky slopes and steep corries, more akin to much of the Highlands than the rest of the Southern Uplands. The hills are generally higher too, with The Merrick reaching 843m, and the walking far tougher, again more like that in the Highlands. The harder rocks of the higher Tweedsmuir Hills give rise to a slightly more rugged landscape than is usual in the Southern Uplands, too.

The valleys are long and winding with several big rivers. The Clyde, the major industrial river of Scotland, on whose banks great ships were once built and the city of Glasgow grew, rises in the Lowther Hills before winding its way north to the Lowlands. Another of Scotland's great rivers runs through the Southern Uplands, this one gentle and rural and known for salmon fishing and the wool products from the sheep that graze the hills and fields around it. The River Tweed begins not that far from the start of the Clyde in the Tweedsmuir Hills then heads east through Peebles, Melrose and Kelso before crossing the border into England to reach the North Sea at Berwick-upon-Tweed. The other two big rivers of the area are the Nith and Annan, which run south to the Solway Firth from either side of the Lowther Hills. Both provide important transport routes along their valleys from the south into central Scotland.

Generally the walking in the Southern Uplands is quite easy, either through heather or on grass. Slopes are usually only steep for short distances. Outside Galloway there are few crags. Navigation can be difficult in poor visibility, however, due to the lack of distinctive features. Although there are a few rock and ice climbs in the Galloway Hills and on outcrops elsewhere, and some scrambles in various places, the Southern Uplands are more hills for the walker than the mountaineer. There are no Munros and only seven summits are high enough for Corbett status; 21 are classified as Grahams.

Running from southwest to northeast the principal ranges in the Southern Uplands are the Galloway Hills, the Carsphairn Hills, the Lowther Hills, the Tweedsmuir Hills, the Moorfoot Hills and the Lammermuir Hills. To the south of these ranges lie the Cheviot Hills, which are split by the Solway Fault, and along which the Scottish–English border runs (although the highest summit, The Cheviot itself, is in England: as The Cheviot and the bulk of the range are in England, the Cheviots are not covered by this book). The last five ranges are part of the region known as the Borders. To the north lie outlying ranges, principally the Pentland Hills, that stretch right into the heart of Edinburgh, and also Tinto in the Clyde valley. Although beyond the Southern Upland Fault and so not technically part of the Southern Uplands from the hillgoers perspective, these hills fit best here.

1:1 THE SOUTHERN UPLAND WAY

Scotland's first and only official coast to coast path runs 340km right through the Southern Uplands, from Portpatrick on the west coast to Cocksburnspath on the east, and takes on average 12–16 days to complete. Walk this path and you will experience every type of landscape the Southern Uplands has to offer. The path was officially opened in 1984 at Tibbie Shiel's Inn by St Mary's Loch, where there is a commemorative plaque.

Coast to coast walks are satisfying and full of purpose. There is a sea to reach, an island to cross, a clear destination. Every day you stride out knowing that you are leaving one coast farther behind while another approaches. On reaching that once distant sea you know that you have crossed the country and seen all that lies in between. Yet

Southern Upland Way (SUW) sign

Walkers on the Minchmuir, SUW

despite the attractions the Southern Upland Way (SUW) is Scotland's most neglected long distance path. Only 2000 walkers are estimated to walk the whole route each year (and rangers along the way reckon the actual number is half that). When I walked the route, at the height of the summer, I was surprised to meet only a couple of other end to end walkers and not many day walkers. On most days I met no one.

Why this is so is unclear. Perhaps it's because the name isn't very inspiring. 'Southern Uplands' hardly stirs the blood or raises the spirits. The route has developed an unjustified reputation for being dull, for spending too much time in dingy conifer plantations and on metalled roads. Whatever the reason, the route's unpopularity is unjustified. The Southern Upland Way is a splendid walk. It won't attract those who like spiky, rocky mountains: rather it is for those who love quiet countryside, a complex, changing mosaic of woods, fields, rivers, lakes, moors and hills. It's not wilderness – human activity is apparent almost everywhere – but it is wild. The interaction of humanity and nature is an integral part of the route. Farming and forestry are the largest and most obvious human manifestations. Cattle, sheep and hay are seen in abundance, as are coniferous plantations, although the

latter are less dull and less extensive than is often thought, and furthermore the Forestry Commission has planted a mix of deciduous species in many places to provide variety and to encourage wildlife. Riparian restoration can be seen along many of the waterways too, from the Water of Trool in the west to the Tweed and its tributaries in the east, with new trees and bushes lining the streams. I found it heartening to see this return of nature. As these trees grow both the forests and the riversides will become more attractive and less monotonous, adding to the pleasures of the walk.

Forests may block some of the views but they – including some plantations – make excellent habitats for wildlife. Many birds live in the woods, including Scottish crossbills, goldcrests, siskins and short-eared owls, although they can be difficult to see among the trees. On the moors and hills kestrels and buzzards are common and hen harriers may be seen. Red grouse are likely to explode from the heather everywhere – some of the moors, especially in the east, are managed for grouse shooting. Smaller birds include wheatear, whinchat, stonechat, skylark and meadow pipit. Dippers live on the rivers, larger water birds such as mallards on the lochs. Animals are less common. I saw a few distant deer and rather more rabbits, plus one large adder lying on the path just a few steps away.

There is much history as well as natural history along the way. Historic buildings, relics and artefacts line the route, from prehistoric standing stones to mines, castles, abbeys and Victorian mansions, and even the least historically inclined walker is likely to find some of them of interest. In the west there are many reminders of the bloody history of the Covenanters in the 1680s, when Presbyterian followers of the National Covenant were hunted down and killed by English government troops. Walking down a quiet forest ride it's a sobering shock to suddenly come upon a memorial to Covenanters who were caught at prayer at this remote spot and shot. Some relics are curious and unexplained, such as the Wells of Rees in Killgallioch Forest, which are small dry stone domes built over tiny springs in the hillside. They are guessed to have had a religious purpose as there is said to have been a chapel nearby, but no one really knows. In total contrast is the great Victorian pile of Abbotsford on the banks of the River Tweed, home of Sir Walter Scott and where he wrote many of his novels. There is much to see in the attractive towns along the way too such as the castle, the tollbooth and Britain's oldest working Post Office in Sanquhar, the mining museum and old mine workings in Wanlockhead and the ruined abbey in Melrose.

Although there are no difficult ascents the route does climb over many hills, reaching 725m on Lowther Hill but mostly staying below 600m. In total end to end walkers will ascend and descend around 9000m. The lack of high summits doesn't mean the SUW is a gentle stroll. It requires stamina and hill knowledge. Mist can quickly cover the higher ground and the route is not all that clear on some moorland stretches despite the regular waymarking posts. The guidebooks are not updated very often either and may be inaccurate in places where the path has been relocated due to forestry operations. Cicerone's *The Southern Upland Way* by Alan Castle (2007) is the most up-to-date.

The Southern Upland Way is both longer and more remote than Scotland's other official Long Distance Routes, despite being the only one not in the Highlands. It is possible to have a warm bed and a hot shower every night, although this does require walking long distances (up to 40km) in places. Baggage transfer and vehicle support is available from Celtic Trails, Make Tracks and Walking Support, and from some of the hotels along the route. There are six bothies on or near

Wild camp on the SUW in the Galloway Hills

the way and wild camping is an option. An annual accommodation leaflet is published by Scottish Natural Heritage, Dumfries and Galloway Council and the Scottish Borders Council.

Portpatrick, at the western end of the path, is a little fishing village grouped round a tiny bay, from where the route heads north along the cliffs, with views over to Ireland and down into little coves and gullies. Seabirds wheel overhead. Starting in the west means the weather is likely to be at your back and the sun won't be in your eyes so this is the way I went, as do most end to end walkers. Soon the route turns inland to wind through a mix of neat sheep-cropped grassland, rough pasture, low moorland and forestry. Ahead the dark outline of the Galloway Hills draws the eye and keeps the feet moving.

The SUW stays low in the Galloway Hills, running through mixed woodland beside the dark pools and swirling eddies of the Water of Trool and then above beautiful Loch Trool with the higher heather-clad, rugged hills rising on the far side. All was calm and peaceful when I walked the Way, unlike my first visit here when I spent two days running round the hills in a big storm on the Karrimor Mountain Marathon. If there is time making a loop off the path, perhaps to Loch Enoch or even the summit of The Merrick, will give a taste of the hill country the SUW bypasses.

Beyond the Galloway Hills the path meanders east, dipping down into little towns and villages, climbing up through fields and forests to moorland hills and following meandering streams. Highlights abound, first the long, shaking suspension bridge over the placid Water of Ken leading into St John's Town of Dalry, then the view of dark hills and dark forest from Benbrack, which is followed by an exhilarating walk over Cairn Hill and Black Hill and along the edge of the forest to High Countam, a passage that gives a feeling of freedom and escape from the confines of the valleys. Then there are the stark ragged ruins of Sanquhar Castle and the high bleak mining village of Wanlockhead, where you can visit the mining museum and the old mines themselves; the dramatic landscape of the Selcloth Burn, a deep ravine where the SUW is just a narrow path high up with unstable slipping hillsides all around and a real mountain feel; and anywhere you might see short-eared owls and hen harriers hunting the forests and moors. Then there are the purple, heather-patched steep hills beyond

the waters of St Mary's Loch, the classic Border country between Traquair and Melrose – purple heather, rolling hills, little towns tucked into folds in the hills, winding rivers, woodland groves, big Victorian mansions – and the Three Brethren on Minchmuir, three huge, beautifully constructed cairns on a hilltop from where there is a splendid view of the eastern Southern Uplands. And there's Melrose Abbey, a gaunt golden Gothic ruin with an atmosphere of dilapidated and ruined grandeur that is attractive and impressive.

Eventually the hills slide away and the route reaches cliffs above a crashing sea, a mirror image of the start of the walk. Cove Harbour is a final point of interest before the last steps inland to the village of Cockburnspath and the finish. The SUW is a rich experience; a complex, interesting and thought provoking mix of nature, landscape and history. I recommend it.

There are regular buses to Portpatrick from Stranraer, which can be reached by train, and from Cockburnspath to Edinburgh and Berwick-upon-Tweed.

FOR MORE INFORMATION

Official website
www.southernuplandway.gov.uk

Luggage Transfer
www.celtrail.com and www.maketracks.net provide luggage transfer for the whole route, while www.walkingsupport.co.uk covers the eastern section.

Guidebooks
The Southern Upland Way by Alan Castle (Cicerone, 2007)
The Southern Upland Way: Official Guide by Roger Smith (Mercat, 2005)
The Southern Upland Way: Recreational Path Guide by Anthony Burton (Auram, 1997)

1:2 THE GALLOWAY HILLS

The finest hills in the Southern Uplands, the Galloway Hills are also the roughest and the wildest, a tangle of gritty boulders, black peat bogs, heather and water with many steep slopes. These are big, bulky, burly hills with broad shoulders and long arms. The walking away from lowland paths is not easy. At the heart of the range lie a series of wild remote lochs ringed by hills and ridges with stirring, evocative, charismatic names – the Rig of the Jarkness, the Rhinns of Kells, Shalloch on Minnoch, the Dungeon Hills, the Range of the Awful Hand, the Wolf Slock and many more. There are three Corbetts here – The Merrick, Shalloch on Minnoch and Corserine – and five Grahams – Craignaw, Mullwharchar, Lamachan Hill, Millfore and Cairnsmore of Fleet.

Much of the area lies in Forest Enterprise's 670km² Galloway Forest Park, which includes many high bare hills as well as forestry plantations. The latter form an awkward barrier in many places, restricting access to the hills to forest roads and those few places not bordered by the dense trees.

There is, sadly, little in the way of public transport in the region. Glentrool Village is accessible by bus from Newton Stewart and St John's Town of Dalry by bus from Dalmellington and Castle Douglas, and the Ayr–Castle Douglas bus service runs along the A713. Otherwise you need a car. The A75 is the main access road, running from Gretna on the M74 away to the east through Dumfries to Newton Stewart, although it stays well

to the south of the hills. The A712, A713, A714 and A762 then take you into the hills. The minor road to Glen Trool leaves the A714 some 14km north of Newton Stewart.

There is a hotel in Bargrennan, just outside Glen Trool, and self-catering and B&Bs plus a caravan and camping site in Glentrool Village. Other accommodation is further afield in the small towns and villages around the edges of the hills, with Newton Stewart and New Galloway the main centres. In the hills there are four bothies – Culsharg, Tunskeen, Backhill of Bush and White Laggan. Note that these are sometimes very busy, making a tent an attractive alternative. Camping in the hills gives more freedom anyway and there are many fine sites: time should be allowed to find dry spots among the bogs.

Glen Trool ☆

Glen Trool, in the southern part of the Galloway Forest Park, provides the main access to the hills and is a worthwhile destination in itself, with some fine natural woodland and beautiful long twisting Loch Trool backed by heather-clad rugged hills. 'Glen' is an appropriate name, as the scene looks more like the Highlands than the Southern

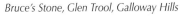

Bruce's Stone, Glen Trool, Galloway Hills

Uplands. A feature to look out for, just beyond the end of the public road, is Bruce's Stone, a massive granite boulder commemorating Robert the Bruce's victory in 1307 when his forces rolled boulders down on the soldiers of the English army as they threaded their way across the rough steep slopes above Loch Trool. This victory marked the turning point in his military campaign, leading seven years later to final victory at the Battle of Bannockburn and independence for Scotland. The Bruce's Stone is set on a knoll looking across Loch Trool to the site of the skirmish. The inscription on the stone reads 'In loyal remembrance of Robert the Bruce, King of Scots, whose victory in this glen over an English force in March 1307 opened the campaign of independence which he brought to a decisive close at Bannockburn on 24th June 1314'.

Glen Trool is the major walking centre for the Galloway Hills with many fine routes. There are several parking places along the road in the glen.

⚪ The Circuit of Loch Trool

This circuit is a pleasant 10km waymarked woodland walk with good views of the hills to the north. Starting at Caldons at the west end of the loch, the route follows the Southern Upland Way, here a narrow path through the oak and pine woods above the southern shore, to the Glenhead Burn 1km beyond the east end of the loch. En route it passes the site of the skirmish commemorated by the Bruce's Stone, marked by a noticeboard. The route leaves the Southern Upland way and crosses the Glenhead Burn to join the private road to Glenhead, which is followed east to the public road. The road can be followed all the way back to the start or else left once past Glen Trool Lodge for a forest trail that stays closer to the loch. The walk takes 2–3 hours.

⚫ The Merrick ☆

The ascent of The Merrick, the highest summit in the Southern Uplands, is the most popular hillwalk in the Galloway area. It lies at the heart of the Range of the Awful Hand, a fanciful name given to the group of hills running north from Glen Trool, whose shape supposedly resembles a hand. Merrick comes from the Gaelic *meurach*, which means branched like fingers. The Merrick is said to be the forefinger of the hand with Benyellary the thumb and Kirriereoch Hill, Tarfessock and Shalloch on Minnoch the other fingers.

Notice about the ascent of the Merrick, Glen Trool, Galloway Hills

A signpost marks the start of the standard and easiest route to the summit at the end of the public road, not far from Bruce's Stone. A clear path climbs steep open slopes past a series of impressive cascades and waterslides on the Buchan Burn before entering conifer forest for a couple of kilometres and passing Culsharg bothy. Beyond the trees the path climbs to the 719m summit of Benyellany and then on to the massive looming bulk of The Merrick. A wind shelter and trig point mark the summit. Below to the east lies Loch Enoch. This wild loch has a ragged, twisting shoreline with many bays and headlands, beaches of coarse white quartz sand and several islets and is set in a fine situation in the heart of the hills. An alternative route to The Merrick from Glen Trool goes via Loch Enoch to the summit. This route is much more arduous, much rougher underfoot and requires good navigation skills in misty weather. However I think it's much more interesting and enjoyable than the standard route, which can used in descent (round trip 14km, taking about 5hrs). The route via Loch Enoch starts with the clear but often muddy path from Glen Trool to Loch Valley and Loch Neldricken. From the last loch a rough intermittent path heads north over rocky, boggy, tussock covered ground to Loch Enoch from where an ascent can be made up pathless boggy broad Redstone Rig, which is quite steep in places and dotted with small rock outcrops, to the summit of The Merrick. A third route to the summit parallels the lochs route to the west over Buchan Hill and the Rig of Loch Enoch, and then also ascends Redstone Rig.

From The Merrick a fine 6km walk leads north to Shalloch on Minnoch (775m) via the summits of Kirriereoch Hill and Tarfessock. The terrain is mostly easier and drier than lower down, although there are some steep sections on loose rock. Shalloch on Minnoch is far from Glen Trool. Unless you are camping or bothying (Tunskeen, the Mountain Bothies Association (MBA)'s first bothy, renovated back in 1965, lies below the eastern slopes of the hill) you will need to retrace your steps, although the final climb back to The Merrick can be avoided by cutting below the summit to the east to Loch Enoch. Shalloch on Minnoch can be climbed on its own from Stinchar Bridge to the north and the Bell Memorial car park to the west. Both start points lie on the minor road from Bargrennan to Straiton.

Many other hills can be climbed from Glen Trool, including the Fell of Eschoncan (c360m), Lamachan Hill (716m), the oddly named Curleywee (674m: the name comes from *cor a gaoith* and means 'point of the wind'), Larg Hill (676m), the Dungeon Hills – Craignaw (645m), Dungeon Hill (620m) and Mullwharcher (692m) – and the Rig of Jarkness and Craiglee (531m). There are also some rock climbs on the south face of Dungeon Hill above the Dungeon Lochs.

⊗ Corserine and the Rhinns of Kells
West of The Merrick lies a long curving ridge almost completely surrounded by forestry plantations. This is the Rhinns of Kells whose high point, Corserine (814m), is the second highest summit in the Galloway Hills. The easiest access to Corserine is from Forest Lodge to the east, which is reached via a minor road that leaves the A713 at Polharrow Bridge, 3.5km north of St John's Town of Dalry. Forest tracks lead from Forest Lodge to Loch Harrow, beyond which the forest is left for an ascent of the North Gairy ridge to the summit. A descent can be made by heading south down the Rhinns of Kells to Meikle Millyea (746m) where you turn northeast and descend to the forest and tracks back to Forest Lodge. Total distance 16km, taking 5–6hrs.

For longer walks along the whole ridge a base in the hills is useful. There is a bothy, Backhill of Bush, in the forest west of the ridge, which can be reached from Glen Trool and from the car park at Clatteringshaws Loch. A tent gives even greater freedom.

1:3 THE CARSPHAIRN HILLS

The Carsphairn Hills are lonely grassy hills rising above boggy valleys to the northeast of the Galloway Hills. The name means 'valley of the alder trees', but today spruce plantations dominate the area, filling the valleys and covering the hills to above 500m in some places. The highest summit and the only Corbett is Cairnsmore of Carsphairn (797m). Two other hills have Graham status – Blackcraig Hill (700m) and Windy Standard (698m). The latter however has been ruined by a massive wind farm that covers the summit and surrounding ridges with concrete and steel windmills and bulldozed gravel roads. This destruction of the loneliness, remoteness and wildness of the hills is destroying the very environment worthy of protection. Is there no value in open space, peace and quiet, in places where the cry of birds, the whisper of the wind in the grass and the patter of rain are the only sounds and green hills, far horizons, clouds and the vast sky the only sights? Industrialisation of any sort has no place on wild land and should be restricted to already developed sites. The wind farm is a virulent eyesore that is the antithesis of everything natural. There is no peace now on Windy Standard and the intrusive wind farm spoils the enjoyment of the other summits.

Most of the area is made up of the greywacke rock that dominates the Southern Uplands. However Cairnsmore of Carsphairn is granite, like the Galloway Hills, and far more rugged than the other summits.

Access to the western side of the hills is via the A75, from the M74 at Gretna, to Dumfries, then up Nithsdale on the A76 to Thornhill and across to Carsphairn on the A702 and B729. For the eastern side of the hills stay on the A76 to Sanquhar. The Cumnock–Dumfries bus service runs along the A76, stopping at Sanquhar, and there is a train station at Kirkconnel just north of Sanquhar. All the villages and small towns around the hills offer accommodation and other services.

ⓘ Sanquhar ☆
This little town is of particular interest as it has the oldest working Post Office in the United Kingdom, dating from 1763, plus a tollbooth built in 1735 and the rather Gothic-looking, ragged ruins of Sanquhar Castle. Most of the remnant walls date from the 16th century but the first castle here was built 200 years earlier.

The ruins of 16th-century Sanquhar Castle, Sanquhar

THE COVENANTERS

Sanquhar was also a centre for the Covenanters and there's an obelisk marking the place where in 1680 the preacher Richard Cameron fixed a declaration renouncing allegiance to King Charles II and called for armed insurrection. Cameron and his followers were objecting to the King's removal of the right of Presbyterians to appoint their own ministers and the imposition of bishops and ministers on the Scottish church. The Covenant itself dated from 1638 and was a declaration that rejected attempts to impose episcopacy and called for independence from the crown and the Anglican Church for Presbyterianism. Before the Restoration of the Monarchy in 1660 the Covenant had been accepted, after the Restoration covenants became illegal and a bloody period known as the 'killing times' ensued from 1678 to 1690 during which government troops hunted down and killed covenanters. Cameron himself was killed by dragoons the same year he made the Sanquhar Declaration. Four years later James Renwick fixed the Sanquhar Protestation in the same place, again disowning the authority of the king. Eventually captured he was hanged in 1688, becoming one of the last of the Covenant martyrs as after the deposing of James VII (James II of England) the same year and the accession of the Protestant William and Mary to the throne persecution of the Covenanters ended. During the killing times Covenanters held meetings and services in remote spots in the hills where they were sometimes found and killed by troops. Every walker in the western Southern Uplands is likely to come upon Covenanter memorials deep in the hills and forests. There are Covenanter grave stones in Sanquhar churchyard.

⊗ Cairnsmore of Carsphairn

This ascent is the premier walk in the region. There are a number of different routes, some taking in other summits, all mostly on grass. The easiest route is from Green Well of Scotland on the A713

6km northwest of Carsphairn village. A track leads up to 420m. From its end the broad southwest ridge can be climbed to the summit where there is a trig point and substantial cairn. Alternatively the track can be left 1km before its end and the summit reached via Dunool, Black Shoulder and the south ridge. The round trip is 12km and takes 4–5hrs. From the east the hill can be climbed from Craigengillan on the minor road beside the Water of Ken, but much of this route lies in forestry plantations. If you want a close encounter with the wind turbines Windy Standard can also be climbed from Craigengillan and the ridge then followed south to Cairnsmore of Carsphairn (20km). This last route has the advantage of taking in the north ridge of Cairnsmore of Carsphairn, which is quite rocky with many granite boulders. The view from the summit in clear weather is excellent, except for those dreadful wind turbines.

⊗ Blackcraig Hill

This hill can be climbed from pretty Glen Afton, which runs south from New Cumnock. It's surprisingly rugged, with a line of broken crags overlooking Glen Afton. The ascent can be made from the glen via the track leading to Blackcraig farm. A path leads east from the farm to Quinton Knowe where you turn south to ascend the north ridge to the summit, which has a trig point and cairn. The return can be made by circling round the head of the Craig Burn valley via Blacklorg Hill to Craigbraneoch Rig, which can be descended

steeply through small crags back to Glen Afton. The distance is 13km and the walk takes 4hrs.

1:4 THE LOWTHER HILLS

The eastern fringes of the Lowther Hills can be seen from the M74, the main road route into Scotland, and the West Coast Main Line to Glasgow, one of the two main rail routes into Scotland. The western edges of the hills rise gently from the A76. Three roads run through the Lowthers as well, the A702, the B797 and the B740, making car access to these hills easy. Buses run along the A76, the A702 and the M74 and from Sanquhar to Wanlockhead.

The walking is mostly easy on these grassy, heathery, rounded hills. On the highest two, Green Lowther (732m) and Lowther Hill (725m), it's particularly easy as roads lead to the summits, the first of which is covered with radio masts and the second with the huge and strange golf balls of a Civil Aviation Authority radar station. This industrialisation makes these hills a destination for those who don't mind such developments in the wilds.

Radio and radar installations are only the latest human intrusions into these hills. Mining took place here for many centuries, perhaps even as far

Lowther Hill and Green Lowther from the east

back as the Romans. Gold was discovered in the Middle Ages but lead has been the main product, although silver and zinc have also been mined. By the 18th century mining was an important local industry and remained so until the 1950s, when the last mines closed.

> Mining is an important tourist attraction in this area. The main centres for mining were Leadhills and Wanlockhead, the highest village in Scotland at 467m. The Museum of Lead Mining in Wanlockhead is very interesting and not a little chilling if you try to imagine how grim conditions for the miners must have been as you view the displays on working and living conditions. Among the geological exhibits is a display of beautiful and colourful crystals. There is an excellent café at the museum. From Easter to September you can take a tour into the Loch Nell Mine. The mining artefacts, including a water-powered beam engine, and spoil heaps strewn along the Wanlock Water valley can be visited at any time.
>
> Leadhills is home to the oldest subscription library in Britain, founded by miners in 1741, which can be visited during the summer.

Away from the mining areas and the developed summits there are many gentle hills and quiet valleys worthy of exploration where few other walkers are likely to be seen. South and east of the A702, which crosses the range via the Dalveen Pass, lies a huge area of remote empty grassy moorland, the Southern Lowthers, whose highest summits are 697m Queensberry and 689m Ballencleuch Law. The Southern Upland Way cuts through the northern edge of these hills.

⊗ The Ascent of Green Lowther and Lowther Hill

This ascent can be combined with a visit to both Wanlockhead and Leadhills on an unusual 12km circuit that takes about 4hrs. From Wanlockhead the Southern Upland Way climbs across heather moorland to Lowther Hill, following the access road to the radar station in places. In misty conditions the giant golf balls can seem quite eerie as they fade in and out of the drifting cloud. A tarmac

road leads from Lowther Hill to Green Lowther, a strange walking experience at 700m. The radar station can arguably be viewed as interesting and even attractive. The collection of radio masts on Green Lowther is just ugly. A descent to the north leads to a reservoir and then a track past old mines to Leadhills. From the village, which has a bar, restaurant and shop, a path leads west of Wanlock Dod (551m) to the Wanlock Water valley where either the road or the Southern Upland Way can be taken back to Wanlockhead, viewing the relics of the mining era along the way.

1:5 THE TWEEDSMUIR HILLS

The Tweedsmuir Hills, which lie in a vast broad horseshoe around the headwaters of the River Tweed, contain the highest summits in the Southern Uplands outside of the Galloway Hills. Broad Law, at 840m, is just 3m lower than The Merrick. The terrain, however, is very different from that of Galloway. Although there are some steep slopes and a few dramatic rock-rimmed corries, especially along the north side of Moffat Dale, these are mostly flat-topped, rolling moorland hills. As well as Broad Law there are two other Corbetts in the range, White Coomb and Hart Fell, and seven Grahams.

Lying immediately to the east of the M74 motorway, the Tweedsmuir Hills mark the start of the Borders country, a region notorious for violence and lawlessness from the 13th to the early 17th centuries, when the Border reivers raided the Lowlands to steal cattle, feuding with their neighbours and with each other. Now the region is quiet, and noted for wool and fishing rather than outlaws and conflict. Moffat on the western edge of the region just off the M74 is the main town. From Moffat the A708 runs northeast up Moffat Dale, a straight glacier-carved U-shaped valley, to St Mary's Loch and Yarrow Water, and then Selkirk. The A72 runs along the northern edge of the region while the western side is cut by the north–south line of the A701. These roads split the hills into three groups. The largest group, containing the highest summits, lies in the rough triangle between the three A roads. To the south of the A708 lie the Ettrick Hills, forming an elongated horseshoe around the Ettrick Water valley, down which runs the Southern Upland Way. Northwest of the A701

The glaciated U-shaped valley of Moffat Dale on the southern edge of the Tweedsmuir Hills

are the Culter Fells. There are buses to Beattock and Moffat and along Moffat Dale. In summer buses run from Peebles and Selkirk to St Mary's Loch.

THE ETTRICK SHEPHERD

The Ettrick area is famous for James Hogg, the Ettrick Shepherd, who lived from 1770 to 1835. Hogg was a poet as well as a shepherd and became friendly with Sir Walter Scott, who brought his work to the attention of the outside world. Today Hogg is best known for his macabre and disturbing novel *The Private Memoirs and Confessions of a Justified Sinner*, said to presage modern psychological thrillers.

White Coomb ☆

The round of the Grey Mare's Tail waterfall, Loch Skeen and White Coomb (821m) is one of the most interesting and scenic walks in the Southern Uplands. The area is owned by the National Trust for Scotland. Above the National Trust for Scotland (NTS) car park in Moffat Dale the Tail Burn tumbles some 100m down from a hanging valley, at first in several cascades then in the single 60m fall of the Grey Mare's Tail, one of the finest waterfalls in Scotland. A footpath climbs steeply up the hillside from the car park on the northeast (true left) side of the burn with spectacular views of the crashing water. Once above the falls the terrain eases, with the path leading on to Loch Skeen, set in a wild situation with craggy slopes rising high above. From the loch you can climb the spur leading northwest above the Midlaw Burn and then over Donald's Cleuch Head and Firthhope Rig to the summit of White Coomb, or can take a longer way round via two more subsidiary summits, Lochcraig Head and Firthybrig Head. The summits of White Coomb and Firthhope Rig lie on the edge of the Carrifran valley, where a new native forest is slowly emerging through a mixture of planting and natural regeneration, and you can look down at the trees slowly spreading across the slopes. The eastern shoulder of White Coomb leads back down to the path on the right bank of the Grey Mare's Tail. The shorter route is 9km with 700m of ascent and takes 3–4hrs: the longer one adds a couple of kilometres and half an hour or so.

Hart Fell

Hart Fell (808m) is the highest summit on the horseshoe of hills ringing the deep, steep-sided, crag-lined Blackhope Burn. The round starts and finishes at Capplegill in Moffat Dale and crosses Nether Coomb Craig (724m), Swatte Fell (728m), Hartfell Rig (739m) and Saddle Yoke (735m). The first ascent and final descent are quite steep but once on the tops the walking is quite gentle, mostly on grass, with wide-ranging views all around. The distance is around 13km with 1030m of ascent, and takes 4–5hrs.

The name of Hart Fell is English rather than Scots or Gaelic, 'fell' coming from the Norse 'fjall', meaning a mountain. Fell is commonly used in Northern English hill names, especially in the Lake District and the Northern Pennines, where it was brought by Norse invaders. 'Hart' is Old English, a now rather old fashioned name for a male deer, especially a red deer. Here there is an Arthurian connection: Hart Fell is said to have been the home of the magician Merlin for a time, and a hart was the animal into which Merlin could turn himself. A shoulder of the hill is called Arthur's Seat, to confirm the link with the British hero.

Broad Law

Broad Law is the second highest summit in the Southern Uplands, but is not the most interesting, being big, bulky and somewhat featureless, except for the radio masts on the summit, which are serviced by a wide track up the western slopes. The quickest ascent is up the broad south ridge from the Megget Stone on the minor road from Tweedsmuir to St Mary's Loch, a distance to the summit of just 3.5km.

1:6 THE MOORFOOT AND LAMMERMUIR HILLS

The northeasternmost ranges of the Southern Uplands are boggy, heathery flat-topped hills, lower in height than those to the west. The highest summits in the Moorfoots are Windlestraw Law (659m), north of Innerleithen, Blackhope Scar (651m), north of Peebles, and, in the Lammermuirs, Meikle Says Law (535m) and Lammer Law (527m). The A7 and A68 roads separate the two ranges. There are many bus services linking the towns of the region.

Away from paths the walking can be difficult in these hills due to peat bogs and deep heather. The scenery is classic Borders, with slow, meandering rivers, purple heather-clad hillsides, small neat towns and sheep everywhere. The main river is the Tweed, famous for its salmon fishing. A new addition to the scenery is the growing profusion of wind farms on the summits.

Windlestraw Law

Windlestraw Law can be climbed from the Tweed Valley to the south from Innerleithen via Kirnie Law, Priesthope Hill and Glede Knowe and from Walkerburn on the A72 east of Innerleithen via the Walker Burn. However the quickest and easiest ascent is from the B709 to the west via the track up Glentress Rig and Wallet Knowe. The round trip is 7km with 375m of ascent and takes 2–3hrs.

Blackhope Scar

This hill can be climbed from the Gladhouse Reservoir, which lies on a minor road running east from the A703 north of Peebles (GR 305543). The route follows a track up the River South Esk valley and then leaves the path to head up a tributary called Long Cleave. Unfortunately the view is dominated by a mass of wind turbines on the hills to the southwest. The return can be varied by following the height of the land north to pick up another track running down the southern slopes of a hill called the Kipp back to the River South Esk. The distance is 12km, with 450m of ascent, and takes 3–4hrs.

Arthur's Seat and Salisbury Crags rising above the city of Edinburgh

1:7 OUTLIERS

The Pentland Hills

The Pentland Hills lie just to the southwest of Edinburgh and can be seen from many parts of the city, so unsurprisingly they are very popular. The Pentlands are made of hard igneous rock and were built by volcanic activity around 400 million years ago. They are a regional park and their 13 reservoirs supply Edinburgh with water. The hills run north-eastwards and are flat-topped and steep-sided. The highest summit is 579m Scald Law ('scabbed hill'), which can be climbed from every direction. A good high-level route is the one from the Flotterstone ranger centre on the A702 to the northeast of the hill, running over Turnstone Hill and Carnethy Hill to the summit and then over East Kip and West Kip. Tracks past Threipmuir Reservoir and Glencore Reservoir lead back to the start. The distance is 20km, with 850m of ascent, and the walk takes 5–6hrs.

Arthur's Seat

Edinburgh is built on the remnants of old volcanoes. Just 1km from the city centre the stumps of one of these volcanoes still thrusts up into the sky: Arthur's Seat (251m) and the adjacent Salisbury Crags. There is an excellent view over the interesting and innovative new Scottish Parliament building (itself worth a visit) to Arthur's Seat from Calton Hill, also a volcanic remnant, just to the north. Arthur's Seat can be climbed from the Palace of Holyroodhouse to the north. A circuit of the area including Salisbury Crags is recommended. From the summit there is an extensive view of Edinburgh and the Firth of Forth.

Tinto

Tinto (707m) is an isolated and distinctive conical hill on the northern edge of the Southern Uplands, clearly visible from much of the Central Lowlands. The River Clyde winds around the eastern side of the hill. Tinto is of volcanic origin and built of a reddish igneous rock called felsite. In the past it was used as a beacon hill and Peter Drummond, in *Scottish Hill Names: Their Origin and Meaning* (Scottish Mountaineering Trust, 2nd revised edition, 2007) reckons the name probably means 'fiery', from the Gaelic *teinnteach*. The standard ascent is from the Tinto Hill Tea Room near Thankerton on the A73 road between Lanark and Biggar. A wide gravel path leads over the heather moorland straight up to the massive summit cairn, which dates from the Bronze Age. There are wide-ranging views over the Lowlands. The return trip to the top is 6.5km with 485m of ascent and takes 2–3hrs.

85

ACCESS, BASES, MAPS AND GUIDES

Access

There is no useful rail access to the Southern Uplands. There are buses to the main towns.

The Galloway Hills The A712 runs along the southern and western edge of the hills, the A713 along the eastern edge.

The Carsphairn Hills The A713 runs along the western edge, the A76 the eastern edge.

The Lowther Hills The A76 runs along the western edge, the M74 motorway along the eastern edge.

The Tweedsmuir Hills The M74 runs along the western edge, the A72 along the eastern edge. The A708 runs east–west along Moffat Dale.

The Moorfoot and Lammermuir Hills These hill groups are split by the A7 and A68 roads.

The Cheviot Hills The A68 runs through the centre of the Cheviots.

Bases

The Galloway Hills Glen Trool, Newton Stewart, St John's Town of Dalry, New Galloway.

The Carsphairn Hills Carsphairn, St John's Town of Dalry, Dalmellington, New Cumnock, Sanquhar.

The Lowther Hills Sanquhar, Thornhill, Wanlockhead, Leadhills, Abington, Crawford.

The Tweedsmuir Hills Moffat, Beattock, Peebles.

The Moorfoot and Lammermuir Hills Peebles, Innerleithen, Galashiels, Melrose, Lauder.

The Cheviot Hills Kirk Yetholm.

Maps

OS Landranger 1:50,000 80, 79, 77, 78, 74, 73, 72

OS Explorer 1:25,000 16 The Cheviot Hills, 309, 310, 311, 312, 313, 318, 319, 320, 321, 322, 323, 324, 327, 328, 329, 330, 331, 335, 336, 337, 338, 339, 344, 345, 346

Harvey Superwalker 1:25,000 Galloway Hills, Cheviot Hills, Pentland Hills

Harvey Walker's 1:40,000 Peebles and the Manor Hills, Lowther Hills, Drumlanrig

Walking Guides

Southern Uplands by Nick Williams (Pocket Mountains, 2005)

The Southern Uplands by Ken Andrew (SMC, 1992)

The Border Country: A Walker's Guide by Alan Hall (Cicerone, 3rd edition 2005)

Walking the Galloway Hills by Paddy Dillon (Cicerone, 1995)

Walking the Lowther Hills by Ronald Turnbull (Cicerone, 1999)

Climbing Guides

Lowland Outcrops by Graeme Nicoll and Tom Prentice (SMC, 1994)

CHAPTER 2: THE SOUTHERN HIGHLANDS

The Campsie Fells, the Ochils, Ben Lomond and the Trossachs National Park, Crieff, Glen Lochay, Bridge of Orchy, Loch Tay and Glen Lyon, plus the southern West Highland Way and the Rob Roy Way

THE SOUTHERN HIGHLANDS: CHAPTER SUMMARY

Location

From the Midland Valley northwards, as far as Glen Orchy, Rannoch Moor, Loch Rannoch and Loch Tummel.

☆ Highlights

☢ LOW-LEVEL/PASSES WALK
- Spout of Ballagan (2:1)
- The Birks of Aberfeldy and Weem Woods, also near Aberfeldy (2:14)

◐ LONG DISTANCE WALK
- The traverse of the Crianlarich Munros (2:9)

⊗ SUMMIT WALK
- Ben Cleugh (2:2)
- Ben Lomond (2:5)
- The Cobbler (2:6)
- The Ben Lui Hills (2:7)
- The traverse of the Crianlarich Munros and Ben More and Stob Binnein (2:9)
- The Corbett Five and the Munro Five near Bridge of Orchy (2:12)
- Numerous routes around Ben Lawers and the Tarmachans (2:13)
- Schiehallion (2:14)

❂ SCRAMBLING
- The Cobbler (2:6)

❋ WINTER CLIMBING
- The Ben Lui Hills (2:7)

❸ SKI TOURING
- The Ben Lawers Traverse (2:13)

ⓘ OTHER HIGHLIGHTS
- Loch Lomond (2:5)
- The Scottish Crannog Centre (2:14)
- The Trossachs (2:8)

Contents

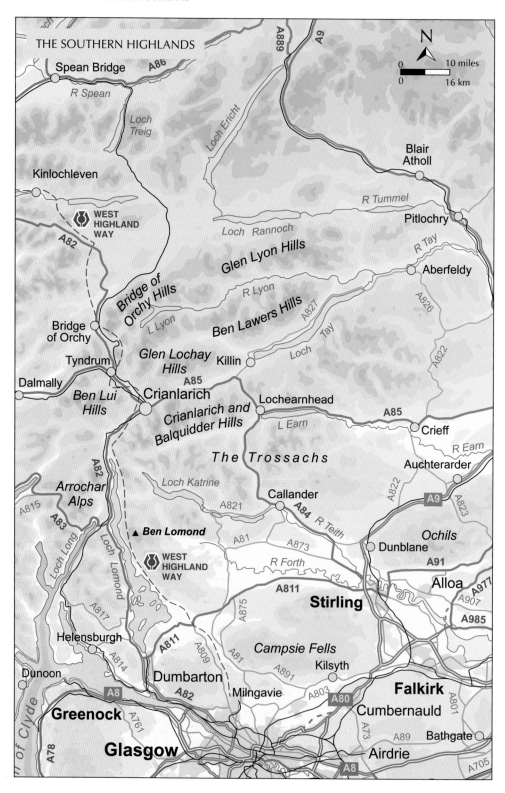

INTRODUCTION

These Hielands of ours, as we ca' them, gentlemen, are but a wild kind of warld by themsells,
full of heights and howes, woods, caverns, lochs, rivers, and mountains,
that it would tire the very deevil's wings to flee to the tap o' them.
Sir Walter Scott, *Rob Roy*

Just a short distance north of the city of Glasgow the southernmost hills of the Highlands rise abruptly above the fields, woods and outlying houses. This sudden change from a gentle lowland landscape to rugged mountain scenery occurs along the Highland Boundary Fault, which cuts right across the country from the Isle of Arran to Stonehaven in a northeasterly direction, and which came into being hundreds of millions of years ago when the original Caledonian mountains were formed. Along the line of the Highland Boundary Fault the soft sedimentary rocks of the Midland Valley abut the hard metamorphic rocks of the Highlands, a change that can be clearly seen in the landscape. There are some hills south of the Highland Boundary Fault: the most significant of these are the Campsie Fells, north of Glasgow, and

the Ochils northeast of Stirling, both volcanic in origin. As these hills lie on the edge of the Southern Highlands I've included them here.

The northern boundary of the Southern Highlands runs along Glen Orchy, the southern edge of Rannoch Moor, Loch Rannoch and Loch Tummel. In the east the high hills fade out as the A9 is reached: in the west they dwindle to lower moors and then the coast. The Southern Highlands are characterised by steep, rocky hills in the west, tightly packed above narrow glens, and more rounded, rolling hills in the east, rising in long ridges above longer, broader, more wooded glens. Rivers in the west are short and fast, those in the east longer and slower. The key river draining the area is the Tay, running from Loch Tay below the Lawers hills out of the Highlands to Perth and the

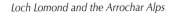

Loch Lomond and the Arrochar Alps

Firth of Tay. Feeding into it are the Tummel, Lyon and Earn; all significant rivers in their own right. In the south the Trossachs area drains into the River Forth. There are many large lochs, most notably Loch Lomond, but also lochs Awe, Katrine, Earn, Tay, Tummel and Rannoch, all freshwater lochs. In the southwest of the area long sea lochs bite into the land, most notably Loch Fyne and Loch Long.

The Southern Highlands mostly consist of Dalradian schists, coarse-grained metamorphosed sedimentary rocks in which creamy white crystals of quartzite and silvery shining specks of mica are common. Although the rocks have been folded and contorted into a complex structure, whose twists and convolutions can in many places be seen, there is a rough pattern, with most rocks paralleling the Highland Boundary Fault. In the south and west the schists are harder than those in the north and east of the region, giving rise to rockier peaks with more cliffs. Here is the region's main area for rock climbing, the Arrochar Alps, centred on the distinctive triple-summited mountain known as The Cobbler. There are no very long climbs, however, and the region doesn't compare with those to the north. When snow and ice conditions are good winter climbing has more scope, again particularly in the Arrochar Alps. Elsewhere Central Gully on Ben Lui is a classic Grade 1 snow climb and one of the best-known winter routes in the Highlands, and there are plenty of high-level walking routes that become mountaineering adventures when snow-covered. The rolling hills in the centre and east of the region are ideal for ski touring when under snow, especially the Ben Lawers range and the Glen Lyon and Glen Lochay hills. For hillwalkers the area contains 46 Munros, 36 Corbetts and 44 Grahams (including outliers like Ben Cleuch in the Ochils).

The Southern Highlands contain one of the most famous lochs in Scotland, Loch Lomond, which is the largest body of fresh water in Great Britain. Above the loch to the east rises one of Scotland's best-known and most popular hills, Ben Lomond, which is also the southernmost Munro. Both hill and loch are protected as part of the Loch Lomond and the Trossachs National Park, which was the first such park thus designated in Scotland. Above the west shore of Loch Lomond rise the Arrochar Alps, a rugged group of steep stony hills, the finest of which – although not the highest – is The Cobbler. North of the Arrochar

Alps lies the Ben Lui group, sometimes known as the Tyndrum Hills. Ben Lui itself is often referred to as the grandest and most beautiful mountain in the Southern Highlands, with two curving ridges rising above the great northeast corrie to a short summit ridge with two tops, the whole creating an almost perfect mountain shape.

West of Ben Lomond lie the Trossachs, an attractive area of craggy hills, mixed forest and shapely lochs, most notably Loch Katrine. The hills here are lower than to the north and west but some are quite distinctive, especially Ben Ledi, one of the southernmost Highland hills, which stands out in views from the Lowlands. Immediately northwest of the Trossachs is a thickly packed line of higher hills, known as the Crianlarich and Balquhidder Hills, with Glen Falloch to the west and Glen Dochart to the north. The two most impressive summits in this group are the twin cones of Ben More and Stob Binnein, which are clearly visible from many parts of the Southern and Central Highlands. Further east a scattering of hills runs just north of the Highland Boundary and the towns of Callander and Crieff. These are known as the Loch Earn and Crieff hills. Most of the area is rolling moorland but two more rocky and mountainous summits, Stuc a'Chroin and Ben Vorlich, rise above the heather and form a distinct skyline visible from many places in the Midland Valley.

The remaining hills of the Southern Highlands lie in a great wedge of land between Loch Rannoch in the north, Loch Tay in the south, the A82 road and the West Highland railway line in the west and Pitlochry and the A9 road in the east. Long, beautiful Glen Lyon runs into the heart of these hills, providing good access. Only one road crosses the area, the B846 from Aberfeldy to Tummel Bridge near the eastern end. All 26 Munros in this region are west of this road. The hills are mostly big and bulky grass- and heather-covered monsters with broad high-level connecting ridges, making this a superb area for long walks over many summits. These hills can be subdivided into four groups. In the southeast the Glen Lochay Hills ring the glen from which they take their name, merging in the west with the Bridge of Orchy Hills to the north. These are dominated by the great cone of Beinn Dorain, a landmark on the journey north from both the West Highland railway and the A82. East of Glen Lochay, between Loch Tay and Glen Lyon, lie the Tarmachan and

Looking west along Loch Tummel to Schiehallion

Ben Lawers massifs, the latter being the biggest single hill group in the Southern Highlands. Ben Lawers itself is the highest peak in the Southern Highlands and one of the best-known and popular hills in Scotland. North of Ben Lawers is another famous and popular hill, Schiehallion, along with the ring of hills rising above Glen Lyon.

The West Highland Way runs for some 77km through the western end of the Southern Highlands, from Drymen to Bridge of Orchy via Glen Falloch and Strath Fillan. Staying low throughout, once past Loch Lomond it's never far from the West Highland railway and the A82, and passes through the villages of Crianlarich and Tyndrum. There is also another long distance path, the Rob Roy Way, which crosses the Southern Highlands from west to east.

2:1 THE CAMPSIE FELLS

Lying just north of the city of Glasgow, the Campsie Fells are a large area of steep-sided, undulating moorland, with few distinct summits. There are some small crags of interest to rock climbers, particularly in the southwest of the area on the slopes of Slackdhu (495m). The Campsies stand out from the nearby Lowlands as they contain some fine corries, particularly the semi-circular Corrie of Balglass on the northern flanks, and have a broken craggy rim. The Campsie Fells are built of basalt lava flows. The name is a mixture of Gaelic and Norse. 'Fell' comes from the Norse 'fjell', a mountain, and is a common name for hills in northern England, especially the Lake District. 'Campsie' is a corruption that Peter Drummond's *Scottish Hill Names: Their Origin and Meaning* (Scottish Mountaineering Trust, 2007) says could come from the Gaelic *cam suidhe*, meaning a seat or level shelf, an apt description, or *cam sith*, a crooked hill.

The high point of the Campsies is Earl's Seat (578m) near the western end, like most of the Campsie tops an undistinguished rise in the moorland. Lower but much more distinctive is the steep little volcanic cone of Dumgoyne ('fort of arrowheads', 427m), lying just to the west of the main moorland mass. Both hills can be climbed from Blanefield or from the Glengoyne distillery on the A81 road. Away from paths the moorland is rough and boggy.

Spout of Ballagan ☆

One of the most interesting walks in the Campsie Fells is the short 700m one from Ballagan House to the east of Strathblane to the ☆ Spout of Ballagan, a fine 21m waterfall in the narrow wooded ravine of Ballagan Glen. An outcrop of many layers of shale, cement stone and sandstone can be seen here. Ballagan Glen is a nature reserve owned by the Scottish Wildlife Trust.

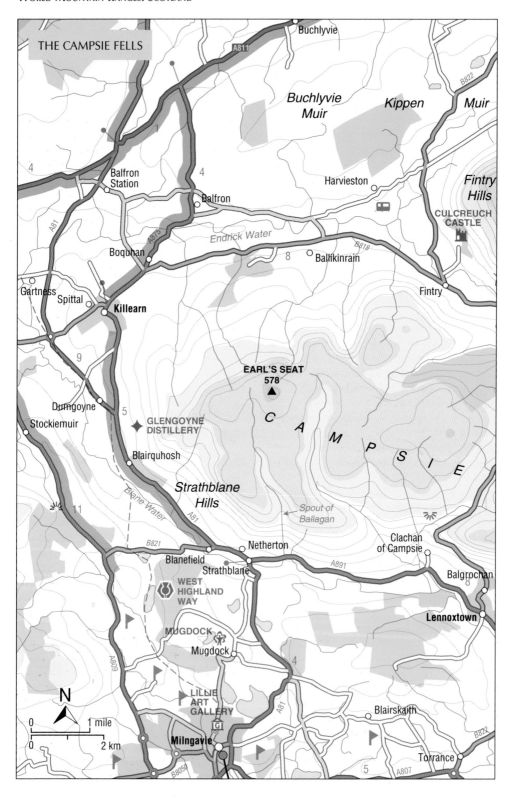

THE CAMPSIE FELLS

Buchlyvie

A811

Buchlyvie
Muir

Kippen

Muir

B822

Fintry
Hills

Harvieston

CULCREUCH
CASTLE

4

Balfron
Station

4

Balfron

Endrick Water

B818

Boquhan

8

Ballikinrain

Gartness

Spittal

Killearn

Fintry

9

EARL'S SEAT
578

Dumgoyne

5

Stockiemuir

GLENGOYNE
DISTILLERY

C
A
M
P
S
I
E

Blairquhosh

Strathblane
Hills

Spout of
Ballagan

Clachan
of Campsie

11

B821

Netherton

Blanefield

Strathblane

A891

Balgrochan

WEST
HIGHLAND
WAY

MUGDOCK

Mugdock

A809

A81

4

Lennoxtown

N

LILLIE
ART
GALLERY

Blairskaith

0   1 mile

0   2 km

G

Milngavie

5

A807

Torrance

B822

B8050

2:2 THE OCHILS

The Ochils present a dramatic steep face split by deep, narrow ravines to the south, clearly visible from the roads around Stirling and Alloa. The A91 runs right along the southern foot of these hills through Dollar, Tillicoultry and Alva – which are known as the Hillfoot Villages, due to their situation – providing good access to the highest summits, including the only one over 700m, Ben Cleuch (721m). To the north above Strathallan the hills are more rounded and rolling as they rise above the busy A9. The Ochils fade slowly into the Lowlands in the east but the main hills lie west of Glen Eagles and Glen Devon, through which runs the A823. In the west the hills drop away quickly to the A9 and the towns of Dunblane and Bridge of Allan. The Ochils are a dissected moorland plateau of fairly even height with only small drops between the many tops. Once up high it's easy to wander widely over many summits, but the most interesting terrain is found in the deep gullies and steep spurs of the southern face of the range. Sadly, the range is being ruined by the erection of wind farms.

The name Ochils comes from the ancient pre-Gaelic Brythonic *uchef*, meaning 'high', and presumably refers to their appearance from the Lowlands to the south, from which they rear up abruptly.

⊗ Ben Cleuch ☆

The highest summit in the Ochils has a Gaelic/Scots name meaning Gully Hill, 'cleuch' having the same derivation as 'clough', a common word for a gully in the hills of northern England. The gully in question is probably that of the Daiglen, a deep slash across the southern flanks of the hill. The ascent of Ben Cleuch is arguably the best walk in the Ochils and can easily be extended to include several other tops. The standard route starts in Mill Glen at the north end of Tillicoultry. Wander through the attractive woods in Mill Glen, then climb the spur between the Daiglen and the Gannel Burn to the subsidiary top of The Law (638m) and on across the high ground to Ben Cleuch. A circuit of the Daiglen can be made by either descending over Ben Ever ('upper hill', 622m) and its southeast spur, or by a circuit of the Gannel Burn by heading east over Andrew Gannel

Hill (670m) to the path that runs above the burn (9.5km, 700m of ascent, 4hrs).

◐ 2:3 THE ROB ROY WAY

The Rob Roy Way runs northeast through the Southern Highlands, from Drymen on the West Highland Way to Pitlochry on the A9. As there are route choices in places, the distance is either 127 or 148km. The route passes through Aberfoyle, Callander, Strathyre, Killin or Amulree and Aberfeldy, and passes Lochs Venachar, Lubnaig and Tay as well as the mountains of Ben Ledi, Ben Lawers and Ben Chonzie.

The idea behind the walk is to explore the area lived in by Rob Roy MacGregor (1671–1734), the famous Highland outlaw immortalised in Sir Walter Scott's classic adventure story *Rob Roy*.

The walk runs through the hills on tracks and footpaths. The going is mostly easy and a week should be ample time. There is plenty of accommodation and eating places along the way and baggage transfer is available.

Information www.robroyway.fsnet.co.uk

Guidebook *The Rob Roy Way* by Jacquetta Megarry (Rucksack Readers, 2003)

2:4 THE WEST HIGHLAND WAY

The West Highland Way begins in the little town of Milngavie, northwest of Glasgow, and runs north for 152km to Fort William. The first 96km, to Bridge of Orchy, lie in the Southern Highlands. This section takes most walkers four to five days. The northern section is covered in Chapter 3. For the first 24km the Way lies south of the Highland Boundary Fault and runs through lowland woods and fields. Beyond Drymen, a useful supply point, the path climbs gently to 360 metre Conic Hill, a superb viewpoint that lies right on the northernmost edge of the Central Belt. Everywhere to the north is in the Highlands, and looks it, being rugged and mountainous. From Conic Hill the Way descends southwest to Balmaha and then follows the eastern shore of Loch Lomond northwards. From Balmaha to Rowardennan there is

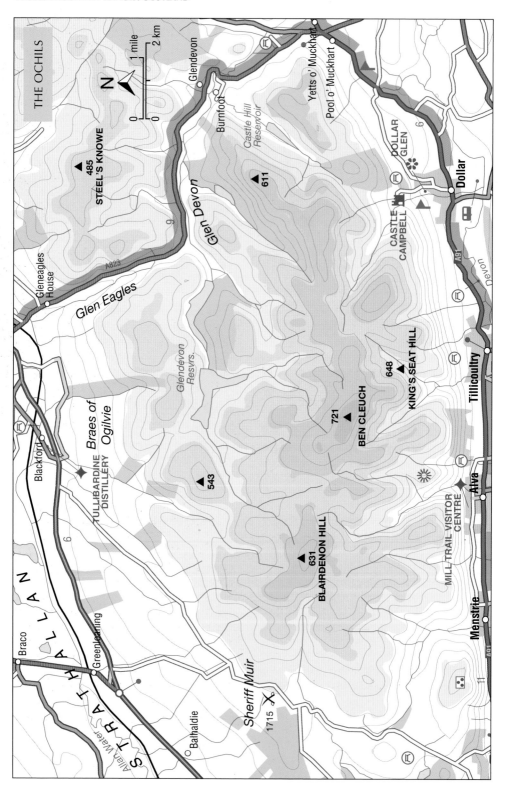

THE OCHILS

N

1 mile
2 km

Glendevon

Glen Devon

Burnfoot

Castle Hill
Reservoir

Yetts o' Muckhart

Pool o' Muckhart

611

STEEL'S KNOWE
485

DOLLAR
GLEN

Dollar

CASTLE
CAMPBELL

Glen Eagles

Gleneagles
House

A823

Glendevon
Resvrs.

KING'S SEAT HILL
648

Braes of
Ogilvie

TULLIBARDINE
DISTILLERY

BEN CLEUCH
721

Tillicoultry

Blackford

543

Alva

MILL TRAIL VISITOR
CENTRE

Menstrie

BLAIRDENON HILL
631

Braco

Greenloaning

Sheriff Muir

1715

Bathaldie

Allan Water

STRATHALLAN

Walkers on the West Highland Way beside the West Highland Line just north of Tyndrum with Beinn Dorain rising into the clouds

a road not far away, along which is a scattering of houses plus a couple of campsites. The road ends at Rowardennan and from here to the north end of Loch Lomond is one of the wildest and most beautiful stretches of the whole West Highland Way. The path winds across steep slopes through natural woodland, with splendid views across the loch to the Arrochar Alps, where the slightly strange-looking triple peaks of The Cobbler are prominent. In spring and summer there are masses of woodland flowers, and in autumn the colours of the fading leaves can be spectacular. Birds are prolific in the rich environment, with its mix of wood, pebble beach and loch. Feral goats may be seen too, grazing in the bracken and scrambling on little crags. The walking is surprisingly rough in places, especially north of Inversnaid, where there is a hotel at the end of a road coming from the east, as the path negotiates tree roots and rocks. At one point a large jumble of boulders blocks the way.

This is Rob Roy country, land once belonging to the Clan MacGregor, and a cavern in this rock pile is marked on maps as Rob Roy's Cave. After he became an outlaw following a falling out with the Duke of Montrose and later due to siding with the Jacobites in 1715 Rob Roy may well have used the cave as a hideout. The cave is also associated with Robert the Bruce, who freed Scotland from English rule at the Battle of Bannockburn in 1314 and who is said to have hidden in it after earlier defeats. Further on the Way passes the site of St Fillan's Priory, which dates back to the 12th century, and Dalrigh, where Robert the Bruce lost a minor battle against the MacDougalls of Lorn in 1306.

At the northern end of Loch Lomond lies Ardleish, where a ferry can be caught across the loch to Ardlui and the A82 road.

From Loch Lomond the West Highland Way runs up Glen Falloch on the western edge of the Crianlarich Hills past Beinglas Farm to Crianlarich, a distance of 10km. Beinglas Farm has a campsite, bunkhouse accommodation in curious wooden wigwams and a small well-stocked shop (www. beinglascampsite.co.uk). The walking is easy along paths and tracks through pastures and patches of forest and this is a good route for stormy days when the tops seem unattractive, especially as the main attraction of the walk is the water, and the wetter it is the more spectacular it is. Glen Falloch is a narrow steep-sided glen with burns pouring into it from either side in a series of waterfalls and cascades, with the wild River Falloch rushing down the centre. The noise of the water can be immense and William Wordsworth called it 'the Vale of Awful Sound'. Today the noise is mainly that of heavy traffic on the A82 just to the west, awful in a different sense to that meant by Wordsworth, although walkers on the West Highland Way can still hear the roar of the river and the waterfalls, especially after heavy rain.

Above Beinglas Farm on a side stream to the east lies Ben Glas Waterfall, an impressive 36m fall in lovely sylvan surroundings. The fall isn't seen clearly from the West Highland Way and requires a short diversion. Dorothy Wordsworth called it a 'fine cascade' in her *Recollections of a Tour Made in Scotland*. Just over 3km further up Glen Falloch the path passes the Falls of Falloch, a series of cascades where the river is squeezed into a narrow gorge. The main fall drops sheer for 10m into a wide wild pool, sometimes called Rob Roy's Bathtub. One of Scotland's most famous mountaineers, W.H. Murray, once almost drowned when trying to jump the gorge above the falls. He made it across but on the return slipped and fell into the water where he 'was seized, whirled round, shot along the gut and hurled twenty feet down to the cauldron' according to *Mountaineering in Scotland* (Baton Wicks, 1997). Once in the whirlpool below the falls Murray was battered by the powerful water and the current prevented him swimming out until, exhausted, he sank and, happily, was washed, still alive, out of the pool by an undercurrent.

Beyond Crianlarich the West Highland Way runs for 10km up Strath Fillan to Tyndrum and then another 11km below the great slopes of Beinn

Odhar and Beinn Dorain to Bridge of Orchy, where it leaves the Southern Highlands. There are facilities in all these little villages. This isn't my favourite section of the route. In my opinion it spends too much time in forestry plantations and close to the road and railway, both of which it crosses several times. There are some good views of the mountains in places, especially back to those around Crianlarich, and ahead to the soaring cone of Beinn Dorain as you ascend gently out of Tyndrum.

2:5 BEN LOMOND AND LOCH LOMOND

Loch Lomond ☆ sits astride the Highland Boundary Fault, with its foot in the Lowlands and its head in the Highlands. The 34km long loch is a stretched triangle in shape – wide at the south, with a long fjordlike tail in the north. As with other glacially-carved lochs it is deepest where it is narrowest, as here the ice moved fastest and so cut down hardest. Near Tarbet at the narrow section the depth is around 180m (600 feet), near the island of Inchmurrin at the widest part of the loch the depth is less than 30m (100 feet). Although 180m is deep it doesn't compare with other lochs such as Loch Morar (see Chapter 5), which at 328m is the deepest loch in Scotland, or Loch Ness, which is 230m deep.

As Loch Lomond narrows, so its shores become more mountainous. From the Lowlands round the southern end of the loch it can be seen tapering into the distance between steep rocky slopes, a wild scene that typifies the rugged yet beautiful Highland landscape. Below the hard stony mountain slopes the banks of the loch are softened by long narrow strips of delightful deciduous woodland, a colourful, complex mix of oak, ash, rowan, hazel, alder and birch. In the broad reaches of the southern loch many attractive wooded islands break up the expanse of water, some of them large enough to have buildings on them: these range from ancient castles and churches to modern houses. These islands mark the line of the Highland Boundary Fault.

Lying just beyond the outskirts of Glasgow Loch Lomond is unsurprisingly very popular, as it can be reached quickly and easily. The A82 runs from the heart of Glasgow up the west side of the loch, where it becomes a narrow, twisting road that is quite scenic but on which traffic can be quite slow when the road is busy. Finding places to park

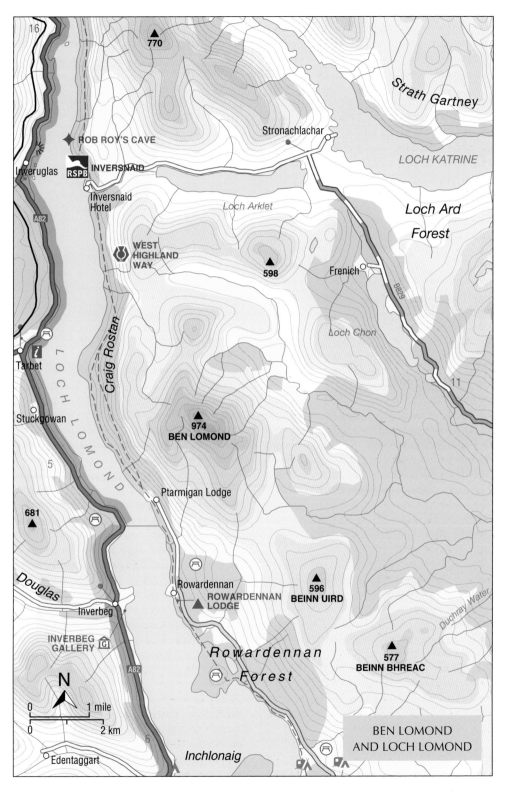

16

▲ 770

Strath Gartney

◆ ROB ROY'S CAVE

Stronachlachar

LOCH KATRINE

RSPB INVERSNAID

Inveruglas

Inversnaid
Hotel

Loch Arklet

Loch Ard

Forest

WEST
HIGHLAND
WAY

A82

▲ 598

Frenich

B829

Craig Rostan

Loch Chon

L
O
C
H

L
O
M
O
N
D

11

Tarbet

Stuckgowan

5

▲ 974
BEN LOMOND

Ptarmigan Lodge

▲ 681

Rowardennan

▲ ROWARDENNAN
LODGE

▲ 596
BEINN UIRD

Douglas

Inverbeg

Duchray Water

INVERBEG
GALLERY

A82

▲ 577
BEINN BHREAC

N

Rowardennan

Forest

0   1 mile
0   2 km

6

Inchlonaig

Edentaggart

BEN LOMOND
AND LOCH LOMOND

View north along Loch Lomond from Rowardennan

can be difficult, and the noise of the traffic negates any sense of peace or tranquillity. On the east side the B837 from Drymen, accessible from the south by both the A811 and A809, reaches the loch at Balmaha from where a minor road follows the east shore as far as Rowardennan. There is no road along the east side of the loch north of Rowardennan (thankfully, as it leaves some of the shoreline free for walkers and those seeking quiet and the sounds of nature) but there is access to Inversnaid, where there is a hotel, via a minor road along Glen Arklet that links with the B829 from Aberfoyle.

It was in his poem 'Inversnaid' that Gerard Manley Hopkins wrote:

What would the world be, once bereft
Of wet and wildness? Let them be left,
O let them be left, wildness and wet;
Long live the weeds and the wilderness yet.

These are oft quoted and popular lines but none the less inspirational for that. They are now inscribed on the walls of the new Scottish Parliament building. Let us hope that they are heeded by the politicians inside.

In summer ferries ply the loch between: Rowardennan and Inverbeg; Inversnaid and Inveruglas; and Ardlui and Ardleish. Cruises on the loch are available from Balmaha, Balloch and Tarbet and are a wonderful way to view the landscape. See www.incallander.co.uk/loch_lomond.htm for information on ferries and cruises.

Plenty of accommodation of every type can be found around the loch including campsites at Luss, Balmaha and Tarbet, a youth hostel at Rowardennan and a bothy at Rowchoish on the West Highland Way.

There is a Loch Lomond and the Trossachs National Park Gateway Centre in Balloch, where the River Leven drains the loch (Loch Lomond was originally called Loch Leven, the current name being taken from Ben Lomond). The Gateway Centre includes a Tourist Information Centre and an interpretation centre. There are also National Park Centres in Balmaha and Luss and a Tourist Information Centre in Tarbet: see www.lochlomond-trossachs.org.

⊗ Ben Lomond ☆

Ben Lomond is an isolated hill and stands out in views north from many parts of Glasgow and the surrounding Lowlands. It's not particularly distinctive however, just a bulky, broad-shouldered, mass rising above lower rounded hills. From the north it is more shapely and mountainous with a steeper pyramid like appearance and it looks very fine from the Arrochar Alps and the north-western shore of Loch Lomond. Ben Lomond is built of mica-schist, a hard crystalline rock. The summit and the area to its south are owned by the National Trust for Scotland.

The meaning of the word 'Lomond' isn't clear but the favourite explanation is that it comes from the old British word 'llumnan' or 'llumon' meaning beacon, which the prominent position of the hill makes very suitable. Peter Drummond says, in *Scottish Hill Names: Their Origin and Meaning* (Scottish Mountaineering Trust, 2007), that it may also derive from the Gaelic 'luimean' or 'luimeanach', meaning a bare hill, and points out that this Gaelic word could itself come from 'llumon' – a bare hill being suitable as a beacon.

Unsurprisingly Ben Lomond is a very popular hill and has been since the first recreational walkers ventured into the Highlands after they became safer for travel following the defeat of the 1745 Jacobite Uprising. Indeed in 1758, just twelve years after the Battle of Culloden ended the Jacobite hopes, the first recorded tourist ascent of Ben Lomond was made by John Symonds, William Beal and John Swan, as described by William Burrell (*Sir William Burrell's Northern Tour*, 1758, edited by J.G. Dunbar, Tuckwell Press, 1997). Burrell himself got 'within a hundred yards of the top' but was 'seized with a dizziness' and so didn't go to the summit. By the last decade of the century Charles Ross in his *Travellers Guide to Loch Lomond* stated that in the summer months 'the summit of Ben Lomond is frequently visited'. Winter ascents came soon afterwards. Ian Mitchell in *Scotland's Mountains Before the Mountaineers* notes that the first recorded account of step cutting on ice in Scotland took place on Ben Lomond in November 1812 when a Colonel Hawker ascended the peak. In his account of the climb the colonel writes that his party 'were literally obliged to take knives and to cut footsteps in the frozen snow'.

Sheet ice on the upper slopes would undoubtedly have led to dangerous conditions and the need for Colonel Hawker's knives. However many early ascensionists tended to describe the climb in dramatic and exaggerated terms. Burrell writes of having 'to crawl on hands and knees' and 'creeping down on all fours' while in 1799 John Stoddart describes the mountain as 'exciting a degree of surprise, arising almost to terror' and as having 'a stupendous precipice of two thousand feet to the bottom' (the cliffs in the northeast corrie are almost 100m high).

Ben Lomond from the north, with the Ptarmigan Ridge on the right skyline

In fact the ascent of Ben Lomond is no more than a steep walk, but a fine one nonetheless, with good views during the climb, while the vista from the summit is arguably the best in the Southern Highlands, encompassing the flat lands to the south and the mountains to the north and of course Loch Lomond. Much of the Southern Highlands can be seen including the craggy Arrochar Alps across Loch Lomond, Ben Lui to the northwest, the ragged wall of the Crianlarich Hills immediately to the north, Ben Lawers to the northeast and the isolated pair of Stuc a'Chroin and Ben Vorlich to the east. When it's very clear Ben Nevis can be seen far to the north.

The standard way up Ben Lomond, sometimes called the tourist route, begins at Rowardennan and follows the broad south ridge before zigzagging up the final steeper slopes to the short, level summit ridge, which curves round the northeast corrie. The walking is easy, the path clear and wide and the views good. The 5.5km with 940m of ascent should take no more than 3hrs. A slightly more adventurous route takes the Ptarmigan ridge, which parallels the south ridge to the west and so gives better and more dramatic views down to Loch Lomond. From the north a longer, much less frequented route runs from Inversnaid along the West Highland Way to Cailness, and then beside the Cailness Burn to the north ridge and the summit.

The northeast corrie is the most distinctive feature on Ben Lomond, a wide bowl in the mountainside ringed with vegetated cliffs below which steep scree and grass slopes drop down to Comer Farm and Gleann Dubh. Although some summer ascents have been done the climbing is generally regarded as poor. Winter climbing is said to be better, when conditions are right, although routes are short. The corrie can be reached from Loch Dubh on the Aberfoyle to Inversnaid road via Gleann Dubh and Comer Farm, and the ridge on the east side followed to the summit. This is the wildest and most rugged approach to the mountain, and feels far from the crowds on the tourist route.

2:6 THE ARROCHAR ALPS

The Arrochar Alps are perhaps the best-known and most popular hills in Scotland due to their visibility and easy access from the Lowlands, the high quality of the landscape and the rocky nature of the mountains. The heart of the group consists

Ben Vorlich in the Arrochar Alps from the south

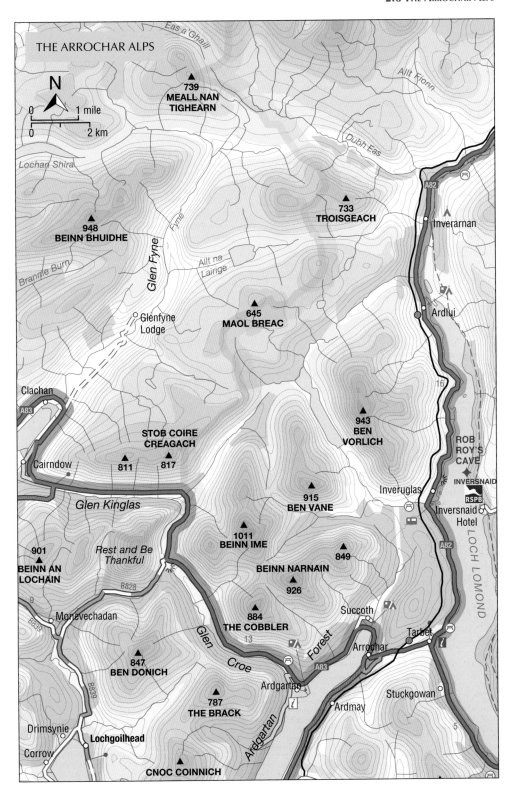

THE ARROCHAR ALPS

N

0 —— 1 mile
0 —— 2 km

Eas a'Ghail

Allt Kionn

▲ 739
MEALL NAN
TIGHEARN

Dubh Eas

A82

Lochan Shira

▲ 733
TROISGEACH

Inverarnan

▲ 948
BEINN BHUIDHE

Glen Fyne

Fyne

Allt na
Lairige

Branne Burn

Ardlui

Glenfyne
Lodge

▲ 645
MAOL BREAC

Clachan

A83

16

▲ 943
BEN
VORLICH

ROB
ROY'S
CAVE

INVERSNAID

RSPB

▲
STOB COIRE
CREAGACH

Cairndow

811   817

Glen Kinglas

▲ 915
BEN VANE

Inveruglas

Inversnaid
Hotel

LOCH LOMOND

▲ 901
BEINN AN
LOCHAIN

Rest and Be
Thankful

▲ 1011
BEINN IME

B828

9

B839

Monevechadan

▲ 849

A82

▲
BEINN NARNAIN
926

B839

Glen

Croe

Forest

Succoth

Tarbet

i

▲ 847
BEN DONICH

13

▲ 884
THE COBBLER

Arrochar

A83

Ardgartan

Drimsynie

Lochgoilhead

Corrow

▲ 787
THE BRACK

Ardgartan

i

Ardmay

Stuckgowan

5

▲
CNOC COINNICH

of five summits – the Munros Ben Vorlich ('hill of the bay'), Ben Vane ('middle hill'), Beinn Ime ('butter hill') and Beinn Narnain (origin unknown, possibly *bhearnan* – 'notches' or 'gaps') plus The Cobbler, a Corbett, which, although lower than the other peaks, is the most dominant and distinctive and has an important place in the history of Scottish mountaineering due to its cliffs and rocky summits. Outside this core group lie another five Corbetts. while further away the isolated Munro Beinn Bhuidhe ('yellow hill') and the isolated Corbetts Beinn Bheula ('hill of mouths') and Meall an Fhudair ('hill of the powder') can be considered outliers. The rock is hard mica schist and the hills are steep and rough with many small crags and stony outcrops. The summits are crammed together above steep-sided narrow glens, creating an enclosed mountain world where the only way to see far is to climb to the summits. The hills are mostly bare, with little natural woodland. However access is hampered in places by extensive forestry plantations. These line some of the main glens in the region, such as Glen Croe and Glen Loin. The latter is also marred by pylons, as is Coiregrogain between Ben Vane and Ben Vorlich.

The Arrochar Alps lie just to the west of Loch Lomond and the A82 up the western side of the loch provides the main road access. From the A82 the A83, running west through Glen Croe and Glen Kinglas, gives access to the southern and western summits. The West Highland Line stops at Tarbet in the south of the region and Ardlui in the north, opening up the possibilities of a walk over the tops between the two with the return by train. The main centres are the small villages of Tarbet and Inveruglas on Loch Lomond and Arrochar on Loch Long. The latter is a sea loch lying only a touch over 2km from the fresh water of Loch Lomond. There are also campsites and a youth hostel at Ardgartan on Loch Long, at the foot of Glen Croe.

The fanciful name 'Arrochar Alps' apparently dates from the 1930s, when unemployed working-class climbers from Clydeside regularly visited the area. The fascinating tale of these times is well told in Alastair Borthwick's entertaining *Always A Little Further* (Diadem, 1983, out of print). Earlier the hills were just known as the Arrochar group or the Arrochar mountains after the village at their foot. Even before modern roads and cars access was easy via steamer from the southern end of Loch Lomond and by the West Highland Line, opened in

1894, so these were among the first hills regularly visited by mountaineers.

The Arrochar Munros

The four Arrochar Munros of Beinn Ime (1011m), Ben Vorlich (943m), Beinn Narnain (926m) and Ben Vane (915m) can be climbed in one long walk, and I have done this a couple of times. The distance isn't great but these are all separate hills with low cols between them and no high-level linking ridges so there is much ascent and descent, often steep. Not needing to return to the start point reduces the time and effort needed – by walking over the tops from Arrochar to Ardlui, for example – while carrying a tent up into the hills gives the option of a high-level camp from which the summits can be climbed in turn. My last round involved walking just over 16kms in just over 10hrs with an ascent of 2400m. I carried camping gear and started at Butterbridge in Glen Kinglas, west of the summits, and finished in Srath Dubh-uisage to the north.

The round can be made easier by omitting Ben Vorlich, which is separated from the other three by the deep trench containing the Loch Sloy reservoir. A circular walk of the three southern Munros, most easily done from Succoth at the head of Loch Long, still involves around 1740m of ascent so it's not an easy day. Leaving Ben Vane for a separate day reduces the ascent to a long but more manageable 1320m over Beinn Ime and Beinn Narnain. The Cobbler could be included in this round.

Ben Vane can be climbed from Inveruglas by the east southeast ridge, a steep 880m climb with some scrambling opportunities on little crags. Ben Vorlich, a long mountain, running some 8km from south to north, and curving to the west at its high point to give it a longbow shape, can be ascended from Inveruglas by the long southeast ridge or from Ardlui by the equally long north ridge. Beinn Ime can also be climbed from Inveruglas via Allt Coiregrogain and the rocky northeast ridge. Shorter but less interesting is the direct ascent of the west face from Butterbridge.

Beinn Ime can be combined with Beinn Luibhean ('hill of the little plants', 857m), a Corbett lying 1.5km to the southwest and separated from it by a 670m col. Beinn Luibhean rises directly above the Rest and Be Thankful Pass at the head of Glen Croe, where there is a large car park. The ascent from here is short but steep. A more scenic and less strenuous route runs up the south ridge from

Glen Croe, starting at the car park at grid reference NN 242 060 (1½–2hrs). This is a good start point for a round of Beinn Luibhean, Beinn Ime, Beinn Narnain and The Cobbler.

There are rock climbs ❻ on the crags of the east face of Beinn Ime, which may be viewed on the ascent from the Allt Coiregrogain, and on Spearhead Buttress at the top of the southeast ridge of Beinn Narnain. These could be places for quiet exploration away from the more popular Cobbler routes.

⊗ ❺ The Cobbler ☆

Although the Arrochar Munros are rugged and attractive none of them are particularly distinctive, and the joy of climbing them lies in the general feel of being in rough mountain country rather than because of the specific appeal of any one peak. The Cobbler, however, is a charismatic mountain with a strange and dramatic rocky outline that draws the eye and, for the mountain lover, the feet. Only in the far northwest, in Torridon and beyond, and in the Cuillin on Skye are there mountains to match the appearance of The Cobbler. Here, among the big blocky hills of the Southern Highlands, it stands out as a striking and unusual aberration, with three jagged rocky summits rippling across the skyline, of which the central one is the highest but the two at either end the most impressive. As the mountain is approached from the east the south and north peaks look higher than the central peak, which is set further back, too.

On many maps The Cobbler is also called Ben Arthur, an old name that was supplanted in general usage a long time ago. Peter Drummond, in *Scottish Hill Names: Their Origin and Meaning* (Scottish Mountaineering Trust, 2007), says Ben Arthur or Beinn Artair may point back to the British King Arthur and points out that the hill is crown-shaped. (There are other Arthurian place names in Scotland, most notably Arthur's Seat in Edinburgh). 'Cobbler' is an English translation of the Gaelic *an greasaiche crom* – the crooked shoemaker. Many writers say that The Cobbler originally referred only to the central peak, going on to quote John Stoddart who, in 1800, in his *Local Scenery and Manners in Scotland, 1799–1800*, wrote that 'its nodding top so far overhangs the base as to assume the appearance of a cobbler sitting at work'. This description applies much more accurately to the overhanging north peak than the central peak, however.

The first known ascent of the central peak was some time in the early 19th century as recorded by John MacCulloch in his four volume 1824 book *Highlands and Western Islands of Scotland*. Ian Mitchell says that MacCulloch, who claimed 'I have ascended almost every principal mountain in Scotland', 'probably deserves the title of Scotland's first peak bagger'. (*Scotland's Mountains Before the Mountaineers*).

At 884m The Cobbler isn't a Munro. That this doesn't stop it being one of the most impressive summits in the Southern Highlands shows the limitations of classifying and, even more, judging hills by their height. The ascent is surprisingly easy considering the intimidating appearance, until, that is, the last few metres are reached. The standard route, and in my opinion the best one, takes the path from a car park at the head of Loch Long through the forest to the Allt a'Bhalachain, which is followed to some large rocks known as the Narnain Boulders (Beinn Narnain lies just to the north). The summit ridge of The Cobbler doesn't come into view until well into the ascent and its startling appearance is a highlight of the walk. Not far past the Narnain Boulders the path crosses the burn and heads into the corrie below the summit and then up steeply to the col between the central and north peaks. The summit ridge is surprisingly wide and grassy and a path leads along it to the central peak, where a little exposed but technically easy scrambling is needed to reach the actual summit sitting on top of a 3m block of rock. The north peak can also be reached by easy scrambling but the south peak is a little steeper and more difficult. It's only 4.5km from the car park to the summit ridge with an ascent of 890m, and the climb shouldn't take more than 2½–3hrs.

Alternative routes include the southeast ridge, which can be climbed from Ardgartan to reach the summit ridge at the South Peak. The most direct and shortest route runs from Glen Croe to the summit, starting at grid reference NN 242 060 and climbing beside the stream to almost 400m then taking a direct line southeast to the summit ridge. This strenuous and not very scenic route takes around 1½hrs. If linking The Cobbler with other hills then it will be climbed from the col with Beinn Narnain, from where the north ridge can be followed to the north peak. When you can tear your eyes away from The Cobbler itself there is a good view from the summit ridge to Ben Lomond.

The Arrochar Alps from the south

● As well as being a superb hill for walkers, The Cobbler is the most important rock climbing venue in the Southern Highlands, with a large number of climbs of varying grades of difficulty, some over 100m in length. The highest route is the traverse of the three summit peaks, graded Difficult if you stick to the crest of the ridge. Below the crest there are climbs on the cliffs of the South and North Peaks, with those on the latter rated the finest. The West Highland Line meant that by the end of the 19th century The Cobbler was easily accessible and many early climbs were made. Then in the thirties and successive decades many more routes were put up by Glasgow climbers who could reach the area in a matter of hours. The climbs are still popular today, especially in dry sunny weather.

⊗ The Brack and Ben Donich

Ben Donich and The Brack are rough and craggy Corbetts with broad ridges that run the length of the southwest side of Glen Croe. Unfortunately so do dense conifer plantations, which also line Gleann Mor north and west of Ben Donich and the shores of Loch Long south of The Brack,

limiting easy access. Happily for hillwalkers paths have been left through the trees in a few places. The easiest way up Ben Donich ('brown hill', 847m) is via the north ridge from the Rest and Be Thankful Pass at the head of Glen Croe, which at 246m means there's only 550m of ascent, the 3.5km taking 1½–2hrs.

Ben Donich can also be climbed from the col with The Brack ('speckled hill', 787m), which lies above Glen Croe at the head of the Allt Coire Odhair. A good waymarked path crosses this col, running for 6km between Glen Croe and Lochgoilhead. All bar 1km of this path are in plantations so it's not a particularly interesting walk in itself. From Lochgoilhead the path runs up beside Donich Water and then the Allt Coire Odhair to the col. On the Glen Croe side it's a bit more complex as the path doesn't start from the road in the glen and there's no easy access through the dense forest. Instead a forest track has to be followed for 4km from the foot of Glen Croe to the beginning of the path (NN 241 047). Once at the high point of the path Ben Donich can be climbed by its east ridge and The Brack by its north ridge.

If climbing just The Brack you only need to walk 2km through the forest from the foot of Glen Croe to where a path climbs beside a stream towards the northeast corrie, and then up onto the north ridge. To make a round, whether climbing both hills or just The Brack, descent can be down the southwest ridge of the latter, to join a good path running from Lochgoilhead to Ardgartan, just above the forest in the Coilessan Glen. This path runs east through the forest down to a forest road in the trees above Loch Long which can be followed back to the start. The circuit of both hills from Glen Croe, ascending to the col between them from the glen and returning via the Coilessan Glen, is an enjoyable walk involving 1500m of ascent, 18km of distance and a time of 7–8hrs.

Once above the col between the hills there are no clear paths on either hill and care is needed with navigation in poor visibility, as the slopes are broad and dotted with knolls, boulders and small crags but without any clear landmarks. The most distinct and interesting features are some curious deep and narrow rocky clefts between big boulders on the lower part of the east ridge of Ben Donich. This area is marked by a large cairn on a boulder just north of the 516m spot height on the OS map (NN 236 042) and is worth the short diversion to see.

⊘ Other Summits

Two steep Corbetts lie either side of Glen Kinglas in the west of this area: Stob Coire Creagach ('peak of the craggy corrie', 817m) to the north and Beinn an Lochain ('hill of the little loch', 901m) to the south. Both can be climbed on the same day from near Butterbridge.

Stob Coire Creagach isn't named on the Ordnance Survey map, although the summit spot height is given. Instead a slightly lower peak with a trig point 1km and a half to the west is named, Beinn an Fhidhleir ('fiddler's peak', 811m). The Scottish Mountaineering Club (SMC) has given the name Stob Coire Creagach to the high point, as it stands at the head of Coire Creagach, which seems sensible to me. Beinn Fhidhleir clearly belongs to the western top and the two summits are far enough apart to have different names. Both lie on the huge long steep hillside that walls the whole northern side of Glen Kinglas. The ascent from anywhere in Glen Kinglas is short and brutal. From Butterbridge you can ascend directly to Stob Coire Creagach, a distance of just 1.5km but a climb of 640m. Allow

1½–2hrs. There are a few small broken crags but these are easily avoided. Once up the ridge can be followed to the west to Beinn an Fhidhleir or northeast to the end of the ridge, and then a steep descent made back into the glen.

Beinn an Lochain was classified as a Munro until the 1981 edition of Munro's *Tables*, when it was demoted, new measurements from the Ordnance Survey showing it to be 14.5m too short. In compensation it goes from being near the bottom of the Munros list to being one of the highest Corbetts. Classification notwithstanding it's a distinctive hill dominating the head of Glen Croe and with a long ridge running down to Butterbridge in Glen Kinglas. The steep east face of the hill facing Loch Restil and the A83 road is quite craggy, although the rocks are mostly broken and vegetated. There's no summer climbing here but when frozen there are winter routes ❄, as there are on the steep north face. The northeast ridge, which is quite narrow in places, is a good ascent route, starting a little way up the road from Glen Kinglas towards Loch Restil in order to avoid plantations. There is a path all the way and the 660m of ascent and 2km distance should take no more than 1½–2hrs. The hill can also be climbed from the Rest and Be Thankful Pass on the A83 by a route of similar length, but which is less interesting than the northeast ridge.

The final hills in this group are three outliers, included here because they fit even less well elsewhere. The Munro Beinn Bhuidhe ('yellow hill', 948m) is one of the most isolated summits in the Southern Highlands, roughly 6km from both the main Arrochar Alps and the Ben Lui group. It's a huge hill, the whole massif filling the land between Glen Fyne and Glen Shira. Set well back from the glens, and buttressed by broad, steep, craggy slopes, the summit isn't easy to see except from distant hills. It's not very distinctive either, being the high point on a long, craggy, bumpy and broad ridge. Beinn Bhuidhe can be climbed from either Glen Fyne or Glen Shira. A long 8km leads up a track from the A83 at the head of Loch Fyne up Glen Fyne to the derelict house at Inverchorachan, from where a direct ascent can be made. Cycling the first 6km of the track reduces the time needed. From Inverchorachan a steep climb up complex slopes leads to the main ridge at a col around 1km northeast of the summit. There is an intermittent path. The total distance is 20km with 950m of ascent and the round trip on foot is likely to be 6½–8hrs. Using a bike would cut this by at least a couple of hours.

Another isolated summit 7km east of Beinn Bhuidhe is Meall an Fhudair (764m), a Corbett. This big rounded hill lies between Glen Fyne and Glen Falloch and is most easily ascended from the latter, starting with the hydro track that zigzags up above Glenfalloch Farm, then up the east ridge of the subsidiary top called Troisgeach, and then across rough ground full of knolls, peat hags and pools – where navigation can be difficult in mist – to the summit. The ascent is 6km long with 800m of ascent and takes 2½–3hrs. The descent can be made by dropping south to the Lairig Arnan and then walking east to the hydro track and Glen Falloch.

The final hill is also quite isolated. The 779m Corbett Beinn Bheula ('hill of the ford') lies west of Loch Goil, well to the south of the other high hills in the area. The east face is quite craggy and rough, that to the west more gentle. Beinn Bheula can be ascended from Lettermay on the minor road between Lochgoilhead and Carrick Castle by a quite interesting route alongside the Lettermay Burn then up the northeast shoulder, a 5km walk with 730m of ascent that should take 2½–3hrs.

2:7 THE BEN LUI HILLS ☆

Ben Lui is regarded as one of the most, perhaps the most, beautiful mountain in the Southern Highlands and one of the loveliest in Scotland. Certainly it has graceful flowing lines and the view from the northeast into the great Coire Gaothaich (corrie of the winds) is magnificent, especially when the mountain is snow-covered. At 1130m Ben Lui is much higher than the surrounding hills, even though three of them are Munros, and quite a distance from them, so it stands out clearly, making it a landmark hill that can be easily recognised from many other summits, some a long distance away. The other Munros are Ben Oss (1029m), Beinn Dubhcraig (978m) and Beinn a'Chleibh (916m). These hills make up the Ben Lui National Nature Reserve, created because of the mountain flowers, such as saxifrage, found on the moist cliffs and outcrops, which are richer here than elsewhere as the soil is less acid. The best time to see these flowers is from May to July. The rock is mica schist, so these hills are rough and craggy.

North of these Munros across the Cononish glen stands a single Corbett, Beinn Chuirn (880m),

Beinn Dubhchraig from Loch Lomond

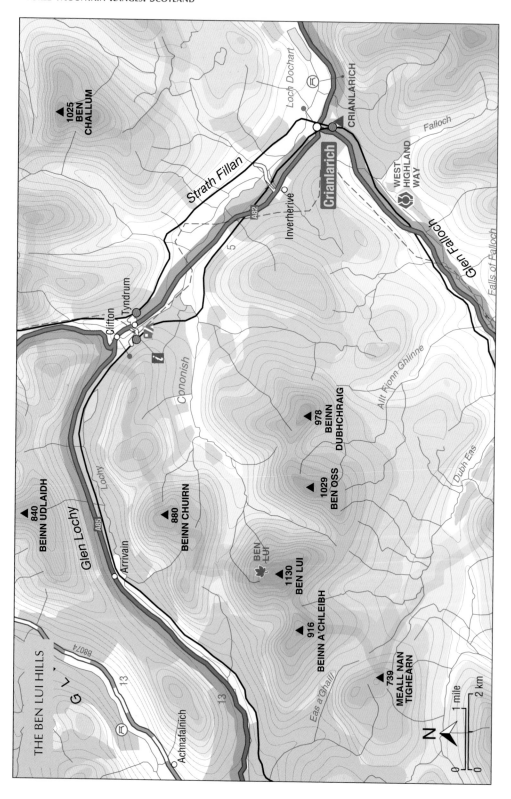

which looks like a smaller version of Ben Lui. The north side of this Corbett and its subsidiary tops presents a steep wall above the gloomy conifer plantations in Glen Lochy. An equally steep hillside rises on the north side of this dark glen, topped by two more Corbetts, Beinn Udlaidh (840m) and Beinn Bhreac-liath (802m).

Ben Lui means 'calf hill', perhaps because the short, curving summit ridge which rises slightly at each end could be said to resemble a calf's head. 'Lui' derives from the Gaelic *laoigh* and the hill is sometimes referred to as Beinn Laoigh. Ben Oss is also named for an animal, the elk (Gaelic *os*), long extinct in the Highlands. Beinn Dubhcraig is the 'hill of the black crag' and Beinn a'Chleibh 'hill of the creel'. The Corbetts all have prosaic names too – Beinn Chuirn is 'cairn hill', Beinn Udlaidh 'dark hill' and Beinn Bhreac-liath 'speckled grey hill'.

Ben Lui is situated in a large roadless block of land (although there are plenty of forest tracks) to the north of the Arrochar Alps. Glen Falloch runs to the southeast of the hills, Strath Fillan to the northeast, with the A82 and the West Highland Line running along these glens. There are railway stations at Crianlarich and Tyndrum. From the latter village the A85 heads west to Oban along Glen Lochy on the northern edge of the hills.

Tyndrum is the main centre for these hills. This tiny village has a Tourist Information Centre, a grocery shop, a café/restaurant, a campsite and accommodation in hotels and B&Bs. The latter are often fully booked however as the West Highland Way runs through Tyndrum and it's a popular overnight stopping place. The complex of services in the Green Welly Stop has a good restaurant and an outdoor shop for any last minute gear supplies (www.thegreenwellystop.co.uk).

⊗ Although the Munros can be climbed singly or in pairs from either Dalrigh on the A82 just south of Tyndrum (NN 344 292) or from Glen Lochy at a car park on the A85 (NN 239 278), from where a path runs up through the forest, the most satisfying walk links all four together by the twisting snake-like ridge that connects them. The approach from Dalrigh up the Cononish glen is by far the finest, as it presents the classic view of Ben Lui rising above Coire Gaothaich. The Glen Lochy approach is shorter but has no other advantages, as it consists of a plod through the forest followed by a slog up the featureless, steep, grassy northwest slopes of Ben Lui. Using this route Ben Lui and Beinn a'Chleibh

can be climbed together (Beinn a'Chleibh hardly justifies an ascent without including Ben Lui) in a relatively short day (9km, 1090m, 4½–5hrs), although including the other two summits and returning to Glen Lochy is inconvenient as much ground has to be retraced. However, if you have a party with two cars, one can be left in Glen Lochy and the other at Dalrigh, to which you can descend from Beinn Dubhcraig. For those with a tent there are many possible sites among these hills and a couple of days can be spent on the ascents.

☆ On the route from Dalrigh you feel as if you are walking into the heart of the mountain as it leads up the Cononish glen past Cononish Farm and right into Coire Gaothaich, from where you can climb south or north to one of the confining ridges, whose rocky slopes can be followed to the summit of Ben Lui. Beinn a'Chleibh is then an out and back route, although the summit of Ben Lui can be avoided on the return by a traverse round the southwest slopes. Once past Ben Lui the route then twists and turns over rough complex terrain full of hummocks and rocks to Ben Oss and Beinn Dubhcraig. From the last summit a descent can be made north into the Coninish glen or, better, down beside the Allt Coire Dubhcraig to Coille Coire Chuilc ('the wood of Corrie Chuilc'), a lovely remnant of Caledonian forest with big Scots pine and rich undergrowth that is in complete contrast to the cramped, dark plantations in Glen Falloch and Glen Lochy. Despite its small size this is a real forest, and unsurprisingly it's a Site of Special Scientific Interest (SSSI). Beyond the trees a track leads back to Dalrigh. The whole route is some 25km long with 1700m of ascent and takes 8–10hrs, making for a long day but one that is well worth the effort.

✳ ☆ The broken crags on these hills don't make for good rock climbing but in winter there are some good routes in Coire Gaothaich on Ben Lui, including one of the classic snow climbs in Scotland, Central Gully. First climbed back in 1892, when this area was a major climbing centre due to the access provided by the railway to Tyndrum, the route goes straight up the centre of the giant bowl of the corrie to the summit ridge, a magnificent line. It's quite straightforward and only Grade I but the situation is dramatic and there can be a large cornice at the top. There are half a dozen other snow routes in the corrie, all Grade I or II.

⊗ Beinn Chuirn can also be climbed from the Cononish glen by way of a zigzag track running up the lower part of the eastern shoulder of the hill (6km, 700m, 2½–3hrs to the summit).

> This track up the eastern shoulder of Beinn Chuirn leads to some old lead mines, opened in 1739 and worked up until 1923. Further exploration, for gold rather than lead, took place as recently as the 1990s and may continue in the future, although, as the area lies in the Loch Lomond and the Trossachs National Park it is to be hoped that the Park Board will prevent this happening. The scars of the recent activity – especially bulldozed roads – are ugly, mar the lower slopes of the hill and should be cleaned up rather than added to.

Beinn Chuirn can be linked with Ben Lui via the 430m col at the head of the Allt an Rund. Descent can also be made back into the Cononish glen from this col.

⊗ The long flat-topped hills Beinn Udlaidh and Beinn Bhreac-liath are hard to access due to the forestry plantations that almost surround them. But there are breaks in the trees, one of these being at the south end of Coille Bhreac-liath, from where Coire Chalein can be ascended from the A82 road (NN 322 337). Steep slopes lead from the corrie to Beinn Bhreac-liath from where it's out and back to Beinn Udlaidh and then down the same way. For a circular route the best starting point is Invergaunan in Glen Orchy to the north (NN 278 368) from where the north ridges of each summit can be ascended or descended (11km, 960m of ascent, 4hrs). There are good views of Ben Lui from these hills.

2:8 THE TROSSACHS ☆

Lying to the northeast of Loch Lomond the Trossachs is a beautiful lake and forest dotted region with some rugged hills, most notably Ben Venue and Ben Ledi. It's often described as being like the Highlands in miniature, although I think the soft loveliness of the wood and water is more akin to the English Lake District. This is a foothills area, a place where the Lowlands and Highlands meet, gentle in the south and gradually becoming more rugged as you travel north. There are no Munros in the Trossachs but there are five Corbetts of which Ben Ledi is the most significant, and some fine lower hills.

Originally the name Trossachs only referred to the small area, barely more than 2km², between Loch Achray and Loch Katrine. The word comes from the Gaelic 'Na Troiseachan', which means the crossing places. Peter Drummond, in *Scottish Hill Names: Their Origin and Meaning* (Scottish Mountaineering Trust, 2nd new edition, 2007) reckons this refers to the fact that boats could be hauled across the low-lying land between the two lochs. Today the Trossachs is normally used to mean the whole area from Aberfoyle and Loch Ard in the south to the hills north of Loch Katrine and Loch Venachar.

The Trossachs area is very popular, hardly surprising given its beauty and the closeness to the Midland Valley. The A81 road runs from Glasgow to Aberfoyle from where the A821 crosses into the heart of the area via 243m Duke's Pass, which gives superb views down to the forests around Loch Achray. From Stirling the A84 runs to Callander where the A821 can be joined again, running west alongside Loch Venachar. All facilities including campsites can be found in the little towns of Aberfoyle and Callander, both of which are good centres for exploring the Trossachs.

The popularity of the area dates back to the early 19th century. Samuel Taylor Coleridge and William and Dorothy Wordsworth visited the area in 1803, as described in Dorothy's *Recollections of a Tour made in Scotland*. In his poem 'The Trosachs' William wrote about the area: 'Rocks, rivers, and smooth lakes more clear than glass untouched, unbreathed upon.' However it was Sir Walter Scott who really popularised the area when he set his first major work, the 1810 romantic poem *The Lady of the Lake*, beside Loch Katrine, and then in 1821 set much of the novel *Rob Roy* in the Trossachs. In the *The Lady of the Lake* Scott writes of the loch:

Loch Katrine lay beneath him roll'd,
In all her length far winding lay,
With promontory, creek, and bay,
And islands that, empurpled bright,
Floated amid a livelier light,
And mountains, that like giants stand,
To sentinel enchanted land.

Today the loch is larger than in 1810, having been dammed in 1859 in order to provide water for Glasgow. One of the last steam-powered passenger vessels in Britain, the S.S. Sir Walter Scott, operates on the loch between Trossachs Pier and Stronachlachar, as it has done for over 100 years.

Much of the woodland in the area makes up the Queen Elizabeth Forest Park. Although there are extensive conifer plantations there are also very attractive semi-natural woods of oak, birch and rowan, some of them ancient.

 There are many walks in the woods and around the lakes in the Trossachs. Particularly recommended for those interested in geology is the Highland Boundary Fault Trail, which starts at the Queen Elizabeth Forest Park Visitor Centre just outside Aberfoyle and runs for 6km through the forest with signs indicating both sides of the fault and a climb to an excellent viewpoint. On this walk you can step from Lowland to Highland and back.

 A much longer walk is that up Glen Finglas ('glen of the white water'). This starts at Brig O'Turk between Loch Venacher and Loch Achray and climbs through woods to Glen Finglas Reservoir. Beyond the reservoir the route does a circuit of Creag Fharsuinn, ascending Glen Finglas then crossing the moorland at its head to descend back to the reservoir by the Allt Gleann nam Meann. The walk is 24km long and ascends 942m to a

height of 600m. It's all on good tracks and takes 6–8hrs. What makes this walk of special interest is the forest restoration scheme being carried out by The Woodland Trust, who bought the Glen Finglas estate in 1996. The Trust is removing non-native conifers, reducing grazing pressures from sheep and deer to allow the forest to regenerate, planting trees where there is no existing seed source and managing the remnants of ancient woodland. The old twisted alder and hazel scattered round the slopes of the upper glen are the largest remaining upland woodland pasture in Britain.

Ben Ledi

Ben Ledi rises to the east of Glen Finglas and can be climbed from that glen. This 879m Corbett is one of the most popular hills in the Southern Highlands and has been so for over two hundred years. In 1794 in the *Old Statistical Account* (the first statistical survey of Scotland, published in 21 volumes between 1791 and 1799) the minister of Callander, one James Robertson, contributed information on Druidical rites on Ben Ledi, writing:

> By reason of the altitude of Ben Ledi and of its beautiful conical figure, the people of the adjacent country to a great distance, assembled annually on its top, about the time of the summer solstice, during the Druidical priesthood, to worship the deity.

Ben Ledi

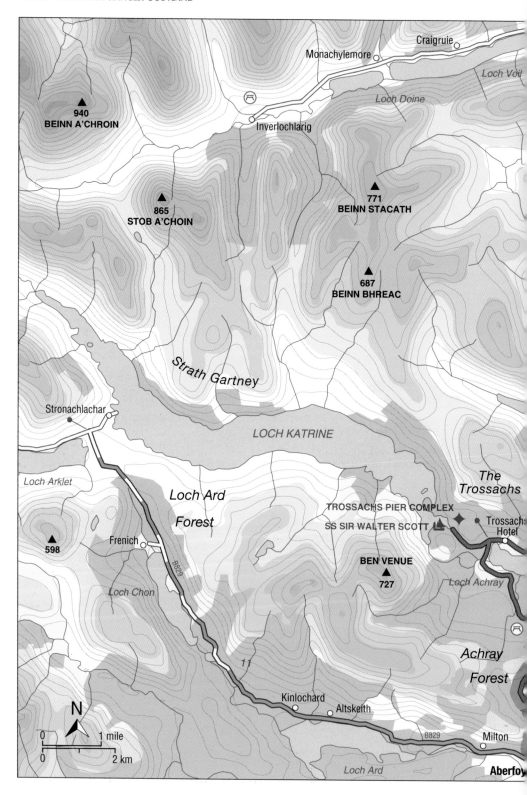

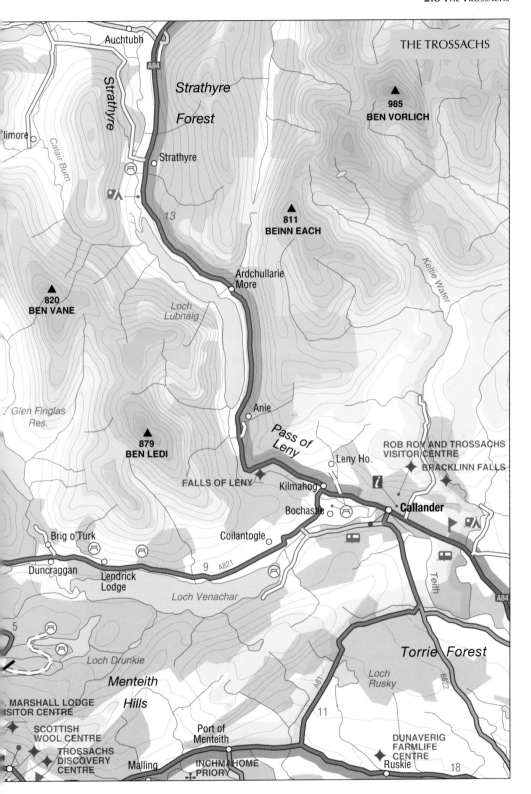

THE TROSSACHS

Auchtubh

Strathyre

Strathyre
Forest

▲ 985
BEN VORLICH

limore

Calair Burn

Strathyre

13

▲ 811
BEINN EACH

Ardchullarie
More

Keltie Water

▲ 820
BEN VANE

Loch
Lubnaig

Glen Finglas
Res.

Anie

Pass of
Leny

ROB ROY AND TROSSACHS
VISITOR CENTRE

▲ 879
BEN LEDI

Leny Ho.

BRACKLINN FALLS

FALLS OF LENY

Kilmahog

Callander

Bochastle

Brig o'Turk

Coilantogle

Duncraggan

Lendrick
Lodge

9   A821

Teith

A84

Loch Venachar

5

Torrie Forest

Loch Drunkie

Menteith

Loch
Rusky

BB22

MARSHALL LODGE
ISITOR CENTRE

Hills

11

SCOTTISH
WOOL CENTRE

Port of
Menteith

DUNAVERIG
FARMLIFE
CENTRE

TROSSACHS
DISCOVERY
CENTRE

Malling

INCHMAHOME
PRIORY

Ruskie

18

Stob a'Choin in the Trossachs

This presumably helped give rise to the idea that the name comes from *Beinn le Dia* and means 'Mountain of God'. Peter Drummond's *Scottish Hill Names: Their Origin and Meaning* (Scottish Mountaineering Trust; 2007) argues against this, however, and says that Ledi is more likely to come from the prosaic *leitir* or *leathad*, meaning a slope, and refers to the southern ridge that rises directly from glen to summit.

⊗ Whatever the name means Ben Ledi is a fine hill, prominently seen from the Lowlands to the south as it rises just north of the Highland Boundary Fault. The east side is craggy, rising steeply out of forestry plantations; the south and west faces are greener and less rough. The standard ascent route is from the east, starting at the car park at NN 586 092 near the bridge over the Garbh Uisge, just 4km from Callander on the A84, and climbing through the forest to the broad southeast ridge and then to the top. The distance to the summit is only 3.75km, with 750m of ascent, and the summit can be reached in a couple of hours. A more interesting ascent from the same start point is via the Stank Glen (don't be put off by the name, it comes from the Gaelic *stang* meaning pool) to the north, reached via a track through the forest. This climbs to the north

ridge and then the summit, a distance of 6km with 826m of ascent, and takes about 2½hrs. I'd suggest going up by the Stank Glen and down by the southeast ridge. Both these routes climb the more rugged side of the hill, although the walking is easy. On the west side there is a route from Brig O'Turk that starts with a walk to Glen Finglas reservoir, as described above, and then up grassy slopes past the new planted woodland to the summit ridge. By this route it's 6.5km to the summit, with 849m of ascent, taking 2½–3hrs.

⊗ Other Trossachs Summits

Ben Ledi is at the southern end of a long wedge of hill running from Loch Venachar to Glen Buckie. The other high summit on this broad ridge is grassy, somewhat featureless Ben Vane ('white hill', 820m), which is also a Corbett, and is easily reached in less than 2hrs from Ben Ledi, a distance of just over 6km with 382m of ascent. En route Lochan nan Corp ('pool of the corpses') is passed; the name commemorates the drowning of a funeral party when the ice on the frozen loch gave way. Ben Vane can be climbed directly by its southern ridge, which runs down to the Glen Finglas reservoir, and from Glen Buckie via the long north ridge.

The other Corbetts in the area are Beinn a' Chroin (770m) west of Loch Katrine, Stob a'Choin (869m) and Beinn Stacath (771m, not named on the OS map although there is a trig point), both north of Loch Katrine. These are knobbly, rugged hills but not very distinctive. They could all be climbed, along with Ben Ledi and Ben Vane, in a two or three day trip with high camps along the way, which would make an interesting traverse across some rough complex country involving around 65km and over 4000m of ascent. Otherwise Beinn a'Choin ('hill of the dog') can be ascended in a circuit of its south and southeastern ridges, Stob a'Choin ('peak of the dog') from the end of the road past Loch Voil and Loch Doine, and Beinn Stacath ('peak hill') from Glen Buckie.

The Corbetts curve round the north side of the Trossachs. Lying at the heart of the area is Ben Venue ('small mountain', 729m), a fine rugged little hill rising above the east end of Loch Katrine. The situation gives Ben Venue a prominence in views of the Trossachs and it could be said to be **the** Trossachs hill. A circular walk to the summit can be made from the west end of Loch Achray, following Achray Water, and then ascending the northeast slopes and descending to Gleann Riabhach. The whole walk should take no more than 3hrs and involves around 9km of distance and 725m of ascent.

2:9 BEN MORE, STOB BINNEIN AND THE CRIANLARICH AND BALQUHIDDER HILLS ☆

North of the Trossachs the higher hills start with a complex line of big, craggy peaks, running west–east to the south of Crianlarich, right in the heart of the Southern Highlands. Seven Munros lie here, most notably the distinctive pair of almost symmetrical cones of Ben More ('big hill', 1174m) and Stob Binnein (possibly 'peak of the anvil', 1165m), which are seen particularly well from Strath Fillan to the northwest and stand out clearly in views from many summits, near and far. Ben More appears as a bulky pyramid. Stob Binnein has a short, flat summit ridge so the top of the cone looks as if it's been sliced off. The other Munros from west to east are Beinn Chabhair (probably 'antler mountain', 933m), An Caisteal ('the castle', 995m), Beinn a'Chroin (probably 'hill of the sheepfold', 940m), Cruach Ardrain ('high heap', 1046m) and Beinn Tulaichean ('hill of the knolls', 946m). Well to the east of the Munros two Corbetts rise above Glen Ogle: Meall an t-Seallaidh ('hill of the view', 852m) and Creag Mac Ranaich ('Mac Ranaich's rock', 809m).

Cruach Ardrain and Beinn Tulaichean (left), Ben More and Stob Binnein (right)

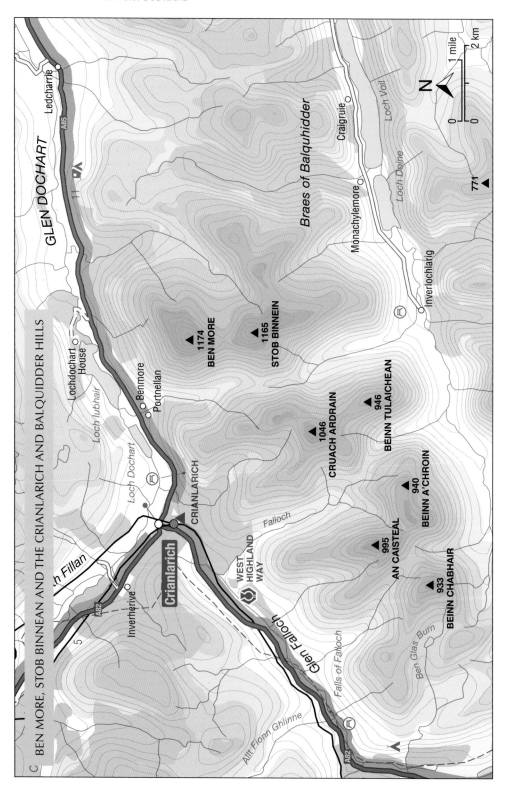

C BEN MORE, STOB BINNEAN AND THE CRIANLARICH AND BALQUIDDER HILLS

GLEN DOCHART

Ledcharrie

Braes of Balquhidder

Craigruie

Loch Voil

Loch Doine

Monachylemore

Inverlochlarig

771

BEN MORE
1174

STOB BINNEIN
1165

Lochdochart House

Benmore
Portnellan

Loch Iubhair

CRUACH ARDRAIN
1046

BEINN TULAICHEAN
946

Loch Dochart

CRIANLARICH

BEINN A'CHROIN
940

Falloch

CRIANLARICH

AN CAISTEAL
995

WEST HIGHLAND WAY

BEINN CHABHAIR
933

Crianlarich

h Fillan

Inverherive

A82

5

Glen Falloch

Falls of Falloch

Ben Glas Burn

Allt Fionn Ghlinne

A82

1 mile

2 km

N

0

0

These hills together make up the big block of roadless land between Glen Falloch in the west, Glen Ogle in the east, Glen Dochart in the north and the River Larig–Loch Voil glen in the south. Roads run along all these glens so access is good. The road alongside Loch Voil is a minor one but all the others are main roads – the A82 up Glen Falloch, the A85 along Glen Ogle and Glen Dochart, although the roads don't quite encircle the hills. Between the road end in the Larig glen and the A82 in Glen Falloch the hills roll unbroken southwards to Beinn a'Choin and the Trossachs tops. Crianlarich, at the junction of the A82 and the A85 and with a railway station on the West Highland Line, is the main centre and has a range of accommodation including a youth hostel, a tea room, bars and a shop. The village lies at the meeting point of three major valleys – Glen Falloch, Strath Fillan and Glen Dochart – and is a key point for access with main roads heading north, south and east. The name means 'low pass'. The modern roads follow the same routes as military roads built in the 1750s – east from Stirling through Callander and along Glen Dochart, and north from Dumbarton along Loch Lomond and Glen Falloch and then north to Fort William and, from Tyndrum, west to Oban. The railway splits in Crianlarich, one branch heading for Oban, the other for Fort William, although the two lines parallel each other until Tyndrum, which has two stations.

For the eastern hills Lochearnhead or Balquhidder, where Rob Roy is buried in a grave marked with the defiant 'MacGregor despite them', are alternatives for a base. There is a superb view along Loch Voil to the hills from Balquhidder.

The Traverse of the Crianlarich Munros ☆

Although the Crianlarich hills are usually climbed singly or in small groups, the best route is the traverse of all the Munros in one trip, as this reveals the character of the whole group and keeps the walker high above the glens on a wonderfully complex, exhilarating and interesting expedition. However this is a long route and requires a good level of fitness to complete in one day. For maximum enjoyment it's best to split it between two or even three days. Starting at Beinglas Farm in Glen Falloch and finishing at Benmore Farm in Glen Dochart, the route is around 26km long, with 3375m of ascent, and requires at least 10–12hrs. In fine weather there are several campsites along

the route. If it's stormy dropping down into one of the corries provides more shelter. The time I walked this route I climbed Beinn Chabhair late one day from Beinglas Farm, then dropped north to camp in Coire a'Chuillin to avoid strong winds. The following day I completed the walk, a distance of 21km with 2700m of ascent, in 10hrs, dropping down east from Stob Binnein into Coire-heathaich to camp (I was continuing on to the Loch Earn hills the next day). Although strenuous the traverse was very enjoyable, a day of sunshine, cloud and clear views when striding out above the world was the most wonderful thing imaginable. The hills are big and craggy, with great bites taken out of them by deep corries, so the route twists and turns, presenting new views at every turn and making for entertaining walking. The walking is mostly rough and stony but not difficult, although in a few places care has to be taken to pick the best route up and down broken, craggy slopes. This isn't one of the well known high-level walks in the Highlands but I think it is one of the best.

Beinn Chabhair, An Caisteal, Beinn a'Chroin, Beinn Tulaichean and Cruach Ardrain

Beinn Chabhair can be easily climbed from Beinglas Farm. There are two routes which can be linked to make a circuit. The most direct starts beside the Ben Glas Waterfall, then follows the Ben Glas Burn to Lochan Beinn Chabhair from where steep grassy slopes lead through rocks to the summit. The other route climbs northeast from Beinglas past the beautifully situated Lochan a'Chaisteil to the summit of Ben Glas at the end of Beinn Chabhair's northwest ridge and along the rough and bumpy ridge to the summit. The round trip is about 11km long, with 1150m of ascent, and takes 4–5hrs.

A big (310m) drop down steep rocky slopes separates Beinn Chabhair from An Caisteal and Beinn a'Chroin, both rather shapeless knobbly hills. The latter two, or the three hills together, can be climbed from Derrydaroch farm in Glen Falloch, where there is a bridge over the river, via the northwest ridge or the north ridge (the unusually-named Twistin Hill) of An Caisteal. From the col south of An Caisteal a path takes a tortuous route through crags to the summit ridge of Beinn a'Chroin. Current maps and guidebooks give the central summit as 942m and the eastern one as 940m. However pre-21st century maps and guidebooks give the eastern top as the higher and so the Munro. Ascending one of An Caisteal's ridges and descending the other gives a round trip of 13km, with 1330m of ascent that takes 5–6hrs. Beinn a'Chroin has a curious twist in its topography that results in the burn running north of the summit, part of the headwaters of the River Falloch, starting 1km south of the Ishag Burn which runs south. Those going on to Beinn Tulaichean need to be careful with navigation here, especially in mist. Tulaichean is really an outlier of the higher Cruach Ardrain to its north, the col between the two is at 820m. The two summits can be climbed from just south of Crianlarich by either the northwest or north ridge of Cruach Ardrain, by far the finest summit of the five western Munros. The round trip is 15km long, with 1450m of ascent, and takes 6–7hrs. There are some winter routes in the corries below the summit of Cruach Ardrain, particularly Y Gully in Coire Ardrain.

⊗ Ben More and Stob Binnein ☆
These are the most distinctive and finest hills in the group, despite being far less rocky, and with smoother, grassier slopes than the others, and are usually climbed as a pair from Benmore Farm in Glen Dochart. You can slog up the unrelentingly steep and monotonous northwest slopes of Ben More from the farm but I think it's preferable to leave these for the descent and to follow the track up the Benmore Glen and then head up the slopes to the east to the Bealach-eadar-dha Bheinn ('the pass between the hills'), the col between the two summits, from where Stob Binnein can be climbed, before returning to the col and traversing Ben More. The views from both summits are extensive and impressive.

All the hills can also be climbed from the glen of the River Larig to the south, although few people do this, leaving this side of the hill for those who like peace and solitude.

⊗ The Two Corbetts
The two Corbetts rising at the eastern end of the range can be climbed from Lochearnhead, Glen Ogle or Balquhidder. The best route is that up Glen Klendrum from Lochearnhead to the col between the summits, which gives a round trip of 17km with 1100m of ascent, taking 5½–6½hrs. This is a pleasant walk but I wouldn't do it in preference to the Munros unless the weather was too bad to go higher.

2:10 THE LOCH EARN AND CRIEFF HILLS

Like Ben Lomond and Ben Ledi, the pointed peaks of Ben Vorlich ('hill of the bay', 985m) and Stuc a'Chroin ('hill of the sheepfold' 975m) are familiar to people in the Midland Valley, their distinctive outlines standing out from many places including the city of Stirling and even Arthur's Seat in Edinburgh. Ease of access means they are popular hills too. The hills lie east of Strathyre, a heavily-forested glen up which the A84 runs from Callander to Lochearnhead, and south of Loch Earn, along which the A85 runs from Crieff and Comrie to Lochearnhead. To the east a minor road runs up Glen Artney from Comrie and Dalginross. North of Comrie is the bulky, isolated Munro Ben Chonzie (931m, probably 'mossy hill'), the highest point on a huge area of moorland lying between Strath Earn and Loch Tay.

Ben Vorlich and Stuc a'Chroin each have an accompanying Corbett – Meall na Fearna ('alder hill', 809m) and Beinn Each ('horse hill', 813m) respectively – which could be climbed along with them, while three more Corbetts – Auchnafree Hill ('hill of the field of the deer forest', 789m), Creag Uchdag ('crag of the hollows', 879m) and Creagan na Beinne ('hill of the crag', 888m) – surround Ben Chonzie, and could again be combined in one long trip.

⊗ Ben Vorlich, Stuc a'Chroin, Beinn Each and Meall na Fearna
Ben Vorlich and Stuc a'Chroin are steep hills with some rocky outcrops and ridges, especially on Stuc a'Chroin, and the round of the pair is an interesting outing. They can be climbed by several different routes. A good circular walk starts at Ardvorlich (NN 633 232) on the minor road on the south side of Loch Earn – a beautiful loch with wooded shores rising to craggy slopes. A path heads up Glen Vorlich and then the north ridge of Ben Vorlich, a steady but easy climb. An alternative is to climb west to Ben Our then up the northwest ridge of Ben Vorlich. A steep stony descent leads to the Bealach an Dubh Choirein, from where the impressive rocky north ridge of Stuc a'Chroin looks quite intimidating. If taken directly it does require the use of hands in places; alternatively there is a narrow path just below the crest on the western side. The view from the summits of both hills is one of contrast. To the

View up Gleann an Dubh Choirean to Stuc a' Chroin

south the Lowlands spread out, gently undulating and featureless. To the north hills spread into the distance, a three-dimensional world of light and shadow. It really feels as if you are on the boundary between two very different worlds. Descent can be made by the northwest ridge of Stuc a'Chroin, from which you can drop down to pick up a path beside the Allt a'Choire Fhuadaraich, leading to Glen Ample, a track to Edinample and Loch Earn, and thence the road back to Ardvorlich (17km, 1270m ascent, 5½–6½hrs).

The track through Glen Ample can also be used to approach the hills from the south. These include Beinn Each, which lies at the end of the southwest ridge of Stuc a'Chroin. The slopes from Glen Ample to Beinn Each are steep but straightforward. Descent could be made from Ben Vorlich down to the Allt a'Choire Fhuadaraich and Glen Ample. (19km, 1500m ascent, 6–7hrs).

The northern Corbett, Meall na Fearna, can be easily climbed from the col with Ben Vorlich. A path runs up Glen Vorlich to this col, and then south to Gleann an Dubh Choirein and on to Callander.

The circuit of all four hills is most easily done from Glen Artney. A number of variations on the circuit are possible but all are long, at least 26km,

with around 1800m of ascent. I'd allow 8–10hrs. Much of the walking is on tracks and paths, but some is cross country over rough and boggy ground. From the end of the road in Glen Artney head for the path in Gleann an Dubh Coirein, which can either be followed to the col between Meall na Fearna and Ben Vorlich, or left for a direct ascent of the former by its south ridge. From Ben Each descent can be made into Coire an Saighead and then down Gleann a'Chroin to Arivurichardich and a track that leads back to the start.

Ben Chonzie and the Three Corbetts

Ben Chonzie probably wouldn't see many ascents if it didn't breach the magic 3000 foot line and have the title of Munro. It's bulky, rounded and heather-clad, with no distinctive features apart from some small grassy crags on its east face and is most noted for the huge numbers of mountain hares that live on its flanks and the surrounding moorland. The three nearby Corbetts are little more distinguished, although Creag Uchdag is at least as worthy of ascent as the Munro. This is sheep farming and grouse shooting country, and many bulldozed roads have been built for these activities. Although these roads speed walking and tend to determine routes they are ugly scars on the landscape and

121

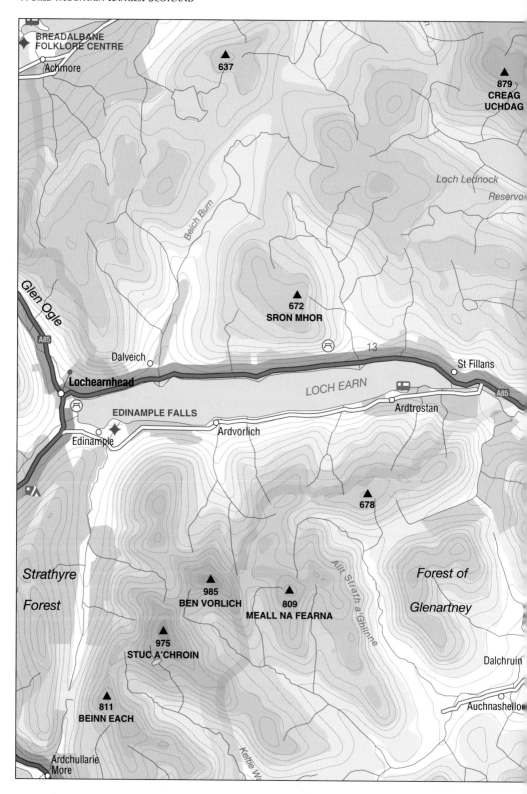

BREADALBANE
FOLKLORE CENTRE

Achmore

▲
637

▲
879
CREAG
UCHDAG

Loch Lednock
Reservo

Beich Burn

Glen Ogle

A85

▲
672
SRON MHOR

Dalveich

13

St Fillans

Lochearnhead

LOCH EARN

Ardtrostan

A85

EDINAMPLE FALLS

Ardvorlich

Edinample

▲
678

Strathyre

Forest of

Allt Strath a'Ghlinne

Forest

Glenartney

▲
985
BEN VORLICH

▲
809
MEALL NA FEARNA

▲
975
STUC A'CHROIN

Dalchruin

▲
811
BEINN EACH

Auchnashello

Keltie W

Ardchullarie
More

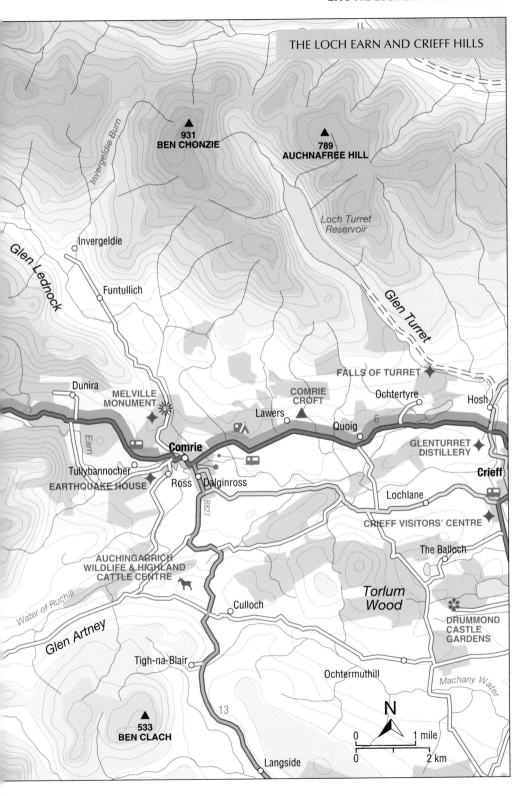

THE LOCH EARN AND CRIEFF HILLS

▲
931
BEN CHONZIE

▲
789
AUCHNAFREE HILL

Loch Turret
Reservoir

Invergeldie Burn

Glen Lednock

Invergeldie

Funtullich

Glen Turret

FALLS OF TURRET ◆

Dunira

MELVILLE
MONUMENT

COMRIE
CROFT

Ochtertyre

Hosh

Lawers

Quoig

6

GLENTURRET ◆
DISTILLERY

Earn

Comrie

Tullybannocher

Ross

Dalginross

EARTHQUAKE HOUSE

B827

Crieff

Lochlane

CRIEFF VISITORS' CENTRE ◆

AUCHINGARRICH
WILDLIFE & HIGHLAND
CATTLE CENTRE

Culloch

The Balloch

Torlum
Wood

DRUMMOND
CASTLE
GARDENS

Water of Ruchill

Glen Artney

Tigh-na-Blair

Ochtermuthill

Machany Water

N

13

▲
533
BEN CLACH

0   1 mile

0   2 km

Langside

detract from the wild appearance of the hills. The walking on the heathery and grassy slopes is mostly easy anyway, unless you get among some of the peat hags found in places, but navigation can be difficult in mist due to the featureless terrain. Under snow these would be good hills for ski touring. The rounded hills are split by long glens, most notably Glen Almond from the east and Glen Lednock from the south. The towns of Crieff and Comrie lie just south of the hills, and Loch Tay is to the north. The A822 and A826 roads run up the east side of the hills from Crieff to Aberfeldy.

⊗ The gentle, obstacle-free slopes mean that these hills can be easily climbed from almost any direction. Ben Chonzie is usually ascended from Glen Lednock or Glen Turret, both of which have reservoirs in them and can be driven up for some way. In Glen Lednock you can park near Invergeldie and follow the bulldozed track beside the Invergeldie Burn, and then a tributary to the track's end at 790m just below the broad south-east ridge, which can be followed to the flat summit ridge. The highest point is at the eastern end. The distance to the top is a little under 7km with an ascent of 725m; 4hrs should be ample for the return trip. The climb from Glen Turret, where you can park by the reservoir dam, is slightly longer at 8km and involves 715m of ascent. This route starts out along the side of the reservoir and then heads up beside the Turret Burn to Lochan Uaine and the summit: 5hrs for the round trip should be enough but most of this time will be on the track beside the reservoir, which is not the most exciting walking (although you could forgo the track and ascend west to the tops and then head north over several minor summits to Ben Chonzie). A bicycle would shorten the time spent on this track considerably. Overall, for those without a bike the Glen Lednock approach is to be preferred. A bike would also be useful for the approach up Glen Almond, as there are 10km of private road to follow from Newton Bridge on the A822 in the Sma' Glen to where a track heads up towards the Mhoine Beag, the col between Ben Chonzie and Auchnafree Hill, from where the summit is easily reached, a distance from Glen Almond of 4.5km with 670m of ascent. On foot the round trip should take around 9hrs, with a bike several hours less. The summit is nondescript but the views are excellent, especially to the north, where the long line of the Ben Lawers massif looks magnificent.

Auchnafree Hill can easily be combined with Ben Chonzie by either the Glen Turret or Glen Almond routes, the walking distance between them being 4.5km. The northern Corbetts are most easily ascended from Ardtalnaig, on the south side of Loch Tay, via a circuit of Gleann a' Chilleine. Clockwise the route goes east up a path from Ardtalnaig onto the tops and then south to Creagan na Beinne, down to Dunan at the head of Glen Almond, west to Creag Uchdag then north towards Tullich Hill, dropping east before the summit is reached to pick up the path beside Allt a'Chliodh that leads back to the start. Total distance is 23km with 1350m of ascent, estimated time 6½–7½hrs.

⊗ ◖ A backpacking trip over all the tops is well worthwhile. There are many possible routes and the start point could be to the south, north or east. As an example, a circular route from Invergeldie in Glen Lednock could go up Ben Chonzie then Auchnafree Hill, down north to Glen Almond, along the glen to the track up Lechrea Hill, up over this hill to Creagan na Beinne, down to Dunan and up to Creag Uchdag, southeast to the Allt Mor, down to the Loch Lednock Reservoir and back to Invergeldie. This route is about 40km long with around 2300m of ascent. A strong, determined walker might manage it in 10–12hrs. Two days would make it a pleasant excursion.

2:11 THE GLEN LOCHAY HILLS

Glen Lochay is a quiet, attractive glen running deep into the hills from the western end of Loch Tay. A road runs most of its length past farms, grassy meadows full of cattle and sheep, lovely birch and alder woods and occasional conifer plantations. The River Lochay is quiet and peaceful, with many deep, dark pools. Beyond the public road, which ends after 11km at Kenknock farm, the glen is boggier and bleaker, with few trees. The area at the head of the glen is also known as the Forest of Mamlorn, which was an ancient deer forest where the Scottish kings once hunted.

To the north of Glen Lochay lies Glen Lyon, to the south Glen Dochart. Ben Challum, at the head of the glen, forms the western boundary. In the east the Lairig Breisleich marks the border with the Tarmachan hills. The northern boundary of Loch Lomond and the Trossachs National Park runs along the southern watershed of Glen Lochay.

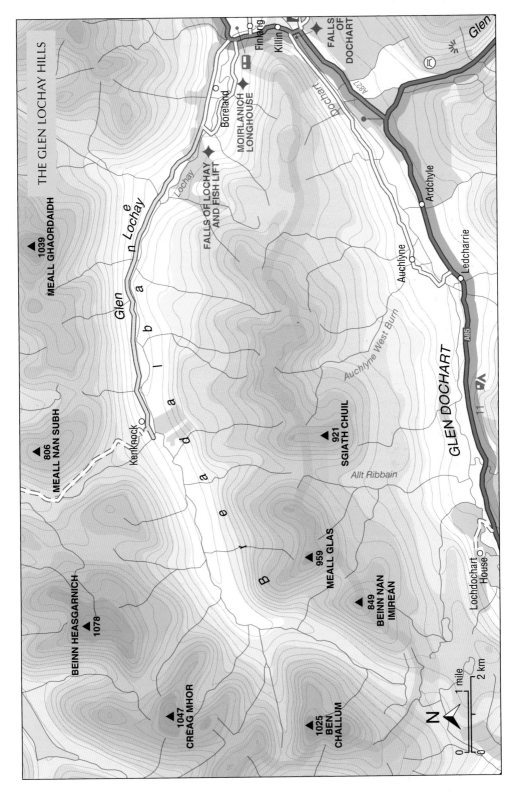

THE GLEN LOCHAY HILLS

MEALL GHAORDAIDH 1039

MEALL NAN SUBH 806

Kenknock

Glen Lochay

Lochay

Falls of Lochay and Fish Lift

Boreland

MOIRLANICH LONGHOUSE

Finlarig

Killin

FALLS OF DOCHART

Glen

A827

Ardchyle

Ledcharrie

Auchlyne

Auchlyne West Burn

A85

GLEN DOCHART

Dochart

BEINN HEASGARNICH 1078

CREAG MHOR 1047

BEN CHALLUM 1025

BEINN NAN IMIREAN 849

MEALL GLAS 959

SGIATH CHUIL 921

Allt Ribbain

Lochdochart House

11

N

0   1 mile
0   2 km

125

Access is from the town of Killin on Loch Tay, itself reached from the east by the A827, which runs from the A9 through Aberfeldy, from the south by the A84, A85 and A827 from Callander and from the west by the A85 and A827 from Crianlarich.

A great horseshoe of hills runs round the glen, consisting of six Munros and three Corbetts, forming its watershed. Running clockwise from the southeast, the Munros are: Sgiath Chuil ('the back wing', 921m); Meall Glas ('grey-green hill', 959m); Ben Challum ('Malcolm's hill', 1025m); Creag Mhor ('big rock', 1047m); Beinn Heasgarnich ('sheltering' or 'peaceful hill', 1078m) and Meall Ghaordaidh (possibly 'the hill of the shoulder' or 'arm', 1039m). The Corbetts are: Beinn nan Imirean ('hill of the ridge', 849m), Meall nan Subh ('raspberry hill', 806m); and Beinn nan Oighreag ('cloudberry hill', 909m). These hills aren't very distinctive and there is much heather and peat bog to cross (although also a fair amount of grass), but they are fairly quiet and lend themselves to long walks, perhaps from a camp in the upper glen. The views from some of the summits are superb. There are a few broken crags and some steep rocky corries, but overall these aren't hills for those who like rock. Under snow they look much more impressive and feel more exciting. Ski touring is probably the best way to see these hills.

🌊 ⛰ A Complete Round of the Loch Lochay Hills

All the hills can be climbed quite easily from Glen Lochay, the only difficulties being navigation in poor visibility. A grand trip would be a circuit of all the summits, starting and finishing at the power station in Glen Lochay (NN 545 351), a distance of around 60km with 4850m of ascent. Given the nature of some of the terrain I'd allow three days for this trip. I've done all the sections but not as a continuous trip.

⛰ Ben Challum

Mostly these hills are climbed singly or in twos or threes. There are many possible routes as there are few obstacles other than peat bogs and deep heather. Ben Challum, which rises as a distinctive pyramid at the head of Glen Lochay, can be climbed by the east ridge that runs down into the glen, a direct route to the summit that is without difficulty, although steep in places. From Kenknock it's 10km with 865m of ascent. The climb should take 3½–4hrs. But the most usual route is from Strath Fillan to the west, starting near Kirkton Farm (NN 357 280) and ascending directly up the grassy northeast slopes to the summit. The distance is only 5.5km, with an ascent of 900m, and shouldn't take more than 2½hrs, but it's a dull slog, far inferior to the Glen Lochay route. The climb

Ben Challum from the northwest

Glen Lyon from Meall nan Subh

leads to the south top, from which a narrow ridge with steep sides leads to the summit. In winter I have seen double cornices on this ridge, which makes the traverse of it potentially dangerous. The best feature on Ben Challum is the steep north face rising above the Allt Challum, the top of which consists of a series of broken crags. The view from the summit is excellent, with the steep pyramids of Ben More and Stob Binnein and the sweeping shapely curves of Ben Lui looking particularly fine. Ben Challum can also be linked with Creag Mhor to the north and Beinn nan Imirean to the east by the connecting passes. These passes can also be used for walks from Strath Fillan to Glen Lochay, perhaps ascending Ben Challum as a side trip en route.

⊗ Beinn nan Imirean, Meall Glas and Sgiath Chuil

Beinn nan Imirean can be climbed on its own from Glen Lochay or from Glen Dochart to its south but only the most committed Corbett bagger is likely to do so as it's a rather dull and uninspiring bump, the good view down Glen Dochart notwithstanding. Combining it with Meall Glas and Sgiath Chuil to the east makes more sense, as it gets three fairly uninteresting summits done in one go. This makes

for a hefty round from Kenknock of some 21km, with 1500m of ascent, and is likely to take 7–8hrs. The round from Auchessan in Glen Dochart to the south is rather shorter at 16km, although the height gain is much the same, so it's steeper. It might take an hour or so less but the featureless slopes hold no interest. Omitting Beinn nan Imirean reduces the distance from Glen Lochy to 17km, with 1275m of ascent, and from Glen Dochart to 15km with 1335m of ascent. Times should be 5½–6½hrs. Of the three hills Sgiath Chuil has the best view – south across Glen Dochart to Ben More and Stob Binnein.

⊗ Creag Mhor and Beinn Heasgarnich

Moving to the north side of Glen Lochy Creag Mhor has the most character of this group of hills, with, steep craggy Coire-cheathaich lying between two long rocky ridges. It can easily be linked with much less interesting Beinn Heasgarnich, although the col between the two is rather boggy. On this round care is needed on the descent of the steep rocky northeast ridge of Creag Mhor. To reach Creag Mhor from Kenknock the private road can be followed to its end at Batavaime, from where the long southeast ridge of the hill can be climbed. Beinn Heasgarnich is a massive hill, the summit taking the form of a long, gently-undulating, quite broad ridge running southwest to northeast. The only real feature is the steep-sided Coire Heasgarnich on the north side of the summit. From Beinn Heasgarnich descend south to regain the track in the glen at Badour. The whole round is some 21km long, with 1400m of ascent, and should take 6½ to 7½hrs.

With all these routes a camp in the upper glen shortens the distance and time considerably. Cutting out 8–10km of track walking saves a couple of hours. From a camp in the glen I've ascended Sgiath Chuil and Meall Glas in the morning, returned to the tent for lunch, then ascended Creag Mhor and Beinn Heasgarnich in the afternoon, a distance of 27km with 2700m of ascent that took almost 12hrs.

⊗ Meall nan Subh
Some 6.5km along the watershed east of Beinn Heasgarnich lies Meall nan Subh, a boggy, bumpy little hill. I don't recommend the walk. It's wet and weary, with soft peat, stream channels, deep heather and tussocks. The best way to climb Meall nan Subh is from the road from Glen Lochay to Glen Lyon, which can be driven at least as far as the sometimes locked gate, a start point at 500m and a climb of just 305m over a distance of 1.5km. The view is worth the effort, with Glen Lyon wending its way east and the huge mass of Beinn Heasgarnich rising to the west.

⊗ Meall Ghaordaidh and Beinn nan Oighreag
Meall Ghaordaidh lies 7.5km along the watershed east of Meall nan Subh. The going is equally as hard as that to Beinn Heasgarnich. Much better is to climb this featureless lump of a hill ('quite the dullest hill in the Southern Highlands', according to Irvine Butterfield), from Glen Lochay or, marginally better, Glen Lyon. A straightforward direct climb up feature-less slopes from Tullich in Glen Lochay (NN 515 367) involves 3km in distance and 870m of ascent.

Some 4km northeast along the watershed from Meall Ghaordaidh lies the last of the Glen Lochay hills, boggy, nondescript Beinn nan Oighreag. The circuit of both tops can be done easily from Duncroisk in Glen Lochay (13km, 1200m ascent, 4½–5hrs) or Stronuich in Glen Lyon (10km, 1075m, 3½–4hrs). If climbing the Corbett alone the easiest route is via the track that leaves Glen Lochay at NN 539 353 and curves round into the Allt Dhuin Croisg glen, from where the south ridge of the hill can be climbed (15km, 800m ascent, 4–5hrs round trip).

2:12 THE BRIDGE OF ORCHY HILLS ☆

West of the A82 road and the West Highland Line lies a compact group of very steep grassy hills with some craggy slopes and deep corries. To the east lies Glen Lyon, to the north Rannoch Moor, to the south Strath Fillan and the Glen Lochay hills. The finest aspect of these hills is the dramatic wall they present to Rannoch Moor, which separates the headwaters of the River Orchy from those of the River Lyon. This 12km long twisting line of steep slopes contains four fine Munros – Beinn Dorain ('mountain of the streamlets', 1076m), Beinn an Dothaidh ('mountain of scorching', 1004m), Beinn Achaladair ('mountain of the farm by the water', 1038m) and Beinn a'Chreachain ('mountain of the bare summit', 1081m). The views over the shining lochs of Rannoch Moor to the Black Mount and Glencoe hills are arguably the finest from any summits in the Southern Highlands. Hidden behind these ramparts is a secretive lower Munro, Beinn Mhanach ('mountain of the monks', 1081m), which is one of the remotest hills in the Southern Highlands.

The Munros are bordered on the southeast by the deep trench of the Auch Gleann (Gleann Ach'-innis Chailein). On the other side of this glen rise five equally steep-sided grassy Corbetts – Beinn Odhar ('dun-coloured hill', 901m), Beinn Chaorach ('sheep hill', 818m), Cam Chreag ('crooked crag', 884m), Beinn nam Fuaran ('hill of the springs', 806m) and Beinn a'Chaisteil ('castle hill', 886m). These hills are so close together that they can be climbed in one outing, albeit one with a great deal of ascent and descent, the only place where this is possible with Corbetts.

Lying directly above the A82 road and the West Highland Line the Bridge of Orchy hills are very accessible from the west. Indeed, their situation and dramatic appearance makes them very well known to travellers heading north by road or rail from Tyndrum. As the pass north of the village is reached one of the great views of the Southern Highlands appears, with the great pyramid of Beinn Dorain towering some 900m over the glen below, and in front of it the smaller but almost identical pyramid of Beinn Odhar. Further north the other three Munros look impressive from the point where the road curves away across the western end of Rannoch Moor. The view from the railway is not

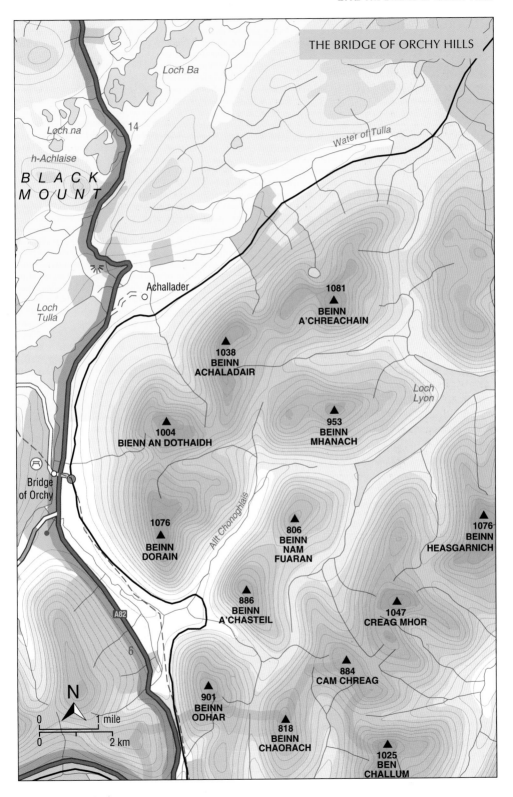

THE BRIDGE OF ORCHY HILLS

Loch Ba

14

Loch na
h-Achlaise

Water of Tulla

B L A C K
M O U N T

Achallader

Loch
Tulla

1081
BEINN
A'CHREACHAIN

1038
BEINN
ACHALADAIR

Loch
Lyon

1004
BIENN AN DOTHAIDH

953
BEINN
MHANACH

Bridge
of Orchy

Allt Chonoghlais

1076
BEINN
DORAIN

806
BEINN
NAM
FUARAN

1076
BEINN
HEASGARNICH

886
BEINN
A'CHASTEIL

1047
CREAG MHOR

A82

6

N

884
CAM CHREAG

0   1 mile

0   2 km

901
BEINN
ODHAR

818
BEINN
CHAORACH

1025
BEN
CHALLUM

quite so good, as it hugs the foot of the mountains closely. In fact the best view is of the railway rather than from it, as it crosses the Auch Gleann on a fine viaduct with the ribbed slopes of Beinn a'Chasteil rising above it. Tyndrum (see The Ben Lui Hills above) and Bridge of Orchy are the main centres, both with railway stations. Bridge of Orchy has a hotel and a small shop at the station, but no more. From the east approaches are long, either beside the Loch Lyon reservoir, along Glen Lochay, or over the tops, and so are best suited to multi-day trips. The east side of these mountains is much less dramatic and imposing, too.

This is the land of Duncan MacIntyre, known as the Glenorchy Bard and Duncan of the Songs, a renowned Gaelic poet who was born near Loch Tulla just to the north of the Bridge of Orchy hills in 1724. After the 1745 Uprising, in which he fought for the Jacobites, he worked as a forester in the Beinn Dorain area and lived in the Auch Gleann. His most famous poem is 'In Praise of Ben Dorain' ('Moladh Beinn Dorain'), one line of which translates as 'O gladly in times of old I trod that glorious ground', and in which the poet describes Ben Dorain as 'the most beautiful mountain I have seen under the sun'.

The Corbett Five ☆

The complete round of these hills is a fine expedition, with varied views and a sense of remoteness and wildness that is surprising so close to a main road and rail line. It's also an arduous undertaking as it involves around 2000m of ascent and 23km of distance, and is likely to take 9–12hrs. The best start point is on the A82 at NN 328 330, where there is space for car parking and the railway can be crossed on the West Highland Way. The steep haul up the big cone of Beinn Odhar starts immediately, at first by an old mine track on the south ridge, then it's down steeply towards the dauntingly steep looking west wall of Beinn Chaorach. It's just a steep climb, however, as are the following ascents of Cam Chreag, Beinn nam Fuaran and Beinn a'Chaisteil. The going is mostly on grass with some peat bogs. There are spacious views from all the summits with Ben Challum a fine bold pyramid and Beinn Dorain a rather blunter, bulkier one. To the southwest Ben Lui stands, graceful and proud. From Beinn nam Fuaran you look right down Glen Lyon and out east, yet from Beinn Odhar the view is all to the west. As Hamish Brown points out, these hills have curious, contorted watersheds. Perhaps the most interesting is Cam Chreag. The actual summit stands above slopes that drain north to Glen Lyon, west to the Auch Gleann and the River Orchy and south to Strath Fillan. However the subsidiary summit, just 1km southeast along the ridge, rises above slopes that drain into Glen Lochay, making this almost, but not quite, one of the Glen Lochay hills. With burns draining ultimately to both the North Sea and the Irish Sea these hills, along with the Munros to the north, are on the watershed of Scotland.

An alternative to a round trip from the A82 is to carry a tent into the hills and camp among them. There are many fine, quiet sites where you can listen to sandpipers calling by the burns, rather than lorries rumbling along the A82, the bulky hills blocking out all sounds of vehicles from the road and railway to the west. On one trip I started from Tyndrum along the West Highland Way, climbed up beside the Crom Allt to the southeast shoulder of Beinn Odhar, left the pack while I went up and down the latter, collected the pack and went on to Beinn Chaorach. The pack was left again at the next col for the ascent of Cam Chreag. Back at the col I descended northwards to the Allt a'Mhaim, beside which I camped before climbing the last two peaks. The whole trip was 19km long with 2050m of ascent and took 10¼hrs.

The Munro Five ☆

The five Munros can be climbed in one long day, but as the main four are strung out in an undulating line there is a long way back to the start. Even if the outlier, Beinn Mhanach, is omitted a round trip from Bridge of Orchy involves 30km and 2100m of ascent. The start or finish along the A82 and the long section beside the Water of Tulla would probably be tedious, too, on such a long day. Far better would be to carry camping gear and spend one or two nights out. The last time I did this I traversed all five hills from Bridge of Orchy then descended east for a high camp near the head of the Allt Learg Mheuran. The distance was 19km with 2000m of ascent and the whole walk took 10hrs.

For enjoyable day walks it's best to climb these hills in two or three separate trips. Beinn Dorain and Beinn Dothaidh make an obvious pair, lying either side of Coire an Dothaidh. The round trip is 13km, with 1380m of ascent, and should take 5–6hrs. The route is T-shaped, with each hill

Allt a'Mhaim and Beinn nam Fuaran ▸

ascended from the col at the head of Coire an Dothaidh and the route retraced to Bridge of Orchy. There is a well-used eroded muddy path and there are no problems, although the going is steep in places and wet in others. Note that the summit of Ben Dorain is at the far end of the ridge. There is a big cairn a few hundred metres before the top that could be assumed to be the summit in mist. A short distance south of the summit there is a dramatic view down to the railway line and the via-duct across the Auch Gleann. On Beinn Dothaidh the middle of the three summits is the highest. Both hills are steep and craggy enough to make interest-ing and exciting outings when under snow. There are some graded winter climbs in the northeast cor-rie of Beinn Dothaidh.

Beinn Achaladair and Beinn a'Chreachain are most easily climbed from Achallader farm (NN 321 442), where a car park is provided for walk-ers. From the farm Beinn Achaladair presents a huge steep curved face that appears quite daunt-ing. The route however goes up a path beside the Allt Coire Achaladair to the col between Beinn an Dothaidh and Beinn Achaladair from where the hill is easily climbed on grassy slopes. The views out over Rannoch Moor and along the crags on the northwest side of the hills to Beinn a'Chreachain are impressive. The walk to Beinn a'Chreachain is quite easy however, as is the descent to the Water of Tulla. The total distance is 18km, with 1300m of ascent, and the walk takes 6–7hrs.

The fifth Munro, Beinn Mhanach, can be included in the round of Beinn Achaladair and Beinn a'Chreachain from the col between Beinn an Dothaidh and Beinn Achaladair, adding an extra 7km and 500m of ascent. If climbed on its own – something only keen Munro baggers are likely to do as it's a rather featureless hill overshadowed by its higher and grander neighbours – the best route is via the Auch Gleann, and involves 19km of walk-ing, mostly on a track, and 870m of ascent. The round trip should take 5–6hrs. The hill appears as a long rounded ridge with gentle summit domes at each end. Beinn Mhanach is the far one, the nearer one being a subsidiary top called Beinn a'Chuirn. Although the hill itself is uninteresting it does offer good views of Beinn Dorain, Beinn Heasgarnich and Creag Mhor and the remote situation is pleas-ing. Beinn Mhanach is the nearest of these hills to the road end in Glen Lyon and it's a 10km round trip along the reservoir, up the east ridge and back.

2:13 BEN LAWERS AND THE TARMACHANS ☆

Ben Lawers is the centre of the largest mountain massif, and also the highest summit, in the Southern Highlands, and is the tenth highest hill in Scotland. There are seven Munros in the Ben Lawers group and the ridge linking them never falls below 750m. The area from the summits southwards has been owned by the National Trust for Scotland since 1950 and forms the Ben Lawers National Nature Reserve, created because the soft schist that makes up the hills is unusually lime-rich and breaks down easily into calcareous soils that support a wide variety of arctic/alpine plants and montane scrub. In 1996 the National Trust for Scotland (NTS) also bought the southern part of the Tarmachans to the east, also in part for the rare flora. Botanists should enjoy these hills in spring and summer.

The hills lie between Loch Tay in the south and Glen Lyon in the north, with the Lairig Breisleich separating them from the Glen Lochay hills to the west. The confluence of the rivers Lyon and Tay forms the eastern boundary. The area is very easy to reach from all directions, with the A827 run-ning south of the hills alongside Loch Tay and the A85 approaching from the west and the east. To the north the minor road along Glen Lyon gives access to this side of the hills. Another minor road runs over the Lochan na Lairige pass, from near the west end of Loch Tay to Glen Lyon, so the Lawers group is completely encircled by roads. The Lochan na Lairige road runs between the Lawers group and the Tarmachans and gives the quickest access to both sets of hills. It's not cleared in winter, however, and so may become impassable due to snow and ice.

Killin is the main centre for the hills and has all facilities including a youth hostel, campsites, a Tourist Information Centre and an outdoor gear shop. Alternatives are Kenmore at the eastern end of Loch Tay and the pretty little town of Aberfeldy, 10km further east down the Tay valley.

The Ben Lawers massif consists of bulky grassy hills with broad shoulders. The main ridge runs roughly southwest to northeast, with many long side ridges running north and south. There are some small crags in high corries but nothing significant for rock climbers. For the hillwalker these are superb hills however, with fine views and interesting high-level walking. From west to

◄ View across Loch Lyon to Beinn a'Chreachain

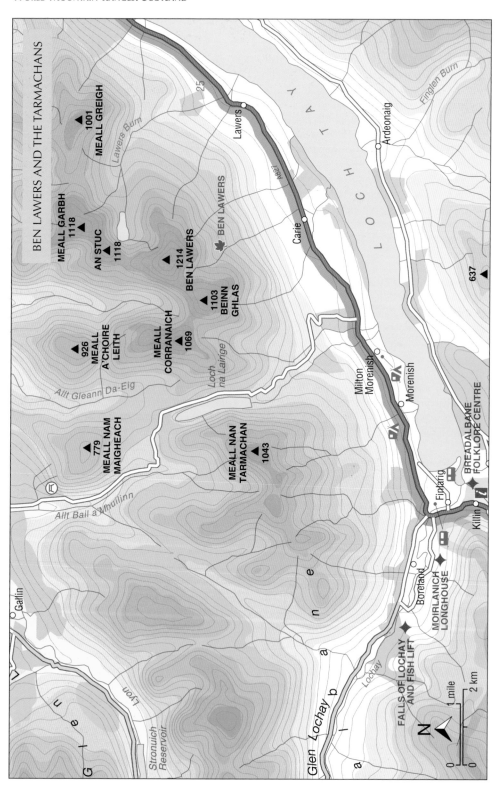

BEN LAWERS AND THE TARMACHANS

MEALL GREIGH 1001

Lawers

25

MEALL GARBH 1118

AN STUC 1118

BEN LAWERS

BEN LAWERS 1214

Carie

BEINN GHLAS 1103

MEALL A'CHOIRE LEITH 926

MEALL CORRANAICH 1069

Loch na Lairige

637

Allt Gleann Da-Eig

Milton Morenish

Morenish

MEALL NAM MAIGHEACH 779

MEALL NAN TARMACHAN 1043

BREADALBANE FOLKLORE CENTRE

Fintarig

Allt Bail a'Mhuilinn

Killin

L O C H   T A Y

Ardeonaig

Finglen Burn

Lawers Burn

BORELAND

MOIRLANICH LONGHOUSE

Gatlin

Lyon

Stronuich Reservoir

Lochay

Glen Lochay

G l e n   L y o n

FALLS OF LOCHAY AND FISH LIFT

N

0   1 mile
0   2 km

The Ben Lawers range from the north

east the Munros are Meall a'Choire Leith ('hill of the grey corrie', 926m), Meall Corranaich ('hill of the sickle', 1069m), Beinn Ghlas ('grey-green hill', 1103m), Ben Lawers (probably 'loud hill', 1214m), An Stuc ('the rocky cone', 1118m), 1118m Meall Garbh ('rough hill', 1118m) and Meall Greigh ('herd hill', 1001m). There is just one Corbett, Meall nam Maigheach ('hill of the hares', 779m), which lies west of Meall a'Choire Leith.

Unlike the Lawers hills the Tarmachans are rough and rocky, a twisting knobbly ridge. Only the highest summit, Meall nan Tarmachan ('ptarmigan hill', 1044m), is a Munro, but the whole ridge is impressive, with four distinct tops.

Ben Lawers and the Tarmachans look impressive from the descent to Glen Dochart from the pass at the head of Glen Ogle on the A85 road and from Ben Chonzie and other summits to the south of Loch Tay. The Ben Lawers massif rises as an undulating line of scalloped green hills with long broad ridges running down to the blue waters of Loch Tay. The Tarmachans look more rugged and rocky, appearing as a stony, spiny ridge with pointed summits.

Back in the days when hills were measured in feet rather than metres 4000 feet was a highly significant elevation. There are only nine Munros

above this height. At 3984 feet (1214m) Ben Lawers just misses out. In 1878 after this awful truth came out with the first accurate measurement of the hill a local man named Malcolm Ferguson paid for a cairn over 20 feet (6m) high to be erected on the summit in order to raise the hill over the magic number. This cairn is long gone, although some of its stones must reside in the current edifice. Now that hills are measured using the metric system Ben Lawers is one of the ten Munros above 1200m.

Ben Lawers played a key part in the development of skiing in Scotland. The Scottish Ski Club built a hut in Coire Odhar below Meall Corranaich and Beinn Ghlas in the 1930s, and held races in the corrie, one of which started from the summit of Beinn Ghlas. In the early 1950s the club erected a rope tow on the col above the hut. Happily no permanent tows were built, and once they were erected elsewhere mass skiing deserted these hills, which were left clear for the ski tourers.

The desolation of a ski resort may have passed the Lawers hills by but a lesser tourist attraction was unfortunately built, by, of all people, the National Trust for Scotland, in the form of a visitor centre at 430m on the Lochan na Lairige road. Unsurprisingly the ascent of Ben Lawers from the centre became very popular, and a wide, eroded path runs from it over Beinn Ghlas to the summit. The visitor centre is now closed. Hopefully the NTS will eventually build a new centre in Killin, as they have done in Glencoe, and restore the path. Before the Lochan na Lairige road and the NTS visitor centre the main ascent route was from Lawers to the southeast of the summit.

Long before the skiers there were people on the mountains. A party organised by an antiquarian called General William Roy made the first recorded ascent of Ben Lawers in 1776 (it's unclear whether Roy himself reached the summit) as part of Roy's study of the use of barometers to measure heights. However it is likely that local people had made the ascent long before this as there are ruins of many shielings (temporary dwellings used when animals were brought up to graze in summer) on the hill, some of them above 600m. There were shielings within 1km of the summit and, as Ian R. Mitchell points out, it seems highly improbable that no one from them ever climbed to the top, whether in search of straying beasts or for the pleasure of the ascent itself.

☾ The Ben Lawers Traverse ☆

The traverse of all seven Munros in the Ben Lawers range is one of the finest hillwalks in the Southern Highlands. As a one day trip it's long and arduous; over two days with a camp en route it's much easier. Because the western summits form a horseshoe around the Allt a' Chobhair glen the best start point for a circuit is to the north, at Camusvrachan in Glen Lyon (NN 619 478). Depending on the exact route taken the whole round involves 28km of walking and 2265m of ascent, and a time of 10–12hrs. A circuit from the high point on the Lochan na Lairige road has the advantage of starting at 570m but the return from the easternmost summit, Meall Greigh, is long. If going this way it would be best to take two days, or else arrange a pickup or leave a car near Lawers on the A827. The whole round involves around the same distance and ascent as the Glen Lyon route, but there is more rough country to cross. Having a car or a lift reduces the distance by 6km.

☾ The Lawers traverse is also a fine ski tour. Indeed, in the SMC's *Ski Mountaineering in Scotland*

(SMC, 1987) it's described as 'undoubtedly one of the three or four best ski-mountaineering expeditions in Scotland'. The route is much the same as the walking one, except that the northeast ridge of An Stuc is best bypassed, either by descending into the Fin Glen to the north or via Lochan nan Cat to the east. All but keen peak baggers (and strong skiers) will probably omit Meall a'Choire Leith.

☾ Other Lawers Range Routes

The two westernmost hills, Meall a'Choire Leith and Meall Corranaich, can be climbed from the high point on the Lochan an Lairige road, a round trip of 10km and 750m of ascent that should only take 3–4hrs. Neither hill is particularly inspiring – indeed Meall a'Choire Leith is really just a rounded bump on the end of the north ridge of Meall Corranaich – but there are excellent views of the rest of the range, especially Beinn Ghlas and Ben Lawers. The Corbett Meall nam Maigheach can be included in this round, an extension of around 5km and 250m of ascent, taking 1½hrs.

A more enjoyable route up Meall nam Maigheach is from Camusvrachan in Glen Lyon, where a track runs up the strangely named Gleann Da-Eig ('glen of the two eggs') to where the eastern slopes can be climbed to the summit then the long north ridge descended back to Glen Lyon (14km, 775m, 4hrs). The ascent of Meall nam Maigheach from Glen Lyon can easily be linked with ascents of Meall a'Choire Leith and Meall Corranaich and arguably the finest route at the western end of the range is the circuit of Gleann Da-Eig, starting with the ascent of the north ridge of Meall nam Maigheach and finishing with the descent of the north ridge of Meall a'Choire Leith (20km, 1450m, 6½–7hrs).

☆ A much more entertaining and exciting walk is the round of the five eastern summits. This can be done from the old NTS Visitor Centre if you don't mind the crowds as far as the summit of Ben Lawers. The distance is 22km with 1740m of ascent if returning to the start point. A quieter way is from the south, from Lawers or Tombreck on the A827. Distances are around 20km, ascents 1650m. Ben Lawers can be ascended directly from the road too. It's just 4km with 980m of ascent to the summit. However none of these southern routes are very interesting until the summits are reached as the southern slopes are fairly uniform and featureless. The many traces of old shielings and the plant life are the main attractions.

Ben Lawers (right) and An Stuc from Meall nam Maigheach

☆ The finest section of any of these routes is from Beinn Ghlas to Meall Garbh, a high-level walk with good views to distant peaks and down into the deep corries to either side. Particularly good is the view down to little Lochan na Cat from the minor summit of Creag an Fhithich, and the ridge round to An Stuc. The latter is the most impressive peak in the Lawers range, a sharp, pointed little grassy summit with steep drops all around. It also has the only difficult section in the whole range, its short rocky northeast ridge being very steep, very loose and, when wet, very slippery. Under ice and snow this ridge requires care and respect. The ground on the Fin Glen side to the north is slightly easier going.

☼ The Tarmachan Ridge ☆

Meall nan Tarmachan can be easily and quickly climbed direct from the Lochan na Lairige dam (1.75km, 560m of ascent to the summit) but this misses almost all that is best about the Tarmachans. To really enjoy and appreciate the hill the bumpy ridge over the subsidiary summits of Creag na Caillich, Beinn nan Eachan and Meall Garbh should be traversed. From near the old NTS Visitor Centre a track runs west across the southern slopes to below the south ridge of craggy Creag na Caillich. Once on the ridge Meall Garbh appears as an impressive steep pinnacle with a narrow arête

below the summit. It's not quite as forbidding as it looks, but nevertheless the ascent does involve a little easy scrambling. From the summit of Meall nan Tarmachan the south ridge leads down to a path that goes back to the track and the start. The distance is 13.5km, with an ascent of 900m, and the walk takes 4–5hrs.

An alternative round starts to the north of the ridge. Meall Garbh lies at the head of Coire Riadhailt and the circuit of this corrie is a good walk, starting at the northern end of Lochan na Lairige and crossing the corrie, ascending over Meall Glas and Beinn a'Bhuic to Meall Garbh and Meall nan Tarmachan, and then descending the north ridge of the latter over Creag an Lochain (11km, 835m, 3½–4hrs).

2:14 GLEN LYON, SCHIEHALLION AND ABERFELDY

Long, beautiful Glen Lyon stretches deep into the hills, running 48km from Strath Tay to its head-waters west of the Loch Lyon reservoir, just 8km from Bridge of Orchy. The glen is narrow and winding, with a mix of forestry plantations, semi-natural woodland of Scots pine, oak and birch, and pastureland through which the lovely River

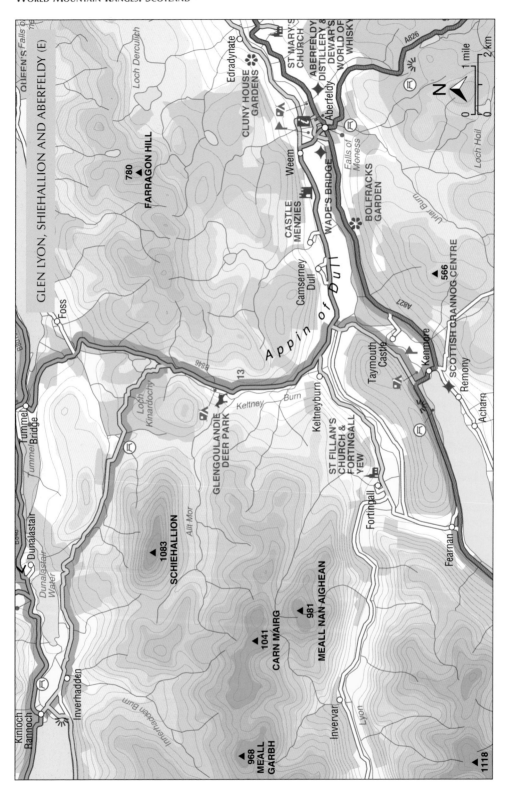

GLEN LYON, SHIEHALLION AND ABERFELDY (E)

Western continuation on p139

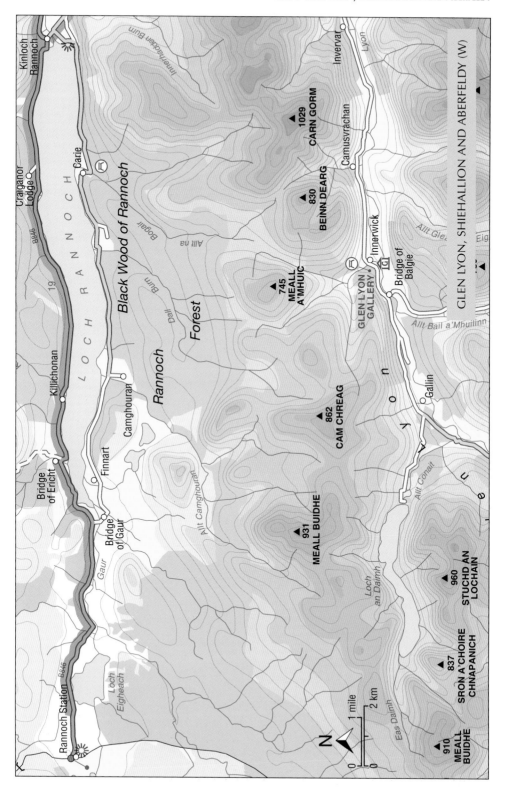

GLEN LYON, SCHIEHALLION AND ABERFELDY (W)

Kinloch Rannoch

Craiganour Lodge

B846

Killichonan

LOCH RANNOCH

Gaur

Bridge of Ericht

Bridge of Gaur

Rannoch Station

B846

Loch Eigheach

Finnart

Camghouran

Carie

Black Wood of Rannoch

Rannoch Forest

Allt Camghouran

Dall Burn

Bogair

Allt na

Innerhadden Burn

▲ 745 MEALL A'MHUIC

▲ 830 BEINN DEARG

▲ 1029 CARN GORM

Camusvrachan

Invervar

Lyon

Allt Glea

Eig

Innerwick

GLEN LYON GALLERY

Bridge of Balgie

Allt Bail a'Mhuilinn

Gallin

Allt Conait

▲ 862 CAM CHREAG

▲ 931 MEALL BUIDHE

Loch an Daimh

▲ 960 STUCHD AN LOCHAIN

▲ 837 SRON A'CHOIRE CHNAPANICH

▲ 910 MEALL BUIDHE

Eas Daimh

N

0   1 mile
0   1   2 km

139

Lyon meanders gently. The journey along the glen reveals constantly changing vistas of wood, hill, moor, meadow and water, a delicious blend of scenery that is both calming and exciting, satisfying and stimulating.

A single track road runs up the glen past farms and hamlets from the B846 Aberfeldy to Tummel Bridge road to finish just below the Loch Lyon reservoir. The only road exit from Glen Lyon along its length is via the Lochan na Lairige road from Loch Tay, which reaches the glen at Bridge of Balgie.

There are several attractive little villages in Glen Lyon. Fortingall at the east end has a hotel and several lovely thatched cottages and is famous for the huge Fortingall Yew, reckoned to be 5000 years old and the oldest living thing in Europe, which can be found in the churchyard. A local legend says that Pontius Pilate was born in Fortingall, but, as the Romans didn't reach here until after AD43 this is clearly fanciful.

A few kilometres up the glen from Fortingall the river narrows and rushes through a deep gorge with big trees on either side. This is called Macgregor's Leap after the feat of Gregor MacGregor, the chief of the clan, who leapt the chasm to escape pursuing enemies in the 1560s.

At pretty Bridge of Balgie in the heart of the glen the Post Office houses a small shop and a café. Beyond Balgie lies Meggernie Castle, a grand edifice dating from 1585 and much modified since, which was once the stronghold of the Campbells of Glen Lyon.

Beyond Meggernie Castle the character of the glen changes and it becomes wilder, harsher and bleaker with moorland running down to the river, although the upper glen isn't untouched: there are two reservoirs with adjacent hydroelectric power stations, little Stronuich and large Loch Lyon.

A long line of moorland hills stretches along the northern side of the glen, continuing above Strath Tay to Pitlochry. These are rolling grass and heather hills, with little exposed rock and few crags. Only one has any real character, famous and popular Schiehallion, and that really belongs to Rannoch rather than Lyon. Apart from Schiehallion this is one area where I think the glens, woods, lochs and rivers are more attractive, interesting and enjoyable than the summits.

There are six other Munros to the north of Glen Lyon apart from Schiehallion, along with four Corbetts, plus two outlying Corbetts between Aberfeldy and Loch Tummel. The remotest

The River Lyon near Camusvrachan

summits are Meall Buidhe ('yellow hill', 910m) and Sron a'Choire Chnapanich ('nose of the knobbly corrie', 837m), which rise above Loch Lyon. Just to their east is one of the few hills in this region with any character, Stuchd an Lochain ('peak of the little loch', 960m), which has a craggy north face overlooking Lochan nan Cat and the Loch an Daimh reservoir, which lies at the head of a short side glen which leads from Glen Lyon. North of Loch an Daimh is another Meall Buidhe, this one a Munro at 931m. Rolling moorland extends east from Meall Buidhe for some 14km to the next Munro. The high points of this moorland are the two rounded Corbetts of Cam Chreag ('crooked crag', 862m) and Beinn Dearg ('red hill', 830m). Finally, above the east end of Glen Lyon, there is some slightly more interesting terrain in the form of a huge semi-circular broad ridge, stretching some 10km from end to end, containing four Munros – Carn Gorm ('blue hill', 1029m), Meall Garbh ('rough hill', 968m), Carn Mairg (perhaps 'rusty hill', 1041m, for whom the group is named) and Meall nan Aighean ('hill of the heifers' or 'hinds', 981m).

As I've said none of the above hills are of any great character. However, just to the northeast of the Carn Mairg group lies one of the most distinctive mountains in the whole of Scotland, Schiehallion, the 'Fairy Hill of the Caledonians' (1083m). This fine isolated peak stands out in views from all over the Highlands south of the Great Glen, often appearing as a soaring pyramid, although it's actually a long curving steep-sided wedge of a hill.

East of Schiehallion the high moorland continues towards Pitlochry over two more Corbetts, Meall Tairneachan ('hill of thunder', 787m) and Farragon Hill ('St Fergan's Hill', 783m). To their south the lovely little village of Aberfeldy in upper Strath Tay makes a good base for the Glen Lyon hills, and has several interesting attractions for days when the weather makes the high tops unattractive including tours of the Aberfeldy Distillery, opened in 1898, and the restored Aberfeldy Water Mill dating from 1825, now a bookshop and café, and a fine stone bridge over the Tay, built in 1733 by General Wade. (Aberfeldy has also given its name to a rather good acoustic music group. The group's founder Riley Briggs named the group after the town because he had enjoyed a holiday there as a youngster).

The Birks of Aberfeldy ☆

The main attraction for walkers in Aberfeldy is the deep ravine running south of the town down which runs the Moness Burn. This damp mossy chasm is heavily wooded with a delightful mix of oak, beech, ash, elm, birch (the 'birks' of the name) and Scots pine. Cascades tumble down the sides of the gorge, and at its head lie the splendid Falls of Moness. After heavy rain the waters are particularly impressive, while the woodland colours are wonderful in spring and autumn.

The ravine used to be called the Den of Moness but is now known as the Birks of Aberfeldy after being made famous by Robert Burns' song of that name, written in 1787, which contains the verses:

The braes ascend like lofty wa's,
The foaming stream deep-roaring fa's,
O'erhung wi' fragrant spreading shaws-
The birks of Aberfeldy.
The hoary cliffs are crown'd wi' flowers,
White o'er the linns the burnie pours,
And rising, weets wi' misty showers
The birks of Aberfeldy.

Good paths run up each side of the ravine, linked by a bridge above the falls. The start is in open woodland, with the gentle burn gurgling through the trees, a pleasant scene that belies the drama to come. The path up the east (true right) side of the burn rises gently at first and then, as the sides of the gorge steepen, zigzags steeply upwards in a series of wooden steps with excellent views down to the rushing waters. At one point a side stream cascades down, to crash into the Moness Burn far below. The main Falls come into view near the top of the path and are in three separate sections, of which the top fall, which drops 15m into a deep rocky amphitheatre, is the most impressive. On the west (true left) side of the burn the path descends more gently, and the views are less grand. The whole walk is only 4km long, with 160m of ascent and can be completed in an hour, although it's better to take longer to enjoy the wildness and beauty of this little gem.

Weem Woods ☆

Just north of Aberfeldy the little village of Weem lies below craggy wooded slopes, where there is an interesting short walk. The wood, now part of the Forestry Commission's Tay Forest Park, is old and contains many fine big trees planted by the

THE SCOTTISH CRANNOG CENTRE

A few hundred metres along the south shore from the foot of Loch Tay lies the fascinating Scottish Crannog Centre (www.crannog.co.uk), where there is a reconstruction of a circular Iron Age lake dwelling, or crannog, built by the Scottish Trust for Underwater Archaeology. There were many crannogs on Loch Tay, built some 5000 years ago, and their remnants can be seen in the form of some of the islands dotting the loch. For anyone interested in the history of the hills and the story of the people who lived here in the past the Scottish Crannog Centre is well worth a visit. Just imagine Loch Tay dotted with crannogs, smoke rising from the roofs, with people grinding grain inside and working on the crops growing in clearings in the forest growing thickly along the shores. Did these people ever climb through the woods and onto the summits? There were no roads but log boats were used on the loch – the remains of a hollowed out oak tree dating from 1500BC plus a steering oar and a paddle blade have been found in the loch – presumably both for fishing and travel between crannogs. As well as visiting the reconstructed crannog, built on wooden posts driven into the loch, you can try your hand at various ancient crafts such as using a bow drill to make holes in a stone and starting a fire by wood friction. The last could be a useful skill in the wilds!

Menzies family, who once owned the estate, in the 19th century. In particular there are some magnificent beeches and Douglas firs, the latter named for one of Scotland's great 19th-century plant collectors, David Douglas, who brought its seeds back from the Pacific Northwest. Another plant collector, Archibald Menzies from Aberfeldy, also introduced some of the trees here. A path climbs through the woods to a shallow cave under an overhanging cliff, where there is a small spring flowing into a basin in the rock known as St David's Well. St Cuthbert, Bishop of Lindisfarne, used the cave as a retreat, probably in 655, but it's named for a son of the local laird, St David, who stayed in it in the fifteenth century. There are many legends about demons and dragons associated with Weem Wood and a log carved into a fine likeness of a sleeping dragon curled round its stolen treasure can be seen beside the path at one point.

The Glen Lyon Hills

All the Glen Lyon hills can be easily climbed from the glen and equally easily linked by long traverses, although the latter can be very boggy in places. As the ascents and descents tend to be fairly tedious plods up and down featureless moorland I think linking the hills in long trips is more enjoyable as you do stay high, with sweeping views over the wide expanse of moorland – when it's clear, that is. In mist navigation can be difficult due to the lack of any distinctive landmarks. An interesting excursion would be a continuous trip, starting with an ascent of Stuchd an

Lochain from the end of the public road below the Loch Lyon dam, and finishing with the descent of Meall nan Aighean to Invervar. This would be a tough and challenging expedition of around 50km, with 4000m of ascent. I'd allow at least two days. The trip would be even better on skis, as all this rolling moorland is ideal for long ski tours, preferably on fairly light cross country gear.

If climbing the hills as day trips then several of them can be paired, which makes sense given the time required to reach the start points for ascents. The two western Corbetts, Meall Buidhe and Sron a'Choire Cnapanaich, can be climbed together from the end of the Glen Lyon road in 4–5hrs, a distance of 14km and an ascent of 950m. Add on 4km, 330m of ascent and another hour and Stuchd an Lochain can be included too.

That said, the most interesting side of Stuchd an Lochain faces north towards Loch an Daimh (which lies at 430m, cutting out some of the ascent) and the best ascent is from this side via the subsidiary tops of Creag an Fheadain and Sron Chona Choirein. The summit is a fine little peak perched right on the edge of the craggy corrie containing little Lochan na Cat. Descent can be made into the corrie from the eastern end, then down to the loch shore (a round trip of 9km with 600m of ascent that takes around 3hrs). This short walk is arguably the best hillwalk in this whole area apart from Schiehallion.

North of Stuchd an Lochain lies Meall Buidhe, which can be climbed on the same day, although only keen Munro baggers are likely to do so as it's

Carn Mairg from the east

quite dull and lacking in character. The direct route from the Loch an Daimh dam is the same length, with around the same ascent, and takes the same amount of time as the one up Stuchd an Lochain, but there's no comparison in terms of quality. There may be moorland flowers of interest on Meall Buidhe, and the view is extensive, but that's it.

East of Meall Buidhe the two equally rounded and undistinguished heather and grass Corbetts of Cam Chreag and Beinn Dearg can each be climbed from Innerwick in Glen Lyon, the first via Allt a'Choire Uidhre, up which a bulldozed road runs, the second, dodging the forestry plantations on the lower slopes, via either its southwestern or western slopes. The Cam Chreag route is 12km long with 660m of ascent, the Beinn Dearg one 9km with 650m of ascent, so both can climbed on the same day, the total time needed being no more than 7–8hrs.

⊗ The Carn Mairg Circuit

The main attraction of this moorland arc is that it includes four Munros. Starting and finishing at Invervar in Glen Lyon, the round is 18km long with 1400m of ascent and takes 6–7hrs. There are no difficulties unless it's misty, when navigation requires care in places. The terrain is mostly grassy,

with some broken mica schist and quartz visible in places. The summits are just rises on the high moorland and the enjoyment of the route lies in staying high up above the glens, with vast space all around and big skies up above, a feeling more akin to that experienced in the Cairngorms to the northeast than elsewhere in the Southern Highlands. To the south runs the rippling line of the Ben Lawers range, to the northeast a great whaleback dominates the view, Schiehallion, looking big and bulky rather than the usual graceful cone.

⊗ Schiehallion ☆

Schiehallion is one of the finest hills in the Southern Highlands. It's also one of the most popular, with thousands of ascents every year, virtually all from the Braes of Foss car park. East Schiehallion, which includes the summit, Gleann Mor to the south and the approach from Braes of Foss, has been owned by the John Muir Trust since 1999. The path from Braes of Foss used to be a wide, eroded scar but the JMT has realigned the route and built a new path, at a cost of over £800,000, that should stand the passage of thousands of feet much better and blend in with the landscape. The JMT is also doing work to restore the old path so that the scar will heal

Schiehallion from the south

in time and become invisible. The old path was slippery and treacherous as well as unsightly. The new path is pleasant to walk, but be aware that the long summit ridge of the mountain is made up of sharp angular blocks of quartzite that have to be crossed.

Unlike most other hills in the Southern Highlands Schiehallion is an isolated hill, surrounded by deep glens and without links to any other summits. It's also a very rocky hill, being mostly made up of hard white quartzite, which shines and glints in sunshine. On the lower slopes there is a band of limestone, forming 'pavements' in places, where there are rich grasslands and also some caves. The vegetation is mostly moorland, even at lower levels, but the JMT is working to reduce grazing pressure so that trees can regenerate.

Although Schiehallion looks impressive from many vantage points perhaps the best view is that from the northwest across Loch Rannoch, from where it appears as an elegant cone curving up above delicate birch woods and the blue waters of the loch, a perfect Highland scene.

Schiehallion is famous for the experiments carried out in 1774 by the Astronomer Royal, Neville Maskelyne, to prove Newton's Law of Gravity by showing that the mountain exerted a gravitational pull on a plumbline dropped from the summit. Maskelyne's work has more than academic interest for hillwalkers as Charles Hutton, one of those who analysed the data, invented the concept of contour lines when mapping Maskelyne's observation points.

The easiest ascent of Schiehallion is up the east ridge from the Braes of Foss by the new JMT path, a round trip of 9km with an ascent of 750m. This route is very popular, so you are likely to be accompanied by many others, but there are plenty of alternative, quieter options. Although there are crags on the sides of Schiehallion these are easily avoided and an ascent can be made almost anywhere, but the south and north faces do involve some quite arduous steep climbing through a mix of heather and boulders. An excellent option is to walk into Gleann Mor, a wide, attractive glen, and climb the south side of the mountain, perhaps descending by the JMT path, a round trip of 11.5km with 800m of ascent. The steep west ridge can be climbed too, a distance of 9km with 850m of ascent. The shortest ascent is the direct route up the north side, involving just 5km and 700m of ascent. The summit can be reached in 3hrs or under by any of these routes, leaving ample time to admire the extensive views, that along Loch Rannoch being particularly fine.

⊗ Farragon Hill and Meall Tairneachan

The block of moorland between Schiehallion and Pitlochry contains the easternmost hills of the Southern Highlands, with two knobbly summits that reach Corbett height, Farragon Hill ('St Fergan's hill', 783m) and Meall Tairneachan ('hill of thunder', 787m). The landscape is surprisingly rugged with many small outcrops and knolls and a scattering of attractive little lochs, but unfortunately the area is sullied by baryte mines high on the sides of the hills, and the accompanying bull-dozed roads (baryte is a mineral from which the element barium comes, and has various industrial uses). Despite the mines the traverse of the hills is quite a pleasant outing involving some 15km of walking and 800m of ascent. The going is on bulldozed roads most of the time, and the walk shouldn't take more than 4–5hrs. If climbing the hills separately, Meall Tairneachan is just 3km and 450m of ascent from the B846 road between Aberfeldy and Tummel Bridge. The top can be reached in 1½hrs. Farragon Hill takes 1hr or so longer to climb. From both north and south there is a bulldozed road to within 1km of the summit. From Edradynate in Strath Tay the distance is 6.5km with 720m of ascent; from Netherton on the south side of Loch Tummel it's 7.5km with 775m of ascent. Away from the roads the terrain is complex and navigation can be tricky in mist. The views from the summits are excellent, with Schiehallion soaring to the west and Ben Vrackie rising to the east.

ACCESS, BASES, MAPS AND GUIDES

Access

This is the most accessible area of the Highlands from Glasgow and northern England, so these are popular hills. The main road from Glasgow to Fort William, the A82, cuts through the heart of the area, running alongside Loch Lomond and then through Crianlarich, Tyndrum and Bridge of Orchy. The Glasgow to Fort William railway line follows a similar route and has many stops useful to hillgoers. The eastern part of the region can also be reached via the A9 Perth to Inverness road and accompanying rail line.

The Campsie Fells A891, A81 and A875 between Milton of Campsie and Killearn. B818 east of Killearn to Fintry. B822 from Lennoxtown to Endrick Water.

The Ochils A91 along the southern edge of the hills through Alva, Tillicoultry and Dollar. A823 through the eastern end of the range from Yetts O'Muckart to Gleneagles. A9 along the northern and western sides of the hills from Gleneagles to Dunblane and Bridge of Allan. Railway stations at Dunblane and Gleneagles.

Ben Lomond and Loch Lomond B837 to Balmaha then the minor road along the east shore of Loch Lomond to Rowardennan.

The Arrochar Alps A82, A83 west to Arrochar, Glen Croe and Glen Kinglas. Railway stations at Tarbet and Ardlui.

The Ben Lui Hills A82, A85 west from Tyndrum down Glen Lochy. Railway stations at Crianlarich and Tyndrum.

The Trossachs A81 Glasgow to Aberfoyle or A84 Stirling to Callander then A821.

Ben More, Stob Binnein and the Crianlarich and Balquhidder Hills A82 to Crianlarich then A85. Railway station at Crianlarich.

The Loch Earn Hills A84 Stirling to Callander and Lochearnhead. A85 to Comrie.

The Glen Lochay Hills A82 to Tyndrum. A9 to Ballinluig then A827 alongside Loch Tay to Killin, A85 and A827 to Killin. Minor road up Glen Lochay from Killin. Railway station at Tyndrum.

The Bridge of Orchy Hills A82. Railway stations at Tyndrum and Bridge of Orchy.

Ben Lawers and the Tarmachans A9 to Ballinluig then A827 alongside Loch Tay to Killin, A82 to Crianlarich then A85 and A827 to Killin. A85 from Perth to A827 to Killin.

Glen Lyon and Schiehallion A9 to Ballinluig, A827 to Aberfeldy, B846 to road along Glen Lyon.

Bases

The Campsie Fells Strathblane, Killearn, Fintry, Lennoxtown.

The Ochill Hills Alva, Tillicoultry, Dollar, Gleneagles, Dunblane, Bridge of Allan.

Ben Lomond and Loch Lomond Inverbeg, Rowardennan, Inversnaid, Balmaha, Balloch.

The Arrochar Alps Ardgartan, Arrochar, Tarbet, Inveruglas, Ardlui.

The Ben Lui Hills Crianlarich, Tyndrum.

The Trossachs Aberfoyle, Callander.

The Ben More, Stob Binnein and the Crianlarich and Balquhidder Hills Crianlarich, Lochearnhead, Balquihidder.

The Loch Earn Hills Lochearnhead, Comrie.

The Glen Lochay Hills Killin, Tyndrum, Crianlarich.

The Bridge of Orchy Hills Bridge of Orchy, Tyndrum.

Ben Lawers and the Tarmachans Killin, Kenmore, Aberfeldy.

Glen Lyon and Schiehallion Kenmore, Aberfeldy, Tummel Bridge.

Maps

OS Landranger 1:50,000: 64, 50, 51, 52, 56, 57, 58

OS Explorer 1:25,000: 364, 365, 368, 377, 378, 379, 386

Harvey's Superwalker 1:25,000: Arrochar Alps; Ben Venue, Loch Ard & Queen Elizabeth Forest Park; Ben Lomond; Ben Lawers; Crianlarich (Ben Lui and Ben More); Ben Ledi; Glasgow Popular Hills

Walking Guides

Southern Highlands by Nick Williams (Pocket Mountains, 2003)

The Southern Highlands by Donald Bennett (SMC, 1992)

Walking Loch Lomond and the Trossachs by Ronald Turnbull (Cicerone, 2009)

Loch Lomond and the Trossachs National Park: East by Tom Prentice (Mica Publishing, 2009)

Loch Lomond and the Trossachs National Park: West by Tom Prentice (Mica Publishing, 2009)

Loch Lomond, the Trossachs, Stirling and Clackmannan (Pathfinder Guide) by John Brooks, Brian Conduit, Neil Coates, and Ark Creative (Jarrold, 2002)

Loch Lomond and the Trossachs National Parks Short Walks edited by Hugh Taylor (Jarrold, 2005)

25 Walks: Loch Lomond and the Trossachs by Roger Smith and John Digney (The Mercat Press, 2004)

The Rob Roy Way by Jacquetta Megarry and Rennie McOwan (Rucksack Readers, 2006)

The Ultimate Guide to the Munros: Volume 1 The Southern Highlands by Ralph Storer (Luath, 2008)

Climbing Guides

Arran, Arrochar and the Southern Highlands: Rock and Ice Climbs by Graham Little, Tom Prentice and Ken Crocket (SMC, 1997)

Highland Outcrops by Kevin Howett (SMC, 1998)

CHAPTER 3: THE CENTRAL HIGHLANDS

Ben Cruachan and Glen Strae, Glen Etive, the Black Mount, Glen Coe and Glen Creran, Rannoch Moor, Ben Nevis and Glen Nevis, Loch Treig and Loch Ossian, Loch Ericht to Loch Laggan, West Drumochter, the Monadh Liath to Glen Roy and the northern West Highland Way

THE CENTRAL HIGHLANDS: CHAPTER SUMMARY

Location

Northwards from Glen Orchy, Rannoch Moor, Loch Rannoch and Loch Tummel, covering the area bordered by the A9 road in the east and Loch Linnhe and the Great Glen in the north

☆ Highlights

☗ LOW-LEVEL/PASSES WALK
- Eas nam Meirleach (3:2)
- Loch Etive and the Trilleachan Slabs (3:2)
- Rannoch Moor (3:7)

◓ LONG DISTANCE WALK
- The West Highland Way (3:4)
- Fort William to Dalwhinnie via Corrour (3:18)

⛰ SUMMIT WALK
- The Ascent of Ben Cruachan (3:1)
- The Glen Strae Hills (3:1)
- The Complete Round of the Ben Starav Hills (3:2)
- Beinn Trilleachan (3:2)
- Ben Starav and Glas Bheinn Mhor (3:2)
- The Northern Black Mount: Meall a'Bhuiridh, Creise, Clach Leathad and Beinn Mhic Chasgaig (3:3)
- The Southern Black Mount: Stob Ghabhar and Stob a'Choire Odhair (3:3)
- The Traverse of Buachaille Etive Mor (3:5)
- The Summits and Ridges of Bidean nam Bian (3:5)
- Beinn a'Bheithir (3:6)
- The Ring of Steall (3:8)
- The Eastern Mamores (3:8)
- The Complete Traverse of the Mamores (3:8)
- The Coire Eoghainn Ridges (3:9)
- The Eastern Grey Corries (3:10)
- The Complete Traverse of the Grey Corries (3:10)
- Leum Uilleum (3:12)
- Ben Alder and Beinn Bheoil (3:13)
- The Aonach Beag–Geal Charn Ridge (3:13)
- Binnein Shuas and Binnein Shios (3:13)
- The Fara (3:13)
- Creag Dhubh (3:15)
- Creag Meagaidh and Coire Ardair (3:16)
- Hills around Glen Roy (3:17)

❸ SCRAMBLING
- Buachaille Etive Mor (3:5)
- Bidean nam Bian (3:5)
- Aonach Eagach (3:5)

- Beinn a'Bheithir (3:6)
- The Carn Mor Dearg Arête (3:9)
- Ben Nevis, North Face: Ledge Route (3:9)
- Ben Alder and Beinn Bheoil (3:13)

◉ ROCK CLIMBING
- The Trilleachan Slabs (3:2)
- Bidean nam Bian (3:5)
- Ben Nevis (3:9)
- Binnein Shuas and Binnein Shios (3:13)

❄ WINTER CLIMBING
- Buachaille Etive Mor (3:5)
- Bidean nam Bian (3:5)
- Ben Nevis (3:9)
- The Aonachs (3:10)
- Coire Ardair (3:16)

❷ SKI TOURING
- West Drumochter Munros Ski Tour (3:14)
- The Monadh Liath (3:15)
- The Creag Meagaidh hills (3:16)

Contents

◀ *Looking up Coire Dhomhain to Sgairneach Mhor, West Drumochter*

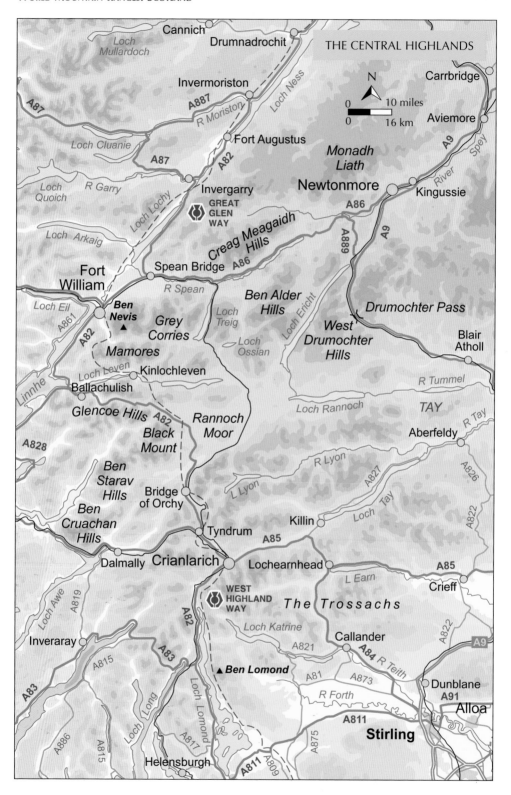

THE CENTRAL HIGHLANDS

N

0   10 miles
0   16 km

Cannich
Drumnadrochit
Loch Mullardoch
Invermoriston
Loch Ness
R Moriston
A887
A87
Carrbridge
Aviemore
A9
Monadh Liath
Spey
Fort Augustus
Loch Cluanie
A87
A82
Newtonmore
River
A9
Kingussie
Loch Quoich
R Garry
Invergarry
GREAT GLEN WAY
A86
Loch Lochy
Loch Arkaig
Creag Meagaidh Hills
A889
Spean Bridge
A86
Fort William
R Spean
Ben Alder Hills
Loch Ericht
Drumochter Pass
Loch Eil
Ben Nevis
Grey Corries
Loch Treig
West Drumochter Hills
Blair Atholl
A861
A82
Mamores
Loch Ossian
Linnhe
Loch Leven
Kinlochleven
R Tummel
Ballachulish
Loch Rannoch
TAY
R Tay
Glencoe Hills
A82
Rannoch Moor
Aberfeldy
Black Mount
R Lyon
A827
A826
A828
Ben Starav Hills
L Lyon
Loch Tay
A822
Ben Cruachan Hills
Bridge of Orchy
Killin
Dalmally
Tyndrum
A85
Lochearnhead
A85
Crianlarich
L Earn
Crieff
Loch Awe
A819
WEST HIGHLAND WAY
The Trossachs
A822
A9
Inveraray
A82
A815
A83
Loch Katrine
Callander
A821
A84 R Teith
Ben Lomond
A81
A873
Dunblane
A83
A886
A815
Loch Long
Loch Lomond
R Forth
A91
Alloa
A817
A875
Stirling
Helensburgh
A811
A809
A811

INTRODUCTION

I have spent numberless weekends on these mountains.
Their charm has never palled, either in summer or winter.
J.H.B. Bell, *Bell's Scottish Climbs*

This region lies at the heart of the Highlands and contains two of the jewels of the Scottish Hills in Glen Coe and Ben Nevis. In the Central Highlands you are surrounded by hills stretching to the horizon in every direction. To the south the area merges with the Southern Highlands but it's clearly defined otherwise, with Loch Linnhe to the west, the Great Glen to the north and the A9 road over the Pass of Drumochter to the east. As with the hills to the south the Central Highlands are steep and rocky in the west, with narrow, steep-sided glens, mostly running southwest to northeast, and are gentler and more rolling in the east, with broader, more open straths.

The Central Highlands are essentially the same range as the Southern Highlands, and like them are mostly built of coarse-grained metamorphic Dalradian schist and other metamorphosed sedimentary rocks, which give rise to rugged and steep but not particularly rocky hills (the main exception to this being the mica schist cliffs of Coire Ardair on Creag Meagaidh). Volcanic action has intruded granites and other cliff-forming rocks at Ben Cruachan, Glen Etive, Rannoch Moor, Glen Coe and Ben Nevis, leading to a rockier landscape, with many cliffs that are the main focus of both rock climbing and winter climbing in the area. Indeed, the Glencoe hills and Ben Nevis are the major climbing centres in Scotland. There are also many fine scrambles on the same hills. When snow-covered there are also ski tours of every standard of difficulty, plus two downhill ski resorts – the Glencoe Mountain Resort at the head of Glencoe and Aonach Mor north of Fort William. For hillwalkers there are 73 Munros, 35 Corbetts and 32 Grahams, and many opportunities for long walks linking these hills.

The region runs in a great sweep from southwest to northeast, starting with the fine peak of Ben

The north face of Ben Nevis from Carn Mor Dearg

Cruachan rising above the Pass of Brander, a long, rugged granite massif containing three Munros. Below Ben Cruachan Loch Awe, at 39km the longest loch in Scotland, runs away to the southwest. To the northeast of Ben Cruachan stretches a wild mass of hills between Loch Etive and Glen Etive in the west, the River Orchy to the east and the flat watery expanse of Rannoch Moor to the northeast. This tangle of summits includes the eastern Etive hills and the Black Mount. Rannoch Moor itself is of great interest, a vast area of lake-dotted blanket bog surrounded by high hills.

Across Glen Etive the western Etive hills merge into the Glen Creran hills and the south Glencoe summits, which include two iconic Highland hills, Buachaille Etive Mor and Bidean nam Bian. Famous Glen Coe itself lies below this last hill, twisting and turning between the huge buttresses running down from the high summits. North of the glen rises the ragged ridge of the Aonach Eagach, whose traverse is a classic scramble and a challenge for hillwalkers. North again, beautiful Loch Leven runs below steep slopes to the little town of Kinlochleven at the foot of the Mamores, a long, undulating ridge containing 11 Munros, one of the finest high-level walks in Scotland. The Mamores face north to Ben Nevis, the highest summit in Scotland, with Glen Nevis, which has lovely woodlands, a magnificent gorge and a superb waterfall, at its foot.

The finest aspect of Ben Nevis lies on the far side from Glen Nevis: the great north face, the biggest cliff in Britain and home to rock, snow and ice climbs of all grades of difficulty. To the east of Ben Nevis lie the big bulky whalebacks of Aonach Beag and Aonach Mor, the latter with a ski resort on its northern flanks, and the more delicate, sinuously curving Grey Corries ridge. This wedge of hills ends at the Loch Treig reservoir, contained in a deep trench through which runs the West Highland Line. East of the loch the hills are bulkier and more rounded. In the big group of hills stretching out to the A9 from Loch Treig Ben Alder stands out, a big steep-sided plateau with some short scrambles on its sides. Pretty Loch Ossian lies in the southwest of this area, not far from remote Corrour Station.

The remaining hills of the Central Highlands stretch out in a long straggling line to the north of Strathspey, Loch Laggan and Glen Spean. In the west, rounded, rolling hills surround deep Glen Roy, which is geologically interesting for the Parallel Roads, the shores of ancient lakes. Moving east the hills rise higher and become more rugged, with Coire Ardair on Creag Meagaidh a major winter climbing venue. North and east of Creag Meagaidh rolling heather moorland dominates the scenery, with the Monadh Liath hills the only distinct summits.

The West Highland Way runs 56km (35 Miles) through the western Central Highlands from Bridge of Orchy to Fort William via the edge of Rannoch Moor, the Devil's Staircase, Kinlochleven, Lairig Mor and Glen Nevis.

3:1 BEN CRUACHAN ☆ AND GLEN STRAE

Ben Cruachan is one of the best-known mountains in the southern half of the Central Highlands, due to its dominant position above Loch Awe on the road to the ferry port of Oban. It's a big mountain almost isolated from surrounding hills by the deep trenches ringing it. Only at the 570m Lairig Noe to the northeast is there any linking high ground. This separation makes Ben Cruachan a distinctive massif that stands out in many views, a conspicuousness aided by its sharp pointed summits. From the road along the southeastern side of Loch Awe it rears up as a steep bulwark of forbidding slopes. The north side, clearly visible from Beinn a'Chochuill, is even fiercer, presenting a series of shattered craggy corries split by rocky spurs and topped by a jagged ridge.

Being so prominent Ben Cruachan became known long before many other Highland hills. Ian R. Mitchell says it was 'one of the first Scottish hills to be mentioned in any written source by name', appearing in a poem called *The Bruce* by John Barbour in the late fourteenth century. The first recorded ascent is generally credited to the geologist John MacCulloch, who appears in Chapter Two as the first ascensionist of the Centre Peak of The Cobbler, who climbed it sometime in the second decade of the 19th century, as described in his book *Highlands and Western Islands of Scotland*, in which he says the ascent is 'tedious, but not difficult' and that the summit 'presents some of the finest and most extensive mountain views in Scotland'. Mitchell however thinks that there had been an ascent or ascents previous to MacCulloch's, possibly by the botanists John Lightfoot and John Stuart in the 1770s, as Lightfoot describes finding plants

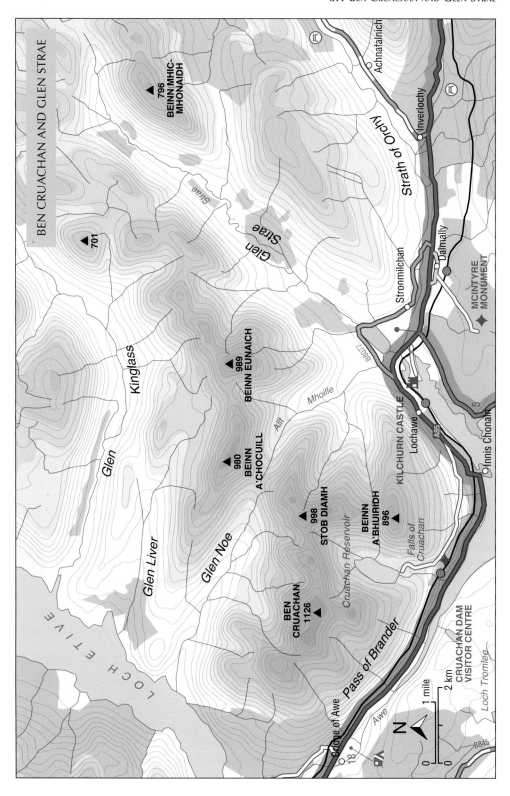

The summit of Ben Cruachan

near the summit in his 1777 book *Flora Scotica*, the first scientific book on Scottish plants.

Cruachan means 'conical hill' and the hill used to be called Cruachan Beinne: Seton Gordon uses this name in his 1935 book *Highways and Byways in the West Highlands* (Birlinn, 1995), meaning 'conical heap on the mountain', which fits the rocky summit cones well.

A legend attached to Ben Cruachan tells how a beautiful goddess lived on the mountain, where she guarded the magic Well of Youth in which she bathed every night to preserve her looks. However one night she fell asleep before replacing the flat stone that covered the well and the waters poured out all night, flooding the glen below and forming Loch Awe. One story says that deprived of the well waters the goddess aged and turned ugly and became the Cailleach Bheur, the old woman or hag of storms, death and winter. Another version says the other gods were furious with her for letting the water escape so they turned her into the Cailleach. The Cailleach turns up in other mountain myths – see the Beinn a'Bheithir section below.

Ben Cruachan takes the form of a long west–east ridge with two long spurs running south from the two main peaks and enclosing the big Coire Cruachan. There are eight summits in total, five of them on the main ridge, two on the subsidiary spurs. From the west those on the main ridge are Stob Dearg ('red peak', also known as the Taynuilt Peak, due to its prominent appearance from Taynuilt village, 1104m), Ben Cruachan (1126m) itself, Drochaid Ghlas ('grey bridge', 1009m), Stob Diamh ('peak of the stag', 998m) and Sron an Isean ('promontory of the chick', 966m). On the ridge south of Ben Cruachan lies Meall Cuanail ('hill of the flocks', 918m); on the ridge south of Stob Diamh lie Stob Garbh ('rough peak', 980m) and Beinn a'Bhuiridh ('peak of the roaring' (of stags), 896m). Of these Ben Cruachan and Stob Diamh are Munros and Beinn a'Bhuiridh is a Corbett. There is another big corrie on the eastern side of the massif, lying between the eastward curving spurs dropping from Sron an Isean and Stob Garbh, and there are also three very rough corries on the northern face of the main ridge separated by short steep rocky spurs. Clearly visible from the east, the curving ridge round the eastern corrie is known as the Dalmally Horseshoe.

Ben Cruachan is a granite mountain, hence the rocky terrain. It's the southernmost part of a granite intrusion that stretches either side of Glen Etive as far as the mouth of Glen Coe. The main ridge is quite narrow in places, especially between Drochaid Glas and Ben Cruachan, and strewn with boulders. Route finding can be tricky in mist and the steep terrain requires care, especially when snow-covered, as some easy scrambling is required in places.

As well as being noteworthy as a mountain Ben Cruachan is known for a huge pumped storage scheme, one of the biggest in the world. The mountain has been hollowed out to accommodate this, while on the surface there is a big reservoir in Coire Cruachan south of the main ridge with roads running up to it. There's a Visitor Centre on the A85 near the power station from where tours can be taken of the vast underground complex.

The pump storage scheme doesn't impinge on the qualities of wildness and natural grandeur found high on Ben Cruachan. Art could do more damage than industry, however, if a scheme to carve huge sculptures into Ben Cruachan, like those of US Presidents on Mount Rushmore in the Black Hills of Dakota, goes ahead. This mad, environmentally destructive and artistically negative idea surfaced a few times in the late 1990s and early 2000s but has hopefully been abandoned, although due to financial constraints, rather than understanding that ruining natural beauty is not a good way for art to proceed.

The A85 from Tyndrum to Oban is the main access road for Ben Cruachan, running through the Pass of Brander below the southern flanks of the mountain. The Oban rail line follows the same route, with three stations near Ben Cruachan, enabling various routes to be done between them, including a complete traverse from Lochawe to Taynuilt.

⊗ The Ascent of Ben Cruachan ☆

Traversing Ben Cruachan is not a light undertaking, as the going is rough and the amount of ascent high, but it is one of the finest expeditions in the Central Highlands. I suggest doing it east–west, as the western approach is unrelentingly steep and not very interesting. Beinn a'Bhuiridh can be climbed first by its long eastern ridge, starting at the junction of the A85 and the B8077, then the ridge followed north to Stob Diamh and then west to the col between Stob Dearg and Meall nan Each. From this col steep grassy slopes can be descended beside the Allt

Gruiniche to Bridge of Awe, where there is a hotel and a campsite. The distance is only 14km but the ascent a hefty 1765m, so the walk is unlikely to take less than 6–8hrs. This route includes all the summits except Sron an Isean. To include this as well adds an extra 1.5km and 200m of ascent. To return to the start point either a bus or train (from Taynuilt, which is 4.8km from Bridge of Awe, which is 14km from the start) can be caught up the Pass of Brander unless you have left a car at either end of the route (or a bicycle at Bridge of Awe).

A circuit of the main ridge can be made from the Cruachan Power Station, starting with the path up beside the burn to the reservoir and then climbing the ridges to west or east and following the circuit of peaks. This involves around 15km of walking and 1800m of ascent and takes 6–8hrs. The peaks can be climbed from the north too, although this involves a walk-in over the Lairig Noe of 8–9km. The north ridges of Ben Cruachan, Stob Dearg and Drochaid Ghlas involve easy scrambling.

❄ Winter climbs on Ben Cruachan
The corries and ridges on the north side of Ben Cruachan offer winter climbs of various grades, the ridges being Grade 1.

⛰ The Glen Strae Hills ☆
Immediately north of Ben Cruachan lie two Munros, Beinn a'Chocuill ('hill of the cowl', 980m) and Beinn Eunaich ('fowling hill, 989m), which can both be easily climbed from the track leading from the B8077 at the mouth of Glen Strae and running north of the Allt Mhoille to the Lairig Noe. The round of the two hills from the B8077 involves 13km of walking and 1250m of ascent and takes 6hrs or so. They can also be ascended without difficulty from Glen Kinglas to the north, which is best done as part of a backpacking trip as this glen is quite remote.

Beinn a'Chocuill is a long sweeping ridge running some 7km from near Loch Etive to the col with Beinn Eunaich. The latter is a very compact, pyramidal hill with three ridges running down from the summit. On the south ridge lies a minor bump called Stob Maol, where Percy Unna, one of the major benefactors of the Scottish mountains, died in 1950. Unna, a one time President of the Scottish Mountaineering Club (SMC), was very rich and donated much of his wealth anonymously to the National Trust for Scotland for the purchase of mountain estates such as Glen Coe,

Dalness (which includes Buachaille Etive Mor) and Kintail, as described in the NTS booklet *The Man Who Bought Mountains* by Rennie McOwan (NTS, 1978). Unna also set out principles of management for the hills designed to keep them wild. These 'Unna Principles' are the basis of the NTS's 2002 Wild Land Policy.

The ascent of the two hills is pleasant but not outstanding. The reward lies in the views of the rugged north side of Ben Cruachan, which are superb.

On the east side of Glen Strae lies the remote Corbett Beinn Mhic-Mhonaidh (796m), which can easily be climbed from the glen via the southwest ridge (18.5km round trip from the B8077 with 830m of ascent, about 5–7hrs). A shorter but less interesting route (much is in forestry plantations) is from Glen Orchy, east of the summit (12.85km, 845m of ascent, 4–6hrs). Being quite isolated, Beinn Mhic-Mhonaidh is an excellent viewpoint, especially for Ben Cruachan, Ben Starav, Stob Gabhar and the Ben Lui hills.

⬤ Loch Etive to Loch Tulla via Glen Kinglas
North of the Ben Cruachan hills lies long Glen Kinglas, separating them from the south Glen Etive hills. There is a good walk from Bridge of Awe up the east side of Loch Etive and then east through Glen Kinglas to a low watershed beyond which lies Loch Dochard and the Abhainn Shira which leads down to Victoria Bridge and Loch Tulla on a minor road from Bridge of Orchy. The walk is 35km long, with a high point of 300m, and is most enjoyably done with a midway camp. The walk takes 10hrs+. Much of the walking is on a wide 4WD vehicle track, with a footpath across the watershed. It's an easy walk with no steep climbs, yet has a wild, remote feel and gives excellent views of the hills to either side.

Rather than going via Loch Etive the walk can be started in Glen Strae, not far from Dalmally. Some 2km up Glen Strae a path heads north to the Lairig Dhoireann, just east of Beinn Eunaich, then descends to Glen Kinglas. This route is 9km shorter than the one from Bridge of Awe but climbs to 615m.

3:2 GLEN ETIVE ☆

Glen Etive is a narrow, steep-sided glen that feels quite wild and remote, despite easy access from the A82 main road at the head of Glen Coe. The

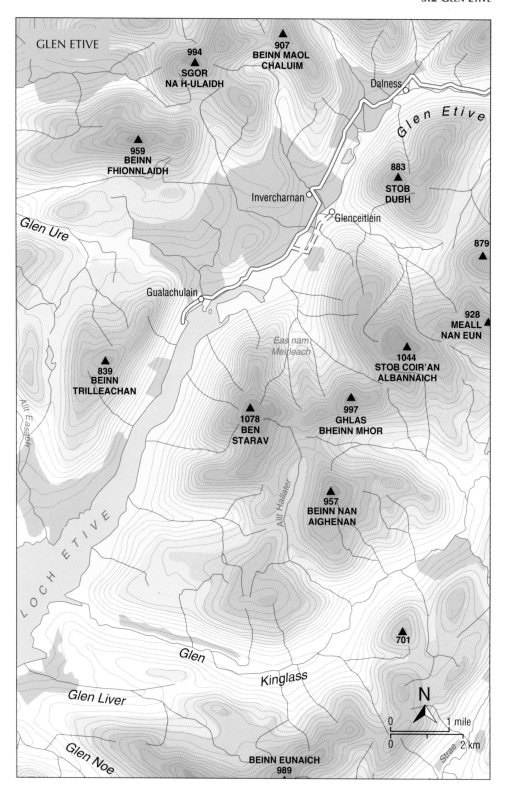

GLEN ETIVE

994
▲
SGOR
NA H-ULAIDH

907
▲
BEINN MAOL
CHALUIM

Dalness

Glen Etive

959
▲
BEINN
FHIONNLAIDH

883
▲
STOB
DUBH

Glen Ure

Invercharnan

Glenceitlein

879
▲

928 ▲
MEALL
NAN EUN

Gualachulain

Eas nam
Meitleach

839
▲
BEINN
TRILLEACHAN

1044
▲
STOB COIR'AN
ALBANNAICH

Allt Easach

1078
▲
BEN
STARAV

997
▲
GHLAS
BHEINN MHOR

Allt Hallater

957
▲
BEINN NAN
AIGHENAN

LOCH ETIVE

701
▲

Glen

Kinglass

Glen Liver

N

0 —— 1 mile
0 —— 2 km

Strae

Glen Noe

BEINN EUNAICH
989
▲

Dusk over the Allt a' Chaorainn and Glen Etive

River Etive tumbles and rushes down the glen over wide pebble banks, rock steps and round boulders, and through dark peaty pools below a forest fringe of alder, birch, holly, rowan and Scots pine. There are no facilities in the glen, just a twisting single track road that runs 20km down the glen to lovely Loch Etive, a long thin arm of the sea reaching deep into the mountains. No roads run beside the 16km long section of the loch from Taynuilt to its head, and like the glen beyond it's quiet and little visited. There are tracks either side of the loch that can be used for access to the hills, or even for a complete circuit of the loch. Loch Etive Cruises run cruises on the upper loch between Easter and October, starting from the jetty on the B845 just north of Taynuilt, a good way to view the mountains. Beinn Trilleachan looks particularly impressive from the loch, with the vast smooth rock sheets of the Trilleachan (Etive) Slabs standing out.

The upper glen runs for 16km from the A82 to Dalness, and has an open moorland feel. The hills here belong to the Black Mount and Glencoe groups and will be described under those headings below. Below Dalness the character of the glen changes and there are many dense conifer plantations, especially on the western side, that impede access to the hills.

Glen Etive was once extensively wooded, but now only remnants of the great forest remain. Much of the wood was used to fuel the Bonawe Iron Furnace, set near the loch just north of Taynuilt. The furnace was set up in 1753, the iron ore being brought from Cumbria, as it was easier to take the ore to places where there was plenty of fuel than to transport the fuel to the mines. Two acres of woodland a day were needed to provide the charcoal to run the furnace. The furnace closed in 1876. It is now owned by Historic Scotland and can be visited from April to September.

🐾 Eas nam Meirleach ☆

Eas nam Meirleach ('The Robber's Waterfall', NN 139 450) is a fine 15m double waterfall on the Allt Mheuran that drops down a dark narrow ravine below an edging of trees on the south side of Glen Etive. It's a 4km uphill walk to the falls from the road in the glen at NN 131 464. The name probably comes from the gorge below the falls having been used to hide stolen cattle or because it was a resting place for the thieves themselves, as it is a good viewpoint for the surrounding area. The best view is across Glen Etive to the bulky massif of Bidean nam Bian.

Ⓐ Loch Etive and the Trilleachan Slabs ☆

Some 300m up the eastern slopes of Beinn Trilleachan lies a great sweep of granite slabs (NN 102 446). These can be reached from the end of the road in Glen Etive, where there is an old rotting pier and some ramshackle buildings, by way of a rough and sometimes muddy path. It's just over 1km (half a mile) to the base of the slabs. Looking up, the sloping granite is impressive and intimidating. It's unusual to see so much smooth rock. Unsurprisingly there are no scrambling routes or easy rock climbs on the slabs. The views across Loch Etive and back up the glen are superb, with Ben Starav soaring upwards from the water, a dark pyramid riven with gullies.

From the slabs a cross country descent can be made southwest through some small birch and oak woods to the path beside the loch. The shore is beautiful and it's worth continuing southwest at least as far as the point of Aird Trilleachan and admiring the birch/oak woods, among which there are some impressively big trees. Once the lochside was clad in woods like these, but much of the forest was cleared to feed the Bonawe Iron Furnace near Taynuilt. Depending on how far along the shore you go the walk is around 8km long and shouldn't take more than 2–3hrs.

Ⓑ The Trilleachan Slabs are set at an angle of 40° and provide 'exciting, but serious climbing', according to the SMT guidebook. There are over 40 different routes, ranging in grade from VS to E3.

Ⓧ ☆ Beinn Trilleachan (a Corbett at 839m) is a big whaleback mountain rising abruptly from the shores of Loch Etive and running for some 5km from north to south. It is a very rocky mountain, with many crags and cliffs apart from the Trilleachan Slabs. The easiest walkers' route is via the northeast ridge, which can be reached from Glen Etive, along the side of the last big plantation before the head of the loch is reached. There is some optional scrambling on the pathless route which visits the 767m top immediately above the Trilleachan Slabs. The views from the small rocky summit are huge and impressive, with a feeling of great space and wildness. Loch Etive lies far below, a dark slash through the mountains, with Ben Starav racing into the sky above it. Down the loch Ben Cruachan rises as two steep-sided peaks. Beyond the loch, to the north, the foot of Glen Etive is a tangle of brown marshes and green pasture threaded by a twisting, braided river. Of the hills visible far up the glen Bidean nam Bian and Buachaille Etive Mor stand out. The easiest descent is to return along the ascent route. Alternatively there is a rough way down from

The head of Loch Etive from Beinn Trilleachan

the col between the summit and the top of the Trilleachan Slabs to Loch Etive. By either descent route the walk is around 8km long with 1000m of ascent and takes 4–5hrs.

Beinn Trilleachan means 'mountain of sandpipers' or 'oystercatchers', both birds likely to be seen beside the loch from which it rises.

The Ben Starav Hills

Lying between Glen Etive and Glen Kinglas, these granite hills run into the Black Mount group in the north but otherwise are a separate group consisting of a line of four Munros running southwest to northeast – Ben Starav (1078m), Glas Bheinn Mhor (997m), Stob Coir'an Albannaich (1044m), Meall nan Eun (928m) – and an outlying, awkward-to-reach Munro to the south, Beinn nan Aighenan (960m), just to make life interesting for Munro baggers.

⊛ Ben Starav and Glas Bheinn Mhor ☆

Ben Starav is the dominant summit of this group, a huge rocky pyramid rising steeply from the shores of Loch Etive. It looks magnificent from the slopes of Beinn Trilleachan on the far side of the loch. Five narrow ridges rise to two summits connected by a curving ridge. The westernmost is the highest. Deep corries lie between the ridges and the hill is rough everywhere.

Ben Starav links easily with Glas Bheinn Mhor to the east, and the two are usually climbed together in a 16km round from Glen Etive. The finest ascent route is up the great north ridge of Ben Starav, which rises in a continuous almost straight line from sea level to the summit (1078m) in just 4km. The climb isn't difficult, just unrelenting, with only two, short, lower-angled sections.

The views from the summit are excellent, especially from the western edge, where there is a startling drop down the steep north face to sea level and Loch Etive, beyond which rises Beinn Trilleachan, with the Etive Slabs shining on its slopes. Elsewhere a mass of hills clamours for attention – Ben Cruachan, Ben Lui, the Bridge of Orchy hills, the Black Mount and the Glencoe peaks.

The meaning of 'Starav' is, according to most sources, unknown. Peter Drummond's *Scottish Hill Names: Their Origin and Meaning* (SMT, 2007) suggests it might come from *starbhanach*, meaning a well-built man, which would accord with Hamish Brown's 'stout or strong hill', or perhaps *starra*,

meaning a block of rock. More likely, Drummond thinks, is *starabhan*, meaning a rustling noise.

From the summit a narrow rocky arête ridge that gives some easy scrambling leads northeast to two rows of pinnacles that can look quite dramatic when they rear up in the mist, like the teeth of a giant shark. From a col at 767m there's an easy walk up the west ridge of Glas Bheinn Mhor ('big grey-green hill', 997m), from where there is a good view back to Ben Starav. A half kilometre or so further east from the summit a descent can be made beside the Allt Mheuran back to Glen Etive. The whole round involves around 16km in distance and 1400m of ascent, and takes 6–9hrs.

⊛ Beinn nan Aighenan

The awkward member of this group is Beinn nan Aighenan, one of the remotest peaks in the Central Highlands, lying 6km in a straight line from Glen Etive and 12km from Victoria Bridge to the east. It's not a particularly distinctive hill and is hidden in most views except those from nearby hills. If combined with Ben Starav and Glas Bheinn Mhor it can be climbed from the col between those peaks. The round trip adds 4.5km and 580m of ascent and takes a couple of hours. The summit can also be climbed from the track between Loch Etive and Loch Tulla in Glen Kinglas (see above) by the southwest or southeast ridge (around 4km and 875m of ascent from Glen Kinglas by either ridge, 2hrs).

⊛ Stob Coir'an Albannaich and Meall nan Eun

These two Munros form the high ground between Glen Etive and Loch Dochard. Stob Coir'an Albannaich ('peak of the corrie of the Scotsman', 1044m) is by far the biggest, a huge mass of a hill stretching some 8km northwest to southeast, with mostly smooth grassy slopes on the western side but much rougher, rockier ones to the north and east. Meall nan Eun ('peak of the birds', 928m) covers a much smaller area but is just as rough and rocky on its eastern flanks. The hills can be climbed from the east but the approaches from Loch Dochard are very boggy and the terrain is very rough. The least wet ascent route is via Coire nam Ban and the southeast ridge of Stob Coir'an Albannaich. Climbing the peaks from Glen Etive avoids the bogs, and the long approach and is my preference. The direct route up Stob Coir'an Albannaich goes straight up the broad western slopes. This is strenuous and not very interesting, except for the views of Ben Starav. A more entertaining and scenic route goes via Eas nam Meirlach (see above) and follows the Allt Mheuran to the col between Glas Bheinn Mhor and Stob Coir'an Albannaich. There is a large cairn on the summit, from where there are extensive views.

The route onto Meall nan Eun twists and turns and can be awkward in mist, when good navigation skills are essential, as there are steep crags below at various points. Descent can be made into the Allt Ceitlein glen, which leads down to Glen Etive. The distance is 17km, with an ascent of 1360m, and the route takes 6–8hrs.

The Complete Round ☆

All five Munros can be climbed in one long walk, perhaps split over two days with a high camp between. Depending on the exact route this involves around 25km and 2650m of ascent, and takes 10hrs or more. The best thing about this round is that it sticks to high ground for most of its length, the lowest point between the summits being 610m.

Two Corbetts: Stob Dubh and Beinn Maol Chaluim

Two hills of Corbett height act as gateways to lower Glen Etive. Although their lower slopes squeeze the glen between them their characters are very different. Stob Dubh is a big, steep pyramid protruding into the glen and prominent in views right down to Loch Etive. A distinguishing feature is the deep gorge cutting across the southern slopes. Beinn Maol Chaluim is a long steep ridge running at right angles to the glen, and not particularly distinctive or noticeable. Both are worth climbing, in particular for the views from their summits. Neither ascent is long and they can be combined in one lengthy day.

Stob Dubh ('the black peak', 883m) is appropriately named, as it looks dark and forbidding. The ascent is steep but mostly on grass. The direct route is up the southwest ridge, which rises 850m in just 2km. Once on top you can continue along a curving ridge to the subsidiary summit Beinn Ceitlein ('hill of concealment', 834m) and then return to Glen Etive via the Allt a'Chaorainn and Allt Ceitlein glens. The round trip from Coileitir, where there is a bridge over the River Etive, is around 14km, with 1100m of ascent (about 5hrs).

Beinn Maol Chaluim ('Malcolm's bare hill' – the name is tautological as both Beinn and Maol mean hill, the latter specifically a rounded, bare hill, 907m) is a higher and more complex hill, and is also harder to reach due to the wall of conifer forest lining the glen below it. However there is a gap in the trees opposite Lochan Urr that allows strenuous access up steep tussocky slopes to the south ridge of the hill. Lochan Urr itself (named on Harvey's Glen Coe map but not on the OS Landranger) is worth a short detour for the splendid views of Buachaille Etive Mor and Buachaille Etive Beag to the northeast, with the perfectly symmetrical glaciated U-shaped Lairig Gartain valley between them. Back on Beinn Maol Chaluim the broad rough south ridge leads via some broken crags where there is optional scrambling to the 1km-long summit ridge and the white quartzite summit, which lies at the far end. During the easy walk along this ridge the fine views of the massive south face of Bidean nam Bian, some 250m higher, can be admired across Gleann Fhaolain. At the head of this glen Beinn Maol Chaluim is linked to Bidean nam Bian by Bealach Fhaolain (705m), and the two hills can be climbed together, although the Bidean side of the pass is made up of steep scree that is arduous to climb, with a descent being made down the southeast face of Stob Coire Sgreamhach back to Glen Etive. Otherwise it's best to descend the ascent route, as all other options on the Glen Etive side run into forestry. If you don't need to return to Glen Etive the mountain can be traversed to the Bealach Fhaolain from where you can descend the Fionn Ghleann to Glen Coe. The return trip to the summit from Glen Etive is 8km with 945m of ascent (about 5hrs).

3:3 THE BLACK MOUNT

The Black Mount is the name of the fine group of granite hills lying to the west of Rannoch Moor that encircle the huge Coire Ba. It is complex both topographically and geologically and divides into two parts, separated by the deep glens of the River Ba in the east and the Allt Coire Ghuibhasan in the west, and connected by the narrow 700m Bealach Fuar-chataidh. To the north of this pass lies the long north–south running Clach Leathad–Creise ridge, with Meall a'Bhuiridh on a spur to the east. South of the pass is Stob Gabhar, with two long ridges stretching out to the northwest. The name Black Mount is a direct translation of the Gaelic Am Monadh Dubh.

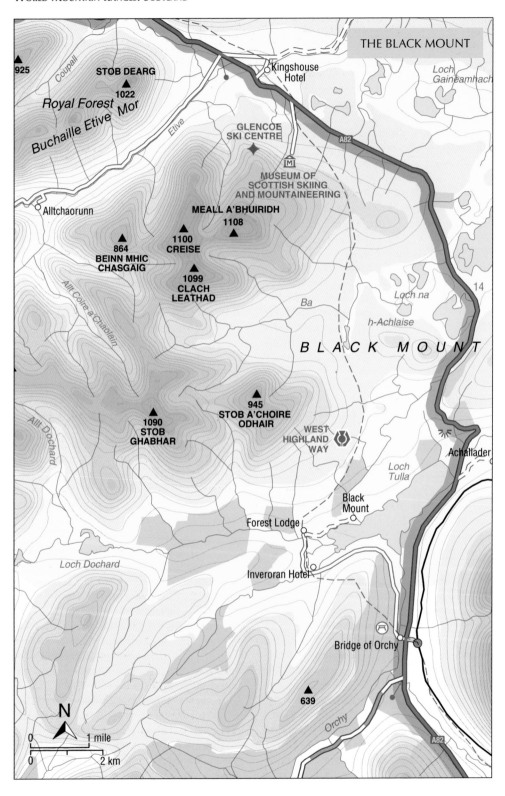

THE BLACK MOUNT

925

Coupall

STOB DEARG
1022

Royal Forest
Buchaille Etive Mor

Etive

Loch
Gaineamhach

A82

Alltchaorunn

GLENCOE
SKI CENTRE

MUSEUM OF
SCOTTISH SKIING
AND MOUNTAINEERING

Kingshouse
Hotel

14

MEALL A'BHUIRIDH
1108

864
BEINN MHIC
CHASGAIG

1100
CREISE

1099
CLACH
LEATHAD

Ba

Loch na
h-Achlaise

B L A C K   M O U N T

Allt Coire a'Chaolain

945
STOB A'CHOIRE
ODHAIR

Allt Dochard

1090
STOB
GHABHAR

WEST
HIGHLAND
WAY

Loch
Tulla

Achallader

Black
Mount

Loch Dochard

Forest Lodge

Inveroran Hotel

Bridge of Orchy

639

N

0   1 mile

0   2 km

Orchy

A82

162

Stob Ghabhar from Aonach Mor

GLENCOE MOUNTAIN RESORT

The northeastern flanks of Meall a'Bhuiridh house the first commercial Scottish ski resort, formerly called White Corries but now Glencoe Mountain (in the hope of diversification from skiing), which is situated at the end of a short spur road from the A82 trunk road. The highest lifts run almost to the summit of the mountain, although not as high as some skiing websites – which give an exaggerated height for Meall a'Bhuiridh – would have you believe! There are seven lifts in total (two chairlifts, five tows), serving 19 pistes of all grades of difficulty, totalling 11km in length, with the longest being 1km. There are two cafés at the resort, which could be of interest to walkers.

The ski resort is not very big but it does sully the northwest flanks of Meall a'Bhuiridh and makes them unsuitable for an ascent for those who don't like walking among the mechanical detritus of a ski resort.

The Black Mount is very accessible as the main Glasgow to Fort William road, the A82, runs past it. There aren't many facilities nearby, however. In the north there are cafés at the Glencoe ski resort when it's open (see above) plus the Kings House Hotel (see under Glencoe below), while to the south lies the historic 19th-century Inveroran Hotel. The nearest villages are Bridge of Orchy and Glencoe.

⊗ The Northern Black Mount:
Meall a'Bhuiridh, Creise, Clach Leathad and Beinn Mhic Chasgaig ☆

With its rocky eastern face curving round deep Coire an Easain Clach Leathad is the most distinctive and outstanding of the three main peaks in the Northern Black Mount. In Munro's *Tables* it's just a subsidiary top of Creise, which is 1m higher, but in reality it's a splendid pointed peak well seen from the A82 road across Rannoch Moor. Clach Leathad is the southern summit on a 3km long ridge running north–south, with Creise in the centre and another subsidiary top, Stob a'Ghlais Choire, at the northern end. The Meall a'Bhuiridh spur juts out from the ridge roughly half way between Creise and Clach Leathad, so the three summits make the form of a capital letter 'T'. To the east lies a Corbett, 864m Beinn Mhic Chasgaig, that presents an unbroken 3km wall to upper Glen Etive, and which can be included in a round of these hills.

Only 9m separates the summits in height, with Meall a'Bhuiridh the highest at 1108m, Creise at 1100m and Clach Leathad at 1099m. As the name

163

suggests (*meall* usually referring to a gentler hill) Meall a'Bhuiridh is, although still rocky and rugged, a more rounded hill than the others. The name means 'hill of the roaring', referring to the bellowing of rutting red deer stags in the autumn. Peter Drummond says, in *Scottish Hill Names: Their Origin and Meaning* (Scottish Mountaineering Trust, 2007), that Creise probably means 'narrow', from an old Gaelic word *creas*. Clach Leathad means 'the stone of the slope'. Beinn Mhic Chasgaig is 'MacChasgaig's Hill'.

These hills can be climbed via the Glencoe ski resort but there are better ways, avoiding the mechanical detritus, which are more in keeping with the wildness of the hills. From the north Creise and Meall a'Bhuiridh form a horseshoe round the steep narrow glen of the Allt Cam Ghlinne. The circuit of this horseshoe is steep and rocky and involves some scrambling. Starting near the head of Glen Etive the route goes up the rock buttress called Sron na Creise, where careful route finding is needed to thread a way through the crags. Once on the main ridge it's easy walking over Stob a'Ghlais Choire to Creise and then the minor top of Mam Coire Easain, from where rougher walking over granite boulders leads to Meall a'Bhuiridh and brief contact with the ski junk. The north ridge of Meall a'Bhuiridh leads above the lifts down to Creag Dhubh and then turns northwest back to Glen Etive. The walk involves 11km of distance and 1200m of ascent and shouldn't take more than 5–6hrs.

To climb all the hills in one trip, and to avoid the ski resort, Alltchaorunn, in Glen Etive is the best place to start. There is a bridge over the river which, before the Land Reform Act of 2003, was notorious for its fortress-like barbed wire defences, both on a high locked gate and along the sides, which made fording the river the only way to gain access to the hills. The new legal right of access has led to the gate being unlocked and it's no longer necessary to get your feet wet, or to turn back if the river is in spate. The path uphill follows the dramatic gorge of the Allt Coire Ghuibhasan, a narrow, steep-sided ravine lined with birch, alder and rowan that ends in a wonderful rock amphitheatre, down which the burn crashes in a beautiful waterfall. The gorge and waterfall are worth a visit in their own right and make a fine short walk of 3.65km with 350m of ascent.

Above the waterfall rough slopes lead up the west ridge of Clach Leathad from where you can head north to Creise, going out and back again to Meall a'Bhuiridh en route. Opposite the ridge to Meall a'Bhuiridh another spur heads west, leading to the bealach with Beinn Mhic Chasgaig, whose flat summit can be confusing in mist. The steep west ridge leads back, with care, to Alltchaorunn.

The views from the summits are good. From Meall a'Bhuiridh the vast watery expanse of Rannoch Moor stretches into the distance to the east, while to the west Creise appears as a flat-topped, steep-sided ridge and Clach Leathad as a more distinctive pointed peak. Meall a'Bhuiridh itself is a red rock pyramid when seen from Creise. Beinn Mhic Chasgaig looks across the deep trough of Glen Etive to the long, snaking ridge of Buachaille Etive Mor.

This walk is only 16km long but it does involve 1700m of ascent and much of the terrain is rough, rocky and steep. I'd allow 7–9hrs.

⊗ The Southern Black Mount: Stob Ghabhar and Stob a'Choire Odhair ☆

Stob Ghabhar ('peak of the goat', 1090m) is a splendid and complex hill with six ridges and eight big corries. Everywhere it is rough and rocky although the southern slopes are less steep and provide the easiest ascent route. Linked to Stob Ghabhar by a 650m-high col is another Munro, Stob a'Choire Odhair ('peak of the dun-coloured corrie', 945m), which, although smaller in area and height, is clearly seen from the A82 and Rannoch Moor.

From Victoria Bridge, by Loch Tulla, at the end of the minor road from Bridge of Orchy, a path leads up into Coire Toaig. This path can be followed all the way to the bealach between Stob Ghabhar and Stob a'Choire Odhair, from where the narrow rocky Aonach Eagach ridge can be climbed, with some optional scrambling, to Stob Ghabhar. There are impressive views into rocky Coirein Lochain to the north from the Aonach Eagach. Returning to the col it's an easy if rough walk up Stob a'Choire Odhair, from where an old stalkers' path can be taken down the south ridge to rejoin the Coire Toaig path. This round is 16km long with 1345m of ascent and takes 6–8hrs. It can easily and pleasurably be extended with either walks along Stob Ghabhar's west ridge to the tops of Sron a'Ghearrain and Stob a'Bhruaich Leith or north to Sron nan Giubhas, perhaps returning via the east ridge of this minor peak and then across Coire Dhearbhadh to the col at the head of Coire Toaig.

Stob a' Choire Odhair from the slopes of Clach Leathad

Stob Ghabhar can also be climbed from Glen Etive via the long Aonach Mor ridge, starting at Alltchaorunn and the Allt Coire Ghuibhasan (see above under Northern Black Mount) and returning via Sron a'Ghearrain and Coire a'Chaolain. This route is also 16km long, with 1285m of ascent, and takes a similar amount of time. There are many other possibilities in this area. A link can be made with the Northern Black Mount via the Bealach Fuar-chataidh and the whole range traversed or a loop made over the Aonach Mor and Stob a'Bhruaich Leith ridges. I'd stay out of big Coire Ba, as it's very wet and boggy, and instead admire it from the rock ridges above.

3:4 ◖ THE WEST HIGHLAND WAY ☆

The West Highland Way runs through the Central Highlands from Bridge of Orchy to its terminus in Fort William, crossing the edge of Rannoch Moor below the Black Mount, skirting the mouth of Glencoe, climbing over the Devil's Staircase to Kinlochleven then rounding the end of the Mamores to Glen Nevis, a total distance of 56km. West Highland Way walkers usually take three days over this stretch, stopping at the Kings House

Hotel near the head of Glencoe (see below under Glencoe) and in Kinlochleven (see below under the Mamores). Near the southern end of this section is the Inveroran Hotel, a good alternative stopping place to Bridge of Orchy.

Beyond Loch Tulla is the finest part of this northern section of the West Highland Way, following the old Glencoe road right under the ramparts of the Black Mount, with the water and bogs of Rannoch Moor stretching away to the east. This is one of the wildest and remotest sections of the way. A highlight is the tumultuous River Ba, which pours out of gigantic cliff-rimmed Coire Ba. Another is the first view of the massive, gully-riven cliffs that make up the pyramidal east face of Buachaille Etive Mor, seen as the way descends past the Glencoe ski resort to cross the A82 to the Kings House Hotel.

Next comes the only real climb on the West Highland Way, the ascent of the Devil's Staircase, along the route of an old military road, built around 1750 by General Caulfeild. This takes you to the highest point on the way, at 548m, before descending to sea level at Kinlochleven, the largest town on the route, and the one with the widest selection of facilities.

The ascent out of Kinlochleven provides good views of the Beinn a'Bheithir horseshoe above

Ballachulish, the distinctive cone of the Pap of Glencoe above Loch Leven, and the spiky pinnacled Aonach Eagach ridge, before these are hidden by Beinn na Caillich and the way runs above the Allt Nathrach to the Lairigmor (big pass) and a final descent into plantations, Glen Nevis and Fort William. This last section is disappointing and dull in my opinion, being mostly in dense conifer forest, and not a fitting end to a fine long distance path. I would rather follow the minor road from Blar a' Chaorainn (NN 100 666) to Fort William as it at least gives views of Loch Linnhe. It's shorter and easier too.

3:5 GLEN COE ☆

The name of this most famous of glens conjures up images of gloom and foreboding in many minds due to the infamous massacre (see below). However for mountain lovers it is a place to celebrate the splendours of the hills, as the glen is one of the most impressive landscapes in Scotland. The rugged, rocky mountains walling the glen offer superb hillwalking, scrambling, rock climbing and snow and ice climbing. Three of Scotland's greatest mountains lie here – Buachaille Etive Mor, Bidean nam Bian and the Aonach Eagach.

The narrow glen runs east to west, dropping some 300m in 13km from its head below Buachaille Etive Mor to Glencoe village and the sea at Loch Leven. The classic, dramatic viewpoint is from the The Study, a large flat rock above the road near the eastern end of the glen (NN 183 564) from where it drops away past three huge buttresses known as the Three Sisters of Glencoe (these are truncated spurs, their ends ground away by the glacier that once ran down the heart of the glen). Opposite the Three Sisters lies the long, steep, unbroken curving wall of the Aonach Eagach, a complete contrast to the complex indented south side of the glen.

Geologically the area consists of volcanic rocks, both lava flows and pyroclastic rock, which accounts for the rocky landscape with its many big cliffs. The rocks were formed during a process known as cauldron subsidence some 400 million years ago in the period of vulcanism that built the Caledonian mountain chain. Great beds of lava spread across the already existing metamorphic rocks and were split by a series of faults that together formed an oval ring fault measuring some 8 by 15km. Much violent volcanic activity took place along the faults. At least eight times, massive eruptions caused the rock inside the faults to collapse and sink deep into liquid magma far below to form a vast caldera, a huge bowl-shaped hole in the earth. Then, as the volcanic activity slowed, molten granite welled up along the line of the ring fault. The rocks thrown up by the volcanoes form the basis of the landscape we see today, but the detailing was carried out by the glaciers of the last ice age. Before

Bidean nam Bian, Gearr Aonach and Aonach Dubh from the lower slopes of Beinn Fhada

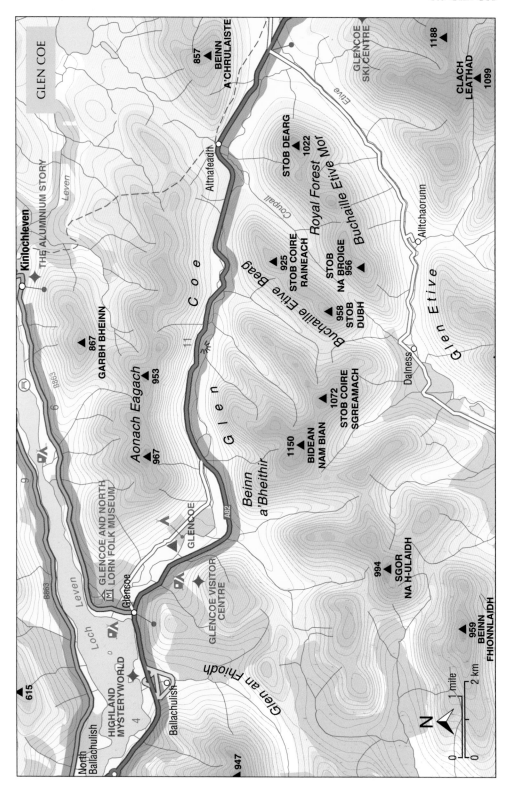

GLEN COE

BEINN A'CHRULAISTE 857

GLENCOE SKI CENTRE 1188

CLACH LEATHAD 1099

STOB DEARG 1022

Etive

Coupall

Royal Forest

Buchaille Etive Mor

Altnafeadh

STOB COIRE RAINEACH 925

STOB NA BROIGE 956

Buchaille Etive Beag

STOB DUBH 958

Alltchaorunn

Glen Etive

THE ALUMINIUM STORY

Kinlochleven

Leven

GARBH BHEINN 867

Coe

Glen

11

953

Aonach Eagach

967

Dalness

STOB COIRE SGREAMACH 1072

BIDEAN NAM BIAN 1150

B863

FC

6

6

Beinn a'Bheithir

SGOR NA H-ULAIDH 994

GLENCOE AND NORTH LORN FOLK MUSEUM

M

Glencoe

GLENCOE

A82

GLENCOE VISITOR CENTRE

BEINN FHIONNLAIDH 959

B863

Leven

Loch

HIGHLAND MYSTERYWORLD

4

Glen an Fhiodh

North Ballachulish

615

Ballachulish

947

N

1 mile

2 km

0

0

that earlier ice ages, along with the effects of rain over millions of years, eroded the rocks, leaving the remnants of ancient volcanic activity for us to view and climb on. Indeed the rocks that sank into the magma now make up the mountains. Cauldron subsidence was first described in detail in Glen Coe and the area is of world wide significance geologically, which has been recognised in its inclusion in the Lochaber Geopark.

Glen Coe is very accessible as the A82 trunk road runs right down the centre. Some might say it is too accessible, and might wish that the road had either followed the West Highland Line, which stays well east and north of the glen, or else the route of the first military roads over the Devil's Staircase at the head of the glen to Kinlochleven (and as for the appalling idea of the Fort William Chamber of Commerce for making the A82 a dual carriageway I'll just quote Ronald Turnbull's excellent *Ben Nevis and Glen Coe* guidebook (Cicerone, 2010) – 'letting us arrive 20 min. earlier at what would no longer be worth visiting'). As it is this is a dramatic road to drive and takes the non-mountaineer right through the heart of some of the most rugged hills in Scotland. Glencoe village lies at the foot of the glen and has all amenities. There are campsites, a youth hostel and other facilities in the lower glen too including the Clachaig Inn (see below). At the head of the glen is the Kings House Hotel.

Since 1935 Glen Coe has been in the care of the National Trust for Scotland which has an excellent visitor centre in the lower glen (www.glencoe-nts.co.uk). Percy Unna (see above under The Glen Strae Hills) was responsible for fund-raising for the purchase from climbing and mountaineering clubs and donated a considerable sum himself. Unna believed in keeping mountains wild and said that Glencoe should be 'maintained in its primitive condition for all time'. The NTS publishes a well-illustrated and useful guide to the glen – *Glencoe* by Lyndsey Bowditch (NTS, 2005).

THE KINGS HOUSE HOTEL AND THE CLACHAIG INN

Glen Coe has two hostelries famous in the annals of mountaineering, the Kings House at the head of the glen and the Clachaig Inn near the foot. Generations of climbers and hillwalkers have gathered in their bars and talked of their adventures on the surrounding hills over pints of beer and glasses of whisky.

The Kings House Hotel dates back to the 1740s, long before the first mountaineers appeared. It was built to provide a stance or resting place for the cattle drovers who brought their herds over the mountains to markets in the Central Lowlands and also as a coaching inn. Because of its remote and wild location in the eighteenth and 19th centuries no rent was charged and the innkeeper was given a government grant. Travellers probably only stayed because they had no other choice. The Wordsworths were guests in 1803 and Dorothy wrote in her journal 'Never did I see such a miserable, such a wretched place ... the floors far dirtier than an ordinary house could be if it were never washed' while the supper was 'a shoulder of mutton so hard that it was impossible to chew the little flesh that might be scraped off the bones, and some sorry soup made of barley and water, for it had no other taste'. By 1841 the food had at least improved according to Charles Dickens, who ate 'a very hearty meal' here. However the hotel was 'still primitive' in the early 1930s according to the mountaineer J.H.B. Bell, who also wrote that 'from one's bedroom one could smell the bacon frying through a hole in the floor' and that 'in another it was said to be necessary to put up an umbrella in bed if the weather was wet'. Later in the decade another leading mountaineer, W.H. Murray, writes of 'a bright fire and hot dinner' at the Kings House after a winter climb on Buachaille Etive Mor, and, in 1941, on leave from the army, of arriving at two in the morning to find 'a fire, hot tea, food and beds – all were waiting for us'. Today the Kings House is a resting place for West Highland Way walkers who have crossed Rannoch Moor, as well as for general tourists and mountaineers. It's in a splendid situation. Just step outside and you are in the wilds, with the vastness of Rannoch Moor sweeping away to the east and the great ribbed and gullied cone of Buachaille Etive Mor towering into the sky to the south. The hotel has a website: www.kingy.com.

The Clachaig Inn also dates back to the 18th century. It's sited in the wooded lower glen not far from the site of the massacre (see below) and near the western end of the Aonach Eagach and has a most impressive view of the great rocky west face of Aonach Dubh to the southwest. The situation may not be quite as dramatic as that of the Kings House but it is still evocative, and also much nearer to other facilities. The inn itself is cosy and friendly and famous for its selection of real ales and malt whiskies. The Boots Bar, which features a log fire, is a gathering place for walkers and mountaineers and has regular live music and talks by well known mountaineers. The Glencoe Mountain Rescue team, one of the busiest in the country, was founded at a meeting in the Clachaig in 1961. The Clachaig has a website at www.clachaig.com.

THE MASSACRE OF GLENCOE

The massacre hangs over Glencoe like a gloomy shadow, a grim darkness reaching out of the past to cast a pall over the glen. Yet the decades and centuries leading up to the massacre were turbulent and violent, with much warfare between clans and many brutal killings and bloodbaths. Why has this one incident among many been remembered so vividly? The general opinion is that it stands out as a particularly nefarious event because it involved a betrayal of trust, the breaking of the loyalty guests owe to their hosts. It also attracted much attention at the time and was used as propaganda by the Jacobites. It then became part of the romantic image of the Highlands in the Victorian era, an illusion in part fostered by Queen Victoria herself as shown in Ian R. Mitchell's excellent book *On the Trail of Queen Victoria in the Highlands* (Luath, 2000).

The event had its origins in the 1689 rising against William of Orange, who had replaced James VII on the thrones of England and Scotland in 1688, which involved many Highland clans including the MacDonalds of Glencoe. The rising was defeated and William offered a pardon to the clans involved if their chiefs swore oaths of allegiance by January 1st 1692. The penalty for not taking the oath was death. MacIain, Chief of the MacDonalds, delayed taking the oath until the end of 1691 and then, for various reasons, was unable to do so until January 6, five days late. However he still felt he was safe and had nothing to fear from the government. He was wrong: the government decided to make an example of the MacDonalds.

At the end of January 1692 a party of government troops arrived in Glencoe and asked for shelter. They were led by a Captain Robert Campbell, and had a number of Campbells in their ranks. The Campbells and MacDonalds were rival clans and had been feuding for decades. Most recently the MacDonalds had raided Campbell lands in Glen Lyon on their way home from the defeat of the 1689 rising. Despite this the MacDonalds gave the soldiers shelter and food. All was fine for ten days, but then Robert Campbell received orders telling him 'to fall upon the Rebels, the MacDonalds of Glencoe, and put all to the sword under 70'. The slaughter began early the next morning and 38 MacDonalds were murdered, including MacIain himself. Around the same number died in the blizzards sweeping the glen. Hundreds more survived and returned to live in the glen.

Buachaille Etive Mor ☆

At the mouth of Glencoe rises one of the great iconic mountains of Scotland, Buachaille Etive Mor. Motorists come face to face with the huge gully-riven pyramid as the A82 curves round the Black Mount and sweeps across the northwestern end of Rannoch Moor, an inspiring sight for mountain lovers. The mountain itself stretches some 7km to the southwest over four summits to finish at Dalness in Glen Etive. Indeed, Buachaille Etive Mor is really a Glen Etive rather than a Glencoe hill, its southeastern slopes walling the upper glen. All the burns on its slopes run into the River Etive too, either directly or via the River Coupall or the Allt Gartain. The name means 'the big herdsman of Etive'. To mountaineers it's just known as 'The Buachaille'.

From northeast to southwest the summits are Stob Dearg ('red peak', 1022m), Stob na Doire ('peak of the oak thicket', 1011m), Stob Coire Altruim ('peak of the corrie of nursing' – probably of deer, 941m) and Stob na Broige ('peak of the shoe', 956m). The first and last are Munros. The first recorded ascent was quite late for such a prominent mountain. It was 1867 when John Stuart Blackie, professor of Greek at Edinburgh University, climbed to the summit. However Duncan MacIntyre, the Glenorchy Bard, (see The Bridge of Orchy Hills in Chapter 2), may well have climbed the hill back in the mid 18th century, as he lived in Glen Etive for many years and wrote in one his poems 'I would love to be on the Buachaille, thigh-deep in snow'.

Soon after Blackie the first mountaineers arrived and Buachaille Etive Mor, or more specifically the northeast face of Stob Dearg, became a major climbing destination, which it has remained ever since.

Buachaille Etive Mor is built of a volcanic lava called rhyolite. This is a beautiful fine-grained rock that appears in striped bands in cliffs, the stripes showing the movement of the molten lava as it rippled over the surface. This is known as flow banding.

⊗ The Traverse of Buachaille Etive Mor ☆
The traverse of the four summits of Buachaille Etive Mor is a fine walk in splendid surroundings. The going is easy once the ridge has been attained, although there is much up and down. The mountain is steep on every side so the ascent to the ridge is strenuous from wherever you start. From the A82 to the north a good path leads into huge Coire na Tulaich, up which a rougher path threads a way through a tangled mass of scree and boulders, with some very easy scrambling in places, to emerge from the corrie onto a broad bealach just west of Stob Dearg. In winter there can be big cornices at the head of Coire na Tulaich, and huge avalanches have swept the corrie so care is required. Cairns mark the route up rocky slopes from the bealach to Stob Dearg's big summit cairn which sits at the apex of the cliffs of the northeast face. It's a dramatic spot with a feeling of great space as the rocks fall away steeply below and the flat expanse of Rannoch Moor, sparkling with water, stretches east to tiny distant summits. Southwest the broad undulating ridge ripples away to Stob na Broige. The walk over the tops is pleasant and easy, although care needs to be taken to turn right (southwest) on Stob na Doire and not take the path south, which leads to dangerous, craggy terrain above Glen Etive. From Stob na Broige there is a stunning view right down Glen Etive to Loch Etive. A steep descent leads directly down the southwest

ridge to Glen Etive, from where a return to the start could be made via the Lairig Gartain to the northwest. This is a long route, however (17km with 1700m of ascent, 8–10hrs). It's shorter to return over Stob Coire Altrum, almost to the next col, and then descend north on a rough path into the Lairig Gartain (13.5km, 1350m ascent, 6–8hrs).

⊗ Scrambles on Buachaille Etive Mor ☆
The massive northeast face of the Buachaille is intimidating and awe-inspiring. Scrambles here are long and mostly serious, in the harder grades. The best-known is the splendid Curved Ridge (Grade 2/3), a fine arête that takes the scrambler fairly easily through stupendous rock scenery with views out across Rannoch Moor. Across the gully to the right of the ridge rises the impressive cliff known as the Rannoch Wall. The 240m route is popular and well worn and follows the jagged crest of the ridge to Crowberry Tower at the top of Crowberry Ridge from where Stob Dearg can be reached.

⊗ ✳ Climbing on the Buachaille ☆
The first rock climb on the Buachaille was made in 1894 by the great Scottish mountaineer Norman Collie and is named after him. Graded Moderate Collie's Climb is 300m long. This was the first of many climbs, both rock and ice, over the following decades that involved leading luminaries of Scottish climbing such as W.W. Naismith, Harold Raeburn, J.H.B. Bell, W.H. Murray, Jimmy Marshall, John Cunningham, Robin Smith, Hamish MacInnes and Dougal Haston. The great cliffs are now laced with routes of all grades and are very popular both summer and winter. Enthralling accounts of pioneering climbs on the Buachaille in the 1930s and 1940s can be found in W.H. Murray's books *Undiscovered Scotland* and *Mountaineering in Scotland* (published together by Baton Wicks, 1997).

A classic and popular route described by Murray is Agag's Groove, which runs up the mighty Rannoch Wall, the eastern face of Crowberry Ridge. First climbed in 1936, it's 105m long and is graded Very Difficult. The route follows the highly visible groove up the face to finish up a nose. The climbing is easy with good belays and is only exposed in a few places, but it feels serious due to the magnificent situation on a big rock face high above Rannoch Moor.

In winter the cliffs of the Buachaille feel even bigger and grander. Gazing out over Rannoch Moor from a snowy perch high on the mountain is a wonderful experience. Curved Ridge becomes a graded climb when under snow and ice (Grade II/III) and is a splendid route. Either side of Curved Ridge are D Gully (150m, Grade II) and Easy Gully (150m, Grade II/III). Arguably the finest winter route is Crowberry Gully (300m, Grade III/IV), first climbed by a party led by Harold Raeburn in 1909, which is generally described as magnificent. It is avalanche prone, however, so conditions need to be right for a safe ascent.

⊗ Beinn a'Chrulaiste

Opposite the northeast face of Buachaille Etive Mor, on the far side of the A82, rises an 857m Corbett called Beinn a'Chrulaiste, a superb viewpoint for the Buachaille. This can be climbed easily by its west and east ridges and a traverse of the hill, with the return being made along the West Highland Way, is a worthwhile and enjoyable outing. The Kings House Hotel lies just south of the east ridge and can be used as a base. The whole circuit is only 10km long with 678m of ascent, and can be done in 3–5hrs. As well as the massive rocky pyramid of the Buachaille, from the summit Rannoch Moor can be seen stretching away southeast to distant hills, the shapely cone of Schiehallion clearly identifiable.

❶ Beinn a'Chrulaiste means 'rocky hill', which hardly seems an appropriate name with the Buachaille, a real rock mountain, just across the way. However there are some crags on the south side of the hill up which a number of easy scrambles can be made. Ascending this side of the hill is more interesting than walking up the ridges at either end.

⊗ Buachaille Etive Beag

Paralleling Buachaille Etive Mor to the west is its lesser relative, Buachaille Etive Beag ('little herdsman of Etive'), which is both smaller and lower. It still makes for a good ridge walk and has a Munro at each end, Stob Dubh ('black peak', 958m) overlooking Glencoe and Stob Coire Raineach ('peak of the corrie of bracken', 925m) overlooking Glen Etive. The latter forms a matching cone with Stob na Broige of Buachaille Etive Mor when seen from Glen Etive, with the classic glaciated U-shaped valley of the Lairig Gartain lying between them.

The easiest ascents to Buachaille Etive Beag's ridge are from the glens either side to the low point between the two peaks, from which both can be easily reached. There is also a steep ascent up the southwest ridge to Stob Coire Raineach from Glen Etive. There are scrambling routes up the craggy northern slopes. One of these, a Grade 2 up the northeast buttress of Stob nan Cabhar ('peak of the rafters'), is described in Noel Williams' *Scrambles in Lochaber* (Cicerone, 2nd edition 2009).

Starting on the path up to the Lairig Eilde from the A82 in Glencoe near The Study the route to the ridge, out and back to both summits and then back the same way is 8km long with 925m of ascent and need only take 3–4hrs.

⊛ The Circuit of the Lairig Eilde and Lairig Gartain

Two glaciated passes lie either side of Buachaille Etive Beag, both 480m high: the Lairig Gartain separates it from its bigger sibling; the Lairig Eilde separates it from Bheinn Fhada and Stob Coire Sgreamhach at the eastern end of Bidean nam Bian. Paths run over both passes and the circuit of the two is a pleasant outing in grand scenery, although it can be very wet and muddy after rain.

The walk starts near The Study in upper Glencoe, where the Allt Lairig Eilde drops in a 20m waterfall into the rocky gorge through which runs the River Coe. The path runs gently up to the broad saddle of the Lairig Eilde, lying between Stob Dubh and the steep rocky northeastern face of Stob Coire Sgreamhach. Lairig Eilde means 'pass of the hinds' and deer are often seen in the area. Beyond the pass the path descends a much steeper glen, in which the burn is also called the Allt Lairig Eilde; this runs down to Glen Etive. Before the woods in Glen Etive are reached traversing paths cut round the southern ridge of Stob Dubh and into the Lairig Gartain. A path beside the Allt Gartain leads to the pass, whose name probably means 'pass of the enclosed field', although it could be 'Gartan's pass'. On the north side of the pass a bigger stream, the River Coupall, speeds down the glen before turning east below the northeast face of Buachaille Etive Mor and running to the River Etive. At the A82 the old road can be followed most of the way back to the start, which avoids the dangers of the speeding traffic. The total distance is 14.5km with 610m of ascent and the walk takes 4–6hrs.

Sunset on Bidean nam Bian from Fraochaidh

Bidean nam Bian ☆

Bidean nam Bian (1150m) is the highest and argu-ably the finest of the Glencoe mountains, yet it is probably the least known to non-mountaineers as it can't be seen clearly from the floor of the glen. However its three great northern buttresses make up the famous Three Sisters of Glencoe and form a major part of the classic view of the glen. Looking down Glencoe they appear as three separate big rocky mountains jutting out into the glen. Behind them rises a higher pyramid that's often mistaken for the highest summit, but isn't: it's a lower top called Stob Coire nan Lochan.

Bidean nam Bian is a big, steep, complex mountain with four summits over 1000m high, two of them Munros, and another five minor summits. Its southern side takes the form of a ridge, running northwest–southeast, on which lie three of the high-est summits, and which presents an unbroken steep rocky face to Gleann Fhaolainn to the south. The north side is much more complicated. At each end of the main ridge arms curve round to the north, the short An-t-Sron ('the nose') in the west and the much longer Beinn Fhada ('long mountain') in the east. Between these arms another ridge juts out to the north from the highest summit and then divides into two spurs called Aonach Dubh ('black ridge') and Gearr Aonach ('short ridge'). These two, together with Beinn Fhada, form the Three Sisters, and are truncated spurs, their ends ground away by the glacier that once ran down Glencoe. Between Beinn Fhada and Gearr Aonach lies Coire Gabhail, an attractive hanging valley often called the Lost Valley; between Gearr Aonach and Aonach Dubh lies Coire nan Lochan, a much rockier, rougher cor-rie; and, finally, between Aonach Dubh and An-t-Sron lies equally rocky Stob Coire nam Beithach. Great cliffs abound on the spurs and the corrie walls, and Bidean nam Bian is a major climbing area, with rock and ice climbs of all grades. The cliffs are built of fine-grained volcanic rock that gives good grip and plenty of holds. Mostly it's pale rhyolite, which is sometimes orange or pink-tinted, but there is some darker andesite too.

Bidean nam Bian is the name of the high-est summit as well as the whole mountain. The name is often translated as 'peak of the mountains' (*Bidean nam Beann*) but Peter Drummond's *Scottish Hill Names: Their Origin and Meaning* (Scottish Mountaineering Trust, 2007) says that it's 'literally the peak of the hides or animal pelts', and also points out that the name on Pont's 16th-century maps is a corruption of *bod an deamhain*, 'penis of the devil', a name also found in the Cairngorms and translated loosely as 'The Devil's Point'. The height is 1150m and the summit is in the centre of the main ridge. The other Munro, which lies at the east end of the ridge, is 1072m Stob Coire Sgreamhach. The name means 'peak of the dreadful corrie', which must refer to Coire Gabhail, although today we think of this corrie as beautiful. The other high summits are 1107m Stob Coire nam Beith ('peak of the corrie of the birches') at the west end of the ridge and 1115m Stob Coire nan Lochan ('peak of the corrie of the little loch'), which lies on the spur running north from Bidean nam Bian.

Surprisingly, given that there are no recorded ascents of Buachaille Etive Mor before 1867, Bidean nam Bian was climbed almost a hundred years earlier in the 1770s by the Presbyterian minister and botanist John Stuart during a botanical expedition with another botanist John Lightfoot, as recorded in the latter's two-volume *Flora Scotica*, published in 1777 (see also Ben Cruachan section). Ian R. Mitchell describes this as an 'astonishing ascent' that wouldn't be equalled for half a century. Anyone who ventures into Bidean's complex, rocky corries and looks up at the great cliffs and high ridges will appreciate the difficulties of an ascent before there were any accurate maps, let alone paths or guidebooks.

⊗ The Summits and Ridges of Bidean nam Bian ☆

A round of the highest summits of Bidean nam Bian is one of the finest walks in the Highlands. The terrain is rocky and complex, the situations thrilling and dramatic, the views superb and there's a wonderful feeling of being in the midst of a big, wild mountain world. Route finding can be difficult in mist, although there are paths, and much of the route is on steep ground. Under snow and ice the walk is potentially hazardous and requires good winter skills. There are a number of different options for a circuit of the tops. Here I've described one running from west to east.

Starting just west of pretty Loch Atriochtan the route passes Achnambeith, a whitewashed farmhouse that has played a major part in mountain rescue in the glen, then heads up into Coire nam Beithach below the huge cliffs of the west face of Aonach Dubh, on a well-constructed path. Coire nam Beithach is a great rocky bowl full of boulders

and scree and ringed with big cliffs. Two particularly noticeable rock buttresses can be seen below the summit of Bidean itself, the Diamond Buttress and the Church Door Buttress. To their left a rough path straggles up steep scree to the col between Stob Coire nan Lochan and Bidean nam Bian. The former can be easily visited from the col before the last steep rocky slopes are ascended to the little pointed summit of Bidean nam Bian, which is situated at the junction of the Stob Coire nan Lochan ridge and the main ridge. All around rise rugged rocky hills. The jagged crest of the Aonach Eagach lies to the north with the bulk of Ben Nevis beyond it and the long Mamores ridge undulating away to its right. East of the summit Bheinn Fhada, both Buachailles and the Black Mount can be seen, while to the south Loch Etive is a long dark slash with Ben Starav and Ben Cruachan prominent among the hills around it. And to the west Beinn a'Bheithir soars above Loch Leven and Loch Linnhe.

Some 700m to the northwest of Bidean nam Bian lies Stob Coire nam Beith from where there is a dizzying view straight down into Coire nam Beith. Returning over Bidean's summit the route continues east along the rocky ridge to Stob Coire Sgreamhach. Below lies Coire Gabhail. To descend into the corrie either return to the col between Stob Coire Sgreamhach and Bidean nam Bian and descend the steep slopes to the flat corrie floor, which is the shortest and easiest route, although steep at the start (look out for a small cairn making the start of the descent), or head along the Beinn Fhada ridge, which involves scrambling and very steep terrain, to a low point before the final top from where a shallow gully can be descended to the corrie floor.

Coire Gabhail is wonderful; a long flat grassy meadow below steep mountain walls with no obvious exit. The name means 'corrie of the booty' and is said to refer to the habit of the MacDonald clan of hiding stolen cattle in the corrie. It would certainly make a good hiding place as it can only be seen from the mountains above. A winding stream trickles across the corrie floor to a narrow gap choked with a chaotic tangle of massive boulders and trees. This is the mouth of the corrie, below which the stream plunges down a steep ravine with a path clinging to its slopes. Once out of the corrie a final walk along the old road down the heart of Glencoe leads back to the start.

Coire Gabhail (the Lost Valley), Bidean nam Bian

Visiting all four 1000+ metre summits and descending from Beinn Fhada involves a distance of 15km with 1650m of ascent. The walk takes 6–9hrs.

⊛ Scrambling on Bidean nam Bian ☆

Bidean nam Bian is a great place for scrambling, with many routes of all grades on the buttresses and corrie walls. Walks on the mountain can easily include optional scrambles. One easy but spectacular scramble is the ZigZags, a Grade 1 that goes right up the steep nose of Gearr Aonach. The route does as the name suggests and zigzags up the face on three slanting ledges. The nose of Gearr Aonach is set right on the edge of the mountain, hanging above Glencoe, and the views back down into the glen and across to the Aonach Eagach are superb. From the top of the ZigZags you can walk along Gearr Aonach and then either descend into Coire nan Lochan or go on to Stob Coire nan Lochan. Another surprisingly easy enjoyable scramble up what appears to be difficult rock is the ascent of Dinnertime Buttress, the northern most buttress on the West Face of Aonach Dubh. The route goes right up the centre of the buttress and reaches the ridge not far from the summit of Aonach Dubh. The ridge can be followed to Stob Coire nan Lochan or a descent made to the lochans in Coire nan Lochan. Dinnertime Buttress is a Grade 1 climb in winter.

❻ ❋ Climbing on Bidean nam Bian ☆

Bidean nam Bian is a major climbing area in summer and winter with well over 200 routes of all grades on its many cliffs. Climbing here has a real big mountain feel, even on easy routes, and many of the situations are spectacular.

One Moderate grade rock climb that bridges the gap between scrambling and climbing is Lower Bow on the East Face of Aonach Dubh above Coire nan Lochan. This 75m climb leads to a terrace from which several more routes head up the steeper cliffs above. The Bow is an obvious curved fault running right up the cliff towards the left end. The continuation of the Bow from the terrace is a deep chimney described as 'usually wet'. The Upper Bow route up this chimney is 60m and long and graded Very Difficult. There is a much better alternative nearby. A superb route starts not far along the terrace, a 60m Difficult called Quiver Rib. This goes up the rib and wall to the right of the Upper Bow chimney. Quiver Rib has good holds and a solid belay half way up but feels serious and exhilarating due to its situation high on a steep wall. The route was first climbed by W.H. Murray and D.B. McIntyre in 1947 and the ascent is described in Murray's *Undiscovered Scotland*, in which he writes 'I did not seriously expect the sheer cliff to go' but later 'an unbroken thread of superb holds curved all the way to the top'. Another good Difficult route, this time on Number 3 Buttress on Stob Coire nam Beith, is the 120m Crack Climb, which goes up the obvious crack at the right edge of the buttress and then via a rib and wall from a ledge belay to easier ground that can be followed to the summit of Stob Coire nam Beith. Further to the right on the same face is a pyramid-shaped buttress up the north ridge, up which runs a good 90m Difficult called The Pyramid.

An example of a good easy winter climb is C–D Scoop, a 150m Grade II up the gully between C and D Buttresses on the West Face of Aonach Dubh that leads to easier ground and the Aonach Dubh ridge.

Aonach Eagach

Walling Glencoe to the north is the long, serrated Aonach Eagach, whose name means 'the notched ridge' and which strikes excitement, anticipation and sometimes fear into the hearts of hillwalkers, as it's both the most sensational and the most difficult ridge on the mainland. Only the Cuillin Ridge on the Isle of Skye and A'Chir on the Isle of Arran are as narrow, exposed and thrilling. The heart of the ridge, the actual Aonach Eagach itself, is a thin twisting line of rock pinnacles, towers and slabs. The name however is now applied to the whole 3km ridge from Meall Dearg in the east to Sgorr nam Fiannaidh in the west. The traverse of this ridge is one of the finest outings in the Highlands.

There are four summits on the ridge, two of them Munros. From the east these are Am Bodach ('the old man', 943m), Meall Dearg ('red hill', 953m), Stob Coire Leith ('peak of the grey corrie', 940m) and Sgorr nam Fiannaidh ('peak of the Fingalians', 967m). The corries referred to in two of the names lie on the little visited north side of the Aonach Eagach. The two Munros, Meall Dearg and Sgorr nam Fiannaidh can be both be climbed separately, without scrambling along the narrow arête between them. Indeed, this is what the first person to climb all the Munros, the Rev A.E. Robertson did, famously kissing first the cairn and then his wife on Meall Dearg, his final Munro, in 1901.

The Aonach Eagach was probably traversed long before the first mountaineers arrived however. The Anderson brothers, from Inverness, in their *Guide to the Highlands and Islands of Scotland*, published in 1827, describe how foxhunters, with their dogs and guns, 'sit astride, and crawl cautiously alongst the narrow ridge'.

❺ The Traverse of the Aonach Eagach ☆

Modern scramblers don't sit astride or crawl along the ridge, but then they don't have to transport dogs or guns either and some definitely like to cling onto the rock very firmly in places. The traverse can be done from either end. East to west is regarded as the easier way, although having done it in both directions I wouldn't say there was much in it. Starting at the east end does involve 150m less ascent as this route starts higher up the glen (of course if you walk up the glen back to the start point you have to regain this height). The scramble is Grade 2 and there is some exposure and a few places where you need to think before you move. It's committing too as there are no safe descent routes down into Glencoe between Meall Dearg and Stob Coire Leith. The Aonach Eagach is one of the finest scrambles in Scotland and very popular. On clear summer days an early start is a good idea to avoid the crowds. In winter it's a Grade II/III climb and a serious undertaking.

At the east end a path climbs steeply up beside the Allt Ruigh to the ridge just below Am Bodach. The scrambling starts not far beyond the summit of the latter with the descent of some very steep outward-sloping polished rock ledges, which are slippery when wet. This section of the ridge is definitely easier west to east, as then you climb the ledges rather than descend them looking down at the big drop below. This is just a taster of what is to come, however, and it's after the next summit, Meall Dearg, that the sustained scrambling begins. The narrow, turreted ridge looks spectacular from Meall Dearg, a contorted snake of tottering and precarious rocks. The scrambling isn't hard however, just exposed in a few places, and the rough volcanic rock feels secure to hand and boot. Beyond a narrow gap that has to be climbed in and out of the terrain eases and it's just a walk to Stob Coire Leith and Sgorr nam Fiannaidh, where you can relax and admire the magnificent view up Coire nam Beithach to Bidean nam Bian and down

Loch Leven to the steep triangle of Garbh Bheinn in Ardgour, across Loch Linnhe.

The slopes down to Glencoe from Sgorr nam Fiannaidh are very steep. It's tempting to descend the mountainside just west of the Clachaig Gully as this leads almost directly to the Clachaig Inn and a well earned drink. However, although there are the remains of a path, this route is extremely loose and eroded, and in places passes right next to big drops into the deep chasm of the Clachaig Gully. A safer and easier route is to go straight down from Sgorr nam Fiannaidh to Loch Achtriochtan. It's a knee-hammering descent but it does leave you just under 3km from the start, and so is the best way down if you have to return up the glen. By far the easiest and most pleasant descent is to continue along the ridge to the col with Sgorr na Ciche and descend the path from there into lower Glencoe; however this does leave you some 7km from the start.

Descending to Loch Achtriochtan and returning up the glen to the start makes for an 11km route with 1285m of ascent and is likely to take 4–6hrs.

⊗ Garbh Bheinn

The north side of the Aonach Eagach is completely unlike the south side, with long spurs and corries making for complex terrain. A long 1.5km ridge runs north from Meall Dearg to a col at 510m, and then rises again to Garbh Bheinn (867m), a Corbett. Although arguably belonging to Kinlochleven – which it dominates, cutting out sunlight to the southern part of the town in midwinter, and looking out across Loch Leven – Garbh Bheinn is an outlier of the Aonach Eagach, and so is included here.

Garbh Bheinn can be easily climbed by its west ridge, which starts near Caolnascon on Loch Leven, where there is a quiet and scenic campsite. From the loch shore Garbh Bheinn looks huge: the best viewpoint is from the far side of the loch from where it rises as a bulky pyramid. The summit is a good viewpoint for the north side of Aonach Eagach and beautiful upper Loch Leven.

⊗ Sgorr na Ciche

The western terminus of the Aonach Eagach ridge is the fine little peak called Sgorr na Ciche, rising as a prominent rounded cone above Glencoe and clearly visible in views along Loch Leven between Ballachulish and Glencoe. Sgorr na Ciche is 742m high and can be climbed in half a day. The name means 'peak of the breast', clearly referring to the shape of the summit. It's often called the Pap of Glencoe, pap being the Scots translation of *ciche*. The path to the summit starts some 800m from

The Pap of Glencoe and Sgorr nam Fiannaidh at dusk

Glencoe village on the old road that runs north of the River Coe. A track that soon becomes a path climbs the hillside to the col between Sgorr na Ciche and Sgorr nam Fiannaidh, from where a short, easy scramble leads up quartzite boulders to the summit.

Situated at the end of the wedge of hills dividing Glencoe and Loch Leven, Sgorr na Ciche is in a fine position and has some of the best views in the Central Highlands. Loch Leven stretches out fjord-like to the east below the undulating line of the Mamores ridge, and westwards to the Ballachulish Bridge and the long ridges of Beinn a'Bheithir. Across Glencoe Bidean nam Bian rises, big, bulky and complex, a tangle of corries, ridges and peaks.

The round trip to the summit is 8km long with 745m of ascent and takes 3–4hrs.

3:6 BEINN A'BHEITHIR AND GLEN CRERAN

West of Glencoe Beinn a'Bheithir, one of the most graceful and attractive hills in the area, rises above Ballachulish. South of Beinn a'Bheithir lies Glen Creran, a remote forested glen with lines of knobbly peaks either side. Other than Beinn a'Bheithir the hills in this area are little visited compared with those of Glencoe, and a good destination for those seeking solitude and quietness. They can all be linked in long walks, and there are many fine high-level campsites on their flanks. Ballachulish on Loch Leven is the best access point for the northern hills of the group. Those to the south can be reached from the minor road that runs up lower Glen Creran from the coast road from Connel to Ballachulish, the A828, at the bridge across the narrows of Loch Creran.

Beinn a'Bheithir ☆

Where the Glencoe peaks are muscular and burly, their brutal and savage rock buttresses and walls glowering over the thin threads of the river and glen below, Beinn a'Bheithir appears graceful, almost delicate, with thin tapering ridges curving up to the neat pointed summits. The mountain takes the form of a huge horseshoe enclosing Gleann a'Chaolais with a minor horseshoe at the east end around the Allt Guibhsachain. There are three summits on Beinn a'Bheithir, two of them Munros. The highest, Sgorr Dhearg ('red peak' – from the reddish granite on its flanks, 1024m) sits at the eastern end of the hill at the apex of three ridges. The other Munro, Sgorr Dhonuill ('Donald's peak', 1001m), is in the centre of the horseshoe. The third summit, Sgorr Bhan ('white peak' – from the white quartzite on its slopes) is the highest point of the easternmost ridge of the mountain. The best view of Beinn a'Bheithir is from the north side of Loch Leven, from where the whole mountain can be seen in perspective.

Beinn a'Bheithir is a lovely mountain but its flanks have been sullied by ugly ranks of conifers that also make access awkward. The trees cover the northern flanks, fill Gleann a'Chaolais and pack Glen Duror to the south of the summits. The Forestry Commission is redesigning the forests to make them more open and with a wider variety of trees, so in time they should become less gloomy. In 2004–2005 the Forestry Commission built two mountain access paths through the trees in Gleann a'Chaolais to give access to the hills.

BALLACHULISH

Ballachulish is an old slate mining village situated on the south shore of Loch Leven just over 1km west of Glencoe. Slate was quarried here for 262 years, from 1693 to 1955, and the industry employed 2000 people in the mid-19th century. Ballachulish means 'village of the narrows' and was originally the name of the village now called North Ballachulish which indeed lies on the narrows of Loch Leven some 3km further west, from where a ferry ran across the loch from 1730 until the bridge was built in 1975. Ballachulish was originally called Laroch, the name of the river that runs through the village, but the quarry was called the Ballachulish Slate Quarry and over time the name was transferred to the village. Today the quarry walls can be seen rising behind the village, silent and calm, while the quarry floors are greening over and returning to nature. There's an interesting display on the slate industry in the visitor centre. Ballachulish offers all facilities except a campsite (there's one in Glencoe).

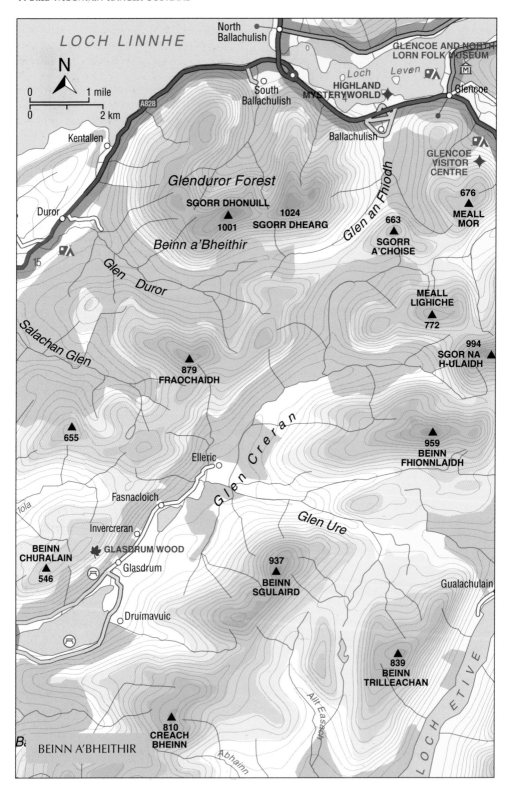

LOCH LINNHE

North Ballachulish

GLENCOE AND NORTH LORN FOLK MUSEUM

Loch Leven

HIGHLAND MYSTERYWORLD

Glencoe

South Ballachulish

A828

Ballachulish

Kentallen

GLENCOE VISITOR CENTRE

Glenduror Forest

Glen an Fhiodh

676
▲
MEALL MOR

Duror

SGORR DHONUILL
▲
1001

1024
SGORR DHEARG

663
▲
SGORR A'CHOISE

Beinn a'Bheithir

Glen Duror

MEALL LIGHICHE
▲
772

Salachan Glen

994
SGOR NA
▲
H-ULAIDH

879
▲
FRAOCHAIDH

Iola

655
▲

Glen Creran

959
▲
BEINN FHIONNLAIDH

Elleric

Fasnacloich

Glen Ure

Invercreran

Gualachulian

BEINN CHURALAIN
▲
546

GLASDRUM WOOD

Glasdrum

937
BEINN
▲
SGULAIRD

Druimavuic

LOCH ETIVE

839
▲
BEINN TRILLEACHAN

Allt Easach

Ba

810
▲
CREACH BHEINN

BEINN A'BHEITHIR

Abhainn

Beinn a'Bheithir's name is tied up with the old mythology of the Highlands as the hill was believed to be the home of the Cailleach Bheithir, the Celtic goddess of storms, winter, death and darkness. The Cailleach ('old woman' or 'hag') was able to cause floods and move mountains, presumably explanations of the heavy rains and black clouds that often enveloped the mountain and which caused flooding and landslides. *Beithir* means a monster, wild beast or serpent or perhaps a thunderstorm or thunderbolt: Beinn a'Bheithir is sometimes translated as 'hill of the thunderbolt (see Ben Cruachan section for more on the Cailleach).

The first recorded ascent of Beinn a'Bheithir was achieved by the same John MacCulloch who climbed Ben Cruachan and The Cobbler, sometime between 1811 and the publication of his book *Highlands and Western Islands of Scotland* in 1824.

⊗ The Beinn a'Bheithir Peaks

The traverse of Beinn a'Bheithir is a fine walk with superb views. A route can be done starting from Ballachulish that avoids all the forestry. The walk starts with an ascent of the north ridge of Sgorr Bhan. From the summit a lovely, graceful arête curves round to Sgorr Dhearg. Under snow this arête is such a perfect mountain feature it almost seems vandalism to mark it with bootprints.

Although the whole ridge has good views those from Sgorr Dhearg are exceptional, with perhaps the finest being southwest down the long sea arm of Loch Linnhe to the Firth of Lorn, distant Ben More on the island of Mull and the twin peaks of the Paps of Jura. Turning the other way rugged waves of mountains stretch out – the Glencoe peaks, the Mamores, Ben Nevis.

Sgorr Dhearg is a pale summit, built from pink quartzite. Looking west the ridge dips and rises to the darker more dome-like summit of Sgorr Dhonuill, a granite hill. It's a rougher peak too, and the east ridge leading up to the summit is bouldery and steep with a little easy scrambling in places. The view west from the summit over Loch Linnhe to the mountains of Ardgour is dramatic.

Beinn a' Bheithir from the east

Any descents to the north end up in the trees. I prefer to go south and angle southeast down the rough hillside from the col between the two Munros to reach Gleann an Fhiodh at the end of the plantation that creeps over the watershed from Glen Duror. A good path leads down Gleann an Fhiodh back to Ballachulish.

By this route the round is about 16km long with 1315m of ascent and takes 5–7hrs.

❺ The East-Northeast Ridge of Sgorr Bhan

Beinn a'Bheithir isn't a very rocky mountain but there is one easy Grade 1 scramble that provides an alternative start to the traverse. This takes the east-northeast ridge of Sgorr Bhan, which can be reached from the path in Gleann an Fhiodh. The ridge consists of slanting shattered slate and quartzite ledges, which can be seen clearly from the north ridge. The route follows the crest of the ridge to its junction with the north ridge.

⊗ Fraochaidh

Immediately south of Beinn a'Bheithir lies 879m Fraochaidh, a Corbett whose name means 'heathery hill'. Despite the name Fraochaidh is a surprisingly rough and rocky hill and its traverse is pleasant, entertaining and likely to be done in solitude. The hill is a curving ridge some 8km long between Glen Duror and Glen Creran. Conifer plantations swathe the lower slopes on most sides but there are gaps to the north and south. The southern approach is long and crosses several intermediate tops and isn't ideal if you want to traverse the whole ridge, as it reaches the ridge part way along. The northern route is a fine one, however. It starts in Ballachulish with the path down Gleann an Fhiodh. Before the plantations running over from Glen Duror are reached the slopes to the south can be climbed to the northeast ridge of Fraochaidh. It's a good 5km to the summit across several small rocky knolls and minor summits to the top, from where there's a good view down Loch Linnhe. Return can be made by the same route, which is no hardship, or else by continuing northwestwards, until the craggy slopes of Coire Dubh to the north of the summit can be skirted round and a descent made into the forest below. A way has to be found through the trees for 1km or so to the track in Glen Duror that leads up the glen and back over the watershed to Gleann an Fhiodh. Returning this way the walk is 21km long with 1250m of ascent and takes 6–8hrs.

⊗ Sgorr a'Choise and Meall Mor

Between Beinn a'Bheithir and the Glencoe peaks lie two little hills with excellent views of their bigger brethren. The walk over them is surprisingly rough and rugged and has the feel of higher hills. There are few paths and fewer people.

Both hills are classified as Grahams, Sgorr a'Choise ('foot-shaped peak') being 663m high and Meall Mor ('big hill') 676m high, but they are completely different in shape, Sgorr a'Choise being a tiny pyramid at the end of a narrow ridge, Meall Mor a bulky hill with a 1km-long summit ridge. Forestry plantations almost surround these hills but can be avoided, although the best walk passes through a section of forest.

This walk starts in Ballachulish, follows the path up Gleann an Fhiodh for 2–3km and then heads up to the southwest ridge of Sgorr a'Choise. This quartzite-dotted ridge is a delight to walk, as it leads up to the little summit perched above steep rocky slopes. Across Gleann an Fhiodh Beinn a'Bheithir looks enormous, it's east face towering high above and sending out long ridges down to Loch Leven. Bidean nam Bian looks huge too, with the summit clearly in view at the end of the rocky wall of Stob Coire nam Beith and An t-Sron. Meall Mor appears as a rounded hump overtopped by the pinnacled Aonach Eagach.

A descent southeastwards leads between two arms of forestry, beyond which you can turn north and climb easy grassy slopes to Meall Mor, from where you can look straight up U-shaped Glencoe, a perfect glaciated valley, and back to the shapely pyramid of Sgorr a'Choise.

An easy descent can be made down open hillsides to lower Glencoe, but this leaves you 5km from Ballachulish and the walking is along the main road, which is both unpleasant and dangerous. Unless a lift has been arranged it's better to risk the forestry north of Meall Mor. Aiming for the communications mast visible on a minor top called Am Meall makes for the shortest time in the trees. Am Meall is only 414m high but it gives a wonderful view west down Loch Leven and over Loch Linnhe. A path leads down from Am Meall past the old slate quarries to Ballachulish.

⊗ Sgor na h-Ulaidh and Meall Lighiche

Hidden away behind the Glencoe giants, and hard to see except from nearby hills, Sgor na h-Ulaidh ('peak of the treasure', 994m) is neglected except by

Munro baggers, which is a shame as it's a fine hill with some entertainingly rough slopes. The whole hill consists of a 3km southeast–northwest undulating ridge with two summits, Sgor na h-Ulaidh and Stob an Fhuarain ('peak of the spring', 968m). Sgor na h-Ulaidh lies at the head of Glen Creran, but the usual ascent is from Glencoe to the north via Gleann-leac-na-muidhe, which gives the best view of the hill. The Allt na Muidhe can be followed almost to the base of the crags of the north face, then left for an ascent to a bealach to the west and a climb to the summit via the minor top of Corr na Beinne. Descent can be made via Stob an Fhuarain to the northwest and the long Aonach Dubh a'Ghlinne, which runs northwards. This route is 11km long, with 1250m of ascent, and takes 5–6hrs.

Sgor na h-Ulaidh can be combined with Meall Lighiche ('doctor's hill', 772m), a Corbett that lies 2km to the northwest and is easy to climb by its north ridge from Gleann-leac-na-muidhe. There is a view from the summit right down Glen Creran to Mull. From Meall Lighiche an easy descent leads to the col below Corr na Beinne. The round of the two summits, with a descent via Aonach Dubh a'Ghlinne, involves 13km in distance and 1400m of ascent, and takes 6–7hrs.

There are routes to both hills from Invercharnan in Glen Etive, via Meall a'Bhuiridh, and also from Elleric in Glen Creran, but they include some forestry walking and neither is as interesting as the northern route.

Beinn Fhionnlaidh

Beinn Fhionnlaidh ('Finlay's hill', 959m) is a big rugged Munro to the south of Sgor na h-Ulaidh. It runs for 3km west to east and is girt with crags on every side. It lies between Glen Etive and Glen Creran and can be climbed from either. From Invercharnan in lower Glen Etive a forestry road weaves a way through the trees to the open hillside, from where the eastern end of the ridge can be reached. Because of the dense plantations lining Glen Etive it's best to return by the same route, for a round trip of 13km with an ascent of 1130m. This takes 5–6hrs.

From Glenure House in Glen Creran the west ridge can be ascended. However a more adventurous and exciting route, involving a little scrambling, follows the Allt Bealach na h-Innsig to the south face of the mountain up which you can scramble to the summit. Ascending this way and

using the west ridge in descent involves 12km of distance and 1050m of ascent, again taking 5–6hrs.

Beinn Sgulaird and Creach Bheinn

The most southerly tops in this group, these hills belong to Glen Creran, with Beinn Sgulaird prominent in views from Loch Creran, and an ascent of both can be made from Druimavuic via the Allt Buidhe into Coire Buidhe, and then up the slopes at the back of the corrie to the col between the summits. Beinn Sgulaird ('hat-shaped hill', 937m), a Munro, lies 2.5km to the north, Creach Bheinn ('hill of spoil', 810m), a Corbett, a little more than that to the south. You can cut the corners in Coire Buidhe and climb more directly to either summit and then do the same in reverse. Doing the walk this way gives a distance of about 15km with 1525m of ascent and takes 6–8hrs. Beinn Sgulaird can also be climbed by its west ridge from Druimavuic.

Lying above the head of Glen Creran, both summits give good views down Loch Creran to the island-dotted Firth of Lorn. There are also fine views of Loch Etive.

From Elleric further up Glen Creran Beinn Sgulaird can be climbed via the track up Glen Ure, an attractive wooded gorge, and then up its northeast ridge, with a descent northwest down rough slopes to lower Glen Ure for a 10km round with 1100m of ascent that only takes half a day (4–5hrs).

3:7 RANNOCH MOOR ☆

Right in the heart of the Central Highlands lies the vast flat expanse of bog, loch and stream called Rannoch Moor, a magical place of light, mist and water which covers some 52km². The moor is roughly triangular in shape, with the apex to the south, just north of Bridge of Orchy. To the west it's walled by the Black Mount, to the east by Beinn Achaladair and then the low hills west of Loch Rannoch. The northern edge is formed by a line of gentle hills running from the Kings House Hotel to Rannoch Station. The West Highland Line crosses the eastern edge of the moor, the A82 the western edge.

Rannoch Moor lies at a height of about 300m. During the last ice age it was the centre for the ice sheet in the Highlands, which was at its thickest here, and the radial drainage patterns of the streams show the movement of the ice outwards

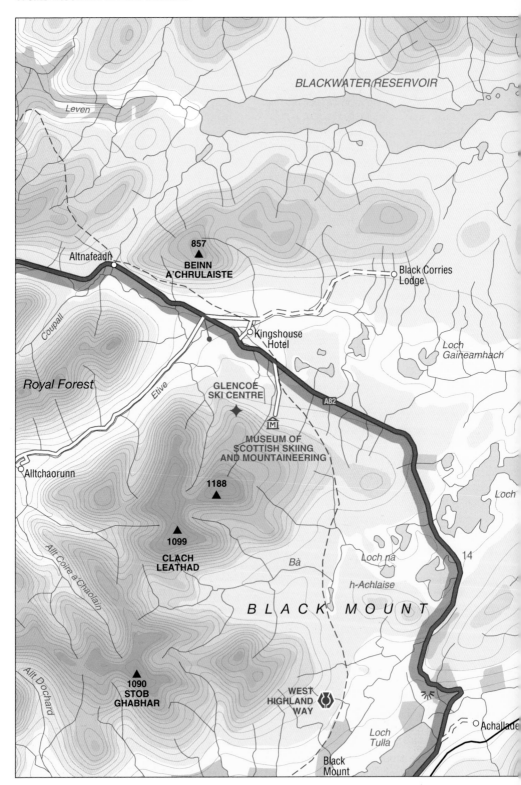

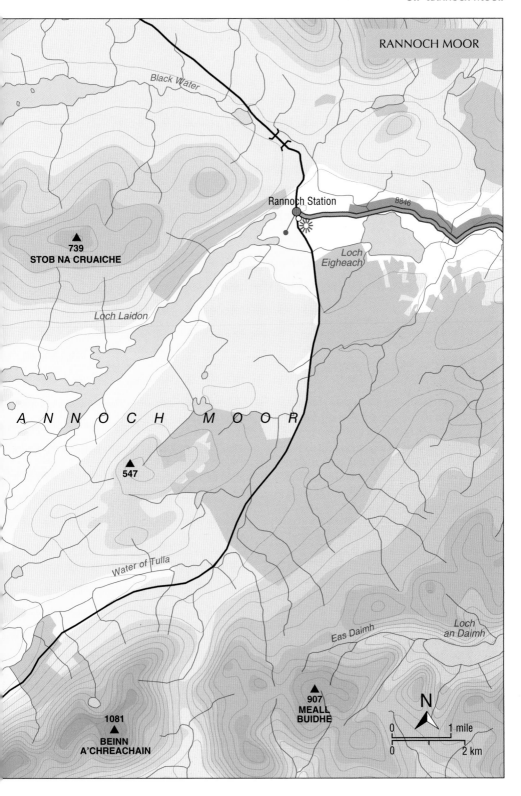

RANNOCH MOOR

Black Water

B846

Rannoch Station

Loch
Eigheach

▲
739
STOB NA CRUAICHE

Loch Laidon

R A N N O C H   M O O R

▲
547

Water of Tulla

Eas Daimh

Loch
an Daimh

N

▲
907
MEALL
BUIDHE

0 _____ 1 mile

0 _____ 2 km

▲
1081
BEINN
A'CHREACHAIN

View across Lochan na h-Achlaise on Rannoch Moor to the Black Mount

from the moor. Once the moor was wooded, and the stumps and roots of ancient trees can be found in the bogs. Now it is covered with deep peat and is a classic and scientifically important example of a blanket bog. The underlying rock is granite and the moor is a basin that was slowly eroded by ice and weather over the millennia. Little of this granite can be seen, however, the knolls on the moor being moraines and made of glacial debris rather than bedrock. Through the heart of the moor from southwest to northeast runs a slow meandering watercourse, much of it consisting of Loch Ba and Loch Laidon, which drains the moor eastwards to Loch Rannoch, the River Tummel, the River Tay and ultimately the North Sea. Despite its closeness to the west coast the mountain barrier prevents water on the moor from heading that way, although this barrier is almost breached in the northwest corner of the moor, where some streams run west to Glen Etive rather than to the Ba–Laidon watercourse.

Crossing the Moor

The West Highland Way crosses the western edge of the moor and it can be seen from many summits round its edge, especially the Black Mount hills.

However to really experience the moor you have to venture into its interior, far from road, railway, hill or house. Out in the centre of the moor it feels astonishingly remote and lonely and there is a tremendous feeling of space and freedom. There are two options for crossing the moor. One follows the Ba–Laidon watercourse right through the centre, the other a track across the northern moor.

Going from Loch Ba to Loch Laidon involves traversing much boggy and tussocky ground. Although flat the going is arduous and wet feet are just about guaranteed unless the ground is frozen or there has been a long dry spell. It's a popular canoe route and that's perhaps the best way to do this trip. On foot there is much meandering round the edges of the lochs and various boggy pools. There's no path. If the north side of the waterway is followed the track across the northern moor can be joined for the last few kilometres. A purer route follows the south side. Either way the distance from the A82 at Loch Ba to Rannoch Station at the foot of Loch Laidon is around 20km. Progress is usually slow so 6–8hrs should be allowed.

The easier route across the moor follows a track from the Kings House Hotel via Black Corries lodge to Rannoch Station. In places the track is quite wet and rough but mostly the walking is easy. The distance is again about 20km and there are 370m of ascent as the track stays above the moor in sections. 5–6hrs should be ample time.

The best way back from Rannoch Station is on foot across the moor. By road it's a very long way as Rannoch lies at the end of a road that runs 65km from Pitlochry on the A9 to the east. The railway is a more viable option as you could catch a train south to Bridge of Orchy.

⊗ Stob na Cruaiche

The highest and most interesting of the hills forming the northern edge of Rannoch Moor is Stob na Cruaiche (739m), a Graham whose name means 'peak of the peat stack'. The ascent can easily be combined with a crossing of the moor and is well worthwhile, as the extensive views from the summit are superb, with a ring of peaks on the horizon encircling Rannoch Moor. The shortest ascent route is from Rannoch Station north, through the forestry on the north shore of Loch Laidon, to Meall Liath na Doire, and then for 4km along the broad northeast ridge to the summit. From the top a descent south can be made to the track from Kings House Hotel. The round trip is 16km long with 675m of ascent, taking 4–6hrs.

3:8 THE MAMORES

The Mamores is the name of the magnificent ridge lying between Glen Nevis and Loch Leven. The Mamores ridge is 11km long in a straight line, twice that on foot, and never dips below 745m. It has 17 summits over 914m, of which 10 are Munros. There are several long spurs jutting out into upper Glen Nevis from the main ridge, and some of the summits lie on these, including the highest peak, Sgurr a'Mhaim. The Mamores are rocky peaks, with narrow ridges and shapely summits rising above big, scalloped corries. Although there is some easy scrambling in places the walking is mostly easy and often on grass. The traverse of the whole ridge from Glen Nevis including all the summits (see below) involves almost 4000m of ascent and 35km in distance, making for a long but highly satisfying trip that is probably the finest ridge walk – as opposed to scramble – in Scotland. Most people take at least 12hrs over this. The record is 6hrs 6mins, set by hill runner Nick Dawes in 1997.

Looking east along the Mamores from Mullach nan Coirean with Sgurr a'Mhaim rising above Coire a'Mhusgain

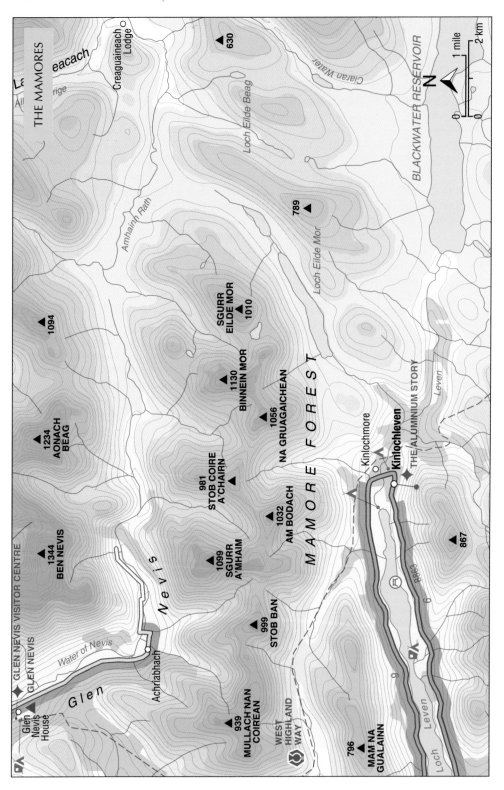

KINLOCHLEVEN

Kinlochleven lies 11km east of Glencoe at the head of Loch Leven, a beautiful fjord-like sea loch stretching deep into the hills. The town grew up around the aluminium smelter, which opened here in 1904. Before the smelter arrived there were just two small villages either side of the River Leven called Kinlochmore and Kinlochbeg. The smelter was built here in order to utilise hydro power for electricity. Vast amounts of power are required to smelt aluminium, and the big Blackwater Reservoir was constructed high in the hills 6km east of Kinlochleven to provide this. Thousands of navvies camped on the bleak moors and built the Blackwater dam – which is over 800m long and 24m high – by pick and shovel between 1904 and 1909. One spin-off from the hydroelectric plant was that Kinlochleven was one of the first towns in Britain to have electric street lighting. The story of the aluminium smelter and the town is told in an exhibition centre in the visitor centre, itself built of aluminium. The smelter closed in 2000 and Kinlochleven has now reinvented itself as an outdoors destination and tourist town. The West Highland Way passes through the town, bringing thousands of walkers every year, and there is now an outdoor centre in the shell of the old smelter with indoor ice climbing and rock climbing walls (the Ice Factor – www.ice-factor.co.uk). The ice wall is the biggest in the world, covering 800m^2, and has every grade of ice climbing, from a simple snow slope to overhanging ice. The centre has a good café and equipment shop and also runs courses, both indoor and outdoor. Kinlochleven has all the other facilities you might want and is superbly situated for the Mamores.

Mamore is sometimes translated as 'big moor', which is obviously not an accurate description of this line of steep mountains. The alternative of 'big breast-shaped or rounded hills' makes much more sense, especially as the second highest top is called Sgurr a'Mhaim – 'peak of the big rounded hill'.

From west to east the 10 Munros are: Mullach nan Coirean ('summit of the corries', 939m), Stob Ban ('white peak', 999m), Sgurr a'Mhaim (1099m), Am Bodach ('the old man', 1032m), Stob Coire a'Chairn ('peak of the corrie of the cairn', 981m), An Gearanach ('the complainer', 982m), Na Gruagaichean ('the maidens', 1056m), Binnein Mor ('big peak', 1130m), Binnein Beag ('little peak', 943m) and Sgurr Eilde Mor ('big peak of the hind', 1010m).

The eastern end of the Mamores is most easily reached from Kinlochleven to the south. The central and eastern sections are equally accessible from Kinlochleven and Glen Nevis.

⊗ The Ring of Steall ☆

Arguably the finest walk in the Mamores, after the complete traverse, is the Ring of Steall, the nicely punning name for the circuit of the great horseshoe of peaks around Coire a'Mhail, which includes four Munros. There is some easy if a little exposed scrambling on the route but it is mostly a walk, albeit an exciting one.

The walk starts at the road end in Glen Nevis, where there is a large parking area. From here a path climbs up through the spectacular wooded Nevis gorge, where the glen is squeezed between the rock walls of Ben Nevis to the north and Sgurr a'Mhaim to the south. Below the path the Water of Nevis roars and crashes down the boulder-choked gorge in a series of cascades. The slopes above the stream are clad in a lovely forest of oak, birch, Scots pine, rowan and aspen.

The path emerges from the gorge into the sudden quiet of a flat meadow, through which the Water of Nevis winds placidly. A three strand wire bridge crosses the river, providing a challenge, especially for those who aren't very tall or have short arms. Unless the river is high it is easily forded above the bridge if you don't fancy the balancing act. The white cottage on the far side is a private mountaineering club hut.

Just beyond the bridge a magnificent waterfall spreads in a white veil over the rocks below the lip of Coire a'Mhail where the Allt Coire a'Mhail pours over the edge. This is An Steall Ban ('the white spout'), better known as Steall Falls, the third highest waterfall in Scotland at 105m.

The area round Steall Falls is steep and potentially dangerous. There have been many accidents, some fatal, to walkers attempting to descend from Sgurr a'Mhaim via Coire a'Mhail. The descent is a terrain trap, with easy ground high up and steep and craggy ground low down, well past the point where climbing back up again is an appealing or even feasible option. The route described here avoids this area completely, and is 16km long with 1800m of ascent, taking 6–8hrs.

About 300m beyond the falls a good stalkers' path, one of the many found in the Mamores, zigzags up the north face of An Gearanach, the first Munro on the walk. From here on until the descent the whole walk is a joy, with splendid views throughout and wonderful terrain underfoot. Across Coire a' Mhail a spiny crest can be seen running from the main ridge to the big cone of Sgurr a'Mhaim. This is the Devil's Ridge and presents the last difficulties on the walk. There is scrambling immediately to hand, however, as beyond An Gearanach the ridge becomes a sharp arête, the top edge of some tilted slabs. This is appropriately called An Garbhanach – 'the rough one'. The scramble along the crest isn't hard but it is exposed as there are big drops on either side. Eventually easier, although still steep, ground leads down to a col beyond which a straightforward ascent leads to Stob Coire a'Chairn on the main ridge. Ahead lies the dark rocky northeast face of Am Bodach,

towering over Corrie na Ba. The climb up the northeast ridge to the summit is steep and rocky but doesn't involve any scrambling. Grassy slopes lead to the next peak, Sgorr an Iubhair ('peak of the yew tree', 1001m), which shows the fickleness of Munro's *Tables* as it was promoted to Munro status in a revision in 1981 then demoted in another revision in 1997. Whether 'officially' a separate mountain or not it's still a fine Mamores summit.

The going turns rocky again as the route leaves the main ridge to head out along the ridge leading to Sgurr a'Mhaim, the longest of the spurs jutting out to the north. After a descent over boulders to a col the Devil's Ridge is reached. This extremely sharp rock arête gives an easy but exciting and airy scramble. The high point of the arête is called Sgurr Coire a'Mhail. Once the crest is crossed broad slopes lead to the summit of Sgurr a'Mhaim.

Sgurr a'Mhaim is the main peak of the western Mamores and it stands out in views up Glen Nevis, the white quartzite of its summit often being mistaken for snow. There is a lovely little scalloped corrie lying just below the summit to the north, that can be seen clearly from Ben Nevis. The views are wide-ranging. Glen Nevis lies at your feet and winds away westwards. Ben Nevis rises directly to

Sgurr a' Mhaim and Stob Ban rising above Glen Nevis

the north, a great dark wall. Eastwards the Mamores ridge twists and turns into the distance.

The descent from the summit is simple, but rather brutal on the legs, straight down the northwest ridge to Glen Nevis, which is reached at the Lower Falls, 1.6km west of the start. At the Lower Falls the Water of Nevis drops 12m round a huge boulder. Up the glen Sgurr a'Mhaim soars into the sky. It's hard to believe you were on the summit so recently. On the north side of Glen Nevis is Polldubh, an area of crags and boulders on the lower slopes of Ben Nevis, where there are many rock climbing routes.

The Eastern Mamores ☆

At its eastern end the Mamores ridge becomes more complex, a tangle of corries, lochans and ridges. The main ridge spreads out in a great curve running south–north around Coire a'Bhinnein, with Binnein Mor at the north end and Sgor Eilde Beag at the south end. East of the latter lies the deep bowl of Coire an Lochain, beyond which rises Sgorr Eilde Mor, the easternmost Mamores peak, which feels cut off from the other peaks as it's separated from them by the lowest point on the ridge, and the view west is blocked by Binnein Mor. North of Sgurr Eilde Mor across big Coire a'Bhinnein is the cone of Binnein Beag, which also feels like an outlier of the main Mamores. A network of excellent stalking paths gives good access to these hills, and they can all be linked along with Na Gruagaichean to the west in one walk from Kinlochleven. It's a long walk, 20km, with 2000m of ascent, and takes 8–10hrs.

From Kinlochleven a path heads northeast to cross the 4WD track from Mamore Lodge, a hotel situated at 200m on the slopes of Am Bodach, to Loch Eilde Mor. Beyond the track the path angles up across the hillside and curves round into Coire an Lochain, a magnificent wild corrie containing a large ragged-edged lochan. Across the lochan is the big, gully-riven, scree and rock cone of Sgurr Eilde Mor. A rough path climbs the quartzite-, scree- and boulder-strewn west ridge to the summit, which feels as if it is perched at the end of the high country, as beyond to the east low rounded hills stretch away to the higher hills around Loch Ossian.

Back down in Coire an Lochain the stalkers' path can be rejoined and followed across Coire a'Bhinnein below the rough rocky east face of Binnein Mor and up to the wide, boggy bealach

between Binnein Mor and Binnein Beag on which there is a small lochan. An arduous ascent up rough scree and boulder-covered slopes leads to the summit of Binnein Beag, from where there is a superb view of Binnein Mor rising as a craggy tent-shaped peak above the lochan on the bealach. Ben Nevis looks imposing too.

There are two options for the ascent of Binnein Mor from the bealach, which can be usefully studied from Binnein Beag. The direct route is a scramble up Sron a' Gharbh-choire, which starts as a rocky buttress above the lochan and becomes a narrow arête higher up. Slightly longer but much easier, mostly a grassy walk in fact, is the northwest ridge, which lies on the far side of the corrie to the north of the summit.

The highest peak in the Mamores, Binnein Mor has a suitably fine summit and superb views, especially along the rest of the Mamores to the west, with the pyramid of Sgurr a'Mhaim prominent, and across Glen Nevis to the huge bulk of Ben Nevis. Sgurr Eilde Mor rises to the east but this peak looks far better from Sgurr Eilde Beag, which, confusingly, is a subsidiary top of Binnein Mor, lying 1km southeast of the South Top. From Sgurr Eilde Beag the view across the depths of Coire an Lochain to the volcano-like cone of Sgurr Eilde Mor has a great feeling of depth and space, the dark waters of the lochan in the corrie looking far, far below. A stalkers' path climbs the south ridge of Sgurr Eilde Beag and makes for a much shorter alternative route that omits Sgurr Eilde Mor and Binnein Beag.

On the main Mamores ridge now twin-topped Na Gruagaichean is soon reached. The Northwest Top looks impressive from the main summit, rising steeply just 300m away above the 60m deep drop separating the two. The going between the two summits is very steep and rocky, with big drops into Coire Easain to the northeast. Care is needed when there is snow and ice on this section.

From the Northwest Top grassy slopes lead down to a wide bealach between Coire Ghabhail and Coire na Ba. A stalkers' path heads down into the latter corrie and descends beside the Allt Coire na Ba down to Kinlochleven. Just above the town it passes a short spur path that leads to the Grey Mare's Waterfall, a worthwhile diversion to one of the most beautiful and spectacular waterfalls in Scotland. In a lovely wooded crag-rimmed gorge the Allt Coire na Ba drops 46m down a sheer cliff into a deep pool.

⊗ The Complete Traverse ☆

The complete Mamores ridge, including all the summits, is a very long and arduous walk. It can be split over two days with an intervening camp, but traversing the whole ridge in one day is more satisfying, in my opinion. You can walk in and camp at the start of the ridge, which does shorten distance and reduce the amount of ascent. In summer with just one overnight this need not mean carrying a heavy pack. My pack weight for trips like this is around 7 kilos. Water needs to be taken into account, especially on hot days, as there is only one source on the ridge between Binnein Mor and Mullach nan Coirean, Lochan Coire nam Miseach between Sgorr an Iubhair and Stob Ban. If heading west it's advisable to fill up water containers from Coire an Lochain below Sgurr Eilde Mor as it's 12km and 1200m of ascent to Lochan Coire nam Miseach. If heading east fill up at Lochan Coire nam Miseach.

The traverse can be done in either direction. Having done both my preference is east to west, as this gives the best views and has the most interesting start. I also prefer the route from Glen Nevis rather than Kinlochleven. The path from the roadhead in Glen Nevis leads up the glen to a ford of the Water of Nevis and an ascent of the northwestern slopes of Binnein Beag. Sgurr Eilde Mor comes next, then a climb over Sgorr Eilde Beag to Binnein Mor. The rollercoaster ridge walk really starts here. You can look west along the summits you'll be crossing in the next hours, including the out and back rocky spurs to An Gearanach and Sgurr a'Mhaim, the most difficult parts of the route, as they involve the only scrambling. From the last summit, grassy, rounded Mullach nan Coirean, which has a great view down Loch Linnhe, a descent can be made down the northeast ridge to the forest and then Lower Falls in Glen Nevis.

⊗ Mam na Gualainn and Beinn na Caillich

These two hills are outliers of the Mamores, separated from the main ridge to the north by the Lairig Mor pass, over which the West Highland Way makes its way from Kinlochleven to Glen Nevis. Situated immediately above Loch Leven the hills give superb views along the loch and across to the hills above the southern shore. Mam na Gualainn ('hill of the shoulder') is the higher at 796m, and a Corbett, but Beinn na Caillich ('hill of the old woman' – it lies opposite Am Bodach – 'the old man', 764m) is the more attractive hill. Mam na

View east to Binnein Mor from Sgurr a' Mhaim

Stob Ban from the east

Gualainn is a rather shapeless lumpy hill with a wide summit area. Beinn na Caillich has three narrow ridges and a small neat summit and it stands out in views from the slopes above Kinlochleven.

The traverse of both summits starts with the West Highland Way, which can be followed over the Lairig Mor to a ruin called Lairigmor, where a path heads southwest across the western slopes of Mam na Gualainn and down to Callert on Loch Leven. This is an old coffin road, along which corpses were transported before being taken by boat out to the island called Eilean Munde in Loch Leven, where they were buried safe from being dug up by wolves. Each clan who buried their dead on Eilean Munde had their own landing place. These were known as the Ports of the Dead. Maclain, Chief of the MacDonalds, who was killed in the Massacre of Glencoe, was buried on Eilean Munde. The island was used for many centuries, the last burials being in the 1950s. The island is named after St Fintan Mundus who built a church on it around AD600.

From 1.5km along the old coffin a road stalkers' path heads up from the broad western slopes of Mam na Gualainn to a height of 518m, from where it is an easy walk to the summit (796m), from where there is a dramatic view of Beinn a'Bheithir across Loch Leven. Beinn na Caillich is just 1.6km away and the walk there is easy, with only 114m of ascent up the west ridge from the col between the two hills. From the summit the dark waters of the Blackwater Reservoir can be seen away to the east, while below lies Ballachulish, Glencoe and Loch Leven. A slightly rough descent continues east, to pick up an old path that zigzags down to the Allt Nathrach glen where the West Highland Way can be rejoined.

The distance is 18km, with 1140m of ascent, and takes 6–7hrs.

❄ Winter Climbing in the Mamores

The steep corries and arêtes of the Mamores make for entertaining and exciting winter mountaineering. An Garbhanach and the Devil's Ridge become much more serious and challenging under ice and snow. Some of the cliffs that are too broken and loose for rock climbing provide good winter climbing, chiefly the northeast face of Stob Ban, on which there are a dozen Grade III and IV routes from 150 to 250m long.

3:9 BEN NEVIS

Ben Nevis is a magnificent mountain, as befits the highest summit (1344m) in the British Isles. The Ben – as it is known to climbers – is rough, rocky and solid, a dense mass of volcanic rock taking the form of a huge steep-sided whaleback that is sliced off abruptly on one side. The summit plateau is quite extensive and there are two subsidiary tops – Carn Dearg NW (1221m) on the northwest spur and Carn Dearg SW (1020m) on the southwest spur. At the end of the huge broad northwest shoulder lies 711m Meall an t-Suidhe. The southern and western slopes are very steep and craggy and split by long gullies, but it's to the north and east that the real glory of the mountain lies, with the great north face, the biggest cliff in Britain, 3km long and up to 610m in height, a rock wonderland of ridges, buttresses, cliffs, gullies and slabs. Unsurprisingly it is a major rock and ice climbing area with hundreds of routes of all grades.

Also unsurprisingly the Ben is very popular with walkers, and some 150,000 people climb it every year. It's not a place for solitude, then, but as the vast majority of walkers use the path known as the mountain track for both ascent and descent it is possible to escape the crowds except on the actual summit. Ben Nevis has been popular for a long time too. The first recorded ascent was by botanist James Robertson in August 1771. Other ascents soon followed and by the early 19th century Fort William had a tourist industry based on climbing Ben Nevis. The poet John Keats climbed the Ben in 1818 and wrote a sonnet on the summit. It's not one of his best poems but some of the lines will bring a wry smile to the faces of all those who've found the summit wreathed in cloud, as it so often is:

Upon the top of Nevis blind in Mist!
I look into the Chasms and a Shroud
Vaprous doth hide them.

The early tourists took the easiest route up the mountain, as most ascensionists do today. It was 1880 before the first mountaineers arrived and started to seek out more challenging ways up the Ben. On 1 May that year W.W. Naismith (he of the Naismith's Rule and a founder of the SMC) and two friends climbed to the summit by the standard route but in thick mist, knee deep snow and without a guide, a feat unheard of at that time. Compass bearings were required to avoid the cliffs and find the summit. By the mid 1880s the first records appear of ascents of snow-filled gullies on the north face. The first rock climb came in 1892, when three members of the Hopkinson family from Manchester climbed part way up Tower Ridge to a feature called the Great Tower. The next day they returned and descended the ridge to the Great Tower and then on to the bottom of the ridge. Then two days later they returned and climbed the Northeast Buttress. The Hopkinsons were unaware of the significance of their climbs and didn't even record them until 1895, when they put a short note in the Alpine Club Journal. The first winter ascent of Tower Ridge was made in 1894 by a party led by Norman Collie. After this climbs were made every year and Ben Nevis was on the way to becoming an international climbing destination.

As well as climbers Ben Nevis soon attracted the attention of runners. Fort William hairdresser William Swan ran up and down the mountain in 1895, taking 2hrs 41mins. Races to the top began in 1899. In 1951 the Ben Nevis Race became an annual event, held every September. The current records for the ascent and descent are 1hr, 25mins and 34secs for men, achieved in 1984 by Kenneth Stuart of Keswick AC, and 1hr, 43mins and 25secs for women, achieved in 1981 by Pauline Haworth, also of Keswick AC. These are astonishing times, as anyone who has walked up the mountain, which takes most people 3–4hrs, will confirm. Whether the race will continue to be held is in question as there are concerns over erosion caused by this and other competitive events involving large numbers of people. In 2009 464 people finished the Ben Nevis Race.

Ben Nevis is the ancient remnant of violent volcanic activity. The lower rocks are granite but

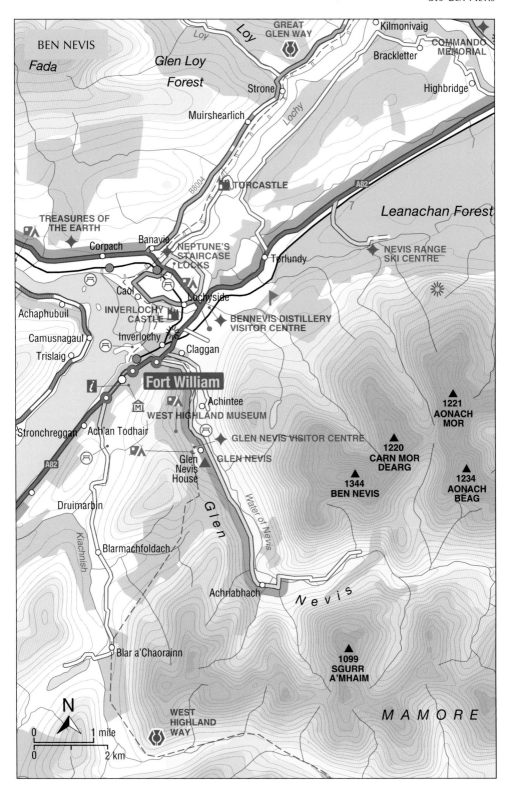

Ben Nevis and Aonach Beag rising above Glen Nevis as seen from the slopes of Sgurr a'Mhaim

the top of the mountain is andesite lava. The mountain was formed by cauldron subsidence, like the Glencoe hills. Putting it very simply ring faults developed and the areas inside the rings collapsed into the liquid granite magma below, forming a plug of andesite. Erosion over millions of years has revealed this plug and it now forms the top 600m of the mountain. So rock that was once underground now sits at the top of the highest mountain in the country. Ice added the final touches as glaciers carved the cliffs and arêtes.

The name Nevis is slightly mysterious, as it has been so corrupted from the original Gaelic that scholars are uncertain as to what it means. It first appears as Neevush in 1532, then Novesh in 1595 and finally Nevis in 1640. The meaning that appears in most books is 'venomous' or 'evil' from *nimheil* or *nibheis*, taken to refer to the bad weather common on the mountain. Peter Drummond, in *Scottish Hill Names: Their Origin and Meaning* (Scottish Mountaineering Trust, 2007), isn't so sure, however,

and among less likely possibilities suggests 'cloud' or 'water' from *neb*, a pre-Gaelic root-word, 'sky' or 'heaven' from *neamh*, 'heavenly' or 'divine' from *neamhaidh* and 'the mountain with its head in the clouds' from *beinn-nimh-bhathais*. Seton Gordon, in *Highways and Byways in the West Highlands*, says that 'popular tradition describes it as the Hill of Heaven'.

The summit of Ben Nevis, and all the rest of the mountain bar the North Face, have been in the care of the John Muir Trust since 2000. The JMT land also includes Carn Mor Dearg, Aonach Beag and the north side of upper Glen Nevis. The North Face and the corrie below it are owned by Alcan, who own the aluminium smelter in Fort William and whose hydroelectric water pipes run under the mountain. For more information on the story of Ben Nevis Ken Crocket's *Ben Nevis: Britain's Highest Mountain* is recommended. There is also a Ben Nevis Visitor Centre in Glen Nevis with interesting displays about the mountain.

THE BEN NEVIS OBSERVATORY

On the summit of Ben Nevis the remains of an old building can be seen below the emergency shelter. This was once a meteorological observatory, opened in 1883 and in continuous operation until 1904. The Scottish Meteorological Society determined to build an observatory on the summit in 1877, and funds were raised from the public for its construction and for building a bridle path to the summit. Before this was done, however, a meteorologist called Clement Wragge offered to climb the mountain every day during the summer of 1881 and make observations. He did so from June to mid-October, regardless of the weather, and repeated the task in 1882.

The observatory was a solid rock building, as it needed to be to withstand the summit storms. The residents could communicate with Fort William by telegraph, as an armoured cable was laid to the summit, replaced by a telephone in 1897. The bridle path, whose route is followed by today's mountain track, was a toll road, a charge of one shilling being made to use it. A room in the observatory served refreshments to visitors in the summer, a practice that continued for 12 years after the observatory closed. There was also an annex offering food and accommodation, run by two young ladies.

After closure the observatory slowly fell into disrepair and was finally dismantled in the 1970s.

The data collected by the observatory is the only continuous meteorological data from a Scottish mountain summit, automatic weather stations having proved unable to operate continuously in Scottish weather. The data show that during those 21 years January was the windiest month and July the calmest. January was also the wettest month with an average 465mm of rain. The driest month was June with 191mm. The annual average rainfall was just over 4m. Unsurprisingly June was also the sunniest month, with a daily average of 4.3hrs. January and December were equal dullest, with just 0.7hrs of sunshine a day. The average annual temperature was -0.3°C, the lowest recorded -17.4°C.

The story of the observatory is told in *The Weathermen of Ben Nevis 1883–1904* by Marjory Roy, available from The Royal Meteorological Society, www.royal-met-soc.org.uk.

Walkers looking across the cliffs of the north face from the summit of Ben Nevis

FORT WILLIAM

The town of Fort William lies at the foot of Ben Nevis and the stories of the two are inextricably bound together. Human beings have been living in the area since at least 2000BC. The first castle, known as Inverlochy Castle, was built in 1270. There were two Battles of Inverlochy here, in 1431 and 1645. The modern town began in 1654 when General Monk, one of Cromwell's officers, built a wooden fortress called 'the Fort of Inverlochy' and garrisoned it with the aim of combating Royalist clans. In 1690 the fort was rebuilt with stone walls and renamed Fort William after the new King who had come to the throne in 1688. The authorisation for the Massacre of Glencoe was signed at the fort in 1692. In 1746 the Jacobite army besieged the fort but failed to capture it. This was the end of the violent period of Fort William's history and by the end of the 18th century the town was starting its development as a tourist destination, with Ben Nevis the prime attraction. This was aided by the first regular steamboat service which began in the 1830s. The sea was the quickest way to reach the town until 1894 when the railway arrived.

The town has an important industrial side too. The Caledonian Canal was built along the Great Glen by Thomas Telford between 1802 and 1822, linking the west and east coasts. The Ben Nevis Distillery opened in 1825 and still makes whisky today. The big industrial development, however, came in 1931 when the British Aluminium Company smelter was opened using hydro power tapped from a huge area of the surrounding hills. A massive tunnel was bored for 24km under the mountains to bring water from Loch Treig to the smelter. The big pipes bringing this water down the mountainside can be seen on the lower slopes of Ben Nevis above the smelter.

Today Fort William describes itself as the 'Outdoor Capital of the UK'. It certainly has all the facilities walkers and mountaineers could want and lies close to major mountain areas. There are cafés, restaurants and bars, outdoor equipment shops, all types of accommodation from campsites, hostels and bunkhouses to luxury hotels and plenty of attractions for bad weather or lazy days such as the West Highland Museum, the Ocean Frontier Underwater Centre, the Ben Nevis Distillery Visitor Centre and the Aluminium Smelter Visitor Centre. Cruises can be taken on Loch Linnhe and there's an annual Fort William Mountain Film Festival held in February. There are always plenty of walkers and climbers in Fort William. The West Highland Way finishes here and the Great Glen Way starts a short distance away while climbers use the town as a base for climbing on the Ben Nevis.

⊗ The Ben Path
By far the most popular way up Ben Nevis is the route up the west slopes from the Glen Nevis Visitor Centre. This follows the line of the original bridle path built to service the observatory and is known variously as the Ben Path, the Mountain Track, Trail or Footpath, the Pony Track and the Tourist Path. The last is a misnomer, for although many people who don't normally climb hills go up Ben Nevis, and ill-shod, ill-clad and ill-equipped walkers regularly make it to the summit, it is a steep rough climb and the conditions on the summit are often cold, wet and windy even in summer. Even by this route Ben Nevis needs to be taken seriously.

Despite its popularity the Ben Path is a boring trudge with little of interest and few views. The lower section from the Visitor Centre to the broad saddle containing Lochan Meall an t-Suidhe (sometimes called the Halfway Lochan, although it's not quite that), between Meall an t-Suidhe and Ben Nevis, does give views of Glen Nevis, but most of the route is up the broad west face of the Ben on a steep zigzag path with views of stone, stones and more stones. Plod on and you'll get to the top eventually, but it's not enjoyable. It's a good descent route, especially in bad weather, but that's about it.

The distance to the top is 8km, with 1340m of ascent, and takes most people 3–4hrs.

⊗ The Coire Eoghainn Ridges ☆
A far better walkers' route is from the road end in Glen Nevis. The Allt Coire Eogbain comes pouring down granite slabs from big Coire Eoghainn, which lies immediately south of the summit of Ben Nevis. The slopes east of the stream can be followed to the spur on the east side of Coire Eoghainn, which leads to final boulder slopes southeast of the summit. There are good views across Coire Eoghainn and

east to Aonach Mor and Aonach Beag. Alternatively climb to the mouth of the corrie and then west up the east ridge to Carn Dearg SW, a top of Ben Nevis, and then follow the ridge above the west side of Coire Eoghainn round to the summit plateau.

These two routes can be combined to give a superb walk in wild country far from the crowds on the Ben Path. The terrain is steep, rough and mostly pathless and good route finding skills are required. The round trip is 7km long, with 1340m of ascent, and takes 4–5hrs.

❾ The Carn Mor Dearg Arête ☆

The North Face cliffs of Ben Nevis make up the southwest side of a huge horseshoe around the Allt a'Mhuillinn and Coire Leis. The northeast side of the horseshoe consists of the steep scree slopes of the long, narrow Carn Dearg ridge, which has three tiny pointed summits. From the high point of this ridge – Carn Mor Dearg ('big red hill', 1220m), the 9th highest Munro – a narrow granite ridge curves round Corrie Leis, forming the back wall of the horseshoe. This is the Carn Mor Dearg Arête and the finest route to Ben Nevis, with superb views of the North Face cliffs. In summer it's a rough walk with some easy scrambling. When snow-covered it's a sensational mountaineering expedition.

There are three possible start points for the Carn Mor Dearg Arête: the North Face car park at Torlundy on the A82, 4km northeast of Fort William, from where a path leads up the Allt a'Mhuillin glen; the Glen Nevis Visitor Centre, from where the Ben Path can be taken to the Lochan Meall an t-Suidhe saddle, from where a path leads into the Allt a'Mhuillin glen; and the road end in Glen Nevis, from where you can walk into upper Glen Nevis and then up Coire Giubhsachan to the east ridge of Carn Mor Dearg. Of the two approaches beside the Allt a'Mhuillin I prefer the one starting in Glen Nevis as the path from the North Face Car Park isn't very interesting lower down and can be boggy. The route from Glen Nevis, with a descent by the Ben Path, is 18km long, with 1850m of ascent, and takes 8–10hrs.

From Lochan Meall an t-Suidhe the path rounds the shoulder of the Ben and heads up the Allt a'Mhuillin. On the right are the huge North Face cliffs, on the left the heather and reddish scree covered slopes of the Carn Dearg ridge, which can be climbed to the northernmost top, Carn Dearg Beag.

THE SUMMIT OF BEN NEVIS

In summer the summit of Ben Nevis comes as a shock if you arrive there by any route other than the Ben Path, as you pass from a feeling of wild rugged mountain landscapes to one of being in a crowded holiday resort. People are everywhere, queuing up to take photographs of each other on the summit cairn, sitting in circles eating picnics, sitting slumped against rocks feeling triumphant but exhausted, and hoping to recover enough to stagger back down, chatting with friends. In mist voices ring round and figures appear and fade in the shifting cloud.

The summit is an extensive stony plateau dotted with cairns. The high point is marked by a big well-constructed cairn topped by a trig point. Nearby a small emergency shelter sits on top of the remnants of the observatory. Just to the north lie the great cliffs, invisible unless you wander over to the edge and look down, something to be avoided in poor visibility or if there is snow, as big cornices build up over the drops. When it's clear the 1km or so stroll round the edge of the cliffs to the top of Carn Dearg NW gives excellent views of the tangle of arêtes, gullies and buttresses below. Across the Allt a'Mhuillin rises the Carn Dearg ridge.

Descending from the summit on the Ben Path is easy when it's clear and the ground is snow-free. However in mist, or when the path is snow-covered, it is easy to go wrong. There are cliffs to the north and south and it's very important to follow the compass carefully. From the trig point walk on a grid bearing of 231° for 150m, then a grid bearing of 282° to the start of the zigzags on the Ben Path. The magnetic variation needs to be added to these bearings. Check your map to see what this is. Be very careful not to stray too far to the south, where there is a notorious terrain trap called Five Finger Gully in which there have been many accidents, some fatal.

Note that the emergency shelter shown on older maps near the summit of Carn Dearg NW has been removed. The only such shelter is the one near the summit cairn of the Ben.

On the Carn Mor Dearg Arête

The narrow stony ridge now leads southwards over Carn Dearg Meadhonach to Carn Mor Dearg, with stupendous views west to the great cliffs, revealed in all their massiveness and glory. Far below a tiny building can be seen beside the Allt a'Mhuillin. This is the CIC Hut, built in 1929 as a memorial to mountaineer Charles Inglis Clark who was killed in the First World War. The hut is owned by the SMC. East of Carn Mor Dearg the long unbroken slopes of Aonach Mor and Aonach Beag can be seen.

The third route to Carn Mor Dearg, from the road end in Glen Nevis, goes through the lovely Nevis Gorge into the upper glen and past the white veil of Steall Falls (see the Ring of Steall section above) to the Allt Coire Giubhsachan, which can be followed up to the bealach between Carn Mor Dearg and Aonach Mor. Coire Giubhsachan is lovely, with the burn rushing down in great sweeps over red and gold granite slabs into cool, dark green pools. From the bealach the east ridge of Carn Mor Dearg leads to the summit. If ascending by this route the best way back to the start is by the east side of Coire Eoghainn (see the Coire Eoghainn ridges above). This round is the least crowded and arguably the most interesting and

beautiful. It's 12km long, with 1475m of ascent, and takes 5–7hrs.

The Carn Mor Dearg Arête curves gracefully round the head of Coire Leis to a broad boulder covered slope that leads up to the summit of the Ben. The traverse of the arête is quite easy with little exposure. There's only a little easy scrambling, and the granite boulders are rough and give good grip. The views and situation are spectacular, and this is one of the finest places in the Scottish mountains. The arête dips down to 1060m, then climbs a little to end abruptly below the boulders of the summit slopes of the Ben. Climbing this massive boulder slope is easy, if arduous. In mist remember that there are big cliffs to the right. The summit plateau comes suddenly as the slope levels out.

❸ Scrambling on the North Face: Ledge Route ☆

The magnificent cliffs of Ben Nevis are worth a close up view even by those who have no intention of scrambling or climbing up them. Just to wander along their base and gaze up at the array of towers, walls and buttresses is exciting and awe-inspiring. However to really get a feel for the cliffs it's necessary to climb them and experience being high up in a vertical world, with space below you and just rock and sky above. The greatest opportunities for this are available to rock climbers, of course, but there are scrambles, some surprisingly easy, which take the non-technical climber into the heart of the rock scenery. A diagram of the cliffs, as found in scrambling and climbing guides, is useful to identify the various features as it's easy to be bewildered by the complex vertical topography. Under snow and ice the routes are much harder and much more serious of course, and are graded winter climbs.

The classic scramble is Ledge Route, which climbs the massive Carn Dearg Buttress. This starts due west of the CIC hut, with an ascent of the lower part of No 5 Gully, and then climbs the crest of the buttress to reach the summit plateau 300m from the summit of Carn Dearg NW. This is only a Grade 1 and the scrambling is easy with little exposure, yet the 450m route takes you right up the cliffs with harder terrain all around and superb views. In winter it's a Grade II climb.

ⓑ ✺ Climbing on Ben Nevis ☆

Rock and ice climbers will find routes of all types and grades on the cliffs of Ben Nevis. Just the names of major features and routes are inspiring – Coire Leis, Northeast Buttress, Little Brenva Face, Observatory Gully, Orion Face, Zero Gully, Point Five Gully, Tower Ridge, Coire na Ciste, Trident Buttress, Carn Dearg Buttress, Castle Ridge. All the major names of Scottish mountaineering have climbed here and put up new routes.

Tower Ridge is the classic route, graded Difficult in summer and III in winter. It's a 600m mountaineering expedition that has been very popular since its first ascent. Tower Ridge is the most distinctive feature on the Ben Nevis cliffs.

Although the cliffs are spectacular in summer and the rock can be inspected closely, it's under snow that there is a really big mountain feel, and a sense of grandeur and awe. Even the easiest routes seem serious and committing. At every belay and every pause the vastness of the cliffs is sensed all around. Just being among this world of white mountains is thrilling, whatever the route.

The North Face of Ben Nevis from the slopes of Carn Mor Dearg

3:10 THE AONACHS
AND THE GREY CORRIES

To the east of Ben Nevis and Carn Mor Dearg a huge, steep mountain wall runs south to north for some 9km from Glen Nevis to the Leanachan Forest. The two major summits on this wall are Aonach Beag ('little ridge', 1234m) and Aonach Mor ('big ridge', 1221m), the seventh and eighth highest Munros. Aonach Mor covers much the bigger area, hence the name, which was given long before the heights of the hills were accurately measured. The east and west sides of this long ridge are craggy and steep.

The Aonachs are big, bulky hills. East of them a finer, more delicate ridge snakes away, the Grey Corries, named for the pale quartzite screes on its flanks. The Grey Corries ridge is 13km long and contains ten summits, four of them Munros. From west to east these are Sgurr Choinnich Mor ('big peak of the moss', 1095m), Stob Coire an Laiogh ('peak of the corrie of the calf', 1116m), Stob Choire Claurigh (probably 'peak of the corrie of clamouring', 1177m) and Stob Ban ('white peak', 977m). The main Grey Corries ridge forms the northwest side of huge Coire Rath. Stob Ban sits at the head of the ridge running down the southeast side of the corrie. Together the ridges form an asymmetrical horseshoe. East of the Grey Corries rise two outlying Corbetts.

These peaks can be reached from Glen Nevis to the south and Glean Spean to the north. A wild camp in upper Glen Nevis makes a good base for exploration and there is a bothy at Meanach that could be used.

⊘ Aonach Beag and Aonach Mor

The ascent of the Aonachs from the south avoids the ski resort and is wild throughout. Starting from the road end in Glen Nevis the route goes through the Nevis Gorge and along upper Glen Nevis, past Steall Falls to the Steall ruins where the path can be left for an ascent of the southwest slopes of Aonach Beag. The most interesting route heads east of Coire nan Laogh to the subsidiary tops of Sgurr a'Bhuic (983m) and Stob Coire Bhealaich (1101m). The latter is a good viewpoint for the east face of Aonach Mor, a ragged wild mix of buttresses, crags and scree tumbling down to the floor of An Cul Choire. The edge of the eastern crags of Aonach Beag can be followed to the summit. To the west Ben Nevis rises above Carn Mor Dearg, and the unrelenting steepness of the southern slope of the Ben can be appreciated. The slope drops 1220m in just over 1.6km to Glen Nevis.

Aonach Mor is just 1.5km away across a narrow dip, with cliffs either side. In winter big cornices can build up on the eastern edge of both Aonachs, and care is needed not to stray on to them. A path runs to Aonach Mor from the col between the summits. The almost level summit ridge is over 1.6km in length. The cairn marking the high point is in the centre of a flat area, so for views you need to walk to the edges. The rock and water complexity of An Cul Choire looks impressive and inviting from above.

Descent can be made back towards the col with Aonach Beag, and then west down a steep spur to the col at the head of Coire Giubhsachan. Those with enough energy can ascend Carn Mor Dearg from here and then traverse the arête and climb Ben Nevis, returning to Glen Nevis via the slopes above Coire Eoghainn. Most people will be

NEVIS RANGE

On the northern side of Aonach Mor lies the Nevis Range ski resort, whose lifts reach almost to 1200m. Access to the pistes is by gondola from the A82 between Fort William and Spean Bridge. There are 12 lifts and 35 runs covering all grades. Nevis Range is newer than Scotland's other ski resorts, having been constructed in the 1980s, and was built with more thought for the environment then the others. Despite this the presence of all the machinery, fencing and buildings still destroys any wild or natural feel and detracts from the mountain landscape. The resort can be used for quick access to Aonach Mor. The gondola is open year round and there are mountain bike courses. For more information see www.nevisrange.co.uk.

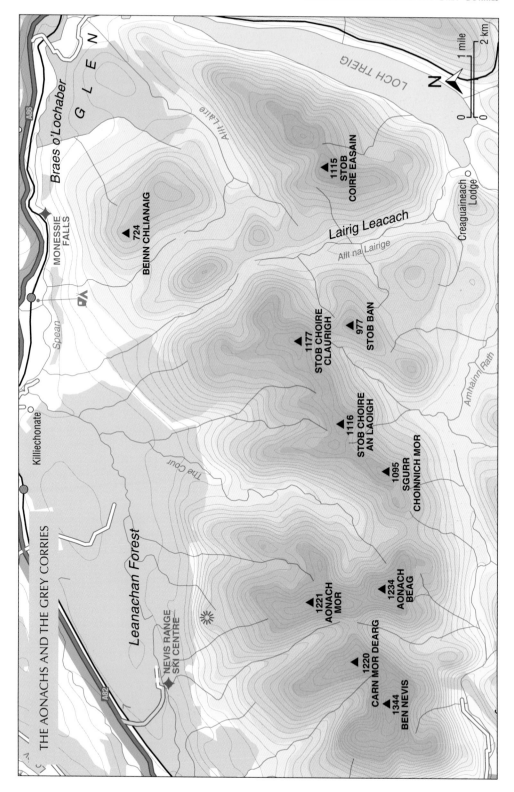

THE AONACHS AND THE GREY CORRIES

GLEN

Braes o'Lochaber

A86

MONESSIE FALLS

Spean

Killiechonate

Leanachan Forest

A82

NEVIS RANGE SKI CENTRE

The Cour

Allt Laire

Lairig Leacach

Allt na Lairige

Amhainn Rath

Loch Treig

Creaguaineach Lodge

BEINN CHLIANAIG
724

STOB COIRE EASAIN
1115

STOB CHOIRE CLAURIGH
1177

STOB BAN
977

STOB CHOIRE AN LAOIGH
1116

SGURR CHOINNICH MOR
1095

AONACH MOR
1221

AONACH BEAG
1234

CARN MOR DEARG
1220

BEN NEVIS
1344

N

0   1 mile
0   1   2 km

201

Aonach Beag from the north

happy to descend beside the Allt Giubhsachan to Glen Nevis.

This route is 16km long with 1550m of ascent, and takes 6–8hrs.

Winter Climbing on the Aonachs ☆

There are many winter climbs on the granite cliffs of Aonach Mor and Aonach Beag, but the rock is too broken to be of great interest for summer climbing. Winter climbing has become more popular on what were once remote cliffs due to easy access via the gondola at the Nevis Range ski resort (see above). Coire an Lochain on Aonach Mor is now the most accessible winter climbing area in Scotland, the top of the cliffs being just 150m from the top ski tow. Most of the 60 plus routes here have been put up since the resort opened. There are climbs of all grades, from 60 to 150m in length. On the long West Face the climbs are much longer, up to 500m, and mostly in the lower grades. This is a quieter area than Coire an Lochain, with a wilder feel. There also many climbs of all grades on the schist cliffs on the north and west faces of Aonach Beag, again mostly put up since the ski resort opened although one, the 460m Grade III Northeast Ridge, was first climbed in 1895 by a party including W.W. Naismith.

The Eastern Grey Corries ☆

The traverse of the eastern Grey Corries is a superb walk along a narrow ridge with great views. The ridge never drops below 1000m and the walking is easy. There is a feeling of remoteness and solitude, however, for these hills are far from towns and roads. The route takes the form of a huge horseshoe round Coire Choimhlidh and crosses eight summits, two of them Munros. The northern edges of the Grey Corries are covered with the vast plantations of the Leanachan Forest. These can be avoided by taking the minor road from the A82 at Spean Bridge along the south side of the River Spean to Corriechoille Farm, and then walking south along a track – an old drove road – that goes to the Lairig Leacach east of the Grey Corries. Once past the edge of the forest the ridge walk starts with an ascent of Stob Coire na Gaibhre (958m), beyond which a steep narrow rocky ridge rises to the first Munro and the highest peak in the Grey Corries, Stob Choire Claurigh. There is a wonderful view west along the line of the Grey Corries to the long unbroken wall of Aonach Beag and Aonach Mor. Just to the south lies Stob Ban, the most isolated of the Grey Corries Munros, which can be climbed from here, although the going is very rough over sharp quartzite boulders and involves 535m extra ascent. Stob Ban can also be climbed by continuing on the track to the Lairig Leachach, where there is a very small bothy, and ascending the northeast ridge.

Although appearing narrow and rocky the Grey Corries ridge provides delightful walking with great views and little sense of exposure, despite the big drops either side. The summits quickly come and go – Stob a'Choire Leith ('peak of the grey corrie, 1105m), Stob Coire Cath na Sine (probably 'peak of the corrie of the battle of the storms' – a fine name, 1079m), Caisteal ('the castle', 1106m), the second Munro Stob Coire an Laoigh (1116m), and finally Stob Coire Easain ('peak of the corrie of the little waterfalls', 1080m). The main ridge continues southwest to Sgurr Choinnich Mor, but this Munro is far from the start point and more easily climbed from Glen Nevis (see below). Unless traversing the whole ridge, maybe with camping or bivi gear, leave the main ridge at Stob Coire Easain and turn north down the long spur running over 1007m Beinn na Socaich and down into the forest, where tracks can be found back to Corriechoille.

⊗ Sgurr Choinnich Mor

The southwesternmost of the Grey Corries Munros can be easily climbed from upper Glen Nevis, reached by the path from the road end in Glen Nevis up the Nevis Gorge. Where the path crosses the Allt Coire a'Bhuic turn up beside the stream to the lochan-dotted 731m bealach between Stob Coire Bhealaich and Sgurr Choinnich Beag and then follow the ridge northeast over Sgurr Choinnich Beag to the fine, pointed summit of Sgurr Choinnich Mor. Unlike the other Grey Corries hills Sgurr Choinnich Mor is built of darker rocks and has greener, grassier slopes. It's the best viewpoint for the long, craggy east face of Aonach Mor and Aonach Beag. Directly to the south Binnein Mor towers over the cone of Binnein Beag.

Descent can be by the same route or south into boggy upper Glen Nevis. From the 731m bealach a descending traverse can also be made across the rough southern slopes of Sgurr a'Bhuic to the Steall ruin. The round trip using this last descent is 18km long, with 1360m of ascent, and takes 6–8hrs.

Stob Ban and the Lairig Leacach Bothy

Loch Treig and Stob Coire Sgriodain

⊗ The Complete Traverse of the Grey Corries ☆

The traverse of the great horseshoe around Coire Rath is a fine and unusual trip involving a long walk the whole length of upper Glen Nevis to the boggy watershed called Tom an Eite. Just across the divide the Abhainn Rath has to be forded. Beyond the stream steep slopes rise to Meall a'Bhuirich (841m) at the end of the easternmost arm of the horseshoe. Easy walking leads along the ridge to Stob Ban, where the terrain changes, becoming much rougher and rockier. The traverse of all the Munros follows, and then finally a descent back into Glen Nevis. The whole round is 27km long, with 2135m of ascent, and takes 9–10hrs.

⊗ Cruach Innse and Sgurr Innse

East of the Grey Corries across the Lairig Leachach rise two Corbetts, Cruach Innse ('island' or 'meadow heap', 857m) and Sgurr Innse ('island' or 'meadow peak', 809m). The names are appropriate, as Cruach Innse is a big, bulky, rather shapeless hill, while Sgurr Innse is a fine distinctive block of rock easily identifiable from many

peaks. Both hills can be easily climbed from the Lairig Leachach, which can be reached from the track from Corriechoille in Glen Spean. From the track climb the heathery northwest ridge of Cruach Innse to the flat stony summit. Continue down the rockier stony ridge to the col between the two peaks, and climb the scree and boulders on the north side of Sgurr Innse. There is some optional easy scrambling on this ascent. There are steep crags on every side of Sgurr Innse and the easiest descent is back down the north side, to the col, and then back down to the Lairig Leacach track. The round trip is 16km, with 1085m of ascent, and takes 5–6hrs.

3:11 LOCH TREIG

Dark Loch Treig lies in a deep narrow trench between steep mountain walls south of Tulloch in Glen Spean. The loch is a reservoir, dammed in 1929 as part of the Lochaber hydroelectric system, which provides power via a 24km tunnel driven through the mountains to the aluminium smelter in

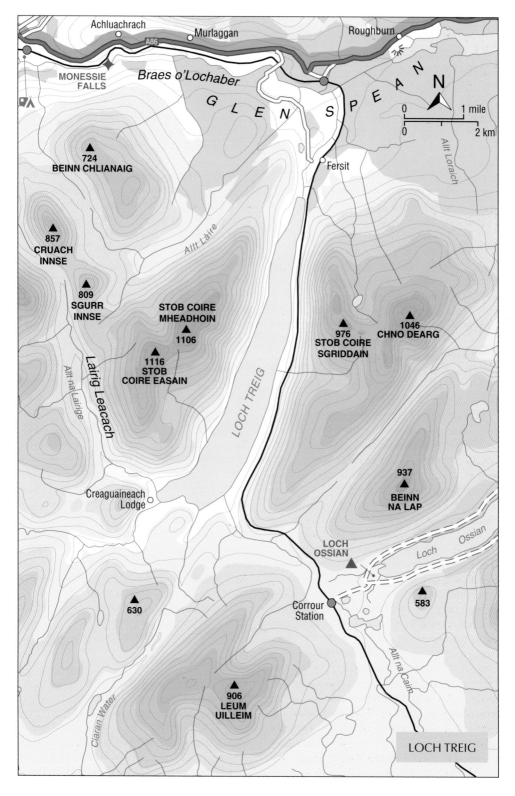

LOCH TREIG

Fort William. The West Highland Line runs down the east side of the loch and there is a station at Tulloch and, to the south, at Corrour. Three Munros rise above the loch. To the west are Stob a'Choire Mheadhoin ('peak of the middle corrie', 1106m) and Stob Coire Easain ('peak of the corrie of the little waterfall', 1116m) – known collectively as the Easains – and to the east are Stob Coire Sgriodain ('peak of the corrie of scree', 976m). The latter peak is linked to another Munro, Chno Dearg ('red hill', 1047m) further east again. The four hills can be climbed together, but this involves descending back to 235m at Fersit at the north end of Loch Treig so they are usually climbed in pairs.

⊗ The Easains
These big, bulky hills form a broad ridge of high ground between the Lairig Leachach and Loch Treig. The easiest ascent is from Fersit to the north from where the 6km long north-northeast ridge leads up to the summits. There are excellent views of the eastern Grey Corries from these hills. The corrie between the peaks can be descended to Coire Lair, for a walk beside the Allt Lair back to the start. The distance is 17km, with 1160m of ascent, and the walk takes 5–7hrs.

The railway can be used to expedite a traverse of the Easains, using the stations at Corrour and Tulloch. A good track leads from Corrour to Creaguaineach Lodge at the southwest corner of Loch Treig. A path continues northwest beside the Allt na Lairige; this can soon be left for a climb up the south ridge of Stob Coire Easain. The traverse is 24km long, with 1350m of ascent, and takes 7–9hrs.

⊗ Stob Coire Sgriodain and Chno Dearg
These two hills, plus an optional intermediate top, Meall Garbh ('rough hill', 977m) make a pleasant circuit from Fersit at the north end of Loch Treig. The north ridge of Stob Coire Sgriodain is rough and rocky but the walking is easy enough. From the summit there's a good view down Loch Treig. The terrain between Stob Coire Sgriodain and Meall Garbh is complex and featureless in places, so in mist care with navigation is needed. The cols between the hills are flat and wide and it's easy to go astray on them. From Chno Dearg there's a view of the northern Ben Alder hills. A descent can be made over the minor tops of Meall Chaorach and Creag Dubh to a track running west to Fersit. The walk is 14km long, with 1155m of ascent, and takes 5–6hrs.

3:12 LOCH OSSIAN

Loch Ossian is a beautiful loch lying just west of Corrour Station on the West Highland Line. It's in a remote, wild situation, perhaps the loneliest in the Central Highlands, and the only access is by train or on foot or bicycle – there are good estate tracks into the area from the north. There is a Youth Hostel at the east end of the loch, run by the Scottish Youth Hostels Association (SYHA) as an eco hostel, with wind power, solar power and dry toilet systems. At the station Currour Station House is a restaurant which offers accommodation, also run by the SYHA. Three Munros lie above Loch Ossian, Beinn na Lap ('dappled hill', 937m) to the north and Carn Dearg ('red peak', 941m) and Sgor Gaibhre ('goat peak', 955m) to the southeast. To the south of the last two lies a Corbett, Meall na Meoig ('whey hill', 868m). East of the railway line is the Corbett Leum Uilleim ('William's leap', 909m).

⊗ Beinn na Lap
Beinn na Lap has a reputation as one of the easiest Munros to climb, as its slopes are even and rounded. However when the wind is so strong you can't stand up and if the hill is coated in ice and hard snow it can still be impossible to reach the summit, as I discovered one December day. Generally, however, the climb of Beinn na Lap is short and uneventful. It's a fairly featureless hill, with a few small crags but little else. From Corrour Station walk to Loch Ossian and then up the southern slopes of the hill to the southwest ridge and on to the summit. To the south Rannoch Moor spreads out flat and vast, a great contrast to the tightly packed ridges of hills lying to the west. Descent can be made down the long northeast ridge to a track that leads back through Strath Ossian, a classic U-shaped glaciated valley, with steep sides and granite crags, then along the shore of Loch Ossian to the start. The round trip is 20km long, with 785m of ascent, and takes 5–6hrs.

⊗ Carn Dearg, Sgor Gaibhre and Meall na Meoig
The first of these two peaks rise above the southeast end of Loch Ossian. They aren't very distinctive, despite steep slopes and a scattering of small crags on the east faces of both, and Sgor Gaibhre, along with its subsidiary top, Sgor Choinnich (929m) to

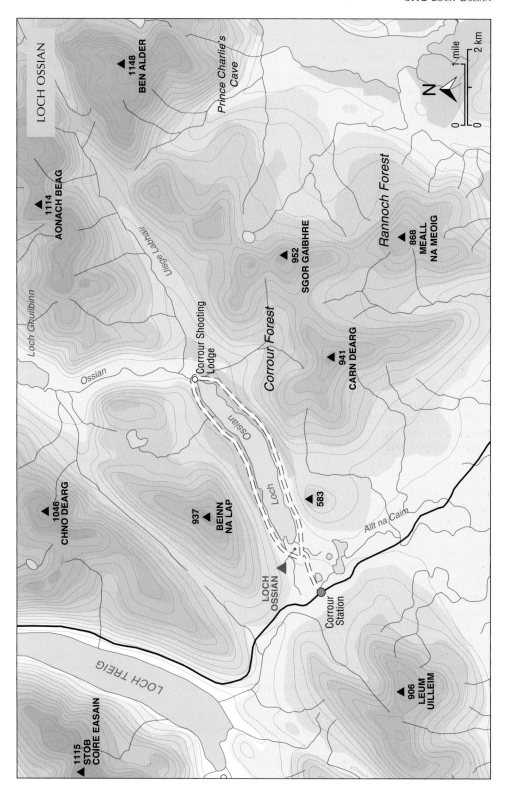

LOCH OSSIAN

1148
BEN ALDER

Prince Charlie's Cave

Rannoch Forest

1114
AONACH BEAG

Uisge Labhair

952
SGOR GAIBHRE

868
MEALL
NA MEOIG

Loch Ghuilbinn

Ossian

Corrour Shooting Lodge

Corrour Forest

941
CARN DEARG

1046
CHNO DEARG

Ossian

937
BEINN
NA LAP

Loch

583

Allt na Caim

LOCH
OSSIAN

Corrour
Station

LOCH TREIG

906
LEUM
UILLEIM

1115
STOB
COIRE EASAIN

N

1 mile

2 km

0

0

View over Loch Ossian and the Youth Hostel to Carn Dearg

the north, looking big and quite impressive from the east. The views from the summits are excellent, and they are worth climbing for these alone. Meall na Meoig lies south of Sgor Gaibhre, and the three hills can be traversed courtesy of the railway, starting at Corrour Station and finishing at Rannoch Station. The walking is easy, much of it on grass and moss. In fact there can be few places where two Munros and a Corbett can be climbed with so little effort. Featureless terrain in places can cause difficulties in poor visibility, however. Carn Dearg can be climbed by its broad western ridge from the path from Loch Ossian to Rannoch Station – the old Road to the Isles. From the summit the U shape of Strath Ossian is clearly seen directly to the north. To the west Binnein Mor and Binnein Beag stand out. Southwest Rannoch Moor stretches out in a great sweep of flat land and water. The walk east to Sgor Gaibhre is easy, and from that summit Ben Alder and Loch Ericht look impressive. A broad ridge leads south to Meall na Meoig and then on over Beinn Pharlagain and down to the Road to the Isles track, and then the B846 2km east of Rannoch Station. The walk is 23km long, with 1200m of ascent, and takes 6–7hrs.

⊗ Leum Uilleum ☆

This hill is in a very isolated position and would be very inaccessible but for the railway station at Corrour. As it is the summit lies less than 4km from the station and the hill can be climbed in an easy half day. Leum Uilleim looks shapely and attractive from the train and is the best reason to stop at Corrour. It's a big, steep hill, with several subsidiary tops and a big corrie, Coire a'Bhric Beag, to the northeast. To the south lies the big Blackwater Reservoir, which supplies hydroelectric power to Kinlochleven. The round of Coire a'Bhric Beag makes a fine short outing from Corrour Station. A stalkers' path leads towards the ridge to the north of the corrie, which can be followed to Beinn a'Bhric (876m). A dip to a col and a short climb then leads to the summit of Leum Uilleim. A great curve of hills sweeps round north of the hill from east to west. Southwards Rannoch Moor sparkles beyond dark Blackwater. The descent back to Corrour is by the northeast ridge, with one steep section down rocky Sron an Lagain Ghairbh, and then over boggy ground to the station. The whole round is 10km, with 575m of ascent, and takes 4–5hrs.

3:13 THE BEN ALDER AND LAGGAN HILLS

A big block of high country runs northeast from Loch Ossian, with Loch Laggan to the northwest and Loch Ericht to the southeast. The A9 cuts across the northeastern corner from Dalwhinnie and the A86 runs along Loch Laggan. However, although these roads give good access from various points, distances to the interior are still long, making overnight trips or the use of a bicycle along the many estate roads worthwhile. There are many fine campsites, both high- and low-level, and the bothies of Culra northeast of Ben Alder and Benalder Cottage on Loch Ericht at the southern end of Ben Alder. The area has nine Munros plus some interesting lower hills. Although the hills are not particularly rocky and the walking is generally easy there are some scrambles and one major rock climbing cliff on Binnein Shuas, plus winter climbing in the Ben Alder corries.

⊗ ❸ Ben Alder and Beinn Bheoil ☆

Ben Alder (1148m) is the dominant summit of the area, a big plateau topped hill with steep craggy sides. Its flat-topped bulk, with the distinctive slash of the Bealach Dubh to the north, is easily identifiable from many other hills and useful for orientation. It lies far from public roads and is one of the remotest hills south of the Great Glen. Ben Alder is on the watershed of Scotland, its streams running to both the Atlantic Ocean and the North Sea. The name is too corrupted from the original Gaelic for the meaning to be clear. It first appears on 17th century maps as Bin Aildir. Peter Drummond's *Scottish Hill Names: Their Origin and Meaning* (Scottish Mountaineering Trust, 2007) says it may come from *ail dobhar*, meaning 'water of rock'.

The first recorded ascent was by the Rev Thomas Grierson, as listed in his book *Autumnal Rambles Among the Scottish Mountains* (James Hogg, 1851). Grierson doesn't give dates but the book was published in 1851 so it was before then. Bonnie Prince Charlie had been on Ben Alder in 1746, while on the run after defeat at the Battle of Culloden, and hid in a cave called Cluny's Cage on the southern slopes. There is however no evidence that he climbed the mountain.

Ben Alder is joined by a neck of land to a lower and smaller Munro, Beinn Bheoil ('hill of the mouth', 1019m), and the two can be conveniently climbed together. Between them lies a deep corrie containing Loch a'Bhealaich Bheithe – the 'mouth' of Beinn Bheoil's name. Ben Alder's slopes are craggy to the north and east. On the eastern side lie two great corries, Garbh Choire and Garbh Choire Beag. They take huge bites out of the summit plateau and are one of the distinguishing features of Ben Alder in views from the north and northeast. Two rocky spurs, the Long Leachas and the Short Leachas, jut out from the northeast corner of the hill and make interesting easy scrambles.

All approaches to Ben Alder are long. From the south a track runs for 12.5km, from the B846 at the west end of Loch Rannoch to Loch Ericht, and then along the lochside to the Alder Burn and Benalder Cottage at the southern end. From the west it's 13km from Corrour Station along the track by Loch Ossian, and then the path beside the Uisge Labhair to the western corner. From Kinloch Laggan, on the A82 to the north, estate tracks lead for 16km beside the River Pattack to Loch Pattack and then onto Culra Bothy in the Allt a'Choire-reidhe glen below the north end. Culra Lodge can also be reached from Dalwhinnie to the northeast, on estate tracks beside Loch Ericht which lead to the pink, confectionery-like Benalder Lodge, with its turrets, and on to Loch Pattack, also a distance of 16km. The last two approaches may be the longest but they are on good tracks and can by easily cycled. Dalwhinnie has a railway station too, on the Edinburgh–Inverness line, and the mountain can be traversed from there to Corrour Station. Ben Alder looks superb from the track to Culra Lodge, rising as a distinct mountain mass with the two Leachas ridges and the rugged eastern flanks standing out.

The finest ascent of Ben Alder climbs one of the Leachas spurs, crosses the summit plateau and descends the southeast ridge to the Bealach Breabag, from where Beinn Bheoil can be traversed and a descent made back to the path running down north from Loch a'Bhealaich Bheithe. The Short Leachas is the southern of the two spurs and can be reached from the path running up to Loch a'Bhealaich Bheithe from Culra Lodge and the Allt a'Choire-reidhe. There are many options for the scramble up the buttress, and any difficulties can be easily avoided. The Long Leachas is reached

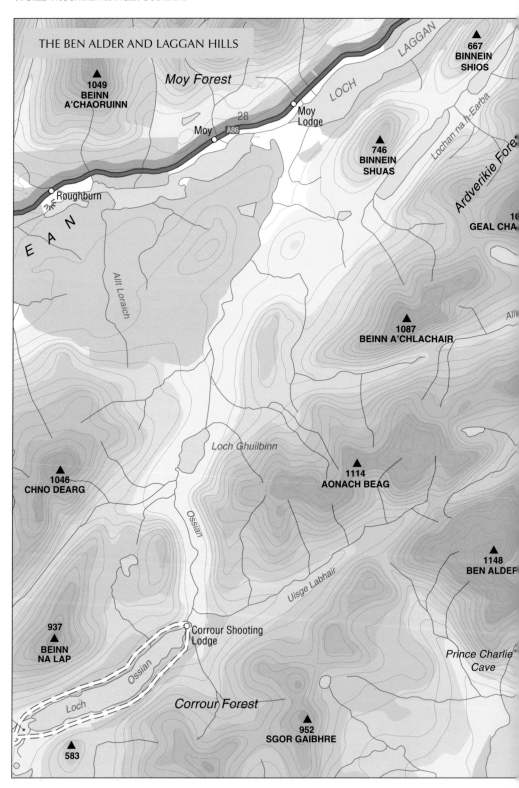

THE BEN ALDER AND LAGGAN HILLS

Moy Forest

LOCH LAGGAN

▲ 667
BINNEIN
SHIOS

▲ 1049
BEINN
A'CHAORUINN

Moy
Lodge

Moy A86
28

▲ 746
BINNEIN
SHUAS

Ardverikie Fore

Lochan na h-Earba

Roughburn

E A N

GEAL CHA

▲ 1
GEAL CHA

Allt Loraich

Allt

▲ 1087
BEINN A'CHLACHAIR

Loch Ghuilbinn

▲ 1046
CHNO DEARG

▲ 1114
AONACH BEAG

Ossian

▲ 1148
BEN ALDEF

Uisge Labhair

937
▲
BEINN
NA LAP

Corrour Shooting
Lodge

Ossian

*Prince Charlie'
Cave*

Loch

Corrour Forest

▲ 952
SGOR GAIBHRE

▲
583

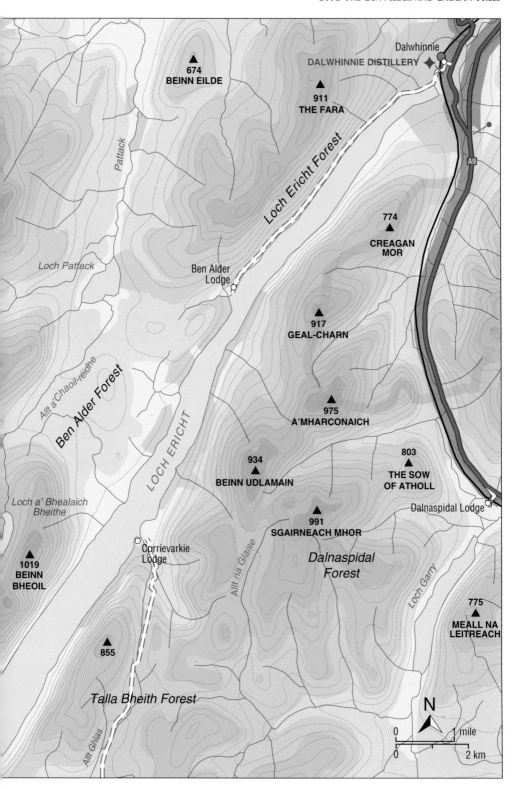

Dalwhinnie

DALWHINNIE DISTILLERY

A9

Loch Ericht Forest

674
BEINN EILDE

911
THE FARA

774
CREAGAN
MOR

Pattack

Loch Pattack

Ben Alder
Lodge

917
GEAL-CHARN

975
A'MHARCONAICH

Allt a'Chaoil-rèidhe

Ben Alder Forest

LOCH ERICHT

934
BEINN UDLAMAIN

803
THE SOW
OF ATHOLL

Dalnaspidal Lodge

Loch a' Bhealaich
Bheithe

991
SGAIRNEACH MHOR

*Dalnaspidal
Forest*

Corrievarkie
Lodge

Allt na Glaise

Loch Garry

1019
BEINN
BHEOIL

775
MEALL NA
LEITREACH

855

Talla Bheith Forest

Allt Ghlas

N

0 ___ 1 mile

0 ___ 2 km

Ben Alder and Culra Bothy

from the path beside the Allt a'Bhealaich Dhuibh that runs from Culra up to the Bealach Dubh. Again there are options, and the scrambling can be Grade 1 or Grade 3. Finding a way up the tangle or blocks and pinnacles of rock is interesting without being exposed or difficult.

From the top of either Leachas it's a walk of about 1km across the plateau to the summit cairn. The plateau is extensive, with some 4km² lying above 1000m. The landscape is a mix of high moorland grasses, patches of gravel and granite boulders, evoking comparisons with the great plateaus of the Cairngorms. The views from the edges are extensive, as you would expect from a big hill lying in the centre of the Highlands. However the most impressive views are close by, down into the rocky depths of Garbh Choire from the eastern edge and across Loch a'Bhealaich Bheithe to the steep scree-clad slopes of Beinn Bheoil. The eastern rim can be followed to the southeast ridge and the descent to the Bealach Breabag. An easy climb now leads over Sron Choire na h-Iolaire to Beinn Bheoil, with a wonderful view of the huge east wall of Ben Alder. 1km or so further along the ridge from the summit of Beinn Bheoil the western slopes can be descended to the path running north to the Allt a'Chaoil-reidhe.

The route from Culra Bothy and back via the Long Leachas is 15km, with 1050m of ascent, and takes 5–7hrs.

✷ Winter Climbing on Ben Alder

The two Leachas ridges are 300m Grade I winter climbs. On the east face Garbh Choire and Garbh Choire Beag hold snow well and big cornices often build up round their upper rims. There are a dozen plus winter routes, mostly in the lower grades. The North Face has more serious routes.

✖ The Aonach Beag–Geal Charn Ridge ☆

North of Ben Alder runs a 14km long ridge containing four Munros, Carn Dearg ('red hill', 1034m), Geal Charn ('white hill', 1132m), Aonach Beag ('little ridge', 1116m) and Beinn Eibhinn ('delightful hill', 1102m). There are several big corries both sides of the ridge plus many small lochans, crags and rocky spurs, making for a complex and interesting massif. The most distinctive individual feature is Lancet Edge, the eastern ridge of a subsidiary top of Geal Charn called Sgor Iutharn. From Culra Bothy Lancet Edge appears as a thin arête running up the centre of a steep, triangular arrowhead-like mountain. There is an easy but excellent Grade 1 scramble up Lancet Edge, which is nowhere as difficult as its spire-like appearance suggests.

Like Ben Alder this ridge is quite remote. The hills can be climbed in pairs from either end, with approaches to the eastern pair from Dalwhinnie or Kinloch Laggan, and to the western pair from Corrour Station or Moy Bridge on the A82 at the west end of Loch Laggan but the finest trip is the traverse of the four Munros in one outing. This can be done from Culra Bothy (see Ben Alder above for approach routes to the bothy) with a return by the Bealach Dubh, a round trip of 19km with 1330m of ascent which takes 6–8 hours. Carn Dearg is a steep but simple climb from Culra – just head for the summit. Heading west along the ridge the eastern slopes of Geal Charn are impressive, a series of crags above deep corries. The corrie south of the ridge holds lonely Loch an Sgoir beyond which rises Lancet Edge. The route goes up the northeast spur of Geal Charn between the crags and corries to a flat grassy summit plateau. It's now an easy dip and climb to Aonach Beag, which has arguably the best views on the ridge, although the views all along the ridge are excellent with Ben Nevis, the Grey Corries, the Mamores, the serrated crest of the Aonach Eagach, Bidean nam Bian, the Black

Mount, Ben Starav, Ben Lui, the Bridge of Orchy hills, Ben More and Stob Binnein, Ben Lawers and Schiehallion all visible. Nearer Ben Alder rises massively above the Bealach Dubh. Stony walking leads from Aonach Beag to the last summit, Beinn Eibhinn, from where a descent can be made down the steep southern slopes to the path leading up to the Bealach Dubh and back to Culra.

⊗ Beinn a'Chlachair, Geal Charn and Creag Pitridh

Northeast of the Aonach Beag–Geal Charn ridge and south of Loch Laggan is a group of three Munros, Creag Pitridh ('Petrie's crag', 924m), Geal Charn ('white hill', 1049m) and Beinn a'Chlachair ('stonemason's hill', 1087m), which can be climbed together from Moy Bridge on the A82 (NN 433 830). The walking isn't as easy as it looks from the relatively gentle profiles of these hills as their upper slopes are covered with rocks and boulders. A track from the highway leads round the south-western shoulder of Binnein Shuas to Lochan na h-Earba, a long double lochan in a narrow trench between the Binnein Shuas–Binnein Shios ridge and Creag Pitridh and Geal Charn. Past the sandy beach at the end of the lochan a path climbs up

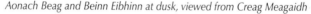

Aonach Beag and Beinn Eibhinn at dusk, viewed from Creag Meagaidh

Beinn a' Chlachair from the north

Coire Pitridh to the Bealach Leambain, beyond which Loch a'Bhealaich Leambain fills a dark hollow between Geal Charn and Beinn a'Chlachair. The path down beside this lochan leads to Loch Pattack.

The path up Coire Pitridh can be left after 1km or so for an ascent of the northeast slopes of Beinn a'Chlachair to the long, bouldery summit ridge. The most impressive feature of the hill is crag-rimmed Coire Mor Chlachair, which lies directly north of the summit. From the top follow the ridge northeast to a final steep descent to the Bealach Leambain. In mist this ridge can seem very long. From the bealach a path cuts across the western slopes of Geal Charn. Once past the crags abutting the bealach turn up the broad, stony slopes and climb to the rocky summit. Descend to the col separating Geal Charn from Creag Pitridh and clamber up the stony cone of the latter, probably wondering why it counts as a separate mountain when it appears just to be a pimple on the side of Geal Charn. It's just 110m of ascent from the col to the summit. From Creag Pitridh it's easiest to descend back to the path between it and Geal Charn and then follow this back to Coire Pitridh.

The walk is 27km long, with 1400m of ascent, and takes 7–9hrs.

⊗ ⓑ Binnein Shuas and Binnein Shios ☆

Between Loch Laggan and Lochan na h-Earba lies a long knobbly ridge clearly visible from the A82 road alongside Loch Laggan. The two summits on this ridge are not high but they are excellent viewpoints, especially for Glen Spean, and are rocky and rough, making for interesting walking. On the south side of Binnein Shuas is a big impressive cliff made of a type of granite called pegmatite, where there are a many rock climbs, including a popular classic slab climb called Ardverikie Wall, graded Severe and 190m long.

The two peaks on the ridge, Binnein Shuas ('upper peak', 747m) and Binnein Shios ('downward peak', 667m), are classified as Grahams. Start the traverse by climbing the southwest ridge of Binnein Shuas from the track from Moy Bridge towards Lochan na h-Earba. There is some optional scrambling on little crags en route to the rocky little summit, from where Binnein Shios rises to the northeast as a neat pyramid rising between the long blue waters of Loch Laggan and Loch na h-Earba. Binnein Shuas is a surprisingly rugged and complex little hill and the descent to the col with Binnein Shios is not obvious or easy. As there are big crags all around careful route finding is required. The easiest way down is via a big trench that almost divides the summit area in two, and which is clearly visible on maps. Descend this trench then traverse across easier ground to the col. The rocks disappear but the going remains tough, as the ascent to Binnein Shios is over tussocky terrain. To return to the start head back along the ridge towards the col then head north towards the trees bordering Loch Laggan and make your way through them to the track beside the loch. The walk along this track through mixed conifer and deciduous woodland is lovely and relaxing.

The walk is 17km long, with 900m of ascent, and takes 5–6hrs.

The Fara ☆

The Fara ('ladder hill') is a fine Corbett that is highly visible from the A9 road as it passes Loch Ericht and Dalwhinnie. It's a huge hill too, stretching some 10km along the north side of Loch Ericht. Despite its size, prominence and accessibility (the summit can be reached in 2hrs from Dalwhinnie) it's not a popular hill, presumably because at 911m it misses Munro status by 3m and is 'only' a Corbett. The easy walk along the ridge is superb however with wonderful views along Loch Ericht to the Ben Alder hills. It fits well into east–west walks across the Highlands and I have traversed it several times on such trips.

The north shore of Loch Ericht is densely forested. However, 2km along the track beside the loch from Dalwhinnie there is a narrow break in the trees and the steep hillside can be climbed to the summit of The Fara. Continue southwest along the ridge over two subsidiary tops, at 901m and 897m, then descend to another gap in the trees northwest of Benalder Lodge. The lochside track

leads back to Dalwhinnie. The distance is 22km, with 985m of ascent, and the walk takes 6–8hrs.

North of the summit of The Fara is a strange, narrow crag-rimmed slot, filled with boulders, called the Dirc Mhor ('big dirk' – a suitable name for this slash in the hillside). This unusual feature, a glacial meltwater channel, can't be seen from The Fara but stands out clearly from 658m Meall nan Egan, a Graham, just to the north. There are some rock climbs on the 90m high buttress called Sentinel Rock at the north end of the ravine. The passage of the Dirc Mhor can be included in an ascent of The Fara, starting on the A889 Dalwhinnie to Laggan road 1km north of Dalwhinnie. Head up beside the Allt an t-Sluic until the crags of the Dirc Mhor can be seen to the south. Meall nan Egan can be climbed from here, a round trip of 1.6km with 200m of ascent. After this diversion clamber through the boulders and thick heather on the floor of the ravine, then head southeast up broad slopes to the summit of The Fara and then down the northeast ridge back to the Allt an t-Sluic. This walk is 12km long, with 650m of ascent, and takes 4–5hrs.

3:14 THE WEST DRUMOCHTER HILLS

Dark, bulky, heather-covered hills rise above the Pass of Drumochter, their heavy, lowering features familiar to travellers on the A9 and the Perth to Inverness railway line, which both cross the pass. These hills form a roughly triangular wedge of land with the apex at Dalwhinnie in the north, Loch Ericht to the west, the A9/Inverness rail line to the east and Loch Rannoch to the south. There are four Munros and five Corbetts in the area. The Munros

DALWHINNIE

Dalwhinnie lies just off the A9 at the dammed head of Loch Ericht (the loch was enlarged for hydro power). The tiny village is a straggling affair, spread out along the A889. At 358m it's the highest village in the Highlands, although nowhere near the highest in Scotland, which is 467m Wanlockhead in the Southern Uplands. The name means 'meeting place', and Dalwhinnie formed in the 1700s around an inn at a junction where drovers' roads came together. In 1724 the first of the military roads came over the Pass of Drumochter to Dalwhinnie, a route which has been used by the main road north ever since.

Dalwhinnie has a mountaineer-friendly hotel, The Inn at Loch Ericht, and a café, but no shop. There is a railway station, which makes it a good place to start or finish cross country walks using the rail network. The most distinctive feature of the little village is the whitewashed Dalwhinnie Distillery with its two pagodas, which was built in 1897. This is the only visitor attraction in the village and is open year round.

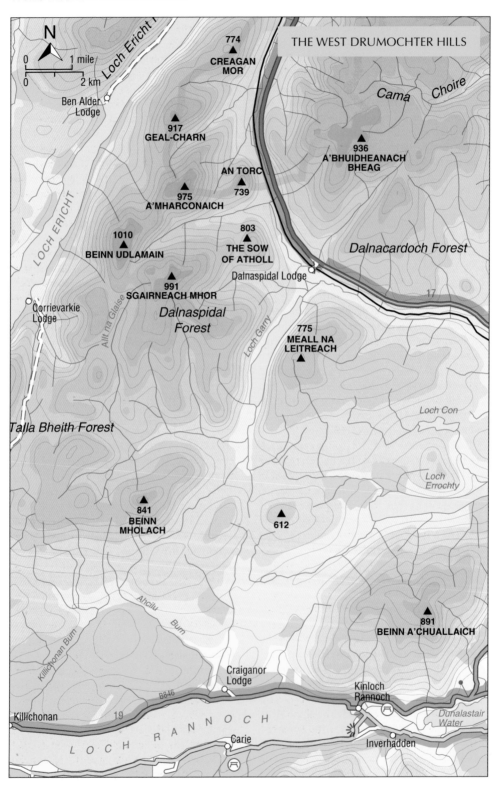

N

0 — 1 mile
0 — 2 km

Loch Ericht

Ben Alder Lodge

LOCH ERICHT

Corrievarkie Lodge

Talla Bheith Forest

Allt na Glaise

774 ▲
CREAGAN MOR

917 ▲
GEAL-CHARN

975 ▲
A'MHARCONAICH

AN TORC
739 ▲

1010 ▲
BEINN UDLAMAIN

991 ▲
SGAIRNEACH MHOR

803 ▲
THE SOW OF ATHOLL

THE WEST DRUMOCHTER HILLS

Cama Choire

936 ▲
A'BHUIDHEANACH BHEAG

Dalnacardoch Forest

Dalnaspidal Lodge

17

Dalnaspidal Forest

Loch Garry

775 ▲
MEALL NA LEITREACH

Loch Con

Loch Errochty

841 ▲
BEINN MHOLACH

612 ▲

Ahcilu Burn

Killichonan Burn

Craiganor Lodge

B846

891 ▲
BEINN A'CHUALLAICH

Kinloch Rannoch

Dunalastair Water

Killichonan

19

L O C H   R A N N O C H

Carie

Inverhadden

lie close together at the northern end of the range and can be climbed together in a round from the A9, made easy by a 450m start point at the Pass of Drumochter. The Corbetts are more scattered, two of them being quite remote. The West Drumochter hills are rounded, with steep sides and flat, stony tops and there are few crags or scree slopes. They are ideal for long walks and ski tours. The hills are fairly featureless, and navigation can be tricky in poor visibility.

⊗ The Munros, The Sow and The Boar

Two steep circular hills hang over the western side of the Pass of Drumochter, known as the An Torc, the Boar of Badenoch (739m) and the Sow of Atholl. *Torc* is the Gaelic for boar and Badenoch is the district to the north, so the anglicised name makes sense. The Sow of Atholl is 'probably a more recent fanciful name', according to Hamish Brown (*Climbing the Corbetts,* published in a compendium with *Hamish's Mountain Walk* by the same author, Baton Wicks, 1996), the original name being Meall an Dobhrachan ('watercress hill'). At 803m high and with a big drop on either side it's a Corbett. The Munros are Sgairneach Mhor ('big stony hillside', 991m), Beinn Udlamain ('gloomy hill', 1010m), A'Mharconaich ('the horse place', 975m) and Geal-charn ('white hill', 917m).

The best starting point for the pleasant round of these hills is the head of long Coire Dhomhain, just south of the Pass of Drumochter, around which all bar one of the hills lie. The railway line has to be crossed and the Allt Coire Dhomhain forded to access the steep but uncomplicated grassy north side of the Sow of Atholl. A steep descent leads to a narrow col beyond which the east ridge of Sgairneach Mhor rises easily to the summit. Further easy walking leads down to the head of Coire Dhomhain, up the south ridge of Beinn Udlamain and on northeast to A'Mharconaich. From Beinn Udlamain there are good views across Loch Ericht to Ben Alder. However, there are even better views in this direction from Geal-charn, which lies just over 2km north of A'Mharconaich and is worth going out and back to for the view down Loch Ericht, as well as to bag the summit. Back on A'Mharconaich a descent east leads to the broad col with An Torc, which is easily climbed by its west ridge. A descent southwards from the summit leads to the track in Coire Dhomhain. The distance is 22km, with 1600m of ascent, and the walk takes 7–9hrs.

Geal-charn and A'Mharconaich can also be climbed in a circuit of Coire Fhar from Balsporran Cottages on the A9, north of the Pass of Drumochter, a much shorter route at 10.5km, with 740m of ascent, which can be done in half a day. The route goes up the northeast ridge of Geal-charn and down the northeast ridge of A'Mharconaich.

❷ West Drumochter Munros Ski Tour ☆

The ski touring on these hills is excellent, and starting at 450m at the Pass of Drumochter makes the need to carry skis to the snow less likely than with lower start points. The same routes described for walkers above can be used, maybe omitting An Torc and the Sow of Atholl for the sake of time. Going anti-clockwise gives the best downhill run at the end of the day, down the northeast ridge of Sgairneach Mhor and then the open slopes to Coire Dhomhain, a drop of 475m in 2.5km. Cornices can build up on the lip of Coire Creagach north of Sgairneach Mhor and on the eastern edge of A'Mharconaich.

⊗ The Drumochter Corbetts

Directly south of the Sow of Atholl lies Meall na Leitreach ('hill of slopes', 775m), a Corbett that is probably the best viewpoint for the Pass of Drumochter. It can be climbed from Dalnaspidal Lodge by its northern slopes. During the ascent and from the summit the glacial origins of the Pass of Drumochter can be clearly seen, with a mass of moraines strewn across the terrain below the Sow of Atholl. The road, railway and pylons look small from up here. The round trip to the summit and back is only 6km, with 400m of ascent, and only takes a couple of hours, leaving plenty of time to climb the Sow of Atholl by its southeast ridge (6.5km, 400m ascent, 2hrs).

South and west of Meall na Leitrach lie two Corbetts rather more awkward of access, Stob an Aonaich Mhor ('peak of the big ridge', 855m) and Beinn Mholach ('shaggy hill', 841m). Stob an Aonaich Mhor is the highest point on the long ridge that runs along the east side of lower Loch Ericht, presenting steep slopes to the loch but gentle ones to the east. This hill is a long way from any access points, lying 12km as the crow flies from both the A9 to the east and the B846 beside Loch Rannoch to the south. From the south a 12km estate road from Bridge of Ericht leads up to the base of the hill. A bicycle is useful on this tarred road, which

Sgairneach Mhor from Coire Dhomhain

would make a tedious walk. Once below the hill the climb to the summit is short and easy (just 1.25km with 230m of ascent). The summit is set right on the edge of the steep slopes above Loch Ericht and gives superb views along the loch.

Beinn Mholach isn't quite so remote, lying 7km from Loch Rannoch and 10km from the A9. It's a rather featureless hill in the middle of a big area of rather featureless boggy moorland. Again an estate track on which a bicycle is useful leads north towards the hill, although a greater distance has to be walked. The shortest round trip from Loch Rannoch, starting at Craiganour Lodge, is 15.5km long, with 700m of ascent, and takes 4–6hrs.

Although practical these ascents from the south spend much time crossing open fairly flat moorland. Far better is the approach from the northeast, along Loch Garry from Dalnaspidal Lodge. A bicycle can be used along the track beside the loch but the walk is enjoyable along the narrow steep-sided trench in which the loch lies. From the end of the loch the northeast ridge of Beinn Mholach can be climbed. To reach Stob an Aonaich Mhor head west over high moorland from Beinn Mholach, over 789m Beinn Bhoidheach, and then north over Meallanan Odhar to the road from Bridge of Ericht. The return to Loch Garry

can be made beside the Allt Feith Gharuiareagan and Allt Shallainn. The walking is not easy in this area, as it's quite boggy and there are no paths. The round trip from Dalnaspidal over both summits is 35km long, with 1160m of ascent, and takes 10–12hrs. As a day trip it's tough, and tiring. However split over two days with a wild camp it's a fine outing into remote, lonely country where few others are likely to be seen.

3:15 THE MONADH LIATH

The Monadh Liath is a huge dissected plateau of lonely and remote rolling hills and high heather moorland stretching from the A9 to the Great Glen. Most of the area is gentle and boggy, however, and not of great interest to mountain lovers, although long Nordic ski tours can be made here and bird watchers will find the area of interest. It's also a great place for practising navigation. One summit in the heart of the area reaches Corbett height – Carn na Saobhaidhe ('cairn of the den', 811m) – but only in the south and west of the area are there many big hills. A line of four Munros and two Corbetts stretches out above Strathspey, while further west three Corbetts lie above the Corrieyairick Pass.

From west to east these hills are Carn a'Chuilinn ('cairn of holly', 817m), Gairbeinn ('rough hill', 896m), Meall na h-Aisre ('hill of the defile', 862m), Geal Charn ('white hill', 926m), Carn Dearg ('red hill', 945m), A'Chailleach ('the old woman', 930m), Carn Sgulain ('hill of the basket', 920m), Carn an Fhreiceadain ('watcher's cairn', 878m) and Geal-charn Mor ('big white hill', 824m). The most impressive hill in the area is lower than any of these, Creag Dhubh ('black crag', 756m), a rugged Graham with imposing cliffs on its south side.

Monadh Liath means 'the grey hills', from the colour of the mica schist rocks and in contrast to the granite Monadh Ruadh – the 'red hills' – the original name of the Cairngorms across Strathspey.

Access to most of the Monadh Liath is from the A86 and A9 roads on the south and east of the range. The Strathspey villages of Laggan, Newtonmore, Kingussie and Aviemore provide all facilities. The northern and western summits can also be reached from Fort Augustus.

The Monadh Liath Munros

Three of the four Monadh Liath Munros can be easily reached from the public road end in Glen Banchor to the northwest of Newtonmore. From the road head north up the Allt a'Chaorainn glen, at first on a track, then a path. The glen can be left for an ascent of the open eastern slopes of A'Chailleach. Carn Sgulain lies north of A'Chailleach. From Carn Sgulain a broad boggy ridge leads over several minor summits to the top of Carn Ban, south of which lies Carn Dearg, perched above steep slopes dropping down into Gleann Ballach. The craggy eastern face of Carn Dearg is one of the few distinctive features in the Monadh Liath. From Carn Dearg return to the col before Carn Ban, descend into Gleann Ballach and traverse the far side to pick up a path leading down the Allt Fionndrigh glen to Glen Banchor. The walk is 24km long, with 1085m of ascent, and takes 7–8hrs.

The fourth Munro, Geal-charn, lies some 10 rather boggy kms from Carn Dearg and is most easily climbed on its own or as part of an overnight trip or cross country walk. The nearest access is from the minor road running west from Laggan village beside the infant River Spey to Garva Bridge and the Corrieyairick Pass. A track from Spey Dam leads up Glen Markie from where the southeast slopes of the hill can be climbed, as long as the Markie Burn can be safely forded (a round trip of 13.5km

and 890m of ascent, taking 4–6hrs). An alternative route goes from Garva Bridge along a path towards Coire nan Dearcag and up the southwest ridge to the summit (12.5km, 650m ascent, 3½–5hrs). East of the summit is a fine corrie containing a lochan and backed by craggy slopes.

The Monadh Liath Corbetts

None of the Corbetts in this region is distinctive or of great interest, although the sense of remoteness is great and some have superb views. Corbett baggers will want to climb them but probably few others. The walking is moorland rather than mountain in feel. Most are much better skied than walked.

Starting in the west Geal-charn Mor just west of Aviemore can be easily climbed from Lynwilg on the A9 by the track running up An Gleannan that leads, initially through some pleasant woodland, to the watershed from where the summit is 1km to the southwest. The view over the Cairngorms is superb. A descent can be made southeast to a path leading to Ballinluig Farm (11.5km, 650m, 3–4hrs).

An even easier walk leads to Carn an Fhreiceadain from Kingussie, further west along Strathspey, as a track runs up to the subsidiary summit Beinn Bhreac and on to the top, while just west of the summit another track runs down the Allt Mor glen. The circuit of these tracks is 15km long, with 800m of ascent, and takes 4–5hrs.

More remote are the two Corbetts lying east of the Corrieyairick Pass, both of which can be climbed from the minor road from Laggan along the River Spey. As the approach is long it's worth climbing both hills on the same day. For Meall na h-Aisre start at Garva Bridge, an impressive old double-arched bridge built by General Wade in 1731, and head north to the southeast ridge. A descent can be made southwards into Coire Iain Oig and the Allt Coire Iain Oig followed back to Garva Bridge (12km, 675m ascent, 3½–5hrs). For Gairbeinn go on to the road end at Melgarve and climb the south ridge, then descend it (7km, 570m ascent, 3hrs). To extend the walk you can head west over Geal Charn to Corrieyairick Hill (probably 'red corrie hill', 891m), once listed as an unusual double Corbett with Gairbeinn, as both were reckoned the same height, but demoted in 1997 when Gairbeinn was discovered to be higher. From Corrieyairick Hill drop down to the Corrieyairick Pass track and follow this to Melgarve (13.5km, 835m ascent, 4–5hrs).

Western continuation on p.222

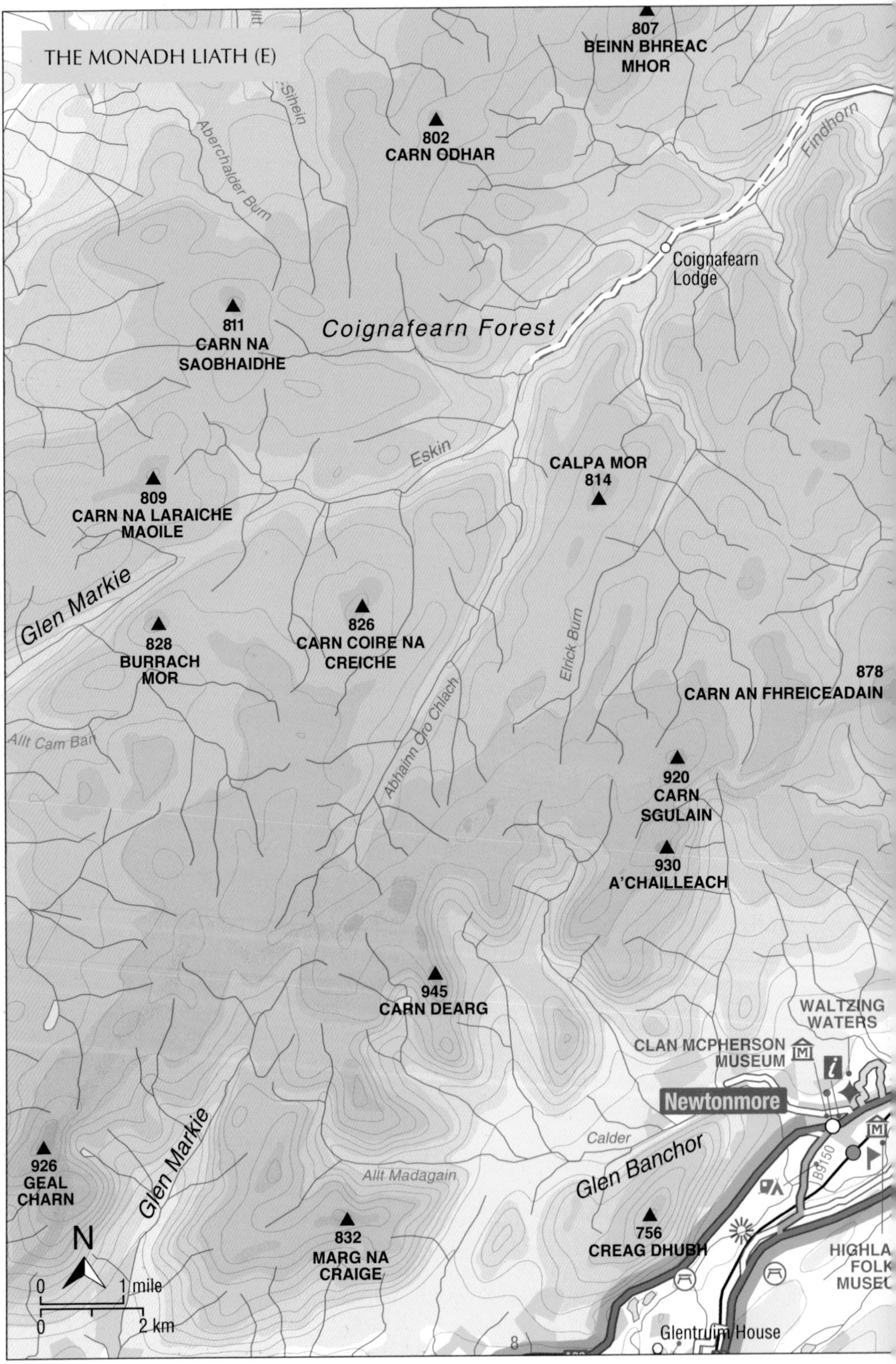
THE MONADH LIATH (E)
807
BEINN BHREAC MHOR
802
CARN ODHAR
Aberchalder Burn
Findhorn
Coignafearn Lodge
811
CARN NA SAOBHAIDHE
Coignafearn Forest
Eskin
CALPA MOR
814
809
CARN NA LARAICHE MAOILE
Glen Markie
826
CARN COIRE NA CREICHE
828
BURRACH MOR
Elrick Burn
878
CARN AN FHREICEADAIN
Allt Cam Ban
Abhainn Cro Chlach
920
CARN SGULAIN
930
A'CHAILLEACH
945
CARN DEARG
WALTZING WATERS
CLAN MCPHERSON MUSEUM
Newtonmore
Calder
Glen Banchor
B9150
926
GEAL CHARN
Glen Markie
Allt Madagain
832
MARG NA CRAIGE
756
CREAG DHUBH
HIGHLA
FOLK
MUSEU
N
0
1 mile
0
2 km
Glentruim House

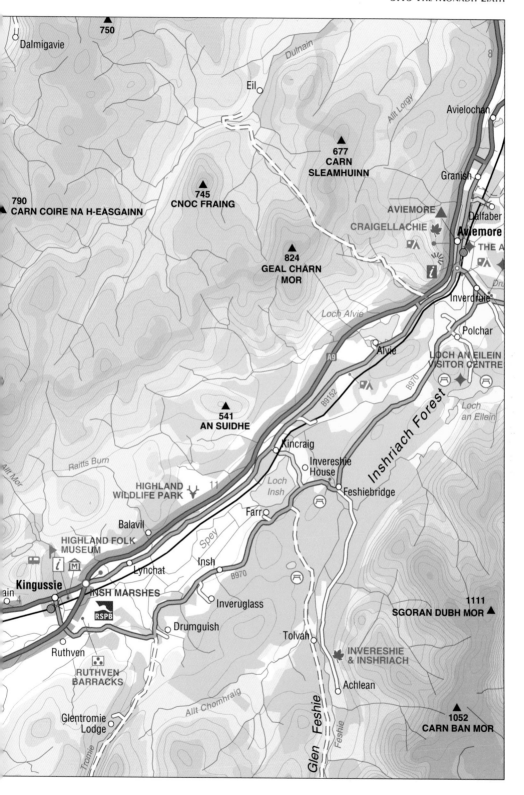

Dalmigavie

▲ 750

Eil

Dulnain

Allt Lorgy

Avielochan

▲ 677
CARN
SLEAMHUINN

Granish

▲ 745
CNOC FRAING

790
▲ CARN COIRE NA H-EASGAINN

AVIEMORE ▲
CRAIGELLACHIE

Dalfaber

Aviemore

THE A

▲ 824
GEAL CHARN
MOR

Inverdruie

Dru

Loch Alvie

Polchar

A9

Alvie

LOCH AN EILEIN
VISITOR CENTRE

B9152

B970

Loch
an Eilein

Inshriach Forest

▲ 541
AN SUIDHE

Kincraig

Raitts Burn

Invereshie
House

HIGHLAND
WILDLIFE PARK   11

Loch
Insh

Feshiebridge

Balavil

Farr

Spey

HIGHLAND FOLK
MUSEUM

Insh

Lynchat

B970

Kingussie
ain

INSH MARSHES

Inveruglass

1111
SGORAN DUBH MOR ▲

RSPB

Drumguish

Tolvah

INVERESHIE
& INSHRIACH

Ruthven

RUTHVEN
BARRACKS

Allt Chomhraig

Glen Feshie

Achlean

Glentromie
Lodge

Tromie

Feshie

▲ 1052
CARN BAN MOR

Allt Mor

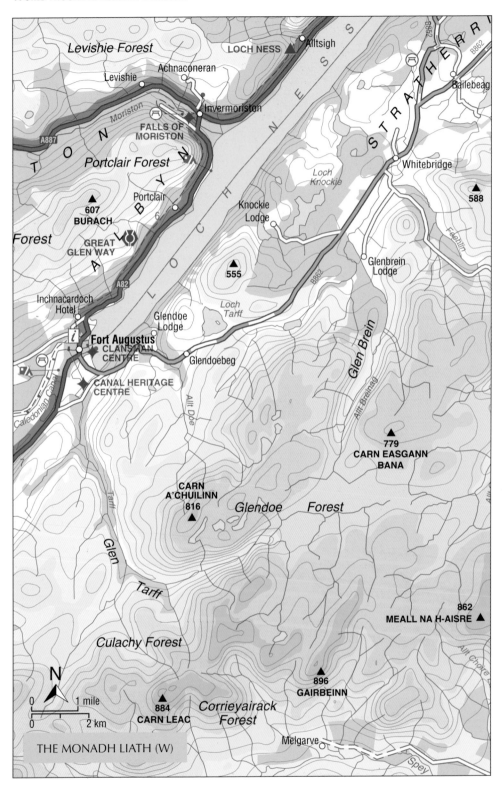

Levishie Forest

LOCH NESS

Alltsigh

Achnaconeran

Levishie

Moriston

Invermoriston

FALLS OF
MORISTON

A887

Portclair Forest

607
BURACH

Portclair

Forest

GREAT
GLEN WAY

A82

Inchnacardoch
Hotel

Glendoe
Lodge

Fort Augustus

CLANSMAN
CENTRE

CANAL HERITAGE
CENTRE

Caledonian Canal

STRATHERR

Bailebeag

Whitebridge

588

Loch
Knockie

Knockie
Lodge

Glenbrein
Lodge

B862

Glen Brein

Allt Breinag

555

Loch
Tarff

Glendoe
Lodge

Glendoebeg

Allt Doe

779
CARN EASGANN
BANA

CARN
A'CHUILINN
816

Glendoe   Forest

Tarff

Glen

Tarff

862
MEALL NA H-AISRE

Culachy Forest

N

896
GAIRBEINN

0   1 mile
0   2 km

884
CARN LEAC

Corrieyairack
Forest

Melgarve

Spey

THE MONADH LIATH (W)

View south from the Monadh Liath

Due north of Corrieyairick Hill lies isolated Carn a' Chuilinn. This is most easily climbed from the north via the tracks in Glen Doe, where there is a new hydroelectric reservoir opened in 2009, on the B862 3km east of Fort Augustus, or Glen Tarff, 1.5km south of the town. The terrain here on the northwestern edge of the range is much rougher, with steeper slopes and more rock than elsewhere in the Monadh Liath. The Glen Tarff approach leads to the western slopes of the hill, Glen Doe to the northern ones. The round trip from Glen Doe is 13km long with 760m of ascent and takes 4–5hrs. The round trip from Glen Tarff is 17km long with 1140m of ascent and takes 5–6hrs. A bicycle can be used on the track up Glen Tarff, which is the start of the Corrieyairick Pass route. The summit of Carn a'Chuilinn is rock rimmed and looks impressive, particularly from the east. There is a good view west to ranks of higher hills while to the east lies a flat tableland dotted with lochans.

There remains one very remote Corbett, Carn na Saobhaidhe. To reach it take the minor road down lovely Strath Dearn, down which the Findhorn River runs through some attractive woodland, from Tomatin or Slochd Summit on the A9 between Aviemore and Inverness to Coignafern

Old Lodge. From here an estate road continues up the glen to Dalbeg, from where paths beside the Allt Creagach and Allt Odhar can be taken to the southeastern slopes of the hill. Once off the paths peat hags make the going difficult. The summit is flat and quite large. The view is extensive, with distant, high peaks to the south and west but none close by. The sense of remoteness is great. The return walk is 28km long, with 600m of ascent, and takes 7–9hrs. However a bicycle can be used for 14km along the track to and from Dalbeg.

A huge wind farm is proposed for Carn na Saobhaidhe which, if built, will destroy this remote and wild area. There is already a wind turbine visible on Beinn Dubhcharaidh to the north and bulldozed roads up from Dumnaglass.

❷ Skiing the Monadh Liath ☆

While walking the Monadh Liath Munros is merely pleasant, skiing them is glorious. The gentle terrain is ideal for light Nordic touring skis, and boggy ground that is slow and tedious when on foot can be swept over easily when the snow is firm. The hills look grander too, especially the eastern corries, which have a real mountain appearance when under snow. The route over the three Munros described above is an excellent ski tour. The only steepish section is down to Gleann Ballach from the col between Carn Dearg and Carn Ban. If conditions are good continuing on to Geal Charn is feasible, returning the same way, which is no hardship when the skiing is easy.

The Corrieyairick Pass

The track over the Corrieyairick Pass between Laggan and Fort Augustus is the remains of the military road built by General Wade in 1731, following the 1715 Jacobite rising, to facilitate the movement of troops for the control of the Highlands. Ironically the road was used by Bonnie Prince Charlie and his army at the beginning of the 1745 uprising. The pass was used long before the 18th century, however. It's situated in wild remote country at a height of 775m. Unfortunately the pleasure of the walk is reduced by the electricity pylons that run beside the track. The pass is steep on both sides and forms quite an impressive notch in the hills.

The meaning of Corrieyairick is unclear, and is given variously as 'rising glen', 'small corrie' and 'red corrie' (*corrie dearg*). Seton Gordon in his 1935 book *Highways and Byways in the Central Highlands* (Birlinn, 1995, first published 1935) calls it Corrieyaireag and says that one of the earliest spellings is Cori Gherrag. Whatever the meaning the corrie of the name lies on the east side of the pass just below the steep climb to the summit.

The complete walk from Laggan to Fort Augustus is 40km long. However the first 15km are on the minor road from Laggan to Melgarve. The whole route can be done in a long day. There are 1000m of ascent.

Creag Dhubh ☆

Although not very high Creag Dhubh is a distinctive hill, towering over the A86 west of Newtonmore, and standing out in views from the A9 and the A889 between Dalwhinnie and Laggan. It's a craggy hill with a pointed summit, much more rugged than the higher Monadh Liath hills just to the north across Glen Banchor. Creag Dhubh or Dubh is a very common mountain name. Peter Drummond, in *Scottish Hill Names: Their Origin and Meaning* (Scottish Mountaineering Trust, 2007) says there are over 70 hills with this name. In views it looks dark, casting a shadow over the road at its base, which is maybe why it's called 'black crag'. It's certainly not due to the rock, which is a pale grey schist with bands of

white quartzite. The lower slopes on the southeast side above the road are covered with a lovely birch wood, Coille na Creige Duibhe ('wood of the black crag').

The big and impressive cliff lies low down on the southwest slopes. To visit the crag start from the small car park on the A86 opposite Lochain Uvie (NN 674 957). A steep path leads up through the woods to the base of the cliff. Traverse west along the base of the cliff until the end can be rounded and the southwest ridge climbed to the summit of Creag Dhubh. There are good views north to the Monadh Liath Munros, which look surprisingly rugged from here. The rocky summit ridge can be followed north to An Torr, from where a rough descent can be made into the woods to the south. A pleasant wander through the woods leads back to the start. The distance is 8km, with 645m of ascent, and takes 3–4hrs.

Rock Climbing on Creag Dhubh

Although low down on the hill and not far from the road the Creag Dhubh crag has the feel of a high mountain cliff. It's steep and imposing and most routes – there are over 100 – are graded Very Severe or harder.

3:16 CREAG MEAGAIDH AND THE LOCH LAGGAN HILLS

1128m Creag Meagaidh is one of the great hills of the Central Highlands, a big, bulky, complex mountain lying just north of Loch Laggan and the A86 road. From a distance the main impression is of a huge steep-sided plateau. However on the east side a great bowl has been gouged out of this plateau to form dramatic Coire Ardair, which contains a lovely lochan and has a back wall of huge mica schist cliffs that are a major winter climbing area, although too broken and vegetated to give good rock climbing. There are smaller attractive corries on the south side too, especially high Coire Moy, where there is a little lochan. The summit plateau is huge, a gently sloping tableland with many dips and hollows. Seven broad blunt spurs run out from the plateau, with deep corries and stream valleys between them. There are four subsidiary tops, all worth visiting.

Creag Meagaidh means 'bogland rock' or 'crag of the bog', perhaps referring to the boggy lands lying to the north around little Loch Spey,

Coire Ardair, Creag Meagaidh

the headwaters of the River Spey. Research by Ian R Mitchell, in *Scotland's Mountains Before the Mountaineers* (Luath, 1999) suggests that the first recorded ascent was made by a Colonel Thomas Thornton who made a tour of Scotland, probably in 1786, with the purpose of killing 'as many animals, birds and fish as he possibly could', which he described in his 1804 book *Sporting Tour*. However Mitchell also suspects that the man Thornton describes as the 'herdsman who knew these mountains', who accompanied the Colonel, 'had already covered the ground Thornton describes many times'.

At the northeast corner of Creag Meagaidh, on the edge of the Coire Ardair cliffs, the ground drops away steeply to a notch call The Window that can be seen clearly in views from distant hills. East of The Window a long ridge curves round the north side of Coire Ardair. Two Munros lie on this ridge – Stob Poite Coire Ardair ('peak of the pot of the high corrie', 1054m) and Carn Liath ('grey hill', 1006m). West of Creag Meagaidh lie two ridges running south–north with big rocky corries on their east sides. The high point on each ridge is a Munro. The easternmost of these is Beinn a'Chaorainn ('hill of the rowan', 1052m), the westernmost Beinn Teallach ('forge hill', 915m). They can be climbed together.

In 1985 the Moy Estate, covering the whole area south of Creag Meagaidh and Carn Liath including Coire Ardair, was bought by the Nature Conservancy Council and became a National Nature Reserve after the UK government refused the owners permission for blanket forestry over much of the area. Creag Meagaidh National Nature Reserve is now owned by Scottish Natural Heritage and instead of becoming yet another area sacrificed to spruce plantations it has become the opposite, a special place that shows that the regeneration of the land is possible. New natural woodland is springing up on the southern slopes of the hills and well up Coire Ardair. The trees are regenerating because deer numbers have been reduced, ending over-grazing. No planting was needed and the new forest has a completely natural spread and natural boundaries. The commonest trees are birch but rowan, willow, oak and alder are also spreading. The mouth of Coire Ardair in springtime is now a lovely place, with the pale green of new leaves spreading up the hillsides. The increase in tree cover creates a better environment for flowers and other plants, too, so the whole ecosystem is richer than when over-grazed. The story of the first ten years of the nature reserve is told in Paul Ramsey's interesting book *Revival of the Land: Creag Meagaidh National*

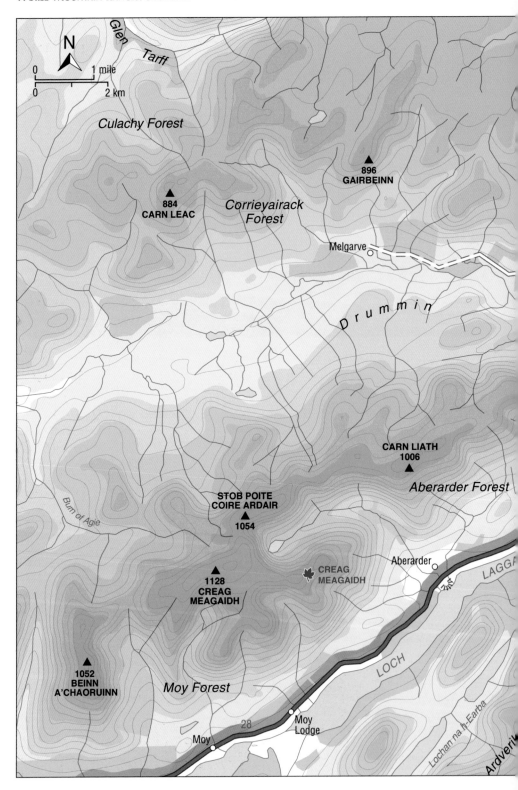

N

0   1 mile
0   2 km

Culachy Forest

▲ 896
GAIRBEINN

▲ 884
CARN LEAC

*Corrieyairack
Forest*

Melgarve ○

D r u m m i n

Glen
Tarff

CARN LIATH
1006
▲

Aberarder Forest

STOB POITE
COIRE ARDAIR
▲
1054

Burn of Agie

▲ 1128
CREAG
MEAGAIDH

CREAG
MEAGAIDH

Aberarder ○

LAGGA

▲ 1052
BEINN
A'CHAORUINN

Moy Forest

LOCH

28

Moy
Lodge

Moy ○   ○

Lochan na h-Earba

Ardverik

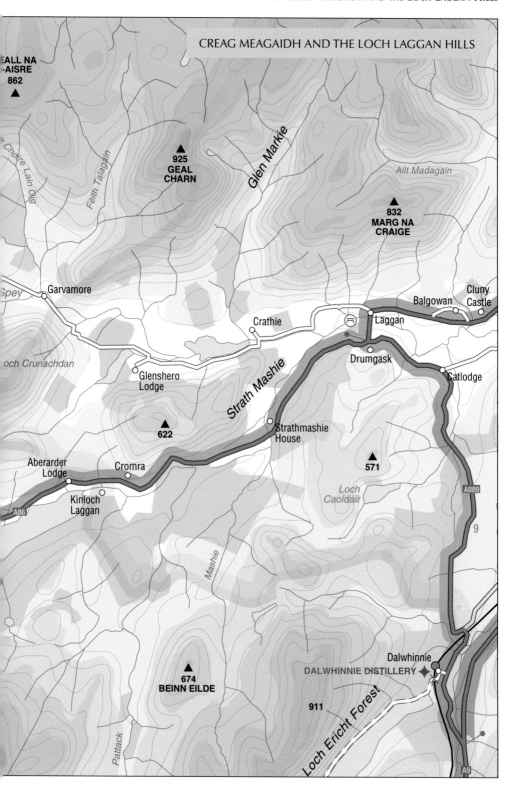

CREAG MEAGAIDH AND THE LOCH LAGGAN HILLS

EALL NA
-AISRE
862
▲

Choire Lain Oig

Féith Talagain

▲
925
GEAL
CHARN

Glen Markie

Allt Madagain

▲
832
MARG NA
CRAIGE

Spey

Garvamore

Loch Crunachdan

Crathie

Laggan

Balgowan

Cluny
Castle

Glenshero
Lodge

Strath Mashie

Drumgask

Catlodge

▲
622

Strathmashie
House

▲
571

A889

Aberarder
Lodge

Cromra

Loch
Caoldair

9

Kinloch
Laggan

A86

Mashie

Pattack

▲
674
BEINN EILDE

Dalwhinnie

DALWHINNIE DISTILLERY ✦

911

Loch Ericht Forest

A9

Winter climbers near the top of the Coire Ardair cliffs, Creag Meagaidh

Nature Reserve (SNH, 1996). There are displays about the reserve at the car park at Aberarder on the A86 at the mouth of Coire Ardair.

⊘ Creag Meagaidh and Coire Ardair ☆

The walk into Coire Ardair and up Creag Meagaidh is one of the best in the Central Highlands. Starting at Aberarder a good path, built of old railway sleepers in boggy areas, curves round through the regenerating woodland in Coire Ardair. As the head of the corrie comes into view the cliffs look small at first, then slowly become more massive and imposing as you approach. From Lochan a'Choire at the base of the cliff the array of buttresses and gullies (known as posts) is dramatic and inspiring. To the northwest the deep and narrow notch of The Window stands out. A rough path ascends the increasingly steep and stony slopes to the boulder-filled gap from where a path climbs steeply onto the plateau. It's still almost 1km and a half across featureless slopes to the summit, which makes for challenging navigation in poor visibility, especially when the ground is snow-covered. The first big cairn seen is called Mad Meg's Cairn, for reasons now unknown. It isn't the summit but is sometimes mistaken for it. The highest point is actually on a ridge west of the broadest part of the plateau. The descent can be made along the rim of the Coire Ardair cliffs (beware cornices in winter and spring) and over the subsidiary tops of Puist Coire Ardair (1071m) and Sron a'Choire, which form the south arm of the Coire Ardair horseshoe, and down east to a bridge over the Allt Coire Ardair and Aberarder. There are superb views over Coire Ardair to The Window from this descent. The walk is 16.5km, with 1090m of ascent, and takes 5–7hrs.

⊘ Carn Liath and Stob Poite Coire Ardair

These two hills can also be climbed via Coire Ardair and The Window as described under Creag Meagaidh above. From The Window climb northeast to Stob Poite Coire Ardair, which lies on the northern edge of Coire Ardair with good views of the lochan and the cliffs. There follows a fine scenic traverse along a gently undulating ridge for 5km to Carn Liath. The walking is easy and the views superb. A descent can be made down the south ridge of Carn Liath to rejoin the path in Coire Ardair. The distance is 16.5km, with 1050m of ascent, and the walk takes 5–7hrs.

Creag Meagaidh can be climbed along with these two summits, ascending over Sron a'Choire to Creag Meagaidh and then down to The Window and along the ridge to Carn Liath, a distance of 19km, with 1300m of ascent and a time of 6–8hrs.

✳ Winter Climbing in Coire Ardair ☆

The cliffs of Coire Ardair are some of the biggest in Britain and second only to Ben Nevis for snow and ice climbing. Much of the climbing is serious and there is often a high avalanche risk. The best-known climbs are the four gullies or posts on the main headwall, known as the Post Face. The gullies are called Last Post (240m, Grade V), South Post (400m, Grade V), Centre Post (400m, Grade III) and North Post (400m, Grade V). Also famous is the Crab Crawl (Grade III/IV), a 2400m girdle of the cliff first climbed, solo, by the famous Scottish climber Tom Patey in 1969.

❷ Ski Touring on the Creag Meagaidh hills ☆

The round of the Coire Ardair horseshoe is a superb ski tour. It's good in either direction, with excellent open slopes and long descents from Sron a'Choire and Carn Liath. In poor visibility care is needed near the rim of Coire Ardair where big cornices can

build up. The tour can be shortened with a descent from The Window, but the slopes can be icy and the boulders near the bottom exposed, making this not a place to slip.

⊗ Beinn a'Chaorainn and Beinn Teallach

These two long ridges form the eastern and western walls of the Allt a'Chaorainn glen and can be easily linked in a circuit of this glen. Dense plantations line the southern slopes but a track runs through these from Roughburn 0.5km east of the Laggan Dam on the A86. Once through the trees the broad southwest ridge of Beinn a'Chaorainn leads to the summit ridge. There are three tops, of which the central one is the highest. The east edge of the ridge lies above steep slopes leading down into Coire na h-Uamha. Big cornices can build up here in winter and care is needed with navigation, as the ridge has kinks in it and doesn't follow a straight line. People have fallen through cornices here. From the ridge drop down to the big cairn on the col at the head of the Allt a'Chaorainn, then ascend the northeast ridge to the summit of Beinn Teallach and descend the south ridge to the track beside the Allt a'Chaorainn. The distance is 17km, with 1280m of ascent, and the walk takes 6–7hrs.

Glen Roy with the Parallel Roads standing out

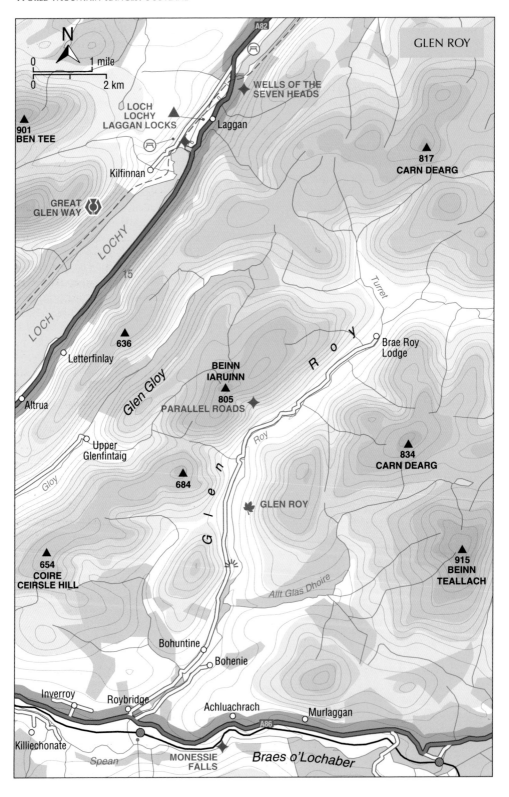

GLEN ROY

N

0   1 mile
0   2 km

A82

WELLS OF THE
SEVEN HEADS

LOCH
LOCHY
LAGGAN LOCKS

Laggan

▲ 901
BEN TEE

▲ 817
CARN DEARG

Kilfinnan

GREAT
GLEN WAY

LOCH   LOCHY

15

Turret

▲ 636

Letterfinlay

Glen Gloy

BEINN
IARUINN
▲ 805
PARALLEL ROADS

Brae Roy
Lodge

G l e n R o y

Altrua

Roy

Upper
Glenfintaig

▲ 834
CARN DEARG

Gloy

▲ 684

GLEN ROY

G
l
e
n

▲ 654
COIRE
CEIRSLE HILL

Allt Glas Dhoire

▲ 915
BEINN
TEALLACH

Bohuntine

Bohenie

Inverroy

Roybridge

Achluachrach

Murlaggan

Killiechonate

Spean

A86

MONESSIE
FALLS

Braes o'Lochaber

3:17 GLEN ROY ☆

Four Corbetts lie round the head of Glen Roy, which runs north for 13km from Roy Bridge in Glen Spean. Three of the summits have the same name – Carn Dearg ('red cairn'). To distinguish them they can be called the East Glen Roy Carn Dearg (834m) and the North and South Gleann Eachach Carn Deargs (817m and 768m), Gleann Eachach being a side glen at the north end of Glen Roy. The fourth Corbett is Beinn Iaruinn ('iron hill', 805m), which lies across Glen Roy from the East Glen Roy Carn Dearg. These are steep-sided, flat-topped, heathery hills.

Glen Roy is best known, and of most interest, for the Parallel Roads, a series of straight lines running across the slopes on either side, which look artificial. In fact they are the old shores of an ancient meltwater loch, created around 10,000 years ago when glaciers in Glen Spean blocked the mouth of Glen Roy. As the ice retreated so the shorelines fell, leaving narrow flat terraces at 350m, 325m and 250m. At first thought to be made by the Celtic mythical hero Fingal and used for hunting their real origins were identified by the great Swiss geologist Louis Agassiz in 1841. The Parallel Roads are internationally known and important geologically, and Glen Roy is a National Nature Reserve, managed by Scottish Natural Heritage, which publishes an interesting booklet, entitled *Glen Roy in the Landscape Fashioned by Geology* series (SNH, 2004). There is a viewpoint for the upper glen 5km up the road.

⦿ Beinn Iaruinn and East Glen Roy Carn Dearg

These two hills can easily be climbed on the same day, as each lies directly above the road in Glen Roy. The ascents cross the Parallel Roads. Beinn Iaruinn is at the head of little Coire Eun and can be climbed in a circuit of the corrie from the road bridge over the stream running out of the corrie. The round is short – just 4km with 600m of ascent – but the going is quite rough over tussocks and bogs. It takes 2–3hrs.

Carn Dearg is a more interesting hill, with two craggy corries facing the road, Coire na Reinich and Coire Dubh, divided by the northwest ridge of Carn Bhrunachain. The ascent starts 3km further up the glen than that for Beinn Iaruinn, at the point

where a bridge crosses the River Roy. Either corrie can be ascended and the other descended. The burns in both lead towards the summit, where there is a view southeast to the Creag Meagaidh hills. The round trip is 7.5km long, with 700m of ascent, and takes 3–4hrs.

⦿ The Gleann Eachach Carn Deargs

These two Corbetts lie beyond the head of Glen Roy and are quite remote. They are rather featureless, and set in an area of rather bleak moorland. The walking, away from paths, is hard, with many tussocks and bogs. However from the end of the public road at Brae Roy Lodge in upper Glen Roy tracks and paths can be linked up Glen Turret and then up Gleann Eachach almost to the col between the summits, which each lie 1km away. It's easiest to return the same way, for a walk of 15km, with 875m of ascent, which takes 4½–5½hrs.

3:18 LONG WALKS

Many high-level long distance walks linking summits are possible in the Central Highlands. One is the round of Glen Nevis via the Mamores, Grey Corries, Aonachs and Ben Nevis. The Loch Treig hills can be added as well, to make a walk of around 100km with almost 9000m of ascent. Astonishingly in 1989 this route was run in 18hrs 23mins by Adrian Belton and 20hrs 24mins by Helene Diamantides. Most walkers will take three days, with two overnight camps. To runners it's known as Charlie Ramsey's Round, after the first person to run it in 1978. Another obvious line is to traverse the hills to the north of Glen Spean and Strathspey from Beinn Teallach across Creag Meagaidh to the Monadh Liath, a distance of around 65km with 3350m of ascent that could be done in two long days but is more comfortable over three.

There are also many glen and pass routes, including the northern section of the West Highland Way (see 3:4) and the Great Glen Way (see Introduction). West to east routes can use the railways to great advantage.

⦿ Kinlochleven to Spean Bridge

This south–north route curves inland from Kinlochleven round the eastern ends of the Mamores and Grey Corries, crossing three passes en route. It takes the walker into remote country and gives a feeling for the vastness of the Central Highlands. The distance is 30km, with 1020m of ascent. There is a path the whole way and the walk can be done in 8–10hrs, but is more enjoyable over two days with an overnight camp and perhaps an ascent of one or two of the peaks, such as Stob Ban in the Grey Corries, along the way. From Kinlochleven the path climbs past the pretty Grey Mare's Waterfall to lochs Eilde Mor and Eilde Beag below Sgurr Eilde Mor. The best view is to the southwest, where the jagged Aonach Eagach rises on the horizon. Beyond the lochs a low watershed is crossed, followed by a gentle descent to the Abhainn Rath. This stream has to be forded, which can be difficult when it's in spate. If the ford looks dangerous you can follow it upstream to look for a safer place. If none appears you can continue west down Glen Nevis to Fort William.

On the far side of the Abhainn Rath lies Meanach bothy, a useful shelter in bad weather. Beyond the bothy the path climbs broad open slopes beside the Allt nan Fang to a boggy saddle, the highest point on the walk at 610m, between the minor top of Meall Mor and the Munro Stob Ban, which looks surprisingly nondescript from here. It looks much more impressive from the tiny Lairig Leacach bothy, to which the path runs from the saddle. This is the finest situation on the walk, with the steep slopes of the Easain Munros rising to the east and the rocky pair of Corbetts, Sgurr Innse and Creach Innse, further north. To the west Stob Ban rises as a pale cone above the narrow wooded gorge of the Allt a'Chuil. There is a rough path up the northeast ridge of Stob Ban.

From the bothy the path rises slowly to the 505m Lairig Leacach pass and then descends beside the Allt Leachdach below the steep slopes of the eastern end of the Grey Corries. Soon the path enters Leanachan Forest and winds through the trees to the Corriechoile farm and the minor road to Spean Bridge besides the lovely tree-lined River Spean.

� Fort William to Dalwhinnie via Corrour ☆
This is a superb station-to-station walk through the heart of the Central Highlands. The West Highland Line is crossed at Corrour Station, where the route can be cut short. The walk is 70km long (if you walk down Glen Nevis from Fort William), with 1885m of ascent, and takes 2–3 days. There are bothies at Meanach and Staoineag beside the Abhainn Rath, a youth hostel at Loch Ossian, another bothy at Culra north of the Bealach Dubh and plenty of lovely campsites.

From lower Glen Nevis the route climbs through the wooded Nevis Gorge to the upper glen, passes Steall Falls, and runs up to the watershed at boggy Tom an Eite, a rather bleak spot but with a great view back west to Ben Nevis. The route runs beside the Abhainn Rath to the head of Loch Treig and then turns south to Corrour Station, from where a 4WD track runs east to Loch Ossian and along the side of the loch to the longest climb of the walk, up to the narrow Bealach Dubh, squeezed between Ben Alder and Geal-charn. The path descends slowly to Culra bothy and then Loch Ericht, whose shores are followed to Dalwhinnie.

ACCESS, BASES, MAPS AND GUIDES

Access

The Central Highlands are ringed by main roads and split by a rail line, with another to the east, so access is good, although the area is a little more distant from the cities of the Central Belt than the hills to the south. The A82 from Glasgow runs through Glencoe, then follows the shores of Loch Linnhe to Fort William and on northeast to Spean Bridge, Fort Augustus and Inverness. The A9 from Perth crosses the eastern edge of the area via the Pass of Drumochter. The two main roads are linked in the north by the A86 from Strathspey to Spean Bridge. In the south the A85 runs west from Tyndrum to Taynuilt and Oban. In the southwest the A828 links the A86 near Oban with the A82 at Ballachulish.

There are good rail connections too with the West Coast Main Line stopping at Rannoch, Corrour, Tulloch, Roybridge and Spean Bridge before finishing at Fort William. The Edinburgh–Inverness line in the east stops at Dalwhinnie, Newtonmore, Kingussie and Aviemore. In the south the Oban line stops at Dalmally, Lochawe, Cruachan and Taynuilt. Bus services are good too, especially along the A9 and the A82.

Ben Cruachan Hills A85 from Tyndrum in the west through the Pass of Brander to Taynuilt. Railway stations at Dalmally, Lochawe, Falls of Cruachan and Taynuilt.

The Glen Etive Hills Minor road down Glen Etive from the A82 near the head of Glencoe.

The Black Mount The A82 across Rannoch Moor on the eastern edge of the hills between Bridge of Orchy and Glencoe.

Glen Coe The A82 runs right down the glen.

Beinn a'Bheithir and Glen Creran The A82 to Ballachulish, A828 from Connel to Ballachulish.

Rannoch Moor The A82 crosses the western edge of the moor. Railway station at Rannoch on the eastern edge.

The Mamores The B863 from the A82 along Loch Leven. Minor road down Glen Nevis from Fort William. Railway station in Fort William.

Ben Nevis Minor road down Glen Nevis from Fort William. A82 northeast of Fort William.

The Aonachs and the Grey Corries Minor road down Glen Nevis from Fort William. A86 along Glen Spean. Railway stations at Roybridge, Spean Bridge and Fort William.

Loch Treig and Loch Ossian A86 along Glen Spean. Railway stations at Corrour and Tulloch.

The Ben Alder and Laggan Hills A86 beside Loch Laggan. A9 to Dalwhinnie. Railway station at Dalwhinnie.

The West Drumochter Hills A9 over the Pass of Drumochter. Railway station at Dalwhinnie.

The Monadh Liath The A9 through Strathspey. Railway stations at Newtonmore, Kingussie, Aviemore.

Creag Meagaidh A86 beside Loch Laggan.

Glen Roy A86 east or west to Roybridge. Railway station at Roybridge.

Bases

Ben Cruachan Hills Dalmally, Lochawe, Bridge of Awe, Taynuilt, Oban.

The Glen Etive Hills Glencoe.

The Black Mount Bridge of Orchy, Glencoe.

Glen Coe Glencoe, Ballachulish.

Beinn a'Bheithir and Glen Creran Ballachulish, Connel.

Rannoch Moor Rannoch, Bridge of Orchy.

The Mamores Kinlochleven, Fort William.

Ben Nevis Fort William.

The Aonachs and the Grey Corries Fort William, Spean Bridge, Roybridge.

Loch Treig and Loch Ossian Roybridge.

The Ben Alder and Laggan Hills Laggan, Dalwhinnie.

The West Drumochter Hills Dalwhinnie.

The Monadh Liath Newtonmore, Laggan, Kingussie, Aviemore.

Creag Meagaidh Roybridge, Laggan.

Glen Roy Roybridge.

Maps

OS Landranger 1:50,000 34, 35, 41, 42, 50, 52

OS Explorer 1:25,000 376, 377, 384, 385, 392, 393, 400, 401, 417

Harvey British Mountain Map 1:40,000 Ben Nevis and Glen Coe

Harvey Superwalker 1:25,000 Ben Nevis, Glen Coe

Harvey Summit 1:12,500 Ben Nevis

Walking Guides

Ben Nevis and Glen Coe by Ronald Turnbull (Cicerone, 2007)

Ben Nevis and Glen Coe Rambler's Guide by Chris Townsend (Collins, 2000)

Ben Nevis and the Mamores (Classic Munros) by Chris Townsend (Colin Baxter, 2009)

Fort William and Glen Coe Walks (Pathfinder Guide) by Hamish Brown (Jarrold/Ordnance Survey, 1992)

Glen Coe (Classic Munros) by Chris Townsend (Colin Baxter, 2008)

Hill Walks Glen Coe and Lochaber by Ruaridh Pringle (The Stationery Office, 1997)

The Central Highlands (Scottish Mountaineering Club District Guide) by Peter Hodgkiss (SMT, 1994)

The Central Highlands by Nick Williams (Pocket Mountains, 2004)

The Ultimate Guide to the Munros: Vol 2 Central Highlands South by Ralph Storer (Luath, 2009)

Scrambling Guide

Scrambles in Lochaber by Noel Williams (Cicerone, 1996)

Climbing Guides

Winter Climbs Ben Nevis and Glencoe by Mike Pescod (Cicerone, 2010)

Ben Nevis Rock and Ice Climbs including Creag Meagaidh, the Aonachs and the Central Highlands by Simon Richardson (SMT, 2002)

Glen Coe by Ken Crocket, Rab Anderson and Dave Cuthbertson (SMT, 2001)

Highland Outcrops by Kevin Howett (SMC, 1998)

General, History and Natural History

Ben Nevis: Britain's Highest Mountain by Ken Crocket and Simon Richardson (SMC, 2007)

Ben Nevis: The Story of Mountain and Glen by Rennie McOwan (Lany Syne, 1990)

Glencoe by Lyndsey Bowditch (The National Trust for Scotland, 2005)

Nevis – the Hill, the Glen, the River by Alex Gillespie (Alex Gillespie Photography, 2007)

CHAPTER 4: THE CAIRNGORMS

East Drumochter, The Gaick and Minigaig, Glen Tilt, Pitlochry and Killiekrankie, Glen Shee, the Angus Glens, Deeside, Strathspey, Lairig an Laoigh, the Cairngorm Plateau, Lairig Ghru, Glen Feshie and the Speyside Way

THE CAIRNGORMS: CHAPTER SUMMARY

Location
The hills east of the A9

☆ Highlights

🅐 LOW-LEVEL/PASSES WALK
- Glen Tilt to Linn of Dee (4:2)
- Jock's Road (4:5)
- Loch an Eilein (4:7)
- Lairig an Laoigh (4:8)
- Walking to Loch Avon (4:9)
- Walking the Lairig Ghru (4:10)
- Walking Glen Feshie (4:11)

🅑 SUMMIT WALK
- Beinn a'Ghlo (4:2)
- Ben Vrackie (4:3)
- The Glas Maol Hills and Caenlochan Glen (4:4)
- Lochnagar (4:6)
- The Dubh Loch, Cairn Bannoch and Broad Cairn (4:6)
- The Complete Round of the Lochnagar Hills (4:6)
- The Ascent of Ben Avon and Beinn a'Bhuird (4:6)
- Meall a'Bhuachaille and Ryvoan Pass (4:7)
- Gleann Einich and the Sgoran Ridge (4:7)
- Ben Rinnes (4:7)
- Bynack More (4:8)
- Beinn Mheadhoin (4:8)
- Derry Cairngorm (4:8)
- Ben Macdui and Cairn Gorm (4:9)
- The Chalamain Gap and Creag an Leth-choin (Lurcher's Crag) (4:9)
- The An Garbh Choire Munros (4:10)
- Mullach Clach a'Bhlair (4:11)

🅒 SCRAMBLING
- Loch Avon to the Cairngorm Plateau (4:9)
- The Northeast Ridge of Sgor an Lochain Uaine (4:10)

🅓 ROCK CLIMBING
- Lochnagar (4:6)
- Creag an Dubh Loch (4:6)
- Beinn a'Bhuird Corries (4:6)
- Creagan a'Choire Etchachan (4:8)
- Cairn Gorm Plateau: Northern Corries (4:9)
- The Loch Avon and Etchachan Cliffs (4:9)
- Coire Sputan Dearg (4:9)
- An Garbh Choire (4:10)

❄ WINTER CLIMBING
- Lochnagar (4:6)
- Creag an Dubh Loch (4:6)
- The Beinn a'Bhuird Corries (4:6)
- Creagan a'Choire Etchachan (4:8)
- Cairn Gorm Plateau: Northern Corries (4:9)
- The Loch Avon and Etchachan Cliffs (4:9)
- Coire Sputan Dearg (4:9)
- An Garbh Choire (4:10)

⛷ SKI TOURING
- East Drumochter (4:1)
- Beinn a'Ghlo (4:2)
- The Glas Maol Hills (4:4)
- Mayar and Driesh (4:5)
- The Lairig an Laoigh Hills (4:8)
- The Cairngorm Plateau (4:9)
- Lairig Ghru (4:10)
- The Cairngorms Five (4:10)
- Glen Feshie and the Moine Mhor (4:11)

🅕 OTHER HIGHLIGHTS
- The Strathspey Pine Forests (4:7)
- Loch Avon (4:9)

Contents

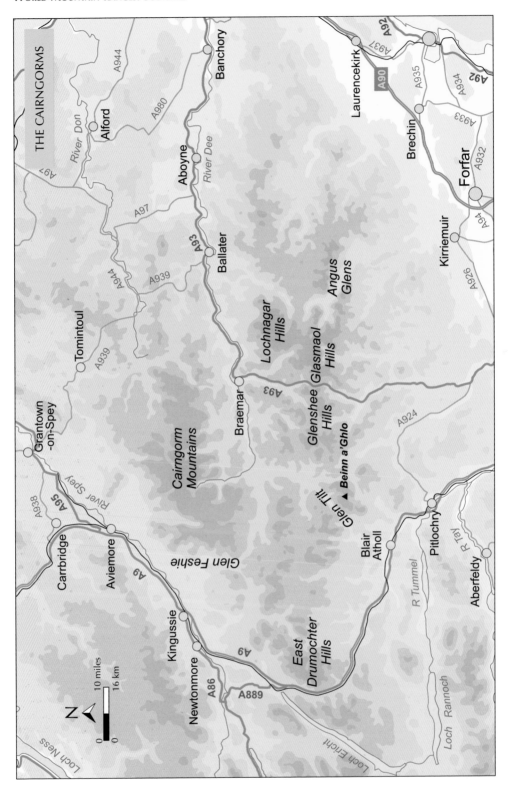

THE CAIRNGORMS

Banchory

Alford

River Don

A944

A980

A97

Aboyne

River Dee

A97

Ballater

A93

A939

A944

A939

Tomintoul

A939

Grantown
-on-Spey

River Spey

A95

A938

Carrbridge

Aviemore

A9

Glen Feshie

Kingussie

Newtonmore

A86

A889

A9

East
Drumochter
Hills

Cairngorm
Mountains

Braemar

A93

Lochnagar
Hills

Glasmaol
Hills

Glenshee
Hills

Angus
Glens

Beinn a'Ghlo

Glen Tilt

A924

Blair
Atholl

Pitlochry

R Tummel

R Tay

Aberfeldy

Loch Rannoch

Loch Ness

Loch Ericht

Laurencekirk

A937

A92

A90

A935

A933

A934

A92

Brechin

A932

Forfar

A94

Kirriemuir

A926

10 miles

16 km

0

N

INTRODUCTION

A place which satisfies and delights my mind's eye with its scale,
its distinctions, its shapes, its wildlife, and especially for its wildness.
Jim Crumley, *A High and Lonely Place*

The Cairngorms are the easternmost mountains in the Highlands, a huge and magnificent area of rolling hills, high plateaus, long passes, deep corries, spreading forests and big rivers. The greater Cairngorms area encompasses all the hill country to the east of the A9, where it links with the Central Highlands. To north, south and east the mountains eventually fade away into foothills and then flatlands, making this a distinct montane bloc. Cairngorm hills are mostly flat-topped but steep-sided. Rather than individual summits – although there are some fine ones – the glory of the Cairngorms lies in ranges of hills, especially the huge high plateaus – the Moine Mhor, the Cairngorm Plateau itself, Ben Avon/Beinn a'Bhuiridh, the White Mounth and Glas Maol – which contain the largest extent of high land in Britain.

The use of the name 'Cairngorms' for this area is relatively new. Originally Cairn Gorm was the name of a hill only. The range containing Cairn Gorm (two Cairn Gorms actually, the second now being called Derry Cairngorm) was Am Monadh Ruadh ('the red mountain') in contrast to the Monadh Liath ('the grey mountain') across Strathspey to the north, names that refer to the colour of the rocks the hills are made from, pink granite for the Cairngorms, grey schist for the Monadh Liath. However in the 19th century the first tourists started calling the whole range the Cairngorms, after the hill that stands out in views from Aviemore and Strathspey, and the name soon started to appear on maps and in guidebooks and became applied to all the ranges east of the A9. The area south of the River Dee used to be called Am Monadh, 'the mountain', which was anglicised to The Mounth. This area is also sometimes known as the Grampians, but the derivation of this name is unknown and it's often applied to larger parts of the Highlands. Today the area is known as the southern Cairngorms to hillgoers.

Like the mountains to the west most of the Cairngorms are built of schist, a metamorphic rock.

However the highest hills are granite and have big cliffs, which are good for climbing, and dramatic rock scenery. This granite welled up under ground as liquid magma some 400 million years ago and cooled beneath the surface, to be revealed after tens of millions of years of erosion and then shaped by glaciers and subsequent weathering to give the dissected plateau landscape of today.

The high plateaus are home to a sub-arctic flora and fauna unique in Britain as nowhere else is there such a vast area above 800m, some 260km^2 in total. Snow lies long at these heights and the plateaus are superb areas for ski touring. Indeed, the region is arguably the best for ski touring in the whole of Scotland. The high snowfall has attracted downhill skiers, too, and three of Scotland's five ski resorts are in the Cairngorms: the Glen Shee Ski Centre on the slopes either side of the Cairnwell Pass at the head of Glen Shee; Cairngorm Mountain in Coire Cas and Coire na Ciste on the north side of Cairn Gorm; and The Lecht in the east of the area, at the high point of the A939 road between Ballater and Tomintoul.

The Cairngorms are also a magnificent area for hillwalkers, especially those who like long distances and remote, wild country, rather than short, steep ascents. There are 50 Munros in the Cairngorms, including five of the six highest. There are also 29 Corbetts and 19 Grahams, mostly round the edges of the higher ground. The long glens and passes between these hills make wonderful and wild through-routes, especially Glen Feshie, Glen Tilt, the Lairig Ghru and the Lairig an Laoigh.

Below the high ground lie some of the last remnants of the old Caledonian pine forest – beautiful natural woods with rich undergrowth and prolific bird life. Two major rivers run through the Cairngorms, the Spey and the Dee, and there are many lovely lochs such as Loch Insh, Loch Morlich, Loch Muick, Loch an Eilean and Loch Einich. One small loch is famous among bird watchers – Loch Garten, near which ospreys nested

View across the Cairngorm Plateau to Cairn Gorm

in 1954, probably for the first time in 40 years (although recent research suggests they may have nested occasionally in Strathspey in the 1930s and 1940s). Loch Garten became an RSPB reserve, and ospreys have bred there ever since. A visit to the Loch Garten Osprey Centre in the spring to view the ospreys at their nest is one of the great events of the Cairngorms. Loch Garten lies in Strathspey to the east of Aviemore in a huge area of Scots pine forest (128km²) that is now the RSPB's Abernethy Reserve where you can see crested tits, capercaillie, red squirrels and other forest wildlife. This is the largest remaining part of the Caledonian forest, and it is regenerating under the RSPB's management.

The majority of the Cairngorms became Scotland's second national park in 2003, and is the largest national park in Britain by far at 3800km². It's not complete, however. Amazingly a large section in the southwest of the Cairngorms was omitted, including Blair Atholl (which should be the gateway to the park), Glen Tilt and Beinn a'Ghlo, and the southern boundary of the park runs along the crest of the mountains, leaving half of them in the park, half outside. That such a magnificent and key part of the Cairngorms was omitted damages the integrity of the park, which will only be complete and the Cairngorms fully protected when it is included in the park. Happily in 2009 the Scottish Government proposed that the park should be extended to cover these areas, but the exact line of the southern boundary is still to be decided.

The Cairngorms take the form of a huge ragged arrowhead, with the point at the Pass of Drumochter in the west and Upper Deeside as the shaft, and with two long barbs on either side. Where the Cairngorms touch the rest of the Highlands at Drumochter the scenery is rolling heather moorland, with steep slopes falling to the pass. From Drumochter the high ground forming the southern half of the Cairngorms sweeps east unbroken for over 100km, a huge tract of land only crossed by one road. The terrain remains one of high moors eastwards across the deep trench of the Gaick Pass and the higher Minigaig Pass. More defined summits lie around Tarf Water and upper Glen Tilt, and on east to Glen Shee and the Cairnwell Pass, where the A93 cuts through the mountains. Across the pass lies one of the great Cairngorm plateaus, the White Mounth, stretching from Glas Maol east to Glen Doll and north to Lochnagar, the most significant peak in the Southern Cairngorms. Beyond these hills the land starts to fall away and becomes more moorland-like in character again until it fades slowly into foothills and farmland.

North of Lochnagar the shaft of the arrowhead, Upper Deeside, cuts deep into the hills. Upper Deeside contains the towns of Braemar and Ballater and the royal palace of Balmoral. North of Braemar is the Ben Avon/Beinn a'Bhuird plateau, with huge corries, high cliffs and granite tors. This plateau is separated from the Cairngorm Plateau to the west by the Lairig an Laoigh, one of the big passes of the Cairngorms running from Speyside to Deeside. The Cairngorm Plateau has the largest single area over 1000m in Britain, at 20km², and contains Ben Macdui, Britain's second highest mountain, as well as many other summits, big corries, spectacular Loch Avon and granite cliffs. Another deep trench separates the Cairngorm Plateau from the Braeriach and Moine Mhor plateau, this one forming the most famous Cairngorm pass, the Lairig Ghru. North of these plateaus are the great pine forests of Rothiemurchus and Glenmore, Loch Morlich, broad Strathspey and the town of Aviemore. West of the Moine Mhor lies beautiful Glen Feshie with some of the finest old pinewoods in Scotland. Beyond Glen Feshie the Cairngorms diminish and narrow, back to the moors overlooking the Pass of Drumochter.

Although the heart of the region lies far from roads and requires long walk-ins, access to the Cairngorms is good. The A9 sweeps round the western and northern edges. The Edinburgh–Inverness railway follows the same route with stations at Pitlochry, Blair Atholl, Dalwhinnie, Newtonmore, Kingussie and Aviemore, and can be used for access to long walks through the glens or over the tops. The southern Cairngorms are split by the A93, which runs over the Cairnwell Pass from Blairgowrie to Braemar and on east to Ballater and eventually Aberdeen. From Braemar a minor road runs west to Linn of Dee, giving access to the centre of the region. West of the Cairnwell Pass long dead-end roads up Glen Clova and Glen Esk lead to the southeast of the area. Along the east of the Cairngorms runs the A939 – a road famous for often being the first to close in Britain when snow falls – from Deeside over The Lecht to Tomintoul and down to Grantown-on-Spey in Strathspey. From the A9 in the north two dead-end roads run south into the hills down Glen More to the Cairngorm Mountain ski resort and down Glen Feshie, both giving access to the northern Cairngorms. The

towns around the edges of the mountains have all facilities. The most popular for mountaineers are Braemar and Aviemore, but those preferring quieter places could well consider Grantown-on-Spey, Kingussie, Newtonmore or Blair Atholl as a base.

4:1 EAST DRUMOCHTER, THE GAICK AND MINIGAIG

A big, undulating, steep-sided moorland plateau stretches northeast for some 14km from the Pass of Drumochter to Loch an t-Seilich. The highest points on this grassy and boggy plateau are the two Munros of A'Bhuidheanach Bheag ('little yellow place', 936m) and Carn na Caim ('cairn of the curve', 941m), but these are no more than gentle rises and can be hard to find in mist. North of these is a much more defined steep-sided circular Munro, Meall Chuaich ('hill of the cup', 951m), and to the east an even steeper Corbett, An Dun ('the fort', 827m), above Loch an Duin and the Gaick Pass. An Dun is matched by an equally steep Corbett on the other side of the pass, A'Chaoirnich ('the rowan hill', 875m). The Gaick Pass is a deep trench (the name means 'cleft') between the Edendon Water glen, which runs north from Dalnacardoch on the A9 in Glen Garry, and Glen Tromie, which runs north to Strathspey near Kingussie. The long heart of the pass is narrow and steep-sided and contains three lochs – Loch an Dun, Loch Bhrodain and Loch an t-Seilich. East of A'Chaoirnich a much higher route crosses the hills, the Minigaig, running from Calvine or Blair Atholl in Glen Garry to Tromie Bridge in Strathspey. The high point of the Minigaig (835m) is less than 2km from the summit of a Corbett, Leathad an Taobhain ('slope of the rafters', 912m). Also accessible from the southern Minigaig route are a Munro, Beinn Dearg ('red hill', 1008m) and a Corbett, Beinn Bhreac ('speckled hill', 912m). Both the Gaick and Minigaig passes have been used for centuries, the latter appearing on maps as early as 1689.

⊗ A'Bhuidheanach Bheag and Carn na Caim
Both these hills can be climbed in one walk from the A9. An old quarry track, a nasty scar on the landscape, climbs almost to 900m from the A9 near the snow gates south of Dalwhinnie (NN 639 821), giving the easiest access to the two summits. The going can be hard on the tussocky ground and

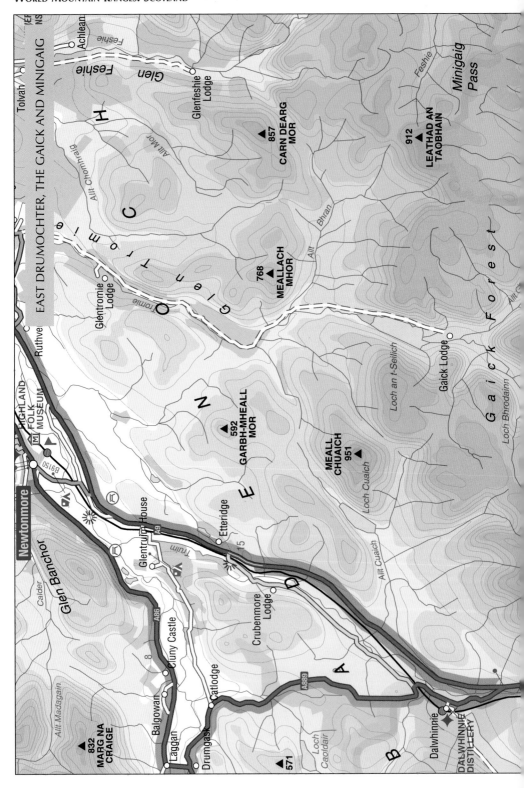

EAST DRUMOCHTER, THE GAICK AND MINIGAIG

Tolvah

Achlean

Feshie

Glen Feshie

Glenfeshie Lodge

Allt Mor

Allt Chomhraig

857
CARN DEARG
MOR

912
LEATHAD AN
TAOBHAIN

Minigaig
Pass

Allt Bhran

768
MEALLACH
MHOR

Glen Tromie

Glentromie Lodge

Tromie

Gaick Lodge

Gaick Forest

Loch an t-Seilich

Loch Bhrodainn

Ruthve

HIGHLAND
FOLK
MUSEUM

592
GARBH-MHEALL
MOR

MEALL
CHUAICH
951

Loch Cuaich

Newtonmore

B9150

Glentruim House

Etteridge

Truim

A9

15

Allt Cuaich

Glen Banchor

Calder

Allt Madagain

Crubenmore
Lodge

Cluny Castle

8

A86

Catlodge

Drumgask

Balgowan

Laggan

A889

Loch
Caoldair

571

832
MARG NA
CRAIGE

Dalwhinnie

DALWHINNIE
DISTILLERY

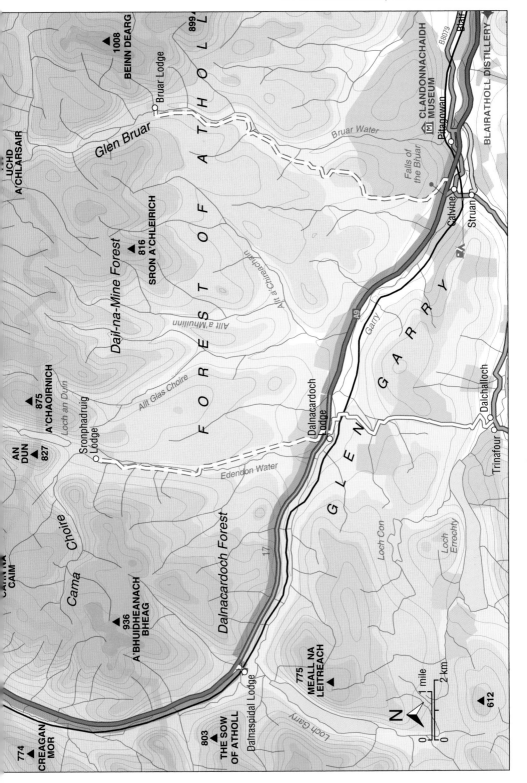

243

it's best to follow the watershed rather than take a direct line between the two hills, due to the loss of height and the boggy ground in between. Compass bearings may be needed even on a clear day. In mist the navigation can be challenging. The walking can't be described as exciting but there are extensive views from the summits. Even so this is probably a walk that will only appeal to Munro baggers. The distance is 18km, with 865m of ascent, and the walk takes 5–6hrs.

⬆ East Drumochter Ski Tours ☆

Under snow the East Drumochter hills are transformed. The grassy plateau only needs a thin covering to be skied and the undulating terrain makes for fast progress on Nordic skis. There are several interesting descent routes back down to the A9. If transport is available the range can be traversed from south to north, starting with an ascent of the southwest slopes of A'Bhuidheanach Bheag and descending west from Carn na Caim. The exact route really depends on where the snow is best. On the plateau many minor summits can be visited. In poor visibility care is needed with navigation as there are some very steep slopes both east and west in places.

⊗ Meall Chuaich

The big solitary dome of Meall Chuaich is visible from many places in Strathspey. Its isolated position makes it a good viewpoint for Strathspey and along Loch Ericht to Ben Alder. A hydro track leads from the A9 east of Dalwhinnie up to Loch Cuaich and a path into Coire Chuaich, which can be left for an ascent of the steep west nose, heathery at first then stony high up, to the summit. Returning the same way the distance is 14.5km, with 600m of ascent, and the walk takes 4–5hrs. Meall Chuaich can also be climbed by its northeast ridge from Bhran Cottage in Glen Tromie. The two routes can be linked to make a traverse of the hill from the railway stations at Kingussie and Dalwhinnie. The distance between the two stations over Meall Chuaich is 30km and the walk takes 8–10hrs.

⚐ The Gaick Pass

The route through the Gaick Pass is a fine long trip, which can be done by bicycle as there are estate tracks for all but the central 5km. In the south the track climbs slowly beside Edendon Water through bleak and featureless moorland past Stronphadruig Lodge to the hulking hills around Loch an Duin. Here in the narrow heart of the pass the steep slopes

Allt Loch an Duin, Gaick Pass

loom over you, and the place can feel oppressive and unfriendly on dull days. The loch fills the glen floor, barely leaving room for the path along its western shore. The steep slopes move back a little as a gentle descent leads past Loch Bhrodain to Gaick Lodge and Loch an t-Seilich. The view back south from Gaick Lodge is excellent, with big bare hills rising steeply from the narrow glen.

These slopes are avalanche-prone in winter and were the scene of one of the earliest recorded avalanche disasters, known as the 'Loss of Gaick'. Early in January 1800 a party of five deer hunters set out for a bothy near Loch an t-Seilich. The next day a huge blizzard raged. When the hunters didn't return a search party went out, only to find the bothy completely destroyed under masses of snow. All the men were dead but some of the bodies weren't found until the snow melted. This is still the only Scottish avalanche incident in which a habitation was destroyed. At the time supernatural forces were believed to have caused the men's death, the Gaick already having a supernatural reputation and popularly believed to be the abode of the Witch of Gaick and a spirit called the Leannan Sith, or 'Fairy Sweetheart'.

Beyond Loch an t-Seilich the terrain eases and the track soon starts to descend into wooded Glen Tromie. The total distance is 32km with 700m of ascent, and takes 8–10hrs.

⊗ An Dun and A'Chaoirnich

This pair of flat-topped Corbetts can be climbed from the Gaick Pass. There are no gentle ways up, the slopes being unrelentingly steep on all sides. Each hill can be ascended from either end and traversed. The circuit of both from Loch an Duin is 7.5km long with 765m of ascent and takes around 3hrs. From the summits there are views east across the flat plateau of the southern Cairngorms.

◗ ⊗ The Minigaig Pass and Leathad an Taobhain

The Minigaig crosses remote and little-visited high and wild country, and takes you far from roads and habitations. The railway is useful for getting back to the start, via the stations at Blair Atholl and Kingussie. From Blair Atholl a track leads across open moorland beside the Allt an t-Seapail to the Allt Scheicheachan, where there is a small bothy, and into Glen Bruar. Steep slopes abut upper Glen Bruar, at the head of which the path climbs up a broad shoulder and across the Caochan Lub burn to the summit of the pass at 835m, from where it's a short walk over grassy tussocks to the top of Leathad an Taobhain. From the pass the path drops down the northwestern slopes of Leathad an Taobhain to the Allt Bhran and Glen Tromie, and a walk out to Tromie Bridge and Kingussie. An alternative is to descend north from Leathad an Taobhain to a track that leads down into Glen Feshie. From Blair Atholl to Kingussie over the Minigaig, including the ascent of Leathad an Taobhain, is a distance of 48km, with 1360m of ascent, which makes for a long day, 11hrs or more for most people. However there are many excellent campsites along the route and this makes a fine two day backpacking trip.

⊗ Beinn Dearg

Beinn Dearg is a granite hill with a distinctive outline rising above Glen Bruar in the middle of an area of featureless peat moorland. Beinn Dearg is quite remote and requires a long walk-in. From the Sheicheachan bothy on the Minigaig Pass walk, described above, a path leads up beside the Allt Sheicheachan and then up the south ridge to the stony summit surrounded by the reddish scree slopes that give the hill its name. The track to the bothy can be cycled, although it is steep and rough. An alternative route from Blair Atholl takes the track beside the Allt Slanaidh and then over Beinn a'Chait to the summit. Using the two routes to make a circuit the distance is 28km, with 1270m of ascent, a long walk that takes 8–10hrs. Beinn Dearg can easily be included in a crossing of the Minigaig Pass with an ascent from Glen Bruar. Beinn Dearg is also part of the Ring of Tarff (see below).

⊗ Beinn Bhreac

Beinn Bhreac lies 4.5km north of Beinn Dearg, on the far side of Tarff Water. It's one of the most remote Corbetts, as well as being the third highest, so not far off Munro status. That doesn't make it interesting or exciting, however: it's a big, rounded, featureless hill that doesn't really justify the long approaches needed. It's better to combine it with other hills such as Beinn Dearg, and it fits well into multi-day cross country routes such as the Minigaig Pass. It can also easily be included in the Ring of Tarff (see below), where it lies on the route between Carn an Fhidhleir and Beinn Dearg. Beinn Bhreac can be climbed from Glen Bruar on the Minigaig route, starting up the path beside the Allt Beinn Losgarnaich and then crossing some rough boggy terrain to its southwest slopes. It's easiest to return the same way, in which case it's a 13.5km walk, with 600m of ascent from Glen Bruar.

4:2 GLEN TILT

Beautiful Glen Tilt is one of the major glens in the Cairngorms, running deep into the hills from Blair Atholl. The upper glen is an amazingly straight, U-shaped glacial trench running 10km northeast without wavering. Lime-rich rocks mean that the scenery is greener and lusher than elsewhere in the Cairngorms. Glen Tilt is geologically important as it was in the bed of the River Tilt that in 1785 James Hutton, the founder of the science of geology, found evidence that granite was injected as molten magma into older rocks from below. Glen Tilt is also important in the history of the struggle for access to the hills. In 1847 the Duke of Atholl tried to close the glen to the public, and barred the route to a Professor John Balfour and a party of botanists. The ensuing court case confirmed the right of way up the glen.

Glen Tilt is walled with steep slopes. Those to the southeast rise to Beinn a'Ghlo ('hill of mist'), a big, complex hill with four summits. Three of these are Munros – Carn Liath ('grey hill', 975m), Braigh Coire Chruinn-bhalgain ('height of the corrie of round blisters', 1070m) and Carn nan Gabhar ('hill of goats', 1121m). On the other side of Glen Tilt rises the thin, steep wedge of Beinn Mheadhonach ('middle hill', 901m), a Corbett, and the tiny pointed summit of Carn a'Chlamain ('hill of the kite', 963m), a Munro.

A major tributary flows east into Glen Tilt, Tarff Water. This lonely moorland stream runs through an area of remote hills. To its north rise two Munros, An Sgarsoch ('place of sharp rocks', 1006m) and Carn an Fhidhleir ('hill of the fiddler', 994m), which test the resolve of Munro baggers.

Blair Atholl is the base for the Glen Tilt hills. This attractive little village, where the River Tilt meets the River Garry, has accommodation – including campsites – as well as cafés and bars, grocery shops and a railway station. The Blair Atholl Water Mill, with its working water wheel,

View southwest down Glen Tilt from above the Falls of Tarf

Braigh Coire Chruinn-bhalgain and Carn nan Gabhar on Beinn a'Ghlo

is interesting and has a nice tea room. The Atholl Country Life Museum is worth a look too. The big visitor attraction is Blair Castle, however, an imposing white building that stands out in views from the west. The tour of the castle, the oldest part of which dates back to 1269, and the grounds, where there are some magnificent trees, is a good option for stormy days.

Glen Tilt to Linn of Dee ☆

The walk up Glen Tilt and over to Deeside is one of the great glen walks in Scotland, taking the walker from the rich woodlands around Blair Atholl, through the impressive upper glen, then over bleak moorlands, with a splendid view of the northern Cairngorms, to the River Dee. The first section, from Blair Atholl to Marble Lodge, is soft and gentle with many trees, including some lovely birches. Then comes the long dramatic upper glen, up which an estate road runs for most of the way, with the River Tilt rippling down over big boulders below unremittingly steep hillsides. Finally the glen curves to the left and Tarff Water is reached. The attractive bridge over the Tarff is called the Bedford Bridge, and was erected in 1886 in memory of a young Englishman who drowned trying to ford the Tilt here in 1879. Just upstream the charming Falls of Tarff can be seen.

The River Tilt begins here at the confluence of Tarff Water and the Allt Garbh Buidhe, beside which the path up Glen Tilt continues out onto open moorland that seems remarkably spacious after the confines of the glen. The watershed is reached at 490m, then the path starts a long, slow descent beside the Allt an t-Seilich to a track beside the Geldie Burn that leads to the Dee at White Bridge, where it turns eastwards to the end of the public road from Braemar at Linn of Dee. The only potential hazard on this walk is the crossing of the Geldie Burn, where there's no bridge and which can be difficult when in spate. The distance is 35km, with 800m of ascent, and could be walked in 9–10hrs. There are many superb campsites along the route, however, and it makes a good two day backpacking trip that could be extended by continuing north through the Lairig Ghru or Lairig an Laoigh or west then north up Glen Feshie.

Beinn a'Ghlo ☆

Beinn a'Ghlo is the finest hill in the southern Cairngorms – apart, arguably, from Lochnagar – and the round of its summits is an excellent high-level walk in splendid scenery with grand views. The mountain forms a broad snaking ridge, cut into by many big corries, which runs for 10km above the southeast side of Glen Tilt. It looks fine

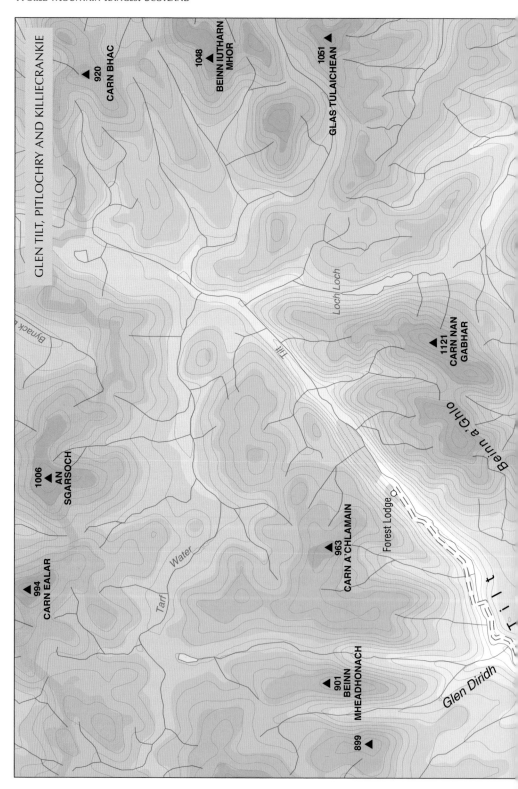

GLEN TILT, PITLOCHRY AND KILLIECRANKIE

CARN BHAC
920

BEINN IUTHARN
MHOR
1048

GLAS TULAICHEAN
1051

Byrack b

Loch Loch

Tilt

CARN NAN
GABHAR
1121

Beinn a 'Ghlo

AN
SGARSOCH
1006

CARN EALAR
994

Water

Tarf

Forest Lodge

CARN A'CHLAMAIN
963

Tilt

BEINN
MHEADHONACH
901

Glen Diridh

899

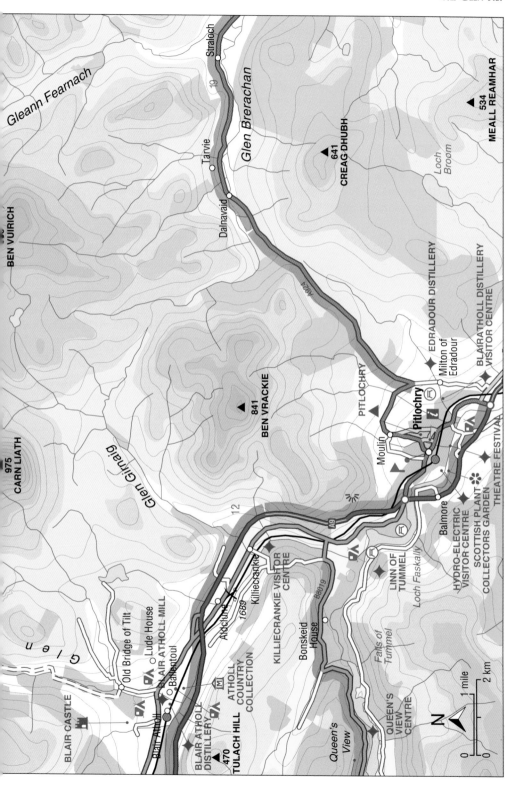

Gleann Fearnach

Straloch

19

Tarvie

Glen Brerachan

Dalnavaid

CREAG DHUBH
641

534
MEALL REAMHAR

Loch Broom

BEN VUIRICH

A924

EDRADOUR DISTILLERY

BLAIR ATHOLL DISTILLERY VISITOR CENTRE

Milton of Edradour

PITLOCHRY

Pitlochry

BEN VRACKIE
841

Moulin

975
CARN LIATH

Glen Girnaig

THEATRE FESTIVAL

SCOTTISH PLANT COLLECTORS GARDEN

12

A9

Balmore

HYDRO-ELECTRIC VISITOR CENTRE

LINN OF TUMMEL

Loch Faskally

Killiecrankie

KILLIECRANKIE VISITOR CENTRE

Aldclune

1689

Bonskeid House

B8019

Old Bridge of Tilt

Lude House

BLAIR ATHOLL MILL

Ballentoul

ATHOLL COUNTRY COLLECTION

Falls of Tummel

Glen

BLAIR CASTLE

Blair Atholl

BLAIR ATHOLL DISTILLERY

TULACH HILL
470

Queen's View

QUEEN'S VIEW CENTRE

N

0   1 mile
0   2 km

from the northern Cairngorms and is also prominent in views from the southwest, the western end of the hill being a landmark on the journey north on the A9 or the Inverness railway line, the first of the big mountains. The great Cairngorms expert Adam Watson, in his *The Cairngorms* (SMC, 6th edition 1992), reckons Beinn a'Ghlo 'one of the most beautiful and mysterious hills of Scotland'. Unsurprisingly for such a visible hill it had an early recorded ascent. General William Roy, who had carried out a survey of Scotland from 1747–1755 in the aftermath of the '45 Jacobite Rebellion led parties making barometrical observations of the heights of the mountains from 1771–1776. One of these parties climbed Beinn a'Ghlo in 1776.

The standard ascent route up Beinn a'Ghlo begins at Loch Moraig northeast of Blair Atholl (NN 905 670). A track leads towards the base of the southernmost summit, Carn Liath, up whose southwest slopes runs a wide, ugly, eroded path. This scar is visible from many miles away. It's not a made path but one that has come into being due to the passage of thousands of pairs of boots. A properly constructed path would climb the hill in zigzags, rather than go straight up. Until such a path is constructed further widening of the current route can be avoided by sticking to the scar and not breaking down its edges. The summit dome of Carn Liath is scattered with grey scree slopes, hence the name.

The lovely walk from Carn Liath over Braigh Coire Chruinn-bhalgain to Carn nan Gabhar is hillwalking at its finest. The terrain is easy, the ridges narrow but not exposed and the views superb, especially down into Glen Tilt. There are big drops between the summits and it's over 6km from Carn Liath to Carn nan Gabhar. From the latter you can descend southwest over the fourth Beinn a'Ghlo summit, stony Airgiod Bheinn ('silver mountain', 1061m), and down to the rough moorland below, which can be traversed southeastwards to the track back to Loch Moraig. The distance is 21km, with 1350m of ascent, and the walk takes 7–8hrs.

⊙ Skiing Beinn a'Ghlo ☆

The traverse of the Beinn a'Ghlo summits on skis is a superb trip. A highlight is the run down from Carn Liath to the col below Braigh Coire Chruinn-bhalgain. The best descent is to reverse the route. If this seems too arduous or the weather is closing in then there's a good more sheltered descent from the col between Braigh Coire Chruinn-bhalgain to

the Allt Coire Lagain. This is a serious tour, with the final summit a long way from the start, and good skiing skills are essential.

⊗ Carn a'Chlamain

Carn a'Chlamain is a distinctive pointed summit sitting on the edge of a large expanse of featureless moorland. It's situated at the head of a deep side glen on the northwest side of Glen Tilt. A fine stalkers' path climbs virtually the whole way to the summit from just beyond Forest Lodge, which lies 11.5km up Glen Tilt on a track that can be cycled. This path zigzags up the steep slopes above the glen to the moorland above, where it heads northwest past the stony summit of Carn a'Chlamain. From Forest Lodge it's an 8km round trip, with 690m of ascent.

Carn a'Chlamain has a place in the history of hillwalking, as the first recorded ascent was made by a party including Queen Victoria in 1844, although it had undoubtedly been climbed by local people before this.

⊗ Beinn Mheadhonach

Beinn Mheadhonach rises as a pointed peak between two deep steep-sided glens when seen from the south. In fact it's a long ridge of a hill when seen from the east or west. A path from Glen Tilt leads to the base of the long south ridge, up which an ascent can be made. The round trip from Blair Atholl is 21km long, with 750m of ascent, and takes around 6hrs.

⊗ An Sgarscoch and Carn an Fhidhleir

These two moorland hills lie on the boggy watershed between the River Feshie, which runs into the River Spey, the Geldie Burn, which runs into the River Dee, and Tarff Water, which runs into the River Garry, in the centre of a wild and remote area. A bulldozed road approaches them from the north however, making the ascent easier than it might appear, although distances are still long. From Linn of Dee it's 12.5km along this track to the ruins of Geldie Lodge. There's only 226m of ascent and the track can be cycled, although it is rough in places. From Geldie Lodge it's a 15km round trip over both summits, with 860m of ascent. A path leads east towards Carn an Fhidhleir, which can be climbed by its north ridge. Follow the southeast ridge down to the col with An Sgarscoch, then the west ridge of the latter to the summit, from where the northern slopes can be descended back to Geldie Lodge. Away from paths the going is tough, with peat bogs, tussocks and deep heather to be tackled except on the summits, which are smoother and covered with grass, moss and stones. There are good views across the Feshie and the Geldie to the northern Cairngorms. In previous centuries the grassy summit of An Sgarscoch was the site of a horse and cattle market. Ian R. Mitchell, in *Scotland's Mountains Before the Mountaineers* (Luath, 1999), suspects that the remote location may have been chosen for dealing in contraband goods and writes 'so we can award multiple repeat ascents of An Sgarscoch to tinkers, cattle thieves, rustlers and the odd honest merchant'.

⊗ The Ring of Tarff

Four Munros lie either side of Tarff Water, An Sgarscoch and Carn an Fhidhleir to the north and Beinn Dearg and Carn a'Chlamain to the south. The circuit of these hills is a tough, challenging walk known as the Ring of Tarff. It's a long day out in remote country, with much boggy and rough terrain, and is best done from a camp in upper Glen Tilt or beside Tarff Water. There's a bothy beside the Tarff, known as the Tarff Hotel, that could be used as a base too. Two Corbetts, Beinn Bhreac and Beinn Mheadhonach, can be included in the round.

Tarff Water can be reached by an ugly bulldozed road from upper Glen Tilt that climbs over a pass between the minor tops of Dun Mor and An Sligearnach. It's 20km from Blair Atholl to the end of this track by Tarff Water. The Ring of Tarff then involves 37km in distance and 2000m of ascent – and that's just for the Munros. The two Corbetts add 3km and 300m of ascent, and 10–12hrs is a good time.

4:3 PITLOCHRY AND KILLIECRANKIE

Pitlochry is an attractive if busy tourist town situated on the southern edge of the Highlands. It's been a tourist destination since Victorian times, and the arrival of the railway in 1863 made it easily accessible from the south. Pitlochry has all facilities and several visitor attractions including the Festival Theatre, two distilleries with visitor centres (Edradour and Blair Atholl) and a Hydroelectricity visitor centre. At the latter there's a 'fish ladder' beside the dam on the River Tummel up which salmon can be seen leaping from May to October.

Between Pitlochry and Blair Atholl lies the beautiful wooded Pass of Killiecrankie. The National Trust for Scotland (NTS) owns the heart of the pass where the River Garry narrows and rushes through a gorge. This was, in 1689, the site of the Battle of Killiecrankie, at which the Jacobite army defeated government forces. There's an interesting National Trust for Scotland visitor centre here, from which paths lead down to the gorge then along the river side below the arched stone viaduct carrying the railway line with above it the concrete stilts bearing the A9 road.

Rising above Pitlochry and the Pass of Killiecrankie is lovely Ben Vrackie ('speckled hill'), an 841m Corbett, that stands out in views from Pitlochry. Much further into the hills and hidden from most views is another Corbett, Ben Vuirich ('hill of roaring', 903m).

⊗ Ben Vrackie ☆

Ben Vrackie is a rugged, craggy hill with superb views from the summit down Strath Tay, west to Schiehallion and north to Beinn a'Ghlo. A good path leads to the top from Moulin in Pitlochry, passing Loch a'Choire en route. There is also a path from the NTS Visitor Centre in the Pass of Killiecrankie. The traverse of the hill using these two paths is excellent. The path beside the River Garry can be used to link the two. The round trip from Pitlochry is 16km long, with 995m of ascent, and takes 5–6hrs.

⊗ Ben Vuirich

Ben Vuirich has superb views of Beinn a'Ghlo, as it lies opposite this hill. It can be climbed from the same start point, at Loch Moraig, as its bigger neighbour, using the same track across the slopes of Carn Liath. Stay with the track past Beinn a'Ghlo then turn up the path above the Allt Coire Lagain to a col beyond which an estate track leads down to Glen Loch. Climb the steep northwestern slopes of Ben Vuirich from this track. An alternative, less steep route runs from the old farm at Shinagag to the southwest of the summit. This route crosses some rough, boggy terrain, however. Going up one way and down the other the round trip is 22km long, with 900m of ascent, and takes 5–6hrs.

Camping beside Loch nan Eun

4:4 GLEN SHEE
AND THE CAIRNWELL PASS

Glen Shee ('fairy glen') is a long glen running north from Bridge of Cally to the Cairnwell Pass, beyond which Glen Clunie runs down to Braemar and Deeside. The A93 runs up Glen Shee, giving good access to the hills either side. And there are plenty of hills, with eight Munros and a Corbett to the west and six Munros and two Corbetts to the east. The Cairnwell Pass at 670m reduces the ascent needed to climb many of these hills. However the ski resort here mars the landscape.

Some 8km west of the Cairnwell Pass lies a compact group of four Munros – Glas Tulaichean ('green hill', 1051m), Carn an Righ ('hill of the king', 1029m), Beinn Iutharn Mhor ('big sharp-edged hill', 1045m), and An Socach ('the snout', 944m). This is complex country, with twisting glens and ridges closely packed together, making for interesting navigation. Lovely little Loch nan Eun lies in the heart of these hills, at the head of long Gleann Taitneach. Carn Bhac ('hill of peat banks', 946 m), an isolated Munro, is 3km north of these hills.

Two Munros – The Cairnwell ('hill of bags', 933m) and Carn Aosda ('hill of age, 917m) – rise above the pass and are now part of the ski resort. Just to their west lies the Munro Carn a'Gheoidh ('hill of the goose', 975m).

East of the Cairnwell Pass a long broad line of hills runs northwards containing four Munros – Creag Leacach ('slabby rock', 987m), Glas Maol ('grey-green hill', 1068m), Cairn of Claise ('hill of the hollow', 1064m) and Carn an Tuirc ('hill of the boar', 1019m). To the east of Glas Maol is impressive crag-rimmed Caenlochan Glen at the head of Glen Isla. East of Cairn of Claise two bumps are also classified as Munros – Tolmount ('hollow mountain', 958m) and Tom Buidhe ('yellow hill', 957m). These hills form the western edge of the huge Mounth plateau, which stretches east to Driesh above Glen Doll and north to Lochnagar above Deeside. There are 13 Munros and three Corbetts on this plateau, all of which can be climbed in a couple of days from a high camp. It's also superb ski touring country.

The three Corbetts in the area are Ben Gulabin ('hill of the curlew', 806m), which rises steeply above the Spittal of Glenshee, Monamenach ('middle hill', 807m), on a ridge between Glen Shee and Glen Isla south of Creag Leacach, and Creag nan Gabhar ('goat crag', 834m) above Glen Clunie, north of Carn an Tuirc.

The main town for the area, with all facilities, is Braemar to the north. There is a café at the ski resort and a hotel with bunkhouse and restaurant at the Spittal of Glenshee.

THE GLENSHEE SKI CENTRE

The Glenshee Ski Centre lies just north of the Cairnwell Pass at the head of Glen Clunie. The area taken over by downhill skiing is large with 21 lifts and 36 runs. Lifts run to the summit of Carn Aosda and close to the summit of The Cairnwell west of the pass and high up on Glas Maol east of the pass. The lifts and bulldozed roads remove any wild feel from the area and are ugly and depressing, especially when there is no snow, which is most of the time.

⊗ The Loch nan Eun Munros

The three Munros around Loch nan Eun, along with An Socach and Carn Bhac, can be climbed together, as they are linked by high cols. There are several possible approaches to these hills. From Spittal of Glenshee it's 9.5km up Gleann Taitneach to Loch nan Eun, at 790m, and the same distance from the A93 in Glen Clunie up the Baddoch Burn to the loch. Bulldozed tracks run most of the way up these glens. There's also a hideous bulldozed track up the south ridge of Glas Tulaichean that reaches almost to the summit. The bulldozed roads in the glens are deplorable, but this disgraceful act of vandalism, which can be seen from miles away, should be condemned by any true lover of wild places. It's another 9.5km from Spittal of Glenshee to Glas Tulaichean by this track. With a 19km round trip just to reach these hills, an overnight camp makes sense. There are many possible sites. Just note that a colony of very noisy gulls nests on an island in Loch nan Eun, and they start shrieking at the first hint of dawn.

Going clockwise from Loch nan Eun, Glas Tulaichean can be climbed by its north ridge. This is the most shapely of these hills, with curving ridges and two fine, deep corries on its east side – Glas Choire Bheag and Glas Choire Mhor. The hill lives up to its name ('green hill'), with soft green turf that makes for delightful walking. The next hill, Carn an Righ, is more rounded and has scree on

its flanks. To reach it descend back down the north ridge of Glas Tulaichean and then cut northwest to a path that runs across the lower slopes of Mam nan Carn to a col below Carn an Righ, from which the latter can be easily climbed. Return to the col, then traverse northeast round Mam nan Carn to a col with Beinn Iutharn Mhor, and ascend the southern slopes of the latter. From Beinn Iutharn Mhor head north across featureless boggy terrain to the stony summit of Carn Bhac then turn southwest for more boggy walking to the long summit ridge of An Socach. The total round from Loch nan Eun is about 26km long, with 1700m of ascent, and takes 8–10hrs.

If climbing the hills separately, Gleann Taitneach or the south ridge of Glas Tulaichean are the best routes for that hill, and Carn an Righ, and Glen Ey running south from Inverey on Deeside, for Carn Bhac, Beinn Iutharn Mhor and An Socach. The latter can also be climbed from the ski resort.

⊗ The Cairnwell Munros

The Cairnwell and Carn Aosda are the easiest to climb of all the Munros. They're also the most disfigured and despoiled, due to the ski resort on their slopes. The Cairnwell is further insulted by two big radio masts on its summit. It does have a good view down Glen Shee to the Lowlands. Carn a'Gheoidh is out of sight of the devastation, and a much pleasanter hill. The two ski-scarred hills can be quickly climbed from the col between them, west of the ski resort. Once this chore is done, the ridge running southwest and then west from the col leads to Carn a'Gheoidh. The round trip over all three summits is 13.5km long, with 745m of ascent, and takes 4–5hrs.

⊗ Ben Gulabin

Ben Gulabin rises as a massive hump above the Spittal of Glenshee, from which it can be climbed by its steep southern ridge, an arduous route. It's easier to take the path 1km further up the A93 (NO 114 714), which runs to a col from where the less steep northern slopes can be climbed. For a hill that looks so steep and pointed the summit is surprisingly flat. It's a superb viewpoint, especially if you walk round the edge. The road in Glen Shee far below looks small and insignificant as it winds its way up to the Cairnwell Pass below the slopes of Creag Leacach and Glas Maol. To the northwest Glas Tulaichean, with its big eastern corrie, looks

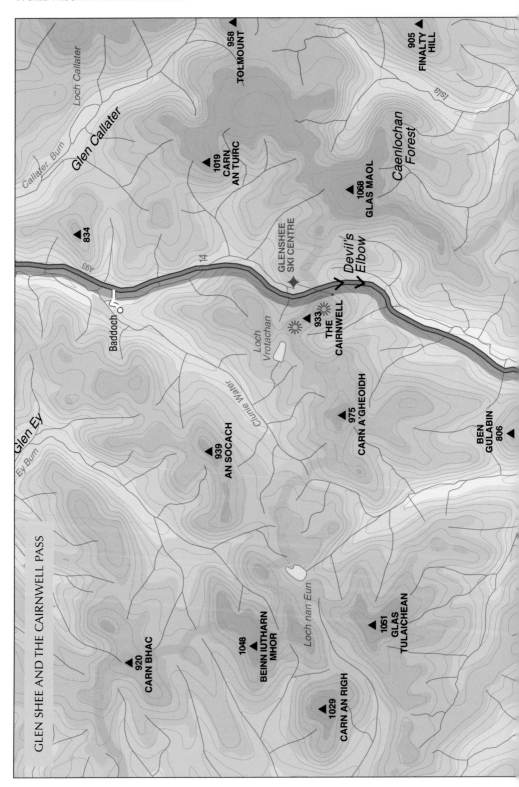

GLEN SHEE AND THE CAIRNWELL PASS

TOLMOUNT 958

FINALTY HILL 905

CARN AN TUIRC 1019

GLAS MAOL 1068

Caenlochan Forest

Loch Callater

Glen Callater

Callater Burn

A93

14

834

GLENSHEE SKI CENTRE

Devil's Elbow

Baddoch

THE CAIRNWELL 933

Loch Vrotachan

Clunie Water

Isla

CARN A'GHEOIDH 975

BEN GULABIN 806

Glen Ey

Ey Burn

AN SOCACH 939

Loch nan Eun

GLAS TULAICHEAN 1051

CARN BHAC 920

BEINN IUTHARN MHOR 1048

CARN AN RIGH 1029

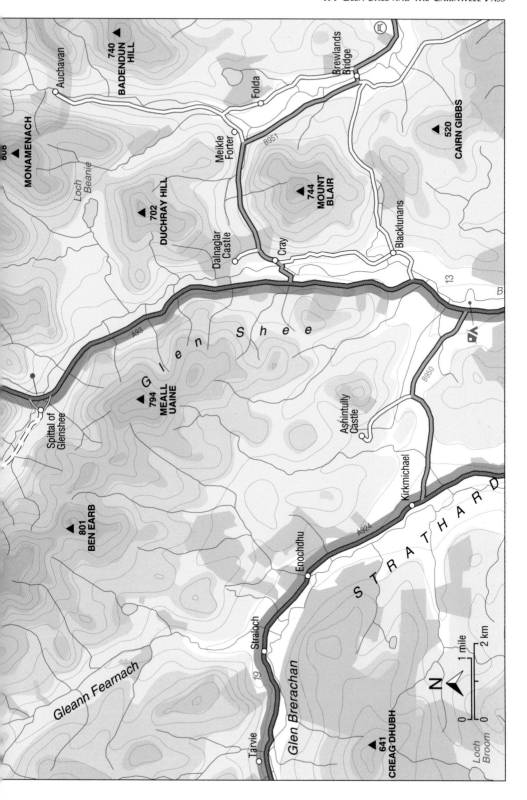

Auchavan

740
BADENDUN HILL ▲

Brewlands Bridge

Folda

808
MONAMENACH ▲

Loch Beanie

Meikle Forter

B951

520
CAIRN GIBBS ▲

702
DUCHRAY HILL ▲

744
MOUNT BLAIR ▲

Blacklunans

Dalnaglar Castle

Cray

13
B

A93

G l e n   S h e e

794
MEALL UAINE ▲

Ashintully Castle

B950

Spittal of Glenshee

801
BEN EARB ▲

Kirkmichael

S T R A T H A R D

Enochdhu

A924

Gleann Fearnach

Straloch

19

Glen Brerachan

Tarvie

641
CREAG DHUBH ▲

Loch Broom

N

0   1 mile
0   2 km

impressive. The return trip is only 5.75km long, with 450m of ascent, and you can be up and down in 2hrs. Ben Gulabin can also be linked with Carn a'Gheoidh by the south ridge of the latter.

The Glas Maol Hills and Caenlochan Glen ☆

These hills can be climbed from the Glenshee Ski Centre, but trudging up through the tows, fences and bulldozed roads is an ignoble way to treat these fine hills. Much better is a traverse from Glen Isla, with a return to the start via the magnificent Caenlochan Glen, the most impressive feature in the area (Caenlochan means 'narrow pass of the lochan', referring to the break in the crags at the head of the glen where there is a small pool). From the end of the public road at Auchavan in upper Glen Isla (NO 191 696) a track climbs west to the southeastern slopes of heathery Monamenach. To the north Craig Leachach and Glas Maol rise, big, bulky and imposing. To reach the first, head northwest over undulating heather moorland to the southwest ridge. The summit is a long quartzite crest that stands out in this area of otherwise grassy, rounded hills. Once the rocks and scree of Creag Leachach are left behind grass predominates, and the climb to the big dome of Glas Maol is easy. Continue north to the col with Carn of Claise, from where a steep descent can be made past the small lochan into wild Caenlochan Glen, or else follow the northern edge of the glen eastwards over Druim Mor to a path that zigzags down into the glen from Caderg. A track leads down Caenlochan Glen to Auchavan. The distance is 23km, with 1230m of ascent, and the walk takes 6–8hrs.

Carn an Tuirc, Cairn of Claise, Tolmount and Tom Buidhe

These four Munros can be climbed together from Glen Clunie to the west or, with more effort, from Glen Callater to the north. From the old bridge over the Cairnwell Burn in Glen Clunie (NO 144 806) a path heads up beside the Allt a'Gharbh-choire, past a little waterfall to the northern slopes of Carn an Tuirc. From the summit of Carn an Tuirc the walking over all the summits is gentle and easy, although navigation can be difficult in mist. Head southeast then south to reach Cairn of Claise, and then northeast to Tolmount, a little summit on the edge of big crags leading down into Glen Callater, from where it looks impressive. Turn south round the head of a stream gully to reach the gentle rise

of Tom Buidhe. Heading back west and skirting Cairn of Claise brings you to a path that descends the Sron na Gaoithe spur and on down to the start. The circuit is 21km long, with 975m of ascent, and takes 6–7hrs.

Ski Touring on the Glas Maol Hills ☆

Once up on the Mounth plateau the ski touring opportunities are great. In good conditions huge distances can be quickly covered. One excellent tour includes five Munros – Glas Maol, Cairn of Claise, Tom Buidhe, Tolmount and Carn an Tuirc. From the Cairnwell Pass ski up through the resort to Glas Maol, then north to Cairn of Claise. Easy skiing now leads east to Tom Buidhe, north to Tolmount and west back to Carn an Tuirc. The exact route can be determined by the state of the snow and how much ascent and descent you want to do. From Carn an Tuirc there is an excellent ski descent down the gully north of the summit to the Allt Garbh Choire, reaching the A93 2km north of the Ski Centre. The tour is roughly 21km long, with 1100m of ascent, and takes 6–7hrs.

Creag nan Gabhar

This little Corbett gives fine views and can be climbed from Auchallater at the mouth of Glen Callater. About 1km up the track in the glen a path climbs steeply west up to Sron Dubh, from where a long ridge runs south to Creag nan Gabhar. Descend southeast to join a track leading into Glen Callater and back to the start. The distance is 13km, with 555m of ascent, and the walk takes 4–5hrs. A much quicker but much less satisfying ascent can be made up the southwest ridge from Glen Clunie, a round trip of just over 3km, with 420m of ascent, which can be done in under 2hrs.

4:5 THE ANGUS GLENS: GLEN CLOVA, GLEN DOLL AND GLEN ESK

The Angus Glens push up into the hills from the Lowlands to the southeast. Glen Clova, a long, U-shaped glacial trench, is a beautiful glen with the meandering River South Esk running down its flat floor among woods and meadows, with steep, rugged hillsides rising either side. At the head of Glen Clova lies Glen Doll, which is walled by impressive cliff-rimmed corries but unfortunately floored by dense conifer plantations. Glen Doll pushes west into the great Mounth plateau, and has big hills on either side. To the south lie a pair of Munros, Driesh ('bramble', 947m) and Mayar (possibly 'high plain', 928m) that are most easily climbed from here. From the head of Glen Doll an old track called Jock's Road crosses the hills to Glen Callater and Deeside.

North of Clova in Glen Clova, where the B955 road turns back on itself (it runs down both sides of the glen here), lie two big rocky corries containing Loch Brandy and Loch Wharral, to the south of which rises Ben Tirran (possibly 'hill of hillocks' or 'hill of lightning', 896m). The corries are high on the hillside and the lochs are invisible from the road.

Glen Esk lies further east, on the edge of the high country, but does give access to the easternmost Munro, and the easternmost Corbett, Mount Keen ('gentle hill', 939m) and Mount Battock (probably 'tufted hill', 778m), both isolated lonely hills. Glen Esk is a lovely long glen with a mix of woods and meadows backed by heather-covered hills, down which runs the River North Esk. At its head Glen Esk splits into two rock-rimmed arms, Glen Lee and Glen Mark.

There are minimal services in Glen Clova and Glen Esk. The Glen Clova Hotel in upper Glen Clova has a bunkhouse, restaurant and bar and is a good base for the Glen Doll hills. The youth hostel and campsite in Glen Doll still marked on some maps are both closed. In Glen Esk there is only the retreat, a restaurant, tea room and gift shop, roughly half way up the glen, 2km east of the little hamlet of Tarfside. The little town of Edzell lies at the foot of the glen.

⊗ Mayar and Driesh

This pair of rounded hills lies at the southeast corner of the great Mounth plateau and can easily be climbed as part of a tour of the whole plateau. If climbed alone the best start point is the end of the public road in Glen Clova at the mouth of Glen Doll. From here a track leads into the dark forest alongside the White Water, then turns up beside the Fee Burn, becomes a path and finally leaves the trees to enter the impressive rocky bowl of Corrie Fee. There are several junctions in the forest, and care needs to be taken to choose the right paths. A path runs up the corrie and climbs the steep headwall past little waterfalls. Once the plateau is reached it's an easy walk over grass south to Mayar and on east to Driesh. There are excellent views

over the Mounth plateau from the summits and east to Mount Keen and south down Glen Clova. To descend head back towards Mayar to intercept a path known as the Kilbo Path, which links Glen Doll with Glen Prosen. Follow this path northeastwards onto a steep-sided narrow spur called the Shank of Drumfollow that juts out into Glen Doll. The path cuts down across the east side of this spur above the Burn of Kilbo to the forest below, through which it descends to the White Water path not far from the start. The walk is 14km long, with 920m of ascent, and takes 4½–5½hrs.

⊕ Skiing Mayar and Driesh ☆

The plateau above Glen Doll makes for delightful ski touring. Ascent can be made by the Shank of Drumfollow from Glen Doll, although skis may have to be carried some of the way. From the top of this ridge it's easy to ski up Mayar and Driesh. From the former you can ski north over easy terrain until past the crags and steep slopes above Corrie Fee and the head of Glen Doll, perhaps all the way to Tom Buidhe if you want to bag a third Munro, or even Tolmount for a fourth. From Tom Buidhe or Tolmount descend east to the upper White Water and then southeast, to pick up the Jock's Road path which leads down into Glen Doll. The descent can be difficult in places, especially if the snow cover is thin, as there are many rocks and boulders. The distance, taking in Tom Buidhe, is 23km, with 1200km of ascent, and the trip takes 7–9hrs.

❄ Winter Corrie and Corrie Fee

The few crags in this area are too broken and vegetated to give much rock climbing, but when under snow and ice they provide some good winter climbs.

On the northeast flanks of Driesh is a big craggy corrie known as the Winter Corrie, overlooking upper Glen Clova and housing a dozen or so winter climbs, mostly in the lower grades and from 60–220m in height. The corrie can be easily reached from the glen. The 200m Diagonal Gully, which runs up the main buttress, is given two stars in climbing guides.

Corrie Fee, to the north of Mayar, high above Glen Doll, has some 10 winter routes ranging from 60–200m, again mostly in the lower grades. Being higher than Winter Corrie it comes into condition more often. Look C Gully, 200m high, was first climbed by the legendary Scottish climber Jimmy Marshall and is given three stars in climbing guides.

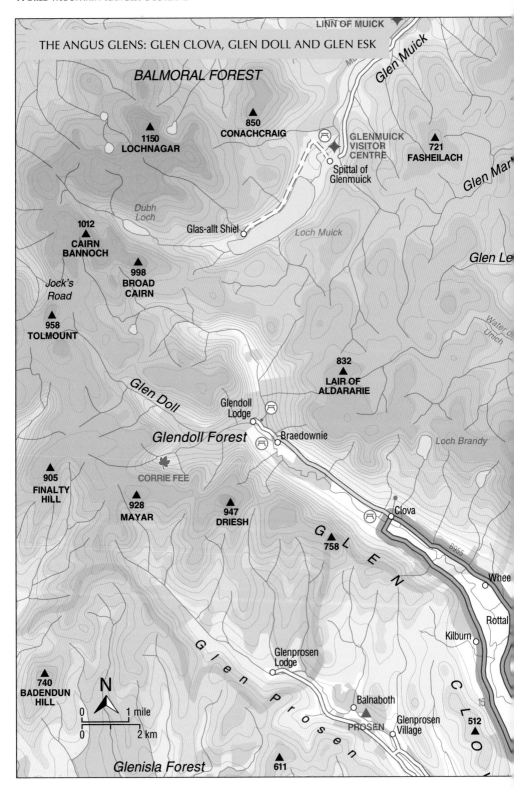

THE ANGUS GLENS: GLEN CLOVA, GLEN DOLL AND GLEN ESK

BALMORAL FOREST

Glen Muick

LINN OF MUICK

▲ 850
CONACHCRAIG

▲ 1150
LOCHNAGAR

GLENMUICK
VISITOR
CENTRE

Spittal of
Glenmuick

▲ 721
FASHEILACH

Glen Mar

*Dubh
Loch*

Glas-allt Shiel

Loch Muick

Glen Le

1012
▲
CAIRN
BANNOCH

▲ 998
BROAD
CAIRN

*Jock's
Road*

▲ 958
TOLMOUNT

*Water o
Unich*

832
▲
LAIR OF
ALDARARIE

Glen Doll

Glendoll
Lodge

Glendoll Forest

Braedownie

Loch Brandy

CORRIE FEE

▲ 905
FINALTY
HILL

▲ 928
MAYAR

▲ 947
DRIESH

Clova

G
L
E
N

B955

▲ 758

Whee

Rottal

Kilburn

N

▲ 740
BADENDUN
HILL

Glen Prosen

Glenprosen
Lodge

Balnaboth

▲
PROSEN

Glenprosen
Village

C
L
O
V

15

512
▲

0   1 mile

0   2 km

Glenisla Forest

▲ 611

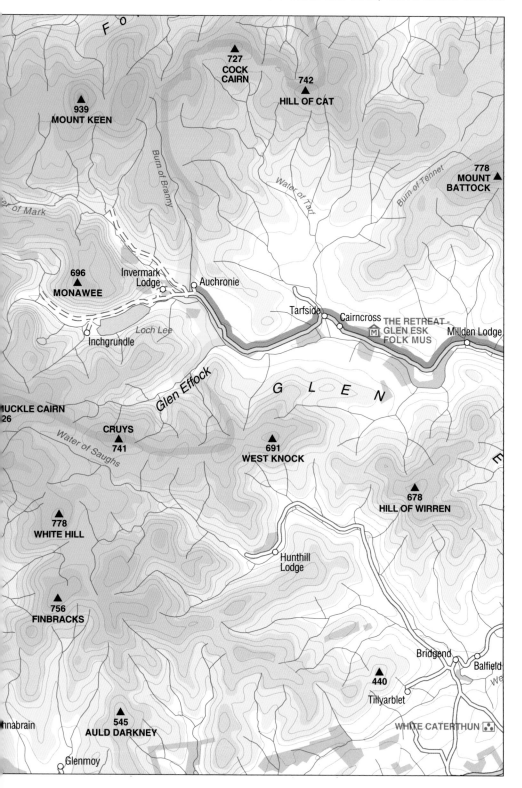

▲ 727
COCK
CAIRN

▲ 742
HILL OF CAT

▲ 939
MOUNT KEEN

778
MOUNT ▲
BATTOCK

Burn of Branny

Water of Tarf

Burn of Tennet

r of Mark

696 ▲
MONAWEE

Invermark
Lodge

Auchronie

Tarfside

Cairncross

THE RETREAT -
GLEN ESK
FOLK MUS

Millden Lodge

Inchgrundle

Loch Lee

Glen Effock

G   L   E   N

MUCKLE CAIRN
26

Water of Saughs

CRUYS
▲
741

691 ▲
WEST KNOCK

678 ▲
HILL OF WIRREN

778 ▲
WHITE HILL

Hunthill
Lodge

756 ▲
FINBRACKS

Bridgend

Balfield

We

440 ▲
Tillyarblet

hnabrain

545 ▲
AULD DARKNEY

WHITE CATERTHUN

Glenmoy

259

⊛ Ben Tirran and Loch Brandy

North of the little village of Clova a steep hillside rises to a big corrie in which is hidden Loch Brandy, a fine body of water set below broken crags and home to a colony of noisy gulls. A well-used path runs up to the southern tip of the loch, then climbs northeast to the corrie rim, and then follows this round to a nose called the Snub, down which it descends back to the loch and on back down to Clova. There are good views of Glen Clova from the corrie edge. The loop path is 8km long, with 660m of ascent, and the walk takes around 2½–3½hrs.

A longer walk climbs to Loch Brandy by the easterly of the two paths and then up to 870m Green Hill, on the corrie rim, from where a moorland walk leads west-southwest to Ben Tirran. The best view is from the lower summit 500m to the southeast, from where you can look down Glen Clova. West of the main summit a path leads down the side of the steep-walled corrie above Loch Wharral, and then down the open hillside, to reach Glen Clova and a pleasant 3km road walk to Clova. The distance is 14.5km, with 790m of ascent, and the walk takes about 5hrs.

ⓐ Jock's Road ☆

Jock's Road is a high path that crosses the Mounth from Glen Clova to Deeside via Glen Doll and Glen Callater. It traverses featureless terrain, reaches a height of 900m and is just as serious a proposition as a summit climb in the area with regard to exposure to the weather and navigation. In fact it passes very close to two Munros, Tom Buidhe and Tolmount, both of which can be easily climbed during the crossing. The name Jock's Road originally only applied to the steep section at the head of Glen Doll, where there is a small shelter called Jock's Bothy, but is now given to the whole route. The path became part of the struggle for access to the hills in the 1880s, when the owner of Glen Doll tried to close it. The Scottish Rights of Way and Recreation Society went to court and in 1888 the right of way along Jock's Road was upheld after it was shown that drovers had long used the route to take sheep from Braemar to market in the Lowlands. Jock's Road is a popular route for long distance walkers, especially those going coast to coast.

Jock's Road begins with a walk through the Glen Doll plantations to leave the trees in upper Glen Doll, a rugged corrie with steep craggy sides.

The path climbs up broken rocky slopes through breaks in the crags and onto the crossing of the high plateau. A steep descent leads into Glen Callater and an enjoyable walk down this impressive steep-sided glen to Loch Callater, and then Auchallater in Glen Clunie some 3.5km south of Braemar. The total distance is 20km, with 800m of ascent, and the crossing can be made in 6–7hrs.

⊛ Mount Keen

Mount Keen is the easternmost of the Munros, a big, domed hill lying some 16km in a straight line east of Lochnagar in the middle of an area of high peat bogs and heather moorland. To the north is Glen Tanar, to the south Glen Mark, and it can be climbed from either glen or traversed from Deeside to Glen Esk. From Invermark at the head of Glen Esk, where the public road ends, a track runs up Glen Mark to the Queen's Well, once visited by Queen Victoria. Soon after the well the track climbs beside the Ladder Burn onto the southern slopes of Mount Keen and splits, the left fork traversing the western slopes of the hill, the right climbing to the granite boulders of the summit, from where there is a good view west to Lochnagar and east to the coast. The easiest way back is by the same route, a total distance of 17km, with 700m of ascent, which takes 4½–5½hrs. The longer route from Glen Tanar runs up the glen through some fine natural pine forest almost to the head of the glen, where a path leads up the northern slopes to the summit. Again it's easiest to return the same way, a trip of 27km, with 850m of ascent, which takes 7–8hrs. Mount Keen can also be climbed from Glen Muick to the west but I don't recommend this route as it involves a great deal of arduous walking through peat bogs. If coming from this direction it's better to descend the Water of Mark, a lovely, twisting, rushing stream, to Invermark, and then ascend from there.

Mount Keen was probably the first Highland mountain to be climbed by a tourist way back in 1618 when a Thames boatman and writer called John Taylor, also known as the Water Poet, toured Scotland, afterwards publishing an account of his trip called *The Pennyles Pilgrimage* (he went with no money, relying on locals to look after him, which they generously did). Of his ascent of Mount Keen Taylor wrote 'when I came to the top of it, my teeth beganne to dance in my head with cold...a most familiar mist embraced me round, that I could not see thrice my length any way: withal, it yeelded so friendly a deaw, that it did moisten thorow all my clothes' (as quoted in Ian R. Mitchell's *Scotland's Mountains Before the Mountaineers*, Luath, 1999).

⊗ Mount Battock

Mount Keen may be the easternmost Munro but Mount Battock really is the easternmost high hill, lying some 14km further east in an area of much lower boggy and heathery hills. It resembles Mount Keen in being a domed hill easily identifiable from afar. There is a feeling of being on the edge of the mountains on the summit, as lower country stretches away to the east while to the west rise higher hills. Mount Battock can be most quickly and easily climbed from Mill of Aucheen in Glen Esk, to the south, from where a bulldozed road, one of many in this area, runs north onto the southeastern slopes of the hill. A descent can be made down the south ridge over Hill of Saughs to another bulldozed road that descends to the ascent track. The round trip is 13.5km long, with 700m of ascent, and it takes around 4hrs.

4:6 DEESIDE

The long valley of the River Dee runs from the heart of the mountains east through moorlands and forest to rich farmland and then the North Sea at the city of Aberdeen. The mountain section, known as Upper Deeside, is a beautiful valley, with many woods either side of the big meandering river. Attractive little stone-built towns lie along the river – Banchory, Aboyne, Ballater and Braemar – offering all facilities and linked by the A93 that runs right down Deeside to Aberdeen.

Deeside is often called Royal Deeside as it contains Balmoral Castle and the Balmoral Estate. Queen Victoria, already in love with the Highlands, bought the estate with her husband Prince Albert in 1848, rebuilt the castle and moved in seven years later. Balmoral has been the Scottish home of the Royal Family ever since. The gardens, various exhibitions, extensive grounds and a small part of the castle are open to the public between April and July. Since Victoria's arrival Upper Deeside has been 'saturated by the presence of the British monarchy', in the words of Ian R. Mitchell (in *On the Trail of Queen Victoria in the Highlands*, Luath, 2000), and it is impossible to travel here without coming across signs of Royalty.

Tourism was already growing on Deeside before Victoria arrived. Her approbation was a gift to the industry, as was the arrival of the railway from Aberdeen at Ballater in 1861. Sadly, the railway was closed in 1966 as part of the infamous, shortsighted and downright stupid Beeching butchery of Britain's railways and most visitors now arrive by car on the A93, either from Aberdeen to the east or over the Cairnwell Pass from the south.

Although many hills lie above Deeside one dominates the area – Lochnagar ('little loch of the noisy sound', 1155m), one of the great hills of Scotland. Lochnagar lies at the northeastern corner of the Mounth plateau, and to its west and south are four more Munros – Carn an t-Sagairt Mor ('big hill of the priest', 1047m), Carn a'Choire Boidheach ('hill of the beautiful corrie', 1110m), Cairn Bannoch (probably 'peaked hill', 1012m) and Broad Cairn (998m). One Corbett lies east of Lochnagar, Conachraig ('abundance of rocks', 865m). One major side valley, Glen Muick, runs southwest into these hills from Ballater. A minor road runs up this glen to Spittal of Glenmuick, where there is a car park and visitor centre. The head of Glen Muick is filled with Loch Muick, a long, dark loch hemmed in by steep slopes, which is the biggest loch in the Cairngorms.

The walking on the Lochnagar hills is excellent and can easily be extended to the hills to the south. There is climbing too, rock and ice, on the granite cliffs of the northeast corrie of Lochnagar and the remoter cliff of Creag an Dubh Loch, between Cairn Bannoch and Broad Cairn, the biggest in the Cairngorms.

West of Braemar the vast Mar Lodge Estate, stretching all the way to Ben Macdui and including the headwaters of the River Dee, Lui Water and Geldie Burn, is owned by the National Trust for Scotland, which has begun removing the many ugly bulldozed tracks that despoil this fine landscape and reducing grazing pressure to allow the regeneration of the fine Scots pine woods found on the estate. Most of the summits aren't Deeside hills, lying too far away. Sgor Mor ('big peak'), an 813m Corbett lying beyond the end of the public road at Linn of Dee, is the westernmost of the Deeside hills.

To the north of Braemar the Mar Lodge boundary runs along the summits of the hills, over the Corbett Carn na Drochaide ('cairn of the bridge',

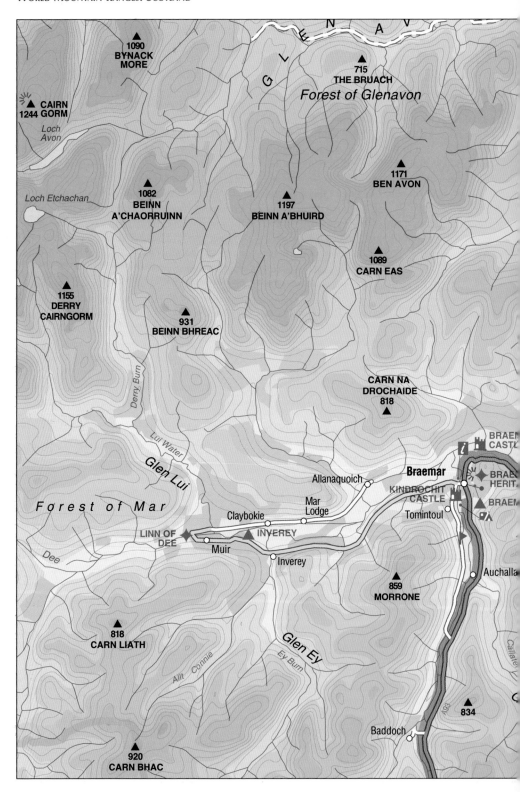

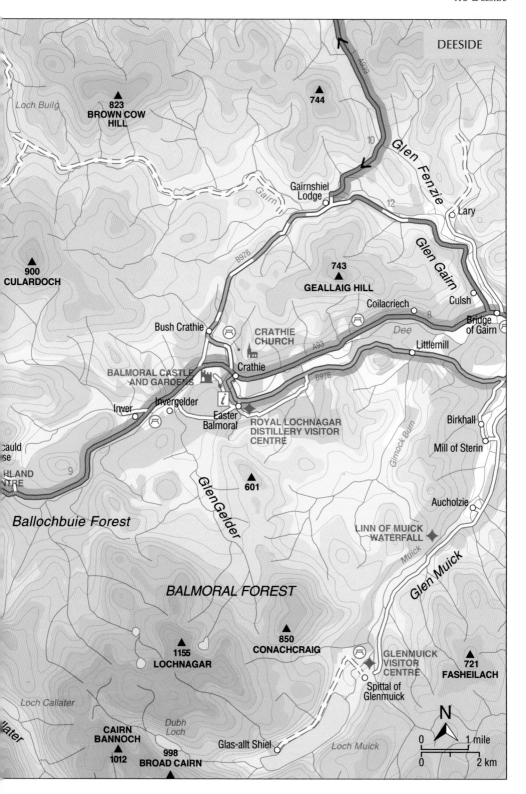

Loch Builg

▲ 823
BROWN COW
HILL

744

Glen Fenzie

10

Gairn

Gairnshiel
Lodge

12

Lary

Glen Gairn

▲ 900
CULARDOCH

B976

▲ 743
GEALLAIG HILL

Coilacriech

Culsh

8

Dee

Bridge
of Gairn

Bush Crathie

CRATHIE
CHURCH

A93

Littlemill

Crathie

B976

BALMORAL CASTLE
AND GARDENS

Inver

Invergelder

Easter
Balmoral

ROYAL LOCHNAGAR
DISTILLERY VISITOR
CENTRE

Birkhall

Mill of Sterin

cauld
se

HLAND
NTRE

9

GlenGelder

▲ 601

Gairnock Burn

Aucholzie

Ballochbuie Forest

LINN OF MUICK
WATERFALL

Muick

Glen Muick

BALMORAL FOREST

▲ 850
CONACHCRAIG

GLENMUICK
VISITOR
CENTRE

▲ 721
FASHEILACH

▲ 1155
LOCHNAGAR

Spittal of
Glenmuick

Loch Callater

Dubh
Loch

N

CAIRN
BANNOCH

▲ 1012

998
BROAD CAIRN
▲

Glas-allt Shiel

Loch Muick

0   1 mile
0   2 km

ater

Lochnagar from the slopes of Cairn an t-Sagairt Mor

BRAEMAR

The pretty little tourist village of Braemar is the main base for the Deeside mountains. It's in a fine location on the south side of the Dee at the point where the A93 leaves Deeside and turns south for the Cairnwell Pass and Glen Shee. Braemar has all facilities, including a Tourist Information Centre, a campsite and a good outdoor shop as well as many tourist shops. Clunie Water rushes through the village on its way to the Dee, an attractive sight among the grey stone buildings. Braemar is at an altitude of 330m and in winter temperatures can be low. The lowest temperature ever recorded in Britain was at Braemar, a chilly -27.2°C. Just east of the town lies the distinctive turreted Braemar Castle, built in 1628 and now open to the public from spring to autumn. West of Braemar a minor road runs down Deeside to the Linn of Dee where it crosses the river and runs along the north side of the valley as far as the Linn of Quoich.

818m) to Beinn a'Bhuird ('hill of the table', 1197m), which with Ben Avon ('hill of the river', 1171m) to the east forms the easternmost plateau of the northern Cairngorms. These two Munros are often referred to collectively as the eastern Cairngorms. Between Ben Avon and Deeside lie two outlying Corbetts, Carn Liath ('grey cairn', 862m) and Culardoch ('back of the high place', 900m).

⊗ Morrone

Braemar's hill is Morrone ('big nose'), an 859m Corbett rising some 3km southwest of the town. It's a rather featureless mound with a summit disfigured by a telecommunications mast and several huts, but does have a good view of the northern Cairngorms from its summit. A good and popular path leads directly from Braemar to the top. There is a fine old birch wood at the start of the walk. The round trip is 7.5km, with 520m of ascent, and takes 2–3hrs. The walk can be extended by following a bulldozed track south then east to Auchallater in Glen Clunie, then following the minor road on the west side of Clunie Water back to Braemar. This is rather a soulless road slog, however. A better descent is to drop down northwards into the birch woods that flank the hill on this side and follow tracks through these back to Braemar.

Lochnagar ☆

The finest hill in the Southern Cairngorms, Lochnagar takes the form of a great horseshoe curving round the corrie holding the lochan for which it is named. The granite cliffs that form the walls of this corrie are some of the most impressive in Scotland, a series of big buttresses split by deep gullies. To the southwest Lochnagar connects with the rest of the vast Mounth plateau, to the north steep slopes fall away over subsidiary tops to the forests of Deeside while to the southeast more abrupt steep slopes drop down to Loch Muick.

Lochnagar is a strange name for a hill. Unsurprisingly it's not the original name, which was Beinn nan Ciochan, 'hill of the breasts', describing the round rocky subsidiary summits now called the Meikle Pap and Little Pap (big and little breasts) according to Peter Drummond, whose *Scottish Hill Names: Their Origin and Meaning* (Scottish Mountaineering Trust, 2nd revised edition, 2007) also records that the name of the loch slowly transferred to the hill above, at first as the Hill of Lochnagar or the Top of Lochnagar. The change of name was confirmed by Lord Byron, who spent his childhood in the area, in his 1807 poem 'Dark Lochnagar' (dark because the northeast cliffs are usually in shadow), which contains lines all mountain lovers will appreciate:

Oh for the crags that are wild and majestic!
The steep frowning glories of dark Lochnagar.

Queen Victoria, who climbed it more than once, called the hill Lochnagar too, which must have settled the name.

The actual summit of Lochnagar is called Cac Carn Beag, often translated as 'little pile of shit', but Peter Drummond says 'cac' is a corruption of *cadha*, meaning slope, so the name is really 'little cairn of the slope'.

The first recorded ascent of Lochnagar may have been in 1771, by the same James Robertson who first climbed Ben Nevis (see Chapter 3). Robertson called it Lochnagan.

⊗ The Ascent of Lochnagar ☆

The standard ascent of Lochnagar is by a wide path from the Spittal of Glenmuick that climbs west across moorland to a sudden and impressive view of the cliffs of the northeast corrie. The best viewpoint, however, is the summit of Meikle Pap, just to the north, a very short and worthwhile diversion. From the Lochnagar/Meikle Pap col the path follows the rim of the corrie, with excellent views down the cliffs to the dark waters of Lochnagar, round to the granite boulder heap of Cac Carn Beag, just west of the cliffs. This is a popular route but also a fine one. The views from the summit are extensive with a wide array of hills on the horizon, especially the northern Cairngorms. The most spectacular views are those of the cliffs during the ascent however.

A good descent is via the Glas-Allt. A path runs southeast beside this burn to Loch Muick, whose shore can then be followed back to the Spittal of Glenmuick. The Glas-Allt is a fine stream, dashing down in a series of waterslides, and there is a dramatic view down to the loch and the steep slopes on the far side. Where the terrain steepens for the final descent to Loch Muick the path passes the Falls of Glas-Allt, an attractive 50m cascade, below which the Glas-Allt runs down a steep gorge.

This circuit is 18.5km long with 1020m of ascent and takes 6–7hrs.

Lochnagar can also be climbed from the west over Carn an t-Sagairt Mor and Carn a'Choire Boidheach (see below) and from the north over Meall Coire na Saobhaidhe. For once I think the standard route is the most scenic and enjoyable.

❺ ❄ Climbing on Lochnagar ☆

The cliffs of Lochnagar's magnificent northeast corrie, a great arc stretching for over 1km and reaching 230m in height, have been a major climbing area since the early days of mountaineering. The great scree cleft known as the Black Spout was first climbed in winter in 1893 by J.H. Gibson and W. Douglas. It's now a popular 250m Grade I. A party led by Harold Raeburn climbed Raeburn's Gully in 1898, now a three star classic Grade II winter climb that is 200m long. The name most associated with climbing here is that of Tom Patey, who put up many winter routes in the 1950s, including the classics Eagle Ridge (250m, Grade VI) and Parallel Buttress (280m, Grade VI). Today there are some 50 winter routes in the corrie, of all grades of difficulty.

Eagle Ridge had first been climbed in summer in 1941 by J.H.B. Bell and Nancy Forsyth. Bell described Eagle Ridge as 'unique amongst long, precipitous mountain ridges in Britain...very steep and narrow, with a symmetrical curving crest'. As a rock climb it's graded VS. Bell also climbed Parallel

The cliffs of Lochnagar

Buttress, with W.H. Murray in 1939, a classic Severe. Although there are other good rock climbs on Lochnagar much of the cliff is loose and grassy, and it's for winter climbing that the mountain is known.

Conachraig
The summit of this sprawling Corbett lies just 1km above the standard route up Lochnagar (see above) and can easily be included on that walk, with the addition of 2km and 185m of ascent.

The Circuit of Loch Muick
A path runs right round Loch Muick and the circuit makes a pleasant walk in grand surroundings from the Spittal of Loch Muick, but it is very popular, especially on sunny summer weekends. The round is 12km long, and can be done in 3hrs.

The White Mounth: Carn an t-Sagairt Mor and Carn a'Coire Boidheach
These two rather undistinguished Munros lie on the plateau west of Lochnagar and are often climbed with it. They can be ascended as a pair from Glen Callater to the west, a round of 23km, with 1050m of ascent, that takes 6½–7½hrs on foot. A bicycle could be used on the track up Glen Callater to the foot of Loch Callater, a round trip of 10km.

From the loch a good path climbs the hillside and traverses upwards to the west slopes of Carn an t-Sagairt Mor, where it can be left for an easy walk to the summit and on over Carn an t-Sagairt Beag to the Stuic, a minor top overlooking the steep crags of Coire Loch nan Eun with a good view down to Deeside. The gentle, almost indistinct rise of Carn a'Choire Boidheach lies directly south. From its rounded summit you can head west to pick up the path left onto Carn an t-Sagairt Mor and follow this back to Loch Callater.

The Dubh Loch, Cairn Bannoch and Broad Cairn ☆
West of Loch Muick lies a high, wild glen in which lie the dark waters of the Dubh Loch below the massive granite cliff of Creag an Dubh Loch, which faces northeast and casts a shadow over the loch, hence the name, which means 'black lake'. A walk through this valley is a splendid excursion that can be combined with an ascent of the two Munros lying just to the south. A path leads up into the glen from the head of Loch Muick past a tumbling waterfall called the Stulan to the Dubh Loch. Once past the loch and the cliffs an ascent can be made southwards to Cairn Bannoch. Easy grassy walking leads southeast to Broad Cairn, beyond whose

266

summit a track leads down to a path that descends Corrie Chash to Loch Muick. The circuit from the Spittal of Loch Muick is 22.5km long, with 970m of ascent, and takes 6–8hrs.

⓫ ✿ Creag an Dubh Loch ☆

Unbroken for 1km, the biggest single cliff in the Cairngorms is a major if rather remote climbing destination for both rock and ice climbers. The cliff is steep and serious and most of the climbs are in the harder grades. The first climbs were made in the 1920s. The cliff is split by the 300m scree chute of Central Gully, an easy clamber in summer, a straightforward Grade I in winter, and a spectacular place in the midst of magnificent rock scenery. There are some 25 other winter climbs on the cliff, and many rock climbs. One of the easier rock routes is the classic Mousetrap (180m, VS), first climbed by J.R. Marshall, R. Marshall and R. Anderson in 1959.

⊗ The Complete Round
of the Lochnagar Hills ☆

The finest hillwalk in the Lochnagar hills is the complete round of the five Munros in the area from the Spittal of Glenmuick. It's a long walk – 28km, with 1360m of ascent – but once the initial climb is over the walking is easy. The round starts with the ascent of Lochnagar described above. From Cac

Carn Beag it's an easy walk west to Carn a'Choire Boidheach and Carn an t-Sagairt, and then south-east to Cairn Bannoch and the walk over that summit and Broad Cairn, also described above.

Ben Avon and Beinn a'Bhuird

These two magnificent Munros are massive sprawling hills covering a huge area, with many wild glens and corries cutting into their flat summit plateaus. They lie between the remote upper reaches of Glen Avon to the north and Deeside, although the latter is far to the south. Glen Gairn cuts into the hills from the east. To the west lie more Munros, and then the Lairig an Laoigh pass and Glen Derry.

Ben Avon is a huge, complex hill stretching some 12km southwest to northeast and 9km from south to north, and with more ground above 900m than any other Scottish hill. On the north and south sides are a series of remote, little-visited, steep-sided corries separated by broad spurs. The big summit plateau is dotted with striking and unusual granite tors, one of which is the highest point. This is called Leabaidh an Daimh Bhuidhe ('bed of the yellow stag', 1171m). An easy scramble leads to the top.

The first recorded ascent of Ben Avon was by the botanist James Robertson in 1771, the same year he also climbed Ben Nevis and, possibly, Lochnagar. It was probably climbed earlier by miners searching for 'Cairngorms' – semi-precious quartz crystals

Ben Avon from Beinn a'Bhuird

– who were active on the hill in the mid-18th century, according to Ian R. Mitchell's *Scotland's Mountains Before the Mountaineers* (Luath, 1999).

Ben Avon is linked with Beinn a'Bhuird by a narrow neck of land called The Sneck ('the notch') at 970m. Beinn a'Bhuird is a very different hill, however; its flat broad summit plateau, for which it is aptly named, runs 3km from south to north with barely any change in altitude. Steep, featureless slopes fall away to the Moine Bhealaidh, a boggy plateau, and the deep Dubh-Ghleann to the west and Glen Avon to the north. The east side is glorious, however, lined with a series of magnificent cliff-rimmed corries that house many climbs, while to the south a broad shoulder rises above the fine stands of old Scots pine beside Quoich Water. The first recorded ascent of Beinn a'Bhuird was in 1810 by the Rev Dr George Skene Keith, who was measuring the heights of hills. He went on to the summit of Ben Avon.

These two hills cover such a vast area and are so complex that an exploration of them can take many days. The area is ideal for camping and for through-routes from one side to the other.

⚑ The Ascent of Ben Avon and Beinn a'Bhuird ☆

There are no short routes to either of these hills, although a bicycle could be used on the approach tracks. The two main start points to the south are the Linn of Quoich west of Braemar and Keiloch near Invercauld Bridge east of Braemar.

From Linn of Quoich, where the Quoich Water runs through a narrow rock cleft, a track runs up the west side of Glen Quoich, a lovely wooded glen with some fine old Scots pine, to the southern end of a long spur of Beinn a'Bhuird called An Diollaid. The bulldozed track used to continue up this spur to finish at 1080m almost on the summit plateau, one of the most hideous scars in the Highlands (and still marked on many maps). However the National Trust for Scotland has removed this track and the ground is slowly recovering. In its place the NTS has constructed a footpath, although this doesn't always follow the line of the track. There are good views from the narrow neck of An Diollaid down into the Dubh-Ghleann. From the end of the path the summit plateau is a short walk east. The North Top, the highest point of Beinn a'Bhuird, lies just under 1.5km to the north. In clear weather the edge of the corries to the east can be followed, with

superb views into their depths. The North Top is around 200m from the edge of Coire nan Clach. The view from the summit and the whole plateau is vast: to the west a huge expanse of hills stretches from south to north, giving an idea of the scale of the Highlands. To descend, head east down to The Sneck between Beinn a'Bhuird and Ben Avon then turn south and go down beside the Glas Allt Mor, and then down the long, wild upper Glen Quoich, turning east with Quoich Water to reach the track running down the east side of the glen. This route is 33km long, with 1190m of ascent, and takes, on foot, 8–10hrs.

If starting at Keiloch a track up Gleann an t-Slugain is followed to Quoich Water, where a path climbs to the plateau. The first 7km of the track can be cycled. In total it's 16km, with 1180m of ascent from Keiloch to the North Top, and takes 5–6hrs.

The same track from Keiloch can be used for the ascent of Ben Avon. When Quoich Water is reached head up Glen Quoich to a huge boulder called Clach a'Chleirich ('stone of the priest') and on beside the Glas Allt Mor to The Sneck between Ben Avon and Beinn a'Bhuird. There's a good view north from The Sneck into the remote wild corrie of Slochd Mor ('the great pit'). Turning east climb up to the Ben Avon plateau and walk across the gravelly terrain to the summit tor. The return can be made by the same route, but it's more interesting to head south across the plateau to its southernmost top, Carn Eas, then descend back to the path in Glen Quoich. The walk is 32km long, of which 14 can be cycled, with 1300m of ascent and takes, on foot, 8–10hrs.

Ben Avon can also be climbed from Tomintoul and Glen Avon to the north, and from Glen Gairn, starting at Gairnshiel Lodge on the A939, to the east. Both routes are long and perhaps best done as two or three day camping trips or else using a bicycle along the estate roads in the glens.

Ben Avon and Beinn a'Bhuird can be climbed together on a long circuit from either Linn of Quoich or Keiloch and Gleann an t-Slugain, linking the routes described above for a round of about 35km, with 1500m of ascent, which is likely to take a minimum of 10hrs.

⑬ ✳ Climbing in the Beinn a'Bhuird Corries ☆

Ben Avon's crags are broken and small and don't provide much in the way of climbing, although there are enjoyable scrambles on the tors on the

The eastern corries of Beinn a'Bhuird

plateau. However the corries of Beinn a'Bhuird harbour many big cliffs, providing give good climbs in wild situations that are as sensational and remote as any in the Highlands. The three main climbing corries are Coire na Ciche and Coire an Dubh Lochain on the eastern side of Beinn a'Bhuird, reached from the path in upper Glen Quoich, and very remote Garbh Choire in Slochd Mor, north of The Sneck. The eastern corries are regarded as being better for snow and ice than rock climbing, but the less broken Garbh Choire cliffs have good rock routes as well as winter ones.

The most famous climb is Mitre Ridge in Garbh Choire. This ridge is a striking 220m rock buttress jutting out from the corrie walls with three towers at the top. Mitre Ridge is a classic climb in summer and winter. It was first climbed in summer in 1933 by E.A.M. Wedderburn, P.D. Baird and E.J.A. Leslie and in winter by W.D. Brooker and Tom Patey in 1953. In summer its graded Severe, in winter V. Another classic is Squareface, a 100m V Diff rock climb in Garbh Choire, first climbed by Tom Patey and J.M. Taylor in 1953, and described by Kevin Howett in *Rock Climbing in Scotland* as 'the superlative of superlatives, continuously exposed and in a remarkable situation'.

Ski Touring on Ben Avon and Beinn a'Bhuird

Some of the best ski touring in the Cairngorms lies on Ben Avon and Beinn a'Bhuird. All the walking routes described above can be done on skis. Although the skiing is mostly easy distances are long and the summits are quite remote, so any ski tour here is serious. Once on the plateaus progress can be quick when snow conditions are good.

The Corbetts: Carn Liath, Culardoch, Carn na Drochaide and Sgurr Mor

These Corbetts are dwarfed by Ben Avon and Beinn a'Bhuird, and while the ascents are pleasant they don't compare with those on the bigger hills, although the views from the summits are excellent. They are all rounded hills, with little sign of rock, and can be climbed from any direction. Carn Liath and Culardoch are usually climbed from the Bealach Dearg between them. The bealach is reached by an estate track that turns north off the Gleann an t-Slugain track from Keiloch, and climbs through trees and then open moorland. The track crosses the western shoulder of Culardoch. From its high point it's just 1km to the summit. Back down at the bealach it's 1.5km to the easternmost summit of Carn Liath. This hill has two summits of equal height, according to the

Ordnance Survey, and the western one is a further 1km. Corbett baggers will probably want to climb them both, just in case one is resurveyed as the higher at some point. Happily, the walk between them is easy and the views are good, especially northwest to Ben Avon. A descent can be made down the southeast slopes of Carn Liath to the outward track. The round trip from Keiloch is 22km, with 1000m of ascent, and takes 6–7hrs.

Carn na Drochaide lies across Deeside from Braemar, and can be climbed in 1½hrs from Linn of Quoich, a distance of 3km, with 485m of ascent, by its steep southwest slopes. From the summit Beinn a'Bhuird and Ben Avon look impressive and there are excellent views of Braemar and Deeside.

Sgorr Mor can be traversed from the Linn of Dee, where the river rushes through a narrow rocky ravine, starting with an ascent of the minor top of Sgor Dubh at the eastern end of the hill and then following the broad ridge to the summit. There are superb views north and west to the northern Cairngorms. From the summit a descent can be made south to the River Dee and a path back to Linn of Dee. The round trip is 15.5km, with 585m of ascent, and takes 4–6hrs.

4:7 STRATHSPEY

The River Spey is one of the great rivers of Scotland. Its wide middle section runs to the north of the Cairngorms through wide, beautiful Strathspey, which is also the busiest tourist area and the most populated part of the Cairngorms, with a string of small towns and villages – Newtonmore, Kingussie, Aviemore, Boat of Garten, Nethy Bridge, Grantown-on-Spey and Carrbridge – that offer all facilities. Access is good, with the A9 and the Inverness railway line running down the strath.

Meall a'Bhuachaille and Ryvoan Pass ☆
North of Glen More lies a line of rolling heathery hills, well seen from the road in the glen. The highest of these lies at the east end, the 810m Corbett Meall a'Bhuachaille ('shepherd's hill'). A fine, popular walk leads through the wooded Ryvoan Pass and up the eastern slopes of the hill. The path starts at the end of the minor road from Glenmore village to Glenmore Lodge, and winds a way through regenerating forest, some in cleared areas where the remains of the old plantations can be seen, to the pass, a V-shaped notch between the

Loch Morlich and the Northern Cairngorms

THE STRATHSPEY PINE FORESTS

Strathspey contains the largest remnants of the Caledonian pine forest and much regeneration is taking place. Rothiemurchus Forest, a privately owned estate south of the Aviemore-Glenmore road, is the most impressive of the old woods, a lovely mix of tree, meadow, river and loch backed by high hills. Immediately northeast of Rothiemurchus is the Forestry Commission's Glenmore Forest Park, running from Loch Morlich to Ryvoan Pass and the lower slopes of Meall a'Bhuachaille. This forest, which had been logged regularly over the centuries, was finally trashed by the Forestry Commission in the twentieth century, the natural woodland having been felled and replaced by dense plantations. Towards the end of the century there was a change in policy, and the Commission started felling the plantations and allowing the old forest to regenerate. This has left a mess, with many ugly cleared areas, but should in time result in the restoration of the natural forest. It is encouraging to see new trees spreading up the hillsides, but it is a pity the Forestry Commission did so much damage in the first place. Glenmore links with Abernethy Forest, an RSPB reserve, to the north. Abernethy contains the largest remaining areas of natural forest in the Highlands, but is situated further from the high hills than the other forests. It is possible to link all these forests in one long walk, perhaps continuing on into Glen Feshie, where there is a mix of plantations and natural woods. Most of the forest consists of Scots pine but there are also many groves of beautiful birches, alders by the streams, plus aspen, rowan, willow and juniper. The Forestry Commission publishes a book on their portion of the woodland – *The Glen with More: A Guide to Glenmore Forest Park* by Kenny Taylor (FCS, 2003).

As well as the forests there are many lochs, marshes and meadows. The bird life is prolific. As Adam Watson says, 'for natural history, Strath Spey is a place for superlatives'.

AVIEMORE

Aviemore is the centre of the tourist trade in the northern Cairngorms and a busy, noisy, bustling town most of the year. Tourism in Aviemore developed in the 19th century, after the arrival of the railway in 1862. 100 years later much development took place with the opening of the ski resort in Coire Cas, as Aviemore was the nearest town. The original Aviemore Centre, a tourist development with go-kart racing, a swimming pool, ice rink, shops and more, built in 60s concrete brutalism style has thankfully been demolished, although some hotels in the same ugly and obtrusive blockhouse design remain. Although there is a new centre – the Aviemore Highland Resort – the life of the town is on the main street where there are shops, cafés, bars, the railway station and a surprisingly large number of outdoor shops.

If the pace and noise of Aviemore seem out of keeping with the quiet of the hills you can walk down to the River Spey and stroll along the bank, or follow the path under the A9 to the birch woods of the Craigellachie National Nature Reserve and spend an hour or two among the trees. Aviemore may be brash, but you can be in peaceful, natural surroundings very quickly.

An interesting book on the history of Aviemore, Rothiemurchus and Glenmore is *The Cairngorm Gateway* by Ann Glen (Scottish Cultural Press, 2008).

ROTHIEMURCHUS–GLENMORE

South of Aviemore a road runs east through Rothiemurchus forest to Glen More ('the big glen'), an area known as the Rothiemurchus–Glenmore corridor. The road is a busy tourist route, taking visitors to Glenmore village, where there are cafés, a shop, a large campsite, a Youth Hostel, a Forestry Commission visitor centre, a Reindeer Centre and not far away Glenmore Lodge, Scotland's national outdoor centre, which is open to the public and has a bar. From Glenmore the road climbs up to the Cairngorm Mountain ski resort. There are regular buses from Aviemore to Glenmore and the ski resort. ▶

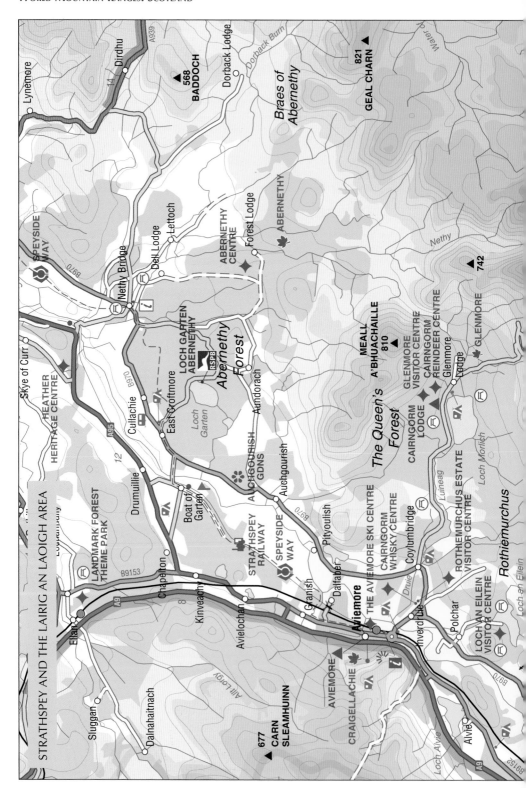

STRATHSPEY AND THE LAIRIG AN LAOIGH AREA

Lynemore

Dirdhu

568
BADDOCH

Dorback Lodge

Dorback Burn

Braes of
Abernethy

821
GEAL CHARN

SPEYSIDE WAY

Skye of Curr

HEATHER
HERITAGE CENTRE

Nethy Bridge

Dell Lodge

Lettoch

Forest Lodge

ABERNETHY
CENTRE

ABERNETHY

Nethy

742

LOCH GARTEN
ABERNETHY
RSPB

Abernethy
Forest

GLENMORE

MEALL
A'BHUACHAILLE
810

GLENMORE
VISITOR CENTRE

CAIRNGORM
REINDEER CENTRE

Glenmore
Lodge

Cullachie

East Croftmore

Loch
Garten

Auldorach

The Queen's
Forest

CAIRNGORM
LODGE

LANDMARK FOREST
THEME PARK

Drumuillie

AUCHGOURISH
GDNS

Auchgourish

Boat of
Garten

STRATHSPEY
RAILWAY

SPEYSIDE
WAY

Pityoulish

Loch Morlich

ROTHIEMURCHUS ESTATE
VISITOR CENTRE

Chapelton

B9153

Kinveachy

Avielochan

Granish

Dalfaber

Coylumbridge

Rothiemurchus

THE AVIEMORE SKI CENTRE

CAIRNGORM
WHISKY CENTRE

Loch an Eilein

LOCH AN EILEIN
VISITOR CENTRE

Polchar

Inverdruie

Aviemore

Ellan

Dalnahaitnach

Sluggan

677
CARN
SLEAMHUINN

AVIEMORE

CRAIGELLACHIE

Alvie

Loch Alvie

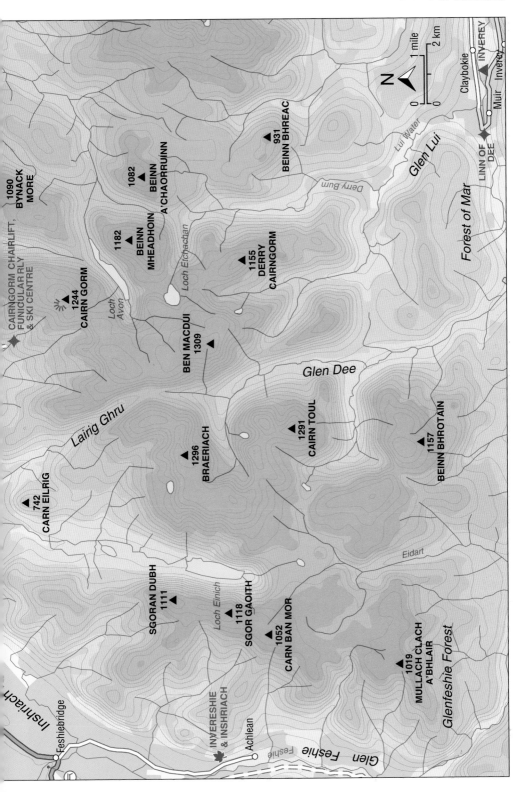

N

0   1 mile
0   1   2 km

Claybokie
INVEREY
Muir Inverey
LINN OF DEE

Glen Lui

Lui Water

Forest of Mar

931
BEINN BHREAC

Derry Burn

1082
BEINN
A'CHAORRUINN

CAIRNGORM CHAIRLIFT,
FUNICULAR RLY
& SKI CENTRE

1090
BYNACK
MORE

1182
BEINN
MHEADHOIN

Loch Etchachan

1155
DERRY
CAIRNGORM

1244
CAIRN GORM

Loch Avon

BEN MACDUI
1309

Glen Dee

Lairig Ghru

1296
BRAERIACH

1291
CAIRN TOUL

1157
BEINN BHROTAIN

CARN EILRIG
742

Eidart

SGORAN DUBH
1111

Loch Einich

1118
SGOR GAOITH

1052
CARN BAN MOR

1019
MULLACH CLACH
A'BHLAIR

Glenfeshie Forest

INVERESHIE
& INSHRIACH

Achlean

Glen Feshie

Feshiebridge

Insh

Inshriach

273

◄ The centrepiece of the Glenmore area is Loch Morlich, a large loch surrounded by pine forest and with a splendid view of the northern Cairngorms. Like other lochs in the area it's a glacial feature known as a kettle hole, which is the hollow formed when a block of ice left behind by a glacier melts. Loch Morlich is a popular place with sailors and canoeists as well as walkers. There are paths right round the loch.

rugged, scree-covered slopes of Creag nan Gall, a distant outlier of Cairn Gorm, and the slightly gentler slopes of Meall a'Bhuachaille. Ryvoan Pass is a lovely spot with many fine old Scots pines, which avoided the destruction of most of the natural Glenmore Forest due a local forester who thankfully didn't follow orders from above to fell them. In the heart of the pass lies An Lochan Uaine – 'the little green loch' – whose waters often are green, as they reflect the light from the trees above, hence the name. Beyond the lochan the path leaves the big trees for moorland, although the numbers of young trees sprouting up through the heather show that the forest will soon accompany the path much further. Soon a small building can be seen ahead, the little Ryvoan Bothy, a useful shelter in a storm. The path up Meall a'Bhuachaille leaves the main path here and climbs the eastern slopes to the summit, where there is a superb view of Loch Morlich, the higher Cairngorm mountains and the broad wooded

expanse of Strathspey. Beyond Meall a'Bhuachaille the path continues over Creagan Gorm ('blue little rock') and an unnamed summit to the last top, Craiggowrie ('goat's crag'), a good high-level walk with splendid views. A path drops southwest from Craiggowrie down into the forest where tracks lead past Badaguish Outdoor Centre to Glenmore village and the start. The walk is 16km long, with 875m of ascent, and takes 4½ to 6½hrs. For a shorter outing (8km, 535m ascent, 2½–3hrs) there is a path down into the forest from the col between Meall a'Bhuachaille and Creagan Gorm.

The path through Ryvoan Pass continues north to Forest Lodge in Abernethy Forest, a distance of 8km, which can be walked in a couple of hours. From Forest Lodge further tracks lead on to Nethy Bridge. On the crossing from Glenmore to Abernethy you can see how the regenerating forest is advancing on both sides and will soon meet. Eventually this will be a forest walk throughout.

An Lochan Uaine, Ryvoan Pass

The summit of Sgor Gaoith

🜂 Loch an Eilein ☆

The jewel in Rothiemurchus Forest is Loch an Eilein ('loch of the island'), a lovely little lake set amid natural pine forest backed by high hills and which, according to Seton Gordon's *Highways and Byways in the Central Highlands* (Birlinn, 1995, first published 1935),'some people consider to be the most beautiful loch in Scotland'. Loch an Eilein is only 5km from Aviemore and a popular spot. Beside the car park there's a small information centre and a small gift and snack shop, open from April to October, plus toilets.

On the little islet for which the loch is named is a romantic and picturesque ruined castle, dating from the 14th century. Immediately south lies smaller Loch Gamhna, in more open surroundings. The 7km walk round the two lochs makes a fine short excursion. There is a good path the whole way.

North of Loch an Eilein lies little Ord Ban ('white hammer'), from whose 428m summit there is a grand view back down to the loch and south to the high mountains. The ascent of Ord Ban can easily be combined with the circuit of the lochs, ascending the east side and descending the south, for a 7km walk with 200m of ascent that takes a couple of hours.

🜂 Gleann Einich and the Sgoran Ridge ☆

Gleann Einich is a long, beautiful glen that runs deep into the mountains from Rothiemurchus Forest just east of Loch an Eilein, starting in lovely natural pine woods and finishing in a stark but magnificent ring of rocky gullies and craggy buttresses above Loch Einich. On the west side of the glen runs the long Sgoran ridge, a broad arm of mountain protruding northwards from the Moine Mhor plateau (see below). To the east lies Braeriach and its northern outliers.

There are four tops on the Sgoran Ridge, of which the highest is a Munro. This is Sgor Gaoith ('windy peak', 1118m), a fine little pointed summit set right on the edge of broken crags falling steeply some 600m to Loch Einich. From the west Sgor Gaoith is a tiny high point on a broad shouldered ridge, while from the east it's a pinnacle atop a mighty cliff. The other peaks on the ridge are Carn Ban Mor ('big white peak', 1052m), Sgoran Dubh Mor ('big dark tor', 1111m) and Creag Dhubh ('black crag', 848m). Sgoran Dubh Mor gives its name to the ridge presumably because it is the biggest and bulkiest of the summits, if not quite the highest.

According to Ian R. Mitchell's *Scotland's Mountains Before the Mountaineers* (Luath, 1999) the first recorded ascent of Sgor Gaoith was probably made in 1804, when Colonel Thomas Thornton took time off from slaughtering as much wildlife as possible on a 'sporting tour' to climb the hill. Thornton describes the ascent in overblown, epic terms and reckons Sgor Gaoith at least 18,000 feet high with a drop of 13,000 feet to Loch Einich. The Colonel also made the first ascent of Creag Meagaidh shortly afterwards (see Chapter 3).

Sgor Gaoith is usually climbed from Glen Feshie (see below), sometimes with Carn Ban Mor or Sgoran Dubh Mor. However the finest ascent route is along Gleann Einich, below the crags, and then back over the summits. A bulldozed track runs up the glen to the loch, which is the water supply for all of Strathspey. A bicycle can be used on this track. The walk can be started at Loch an Eilein, or at Whitewell not far to the east, at the end of a minor road from Inverdruie just outside Aviemore. From Loch an Eilein it's 12km and 250m of ascent to Loch Einich. The stream in the glen, called Am Beanaidh, runs through a narrow ravine at the mouth of the glen, squeezed between the northernmost outliers of the high hills to the south, Cadha Mor and Carn Eilrig. Beyond this lovely narrow section the trees are left behind and the glen widens out. It is in fact a classic glaciated U-shaped valley with a flat bottom and steep sides. The glen floor is boggy and wet – einich means 'marsh'. From the foot of Loch Einich a somewhat indistinct old path called Ross's Path runs about two thirds of the way along the west shore, then traverses up the steep eastern slopes of Sgor Gaoith to a height of 710m, from where a route can be made between broken crags to the Fuaran Diotach, or 'dinner well', a beautiful spring, and then the col between the rounded hump of Carn Ban Mor and the pointed summit of Sgor Gaoith. A well-used path runs up to Sgor Gaoith from the col. The view straight down to Loch Einich from the tiny summit cairn is startling and impressive, as is the view across the loch to the bulky shoulders of Braeriach. A splendid easy ridge walk now follows over Sgoran Dubh Mor to Creag Dhubh and Cadha Mor. On the southern slopes of Creag Dhubh there are several granite tors, the most prominent of which is known as Clach Mhic Cailein or the Argyll Stone. From Cadha Mor the easiest descent is east down to the track in Gleann Einich, but it is also possible to descend north and make a way through the forest to the track near Loch an Eilein. From Loch an Eilein the whole walk is 30km long, with 1300m of ascent, and takes 9–10hrs.

⊘ Ben Rinnes ☆

On the edge of the mountains just south of the confluence of the rivers Avon and Spey, and to the northeast of the main Cairngorms, lies Ben Rinnes, an 840m Corbett. The name means 'headland hill' and it does stand out, a distinctive and lovely cone easily identifiable from afar. Ben Rinnes stands in the middle of malt whisky country and is literally surrounded by distilleries, including Glenfarclas, The Macallan, Balvenie, Glenlivet, Glenfiddich and Benrinnes itself, which is in the town of Charlestown of Aberlour, which lies north of Ben Rinnes. Dufftown to the northeast boasts seven distilleries. To the south lies the Glenlivet distillery. An ascent of Ben Rinnes can be easily combined with a distillery visit or two. If there's a whisky hill this is it. The Glenfarclas distillery lies on the lower slopes of the hill itself and is made with water from Ben Rinnes. The slopes of Ben Rinnes are mostly heather-clad and of even steepness so it can be climbed just about anywhere. The easiest and most popular route is that up the east ridge. This starts at Glack Harnes on the minor road running northwards to Edinvillie from the B9009 southwest of Dufftown. A wide path runs over Round Hill and Roy's Hill to the granite tor on the summit, which has the splendid name of Scurran of Lochterlandoch. There are grand views north across the Moray Firth to distant hills. The return walk is 7km long, with 550m of ascent, and takes 2–3hrs.

4:8 THE LAIRIG AN LAOIGH AREA

The Lairig an Laoigh is the easternmost of the great passes of the Cairngorms, linking Strathspey with Deeside and useful for access to many hills. The name means 'calf's pass', and this is an old drove road along which cattle were taken south to market.

The Lairig an Laoigh path runs past five Munros – Bynack More (possibly 'the big cap', 1090m), Beinn Mheadhoin ('middle hill', 1182m), Derry Cairngorm ('blue hill of the woods', 1155m), Beinn a'Chaorainn ('hill of the rowan', 1083m) and Beinn Bhreac ('speckled hill', 931m) – and one Corbett, Creag Mhor ('big crag', 895m). Paths from the Lairig an Laoigh run up to Loch Avon and Loch Etchachan in the heart of the northern Cairngorms.

Lairig an Laoigh ☆

The crossing of the Lairig an Laoigh is a superb walk that takes you from Glenmore Forest up into wild, remote mountain country, and then down Glen Derry into the fine pine forests of Deeside. It's 29km from Glenmore to Linn of Dee, with 860m of ascent, a walk that takes 8–10hrs. Starting in Glenmore the route runs through Ryvoan Pass (see above) then turns east to round the northern extremities of Cairn Gorm to the River Nethy and a view straight up long narrow steep-sided Strath Nethy. The shelter beside the River Nethy, called Bynack Stable on maps, blew down in winter storms in 2005 and has not been rebuilt. From the River Nethy the path climbs over the northern shoulder of Bynack More, reaching a height of 790m, then descends rounds the eastern side of this hill to reach the Fords of Avon, where there is a very small refuge shelter. There are stepping stones across the River Avon here but they are often covered, and the river has to be waded. When in spate this may be too dangerous to attempt. You are now in the heart of the mountains, far from signs of civilisation. From the River Avon the path climbs past the dark waters of the Dubh Lochan pools, between the steep craggy slopes of Beinn a'Chaorainn and Beinn Mheadhoin, to the top of the Lairig an Laoigh at 740m. Straight ahead lies long Glen Derry, down which the path runs to the

pine forest and Derry Lodge, where it turns east down Glen Luibeg to the Linn of Dee.

Skiing the Lairig an Laoigh Hills ☆

This is a great area for ski touring, and all the walking routes described in this section can be skied. The crossing of the Lairig and Laoigh itself is a wonderful ski tour that takes the skier through very remote country. On Bynack More the best ascent route is from the Lairig an Laoigh path to upper Choire Dhuibh, and then the col between the summit and Bynack Beag rather than via the rocky north ridge. This makes a great descent route too, as the corrie holds snow well. Beinn a'Chaorainn and Beinn Bhreac are both good ski hills and the Moine Bhealaidh between them is much more easily crossed when the peat bogs are frozen and snow covered. A good ascent route from Glen Derry is up Coire an Fhir Bhogha to Craig Derry to the northwest of Beinn Bhreac from where you can head north to Beinn a'Chaorainn before returning over Beinn Bhreac. The shallow corrie southeast of Beinn a'Chaorainn is an excellent descent route back to the Moine Bhealaidh.

Bynack More ☆

Bynack More is an isolated mountain, separated from the other high hills by Strath Nethy and upper Glen Avon. It takes the form of a steep-sided ridge.

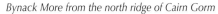

Bynack More from the north ridge of Cairn Gorm

From the north, looking end on to the ridge, it appears as a fine conical peak; from east and west it's a steep-sided wedge. The standard ascent route is from the high point of the Lairig an Laoigh path across the northern shoulder of the hill, from where the narrow rocky north ridge can be climbed to the jumble of boulders that makes up the summit. The approach is long but this is the most impressive ascent route (9.5km with 800m ascent). There is a tremendous view southeast to the northern slopes of Beinn a'Bhuird and Ben Avon from the summit. South of the summit lie some curious big granite tors, known as the Barns of Bynack, which are worth a close inspection.

There are a number of options for the return. An interesting and rugged one is to head northeast to the top of Bynack Beag then descend the steep northwest ridge into Strath Nethy, where the river can be forded, if not in spate, and the ridge above crossed to the west of Stac na h-Iolaire ('eagle's precipice'), a broken cliff rising above a cleft in the hillside, from where a descent can be made into the trees and the Ryvoan Pass path. This return route is 7km long, with 230m of ascent. Alternatively, once down in Strath Nethy a muddy path can be followed down this valley to the Lairig an Laoigh path where it crosses the River Nethy.

Strath Nethy can also be descended from the col called The Saddle at its head, between Bynack More and Cairn Gorm. The Saddle is reached from Bynack More by heading southwest over the top of A'Choinneach ('the moss'), which was once classified as a Munro, from where there is a magnificent view along Loch Avon to the cliffs ringing its head. From The Saddle you can also climb Cairn Gorm.

⊗ Creag Mhor

This rather remote Corbett, which lies southeast of Bynack More, is easy to climb but takes a while to reach. The quickest route is from Glenmore along the Lairig an Laoigh to Lochan a'Bhainne at the start of the descent to the Fords of Avon. The summit of Creag Mhor is just under 1km and 160m of ascent east of the lochan and can be reached in under half an hour. However it is 11.5km, with 625m of ascent, from Glenmore to Lochan a'Bhainne. The distance means that it makes sense to climb Creag Mhor during a crossing of the Lairig an Laoigh, or in combination with Bynack More. There is a granite tor on the summit and a good view of Bynack More.

⊗ Beinn a'Chaorainn and Beinn Bhreac

Beinn a'Chaorainn is a remote Munro lying directly above the high point of the Lairig an Laoigh. It's a shapely, conical hill with steep sides and is linked to the rather more featureless and nondescript Beinn Bhreac by the boggy, pool-dotted Moine Bhealaidh ('broom moss') plateau at a height of 850m and the two hills are easily climbed together from the Lairig an Laoigh path in Glen Derry. The Linn of Dee is the nearest road end. From Glen Derry an ascent can be made to the col between Meall an Lundain and Beinn Bhreac, from which the latter is an easy walk. Head north across the Moine Bhealaidh, where it is very easy to go astray in mist, and up the southern slopes to Beinn a'Chaorainn, then down southwest to the path at the head of Glen Derry. The round trip from Linn of Dee is 29km, with 1000m of ascent, and takes 8–9hrs. The best views on the trip are up Coire Etchachan from the Moine Bhealaidh (which Adam Watson's *The Cairngorms* (SMC, 6th edition 1992) describes as 'one of the fine wildernesses of the Cairngorms').

⊗ Beinn Mheadhoin ☆

Beinn Mheadhoin (1182m) is a remote hill, awkward to reach, and lives up to its name, 'middle hill', as it does indeed lie amid other hills. It's often climbed from the Cairngorm ski resort, but this involves crossing the Cairngorm Plateau and descending to Loch Avon first. The only direct route to the hill, without crossing any other hills, is via Glen Derry and Coire Etchachan. Beinn Mheadhoin looks magnificent from this direction too, rising as a steep rocky pyramid at the head of Glen Derry. From Linn of Dee follow the path up Glen Derry and then the fork that leads west past the little Hutchinson Memorial Hut, a useful shelter in bad weather, and up to Loch Etchachan, which lies in a splendid dramatic situation at a height of 925m, with rocky slopes and crags all around. From the loch steep slopes lead to the gravelly summit plateau. The highest point is a granite tor. A short easy scramble leads up the latter. The extensive summit plateau restricts the views from the top. Much better views are to be had from the northern side of the plateau, where you can look straight down to Loch Avon and across to the unspoiled wild side of Cairn Gorm. There is an even better view of Loch Avon and the crags round its head from the minor top of Stacan Dubha, which is a worthwhile short diversion. Retracing the ascent route is the best

Derry Cairngorm from the Coire Sputan Dearg cliffs ▶

option for descent route, making a round trip of 31km, with 1000m of ascent, that takes 9–10hrs.

🌑 Derry Cairngorm ☆

Boulder-covered Derry Cairngorm is one of the stoniest hills in the Cairngorms. From Glen Lui to the south it appears as a big cone, quite elegant in contrast to bulky Beinn Mheadhoin. From east and west it's more of a curving wedge. It is often climbed with Ben Macdui, but is a worthwhile ascent on its own and can also be combined with Beinn Mheadhoin. As for the latter, ascend Glen Lui and Glen Derry from Linn of Dee and then the path up to Loch Etchachan. From the loch it's just 2.5km and 300m of ascent to the summit of Derry Cairngorm, and a good view across Coire Sputan Dearg to Ben Macdui. The long south ridge of the mountain can be descended back to Derry Lodge, for a walk of 27km, with 1100m of ascent, which takes 8–9hrs.

The first recorded ascent of Derry Cairngorm, in 1830, was by accident, when a party led by the naturalist William MacGillivray, descending in mist

after climbing Ben Macdui, traversed the hill rather than descending steep rocky slopes in the dark.

🌓 ❄ Climbing on Creagan a'Choire Etchachan ☆

Creagan a'Choire Etchachan is a minor summit to the north of Derry Cairngorm. On its north face is the 120m granite cliff for which it's named, hanging over upper Coire Etchachan. This is a remote crag in a fine situation. The approaches are long. It can be reached most easily from the path up Coire Etchachan from Glen Derry, and has good winter and summer routes in a wide range of grades. Rock routes range from the easy Quartzvein Edge, a 108m Moderate first climbed by K. Winram, G.C. Greig and M. Smith in 1952 (Grade III in winter), through The Talisman, a 90m Hard Severe first climbed in 1956 by W.D. Brooker and K.A. Grassick (Grade IV in winter), to the serious King Crimson, a 123m E3, first climbed by A. Ross and G.S. Strange in 1984. Winter routes range from the straightforward Forked Gully, a 120m Grade 1, through Central Chimney, a 120m Grade III, first

Beinn Mheadhoin and Carn Etchachan rising above the Loch Avon basin

Walkers ascending Cairn Gorm from the Cairngorm Plateau with Coire an t-Sneachda and Cairn Lochan behind them and Cairn Toul, Sgor an Lochain Uaine and Braeriach on the horizon

climbed by a party led by Tom Patey in 1955, to the hard Switchblade, a 160m Grade VI, first climbed by J. Lyall and A. Nisbet in 1991.

4:9 THE BEN MACDUI AND CAIRNGORM PLATEAU

The great plateau containing Ben Macdui and Cairn Gorm, usually known as the Cairngorm plateau, is the biggest area of sub-arctic tundra-like terrain in Scotland with 20km² above 1000m and 33km² above 900m: a vast expanse of undulating stony terrain made up of gravel screes, boulders and arctic-alpine vegetation. The plateau lies in the centre of the northern Cairngorms, between the Lairig an Laoigh and Lairig Ghru passes, with Glen More to the north and Glen Luibeg to the south. In the west steep slopes run unbroken for 12km above the Lairig Ghru. To the north the plateau ends in big rocky corries, the Northern Corries of Cairn Gorm, with long ridges running down to Glen More. The only big intrusion into the plateau is to the east, where Loch Avon lies in a deep glacial trench below steep slopes and big cliffs, arguable the finest place in the Cairngorms and one of the most spectacular in Scotland. Big waterfalls and water

slides crash down from the plateau into the Loch Avon basin.

Ben Macdui is a big, bulky hill, buttressed by outliers and far from any roads, and thus hard to see from the valleys, and is less known than many lower summits. At 1309m it's the second highest summit in Scotland. In the early 19th century it was believed to be the highest and when it was proved not to be so plans were made by indignant locals to build a cairn on the summit to raise Ben Macdui above Ben Nevis. The man who measured the height of Ben Macdui, the Rev Dr George Keith, also made the first recorded ascent of the hill in 1810. The height was confirmed in 1847 when the Ordnance Survey set up a trigonometrical station on the summit. Just east of the summit the remains of the surveyor's stone hut, often called the Sappers' Bothy, can still be seen.

As with Ben Nevis the meaning of the name is unclear. It could be 'hill of the black pig' or, more likely, 'MacDuff's hill', the MacDuff estates having included the mountain. To the south of Ben Macdui a long narrow ridge, an unusual feature in the Cairngorms, runs out to another Munro, Carn a'Mhaim (1037m). The name is often translated as 'peak of the large rounded hill', which doesn't really apply unless the rounded hill is Ben Macdui.

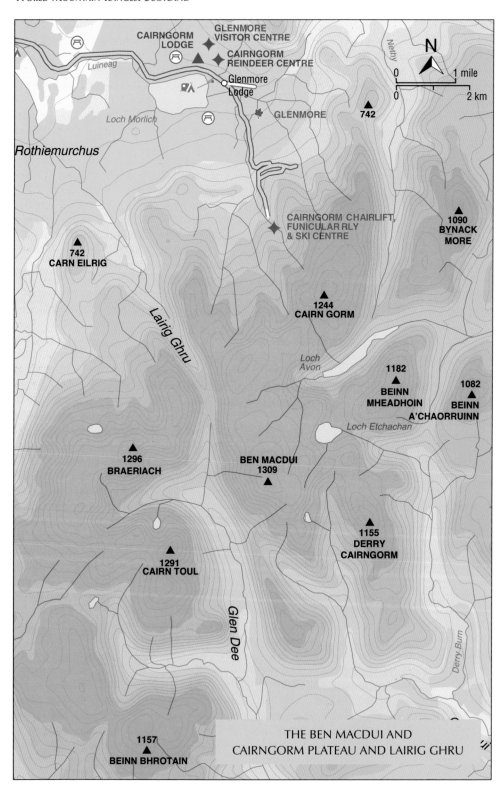

THE BEN MACDUI AND
CAIRNGORM PLATEAU AND LAIRIG GHRU

Peter Drummond's *Scottish Hill Names: Their Origin and Meaning* (Scottish Mountaineering Trust, 2nd revised edition, 2007) reckons it's more likely to be 'cairn above the pass' due to its position above the southern end of the Lairig Ghru. 'Mhaim' is from *mam*, which means a breast, and is used for rounded hills but also for a pass between two hills.

Ben Macdui is reputed to be haunted by a spectral figure, Am Fear Liath Mor, the 'Big Grey Man'. The legend goes back to at least the early 19th century when James Hogg, the Ettrick Shepherd (see Chapter 1), wrote verses about this phantom, but the story gained more credence when the leading mountaineer Norman Collie described, in 1891, hearing giant steps following him, being seized with terror and running down the mountain. Other bizarre stories to do with Ben Macdui being a home to spacemen or a holy Buddhist being have appeared. These and other far fetched beliefs are described in Affleck Gray's book *The Big Grey Man of Ben Macdhui* (Birlinn, 2000). I have been alone on the summit of Ben Macdui many times, often in mist, and have never noticed anything unusual. It is a wonderful, wild, awe-inspiring place without the need for supernatural figures to enhance it.

Cairn Gorm is a domed hill rising south of Glen More and clearly visible from Aviemore and much of Strathspey, although the Northern Corries to the west look more impressive than the summit. It's the sixth highest mountain in Scotland at 1244m. The name means 'blue hill'. Just southwest of Cairngorm are two significant subsidiary summits, Stob Coire an t-Sneachda ('peak of the corrie of the snow', 1176m) and Cairn Lochan ('cairn of the little loch', 1215m). (In my opinion the latter should really be classified as a Munro as it lies 2.5km in a straight line from Cairn Gorm, with a reascent of over 100m. It's even further from Ben Macdui, with a reascent of 90m). Below these summits lie the cliff-rimmed Northern Corries, which are two of the most popular climbing areas in Scotland, especially in winter, due to easy access from the high car park in Coire Cas. The first recorded ascent of Cairn Gorm was by James McIntyre, who'd fought with Bonnie Prince Charlie at the battle of Culloden in 1746, where the Jacobite army was defeated, and who raised the standard he'd carried on the summit in the years following the battle. Ian R. Mitchell, in *Scotland's Mountains Before the Mountaineers* (Luath, 1999), reckons this would have been in the 1750s, as doing so in the years immediately following Culloden would have been punishable by death.

CAIRNGORM MOUNTAIN SKI RESORT

The north side of Cairn Gorm has been lost to lovers of wild country, as an ugly and depressing ski resort fills Coire Cas and Coire na Ciste, the two corries immediately below the summit. The first lifts were erected in 1961. The most recent construction is a funicular railway, opened in 2001, which runs to a restaurant and visitor centre just 120m below the summit and is open year round. The building of the funicular involved a great deal of destruction and damage, making the mess already created by the lifts and bulldozed roads even worse. Cairngorm Mountain, the company running the resort, which is publicly owned and was built with public money, makes great play of its environmental credentials, calling it a National Centre for the Mountain Environment. The only genuine way to improve the environment here would be to remove the whole hideous lot and allow the mountain to recover. There should be no place high on a wild mountainside for mass industrial tourism. A National Centre for the Mountain Environment is a great idea, but it should be in Aviemore, not near the summit of a mountain.

To protect the land around the top station, those who use the funicular are not allowed to leave, as such easy access for large numbers of people would lead to damage to the fragile surrounding terrain. As it is, the road that runs from Glenmore to the car parks at the bottom of the resort in Coire na Ciste and Coire Cas makes access to Cairn Gorm and the Northern Corries much quicker than it would be otherwise.

The resort has 15 lifts, apart from the railway, and more than 20 interlinking runs of all grades. However it seems likely that some of these lifts will be removed in the years to come.

Ben Macdui from Braeriach

⊘ Ben Macdui and Cairn Gorm ☆

These two hills can be climbed separately but the finest walk is across the plateau between them, which gives a real feel of the northern sub-arctic nature of the area. It is a popular route and the walking is easy, which can make it seem safe and gentle on a warm sunny day. However the plateau is big and ringed by very steep, dangerous terrain, and when the mist comes down navigation can be difficult and care is needed. In winter, white-outs, blizzards and very strong winds can make the plateau a very hazardous place.

⊘ Ascending Cairn Gorm

From Glenmore there are a number of approaches to Cairn Gorm. The one to be avoided is the dismal plod up through the ski resort to the top station, from where a line of posts leads to the summit. This does make a safe descent route in bad weather however, especially in winter. A much better route is the ascent of the broad ridge immediately west of Coire Cas, the Fiacaill a'Choire Chais. This ridge narrows and becomes stonier towards the top, finishing at a big cairn at 1141m on the edge of the plateau. The views from the ridge are a great contrast. On one side lies the ski resort in tamed Coire Cas, with the funicular railway running

up the centre, while on the other lies Coire an t-Sneachda, a rugged wild mountain corrie backed by high cliffs. It's 2.5km with 500m of ascent to the plateau by the Fiacaill a'Choire Chais, and then just 0.5km and 100m of ascent east to the summit of Cairn Gorm, where there is a weather station and a large cairn. The view from the latter down to Loch Morlich and the forests of Glenmore and Rothiemurchus stretching out to Strathspey is tremendous. Unfortunately further to the north and east the jarringly unnatural white spikes of wind turbines draw the eye, dominating the quieter, subtler flowing lines of the natural landscape.

To avoid the ski resort altogether and gain a close look at Coire an t-Sneachda, one of the finest corries in the Highlands, take the path leading southwest from the Coire Cas car park, which soon rounds a corner and leaves the sight and sound of the resort behind. The path curves south into the boulder-filled corrie, then climbs to two little pools lying below the cliffs that form the back wall of the corrie. There is a stretcher box here in case of emergency. From the lochans the quickest route to Cairngorm is up the steep slopes at the east end of the cliffs which lead to the plateau close to the top of the Fiacaill a'Choire Chais (4km, 520m of ascent from Coire Cas, around 2hrs). A more interesting route is the Goat Track, a path which zigzags south-west up steep broken ground to emerge abruptly on the plateau at the col between Cairn Lochan and Stob Coire an t-Sneachda (3.5km and 500m ascent from Coire Cas, around 2hrs). The latter peak has to be crossed to reach Cairn Gorm, which lies 2.25km and 200m of ascent to the east (1½–2hrs). If ascending the Goat Track it's best to head for Ben Macdui first, returning over Cairn Gorm.

The west wall of Coire an t-Sneachda, sepa-rating it from Coire an Lochain, is the impressive rocky Fiaciall Coire an t-Sneachda, an easy Grade 1 scramble that reaches the plateau just east of the summit of Cairn Lochan.

The easiest, least steep but longest route to the plateau from Coire Cas takes the path across the bottom of the Northern Corries and then climbs the broad stony ridge forming the west side of Coire an Lochain, reaching the plateau on the southwestern slopes of Cairn Lochan, from where it continues south to Ben Macdui's stony summit. From Coire Cas to Ben Macdui is 8km, with 750m of ascent. The return over Cairn Lochan and Stob Coire an t-Sneachda, with a diversion to Cairn Gorm and descent by the Fiacaill a'Choire Chais, is 10km with 330m of ascent. The return trip from Coire Cas

takes 6–7hrs. The plateau walk is stony but gentle. At the dip between Cairn Lochan and Ben Macdui the route passes the highest named pool in Britain, Lochan Feith Buidhe (1120m), which drains east-wards into Loch Avon.

There is a large cairn topped by a trig point on Ben Macdui plus a panoramic indicator, built by the Cairngorm Club in 1925. A wide range of hills can be seen, showing the extent of the Highlands, but the best view is from some 200m west of the summit, where there is a tremendous vista across the deep trench of the Lairig Ghru to Braeriach and Cairn Toul, with the vast rocky bowl of An Garbh Choire lying between them.

Cairn Gorm can also be climbed by its steep southeastern slopes from the Saddle at the head of Strath Nethy, which can be reached by walking up the boggy strath from the Lairig an Laoigh path or, more pleasantly and interestingly, over Bynack More and A'Choinneach. From The Saddle you can also descend to the path alongside Loch Avon, then climb the steep path into Coire Raibert and then up the southwest slopes of Cairn Gorm. Beyond the head of the loch another path leads up Coire Dhomain to the col between Cairn Lochan and Stob Coire an t-Sneachda. These routes are all on

Stob Coire an t-Sneachda

the wild, unspoilt side of Cairn Gorm and avoid the ski resort completely.

⊗ Ascending Ben Macdui

Ben Macdui can be climbed from the south and the east. A path leads from Loch Etchachan (see Beinn Mheadhoin above) southwest to the summit. A fine route runs up the long Sron Riach ridge from Glen Luibeg, passing the edge of the impressive crags in Coire Sputan Dearg. The return could be made over Carn a'Mhaim and down south, to pick up the Lairig Ghru path that leads back east to Glen Luibeg. The distance is 30km, with 1400m of ascent, and the walk takes 9–10hrs.

⊗ The Chalamain Gap and Creag an Leth-choin (Lurcher's Crag) ☆

On its western side the Cairngorm Plateau ends where the slopes of Cairn Lochan run northwest down to a flat, wet area known as Lurcher's Meadow. To the north rises a steep rocky ridge, a 1053m top called Creag an Leth-choin ('Lurcher's Crag'), whose western slopes are a steep craggy wall rising above the Lairig Ghru and whose northern slopes run down to a narrow rocky ravine called the Chalamain Gap. Creag an Leth-choin looks very impressive from the north, rising as a pointed peak above the notch of the Lairig Ghru. From Lurcher's Meadow a wide gully runs north. This is Lurcher's Gully, the site of a major struggle between environmentalists and developers in the 1980s, when there were proposals to extend the ski resort here. Happily these plans were rejected by a public enquiry and the area has remained wild and natural.

An enjoyable circuit of the Chalamain Gap and Lurcher's Crag can be made from the Sugar Bowl car park, which lies part way up the ski road to Coire Cas (NH 985 074). From the Sugar Bowl a path runs southwest, with good views south to the Northern Corries and Cairn Gorm, to the Chalamain Gap. The gap is a 450m long canyon full of granite boulders, and with steep rocky sides. It's a glacial feature, a meltwater channel where a stream full of rubble ran under the ice, cutting through the rock. The path fades away at the mouth of the gap, leaving an awkward boulder-hopping passage through the gap. The impressive surroundings make up for the rough walking. Once out of the ravine head up the steep northern slopes to the northern summit of Creag an Leth-choin then along the rocky ridge to the higher southern summit. Just south of the

summit is an amazing and dramatic view along the huge cleft of the Lairig Ghru. A short descent leads south from the summit to Lurcher's Meadow, from where you can descend Lurcher's Gully to reach the outward path northeast of the Chalamain Gap. The round trip from the Sugar Bowl is 11km long, with 750m of ascent, and takes 3½–4hrs.

⊙ Ski Touring on the Cairngorm Plateau ☆

The Cairngorm Plateau and surrounding corries are wonderful areas for ski touring. Coire an t-Sneachda and Coire an Lochan are good for short tours, as they can be reached quickly from the Coire Cas car park yet have a wild, remote feel and splendid cliffs. Just west of them Lurcher's Gully provides a superb downhill run and can also be used to reach the plateau by the southwest slopes of Cairn Lochan. The classic tour is from Cairn Gorm to Ben Macdui. Cairn Gorm can be climbed from Coire Cas by way of the Sron an Aonaich between Coire Cas and Coire na Ciste, which leads to the top of the resort from where Cairn Gorm is easily reached. The Fiacaill a'Choire Chais is another option but this is rockier and narrower and doesn't hold the snow as well as the Sron an Aonaich. From the summit of Cairn Gorm the ski across the plateau to Ben Macdui is easy in good weather, and the surroundings have an arctic appearance and sense of vastness. It's a long way back from Ben Macdui however and blizzard conditions can make skiing dangerous and difficult. The skiing may be undemanding but this is a serious tour, taking the skier into remote country, and will take in the region of 5–8hrs. A good circuit is to ascend by the Sron an Aonaich, ski the plateau, then descend by Lurcher's Gully.

⓫ ✳ Climbing in the Northern Corries

Quick access from the Coire Cas car park makes the cliffs in Coire an t-Sneachda and Coire Lochain very popular for both rock climbs and snow and ice climbs, but these corries are better known for the latter. Coire an t-Sneachda in particular can be very crowded on good winter days. Climbers were here long before the road and ski resort however with a party led by Harold Raeburn climbing Pygmy Ridge in Coire an t-Sneachda in 1904. This rock climb is 100m long and is graded Moderate. In the same year T.E. Goodeve and A.W. Russell made a winter ascent of Central Gully in Coire an t-Sneachda (135m, Grade 1). Other easy snow climbs in the same corrie such as Jacob's Ladder (90m, Grade I/II) and Aladdin's

The cliffs of Coire an t-Sneachda

Couloir (180m, Grade I) were first climbed in the 1930s. As well as the ease of access a main attraction of Coire an t-Sneachda is the wealth of lower grade winter climbs. Out of some 50 routes half are Grade III or lower. The routes are fairly short too, most being between 100 and 150m long. Coire an Lochan has slightly fewer winter routes but more of these are in the harder grades. One of the classic climbs in the Cairngorms is 90m Savage Slit, a Very Difficult rock climb and a Grade V winter climb that goes up an easily identifiable crack in a prominent corner.

In winter and spring avalanches and cornice collapses are a danger in both corries, but especially Coire an Lochan, where the Great Slab, a huge piece of pink granite, avalanches regularly.

Loch Avon ☆

The Loch Avon basin is one of the wildest and most impressive places in the Cairngorms and indeed all of the Highlands. The naturalist Seton Gordon reckoned there was 'no more splendid loch in all Scotland' in *Highways and Byways in the Central Highlands* (Birlinn, 1995, first published 1935). The glacially-carved basin is a deep, steep-sided trench with a magnificent ring of grand cliffs at its head, lying at an altitude of 720m. To the north is Cairn

Gorm, to the south Beinn Mheadhoin, to the west the Cairngorm Plateau and the northeastern slopes of Ben Macdui. Although the Cairngorm ski resort can be used for fairly quick access to Loch Avon it's still a remote place, and one that can be difficult to escape from in bad weather, especially in winter. The loch itself is 2.5km long, 300m at its widest and up to 35m deep. At either end, and in places along the sides, there are beautiful gold and white sandy beaches. Beyond the head of the loch there's a small flat meadow below the great cliffs of Hell's Lum, the Shelter Stone Crag and Carn Etchachan, and the rushing water slides of the Garbh Uisge ('rough water') and the Feith Buidhe ('yellow bog-stream'), which merge as they reach the floor of the basin. The best view along the loch to the cliffs is from the southwestern slopes of A'Choinneach and The Saddle to the northeast. From above there is a fine view of the loch from Stacan Dubh, on the edge of Beinn Mheadhoin, and from the eastern edge of the Cairngorm Plateau. There are rough paths along both sides of the loch.

🚶 Walking to Loch Avon

There are a number of ways to reach Loch Avon. From Glenmore the Lairig an Laoigh path (see

287

above) leads to Strath Nethy. The walk up this long, narrow, almost claustrophobic boggy glen leads to the col called The Saddle from where you can descend to the loch shore, a distance from Glenmore of 12.5km, with 590m of ascent, taking 3½–4hrs. It's another 2km to the head of the loch. A longer but less boggy route stays with the Lairig an Laoigh path to the Fords of Avon, then follows the River Avon up to the loch, a distance of 15km with 650m of ascent from Glenmore to the foot of the loch, which takes 4–5hrs. The shortest routes to Loch Avon are the steepest and highest, as they involve crossing the Cairngorm Plateau. From Coire Cas the Fiacaill a'Choire Chais (see above) can be climbed to the plateau and then Coire Raibert immediately to the south descended to Loch Avon, a distance of just 4.6km with 500m of ascent. This route brings you out 500m from the head of the loch. To reach there directly you can climb the Goat Track in Coire an t-Sneachda and then descend Coire Domhain, a distance from Glenmore of 5km with 500m of ascent. By either of these routes you can reach Loch Avon in a couple of hours. The terrain is steep and these are not suitable as escape routes in storms, especially in winter. Far better the long walk out via Strath Nethy than risk crossing the plateau in a blizzard.

⬦ Loch Avon to the Cairngorm Plateau ☆

The climb out of the Loch Avon basin to the Cairngorm Plateau is an easy but spectacular scramble and one of the finest routes in Scotland, passing through glorious rock scenery beside beautiful cascades. There are many route options and most of the scrambling can be avoided. The grade is 1 or 2 depending on the route chosen. The scramble ascends the tiers of easy angled slabs lying between the Feith Buidhe and the Garbh Uisge streams. These crash down in a series of cataracts and slides, a magnificent sight. The Garbh Uisge cataracts fall 110m, the last 30m being one impressive unsupported fall just above the boulder-filled floor of the basin. The Feith Buidhe cataract is even longer at 250m, but is more a series of water slides than waterfalls, as the water glides over smooth granite slabs. In spate both streams are awesome and powerful, great torrents of surging white water. The routes to the plateau meander up the slabs beside the Feith Buidhe. In places you can even walk up the water. Once the terrain has eased and the plateau is reached you can continue west to the Lochan Buidhe, turn south for Ben Macdui or north for Cairn Lochan.

An alternative scramble is via the big scree chute called Castlegates Gully between Carn Etchachan and the Shelter Stone Crag. This is a straightforward Grade I snow climb in winter.

Loch Avon from the Cairngorm Plateau

Carn Etchachan and the Shelter Stone Crag rising above the head of Loch Avon

THE SHELTER STONE

*The Shelter Stone
in the Loch Avon basin*

The most distinctive and impressive of the cliffs around the Loch Avon basin is the great flat-topped block of the Sticil or Shelter Stone Crag. Below this massive rock, which lies on the south side of the basin, a wild jumble of boulders spills down the hillside, the results of an ancient and enormous rockfall. The largest of these boulders is the Shelter Stone or Clach Dhion ('stone of the shelter'), a huge block resting on smaller ones with a space beneath it and one of the most famous refuges in Scotland. Estimates of the weight of the stone range from 1300 to 1700 tons. The dark chamber below the Shelter Stone has been a refuge for many centuries. It was used 'as a sleeping place for hunters of the red deer' according to Seton Gordon (*Highways and Byways in the Central Highlands* (Birlinn, 1995, first published 1935). However other accounts say it was used by bandits and could hold 'eighteen armed men'. It would certainly have made a good hiding place but it would be a squeeze for 18 people, as the floor only measures around 4m by 3m, which is just comfortable for five or six walkers plus gear. There isn't room to stand up straight but you can crouch and there's ample room to sit. The floor is covered with orange plastic sheets (mostly survival bags split down the sides), heather and dirt. Gaps in the sides of the shelter have been stuffed with stones, heather and clods of earth to make it quite windproof and dry. The entrance is a narrow crack that keeps out the weather but easily gets snowed up in winter. The Shelter Stone is quite easy to locate as there is a cairn on top and paths to it from below. It's a popular shelter and can be full. Due to this there are less cosy and effective shelters under other boulders close by, some of them only big enough for one person.

The Shelter Stone has been used by mountaineers since the early days and the first climbing club in Scotland, the Cairngorm Club, was founded at the Shelter Stone in 1887. There is a visitors' book in a tin box, as there has been since the Cairngorm Club placed the first one there in 1924.

ⓒ ✸ Climbing on the Loch Avon and Etchachan Cliffs ☆

The Loch Avon basin is one of the most magnificent climbing arenas in Scotland, with superb rock and ice climbs on Hell's Lum, the Shelter Stone Crag and Carn Etchachan.

Hell's Lum is a south-facing crag high up on the mountainside, at a height of 850m. The name comes from big Hell's Lum Gully on the left side of the crag, *lum* being Scots for chimney. Hell's Lum is often wet; in winter freezes there are excellent ice routes, mostly in the higher grades. In summer a classic rock climb is another prominent gully, Deep-Cut Chimney, a 135m Very Difficult, first climbed by I.M. Brooker and Miss M. Newbigging in 1950. In winter Deep-Cut Chimney is a Grade IV, first climbed by Tom Patey and D. Holroyd in 1958. Hell's Lum Gully itself runs with water in summer, but is a 150m Grade II/III when frozen, and was first climbed in 1956 by G. McLeod and I. Brown.

The mighty Shelter Stone Crag faces north and rises 240m above an apron of boulders. Harold Raeburn came here and climbed his eponymous Raeburn's Buttress in 1907 but there were no other ascents for 40 years. Raeburn's Buttress is described as 'a dangerously vegetated pioneer route' (*Cairngorms* Guide, SMT, 2007). In winter it's a 240m Grade IV, first climbed in 1971 by W. March and J. Hart. In general the Shelter Stone Crag is steep and serious, with most routes in the higher grades, including an E7 rock climb (Realm of the Senses, 139m, first climbed by R. Campbell and G. Latter in 1993) and a Grade VII winter climb (Citadel, 270m, first climbed by M. Hamilton and K. Spence in 1980) that goes up the centre of the main face. As a rock climb The Citadel is graded VS and was first climbed by Ronnie Sellars and G. Annand in 1958.

The third of the great trio of cliffs around the head of Loch Avon is Carn Etchachan, a complex pointed crag that is one of the biggest in the Cairngorms. It's 240m high and faces north. Winter routes range from Grade II/III to Grade VI. A classic is Route Major, a 285m Grade IV that runs up the centre of the face. It was first climbed by Tom Patey and M. Smith in 1957. Another classic Patey route on Carn Etchachan is Scorpion, a 240m Grade V. Scorpion is a Very Difficult grade rock climb.

ⓒ ✸ Climbing on Coire Sputan Dearg ☆

Coire Sputan Dearg is the only crag that actually belongs to Ben Macdui rather than a subsidiary top. It lies 1km east of the summit at the head of Glen Luibeg at a height of 990m. Facing south gives it a sunnier more open feel than many cliffs. The routes are mostly in the easier grades but climbing here is still serious due to the remoteness and the long walk in. The easiest access is from Linn of Dee up Glen Luibeg. A classic rock route is Crystal Ridge, a 90m Difficult first climbed in 1948 by R. Still and J.E. Lawrence, which runs up the narrow crest of a huge slab. In winter it's a Grade III and was first climbed by W.D. Brooker and M. Smith in 1949.

4:10 LAIRIG GHRU

The Lairig Ghru is one of the finest and best-known high mountain passes in the Highlands, linking Strathspey with Deeside through the heart of the Cairngorms. From Strathspey to the north the pass appears as a huge, steep-sided cleft between Creag an Leth-choin and Sron na Lairige. The Lairig Ghru runs from the fine old pines of Rothiemurchus Forest in Strathspey up into wild rocky country, reaching 835m, then down Glen Dee to the pine forest around the Linn of Dee. The east side of the pass is an almost straight, unbroken wall of rock and scree stretching some 13.5km from the northern slopes of Castle Hill to the southern slopes of Carn a'Mhaim, a wall topped by Ben Macdui.

The west side is completely different, with the huge An Garbh Choire ('the rough corrie'), the biggest and most impressive corrie in the Cairngorms, biting back into the mountains. There are four Munros on this western side, including the third, fourth and fifth highest, all most easily climbed from the pass. From north to south these are: Braeriach ('brindled upland', 1296m), Sgor an Lochain Uaine ('peak of the little green loch', 1258m), Cairn Toul ('peak of the barn', 1291m) and The Devil's Point (1004m). The last name is a Victorian euphemism, the Gaelic being Bod an Deamhain, which means 'devil's penis'. Sgor an Lochain Uaine is sometimes called the Angel's Peak, as a contrast to the Devil's Point. Set further back from the pass, around the side valley of Glen Geusachan are two more Munros, Monadh Mor ('big hill', 1113m) and Beinn Bhrotain ('hill of

View from Ben Macdui to Cairn Toul and Sgur an Lochain Uaine rising above the Lairig Ghru

the mastiff Brodan', 1157m), which are also most easily climbed from the Lairig Ghru.

Braeriach is a massive hill with many corries and broad shoulders, and has a long, flat summit plateau. Sgor an Lochain Uaine and Cairn Toul are much smaller in area, the former with a fine pointed summit, the latter with a short, sloping summit ridge that makes for a distinctive profile when seen from the west. However from the south-east it's a lovely, pointed cone with a little corrie just below the summit.

The slopes on the Lairig Ghru side are all steep and rocky, but gentler, greener slopes fall away to the Moine Mhor ('big moss') to the west. The Devil's Point is a stubby pyramid paved with big overlapping slabs on its south and east faces.

The first recorded ascent of Braeriach and Cairn Toul (and presumably Sgor an Lochain Uaine, as it lies between them) was by the Rev Dr George Keith on the same 1810 journey on which he made the first ascents of Beinn a'Bhuird and Ben Macdui (see above). His ascent of Braeriach and Cairn Toul was quite an epic, with thick fog, torrential rain, strong winds, a scramble up the rocks beside the Falls of Dee – which counts as one of the earliest recorded rock climbs – and a descent in the dark during which the party became lost. When

they finally arrived at a shieling where there were a couple of shepherds Keith said they were 'completely exhausted with hunger and exertion'. All the shepherds had to offer them were thick oatmeal bannocks, which Keith said were 'the best I have ever tasted'. Keith's account of the ascent is quoted in Ian R. Mitchell's *Scotland's Mountains Before the Mountaineers* (Luath, 1999).

Lairig means 'pass' but the meaning of 'Ghru' is obscure, an 'enigma' according to Seton Gordon's *Highways and Byways in the Central Highlands* (Birlinn, 1995, first published 1935). Peter Drummond, in *Scottish Hill Names: Their Origin and Meaning* (Scottish Mountaineering Trust, 2nd revised edition, 2007), gives it as 'gloomy', but Adam Watson says it is probably from *drudhadh* meaning 'oozing' (*The Cairngorms*, SMC, 6th edition 1992).

The pass was once a drove road used to take cattle and sheep south to Braemar. Seton Gordon says that the path was kept in good repair, and was once not rough and rocky at the watershed, as it was when he wrote about it in 1935, and as it is now. Gordon reports that women from Rothiemurchus used to cross the pass with baskets of eggs on their heads to sell in Braemar, something that would be very difficult to do now.

291

The Lairig Ghru is not a gentle place and the weather can be harsh, with winds picking up speed as they are funnelled through the narrow defile. Sometimes cloud can be seen boiling up in the pass when the tops either side are clear. Over the years there have been many accidents involving walkers in the Lairig Ghru, often due to exhaustion or hypothermia. One of the best known, although undated, is the story of three tailors who took a bet that one New Year's Eve they could dance a reel in Abernethy, Rothiemurchus and Braemar. They had crossed the pass and were heading down Glen Dee when a blizzard blew up and they died trying to shelter behind a pile of rocks halfway between the Allt Clach nan Taillear and Corrour Bothy. This is now known as the Clach nan Taillear – 'stone of the tailors'.

◑ Walking the Lairig Ghru ☆

The record time for the Lairig Ghru is 3hrs 11mins for men, set by D. Brown in 1984, and 3¾hrs for women, set by Helene Diamantides in 1992. Most people will take around 12hrs for the whole route, however, which can easily be split over two days, with an overnight camp or a stay in Corrour Bothy, a small and often crowded shelter roughly halfway that was built in 1877 as a deer watcher's house, but has been used by mountaineers and walkers since the 1920s.

Once through the Lairig Ghru there is the problem of returning to the start. Unless a lift has been arranged the easiest way is to walk, as there is no direct public transport. Even with a car the journey is at least a couple of hours over the A939. Walking back can be done over the summits, via the Lairig an Laoigh or via Glen Feshie.

The most scenic way to walk the Lairig Ghru is north to south, as the finest section is that from Rothiemurchus Forest into the giant maw of the pass, a journey from the soft green of the forest into the harsh rocky heart of the mountains. The walk starts at Coylumbridge, 2.5km east of Aviemore, where a track heads south through the forest beside the Am Beanaidh burn to the confluence with the Allt Druidh, which is then followed upwards through pines that gradually diminish, in both size and numbers. Slowly the slopes on either side close in and steepen. Winds whistle through the pass, and I have been turned back in winter when blowing snow and hurricane-force blasts made progress impossible. As the top of the pass

is approached the terrain becomes stonier, with many boulders through which the path threads a way. Just beyond the pass lie the bleak yet lovely Pools of Dee, from which you can look down at Glen Dee broadening out to the south, with the dark blunt pyramid of The Devil's Point prominent. Descending Glen Dee there are superb views up huge crag-rimmed An Garbh Choire and to the distinctive, sloping-topped Cairn Toul. Corrour Bothy lies across the river close to the foot of The Devil's Point. From Corrour there are two options. Either stay beside the River Dee south to White Bridge and then east to the Linn of Dee, or take the path curving east to Glen Luibeg and Derry Lodge, and then down Glen Lui to Linn of Dee.

◑ The An Garbh Choire Munros ☆

The four Munros ringing An Garbh Choire can be climbed together in one great circuit of the rim of the corrie, which is one of the finest high-level walks in the Cairngorms (Adam Watson says 'perhaps the finest high-level hillwalk in Britain'). It's long, however, and perhaps best done from a camp or from Corrour Bothy in the Lairig Ghru – or even, in good weather, a camp high on the tops. The nearest starting point is the Sugar Bowl car park on the ski road from Glenmore to Coire Cas. From the Sugar Bowl take the path through the Chalamain Gap (see above) and down into the Lairig Ghru. A path climbs up Sron na Lairige, a subsidiary top of Braeriach, on the far side, then curves round to the summit of this big, burly hill. Braeriach is an S-shaped mountain, running south, then west, then south again. There are rugged corries to every side except the southwest. The summit cairn lies not far from the edge of Coire Bhrochain on the north side of An Garbh Choire. There are fantastic views down into the corrie, across to Cairn Toul and over the Lairig Ghru to Ben Macdui.

The splendid views continue on the walk round the rim of An Garbh Choire to Sgor an Lochain Uaine and Cairn Toul. On the descent from Braeriach there is a view of the Falls of Dee, the infant river tumbling down granite slabs into An Garbh Choire from its source at the Wells of Dee at 1220m. From Cairn Toul the route descends over the subsidiary top of Stob Coire an t-Saighdeir ('peak of the corrie of the soldier') to the head of Coire Odhar, where a path leads down to Corrour Bothy and the Lairig Ghru. The Devil's Point is an easy 500m walk, with 120m of ascent from the top

Braeriach from the Cairngorm Plateau

of Coire Odhar. The whole walk from the Sugar Bowl over all four Munros is 36km long, with 2200m of ascent, and takes at least 10–12hrs.

Braeriach can also be climbed from An Garbh Choire via the south ridge of Coire Bhrochain, an exciting route with a touch of adventure and exploration about it, from long Gleann Einich to the northwest and across the Moine Mhor from Glen Feshie to the west, from where Cairn Toul and Sgor an Lochain Uaine can be climbed as well.

❥ The Northeast Ridge of Sgor an Lochain Uaine ☆

A high hanging corrie lies between Sgor an Lochain Uaine and Cairn Toul containing the beautiful lochan from which the former takes its name. The ridge that forms the western rim of the corrie is narrow and rocky and an excellent easy Grade 1 scramble. To reach Lochain Uaine head up An Garbh Choire to the very small Garbh Choire Refuge (it just sleeps three in its windowless dark and damp confines) then turn south and find a way up the steep slopes above to the lip of the corrie, where a waterfall pours down granite slabs, and a sudden view of the lochan with the two peaks rising either side, steep pointed Sgor an Lochain looking much the finer. The 300m northeast ridge

is a lovely arête, one of the few like this in the Cairngorms, and leads straight to the summit. There are many boulders on the ridge but no really exposed scrambling. In winter it's a Grade 1 climb.

☸ The Glen Geusachan Munros

Beinn Bhrotain and Monadh Mor are easily climbed together. They are wild and remote, but less dramatic – and therefore less visited – than the An Garbh Choire hills just to the north. Beinn Bhrotain is a huge, sprawling, rather shapeless hill with many broad ridges. To the west a narrow neck of land separates it from Monadh Mor, which takes the form of a broad ridge running south–north. The steepest, rockiest and most impressive side of these hills is that facing Glen Geusachan, and the most interesting ascent is up this beautiful glen to its head and then over the summits. Starting at Linn of Dee the Lairig Ghru path can be followed up Glen Dee to Glen Geusachan. The latter glen can be quite boggy, but the magnificently wild surroundings of crags, slabs, screes and streams makes up for any discomfort. The climb out of the head of the glen leads to high, wild Lochan nan Stuirteag, from where you can cross the stony summits to descend via the subsidiary top of Carn Cloich-mhuillin ('millstone hill') – which was Sir Hugh

Loch Einich and Braeriach from Sgor Gaoith

Munro's intended final summit (he classified it as a separate mountain) but he died with it unclimbed – and back down to Glen Dee. From Linn of Dee this is a 35km walk, with 1200m of ascent, and takes 9–10hrs.

Climbs in An Garbh Choire ☆

The high corries hanging above An Garbh Choire hold masses of snow, especially Garbh Choire Mhor, in which a small snowfield is said to have disappeared only three times in the 20th century. This is remote country – it take 2½hrs just to walk from the Lairig Ghru up An Garbh Choire to its head – so any climbing here is a serious venture. There are over 50 routes, many of them in the lower grades. There are rock climbs but the area is more noted for the winter climbing. Two highly-regarded routes in upper Garbh Choire Mhor are 120m She-Devil's Buttress, a Very Difficult rock climb and a Grade V winter climb, and 140m Vulcan, a VS in summer and a Grade V in winter.

Around the Falls of Dee lie the crags of Garbh Choire Dhaidh. The classic route here is the dark 140m chimney in the centre of the cliffs called the Great Rift, which is a Very Difficult rock climb and a Grade V winter climb. In Coire Brochain, directly

below the summit of Braeriach, is the 80m Ebony Chimney, a three-star Grade VI winter route.

Lairig Ghru Ski Tours ☆

This is a fine area for ski touring, although the long approaches from low ground mean that skis may have to be carried a fair way. Skiing right through the Lairig Ghru itself is a grand tour when there is enough snow. The steep slopes overlooking the Lairig Ghru don't make for easy approaches to the summits, however, and these are usually skied over the Moine Mhor from Glen Feshie to the east (see below). Braeriach can be skied from the Lairig Ghru via the Sron na Lairige, however, and Beinn Bhrotain and Monadh Mor reached from the head of Glen Geusachan.

Skiing the Cairngorms Five ☆

The round of Cairn Gorm, Ben Macdui, Cairn Toul, Sgor an Lochain Uaine and Braeriach is one of the great ski tours, passing through magnificent scenery and climbing the five highest summits in the Cairngorms. The skiing is very varied, with steep ascents, easy, fast plateau traverses and exciting steep descents. It's a major expedition that's 32km long, with 2100m of ascent, and takes 12–15hrs, making it best done in spring rather than winter in order to have more daylight hours. The tour can be done from Linn of Dee to the south, or Whitewell or Loch an Eilean to the north, but these involve long low-level approaches where skis will probably have to be carried. The highest start point is the Coire Cas car park, from where Cairn Gorm can be climbed via Sron an Aonaich and then the plateau crossed to Ben Macdui. The most difficult, but also the finest downhill skiing comes next, with the steep 700m descent into the Lairig Ghru. Care is needed, as there can be avalanche danger here. If safe the Allt Clach nan Taillear ('burn of the tailor's stone') can be descended. Alternatively the broad shoulder south of the burn can be skied. Once across the Lairig Ghru there is an ascent of Coire Odhar – which is quite steep and can be icy at the top, sometimes requiring crampons – to the southern slopes of Cairn Toul and a ski over the three summits east of the Lairig Ghru. From Braeriach there is a wonderful ski over Sron na Lairige and down Coire Gorm to Lochan Odhar, where you can turn east, cross the Lairig Ghru again, and then ski through the Chalamain Gap and across the foot of the Northern Corries back to Coire Cas.

4:11 GLEN FESHIE

Glen Feshie is one of the loveliest glens in the Cairngorms, with a wide variety of scenery, including fine old Caledonian forest, a narrow rocky ravine, and a wide boggy upper section that feels very lonely and wild. Insensitive plantations, bulldozed roads and over-grazing have damaged the glen but it still retains enough wildness and beauty to be a wonderful place. Glen Feshie has changed hands many times over the years and how well it has been cared for has depended on the whims of the owner, a disgraceful situation for such an important part of the natural heritage of Scotland.

There are few habitations in Glen Feshie today. There were far more in the past, and there are traces of many dwelling places in the glen, some dating back 400 years. An interesting study of the glen's history is Meryl M. Marshall's *Glen Feshie: The History and Archaeology of a Highland Glen* (North of Scotland Archaeological Society, 2006).

Glen Feshie is a long glen, stretching some 32km from Feshiebridge in Strathspey to the headwaters below Leathad an Taobhain (see above). From Feshiebridge, which lies on the B970 road

to the south of the River Spey, a single track road runs south through forestry plantations down the east side of the glen for 8km to Auchlean. Halfway along the road is Glen Feshie Hostel at Balachroick House, a friendly independent hostel that makes a good base for exploring Glen Feshie and the surrounding hills. No parking is allowed at Auchlean but 1km before the road end there's a car park. There is a road on the west side of the glen but this is only a public road for 4km, after which it becomes a private estate road leading to Glenfeshie Lodge. Bikes can be used on this road, giving quick access to the upper glen. The lower glen south of Auchlean is a wide glaciated U-shaped valley with a flat floor and steep sides.

From Auchlean a path runs on heather-covered shelves above the rushing river, past forest plantations, to join a bulldozed track opposite the buildings at Carnachuin, the most southerly permanently inhabited buildings in the glen. To the east the mouth of a deep-sided glen can be seen. This is Coire Garbhlach, a narrow twisting corrie hidden by steep, craggy sides. A rickety wooden bridge used to cross the river at Carnachuin but this was washed away in a flood in September 2009. There is supposed to be a new bridge here but at the time of writing this has not been built and the bridge 2.8km down the glen at NN 850 964 should be used if you need to cross the Feshie. The finest part of the lower glen lies ahead, with many magnificent old Scots pine and large junipers scattered among grassland, through which the wide braided river runs over shingle banks. There is a large and popular bothy here, called Ruigh-aiteachain, with an outside toilet. Nearby is a ruined stone chimney, probably the last remnant of a building built by the Victorian artist Sir Edwin Henry Landseer, famous for the sculptures of lions in Trafalgar Square in London and the romantic painting of a red deer stag called *The Monarch of the Glen*. Queen Victoria visited the glen in 1861 and wrote that she 'went into one of the huts to look at a fresco of stags of Landseer's over a chimney-piece'. In the 1930s the remains of these frescoes could still be seen on the walls according to Seton Gordon's *Highways and Byways in the Central Highlands* (Birlinn, 1995, first published 1935), which says the building was a chapel. Ruigh-aiteachain means 'shieling of the junipers', and there are indeed many big juniper bushes nearby.

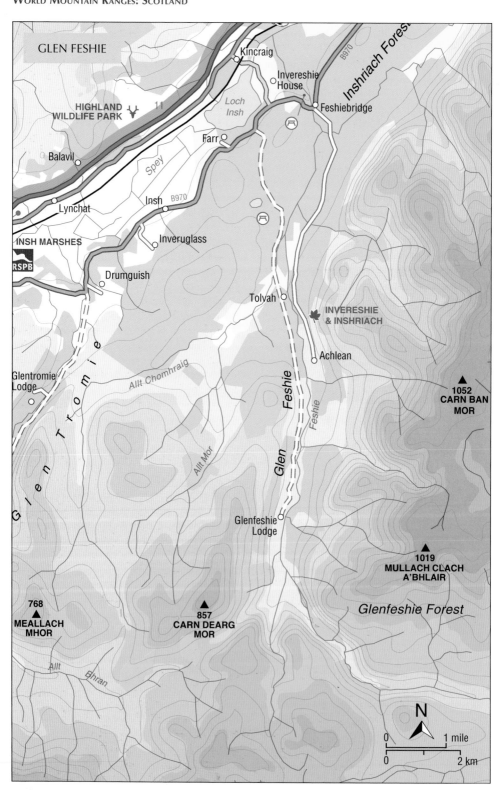

South of the bothy the glen starts to turn to the southeast, and here its character begins to change, as it narrows and is hemmed in by steep craggy slopes, wilder and more rugged than the broader glen to the north. Waterfalls rush down the steep slopes either side and there are stands of ancient twisted birches and pines. Soon the woods are left behind and the glen becomes a moorland valley. A major tributary, the River Eidart, joins the Feshie from the north. The Eidart runs deep into the Moine Mhor, making for a wonderfully wild and remote way to the summits. Not far beyond the confluence with the Eidart the Feshie makes a dogleg turn to the west and the broad, boggy and little visited upper glen. At the dogleg only a few hundred metres and a gentle almost unnoticeable rise separates the Feshie, running north to the Spey, from the infant River Geldie, which runs east to the Dee.

Lower Glen Feshie is walled by the broad shoulders of the Sgorans ridge on the east (see above) with gentler, wooded hills to the west. South of the Sgorans lies the vast expanse of the Moine Mhor, rising to a high point at 1019m Mullach Clach a'Bhlair ('summit of the stone of the plain' – the plain being the Moine Mhor), a massive bulky Munro. Carn an Fhidhleir, An Sgarscoch

and Beinn Bhreac (see above) lie to the south of the upper glen. Rising to the west above the braided river and the old pines south of Ruigh-aiteachain is an 857m Corbett, Carn Mor Dearg ('big red cairn'), which can be linked with another Corbett further west still, 769m Meallach Mhor ('big hump').

According to Adam Watson's *The Cairngorms* (SMC, 6th edition 1992) Glen Feshie is an anglicisation of Gleann Feithisidh, which means 'boggy-haugh glen', a haugh being a low-lying meadow, of which there are many in the glen. However Meryl M. Marshall's *Glen Feshie* says it 'is thought to mean "fairy water" from the Gaelic "*feith sithean*"' but that it might also be Pictish or Celtic in origin, from the root *ved*, which means wet.

Walking Glen Feshie ☆

Glen Feshie is the easiest walking route from Strathspey to Deeside, the crossing over to the Geldie Burn being far less mountainous than the Lairig an Laoigh or Lairig Ghru. It's 33km with 700m of ascent from Auchlean to Linn of Dee. There's a path all the way and this is a fine through-route. The Glen Feshie section is the best part of it, however, and is enjoyable in both directions, so is a good there and back route. Indeed, I think this is one of the best

Upper Glen Feshie

glen walks in the Highlands. A fitting turning point is the ruined sheiling at Ruighe nan Leum, where the Allt Coire Bhlair rushes down a narrow rock-rimmed gorge from the Moine Mhor to the north and then wanders across a pleasant green sward to the Feshie. The walk from Auchlean to Ruighe nan Leum takes you through the forests of the lower glen, into the narrow craggy section and up to the edge of the bare open moorland of the upper glen, a transition from green softness to brown harshness, with, all the time, the sparkling river dancing along close by. The round trip from Auchlean is 24km long, with 600m of ascent, and takes 7–8hrs.

⊗ Mullach Clach a'Bhlair ☆

Mullach Clach a'Bhlair is Glen Feshie's Munro, the only one that really belongs to the glen. Sgor Gaoith sends down bulging shoulders to Glen Feshie, but the summit and the crags abutting it overlook Gleann Einich. Mullach Clach a'Bhlair however presents its steepest slopes to Glen Feshie, dominating the east and north side of the glen for some 10km. To the north Mullach Clach a'Bhlair fades away gently into the Moine Mhor, while to the east it drops steeply to the River Eidart, a tributary of the Feshie.

Mullach Clach a'Bhlair has a reputation as a rather dull hill, probably because the standard way up follows the ugly bulldozed road above the Allt Coire Chaoil and then south across the Moine Mhor almost to the summit. This is only a good route when the road is buried by snow and skis can be used. As a walk it does a disservice to Mullach Clach a'Bhlair. There are two far better ways that can be linked to make a grand circuit that is actually one of the most interesting walks in the Cairngorms and includes a visit to secretive Coire Garbhlach, whose mouth is passed by many walkers who have no idea of the wild and glorious scenery lying just a short distance away.

To reach the corrie leave the path down the glen at the Allt Garbhlach and follow the stream upwards. The going is rough at first, with much heather and some peat bog, but gets easier as the corrie is entered, where traces of a path appear. The 2km long floor of the corrie is narrow, and twists between steep scree and heather slopes topped by ragged, broken crags, showing why this corrie's name translates as 'the Rough Corrie'. The stream speeds up, crashing down in a fine waterfall near the mouth of the corrie and then twisting and turning over boulders in the chaotic heart of the corrie. Each turn of the corrie reveals yet more steep crags and scree, and soon you are surrounded by the steep slopes, with the entrance to the corrie hidden. A final turn and a fine waterfall appears, tumbling a hundred metres or so down the corrie headwall. There are various ways to climb out of the corrie, all of them steep and arduous. The easiest is via Fionnar Choire, a grassy side corrie lying to the north, although if this is taken the headwall waterfall will be missed. Instead you can scramble up beside the waterfall, which involves some easy Grade 1 scrambling, or take the somewhat easier slopes either side.

Once on the gentle slopes above the corrie it's an easy walk south to the summit of Mullach Clach a'Bhlair, some of it on the vehicle track, which is hard to avoid. From the rounded summit, the highest point of which can be hard to find in mist, there are views across the Moine Mhor to Braeriach. To descend head down the southwest ridge over Druim nam Bo and on down to Lochan nam Bo, which lies in a narrow notch in the hillside, and then the little cairned summit of Creag na Gaibhre from where there is a superb view down steep craggy slopes to Glen Feshie. Just below the summit to the northwest an old and little-used stalkers' path zigzags down the hillside, then cuts north to eventually reach the glen floor not far from Ruigh-aiteachain. This is a lovely path but one that is hard to follow in places.

⊗ Carn Dearg Mor, Meallach Mhor and Leathad Taobhain

Facing Mullach Clach a'Bhlair across Glen Feshie lies the sprawling, rounded, heather-covered mass of Carn Dearg Mor, a rather isolated Corbett with good views. This hill can be easily traversed from Glen Feshie or combined with Meallach Mhor, an even remoter and less visited Corbett that is also rounded and heathery, lying 5km to the east above Glen Tromie, or with Leathad an Taobhain (see above), 5km to the south. The route from Auchlean runs down Glen Feshie to Carnachuin, then takes an estate track northwest to the north ridge, which runs up to Carn Dearg Beag, where there is a trig point, and then gently southwards to Carn Mor Dearg with a superb view all around. To the north the Monadh Liath looks almost flat-topped, a long, straight ridge above Strathspey. To the south the rolling, rounded southern Cairngorms are equally undistinguished. To the west, however, Creag Meagaidh is big and impressive, with the gash of The Window prominent. The best view lies to the east, however, especially if you walk 100m or so in that direction, from where you can look down to the braided River Feshie far below, with Mullach Clach a'Bhlair rising on the far side, massive and ponderous. From here it's possible to see just how dominant and complex a hill it is. Beyond the Mullach flat-topped, steep-sided Cairn Toul, the asymmetric pyramid of Sgor an Lochain Uaine and bulky Braeriach rise on the far side of the Moine Mhor.

From Carn Mor Dearg a short descent leads southwest to a track that can be taken east through a narrow glen, past little Lochan an t-Stuic and down to Glen Feshie, where it continues north up the west side of the glen to Carnachuin. The round trip from the Auchlean car park is 21.5km long, with 645m of ascent, and takes 5–7hrs.

Just west of Lochan an t-Stuic the track forks. The southern branch leads for just over 5km, with 450m of ascent, to Leathad an Taobhain. The return can be made by heading west to join the Minigaig path (see above) which leads down to the track between the Allt Bhran and Glen Feshie that runs past Lochan an t-Stuic.

If climbing both Meallach Mhor and Carn Mor Dearg, the track from Carnachuin running northwest and then southwest to the Feith Mhor leads up to the 540m high col between the two hills, from where Meallach Mhor is 1hr walk to the west (2.5km and 270m of ascent). Back at the col Carn Dearg Mor can be climbed and the north ridge descended back to Glen Feshie, for a round trip from Auchlean of 32km, with 1000m of ascent, which takes 8½–9½hrs.

❷ Glen Feshie and the Moine Mhor Skiing ☆

The Moine Mhor provides some of the best ski touring in Scotland and holds the snow well, often long into the spring. Mullach Clach a'Bhlair is a fine hill to ski, and once on the plateau many other peaks can be reached – Sgor Gaoith, Braeriach, Cairn Toul, Monadh Mor. Perhaps the classic tour is from Mullach Clach a'Bhlair to Sgor Gaoith, along the western edge of the Moine Mhor. The western slopes of Mullach Clach a'Bhlair can be climbed to the summit from Carnachuin. This is ideal if there is enough snow to ski down the glen; if not the track above the Allt Fhearnagan can be climbed to reach the Moine Mhor just south of Carn Ban Mor, from where you can go north to Sgor Gaoith and south to Mullach Clach a'Bhlair. The best descent route depends on where the snow lies. The gullies of both Coire Gorm and Coire Ruadh, which lie either side of the Allt Fhearnagan track, are excellent ski descents when full of snow. Depending on the exact route chosen this route is around 24km long with 1000m of ascent, and takes 7–9hrs.

4:12 THE SPEYSIDE WAY

The Speyside Way runs from the coast into the northern Cairngorms. It's an approach route rather than a mountain route and is covered in the Introduction.

ACCESS, BASES, MAPS AND GUIDES

Access

East Drumochter, The Gaick and Minigaig The A9 over the Pass of Drumochter to Dalwhinnie. Railway stations at Blair Atholl, Dalwhinnie and Kingussie.

Glen Tilt A9 to Blair Atholl. Railway station at Blair Atholl.

Ben Vrackie A9 to Pitlochry. Railway station at Pitlochry.

Glen Shee A93 from Blairgowrie to Braemar.

Glen Doll B955 up Glen Clova from Kirriemuir.

Lochnagar The A93 from Braemar to Ballater. Minor road from Ballater along Glen Muick to the Spittal of Glenmuick.

Mount Keen Minor road up Glen Esk from the B966 north of Edzell. Minor road up Glen Tanar from the Bridge of Ess on the B976 southwest of Aboyne.

Ben Avon and Beinn a'Bhuird Invercauld Bridge on the A93 east of Braemar. Linn of Quoich on the minor road on the north side of Glen Dee west of Braemar. Minor road up Glen Avon from Tomintoul on the A939.

Lairig an Laoigh Linn of Dee on the minor road along Glen Dee west of Braemar. Glenmore Lodge on the minor road from Aviemore to Coire Cas.

Ben Macdui and Cairn Gorm Linn of Dee on the minor road along Glen Dee west of Braemar. Glenmore village on the minor road from Aviemore to Coire Cas. Cairngorm Mountain resort at Coire Cas.

Lairig Ghru Linn of Dee on the minor road along Glen Dee west of Braemar. Minor road from Aviemore to Coire Cas.

Glen Feshie Minor road from Feshiebridge on the minor road from Inverdruie to Kingussie on the south side of Strathspey.

Bases

East Drumochter, The Gaick and Minigaig Blair Atholl, Dalwhinnie, Kingussie.

Glen Tilt Blair Atholl.

Ben Vrackie Pitlochry.

Glen Shee Glenshee Ski Centre, Spittal of Glen Shee, Braemar.

Glen Doll Clova, Kirriemuir.

Lochnagar Braemar, Ballater.

Mount Keen Ballater.

Ben Avon and Beinn a'Bhuiridh Braemar.

Lairig an Laoigh Aviemore, Glenmore, Braemar.

Ben Macdui and Cairn Gorm Aviemore, Glenmore, Braemar.

Lairig Ghru Aviemore, Glenmore, Braemar.

Glen Feshie Kincraig, Aviemore, Kingussie.

Maps

OS Landranger 1:50,000 35, 36, 42, 43, 44, 52

OS Explorer 1:25,000 387, 388, 402, 403, 404, 405

Harvey's Superwalker 1:25,000 Cairn Gorm

Harvey's Superwalker 1:25,000 Lochnagar and Glen Shee

Harvey's 1:40,000 Cairngorms and Lochnagar British Mountain Map

Walking Guides

Walking in the Cairngorms by Ronald Turnbull (Cicerone, 2005)

The Cairngorms by Adam Watson (SMC, 6th edition 1992)

The Cairngorms by Nick Williams (Pocket Mountains, 2003)

The Cairngorms Classic Munros by Chris Townsend (Colin Baxter, 2008)

Cairngorms Walks by John Brooks (Jarrold, 1996)

Climbing Guides

The Cairngorms: Scottish Mountaineering Club Climbers' Guide by Andy Nisbett, Allen Fyffe, Simon Richardson, Wilson Moir and John Lyall (SMC, 2007)

Winter Climbs in the Cairngorms by Allen Fyffe (Cicerone, 2000)

Natural History and History

The Nature of the Cairngorms: Diversity in a changing environment by Philip Shaw and Des Thompson (The Stationery Office, 2006)

The Cairngorms: Their Natural History and Scenery by Desmond Nethersole-Thompson and Adam Watson (Collins, 1974)

The Life and Times of the Black Pig: A Biography of Ben Macdui by Ronald Turnbull (Millrace, 2007)

CHAPTER 5: THE WESTERN HIGHLANDS

Ardgour, Morvern, Sunart and Moidart, Glenfinnan and Loch Eil, the Great Glen including Loch Ness and the Great Glen Way, Loch Arkaig and Knoydart to Glen Shiel, Kintail, and Glen Affric to Glen Carron

THE WESTERN HIGHLANDS: CHAPTER SUMMARY

Location

Hills north and west of Loch Linnhe and the Great Glen, as far as the Dingwall–Kyle of Lochalsh railway line

☆ Highlights

🔵 LOW-LEVEL/PASSES WALK
- Glenfinnan to the head of Loch Arkaig (5:2)
- Loch Morar via Glen Pean and Glen Dessary (5:4)
- Walking to Knoydart (5:5)
- Kinloch Hourn to Glenelg via Gleann Beag (5:6)
- The Circuit of Beinn Fhada (5:8)
- The Falls of Glomach (5:8)
- Glen Affric to Loch Duich (5:9)

🟤 LONG DISTANCE WALK
- The Great Glen Way (5:3)
- The Cape Wrath Trail (5:11)

🔵 SUMMIT WALK
- Garbh Bheinn (5:1)
- Sgurr Dhomhnuill (5:1)
- Sgurr Ghiubhsachain (5:1)
- Beinn Resipol (5:1)
- The Moidart Corbetts (5:1)
- Streap (5:2)
- Sgurr Thuilm and Sgurr nan Coireachan (5:2)
- Druim Fada (5:3)
- Meall Fuar-mhonaidh and Glas-bheinn Mhor (5:3)
- The Three Strathan Corbetts (5:4)
- Bidean a'Chabair and Carn Mor (5:4)
- The Sgurr nan Coireachan–Sgurr na Ciche Ridge (5:4)
- The Circuit of Gleann na Guiserein (5:5)
- Luinne Bheinn and Meall Buidhe (5:5)
- Beinn Buidhe (5:5)
- Sgurr a'Choire-bheithe, Sgurr nan Eugallt and Slat Bheinn (5:5)
- Meall nan Eun (5:5)
- The Ascent of Beinn Sgritheall (5:6)
- Beinn na h-Eaglaise and Beinn nan Caorach (5:6)
- Sgurr Mhic Bharraich and the South Glen Shiel Ridge (5:7)
- Sgurr a'Mhaoraich (5:7)
- Gleouraich and Spidean Mialach (5:7)
- The North Glen Shiel Ridge (5:8)
- Am Bathach (5:8)

- Beinn Fhada and A'Ghlas-bheinn (5:8)
- The Cluanie Horseshoe (5:9)
- The North Glen Affric Ridge (5:9)
- Sgurr nan Ceathreamhnan, An Socach and Mullach na Dheiragain (5:9)
- The Sgurr na Lapaich Four (5:10)
- Sgumain Coinntich, Faochaig and Aonach Buidhe (5:10)
- The Strathfarrar Four (5:10)
- Maoile Lunndaidh, Sgurr a'Chaorachain and Sgurr Choinnich (5:10)
- Beinn Tharsuinn, Bidein a'Choire Sheasgaich and Lurg Mhor (5:10)

🏃 SCRAMBLING
- Garbh Bheinn (5:1)
- Ben Aden (5:4)
- Ladhar Bheinn (5:5)
- The Saddle (5:7)

🔵 ROCK CLIMBING
- Garbh Bheinn (5:1)

❄ WINTER CLIMBING
- Sgurr na Feartaig (5:10)

🔵 SKI TOURING
- The Mullardoch Hills (5:10)
- The Strathfarrar Four (5:10)

🔵 OTHER HIGHLIGHTS
- Glenfinnan (5:2)
- Eas Chia-aig (5:3)

Contents

◀ *Sgurr Thuilm and Lochan a' Chomhlain from Braigh nan Uamhachan*

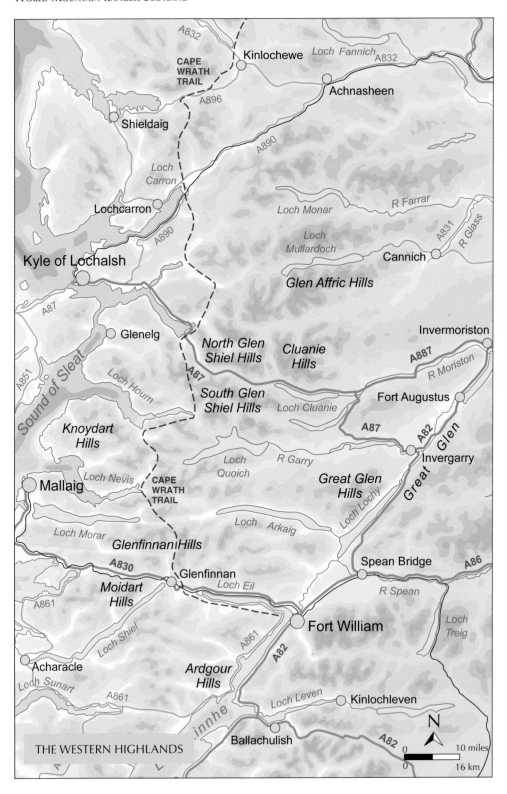

THE WESTERN HIGHLANDS

INTRODUCTION

A wild country of dark sea lochs and gloomy hills, often mist-shrouded.
Seton Gordon, *Highways and Byways in the West Highlands*

The Western Highlands run in a great sweep from the big peninsular lying west of Loch Linnhe in the southwest to the fertile Lowlands around the Cromarty and Beauly firths in the northeast. The southern boundary is the Great Glen and Loch Linnhe, the northern boundary the break in the hills formed by lower Strath Conon, Strath Bran and Strathcarron, a through-route along which runs the Dingwall to Kyle of Lochalsh railway line and the A835, A832 and A890 roads.

The Western Highlands are characterised by long, steep ridges with many summits running west to east, split by long deep glens. The hills are all of similar height, as the area is basically a dissected plateau. The coastline along the western edge is complex and beautiful and there are many long, glacier-gouged sea lochs running deep into the mountains, the biggest being, from the south, lochs Sunart, Nevis, Hourn, Alsh, Duich and Carron. Along the western fringe the hills are rocky and rough and packed tightly together, rising steeply, often from sea level. Further inland the hills, while still steep, are less rocky, greener and more widely spread out. The region is characterised by high rainfall, especially in the west. The watershed is close to the coast, so the rivers on this side are short and fierce, rising rapidly after heavy rain. East of the watershed the rivers are quieter but much longer, meandering away down the glens.

As with the hills to the south the main rocks of the Western Highlands are coarse-grained metamorphic schists. Here they are part of the series known as the Moine schists and glisten with white and black mica flakes. These schists form steep but not particularly rocky hills. In the west of the region there are granite intrusions and areas of gneiss, a hard metamorphic rock made of quartzite and feldspar, like granite, which form rockier hills with bigger cliffs, such as Garbh Bheinn of Ardgour. Mostly, however, these are not hills for rock and ice climbers but are more suited to walkers, winter mountaineers and ski tourers, especially those who

like long distances and remote, wild mountains. The region holds 62 Munros, 61 Corbetts and 43 Grahams. The walking is unusual in that the hardest walking away from paths is often in the glens and on the lower slopes of the hills, as these are usually boggy and covered in tussocks. Higher up the terrain is drier and grassier and the walking much easier. The opportunities for long distance walks are great and there is one official long distance path in the region, the low-level Great Glen Way (see Introduction). Much more challenging and exciting is the unofficial Cape Wrath Trail, the first part of which runs through the West Highlands from Fort William to Achnashellach.

The southwesternmost hills of Ardgour, Moidart and Sunart lie across Loch Linnhe from Fort William and Loch Leven. These are rough, steep hills, rising in small groups above long sea lochs and split by long freshwater Loch Shiel, which separates Moidart from Sunart and Ardgour. There are 16 Corbetts here but no Munros, and the region is usually quiet, despite its closeness to Fort William and the presence of one of the finest hills in the Western Highlands, Garbh Bheinn of Ardgour. West of this region is the lower Ardnamurchan peninsula. The Point of Ardnamurchan, where there is a big, distinctive lighthouse, is the most westerly spot in mainland Britain and a favourite place for starting or finishing coast-to-coast walks (Keith Inch in Peterhead is the easternmost point in mainland Scotland, Lowestoft Ness in Suffolk the easternmost in mainland Britain).

North of Ardgour and Moidart lie a long line of hills between the Road to the Isles (A830 Fort William to Mallaig) and Lochs Morar and Arkaig. Loch Morar is the deepest freshwater loch in Britain and is said to be home to a monster, called, unsurprisingly, Morag. The hills around Loch Morar gradually increase in height from west to east, with the highest hills just beyond its head. Big hills then continue eastwards to the Great Glen, slowly declining in roughness and height.

The view down Gleann Sron a' Chreagain to Loch Linnhe,
Ben Nevis and the Mamores from Stob Coire a' Chearcaill

North of Loch Morar is Loch Nevis, one of the most beautiful sea lochs, which forms the southern boundary of the remote peninsular of Knoydart, containing some of the most wonderfully rugged terrain in Scotland, a complex tangle of narrow steep-sided glens and rocky peaks, of which the finest is Ladhar Bheinn. Again the high hills running eastwards to the Great Glen become less rocky and less rough the further they are from the coast. Two big lochs, Arkaig and Quoich, the latter dammed to form a reservoir, split these hills. To the north Knoydart is bounded by another wild and attractive arm of the sea called Loch Hourn.

The hills north of Knoydart and the Arkaig–Quoich hills are less tangled and more orderly, typically forming long ridges running west to east– the South Glen Shiel Ridge, the North Glen Shiel Ridge (including the famous Five Sisters of Glen Shiel), Beinn Fhada, the North Glen Affric hills, the Loch Mullardoch hills, the Glen Strathfarrar Four – split by the long wide glens of Glen Shiel, Glen Affric, Glen Cannich, Glen Strathfarrar – and long lochs – Loch Cluanie, Loch Affric, Loch Beinn a'Mheadhoin, Loch Mullardoch, Loch Monar – many of which have been enlarged to form reservoirs for hydroelectricity. This is big, open country

with a sense of space and distance completely different to the closed-in feel of the Knoydart hills. The region from Glen Shiel north to Glen Carron is unbroken by any roads, a vast area of wild land in which backpackers can lose themselves for many days. The straight line distance south to north across the heart of this area is 40km. The highest hills north of the Great Glen are here – Mam Sodhail and Carn Eige – but the real glory of the region is in the long ridges and glens rather than individual peaks. Ski touring can be excellent here when the snow lies deep.

5:1 ARDGOUR, MORVERN, SUNART AND MOIDART

The southernmost hills in the Western Highlands lie in the districts of Ardgour, Morvern, Sunart and Moidart, an area bounded on the west by the coast, on the east by Loch Linnhe and to the north by Loch Eil and the glens holding the Fort William–Mallaig railway and the A830. To the south the hills fade away into the Lowlands of Morvern. The latter district lies south of Glen Tarbet and Loch Sunart with Ardgour and Sunart immediately to the north. Moidart is north of Sunart, separated from it and Ardgour to the east by 32km long Loch Shiel, which is freshwater but only separated from the sea at Loch Moidart at its foot by 3.25km and from the sea at Loch Eil at its head by 6.25km, which shows how nearly an island the Ardgour, Morvern and Sunart peninsula is.

The landscape is complex, with many individual hills separated by long glens and low passes. The scenery is very rugged, rocky and impressively wild. The lack of Munros makes the area much less visited than many that are less attractive. For solitude, wild camps, hillwalking over splendid summits and a feeling of remoteness this region can't be bettered. The walking here is some of the roughest in Scotland, however, with few paths and many tussocks, bogs and steep slopes.

The best access to the southern hills of the area is via the Corran Ferry across the narrows of Loch Linnhe, just north of Onich on the A82 Fort William road. The Corran Inn is a good hostelry that welcomes mountaineers. Although the Corran crossing is short the smell of the sea and the sight of seabirds and seaweed give the feeling of travelling to an island, that magical feeling of crossing water to a different land, a special place cut off from life

on the mainland. Indeed, these days this seems more like an island than the Isle of Skye, with its solid, soaring bridge. As the ferry makes its curving way across the strong tidal waters the view south down Loch Linnhe opens out, a spreading seascape of wide water and low islands. The splendidly situated and attractive Corran Lighthouse draws attention as the ferry comes in to the slipway at Ardgour. Above the harbour is the Inn at Ardgour, one of the few places for refreshment for many miles on this side of Loch Linnhe (another is the new Boat House Restaurant at Kingairloch on the shores of Loch a'Choire).

From the ferry the A861 heads south along the coast then west along Glen Tarbet, a steep-sided and rugged glen, to the village of Strontian on Loch Sunart where there are shops, a hotel and a campsite. Strontian was built in 1724 to provide housing for miners working local lead mines, which were open until 1790 and then intermittently until 1980, when they closed for good. The village is most famous for giving its name to the element strontium, which was discovered in the mines.

From Strontian the A861 continues alongside Loch Sunart to Salen, then turns north to the long, strung-out village of Acharacle at the foot of Loch

The Ardgour hills from Braigh nan Uamhachan

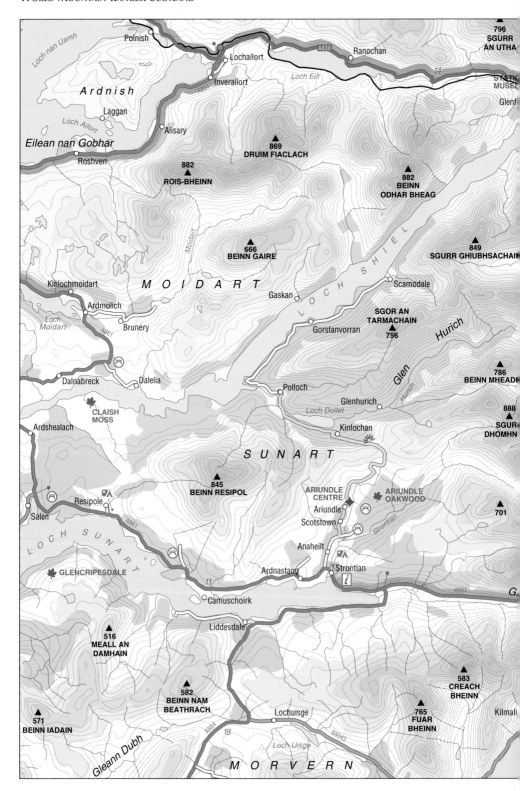

796
SGURR
AN UTHA

Loch nan Uamh

Polnish

Lochailort

A830

Ranochan

14

Inverailort

Loch Eilt

STATIC
MUSEI

A r d n i s h

A861

Glenf

Laggan

Loch Ailort

Alisary

Glenf

Eilean nan Gobhar

Roshven

869
DRUIM FIACLACH

882
ROIS-BHEINN

882
BEINN
ODHAR BHEAG

Moidart

666
BEINN GAIRE

849
SGURR GHIUBHSACHAI

M O I D A R T

Scamodale

Kinlochmoidart

Gaskan

L O C H   S H I E L

Ardmolich

Gorstanvorran

SGOR AN
TARMACHAIN

756

Hurich

Loch
Moidart

Brunery

A861

Glen

786
BEINN MHEAD

Dalnabreck

Dalelia

Polloch

Glenhurich

Hurich

888
SGUR
DHOMHN

CLAISH
MOSS

Loch Doilet

Kinlochan

Ardshealach

S U N A R T

845
BEINN RESIPOL

ARIUNDLE
CENTRE

ARIUNDLE
OAKWOOD

701

Resipole

Ariundle

L O C H   S U N A R T

Salen

Scotstown

Strontian

Anaheilt

GLENCRIPESDALE

Ardnastang

Strontian

i

A861

G.

11

Camuschoirk

516
MEALL AN
DAMHAIN

Liddesdale

583
CREACH
BHEINN

582
BEINN NAM
BEATHRACH

Lochuisge

765
FUAR
BHEINN

Kilmali

571
BEINN IADAIN

A884

18

B8043

Gleann Dubh

Loch Uisge

M O R V E R N

308

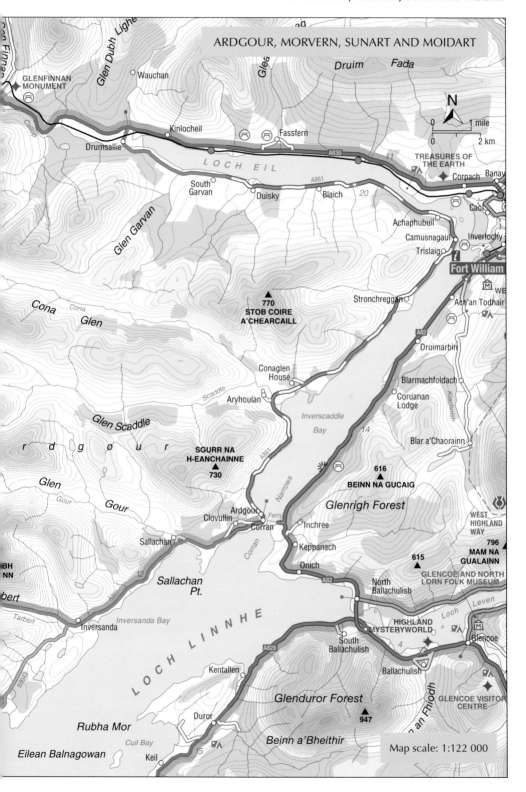

ARDGOUR, MORVERN, SUNART AND MOIDART

Glen Dubh Lighe

Druim Fada

GLENFINNAN MONUMENT

Wauchan

Kinlocheil

Fassfern

Drumsallie

LOCH EIL

A830

TREASURES OF THE EARTH

Corpach

Banay

South Garvan

Duisky

A861

Blaich

20

Achaphubuil

Caol

Glen Garvan

Camusnagaul

Inverlochy

Trislaig

Fort William

Cona

Cona

Glen

STOB COIRE A'CHEARCAILL
770

Stronchreggan

Ach'an Todhair

Druimarbin

A82

Conaglen House

Blarmachfoldach

Scaddle

Aryhoulan

Coruanan Lodge

Glen Scaddle

Inverscaddle Bay

Blar a'Choirainn

r   d   g   o   u   r

SGURR NA H-EANCHAINNE
730

14

BEINN NA GUCAIG
616

Glen

Gour

Glenrigh Forest

Glen

Gour

Narrows

WEST HIGHLAND WAY

Ardgour

Ferry

Inchree

Clovullin

Corran

MAM NA GUALAINN
796

Sallachan

Corran

Keppanach

615

GLENCOE AND NORTH LORN FOLK MUSEUM

BH NN

Onich

A82

Sallachan Pt.

North Ballachulish

Loch

Leven

Inversanda Bay

HIGHLAND MYSTERYWORLD

Tarberi

Inversanda

South Ballachulish

4

Glencoe

Kentallen

A828

Ballachulish

Glenduror Forest

GLENCOE VISITOR CENTRE

LOCH LINNHE

Rubha Mor

Cuil Bay

Duror

Beinn a'Bheithir
947

Eilean Balnagowan

Keil

15

Map scale: 1:122 000

Shiel. Both Acharacle and Salen have accommodation, shops and eating opportunities. From Acharacle the road winds northwards to Loch Moidart and then Loch Ailort, whose shores it follows to the A830 at Lochailort, where there is an inn and a railway station. Going north from the Corran Ferry the A861 runs alongside Loch Linnhe and then west along Loch Eil to join the A830 at the head of the loch. Thus the A861 and A830 together make a complete circuit of the hills of Ardgour, Sunart and Moidart. Few roads run into the hills, the only one of any significance being the minor road that runs north from Strontian then east to Polloch, giving access to the eastern Ardgour hills. The northern hills of Ardgour and the Moidart hills are most easily accessed from Glenfinnan and Lochailort on the A830. The Morvern hills can be accessed from Glen Tarbet to the north.

⊗ The Morvern Hills: Fuar Bheinn, Creach Bheinn and Beinn Mheadhoin

A horseshoe of hills encircles Glen Galmadale, which runs north from the B8043 road beside Loch Linnhe south of Glen Tarbet. The high points of this horseshoe are the two highest hills in Morvern and the only Corbetts – Fuar Bheinn ('cold hill', 766m) and Creach Bheinn ('hill of spoil', 853m). To the south of these hills lies another fine horseshoe, running round three big corries feeding the Abhainn na Fearna. The highest point is Beinn Mheadhoin ('middle hill', 739m), a Graham. Both horseshoes are rocky, with many granite outcrops and rough corries on their flanks. Beinn Mheadhoin is rather spoiled, however, by the gigantic Glensanda granite quarry, one of the largest in the world, which lies on its southeastern flanks.

The round of Glen Galmadale involves a great deal of ascent and descent – some 1500m in total – as it crosses five minor summits as well as the two Corbetts. The circuit is started at the bridge over the Glengalmadale River on the B8043. The walking is on broad stony ridges and there are no difficulties. The best views are east across Loch Linnhe. The distance is 15km, and the walk takes 5½–6hrs.

The Beinn Mheadhoin horseshoe faces east to Loch a'Choire, a short arm of Loch Linnhe. The round can be done from the B8043 near Tigh Ghardail and starts with a ford of the Abhainn na Coinnich. There are good views across Loch Linnhe and south to Mull from the summit. The walking is again on broad ridges, mostly grassy. The distance is 14km, with 1075m of ascent, and the walk takes 5½–6hrs.

☆ Garbh Bheinn of Ardgour

One of the great mountains of the Western Highlands, 885m Garbh Bheinn of Ardgour (so titled to distinguish it from the two other peaks called Garbh Bheinn in the Western Highlands) rises across Loch Linnhe opposite the mouth of Loch Leven and is well seen from Glencoe village and, especially, the Ballachulish Bridge from where it appears as a ragged dark pyramid. Garbh Bheinn forms the southwestern side of a big horseshoe around Coire an Iubhair. The big northeast face of the mountain looming above the corrie is impressively steep and craggy, harbouring many rock and ice climbs. Garbh Bheinn means, appropriately, 'rough mountain'. The southwestern slopes above Glen Tarbet are more uniform and less rocky and lacking in much interest. Ascents on this side are strenuous but without difficult. Garbh Bheinn is mainly built of gneiss, a rough metamorphic rock that is excellent for climbing. It's also very attractive, with black and grey rippled banding.

⊗ ➌ The Ascent of Garbh Bheinn ☆

The finest walking route on Garbh Bheinn is the round of Coire an Iubhair. Starting by the bridge over the Abhainn Coire an Iubhair on the A861, rough slopes lead eastwards to the long Druim an Iubhair ridge, which walls the east side of Coire an Iubhair and leads northwards to the first summit, Sgorr Mhic Eacharna (650m). Turning to the west the ridge now dips a little then rises to Beinn Bheag (736m), beyond which there is a steep drop southwards to the little Lochan Coire an Iubhair on the Bealach Feith'n Amean at the head of Coire an Iubhair. Throughout this walk there are superb views across Coire an Iubhair to the buttresses, gullies and crags of the east face of Garbh Bheinn.

The steep rocky north ridge of Garbh Bheinn rises above the Bealach Feith'n Amean. It looks more fearsome than it is and the ascent is an easy and quite straightforward scramble. In descent it can be hard to find the easiest route, however, a reason for doing this circuit in an anti-clockwise direction. The summit, a small flat area on the edge of the east face, gives a dramatic view straight down into Coire an Iubhair and wide-ranging views over the surrounding area. The most impressive views are of Garbh Bheinn, rather than from it, however.

The summit of Garbh Bheinn of Ardgour

From the summit steep rocky slopes lead down to a col at 748m and then up to the 823m summit at the top of the Sron a'Ghairbh Choire Bhig ridge. This is a great viewpoint for the intimidating rock sculpture of the east face of Garbh Bheinn, which towers, dark and forbidding, over the corrie far below. The Sron ridge runs southeast down rocky slopes to the start, and makes for a rough but direct route down. An alternative descent is from the 748m col, from where a rough path leads steeply through the rocks to Coire an Iubhair and a better if very wet path that runs down to the bridge. Although rough initially this descent does give magnificent views of the east face of Garbh Bheinn.

🔰 Scrambling on Garbh Bheinn ☆

There are few scrambling routes on the steep and serious rock of Garbh Bheinn aside from the simple north ridge route described above, but there is one that is regarded as a classic and receives two stars in the scrambling guidebooks – Pinnacle Ridge. This lies at the northern end of the cliffs above Coire an Iubhair to the right of the two most obvious features – a big ravine called Great Gully and the massive Great Ridge, which soars some 300+m to the summit. Pinnacle Ridge curves up to the

summit ridge over two rocky pinnacles, the first of which gives the hardest scrambling. The grade is 3(S), which is the upper end of difficulty and seriousness for scrambling, so this is a route for those confident on steep exposed rock.

🔰 Rock Climbing on Garbh Bheinn ☆

The cliffs, buttresses and ridges of the northeast face of Garbh Bheinn host a range of rock climbs of all grades in a magnificent high mountain setting. The classic and most obvious line is the Great Ridge, which rises 325m to the summit. This long climb is graded V Diff and was first ascended by J.H. Bell and W. Brown in 1897. High on the side of the Great Ridge is the impressive cliff known as the South Face, up which goes 106m Butterknife, a VS first climbed by a party led by J.R. Marshall in 1956. This is described as 'in an intimidating situation' by Kevin Howett, in *Rock Climbing in Scotland* (Francis Lincoln, 2004). It certainly looks it from below. There are much harder routes on the South Face however, such as the 105m E2 The Golden Lance (first climbed by R. Anderson and A. Russell in 1984) and the 45m E4 6a White Wall (first climbed by P. Whillance, E. Anderson and M. Hamilton, also in 1984). The huge dark gash of Great Gully, which cuts down through the cliffs directly from the summit was first climbed by W.H. Murray and Douglas Scott in 1946, an ascent described in Murray's classic book *Undiscovered Scotland*.

⛰ The Other Hills of Ardgour

North of Garbh Bheinn a tangle of rough hills runs north to Loch Eil and Glenfinnan. One of the most prominent of these is Sgurr na h-Eanchainne. It's only 730m high, but the situation of this distinctive gentle-sided cone on the west side of Loch Linnhe just north of the Corran ferry means it can be clearly seen from the A82 between Ballachulish and Fort William. This lochside location gives superb views from the summit, especially up Loch Linnhe to Ben Nevis and the Great Glen. Sgurr na h-Eachainne (which has the odd meaning of 'peak of the brains') is actually only the end of a ridge curving round the corrie called Coire Dubh, whose highest and rather undistinguished point lies some 2km away. Generally known as Druim na Sgriodain ('ridge of the stony ravine') this 734m Graham is also named Meall Dearg Coire nam Muc on the OS 1:50,000 map. The circuit of Coire Dubh over the two summits can be easily made from Ardgour.

To the north and south of Druim na Sgriodain the long arms of Glen Gour and Glen Scaddle stretch deep into the hills from Loch Linnhe. Between these valleys lies the 762m Corbett Beinn na h-Uamha ('hill of the cave'), a very rocky hill and the highest part of a ridge stretching some 4km above the watershed between Glen Gour and Glen Strontian. Beinn na h-Uamha is most easily climbed by the southeast ridge in Glen Gour, which can be reached from Sallachan at the foot of the glen. If the return is made by descending steeply south back into Glen Gour this gives a round trip of 15km, with 900m of ascent, which takes 5–6hrs. If there's time it's worth continuing along the ridge to Sgurr a'Chaorainn, which is just a metre lower, and then descending to the head of Glen Gour – which adds an extra 5km and around 1½hrs – or down to the Strontian Glen and a walk out to Strontian village, where buses can be caught back to Ardgour, which makes for a 20km walk.

☆ Sgurr Dhomhnuill, the highest peak in Ardgour at 888m and the most impressive after Garbh Bheinn, lies 2km north of Sgurr a'Chaorainn. The pyramidal shape of Sgurr Dhomhnuill ('Donald's peak') is a distinctive landmark from many directions although it stands at the head of the Strontian Glen in the heart of Ardgour in quite

a remote situation. It can be ascended from the Strontian Glen via the Druim Leac a'Sgiathain ridge and the subsidiary top of Sgurr na h-Ighinn (15.5km there and back with 1200m of ascent, around 5–6hrs), a route that starts with a walk through the lovely oak and pine woods of the Ariundle Nature Reserve. An alternative, shorter but less interesting route starts at the high point of the minor road from Strontian to Polloch, climbs the rather featureless Druim Garbh ridge and then the northwest ridge to the summit. The return can be made via Druim Leac a'Sgiathain then west over Druim Glas for a round trip of 12.5km, with 1000m of ascent, which takes about 5hrs.

Directly north of Sgurr Dhomhnuill, across the head of lonely Gleann na Cloiche Sgoilte, lies the long and in places narrow ridge of Beinn Mheadhoin, the highest point of which, Carn na Nathrach ('cairn of the adders', 786m), is a Corbett. Beinn Mheadhoin means 'middle hill', an appropriate name as it lies in the centre of Ardgour, making it one of the remotest hills in the region. Beinn Mheadhoin isn't as distinctive as nearby hills and is a long way from the nearest road, so it's a quiet hill on which you are unlikely to meet anyone else. It stretches some 9km west to east, from Glen Hurich to Glen Scaddle, and the best route is to traverse it as part of a long walk right across Ardgour to Loch Linnhe. The distance is 22.5km from Kinlochan to Inverscaddle Bay, with 900m of ascent, and the walk is likely to take 7–9hrs. The shortest approach to Carn na Nathrach is from Kinlochan on the narrow, winding road from Strontian to the little village of Polloch. A forest track runs up through the plantations in Glen Hurich and across the River Hurich (this section could be cycled) for 3km to the foot of the southwest ridge of Beinn Mheadhoin. It's then 4.5km walk to Carn na Nathrach. There are 825m to climb and the ascent is likely to take 3–4hrs unless a bicycle is used on the forest track. Descent can be made the same way, or by dropping steeply north into upper Glen Hurich and the forest track.

A walk linking Carn na Nathrach with both Sgurr Dhomhnuill to the south and Stob a'Bhealach an Sgriodain to the north is an outing for those who like tough days and rugged terrain, as the slopes involved on all three hills are very steep and very rough. Oddly Stob a'Bhealach an Sgriodain ('peak of the pass of the screes') isn't named on the O.S.1:50,000 map, although the summit height of 770m is marked as is the Bealach an Sgriodain and the ridge to the northwest (Druim Tarsuinn), as well as a lower peak just to the east (Meall Mor). Stob a'Bhealach an Sgriodain is the highest point on a the massive ridge that runs between long Cona Glen to the north and Glen Scaddle and Gleann an Lochain Duibh to the south almost the whole way from Loch Linnhe to Loch Shiel, a straight line distance of 16km. Stob a'Bhealach an Sgriodain is another remote hill, the shortest routes to the summit both being 9.5km long, from the car park beside the Callop River 2km east of Glenfinnan to the north and Kinlochan in Glen Hurich to the south, with ascents of 1000 and 885m respectively (and times of 6–7hrs for the return trip). The northerly route is the most scenic, the southerly one being in forest much of the way. The northerly route can also be combined with an ascent of two more Corbetts, Sgurr Ghiubhsachain ('peak of the pine wood', 849m) and Sgorr Craobh a'Chaorainn ('peak of the rowan tree', 775m) (22km, 1600m of ascent, 7–9hrs). Although there are few trees on the hills themselves the names are still appropriate in a way, as on the northern fringes lies the Glenfinnan Native Woodlands Regeneration scheme, with a restored forest consisting mostly of Scots pine with some sessile oak.

☆ Sgurr Ghiubhsachain is one of the finest hills in the Western Highlands, rising as a ragged pyramid above Loch Shiel. It's clearly visible from Glenfinnan, from where it forms a pair with Beinn Odhar Bheag (see below) in the magnificent view down Loch Shiel. The best ascent is by the long rough and rocky east-northeast ridge, reached by a scenic walk alongside Loch Shiel from the Callop car park. There are scrambling options on the ridge, although these are easily avoided. The views along Loch Shiel from the summit are superb. It's easy to continue on to Sgorr Craobh a'Chaorainn – from where there is a good view back to Sgurr Ghiubhsachain – and then down into the Allt na Cruaiche glen and some impressive old birch and pine woods for the return to Callop, to give a circuit of 17km, with 1100m of ascent, which takes around 6–8hrs.

The final Corbett in Ardgour, Stob Coire a'Chearcaill ('peak of the circular corrie', 771m) lies in the northeast of the region, far from any of the other high hills. Its craggy summit stands out in views from Fort William and the A82. Its position across Loch Linnhe means it's not that easy to reach, making it a hill that is admired far more often than it's climbed, but the ascent is worth the

Sgurr Ghiubhsachain from Sgorr Craobh a' Chaorainn

effort for the superb views of Ben Nevis and Fort William from the summit, where there is a trig point and a very large, tumbledown cairn. The quickest way up is from the A861 just east of the Doire na Muice plantation, on the south side of Loch Eil, from where the open hillside can be climbed to the summit ridge (9km for the round trip with 770m of ascent, 3–4hrs). This route is a pretty tedious slog up featureless boggy slopes, the only views being back across Loch Eil to bulky Gulvain, and a far better route is from Loch Linnhe west up Gleann Sron a'Chreagain and onto the east-northeast ridge of Braigh Bhlaich. This route gives good views of Coire a'Chearcaill and the broken crags below the summit (13km and 800m of ascent for the round trip, 4–5hrs).

Beinn Resipol ☆

The district of Sunart lies west of Ardgour, between salt Loch Sunart and freshwater Loch Shiel. It's a fairly small region, really just a westerly extension of Ardgour, and boasts just one big hill, Ben Resipol (845m). This is a big, rugged hill with a craggy north face that looks impressive from Loch Shiel. Isolated from other high hills and with no higher ground between it and the coast Beinn Resipol gives superb views, with a sweep of islands and sea from Mull to Skye and to the north and east the wild jumble of the hills of Moidart and Ardgour, with Ben Nevis rising beyond the latter. The meaning of the name 'Resipol' seems unclear. The 1973 edition of the Scottish Mountaineering Club (SMC) District Guide *The Western Highlands* by G.Scott Johnstone says the meaning is doubtful and gives *pol* as 'Old Norse – bol, bolstaor, a homestead'. There is a farm called Resipole at the foot of the hill, so it perhaps it was named after this. The SMC guidebook writers obviously decided that 'homestead' was good enough as in The Corbetts and Other Scottish Hills (1990 and 2002) it says 'from Old Norse homestead' without any qualification, while in the *North-West Highlands* (2004), the replacement for the old District Guides to the Western and Northern Highlands, it says 'hill of the horse farm or hill of the homestead'. However Peter Drummond's *Scottish Hill Names: Their Origin and Meaning* (Scottish Mountaineering Trust, 2nd revised edition, 2007) says that this meaning would be an unusual one as hills are rarely named for farms at their bases. Drummond points to the broad River Polloch to the north of the hill, whose

name comes from the Gaelic *poll* meaning a pit or pool and suggests 'hreysi poll' – the cairn above the pool.

Whatever the name means Beinn Resipol is a fine hill and quite easy to climb from both east and west with a traverse of the hill being the finest expedition. From the east an ascent can be made from the minor road 2km north of Strontian, starting with an old miners' track and leaving this at its high point to cross Meall an t-Slugain and climb the east ridge to the summit (6.5km, 800m ascent, 2½–3hrs). The western ascent starts at Resipole, where there is a campsite, and follows the Allt Mhic Chiarain, at first through some attractive oak and birch woodland, to the west ridge of Beinn Resipol (5km, 850m, 2½–3hrs).

The Moidart Corbetts ☆

The final hills in this complex area lie between Loch Shiel and the sea at Loch Ailort in northern Moidart. The westernmost hills rise above Loch Ailort and give wonderful views out to sea to the islands of Eigg and Rum. A twisting, rocky ridge links the rough and rugged summits and makes for a superb high-level circuit around Coire a'Bhuiridh, one of the best ridge walks in the West Highlands. The main hills are three Corbetts: An Stac ('the stack', 814m), Rois-Bheinn ('horse hill', 882m) and Sgurr na Ba Glaise ('peak of the grey cow', 874m). The circuit also includes the subsidiary but still excellent peak of Druim Fiaclach ('toothed ridge', 869m), which actually gives the most exciting walking. The walk starts at Lochailort on the A830 at the head of Loch Ailort. Going anticlockwise, it crosses the Allt a'Bhuiridh and climbs an open hillside to the col between Beinn Coire nan Gall and Druim Fiaclach, where there is a little lochan, then ascends the steep, rocky northern side of Druim Fiaclach. Stretching out to the east from the summit is the turreted ridge that gives the hill its name. To the south very steep slopes drop into Coire Reidh. Descend via the narrow southwest ridge to the Bealach an Fhalaisg Dhuibh and then ascend the narrow ridge of An t-Slat Bheinn. A broader ridge leads from the summit of the latter to Sgurr na Ba Glaise, whose craggy north face is in view from Druim Fiaclach. A descent to the Bealach an Fhiona and a final climb leads to the trig point on the highest summit, Rois-Bheinn, which rises directly and steeply from sea level on Loch Ailort. The views are breathtaking, especially

Backpackers on a traverse of the Moidart hills

from the slightly lower 878m western summit, which lies 700m further on. To reach the final summit, An Stac, retrace your steps to the Bealach an Fhiona then turn north for a steep descent and then a steep rocky ascent to the summit. Continue north down the ridge to reach the path to Lochailort (16.5km, 1600m, 7–9hrs).

To the east of the Coire a'Bhuiridh horseshoe is the lowest and least noticeable of the Moidart Corbetts, 783m Beinn Mhic Cedidh ('MacCedidh's hill'), a rounded, compact hill with a narrow rocky north ridge that looks impressive from the A830 along side Loch Eilt. Much more massive and distinctive is Beinn Odhar Bheag ('little dun-coloured hill', 882m) which, with its subsidiary summit 870m Beinn Odhar Mhor ('big dun-coloured hill'), rises dramatically in steep craggy slopes from the shores of Loch Shiel and dominates the views down the loch from Glenfinnan (presumably the names were given long before surveys of the heights were made, because Odhar Mhor was thought to be the higher when viewed from below). The twin summits look very impressive when viewed across the loch from Sgurr Ghiubhsachain. An ascent of the two Corbetts can be made from the A830 2km east of Loch Eilt, where there is a bridge across the Allt Lon a'Mhuidhe next to the railway line,

which also has to be crossed. Climb rough tussocky ground southwest to the broad north-northwest ridge of Beinn Odhar Mhor, which leads up to the trig point. A complex, meandering ridge drops to a 750m col beyond which a narrower rockier ridge leads without difficulty to the little summit of Beinn Odhar Bheag. Another broad ridge leads down to the Bealach a' Choire Bhuidhe, from where a rather relentless slope rises to Beinn Mhic Cedidh. Descent can be made either via the north ridge, which takes you to the railway a couple of kilometres west of the start point, or by returning to the Bealach a' Choire Bhuidhe, descending into Coire Buidhe and traversing over the northwest and north-northwest ridges of Beinn Odhar Mhor to the outward route. This is complex terrain and good route finding skills are needed in poor visibility. Returning via Coire Buidhe the walk is 11km long, with 1300m of ascent, and takes 6–7hrs.

The finest hillwalk in Moidart is the traverse of all the Corbetts, a long, tough expedition that could be split over two days. Note that campsites are more easily found high up than in the boggy glens and corries. There are railway stations at Glenfinnan and Lochailort, so a train could be caught back to the start. The route described above can be followed to Beinn Mhic Cedidh then the western slopes of this hill descended to a wide flat marshy col and the narrow pinnacled east ridge of Druim Fiaclach climbed to join the ridge walk over the western summits. The straight line distance is 22km, although many more will be walked on the ground, and the ascent around 2600m. Expect to take 9–12hrs.

Low-level Walks

The long glens of this region make for excellent through-routes, giving good views of the summits and taking the walker through wild, remote country. Starting in the south of Ardgour there is a fine route up Glen Gour, from Sallachan on Loch Linnhe, to a narrow 195m pass between Sgurr na Laire and Sgurr nan Cnamh, and then down beside the Strontian River through the lovely Ariundle Nature Reserve woodland to Strontian, a distance of 20km (4–6hrs). The middle section of this route is pathless and quite tough going. From Ardnastang, 2.5km west of Strontian, a path leads over the hills, reaching 395m, to one of the old mines and the forest around Loch Doilet, from where a track runs past Polloch down to Loch Shiel and then along the loch to Callop just east of Glenfinnan (31km, 8–9hrs). Another route to Callop goes 13km up the Cona Glen from Inverscaddle Bay on Loch Linnhe, 6km north of the Corran Ferry, and then climbs to the 390m col between Meall na Damh and Glac Gharbh and descends the glen of the Allt na Cruaiche to Callop (21km, 5–6hrs). These routes can be linked to form loops, and other glens and passes can be included.

Long Distance Walks

There are no waymarked long distance routes in this area but many can be done by linking summits and glen and pass routes. As an example here's a description of a mostly pathless two day walk across Moidart over five summits that I undertook one October with two companions. We began late one afternoon at Brunery at the mouth of Glen Moidart, 1.5km east of Ardmolich on the A861, and walked up the glen to Glenforslan where we turned east and climbed up to the loch in Glenforslan, above which we camped. To the north and west lay a big, sprawling, rather shapeless hill mass, the highest point of which is Beinn Gaire ('laughing hill', 666m), a Graham, which we traversed the next day, enjoying excellent views of Loch Shiel and many hills including Garbh Bheinn, to the

Bealach a'Choire Mhoir. Above the bealach rises another Graham, Croit Bheinn ('croft hill', 663m), which is completely different, being a compact and distinctive cone. We climbed Croit Bheinn, then made a very steep descent down boggy tussocks ('controlled falling', one of the party called it) into Glen Alladale, where we failed to find a campsite, as it was too boggy, and so climbed up towards the Bealach a'Choire Bhuidhe to a dry if bumpy site on a small island in the Allt a'Chairn. The following morning we finished the climb to the bealach, where we left our packs to make an ascent of Beinn Mhic Cedidh, which lay to the west. Retrieving our loads we turned southeast to climb Beinn Odhar Bheag and then north to Beinn Odhar Mhor, crossing these summits in mist and rain. The hardest part of the walk came next – locating a route down to the bridge across the Allt Lon a'Mhuidhe, beyond which we'd left a car beside the A830. The terrain is complex and rough here, and in the thick mist it took careful navigation to find a sensible way down. On the map the route was only 22km long but I reckon we covered twice that distance zigzagging about to avoid bogs, pools and crags. The walk involved 2200m of ascent and the total walking time was 13hrs 10mins.

5:2 GLENFINNAN AND LOCH EIL

Glenfinnan is a small settlement at the head of Loch Shiel. Both the Road to the Isles from Fort William to Mallaig, built by Thomas Telford in 1812, and the West Highland railway line pass through Glenfinnan, so it's very accessible. Loch Eil is a continuation of Loch Linnhe, a dogleg running west from Fort William and taking the sea deep into the mainland.

Between the Road to the Isles and Glen Pean and Loch Arkaig to the north lie three Munros and four Corbetts that are usually climbed from Glenfinnan or nearby. From east to west the Munros are Gulvain (987m), Sgurr Thuilm (963m) and Sgurr nan Coireachan (956m). The Corbetts are Meall a' Phubuill (774m), Braigh nan Uamhachan (765m), Streap (909m) and Sgurr an Utha (796m). All are fine rough hills in splendid situations and all can be linked to make several circuits or one multi-day trip.

GLENFINNAN

Glenfinnan is famous as the place where Prince Charles Edward Stuart (Bonnie Prince Charlie) raised his standard in August 1745, after crossing to Scotland from France, thus beginning the last attempt by the Stuart dynasty to wrest back the British crown. In 1815 a monument was built at Glenfinnan to commemorate the clansmen who rallied to the Jacobite cause and formed the prince's army, many dying far from home. The tall tower, prominent in views along Loch Shiel, is topped by a statue of a Highlander in a kilt. The monument is now in the care of the National Trust for Scotland which has a visitor centre, including a small café, just across the A803 from the monument. After defeat at the battle of Culloden near Inverness in April 1746, just eight months after arriving at Glenfinnan, the prince went on the run in the Highlands. By July he was back in the Glenfinnan area, hiding among the hills and adding another, albeit minor, note to his story by climbing some peaks.

Glenfinnan is also known for the Glenfinnan Viaduct, built between 1897 and 1901, whose curving concrete span carries the West Highland railway line high above the glen. The viaduct is 380m long and has 21 arches, the tallest of which is 30m high. It's an impressive structure in an impressive situation and has been used in several television programmes and cinema films, most notably the Harry Potter series, where the Hogwarts Express is seen crossing the viaduct. Loch Shiel also features in the films as the lake outside Hogwarts and viewers can spot several of the hills around the loch in some of the scenes. To the west of the viaduct secretive Glenfinnan station lies in a cutting. There is a café and self-catering accommodation in dining cars at the station, plus a railway museum.

ⓐ Glenfinnan to the head of Loch Arkaig

This through-route links Loch Shiel with Loch Arkaig via 471m Bealach a'Chaorainn and gives access to the Sgurr nan Coireachan–Sgurr Thuilm circuit and to Streap (see below). Linked with the Loch Arkaig–Inverie route (see below) it makes for a good 2–3 day route into Knoydart, with public transport links at the finish, from where you can

Loch Shiel, the Glenfinnan Viaduct and Sgurr Thuilm

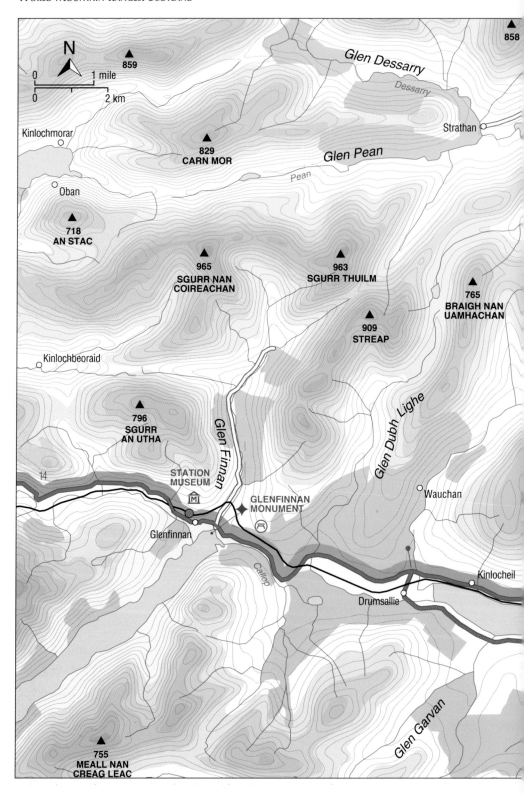

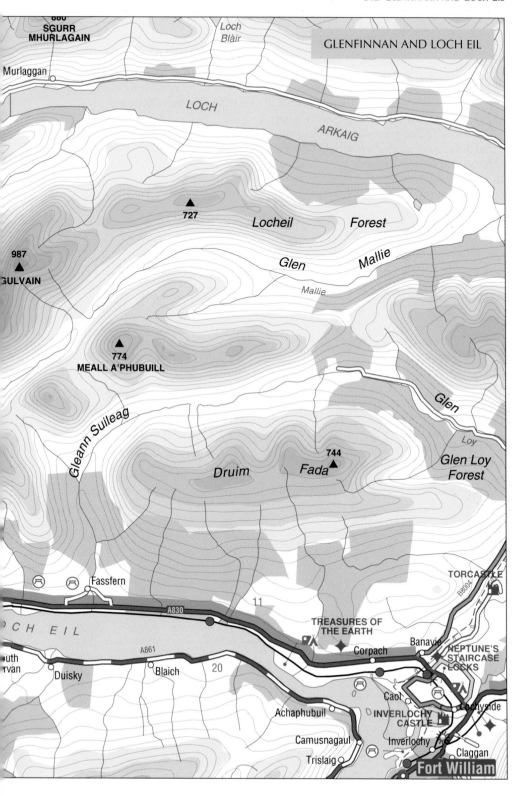

GLENFINNAN AND LOCH EIL

660
SGURR
MHURLAGAIN

Loch
Blàir

Murlaggan

LOCH
ARKAIG

Locheil   Forest

727

Glen   Mallie

Mallie

987
GULVAIN

774
MEALL A'PHUBUILL

Glen

Loy

Gleann Suileag

Glen Loy
Forest

744

Druim   Fada

TORCASTLE

B8004

Fassfern

A830

11

TREASURES OF
THE EARTH

Banavie

NEPTUNE'S
STAIRCASE
LOCKS

LOCH EIL

A861

Corpach

uth
rvan

Duisky

Blaich

20

Caol

INVERLOCHY
CASTLE

Achaphubuil

Camusnagaul

Inverlochy

Claggan

Trislaig

Fort William

catch a ferry to Mallaig and then the train from Mallaig to Glenfinnan. The walk itself is pleasant without being dramatic. It starts on the wide track up Glen Finnan, running underneath the Viaduct and through plantations to Corryhully Bothy, on the hillside above which rises Glenfinnan Lodge, an incongruous modern house that sits badly in this wild location, a building seemingly designed not to fit into its surroundings. Beyond the bothy the track becomes rougher and then ends at the mouth of big Coire Thollaidh, above which rises the curving Sgurr nan Coireachan–Sgurr Thuilm ridge. To the northeast lies the pass, a graceful glaciated curve between Sgurr Thuilm and Streap. The path climbs the narrow glen to the bealach then descends Gleann Cuirnean to Glen Pean, from where a forest track leads to Strathan and Loch Arkaig. The distance is 15km, with 600m of ascent, and it can be walked in 4–5hrs.

The Glenfinnan and Loch Eil Hills from East to West

⊗ Meall a'Phubuill

Meall a'Phubuill ('hill of the tent', 774m) is the highest of the group of steep-sided, rounded-topped, grassy hills lying north of Loch Eil. It rises above the heads of four glens – Gleann Suileag to the south, Glen Loy to the east, Glen Mallie to the north, Gleann Fionnlighe to the west – and an ascent can be made from any of them. The easiest and quickest route is from Fassfern to the south up Gleann Suileag. An estate track runs for 4.5km up the glen, through forest at first and then across open hillside to a bridge over the An t-Suileag stream. This section could be cycled. Just beyond the bridge lies Glensulaig bothy, with the dome of Meall a'Phubuill rising above it. A path leads up the lower slopes but soon disappears, leaving a steady pull straight up broad slopes to the summit where there are extensive views of the surrounding hills, especially Gulvain, whose long dipping summit ridge and east face look grand. The round trip from Fassfern is 14km long, with 800m of ascent, and takes 6–7hrs.

Meall a'Phubuill can be linked with the next hill, Gulvain, by descending northeast to the boggy 300m pass between Gleann Suileag and Glen Loy, where a small lochan appears to feed the streams running down both glens. From the pass there's a 687m ascent up the southeast slopes of Gulvain.

The distance between the two summits is 3.5km. If combining the two hills it makes sense to climb Meall a'Phubuill from Gleann Fionnlighe, and then descend this glen from Gulvain. It's 11.5km with 850m of ascent up Gleann Fionnlighe to the summit of Meall a'Phubuill (4–5hrs).

⊗ Gulvain

Gulvain is a big, bulky hill running along the northwest side of Glen Mallie, which cuts into the hills from near the east end of Loch Arkaig, and Gleann Fionnlighe, which runs northeast from the Road to Isles 1km west of the head of Loch Eil and 7km east of Glenfinnan. Gulvain can be climbed from Glen Mallie, but the approach is long and not that interesting and it is most enjoyably climbed from the south via Gleann Fionnlighe. The meaning of Gulvain is unclear. It's often given as *gaor bheinn* – 'filthy hill' – but Peter Drummond's *Scottish Hill Names: Their Origin and Meaning* (Scottish Mountaineering Trust, 2007) says it possibly comes from *gailbhinn* – 'rough hill' – which, as he says, is a more apt description. Gulvain runs roughly south to north and has two summits 1.3km apart. The northern one is the highest but it's the southern one that has the trig point. Gulvain is much higher than neighbouring hills, and stands out in many views. From the east and west it has a distinctive shape, with a curving saddle between the two summits. From the north and south it appears more as a pyramid, the long summit ridge being hidden. It's a mostly grassy hill with little visible rock, although there are some steep slabby outcrops on the western slopes, and the walking is fairly easy.

A rough wide track runs up Gleann Fionnlighe through some plantations almost to the foot of the south-southwest ridge, a distance of 6km that could be cycled. The ascent of the ridge itself is arduous, as it is unrelentingly steep for 700m to a subsidiary top at 855m, where it eases off before the south top is reached. The ridge between here and the main summit is the finest part of the mountain. It's narrow without being exposed and has splendid views all around. The best way back is by the outward route, for a round trip of 21km, with 1200m of ascent which, without a bicycle, takes 7–9hrs.

To link Gulvain with Braigh nan Uamhachan, which lies 3km to the west-southwest, descend west to the long 520m saddle between Fraoch Mor and the Allt a' Choire Raidh, and then climb the

Gulvain from Braigh nan Uamhachan

west ridge and turn south to the summit. There are 250m of ascent.

🌐 Braigh nan Uamhachan

Directly west of Gulvain lies another long ridge, running south–north and separating Gleann Fionnlighe – 'glen of the pale stream' – from Gleann Dubh Lighe – 'glen of the dark stream'. The high point of this ridge, which lies at the northern end, is called Braigh nan Uamhachan – the slope of the caves. Where the caves may be I don't know, never having found them nor seen them from nearby hills. As they aren't mentioned anywhere else others seem to have had the same difficulty. Wherever the caves may lie Braigh nan Uamhachan is a fine hill. It can be climbed from either Gleann Fionnlighe or Gleann Dubh Lighe. The route up the latter follows the track for 6km, as for Gulvain, after which a rising traverse can be made northwards to the summit ridge, a distance of 9km, with 790m of ascent, which takes 3–4hrs. Descent can be made the same way or by following the ridge southwards and then descending west, to reach Gleann Dubh Lighe above the forest that blankets the lower glen. Continuing south down the ridge is inadvisable as there is dense forest on the lower southern flanks of the hill. The ascent via Gleann Dubh Lighe is

8.5km long, with 850m of ascent. There is a small bothy in the forest in the glen.

Braigh nan Uamhachan connects with Streap, which lies 3km away just south of west, by a 350m pass between Gleann Dubh Lighe and Gleann Camgharaidh. The re-ascent of 650m goes over the subsidiary top of Streap Comhlaidh.

🌐 Streap ☆

Sharp-topped and narrow-ridged Streap is the most impressive hill in this area with a distinctive and exciting summit, and the ascent is the finest hill-walk around. Streap is the highest point on the twisting, craggy ridge between Gleann Dubh Lighe and Glen Finnan. The terrain is rougher and rockier than on the hills to the east, the first touch of the harshness of Knoydart to the northwest. The ground is more complex, too, with some big corries biting into the ridge. Streap means 'climbing hill', and it does climb steeply from every direction. An ascent can be made from either glen, but that from Gleann Dubh Lighe is by far the most interesting and allows a circuit of the big corrie south of the summit. A forest track runs up to the edge of the trees from the main track a few hundred metres before the bothy. Once out of the forest rough slopes can be climbed to Beinn an Tuim, and then the undulating rocky

Looking towards Sgurr Thuilm from Braigh nan Uamhachan

ridge followed north over Meall an Uillt Chaoil and Stob Coire nan Cearc to the final exciting, steep, narrow and exposed crest leading to the tiny summit of Streap, a wonderful situation with splendid views. Continue east to Streap Comhlaidh along an excellent narrow ridge then descend the long grassy south ridge of the latter back to Gleann Dubh Lighe. The round is 16.5km long, with 1200m of ascent, and takes 7–8hrs. The views throughout the ridge walk are superb.

The ascent of Streap from Glen Finnan is perhaps easier, with more track walking, but omits much of the high-level traverse. The wide track up Glen Finnan runs underneath the viaduct and through plantations to Corryhully Bothy, where there is a break in the trees that gives access to the western slopes of Meall an Uillt. From this top follow the ridge to Streap. A direct descent into Glen Finnan from the summit is inadvisable, as the slopes are extremely steep and broken. Instead go back down the narrow arête and then make a descending traverse to rejoin the track in the glen

just above the forest. This route is 17km long, with 1200m of ascent, and takes 7–8hrs.

Just 2km northwest of Streap rises imposing Sgurr Thuilm. Between the two is the 471m Bealach a'Chaorainn, a classic glaciated U-shaped pass with very steep slopes either side. Rather than attempt a direct line between the two summits it is easier, safer and less arduous to descend into Glen Finnan and then ascend Sgurr Thuilm via the Druim Coire a'Bheithe.

✪ Sgurr Thuilm and Sgurr nan Coireachan ☆

These two Munros lie 4km apart on a long, steep-sided rocky ridge that curves around the huge arena of little Coire a'Bheithe and big Coire Thollaidh, and are usually climbed together. The hills rise above upper Glen Finnan, from where they look dramatic. The terrain is rough and rocky, similar to that of Knoydart to the north. Sgurr nan Coireachan means 'peak of the corries', which is appropriate as it stands at the head of Coire Thollaidh, as well as above the equally massive Coire Odhar Mor to the southwest, and also Coire a'Bheithe to the north. Sgurr Thuilm however means peak of the knoll or rounded hill, which seems a rather poor name for this fine hill. Presumably it has this name because it is not quite as rugged as nearby summits.

Research by Ian R. Mitchell, carefully detailed in *Scotland's Mountains Before The Mountaineers* (Luath, 1999), shows that the first recorded ascent of these peaks was by Prince Charles Edward Stuart and supporters in July 1746, during his journey through the Highlands in hiding from government troops. Mitchell does point out however that the party was accompanied by one Donald Cameron of Glenpean, who knew the way, so presumably had been on the summits before.

The round of the Thuilm–Coireachan horseshoe (perhaps it should be the Coire Thollaidh Horseshoe) follows the track up Glen Finnan through the forest to Corryhully bothy. After another 1km a stalkers' path leads up to the narrow and rocky south ridge of Sgurr nan Coireachan, which can be followed over the minor top of Sgurr a'Choire Riabhach to the summit. The ridge on to Sgurr Thuilm over two more minor tops – Meall nan Tarmachain and Beinn Gharbh – is rugged and complex, with many knolls and pools, but a line of old fence posts greatly assists navigation. Descend by the southwest ridge of Sgurr Thuilm, Druim Coire a'Bheithe. Throughout the horseshoe walk there are tremendous views into the deep corries below and across to nearby hills. From the Thuilm–Coireachan ridge the densely-packed, ragged hills of Knoydart can be seen to the north, a splendid vista. The round is 22km long, with 1450m of ascent, and takes 8–10hrs.

Sgurr Thuilm and Sgurr nan Coireachan can be climbed from Glen Pean – which is gloomy with plantations but does have a useful bothy – to the north via the long northeast ridge of the former. This side of the mountains is steep, complex and rocky, and any descent from the Sgurr nan Coireachan end of the ridge is arduous and requires careful route-finding. Perhaps the best way down is from Meall nan Tarmachain northeast over the 406m spot height on the OS map. It's all rough, however, and progress will be slow. Streams in this area rise fast during and after rain and the River Pean can be dangerous to cross, so this is not a route for times of heavy rain. Unfortunately the paths and tracks in the glen all lie on the north side of the river. There is a footbridge at the foot of the northeast ridge of Sgurr Thuilm but there are no bridges further up the glen. There are some stepping stones near the bothy. Using the bothy as a base I climbed the hills during a period of very wet weather on my Munros and Tops walk and found the stepping stones just covered as I set out but deep in rushing water on my return, and I had to go downstream a little way to where the river was wider and I could make a knee-deep ford via a spit of gravel. On that occasion I climbed to the ridge just east of Sgurr nan Coireachan and descended directly to the bothy from Sgurr Thuilm. Ragged, swirling clouds, in which peaks appeared and disappeared like dark phantoms, blasting hail that stung my face, a gusting wind that almost blew me over several times and the ground bursting with explosive burns made for an interesting if sodden day. From the bothy my trip took 5hrs – it wasn't a day for stopping, and I had just one brief rest to eat a chocolate bar in the shelter of the cairn on Sgurr nan Coireachan. From the end of the public road along Loch Arkaig the distance is around 20km, with 1600m of ascent, and the walk takes 7–8hrs.

5:3 THE GREAT GLEN

The Great Glen forms the southern boundary of the West Highlands and is a major transport artery, with the A82 running its length from Fort William to Inverness, a fairly slow road due to all the double bends and blind corners. There's a string of towns and villages along the glen, so facilities are many and frequent. The Great Glen Way runs the length of the glen and is an easy long distance path. The hills around the glen are mostly rolling moorland, with few distinctive summits. The highest are at the southwestern end of the glen where there are two Munros – Meall na Teanga (918m) and Sron a'Choire Ghairbh (937m) – and five Corbetts, Ben Tee (904m), Meall na h-Eilde (838m), Geal Charn (804m), Beinn Bhan (796m) and Meall a'Phubuill (774m). There are also five Grahams along the glen of which three stand out for their situation and views – Druim Fada (744m), above the southwestern end of the Great Glen, and Meall Fuar-mhonaidh (699m) and Glas-bheinn Mhor (651m), both halfway along Loch Ness.

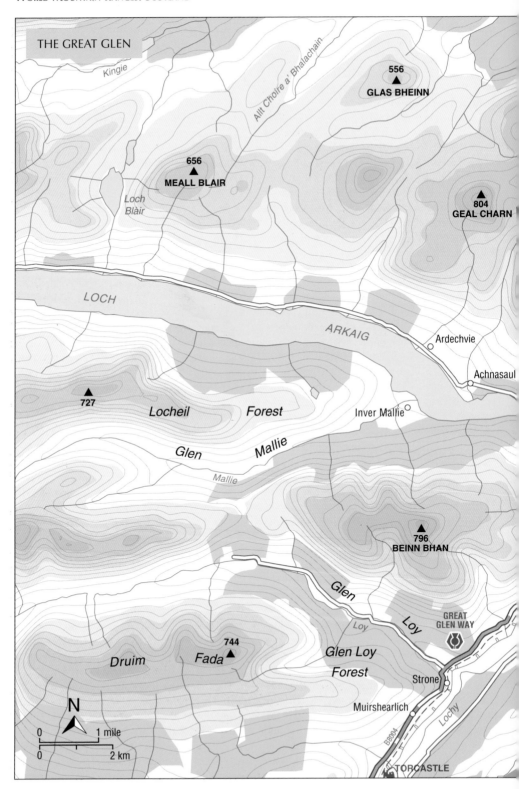

THE GREAT GLEN

Kingie

Allt Choire a' Bhalachain

556
▲
GLAS BHEINN

656
▲
MEALL BLAIR

Loch
Blàir

804
▲
GEAL CHARN

LOCH

ARKAIG

Ardechvie

Achnasaul

727
▲

Locheil   Forest

Inver Mallie

Glen   Mallie

Mallie

796
▲
BEINN BHAN

Glen

Loy

GREAT
GLEN WAY

Loy

Glen Loy

Druim   Fada

744
▲

Glen Loy
Forest

Strone

N
▲

Muirshearlich

Lochy

B8004

0   1 mile
0   2 km

TORCASTLE

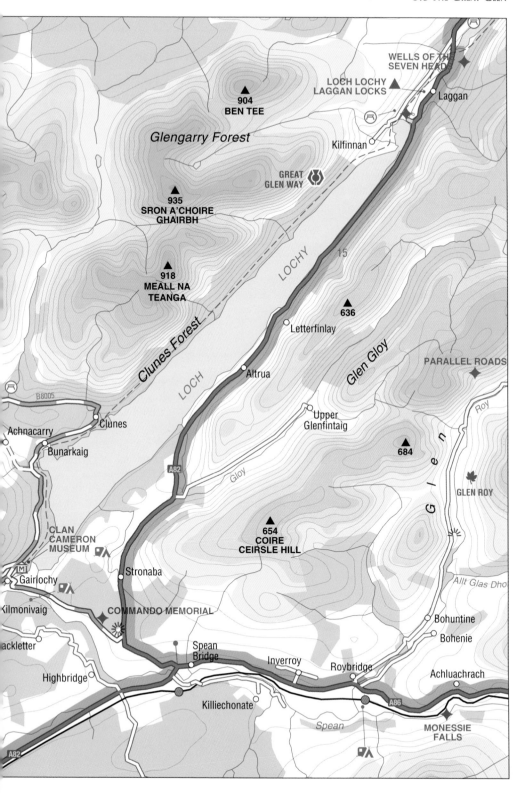

WELLS OF THE
SEVEN HEADS

LOCH LOCHY
LAGGAN LOCKS

Laggan

904
BEN TEE

Glengarry Forest

Kilfinnan

GREAT
GLEN WAY

935
SRON A'CHOIRE
GHAIRBH

LOCHY

15

918
MEALL NA
TEANGA

636

Clunes Forest

Letterfinlay

Glen Gloy

PARALLEL ROADS

LOCH

Altrua

Upper
Glenfintaig

Roy

684

B8005

Clunes

GLEN ROY

Achnacarry

Gloy

Bunarkaig

G l e n

A82

CLAN
CAMERON
MUSEUM

654
COIRE
CEIRSLE HILL

Allt Glas Dho

Gairlochy

Stronaba

Kilmonivaig

Bohuntine

COMMANDO MEMORIAL

Bohenie

ackletter

Spean
Bridge

Inverroy

Roybridge

Achluachrach

Highbridge

A86

Killiechonate

Spean

MONESSIE
FALLS

A82

THE GREAT GLEN GEOGRAPHY AND GEOLOGY

An Gleann Mor – the Great Glen – is the most distinctive geographical feature in Scotland, a giant slash cutting the Highlands in two. The Great Glen runs for 90km southwest to northeast coast to coast, from Corpach near Fort William to Inverness, a low defile with a high point of only 35m. The Great Glen is a geological fault line, formed some 420–400 million years ago during the creation of the Caledonian mountains, when the land mass on the north side of the glen slipped sideways and moved to the southwest. This took place over millions of years, of course: in fact it is still going on, as around three earthquakes a year are recorded in the glen, showing that the fault is still active. During the ice age the glen was filled by a vast glacier which gouged huge hollows in the base of the glen. These became a chain of lochs when the ice melted and left the Great Glen as a huge U-shaped valley. Loch Linnhe is a continuation of the Great Glen fault, which extends under the sea all the way to Ireland.

LOCH NESS

The biggest of the lochs in the Great Glen is the world-famous Loch Ness, the second biggest loch in Scotland by area and the biggest overall in volume. Loch Ness is 37km long and its foot is just 8km from the sea at the Moray Firth. It's an extremely deep loch, reaching 226m at one point. The size and depth, along with the murkiness of the water due to peat in the streams that run into the loch, helps explain how the legend of the Loch Ness Monster arose – it's hard to see just what exists in the gloomy depths. This legend goes back at least to the time of St Columba, who came to Inverness in the late 6th century and is said to have driven the monster away with the sign of the cross when it attacked a swimmer in the loch. No one wants to drive the monster away today, as it's the heart of a flourishing tourist industry. There are two Loch Ness Monster Visitor Centres in Drumnadrochit for those who wish to find out more.

Loch Ness has far more attractions than just the legendary monster of course, with Urquhart Castle the most impressive (and popular) of the other human attractions. This romantic ruined castle stands in a magnificent situation on the promontory of Strone Point almost half way along the loch, with fine views up and down the dark waters. There has been a castle on the site since at least the 13th century. Its history is bloody, as it was besieged and changed hands many times until a final bout of warfare in 1689, when it was held by supporters of William and Mary against the Jacobites. When the soldiers left in 1693 they blew the castle up to prevent it being used by the Jacobites, and it has been a ruin ever since.

These attractions aside, for many of us it's the birds on the water, the forests gracing the banks, the moorland rising above, the burns tumbling down the hillsides, the play of sun on the water, the whole natural world in fact that makes Loch Ness worth visiting.

THE CALEDONIAN CANAL

A canal linking the Irish and North Seas via the Great Glen was first proposed by James Watt, of steam engine fame, in 1773. It was an obvious route, as it would mean that ships could avoid the long journey round the treacherous storm-swept north coast of Scotland. The Caledonian Canal was eventually built by the famous Scottish civil engineer Thomas Telford and opened in 1822. Many locks were required on the canal, the most impressive being those of Neptune's Staircase, at the southwest end of the glen, where eight locks raise the canal 19.2m in a distance of just 550m. The canal itself is 35km long, linking the navigable lochs Lochy, Oich and Ness. Originally it was a trade route, but today cruises on the canal and the lochs are popular.

The Caledonian Canal above Neptune's Staircase in the Great Glen

The Great Glen Way

The Great Glen Way runs 117km along the length of the Great Glen from Fort William to Inverness, mostly on the northwest side. It's mostly a pleasant and gentle walk. I'd skip the first section from Fort William to Banavie however, as it's a not very attractive urban route past a supermarket and through a housing estate. Far better to start at the southwestern terminus of the Caledonian Canal at Banavie. The Great Glen Way is a low-level route, the highest section being around 275m above sea level, and the walking is quite easy along woodland tracks, canal towpaths and some moorland and farmland paths. The route runs beside the Caledonian Canal, beautiful Loch Lochy and Loch Oich – the highest part of the Great Glen, at just 35m above sea level – and finally the huge slash of Loch Ness. The Great Glen Way climbs 275m above Loch Ness at one point to give good views along the long, dark water. There are many settlements along the route, including Fort Augustus and Drumnadrochit, providing ample accommodation and supplies. Many mountains can be seen from the walk, especially at the western end where Ben Nevis looms over the Great Glen, and diversions could be made to climb some of these. Without side trips the walk takes 4–6 days. As well as the scenery there is much historical interest along the way, primarily the Caledonian Canal. Inverness and Fort William are both on main rail lines, so access to the walk is easy. Baggage transfer is offered by taxi. For further information on guidebooks and so on see the Introduction.

Eas Chia-aig ☆

These falls lie just west of the Great Glen at the end of the section of road running to Loch Arkaig known as the Mile Dorcha – Dark Mile – so-called for the avenue of thick woodland that shades it. Just above the road bridge the Abhainn Chia-aig crashes down a rocky bowl set in dense coniferous forest in two waterfalls of some 12m and 6m in height, a splendid scene. At the foot of the falls is a dark pool called the Witch's Cauldron after a local folk tale that tells of the death of a witch by stoning here. Louis Stott describes this as a 'charming fairy story' in *The Waterfalls of Scotland* (Aberdeen University Press, 1987). Grim and disturbing sound more appropriate descriptions to me.

The Great Glen Hills from South to North

Druim Fada ☆

Druim Fada (744m) is the most southerly of the hills along the Great Glen. The name means 'long

327

Dawn over the Ardgour hills from Stob a'Ghrianain

ridge' and the hill is indeed lengthy, stretching from the Great Glen west to Gleann Suileag, a distance of some 12km. Loch Eil lies to the south, Glen Loy to the north. Druim Fada is a grassy, undulating hill that isn't particularly distinctive but is worth climbing because of the superb views, especially of Ben Nevis, Fort William and the southern section of the Great Glen. The summit area, which lies towards the eastern end of the ridge and is named Stob a'Ghrianain on the OS map, is quite extensive and has a few small pools, as well as several cairns. I camped here the night of the full moon one September and sat watching the great bulk of Ben Nevis slowly darkening to a silhouette as the red and pink sunset turned to grey, Fort William fading into a blackness dotted with bright lights and a huge orange moon rising over the Great Glen. When the wind dropped I could hear traffic down in the busy world below, a mechanical intrusion into a world of whispering wind in the grass, the dark shapes of nighttime hills and the cold light of stars.

The best and quickest ascent route is from Glen Loy along the track to Puiteachan and then through the lovely old pine and birch trees of Coille Phuiteachain and up boggy slopes to the summit, a distance of 2.5km with 630m of ascent, which

takes 2–3hrs. Descent can be made by the same route, but a better option is to walk west along the ridge, with good views of the Glenfinnan hills, descend to Gleann Suileag and then return down Glen Loy. The round trip is then 16.5km, long with 800m of ascent, and takes 5–6hrs. An alternative is to climb Meall a'Phubuill (see above) from Gleann Suileag, and then to traverse the long eastern ridge of this hill before descending to Glen Loy.

⊗ Beinn Bhan

Beinn Bhan ('white hill', 796m) lies on the far side of Glen Loy from Druim Fada. Combining the two hills is difficult due to the extensive forestry plantations in Glen Loy. Beinn Bhan's long flat summit ridge curves round big south-facing Coire Mhuillin and the best walk on the hill is the circuit of this corrie. The high point lies at the eastern end of this horseshoe. The best start point is Inverskilavulin in Glen Loy, from where steep open slopes lead up to the southern edge of the corrie. Easy walking leads round the rim to the trig point on the big flat summit, which can be hard to locate in mist, from where a descent can be made back to the start point for a round of 8km, with 750m of ascent, which takes 3–4hrs. There are good views of Ben Nevis, the Grey Corries and the Great Glen from the summit. Beinn Bhan can be ascended directly from the Great Glen, but this is an arduous and not very scenic route (the views are behind you).

Sron a' Choire Ghairbh and Meall na Teanga

These two Munros are the highest points in the big tangle of ridges and corries rising up from the west shore of Loch Lochy. They are bigger and more complex than any nearby hills, standing out in views across the loch. Their distinctive and prominent shapes are reflected in their names, Sron a' Choire Ghairbh (937m) meaning 'nose of the rough corrie' and Meall na Teanga (918m) 'hill of the tongue'. The two hills are usually climbed together from the Cam Bhealach that lies between them at a height of 610m. I once camped on this pass and sat in the tent doorway watching a pink sunset fading over the rippling hills to the west and listening to the gentle swish of a breeze in the grass, the trickle of a burn and the occasional guttural bark of a red deer, before falling into a deep and restful sleep, the sort that only comes after a day in the hills and in the quiet of nature.

The Cam Bhealach can be reached from Loch Lochy or, more enjoyably, from the Mile Dorcha between the Great Glen and Loch Arkaig. The Loch Lochy route begins at Kilfinnan at the terminus of the public road at the north end of the loch from where forestry roads run southwest through the plantations that blanket the lower slopes of these hills. From the upper forest road a path leads westwards up the steep-sided glen of the Allt Glas-Dhoire to the pass. The Mile Dorcha route begins beside the Eas Chia-aig (see above), where a path and track runs northwards up Gleann Chia-aig through the forest to the open glen which can be followed to the pass. From the Cam Bhealach an old zigzag stalkers' path climbs north towards Sron a' Choire Ghairbh, which is an easy walk from the end of the path. There is no path heading south and the ascent of Meall na Teanga is somewhat rockier, although still quite easy. The views over Loch Lochy from both summits are excellent. If ascending from the Mile Dorcha, rather than returning to the Cam Bhealach a descent can be made west over Meall Odhar and down to Gleann Chia-aig. If the ascent is made from Loch Lochy the long northeast ridge can be descended over Sean Mheall and Meall nan Dearcag. Both routes are 16–18km, long with about 1400m of ascent. A fine expedition would be the traverse of both hills from Kilfinnan to the Eas Chia-aig.

Meall na h-Eilde and Geal Charn

West of the two Munros are two Corbetts situated on a long high ridge between Loch Arkaig and Glen Garry. Meall na h-Eilde ('hill of the hinds', 838m) and Geal Charn ('white cairn', 804m) are connected by a 3.3km, curving grassy ridge and are usually climbed together, as the walk between them is easy. These hills are pleasant but not distinctive, although Meall na h-Eilde looks attractive when seen from Glen Garry. The best ascent route is from Loch Arkaig. The same route as for the Munros can be taken from the Mile Dorcha up Gleann Chia-aig, leaving the glen where it splits and continuing north up to the Bealach an Easain, from where it's less than 1km northwest to Meall na h-Eilde. The ridge, which has spacious views, can now be followed over Meall Coire nan Saobhaidh – once thought higher than Meall na h-Eilde and so the Corbett – to the final steeper slopes to Geal Charn. Descend to the glen of the Allt Dubh, where a track leads down to Achnasaul above Loch Arkaig and a 2.5km walk along the road to the start (18km, 1080m of ascent, 6–8hrs).

Ben Tee

Ben Tee ('fairy hill', 774m) is a distinctive symmetrical cone lying to the north of Sron a' Choire Ghairbh. The views from the summit to the west and northeast are superb, as there are no other hills approaching the height of Ben Tee for many kilometres in these directions. Ben Tee is easily climbed from Kilfinnan at the north end of Loch Lochy, via the slopes to the northeast of Kilfinnan Burn which level out to undulating moorland then rise again to the stony summit. Return the same way for a there and back again walk of 9km and 890m of ascent, which takes 4–5hrs, or else descend southwest to a col and then climb Meall a'Choire Ghlais, the northeast spur of Sron a'Choire Ghairbh, and follow the ridge round to the Munro before descending to the Cam Bhealach and Loch Lochy (see above). This Munro and Corbett combination is 15.5km, long with 1650m of ascent, and takes 6–8hrs.

Meall Fuar-mhonaidh and Glas-bheinn Mhor ☆

Few hills of any note rise above Loch Ness. Perhaps the most distinctive is Meall Fuar-mhonaidh 'hill of the cold slopes'), which rises above the western shore about half way along the loch and can be clearly identified in views down the Great Glen. The situation of this little hill makes it a magnificent viewpoint for virtually the whole of the Great Glen, clearly seen as a long, ruler-straight defile. The bigger hills of the glens to the west and north – Affric, Cannich and Strathfarrar – look impressive too. The views from Glas-bheinn Mhor ('big green hill'), which lies northwest of Meall Fuar-mhonaidh, are not quite so good (the Great Glen can't be seen) but the situation is wonderfully remote and isolated, with rolling moorland on every side. These two Grahams can easily be climbed together from Balbeg near the end of a minor road from Borlum Bridge near Drumnadrochit that crosses the moorland above Loch Ness. A signposted path leads to Meall Fuar-mhonaidh through woodland and then heather moorland. The summit ridge has crags on the northwest side that drop down to Loch nam Breac Dearga, across which the little ragged cone of Glas-bheinn Mhor can be seen. To reach it descend the southwest ridge of Meall Fuar-mhonaidh until the crags have faded away (about 1km) and descend past the loch, which is in a lovely wild situation itself, then ascend Glas-bheinn Mhor, whose summit has a trig point. Return can be made via the northern end of Loch nam Breac Dearga and then across the northern slopes of Meall Fuar-mhonaidh. The round trip is 13.5km long, with 750m of ascent, and takes 4–6hrs.

5:4 LOCH ARKAIG, GLEN KINGIE, GLEN PEAN AND GLEN DESSARY

Loch Arkaig is a long loch running east–west that lies just west of the southern part of the Great Glen. Loch Arkaig leads from gentle wooded terrain into harsher, bleaker moorland. At its head two rugged narrow glens – Pean and Dessary, both unfortunately damaged by vehicle tracks and insensitive forestry in their lower reaches, lead off into steep, rocky hills and passes that give access to Loch Morar and Loch Nevis, one of the most lovely sea lochs. The next valley north from Loch Arkaig is Glen Kingie, which leads into Glen Garry. As Loch Quoich blocks access to the Glen Kingie hills from the north and they share much in character with the Loch Arkaig hills – and indeed link with some of them – I'm including them here. There are five Munros strung out on a long east–west ridge (whose complete traverse over a day or two would make a superb

expedition) – Gairich (919m), Sgurr Mor (1003m), Sgurr nan Coireachan (953m), Garbh Chioch Mhor (1013m) and Sgurr na Ciche (1040m) – and six Corbetts rather more randomly scattered – Sgurr Mhurlagain (880m), Fraoch Bheinn (858m), Sgurr Cos na Breachd-laoigh (835m), Carn Mor (829m), Bidean a' Chabair (867m) and Sgurr an Fhuarain (901m). The whole region is rough, rocky and steep, with some of the most impressive scenery in Scotland. Even the glen and passes routes are rugged and have a feeling of seriousness about them.

Access to this remote region is at the western end of the winding, undulating 21km single track road along the north side of Loch Arkaig. The increasingly splendid views make this a marvellous drive – for passengers. The twisting nature of the road, with many little blind summits beyond which lie sharp bends, means that drivers need to keep their eyes on the road if they want to stay on it. The area can also be reached on foot from Inverie in Knoydart to the west (see below), from Glenfinnan to the south and Glen Garry to the northeast. These approaches are most suited to multi-day trips. There are no facilities other than some basic bothies in the area: the nearest are in Inverie.

ⓐ Loch Morar via Glen Pean and Glen Dessary ☆

Although a low-level route – the highest point is 215m – this circuit is rougher and rockier, and a more serious undertaking, than many ascents. It's a glorious route too, taking the walker into wild, remote and outstandingly spectacular country. From Strathan, 1km from the end of the public road along Loch Arkaig, the route starts easily if dully with a stroll down Glen Pean on a forest road through ranks of conifers for 4.5km. Once out of the plantation the walk improves instantly. Pean Bothy, in a splendid situation facing south to the rugged slopes of Sgurr Thuilm, lies just beyond the forest fence. Although a path continues along the north side of the River Pean it's best to cross the river by the stepping stones below the bothy and make a way along the boggy tussocks of the far shore. If the river is in spate it may be too dangerous to ford. A couple of kilometres further little Lochan Leum an t-Sagiart is reached, filling the glen. The northern slopes are very steep, the reason for having forded the river at the stepping stones. There is a feeling here of being hemmed in by the steep craggy slopes towering overhead.

View over Loch Quoich to Sgurr Mor, Sgurr na Ciche, Garbh Chioch Mhor and Sgurr nan Coireachan from Gleouriach

This feeling grows as the lochan is passed, the slopes close in all around and the view ahead is of a narrow, boulder-choked notch. This is the pass between Glen Dessary and Morar. Once through this dramatic defile, where there is a little lochan and some scattered trees, a path reappears and winds its way down Glen an Obain Bhig to the eastern end of Loch Morar, the deepest piece of fresh water in Britain and the seventeenth deepest in the world, with a maximum depth of 328m and a mean depth of 86m. Loch Morar is 19km long and its head is less than 1km from the sea. Only some hard rocks that resisted the glaciers that ground out its deep basin prevent Loch Morar from being a sea loch. At its wild eastern end, surrounded by rugged mountains whose slopes descend into the loch, the coast seems far away.

Just over 500m along the south shore of Loch Morar is Oban bothy, useful if a shelter is needed and in a wonderful situation looking out across the loch. Our route lies round the eastern end of the loch, however, to a ford of the Abhainn Ceann Loch Morar beyond which a path runs up Gleann an Lochain Eanaiche to an extremely narrow defile with steep rocky slopes rearing up either side to the Corbetts of Carn Mor and Bidean

a'Chabair. Lochan Eanaiche lies in this chasm, one of the most dramatic situations for a lochan anywhere. Beyond the lochan the glen widens out a touch and runs up to a pass on the far side of which the plantations in Glen Dessary can be seen. Once in the trees there's a path that runs alongside the River Dessary to a forest road that leads back to Strathan. From the end of the Loch Arkaig road the circuit is 29km long and, given the rough nature of much of the terrain, is likely to take at least 8hrs.

The Three Strathan Corbetts ☆

To the north of the western end of Loch Arkaig and lower Glen Dessary three bulky hills dominate the view, separated by deep, steep-sided glens through which paths lead to Glen Kingie. These three Corbetts – from east to west Sgurr Mhurlagain ('peak of the bays', 880m), Fraoch Bheinn ('heather hill', 858m) and Sgurr Cos na Breachd-laoigh ('peak of the hollow of the speckled calf', 835m) – are the first of the rough hills of this area. They can be climbed together on a long day, as pairs or separately. All three send down long ridges to Strathan just west of the head of Loch Arkaig and can be climbed from here. The round of all three Corbetts

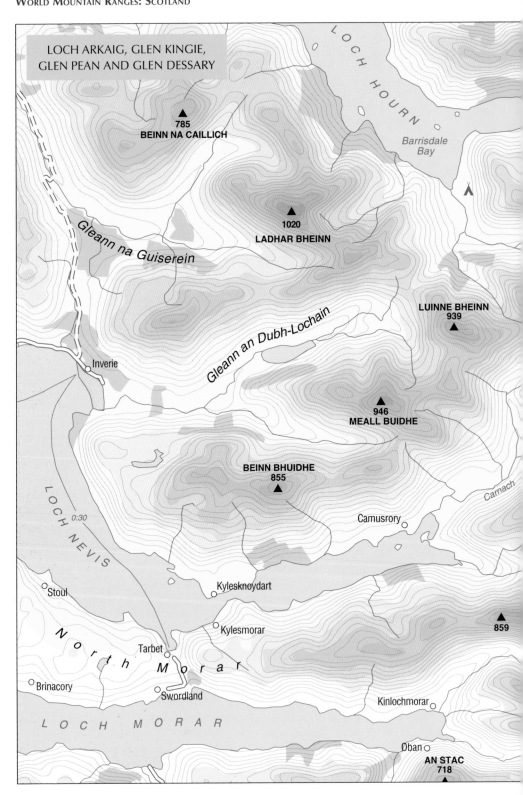

LOCH ARKAIG, GLEN KINGIE,
GLEN PEAN AND GLEN DESSARY

LOCH HOURN

Barrisdale
Bay

▲
785
BEINN NA CAILLICH

Gleann na Guiserein

▲
1020
LADHAR BHEINN

LUINNE BHEINN
939
▲

Gleann an Dubh-Lochain

Inverie

▲
946
MEALL BUIDHE

Carnach

BEINN BHUIDHE
855
▲

Camusrory

LOCH NEVIS

0:30

Stoul

Kylesknoydart

▲
859

Kylesmorar

North Morar

Tarbet

Brinacory

Swordland

Kinlochmorar

LOCH MORAR

Oban

AN STAC
718
▲

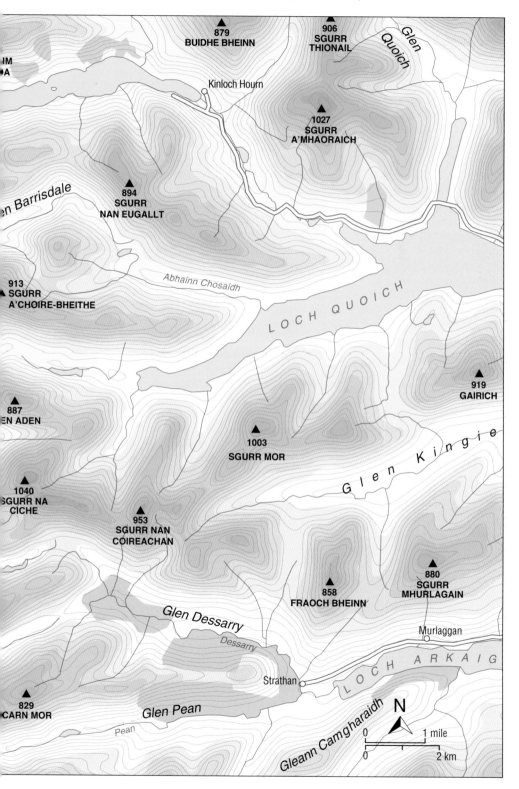

▲
879
BUIDHE BHEINN

▲
906
SGURR
THIONAIL

Glen
Quoich

IM
A

Kinloch Hourn

▲
1027
SGURR
A'MHAORAICH

en Barrisdale

▲
894
SGURR
NAN EUGALLT

Abhainn Chosaidh

913
SGURR
A'CHOIRE-BHEITHE

LOCH QUOICH

▲
919
GAIRICH

▲
887
EN ADEN

▲
1003
SGURR MOR

Glen Kingie

▲
1040
SGURR NA
CICHE

▲
953
SGURR NAN
COIREACHAN

▲
880
SGURR
MHURLAGAIN

▲
858
FRAOCH BHEINN

Glen Dessarry

Murlaggan

Dessarry

LOCH ARKAIG

Strathan

▲
829
CARN MOR

Glen Pean

Gleann Camgharaidh

N

Pean

0   1 mile
0   2 km

is 20km long with a strenuous 1900m of ascent. It'll take 8–9hrs.

⊗ Sgurr Mhurlagain

Sgurr Mhurlagain's southern flanks are steep and fairly featureless. An ascent would be strenuous and probably not that interesting. The long more gently angled southwest ridge is a better route. This can be climbed from the glen or by taking the path beside the Dearg Allt for a few kilometres and then climbing up to the ridge. Descending the same way, this makes for an 11km walk, with 860m of ascent, which takes 3–4hrs. Sgurr Mhurlagain is situated on the boundary between the rugged hills of the west and the smoother rolling hills stretching out east to the bulk of Aonach Mor and Ben Nevis, and the views show the distinction clearly. Three long ridges stretch down to Glen Kingie, from where the hill looks more impressive than from the south. Any of these ridges can be climbed but approaches from the north are long, and best undertaken as part of a multi-day trip.

⊗ Fraoch Bheinn

Fraoch Bheinn presents its more interesting side – two rocky spurs and a big corrie – to the north but is usually climbed from the south. From the south it rises as a steep pyramid and is the most impressive-looking of the three Corbetts. A 450m col links Sgurr Mhurlagain with Fraoch Bheinn to the west and can be used to traverse the two hills. Otherwise Fraoch Bheinn can be climbed from Strathan by its long southerly ridge. The view from the summit is similar to that from Sgurr Mhurlagain, but it's surprising how much closer the big Knoydart peaks look. The islands of Eigg and Rum are visible too, with patches of sea. The round trip from the end of the Loch Arkaig road is 8km long, with 850m of ascent, and takes 3–4hrs.

⊗ Sgurr Cos na Breachd-laoigh

While the other two Corbetts only give the option of going out and then back by the same route if approached from the south, Sgurr Cos na Breachd-laoigh has a narrow curving ridge marked by a squat pinnacle that can be traversed from the subsidiary summit of Druim a'Chuirn above big Coire Chicheanais. There is a 3km walk up Glen Dessary to Glendessary Lodge first, however. From the lodge the circuit is 8km with 860m of ascent, taking 3 hrs or so.

⊗ Bidean a'Chabair and Carn Mor ☆

These two Corbetts tower over the narrow notch of the Gleann an Lochain Eanaiche, which runs between Loch Morar and Glen Dessary. The circuit of the two from the head of Loch Arkaig is a fine, rugged expedition some 26km long with 2000m of ascent. Strong walkers will do it in 9–10hrs. A more relaxed approach is to take two days and have a camp between the two summits.

Bidean a'Chabair ('pinnacle of the hawk', 886m) is the more distinctive of the two hills, forming a long rough ridge between Gleann an Lochain Eanaiche and Mam na Cloich' Airde and looking superb from Glen Dessary, a soaring steep cone. It has two summits, some 800m apart. For many years the westernmost, Sgurr an h-Aide ('peak of the hat'), was thought to be the higher and it is listed as the Corbett in older books. However the eastern summit is in fact 8m higher. Carn Mor ('big peak', 829m) forms a broader, less rocky ridge between Glen Pean and Glen Dessary.

The walk starts with a stroll through the Glen Dessary plantations. Once out of the trees the west northwest ridge of Bidean a'Chabair can be traversed over Meall na Sroine and Druim Coire nan Laogh to a final easy scramble to the summit. This fine ridge is undulating, convoluted and replete with crags and rocks that turn the walker this way and that. I walked it one October among snow and hail showers and flashes of bright sunlight and relished the feeling of remoteness and high mountain grandeur. There are dramatic views of the surrounding hills, packed tightly together, and down to shining Loch Nevis and tiny Sourlies bothy on its bright green sward. A steep, knee-hammering descent leads down very rough tussock, bog and rock slopes to Gleann an Lochain Eanaiche west of the lochan. Once down there's a short respite from the steepness on the walk east past the lochan. Then it's up more steep tussock, bog and rock to Carn Mor. Again the hills all around crowd in, a grim yet magnificent mountain world. There's also a tremendous view down into Glen Pean to the south. Below the summit on this side is a huge landslip, said to be one of the biggest in the Highlands. From the summit a 7.5km ridge undulates eastwards down to 478m Monadh Gorm. The ridge is grassy and the walking easy until the final descent from Monadh Gorm, which is steep and tussocky and ends with a short struggle through the plantations to the track and Strathan.

Sgurr na Ciche, Garbh Chioch Mhor and Sgurr nan Coireachan from the south

⊗ The Sgurr nan Coireachan–
Sgurr na Ciche Ridge ☆

This is undoubtedly one of the great ridge walks of the Highlands and arguably the finest high mountain walk in the Western Highlands, both for the challenge of the terrain and for the views. It traverses three Munros, Sgurr nan Coireachan ('peak of the corries', 953m), Garbh Chioch Mhor ('big rough place of the breast', 1013m) and Sgurr na Ciche ('peak of the breast', 1040m), whose names give an inkling as to the nature of the summits and the terrain. Although not geographically part of the Knoydart Peninsula these hills are just as steep, rocky and rugged as the true Knoydart hills and are often considered as part of the Rough Bounds of Knoydart. Sgurr na Ciche is a fine, pointed pyramid and one of the most distinctive hills in the West Highlands.

There are a few touches of easy scrambling but overall, outside of winter conditions, this is a rough walk not a scramble. Under snow and ice it's a much more serious proposition, as the slopes fall away steeply on either side. The area is remote, with a 7km walk up Glen Dessary needed just to reach the start of the ascent. Although it can be done as a day walk from the road end it's more enjoyable and less strenuous to take two days, with an overnight by Loch Nevis, perhaps at Sourlies Bothy if it's not too crowded, or else camping on the soft turf nearby (see Glen Dessary to Inverie in the Knoydart section below). The remoteness lends an air of wildness and seriousness to the walk not found on hills closer to roads and buildings. After the walk up Glen Dessary the climbing starts with a very steep, arduous haul up the grassy south ridge of Sgurr nan Coireachan. From the summit a steep descent leads to the Bealach Coire nan Gall, above which rocky slopes lead to the complex, twisting rocky ridge of Garbh Chioch Beag and Garbh Chioch Mhor. The traverse of this ridge is entertaining throughout, with a succession of rocky knolls to cross, many stunning situations and wonderful views into the stony depths of Coire nan Gall to the north. A dry stone wall follows the crest, making navigation easy. A steep drop leads from Garbh Chioch Mhor to the pass of Feadan na Ciche, above which a final chaotic mountainside of boulders and little crags leads to the tiny summit of Sgurr na Ciche. The views are stupendous, with Loch Nevis stretching out to the open sea and the Isle of Skye and the tiny silver thread of the River Carnoch far below to the northwest surrounded by incredibly knobbly, rocky hills. This really is one of the most complex, rugged landscapes imaginable.

From Sgurr na Ciche there are two options. The finest is to take the long west ridge right down to sea level on the shores of beautiful Loch Nevis. The views of the loch during the descent are magnificent. However if returning to Loch Arkaig it's best to go back to the Feadan na Ciche, descend the gully to the southwest and then cut southeast, below Garbh Chioch Mhor, to Bealach an Lagain Duibh at the head of Glen Dessary. From Loch Arkaig to Sourlies is 16km. The return trip to Loch Arkaig via the Feadan na Ciche is 24km. Both routes involve around 1600m of ascent. Walking times are at least 7–10hrs for each route for most walkers, which may seem long but aren't when the nature of the terrain is taken into account. You simply can't move as fast over ground this rugged as you can over gentler terrain.

❸ Ben Aden ☆

Immediately north of Sgurr na Ciche lies the equally rugged Corbett of Ben Aden ('hill of the face', 887m), a wild, beautiful mountain. Lying between the heads of Loch Nevis and Loch Quoich Ben Aden is a remote hill in the midst of very rough terrain that makes its ascent challenging. Navigation can be difficult, especially in poor visibility, due to the tangle of little crags, knolls and boulders that cover its steep slopes on all sides. Just reaching the base of the mountain involves a fairly long walk from any direction and the hill is normally climbed from a camp or Sourlies Bothy rather than as a day walk from a road. Sourlies and the head of Loch Nevis lie some 14km from Loch Arkaig. From Sourlies it's another 7km, with 900m of ascent to the summit, which takes about 3hrs. The route from Loch Nevis follows the rough and often wet path beside the River Carnoch to the Allt Achadh a'Ghlinne, from where it climbs the southwest face of Ben Aden, cutting north below the summit crags to the northwest ridge. Ben Aden can also be climbed from the west end of Loch Quoich via 740m Meall a'Choire Dhuibh and the east ridge (4km, 825m of ascent, 2hrs one way). The views from the summit of the surrounding higher hills is magnificent.

Combining Ben Aden with Sgurr na Ciche makes for a superb day, one of the best in the West Highlands, with rough terrain and fantastic scenery throughout. The circuit is 15km long with 1540m of ascent and takes 6–7hrs.

⊗ Sgurr Mor

Sgurr Mor ('big peak', 1003m) lies between Loch Quoich and Glen Kingie, on the long ridge that runs from Gairich to Sgurr na Ciche. The name is a good one as it's a big, bulky hill presenting a long steep wall of unbroken grassy slopes to the south, which add to the desolateness of Glen Kingie. On the north side two spurs enclose Coire Buidhe. A curving ridge connects Sgurr Mor with a subsidiary top, Sgurr an Fhuarain ('peak of the spring', 901m), to the east. Although the north side is the more impressive, especially when viewed across Loch Quoich, ascents from this side are rare as the walk in is long, some 10km from the Quoich dam up Glen Kingie. In fact, although other hills lie in between, Sgurr Mor is most easily reached from the head of Loch Arkaig and Glen Dessary, although this means crossing a pass and descending into Glen Kingie. From Glendessary Lodge a path runs northwards between Fraoch Bheinn and Druim a'Chuirn to a height of 360m before descending into Glen Kingie, a wide, boggy and, it must be said, rather featureless glen. The path curves east and runs along the southern side of the glen to Kinbreack bothy, which could be used as a base for Sgurr Mor, Gairich and the hills to the south. However if heading directly for Kinbreack there is a more direct route from Strathan via the Dearg Allt. For Sgurr Mor leave the path from Glendessary Lodge where it starts to turn east and head northwest across the bogs to the River Kingie, which must be forded. This can be difficult or impossible when the river is spate. Then you need to follow the river upstream until a safe crossing point is found or else retrace your steps and come back another day. On the north side of the river an excellent well-made stalkers' path runs along Glen Kingie and then climbs steep slopes to the southwest ridge of Sgurr Mor and over the minor top of Sgurr Beag to Sgurr Mor itself, from where it continues along the graceful ridge to Sgurr an Fhuarain. Here it turns north and descends to disappear into Loch Quoich, having been made before the reservoir was created. It's best to leave the path on Sgurr an Fhuarain and either make a steep descent south or follow the east southeast ridge down into Glen Kingie and then take the path past Kinbreack bothy, over the pass between Sgurr Mhurlagain and Fraoch Bheinn and back to Strathan and Loch Arkaig. The round trip is some 24km long, with 1790m of ascent, and takes 8–10hrs.

⊗ Gairich

The easternmost of the Munros in this group, Gairich is also the most accessible and the easiest to climb. It's quite an isolated hill, separated from Sgurr an Fhurain to the west by a broad low 360m col. Gairich stands out from Glen Garry but isn't so noticeable once you are in the hills. The northern and southern slopes are steep but the long east ridge is quite gentle until the final rocky section. A stalkers' path runs up this ridge, and this can be reached from the path heading south from the Loch Quoich dam. It's best to return the same way, for a 15km walk with 970m of ascent, that takes around 5hrs.

5:5 KNOYDART

The Knoydart Peninsula is legendary among hill-walkers for its wild beauty, ruggedness and inaccessibility. No roads penetrate into this mountain fastness and approaches on foot are long and rough. There's one village in Knoydart, Inverie on the northern shore of Loch Nevis, which is the only village on the British mainland to which there is no access by road, just by sea or on foot. The Mallaig to Inverie ferry is a scheduled service, running several days a week year round (www.knoydart-ferry.co.uk). Another ferry (www.arnisdaleferryservice.com) can be booked in advance. This runs from Arnisdale on the north shore of Loch Hourn to Barrisdale on the northeastern edge of Knoydart, where there is a bothy, campsite and self-catering accommodation (www.barisdale.com). Both ferries are wonderful ways to reach Knoydart, with superb views of the mountains in clear weather. The nearest points

Luinne Bheinn and Meall Buidhe from the north

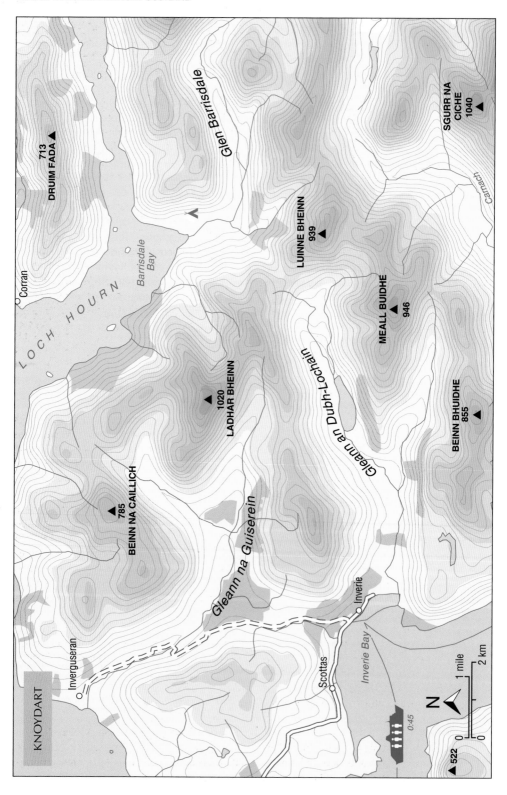

KNOYDART

DRUIM FADA 713 ▲

Glen Barrisdale

SGURR NA CICHE 1040 ▲

Corran

Barrisdale Bay

LOCH HOURN

LUINNE BHEINN 939 ▲

Carnach

MEALL BUIDHE 946 ▲

LADHAR BHEINN 1020 ▲

Gleann an Dubh-Lochain

BEINN BHUIDHE 855 ▲

BEINN NA CAILLICH 785 ▲

Gleann na Guiserein

Inverie

Inverguseran

Scottas

Inverie Bay

N

522 ▲

0:45

0 1 mile
0 2 km

Sgurr a' Choire-bheithe and Luinne Bheinn from Sgurr nan Eugallt

by road are at Kinloch Hourn at the end of a long single track road from Glen Garry and the head of Loch Arkaig, at the end of another long single track road. Inverie offers accommodation ranging from bunkhouse to guest house, a Post Office and shop, a café and a wonderful pub, The Old Forge, on whose website it says enticingly 'Munro baggers, deer stalkers, hill climbers, anarchists and hippies all intermingled with a generous helping of musicians are the norm' (www.theoldforge.co.uk).

Since 1999 a large part of Knoydart, including Inverie, has been owned by the Knoydart Foundation (www.knoydart-foundation.com), a partnership of local residents, the Highland Council, Chris Brasher Trust, Kilchoan estate and the John Muir Trust, whose aim is 'to preserve, enhance and develop Knoydart for the well being of the environment and the people'. The John Muir Trust also owns the Li and Coire Dhorrcail Estate, making up the summit and the superb north side of Ladhar Bheinn, which was its first property, purchased in 1989.

The Knoydart Peninsula lies between the long fjord-like sea lochs Nevis and Hourn (the name Knoydart has a Norse derivation and comes from 'Knut's Fjord') and is bordered to the east by Loch Quoich. There is no low ground between the Knoydart hills and those immediately to the east, between the River Carnoch glen and the minor road to Kinloch Hourn, so it's logical to include these with the Knoydart hills. There are three Munros in Knoydart (although Sgurr na Ciche is often included as well) – Luinne Bheinn (possibly 'sea-swelling mountain', 939m), Meall Buidhe ('yellow hill', 946m) and Ladhar Bheinn ('hoof hill', 1020m) – and five Corbetts, Beinn Buidhe ('yellow hill', 855m), Sgurr Coire Choinnichean ('peak of the mossy corrie', 796m), Beinn na Caillich ('peak of the old woman', 785m), Sgurr a'Choire-bheithe ('peak of the birch corrie', 913m) and Sgurr nan Eugallt ('peak of the furrowed rocks', 898m). On the edge of the area are two interesting Grahams – Slat Bheinn ('rod hill', 700m) and Meall nan Eun ('hill of the birds', 667m).

Walking to Knoydart ☆

Two superb walking routes lead to Knoydart from the road ends at Loch Arkaig and Kinloch Hourn. These are usually used as the start of multi-day trips in the region.

ⓐ Glen Dessary to Inverie via the Mam na Cloich' Airde and the Mam Meadail

This is one of the finest through-routes in the Highlands, threading a way up narrow glens and over wild passes from Loch Arkaig to Inverie at the mouth of Loch Nevis. Crossing two passes at 310m and 550m, with a drop to sea level between them and with much rough, rocky terrain, this 27km walk is harder than many hill climbs and not to be underestimated. It starts easily enough, as there are vehicle tracks running along each side of Glen Dessary, either of which can be followed from Loch Arkaig. The one on the northern side is less constrained by the plantations that bedevil the glen (a disgraceful legacy of a previous owner who, as the chair of the then Countryside Commission, should have known better) and so provides better views. There is a bothy, A'Chuil, on the southern side. The tracks eventually become paths that link up and continue into the wild, unspoilt upper glen and up to the first pass, 310m Bealach an Lagain Duibh, which is hemmed in by steep rocky slopes. The descent goes past Lochan a' Mhaim and through the long narrow boulder-strewn cleft of the Mam na Cloich' Airde, and then down to the head of Loch Nevis and little Sourlies Bothy. This is one of those magical places in the Highlands that feels special and splendid, bringing a feeling of joy to lovers of wild nature. The narrow loch runs out to the west between steep hills. The open sea cannot be seen but the seaweed and tide lines on the shore and the smell of sea spray show that this is salt water. Above the sandy shore lies a stretch of green turf and then the long Druim a'Ghoirtein ridge rising steeply to Sgurr na Ciche. Seabirds whirl and call along the shoreline and in spring and summer flowers dot the ground, including big irises in the wetter areas. This is a place to relax and absorb the atmosphere before continuing the rugged journey. When the tide is high the headland northwest of Sourlies has to be crossed. At low tide you can stroll along the sandy shore round to the mouth of the River Carnoch from where a vague path crosses salt marshes to a footbridge leading to some ruins marked as Carnoch on the map. From Carnoch the path climbs steeply northwest to Mam Meadail through splendidly rough terrain then descends Gleann Meadail to the Inverie River and a vehicle track to Inverie village.

ⓐ Kinloch Hourn to Inverie via Barrisdale

Kinloch Hourn lies at the end of a scenic 35km long single track road that runs from the A87 west of Invergarry alongside Lochs Garry and Quoich. There's not much at Kinloch Hourn – just a few houses, a farm, two car parks (one for day visitors, one for long stay) and some jetties. There is accommodation and a tearoom at Kinlochhourn Farm (www.kinlochhourn.com). The situation is glorious, with steep rugged slopes rising out either side and the loch stretching out into the distance. Upper Loch Hourn is quite narrow and hemmed in by steep hills. The name means 'loch of hell', presumably reflecting the difficulties and dangers of navigation. The head of the loch is known as Loch Beag – 'little loch'. The path to Barrisdale, where the loch opens out and you can look west to the Isle of Skye, runs along the south side of Loch Hourn and although always clear is often steep and muddy, as it crosses little headlands and marshy meadows. It's wonderful walk with splendid views throughout. The distance to Barrisdale is 10km and the walk takes around 3hrs. Most people will want to stay at Barrisdale for a day or two (and I certainly recommend this – it's too beautiful a place to breeze through) but the walk can be continued on a good path over 450m Mam Barrisdale and down Gleann an Dubh-Lochain to Inverie, a distance of 13km, with 500m of ascent, which takes around 4hrs. This walk isn't quite as scenic as the route to Barrisdale and passes beneath slopes which, for Knoydart, are rather plain and featureless.

Ladhar Bheinn ☆

❸ Scrambling on Ladhar Bheinn ☆

Ladhar Bheinn (1020m) is generally recognised as one of the most superb mountains in Scotland. It's the westernmost Munro on the mainland and forms a ragged-edged V or arrowhead shape, with a long southeast to northwest ridge, on which the summit lies, and an equally long subsidiary northeast to southwest and west ridge. On the north side long narrow rocky spurs run out between deep craggy corries above the dark waters of Loch Hourn, a magnificent wild sight. The south side is unbroken and of less interest. The name, which means 'hoof' or 'claw mountain', probably comes from the shape of the corries and spurs. Peter Drummond in *Scottish Hill Names: Their Origin and Meaning* (Scottish Mountaineering Trust, 2nd revised

Ladhar Bheinn and Loch Hourn

edition, 2007) points out that the word order, with Bheinn unusually coming second, is Norse, showing whose territory this once was.

The finest route on Ladhar Bheinn is the circuit of spectacular Coire Dhorrcail from Barrisdale, starting with the ascent of Creag Beithe, the easternmost of the northward trending ridges, from the path into the corrie. This ridge leads to a steep Grade 1 scramble up Stob a'Chearcaill, which looks impressively steep and elegant from Barrisdale, and then continues on to the summit of Aonach Sgoilte ('split ridge'), at the apex of the arrowhead. The route turns onto the main ridge here and descends to the Bealach Coire Dhorrcail from where it ascends over rocky knolls to the summit, which is some 300m before the 10m lower trig point. Descent can be made over Stob a'Choire Odhair, which is steep and quite exposed, and down Druim a'Choire Odhair from where you can drop into the mouth of Coire Dhorcail. Throughout the circuit there are superb views of the cliffs of

Coire Dhorrcail and out across Loch Hourn. The distance is 15km, with 1400m of ascent, and takes 6–8hrs. Under snow and ice this is a serious expedition with some exposed sections.

✽ Winter Climbing on Ladhar Bheinn

Ladhar Bheinn's cliffs are vegetated and loose, making them unattractive for rock climbing. However in winter conditions there are many highly rated climbs, dating right back to 1897 when Harold Raeburn climbed the big gully in Coire Dhorrcail now named after him. Since then many climbs of different grades have been made, ranging in length from 200 to 350m. However the remoteness of Ladhar Bheinn and the unpredictability of the weather, with good winter conditions rare, mean that few climbers actually venture onto its cliffs.

⬨ Sgurr Coire Choinnichean

Rising from the shores of Inverie Bay Sgurr Coire Choinnichean appears as a conical peak when viewed from the ferry or Inverie. However this is the end-on view. From the side it's a long flat-topped ridge, the end, in fact, of the 5.5km long ridge running southwest from Ladhar Bheinn that forms the southern wall of Gleann na Guiserein. Sgurr Coire Choinneachan can be most easily climbed via the corrie of the same name. A band of dense forestry covers the lower slopes above Inverie. To get through this take the track heading north towards the Mam Uidhe until out of the trees, then climb east into Coire Choinneachan then southeast to the narrow southwest ridge, which is followed to the summit (7.5km, 790m ascent, 2–3hrs). Sgurr Coire Choinneachan is marvellously situated with tremendous views of mountains on three sides and the sea and islands on the other. The walk can be continued onto Ladhar Bheinn via the Mam Suidheig and the Aonach Sgoilte, another 8km and 950m of ascent.

⊗ Beinn na Caillich
To the northwest of Ladhar Bheinn lies remote Beinn na Caillich. The two summits are linked by 6km of complex terrain, with a low point on the Mam Li at 665m. To climb Beinn na Caillich take the Mam Uidhe track from Inverie, then the eastern fork into Gleann na Guiserein, from where the southern slopes of Meall Coire an t-Searraich can be ascended and the ridge followed northeast to Beinn na Caillich (10km, 900m, ascent, 3–4hrs). The view of Ladhar Bheinn and Loch Hourn is excellent.

⊗ The Circuit of Gleann na Guiserein ☆
One of the finest long hillwalks in Knoydart is the circuit of upper Gleann na Guiserein over Beinn na Caillich, Ladhar Bheinn and Sgurr Coire Choinnichean. From Inverie this involves 27km of distance and 2415m of ascent, much of it on very rough terrain. It could be split over two days with a high camp en route.

⊗ Luinne Bheinn and Meall Buidhe ☆
Ladhar Bheinn is the finest mountain in Knoydart but the true heart of the region lies in the complex terrain, containing Luinne Bheinn (939m) and Meall Buidhe (946m) that lies between Gleann Meadail in the southwest, Gleann an Dubh-Lochain in the northwest, Gleann Unndalain in the northeast and the River Carnoch glen in the southeast. This is some of the roughest country in Scotland, a mass of rocks, crags, gullies, tussocks and knolls. Ridges twist and turn in every direction and route finding can be difficult even in clear weather. Meall Buidhe is the biggest in area of the two hills, and forms the north wall of Gleann Unndalain. The summit itself is not particularly distinctive, and the grandeur of the mountain lies in its overall size and ruggedness rather than its shape. Luinne Bheinn, which forms the southwest wall of Gleann Meadail, is smaller in area, with a better defined summit that appears as an elegant steep cone from some places, such as Lochan nam Breac to the southeast.

The two Munros can be climbed together from Inverie or Barrisdale or, on a multi-day trip, from Loch Nevis. From Inverie take the path to Gleann Meadail then climb the long western ridge of Meall Buidhe to the summit, from where there is a splendid view across Choire Odhair to Luinne Bheinn. The route now follows the convoluted edge of Choire Odhair to Luinne Bheinn via the east top of Meall Buidhe, the Bealach Ile Coire, Meall Coire na Gaoithe'n Ear and Luinne Bheinn's east top. The views from Luinne Bheinn are superb, back across Choire Odhair to Meall Buidhe, north to Ladhar Bheinn, southeast to Ben Aden and Sgurr na Ciche and west to the Cuillin on Skye. From Luinne Bheinn descend the northwest ridge to the Mam Barrisdale, then take the path down Gleann an Dubh-Lochain back to Inverie. This walk is 26km long, with 1800m of ascent, so at least 8–9hrs should be allowed, especially given the rough terrain and the difficult navigation.

⊗ Beinn Buidhe ☆
Opposite Meall Buidhe lies huge Beinn Buidhe (855m), forming the south wall of Gleann Meadail. This mountain is some 7km long in a straight line but considerably longer to walk, as its long ridge forms a shallow curve round a succession of corries that bite into the rocky northern flanks. To the south more uniform, less interesting slopes run down to Loch Nevis. There are a series of summits on the ridge, the highest lying just about in the centre. The shortest ascent route is up the ridge from the west, returning the same way, but it's much better to traverse the whole ridge. From Inverie follow Gleann Meadail to the Mam Meadail, then turn southwest and ascend the first peak on the Beinn Buidhe ridge, 718m Meall Bhasiter. A typically Knoydart, undulating walk over rough terrain now leads for almost 3km to the summit of Beinn Buidhe. Continue on along

View up the northeast ridge to Sgurr nan Eugallt

the ridge another 2km to Sgurr Coire nan Gobhar (787m). The ridge divides here. Take the branch running north to Sgurr nam Feadam, then descend west to Loch Bhraomisaig, from where you can head north again to a bridge over the Inverie River and the track back to Inverie. All the way along the ridge there are magnificent views down to Loch Nevis and to the sharp spire of Sgurr na Ciche rising at its head. The traverse of the ridge from Inverie is 22km long, with 1500m of ascent, and takes 7–8hrs.

⊗ Sgurr a'Choire-bheithe, Sgurr nan Eugallt and Slat Bheinn ☆

A 10km long, rugged and steep-sided ridge called Druim Chosaidh stretches from Loch Quoich to Barrisdale Bay. Sgurr a'Choire-bheithe (913m) is the highest point on this ridge. To the north across Glen Barrisdale and Gleann Cosaidh a ridge of equal length, ruggedness and steepness forms a great curve between upper Loch Hourn and Loch Quoich. Slat Bheinn is a squat little peak lying between the two Corbetts. The three peaks can be climbed together in a two day backpack, or one long, tough day from either Barrisdale or Coireshubh on the road between Loch Quoich and Loch Hourn, from where a stalkers' path climbs to 500m on Sgurr nan Eugallt. The whole route is 25km long, with 2525m of ascent, and would take a strong walker 9–10hrs. The terrain is the usual Knoydart mix of crags, gullies, knolls and bogs and the route-finding is complex in places. The rocks can be scrambled over or mostly avoided by the careful selection of grassy rakes. The three summits all offer splendid views. From Sgurr nan Eugallt Lochs Hourn and Quoich look big and distant, shining far below. Ladhar Bheinn rising as a slanting ridge above the

343

The summit of Sgurr nan Eugallt with the Skye Cuillin on the horizon left of the trig point and Beinn Sgritheall on the horizon to the right

steep walls of Coire Dhorrcail is the most impressive mountain in view. Note that the actual high point on Sgurr nan Eugallt (898m) is some 600m northwest of the trig point. Slat Bheinn (700m), a blocky peak ringed by little crags and shattered rock ridges, gives views of the massive southwest and northeast walls of the two higher peaks, as well as Ladhar Bheinn and Loch Quoich. Sgurr a'Chouire-bheithe has similar views to Sgurr nan Eugallt, although not quite as fine in my view.

⊗ Meall nan Eun ☆

Meall nan Eun (928m) may be dwarfed by the bigger peaks round about and easy to overlook but it's ascent is well worthwhile, as it has arguably the best view of Loch Hourn and one of the finest of Ladhar Bheinn. Meall nan Eun is situated immediately south of upper Loch Hourn, just east of the narrows of Caolas Mor, and its steep northern slopes can be quickly climbed from the path to Barrisdale (2.7km, 667m ascent and 2–3hrs for the return trip). A longer circuit can be made from

Loch Hourn via the minor summits of Carn Mairi (502m), Beinn Bhuidhe (569m) and An Caisteal (622m) (8km, 975m ascent, 3–5hrs).

5:6 THE GLENELG PENINSULA

The broad Glenelg Peninsula juts out into the Sound of Sleat between Loch Hourn and Loch Duich. Little villages dot the coastline, the principle one being Glenelg, where there is a ferry to Skye (see Chapter 7) plus shops, an inn and accommodation. Glenelg is reached by a narrow road from Shiel Bridge that climbs over the steep 339m Bealach Ratagan, which has tremendous views back over Loch Duich to the Five Sisters of Kintail (see Kintail and Glen Shiel below). Macrae Kintail of Glenelg offer an inexpensive taxi service from Shiel Bridge to Glenelg and other places on the peninsula and will meet scheduled buses (☎ 01599 511384).

The Glenelg Peninsula only has one Munro but it is a splendid one with some of the best views in

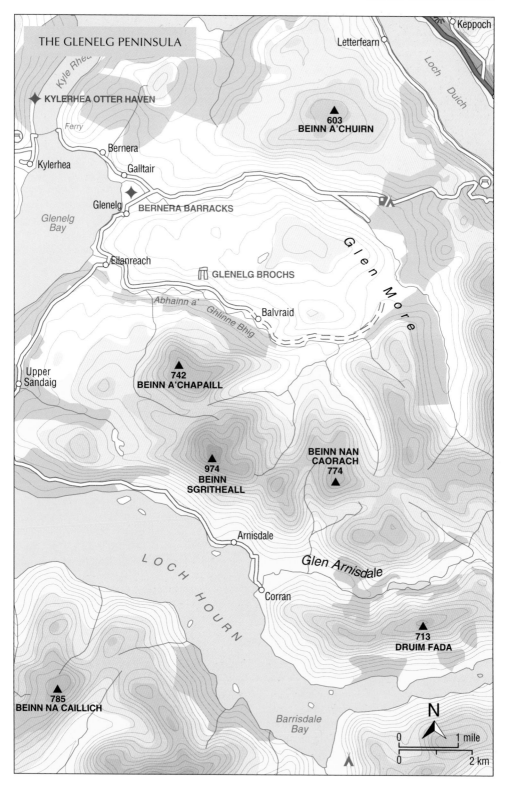

THE GLENELG PENINSULA

Keppoch

Letterfearn

Loch Duich

Kyle Rhea

✦ KYLERHEA OTTER HAVEN

Ferry

Bernera

Kylerhea

Galltair

Glenelg

✦ BERNERA BARRACKS

Glenelg Bay

Ellanreach

▲ 603
BEINN A'CHUIRN

Glen More

🏛 GLENELG BROCHS

Abhainn a' Ghlinne Bhig

Balvraid

Upper Sandaig

▲ 742
BEINN A'CHAPAILL

▲ 974
BEINN SGRITHEALL

BEINN NAN CAORACH
▲ 774

Arnisdale

Glen Arnisdale

Corran

L O C H   H O U R N

▲ 713
DRUIM FADA

▲ 785
BEINN NA CAILLICH

Barrisdale Bay

N

0 _____ 1 mile
0 _____ 2 km

the Highlands. Beinn Sgritheall (maybe 'scree hill', 974m) lies on the north side of Loch Hourn and has two fine Corbetts as outliers – Beinn na h-Eaglaise ('hill of the church', 805m) and Beinn nan Caorach ('hill of the rowan berries', 774m). Beinn Sgritheall rises directly from the loch, its steep slopes a mass of scree, boulders and broken crags.

The little village of Arnisdale, a long strip of white-painted houses, lies at its foot, near the end of a 16km single track road running round the coast from Glenelg. To the north of the hills is Gleann Beag, running inland from Glenelg. In Gleann Beag are three of the circular stone towers called brochs, one of which, Dun Telve, is the most intact broch on the Scottish mainland. These brochs were built by the Picts some 2000 years ago and are amazing structures built with dry stone techniques. Visiting the brochs can be combined with an ascent of Beinn Sgritheall by its more interesting and complex northern side.

Also of historical interest are the Bernera Barracks in Glenelg, built in the early 1720s to house soldiers after the 1715 Jacobite rebellion. The barracks can be seen but not visited, as they are on private land and in a dangerous condition. The road over Bealach Ratagan to Glen Shiel was originally a military road, built by General Wade to service the barracks.

Between Glenelg and Arnisdale is Sandaig, on the westernmost part of the peninsula. Sandaig was made famous by the writer Gavin Maxwell, who lived here for many years, calling the bay Camusfearna in his book *Ring of Bright Water*, about his life and the otters he shared it with. A short (2km) walk runs on forest roads through plantations from Upper Sandaig to Sandaig Bay and the site of Maxwell's house. It's a popular stroll for enthusiasts for Maxwell's books.

Kinloch Hourn to Glenelg via Gleann Beag ☆

Glenelg can be reached from Kinloch Hourn by an interesting and intricate route that follows a fault line across the hills that can be clearly seen on the geological map on the back of the British Mountain Map for Knoydart, Kintail and Glen

Affric. There is a path, often muddy, the whole way to the road in Gleann Beag. The route is varied and scenic with excellent views of Loch Hourn at the start but marred by the line of electricity pylons that accompany it. Despite this ugly intrusion it's well worth walking. From Kinloch Hourn the path climbs steeply through woods and then up open hillside before easing off, crossing flat ground at the mouth of Coire Reidh then climbing out of upper Gleann Dubh Lochain (which can be descended to Arnisdale) and following the Allt an Tomain Odhair up to the high point of the route, 474m Bealach Aoidhdailean. The path then descends Gleann Aoidhdailean to Gleann Beag. The minor road down Gleann Beag to Glenelg is quiet and visits can be made to the brochs. The route is 23km long and takes 6–7hrs.

The Ascent of Beinn Sgritheall ☆

The long, unbroken, steep south face of Beinn Sgritheall looks forbidding from Arnisdale and any direct ascent would be arduous and difficult. However it can be approached from either flank, and the combination of these makes for a good round trip. The start can be made some 2.5km northwest of Arnisdale, near Creag Ruadh, with a climb through woods on a sketchy path to a little lochan at the foot of the west ridge, up which a path leads to the summit. Continue on the path along the fine curving ridge over the east top then descend steeply to the Bealach Arnasdail where the path follows a burn down to Arnisdale. The whole round, including the road walk back to the start, is 9km long, with 1120m of ascent, and should take no more than 4–5hrs.

The north side of Beinn Sgritheall is very different to the south, with three long rocky spurs running out from the main ridge divided by big corries. This is complex country without paths, so ascents on this side require good route finding abilities, especially in poor visibility. There are a number of options for an ascent, all starting at Balvraid at the end of the public road down Gleann Beag. Continue along the track in the glen to a footbridge over the Abhainn a'Ghlinne Beag, just before the little wood of Srath a'Chomair. Cross a low col to the Allt Srath a'Chomair, from where any of the spurs can be ascended or the passes at either end of the mountain – the Bealach na h-Oidhche and Bealach Arnasdail – reached and the ridges from these climbed. I like the climb up the longest spur,

The summit of Beinn Sgritheall

the northeast, which gives superb views into Coire Dubh and Coire Min, and leads directly to the summit. The descent can be made via the Bealach Arnasdail. This route is 16km long, with 1215m of ascent, and takes 5–7hrs.

The views from the summit of Beinn Srgitheall across Loch Hourn to Ladhar Bheinn and west to the Cuillin on Skye are spectacular. All around are vistas of rugged mountains, islands and sea. This is a summit on which to linger.

⊗ Beinn na h-Eaglaise and Beinn nan Caorach ☆

Beinn Sgritheall's adjacent Corbetts can be climbed in conjunction with the Munro, but this makes for a very long day, with some 1550m of ascent and 15km of distance, much of it on rough, pathless terrain. The slopes of Beinn na h-Eaglaise above the Bealach Arnasdail, which links it with Beinn Sgritheall, are very steep and rocky, with crags that need circumventing. It's much easier to find a route in ascent than descent so if linking the Munro and Corbett it's best to start with Beinn Sgritheall, possibly ascending from and then returning to the Bealach Arnasdail. Just to the north of the Bealach

Arnasdail a shallow grassy gully runs up the face of Beinn na h-Eaglaise. This gully is very steep, but avoids all the rocks, and so is probably the easiest ascent route from this side.

The two Corbetts are fine, shapely hills in their own right, and the circuit of the two is an excellent walk with superb views of Loch Hourn, the Knoydart hills and Beinn Sgritheall. The walk starts at Corran at the end of the road along Loch Hourn and takes the track up Glen Arnisdale. Leave the glen after 1.25km and cross the river on a bridge, then take the path above the Allt Utha to the mouth of Coire Chorsalain. Cross the river here and climb the south-southwest ridge of Beinn nan Caorach. Deep Coire Dhruim nam Bo lies between the two Corbetts so it's necessary to head northwest to Bealach nam Bo ('pass of the cattle', 586m) between them, then over the little rise of Dhruim nam Bo, before climbing the northeast ridge to the summit of Beinn na h-Eaglaise. Fence posts run along the watershed between the summits, useful in mist. From Beinn na h-Eaglaise descend south-southeast over Beinn Bhuidhe then south-southwest down to the road, with excellent views of Loch Hourn throughout.

The Skye Cuillin from Beinn Sgritheall

This route is 10km long, with 1080m of ascent, and takes 4–5hrs.

5:7 NORTH LOCH QUOICH AND SOUTH GLEN SHIEL

North of Loch Quoich the hills are less crammed together than in Knoydart and the glens are wider and more open. There are twelve Munros here, seven of them on the South Glen Shiel Ridge, plus four Corbetts. Immediately above Loch Quoich are three Munros separated by an inlet of the loch that fills Glen Quoich. To the east of this are Spidean Mialach (probably 'peak of the deer' although literally 'lousy peak', 996m) and Gleouraich ('roaring' – presumably from the sound of rutting stags, 1035m), while to the west rises the massive Sgurr a'Mhaoraich ('peak of the shellfish', 1027m). North of these peaks run three long, lonely glens – Glen Loyne, Easter Glen Quoich and Wester Glen Quoich, with the vast wall of the South Glen Shiel Ridge rising above them. The Munros on this ridge are, from east to west, Creag a'Mhaim ('rock of the breast', 947m), Druim Shionnach ('ridge of the fox', 987m), Aonach air Chrith ('ridge of trembling',

1021m), Maol Chinn-dearg ('bald red hill', 981m), Sgurr an Doire Leathain ('peak of the broad oak grove', 1010m), Sgurr an Lochain ('peak of the little loch', 1004m) and Creag nam Damh ('rock of the stags', 918m).

A high pass, the Bealach Duibh Leac ('pass of the black slab', 721m), separates the South Glen Shiel Ridge from the hills to the west (thought it can be argued that they are all a continuation of the ridge) and provides a route from Wester Glen Quoich to Glen Shiel. Immediately above the pass to the west is one summit of a curious double-topped Corbett, Sgurr a'Mhac Chaolais ('peak of the hollow of the narrows', 885m). Around the rim of Coire Reidh, 3km away, is Buidhe Bheinn ('yellow hill') at exactly the same height of 885m. The drop between them isn't enough to make them two Corbetts so they count as one. West of Sgurr a'Mhic Chaolais is Sgurr na Sgine ('peak of the knife', 946m), whose subsidiary, steeply pointed top Faochag ('the whelk', 909m) looks very impressive from Glen Shiel.

West again from Sgurr na Sgine lies the most impressive mountain in this area, 1010m The Saddle (from the Gaelic *An Diollaid*) which has a long rocky spur, called the Forcan Ridge, running down towards Glen Shiel.

North of The Saddle is an isolated Corbett, Sgurr Mhic Bharraich ('peak of the son of Maurice', 779m) while far to the east above Glen Garry is an even more isolated Corbett, Meal Dubh ('black hill', 789m). Both these Corbetts are wonderful viewpoints. The last Corbett of the area is Beinn Loinne ('elegant hill', 790m), which forms a long moorland ridge between Loch Loyne and Loch Cluanie.

The walking in this area is easier than in Knoydart as the hills are grassier and less rough. There are many excellent stalking paths, not all marked on maps.

Glen Shiel

Glen Shiel is one of the major glens of the Western Highlands. In conjunction with Strath Cluanie and Glen Moriston it provides a route from the east through the mountains to the coast. The A87, running from the Great Glen to the Isle of Skye, runs through the glen. This road past Loch Cluanie and through Glen Shiel is dramatic as it sweeps across open moorland, with the mountains growing in size to the west, and then sweeps down the steep, narrow glen to Loch Duich. At Shiel Bridge at the

foot of the glen there's a combined shop/café/campsite/petrol station.

⚑ Through-routes: Kinloch Hourn to Glen Shiel and Glen Garry to Glen Shiel

There are walking routes to Glen Shiel from Kinloch Hourn to the south and Glen Garry to the east by way of Easter and Wester Glen Quoich and the Bealach Duibh Leac. Both routes are ideal as parts of multi-day trips.

The route from Kinloch Hourn starts at the north end of Loch Coire Shubh, on the public road just over 1.5km east of Kinloch Hourn, where a path heads north then northeast into Coire Sgoiredail. The path then crosses a pass at the head of the corrie and drops into Wester Glen Quoich, where it joins the path along the glen. At the junction turn up the glen (northwest) and climb the head of the corrie to Bealach Duibh Leac. The path fades away during this ascent, and its continuation on the broad saddle above can be hard to find in poor visibility (the author went astray here once, descending awkward slopes for some distance before happening on the path). The path is faint at the top but becomes more

Wild camp in Easter Glen Quoich looking towards Sgurr a' Mhaoraich

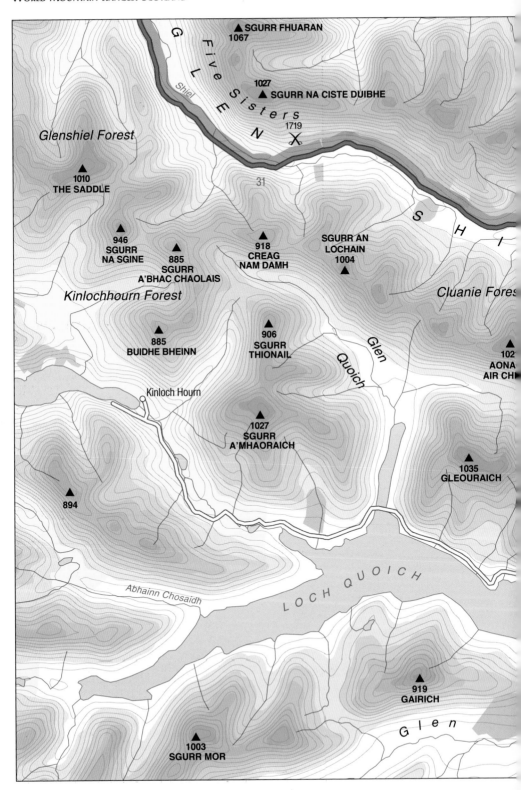

▲ SGURR FHUARAN
1067

GLEN

Five Sisters

Shiel

1027
▲ SGURR NA CISTE DUIBHE

N

1719
✗

31

S H I

Glenshiel Forest

▲
1010
THE SADDLE

▲
946
SGURR
NA SGINE

▲
885
SGURR
A'BHAC CHAOLAIS

▲
918
CREAG
NAM DAMH

SGURR AN
LOCHAIN
1004
▲

Cluanie Fores

Kinlochhourn Forest

▲
885
BUIDHE BHEINN

▲
906
SGURR
THIONAIL

Glen

Quoich

▲
102
AONA
AIR CH

Kinloch Hourn

▲
1027
SGURR
A'MHAORAICH

▲
1035
GLEOURAICH

▲
894

Abhainn Chosaidh

LOCH QUOICH

▲
919
GAIRICH

▲
1003
SGURR MOR

G l e n

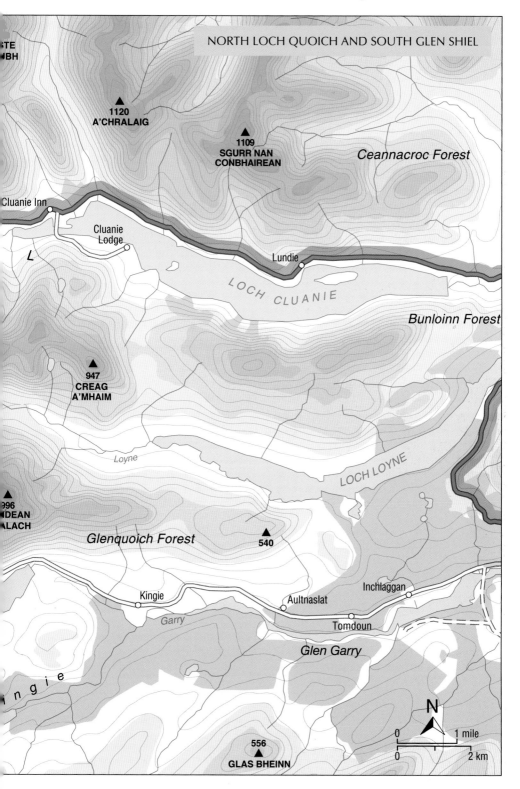

NORTH LOCH QUOICH AND SOUTH GLEN SHIEL

TE
BH

▲ 1120
A'CHRALAIG

▲ 1109
SGURR NAN
CONBHAIREAN

Ceannacroc Forest

Cluanie Inn

Cluanie
Lodge

L

Lundie

LOCH CLUANIE

Bunloinn Forest

▲ 947
CREAG
A'MHAIM

Loyne

LOCH LOYNE

▲ 996
DEAN
ALACH

Glenquoich Forest

▲ 540

Inchlaggan

Kingie

Aultnaslat

Garry

Tomdoun

Glen Garry

n g i e

N

0   1 mile
0   2 km

556
▲
GLAS BHEINN

351

defined as it zigzags down steep slopes from the bealach to the Allt Coire Mhalagain, which is followed to reach the A87 in Glen Shiel 6km from Shiel Bridge. The route is 12km long, with 835m of ascent, and takes 4–5hrs. It's been used as way through the hills for centuries. Bonnie Prince Charlie came this way in 1746, on the run from government troops, crossing the Bealach Duibh Leac in darkness.

The route from the east starts on the road to Kinloch Hourn in Glen Garry, where a path climbs up beside the Allt a'Ghobhainn (NH 112 018). This path crosses a 475m pass called Mam na Seilg and descends to Glen Loyne. Head up the glen to the broad saddle with Easter Glen Quoich and continue on up this glen and Wester Glen Quoich to join the route from Kinloch Hourn, described above, below the Bealach Duibh Leac. The route is 23km long, with 1100m of ascent, and takes 6–8hrs.

☺ The Saddle ☆

The Saddle is one of the great hills of the Western Highlands and the ascent by the Forcan Ridge is one of the finest scrambles. The Saddle forms a long summit ridge with three ridges running north from it, cradling two big corries, Coire Uaine in the west and Coire Chaoil in the east. All the ridges are narrow and rocky. The narrowest and rockiest of all, the Forcan Ridge, runs east from the summit ridge over Sgurr na Forcan. This knife-edge ridge is dramatic and exposed but the scrambling isn't very difficult or prolonged. If the hardest sections are taken direct it's a Grade 2 scramble. Easier options reduce it to Grade 1.

Although there is much rock on The Saddle none of it is very continuous and there is a surprising amount of green between the little slabs and splintered crags. Although there are some routes on the crags it's not a popular hill for rock climbing.

The ascent of The Saddle by the Forcan Ridge starts in Glen Shiel at NG 968 142, where a stalkers' path climbs up to the 490m col between Meallan Odhar and Biod an Fhithich. A well-used path runs south and southwest from the col to the foot of the Forcan Ridge. Once on the ridge the feeling of exposure is great, with steep slabs falling away into Coire Mhalagain to the south. Apart from one knife-edge section most of the exposure and the hardest scrambling can be avoided on paths just below the crest. The view to Sgurr na Forcan along the arête is sensational, as is that from Sgurr na Forcan to The Saddle.

Beyond Sgurr na Forcan the hardest scrambling comes with a short, steep descent. Gullies either side give easier options. After this descent the narrow ridge continues to the East Top and then broadens out for the final, almost level walk to the summit of The Saddle. The highest point, by about 1m, is the cairn 100m east of the trig point. The trig point and the east top used to be listed as subsidiary Tops in Munro's Tables until the 1997 revision, which made them the easiest Tops to do as there's no ascent and hardly any distance involved. Sgurr na Forcan, by contrast, deserves its status as a Top.

In winter conditions the Forcan Ridge is a Grade 1 or 2 climb, depending on the route taken, and is regarded as a classic alpine ascent.

The Forcan Ridge can be avoided by a traverse beside an old stone wall above Coire Mhalagain to the Bealach Coire Mhalagain, which harbours a little lochan. From the bealach head northwest to the summit. This route can also be used as the descent after an ascent via the Forcan Ridge. The round trip is 10km long, with 1142m of ascent, and takes 4–6hrs.

⊗ Sgurr na Sgine and Sgurr a'Bhac Chaolais/ Buidhe Bheinn

South of The Saddle, across the Bealach Coire Mhalagain, lies a much smaller and less spectacular Munro, Sgurr na Sgine (946m). This hill presents steep but fairly featureless and easily ascended slopes to the Bealach Coire Mhalagain. The most impressive feature lies on the far side, the southeast face, a pyramid of rotten crags and loose gullies. Sgurr na Sgine is often climbed with The Saddle, but I think this rather reduces it to an afterthought, and the most interesting route on the mountain becomes the descent route, at the end of a long day, when it is unlikely to be appreciated. I think Sgurr na Sgine is best climbed alone or with the double-Corbett of Sgurr a'Bhac Chaolais/Buidhe Bheinn. This makes for an interesting round of Coire Toiteil with an optional out and back again to Buidhe Bheinn.

The direct climb of Sgurr na Sgine starts at the bridge over the Allt Mhalagain, where a stalking path heads up the northeast of Faochag, a straight line to the summit. From Faochag an easy but airy ridge leads to Sgurr na Sgine. There is an excellent view of the Forcan Ridge from this ascent. The southeast face bars a direct descent to the col linking Sgurr na Sgine to Sgurr a'Bhac Chaolais,

Bealach an Toiteil (692m). To reach the bealach safely descend the southwest ridge of Sgurr na Sgine to the end of a stone wall at 780m (marked on the Harvey's British Mountain Map but not the OS map), which can be followed just north of east almost all the way to the bealach. A rocky ascent to Sgurr a'Bhac Chaolais follows. Here a decision has to be made as to whether to go out and back to Buidhe Bheinn. The connecting ridge makes a fine walk and the views down Loch Hourn from Buidhe Bheinn are wonderful, but it does add 6km of distance and 580m of ascent. Including Buidhe Bheinn this route is 17km long, with 1800m of ascent, and takes 6–8hrs.

Sgurr Mhic Bharraich ☆

This little Corbett rises directly above Shiel Bridge, and gives good views of Loch Duich and the Isle of Skye. The direct return trip to the summit only takes 3–4hrs at most. A more interesting circular route takes a little longer. From the campsite in Shiel Bridge take the good path up Gleann Undalain and on up to Loch Coire nan Crogachan, from where a climb leads north to the summit. Descent can be made down the east ridge back into Gleann Undalain. This route is 8.5km long, with 810m of ascent, and takes 4–5hrs.

The South Glen Shiel Ridge ☆

The magnificent high-level traverse of the seven Munros of the South Glen Shiel Ridge is one of the classic ridge walks of the Highlands. The actual summits are of less significance than the ridge as a whole. Going east to west gives the best views and slightly less ascent but the walk is still 25km long, with 2200m of ascent, and can be expected to take at least 9hrs. The finish leaves you 12km down the busy A87 from the start. Aside from the extra distance the road walk would be unpleasant and potentially dangerous so transport arrangements need to be made if you need to return to the start. Backpackers don't need to worry about this and can split the walk over two days with a high camp en route, while some walkers may choose to stay in Shiel Bridge after the walk. Buses do run down the glen so if the times are suitable one can be caught to the start. Otherwise a party with two cars can leave one at either end or bicycles can be left at one end (in which case a west–east traverse would mean a downhill cycle ride at the end of the day). As a last resort hitch-hiking is an option.

If the whole ridge in a day seems a daunting prospect the eastern and western parts of the ridge can be climbed separately, with Maol Chinn-dearg as the dividing point.

The South Glen Shiel Ridge from the south

From the easternmost summit, Creag a'Mhaim, to the westernmost, Creag nam Damh, is a distance of 12km. Much of the ridge is above 900m and it only dips below 800m at one point, 729m Bealach Fraoch Choire. To the south it presents an almost uniform wall of grass and scree rising above Wester and Easter Glen Quoich and upper Glen Loyne. To the north a succession of steep ridges runs down to Glen Shiel with deep, scooped corries between them.

The traverse begins just east of the Cluanie Inn, where a wide track heads south round the eastern end of the ridge. From the 476m high point a stalkers' path climbs the southeast ridge of Creag a'Mhaim almost to the summit. The ridge walk itself, although airy and narrow in places, is without difficulty and there is a well-worn path the whole way. The only Munro not on the main ridge is Sgurr an Doire Leathain, which lies 100m to the north. If the walk is being split over two days a descent can be made from Maol Chinn-dearg down Druim Coire nan Eirecheanach then a renascent up the Druim Thollaidh to Sgurr Coire na Feinne, a minor top just west of Maol Chinn-dearg.

Throughout the walk there are excellent views of the hills north of Glen Shiel and the hills to the south above Loch Quoich. Ahead The Saddle draws the eye.

✺ Winter Climbing in Coire an t-Slugain

Coire an t-Slugain lies on the north side of the South Glen Shiel Ridge between Druim Shionnach and Aonach Air Chrith, and is easily and quickly accessible from the Cluanie Inn. The corrie houses two crags – the West Face of Druim Shionnach and Creag Coire an t-Slugain – on which there are many winter climbs at all grades. The routes are described as 'turfy mixed climbing' in the SMC *Scottish Winter Climbs* and while many receive one or two stars none receive three or four.

North Loch Quoich

☒ Sgurr a'Mhaoraich ☆

Sgurr a'Mhaoraich is a massive, complex hill, measuring 6km from both south to north and east to west. Long curving ridges run south, north, northeast and east and there are half a dozen corries biting into its slopes. The most interesting, craggy side of the hill faces north and east, hidden from the road alongside Loch Quoich, which is probably why it's not that well known.

The southern side, facing the road, is grassy and rather featureless.

The quickest but least interesting route up the mountain is by the south ridge (a round trip of 6km, 810m ascent, 3–4hrs) but this misses most of the interesting terrain. A much better route is to climb the subsidiary top of Sgurr Coire nan Eiricheallach first. This takes a stalking path from the road 1km west of the bridge over an arm of Loch Quoich, and climbs Bac nan Canaichean to Sgurr Coire nan Eiricheallach and the east ridge. This entertaining ridge is rocky, with three towers, and provides some optional scrambling although there is an ingenious path that threads a way across the rocky slopes south of the towers, twisting and turning round gullies, slabs and crags. The ascent is 5km long, with 915m of ascent, and takes about 3hrs.

The summit gives good views south and west to the hills across Loch Quoich and west to Sgurr na Ciche. To the north the South Glen Shiel Ridge presents a somewhat bland unbroken and mostly grassy wall.

There are two options for the descent. One is via the south ridge as described above, giving a total of 8km and 915m of ascent, which takes 4–6hrs. Longer but better is to head north across the Bealach Coire a'Chaorainn to the spur of Am Bathaich, down which a stalking path runs to a track in Glen Quoich, beside the inlet of Loch Quoich, which can be taken back to the road. This route makes a circuit of the fine Coire a'Chaorainn, and gives good views into this corrie and into Coire Glas north of Am Bathaich. The round is 13km long with 1100m of ascent, and takes 5–6hrs.

☒ Gleouraich and Spidean Mialach ☆

These two Munros are the high points of a superb undulating ridge running between Loch Quoich and Easter Glen Quoich. As with Sgurr a'Mhaoraich the finest side of these hills lies to the north – a wonderful tangle of rocky ridges and deep, boulder-strewn corries. The public side, facing the road, is grassy and gently indented, with no particular features of interest. Because of the situation most ascents are via the southern side, but those with time and an exploratory instinct are encouraged to head for the north side. Good stalking paths take the sting out of the steep ascent and descent of the southern slopes. These paths leave the road just 370m from each other, thus minimising the road walking.

View along the ridge from Spidean Mialach to Gleouriach, with Sgurr a' Mhaoraich in the background

The path to Gleouriach starts beside the Allt Coire Peitireach just west of a small wood, and climbs the southwest ridge, with dramatic views down very steep slopes to Loch Quoich, before turning east and running almost to the summit. The 2.75km ridge walk to Spidean Mialach over several subsidiary tops is easy with a path much of the way. It skirts the edge of three deep corries to the north and gives wonderful views all around. The contrast between the two sides of the mountains can be clearly seen during this walk with smoother, easier angled grassy slopes running south and rougher, steeper, rocky slopes running north. From Spidean Mialach descend southwest above Loch Fearna to join the eastern stalkers' path at Allt a'Mheil and follow it across Coire Mheil and back down to the road. This route is 10km long with 1185m of ascent and takes 4–6hrs.

❷ Ski Touring on Sgurr a'Mhaoraich, Gleouriach and Spidean Mialach

The three hills north of Loch Quoich make good ski tours for experienced ski mountaineers. Sgurr a'Mhaoraich is easier than the pair to the east, although still steep in places. The recommended route goes up Coire nan Eiricheallach to the East ridge. If there's enough snow descent can be via the south ridge. Otherwise use the ascent route.

The traverse of Gleouriach and Spidean Mialach is a serious expedition, with steep ascents and descents. The SMC's *Ski Mountaineering In Scotland* (SMC, 1987) calls it 'one of the finest traverses in the Western Highlands'. The recommended route climbs from Loch Quoich into Coire Mheil and then Coire Peitireach and the ridge west of Gleouriach. Descend from Spidean Mialach above Loch Fearna into Coire Mheil.

⊗ Meall Dubh

Meall Dubh (788m) is a real outlier, far from any other high hills. This makes it a superb viewpoint (one of the finest in Scotland, according to Hamish Brown) although as a hill it's unexciting, being no more than the high point on an area of rolling boggy moorland. This is a hill for a fine day. It lies well to the east of Loch Loyne and Loch Cluanie and is included here simply for want of anywhere else to place it. Probably the most interesting route is from the A87 at the dam at the end of Loch Loyne. Climb to Clach Criche, then follow the ridge past several lochans to Meall Dubh. From the summit a vast sweep of the Highlands can be seen, from the Grey

Corries and Ben Nevis round to Sgurr na Ciche, the Loch Quoich hills, the Glen Shiel ridges, the Affric hills and back round over the western Monadh Liath, a tremendous panorama. The return walk is 10.5km long, with 690m of ascent, and takes 3–4hrs.

5:8 KINTAIL AND NORTH GLEN SHIEL

Kintail covers the area lying north of Glen Shiel and stretching as far as Strath Croe and the Falls of Glomach, with an eastern boundary running from Loch Cluanie along a line of connecting glens to the Falls of Glomach. The famous and distinctive Five Sisters of Kintail form a serrated ridge of steep pointed peaks rising above Glen Shiel. The classic view of the Five Sisters, immortalised in a myriad photographs and postcards, is from the south side of Loch Duich. The original Gaelic name of the Five Sisters is Bheinn Mhor – 'big mountain'. Where the name Five Sisters comes from is unknown but it seems fairly modern. Peter Drummond in *Scottish Hill Names: Their Origin and Meaning* (Scottish Mountaineering Trust, 2nd revised edition, 2007) says it was 'widely used by the late 1930s'.

Much of Kintail, including the Five Sisters and the spectacular Falls of Glomach, is owned and managed by the National Trust for Scotland (NTS), which has an unstaffed Countryside Centre at Morvich, open from April 1 to September 30. In the east this estate borders West Affric, also owned by the National Trust for Scotland, making a large area of wild mountain land under conservation ownership. The Kintail and Morvich estate was purchased for the NTS by Percy Unna in 1944.

Three of the Five Sisters are Munros – Sgurr na Ciste Duibhe ('peak of the dark chest', 1027m), Sgurr na Carnach ('rocky peak', 1002m) and Sgurr Fhuaran (uncertain but not, according to Peter Drummond, 'the peak of the wolf', as claimed in several books, 1067m). The other Sisters are Sgurr na Moraich ('majestic' or 'mightiness peak', 876m) and Sgurr nan Saighead ('arrows peak', 929m). The Five Sisters make up the western part of the long North Glen Shiel Ridge. Three Munros sometimes known as the Three Brothers lie on the eastern part of this ridge. These are Aonach Meadhoin ('middle ridge', 1001m), Sgurr a'Bhealaich Dheirg ('peak of the red pass', 1036m) and Saileag ('little heel', 956m). To the north of Aonach Meadhoin is a remoter Munro, Ciste Dhubh ('dark chest', 979). The Brothers and Sisters can be combined in one very long but glorious high-level walk. The fit and ambitious will include Ciste Dhubh as well. East of Ciste Dhubh is a fine steep Corbett, Am Bathach ('the byre', 798m).

The North Glen Shiel Ridge presents a very steep, fairly uniform face to Glen Shiel, with only a few small corries and short spurs. It's the steepness and height that are impressive. One of the longest continuously steep slopes in Scotland falls from the summit of Sgurr na Ciste Duibhe southwest into Glen Shiel, dropping some 925m in 1.5km. The north side is much more complex with five long spurs and a series of deep, rough corries. The best viewpoint for this side is the southern edge of Bheinn Fhada.

North of the Sisters and Brothers ridge Gleann Lichd and the Fionngleann provide a low-level route through the mountains. A huge mountain wall, Beinn Fhada ('long hill', 1032m), runs along

---

THE BATTLE OF GLEN SHIEL

Glen Shiel is notable as being the site of the last battle on the British mainland between the British army and a foreign army. This occurred in 1719, when a force of Jacobites and Spanish soldiers was defeated in the glen. The Spanish soldiers were meant to be an advance guard for a fleet from Spain which was wrecked in a storm. The battle was brief and casualties few. After their defeat the Spanish retreated up the hills north of the glen, one of which is called Sgurr na Spainteach ('peak of the Spaniards'). There's also a Leac nam Spainteach ('flat stone of the Spaniards'), Bealach nam Spainteach ('pass of the Spaniards') and Coirean nan Spainteach ('hollow of the Spaniards'). Ian R. Mitchell, in *Scotland's Mountains Before the Mountaineers* (Luath, 1999) says that the Spanish soldiers did climb the hill named after them, writing that it was 'in all probability, the biggest mass-ascent of a Scottish mountain before the era of club outings a couple of centuries later'. A plaque with information on the battle can be found beside the A87 below Sgurr na Spainteach in Glen Shiel.

the north side of these glens, stretching 10km from Morvich at the foot of Gleann Lichd in the west to the head of Glen Affric in the east. The name is sometimes anglicised to Ben Attow. The final Munro in Kintail lies to the north of Beinn Fhada, A'Ghlas-bheinn ('grey-green hill', 918m).

Just outside Kintail to its northwest is a lower although still very rugged area containing the 841m Corbett Sgurr an Airgid ('silver peak') and the remote Graham Carnan Cruithneachd ('wheat cairn', 729m), which can be climbed in combination with a visit to the Falls of Glomach (see below).

The only facilities in the area lie on the western coastal fringe apart, an exception being the Cluanie Inn at the head of Loch Cluanie. There are campsites at Shiel Bridge and Morvich, a shop, petrol station and café at Shiel Bridge and the Kintail Lodge Hotel, with bar and bunkhouse, at the head of Loch Duich. Along the highway beside Loch Duich there's a scattering of cafés and accommodation in little villages like Inverinate, all the way to the larger settlement of Dornie, which lies opposite romantic Eilean Donan Castle, one of the classic, not to say clichéd, images of the Highlands.

⊗ The North Glen Shiel Ridge ☆
The traverse of the whole North Glen Shiel Ridge from Loch Cluanie to Loch Duich is a magnificent walk. However, as it's 26km long, with 2750m of ascent, it's a major undertaking that is likely to take at least 11–12hrs. Starting at Loch Cluanie at 223m saves a little climbing, so I'd recommend an east–west traverse. From the loch the walk goes up the An Caorann Beag glen to Bealach a'Choinich from where Ciste Dhubh can be ascended before the traverse of the ridge proper begins to give a total of seven Munros. Set back to the north of the other hills, Ciste Dhubh is a fine, pointed peak that gives a good view of the main ridge, which runs west over the Brothers and then turns northwest over the Five Sisters. Once on the ridge the summits come in quick succession and it's easy to forget which is which as it's the joy of striding out high above the world in a wild mountain landscape, rather than the individual summits, that makes this walk so wonderful. The views throughout are superb. All the peaks lie on the ridge itself except Sgurr a'Bhealaich Dheirg, which lies at the end of a short rock arête just to the north. The

most dramatic and rugged section of the traverse is from Sgurr na Ciste Duibhe, which has a tremendous view across the depths of craggy Coire Dhomhain, to Sgurr Fhuaran, but it's all highly enjoyable.

Most people climb the North Glen Shiel peaks in two trips, with the Bealach an Lapain between Saileag and Sgurr nan Spainteach as the dividing point. The traverse of Ciste Dhubh and the Brothers from Loch Cluanie via the Bealach a'Choinich, finishing with a descent from the bealach, gives a walk of 15km, with 1800m of ascent, which takes 6–8hrs. The Five Sisters traverse starts with a climb to the Bealach an Lapain and finishes with a descent southwest to Glen Shiel from the westnorthwest ridge of Beinn Bhuidhe, for a walk of 11km, with 1600m of ascent, which takes 6–8hrs.

All traverses on the ridge leave the walker some distance from the start point so utilising buses, two cars or bicycles is necessary to avoid a long road walk. Or, of course, camping gear can be carried and a night spent out in the hills.

❄ Winter Climbing on the North Glen Shiel Ridge
The northern corries of the North Glen Shiel Ridge hold snow well and there are a number of easy to mid-grade winter climbs such as Resolution Gully (150m, Grade III) in the Ghlas Choire of Sgurr a'Bhealaich Dheirg and Trident Gully (220m, Grade II/III) on the north face of Sgurr Fhuaran.

⊗ Am Bathach ☆
Am Bathach is unusual in not lying on a long ridge but being a separate summit divided from neighbours by two deep glens – An Caorann Mor and An Caorann Beag – and the Bealach a'Choinich. Being so isolated makes it a good viewpoint, especially for Ciste Dhubh. Am Bathach looks impressively steep and pointed from Cluanie. The long curving whaleback of Am Bathach can be ascended directly from Glen Shiel, starting beside Loch Cluanie just west of the bridge over the Allt a'Chaorainn Mhoir. The main ridge is grassy but also very narrow, giving a feeling of walking on air. The summit lies at the far end of the ridge. A descent can be made northwest to the Bealach a'Choinich, from where Ciste Dhuibh can easily be ascended, and then down An Caorann Beag. The walk is 8.5km long with 675m of ascent and takes 3–4hrs, making it a good choice for a half day.

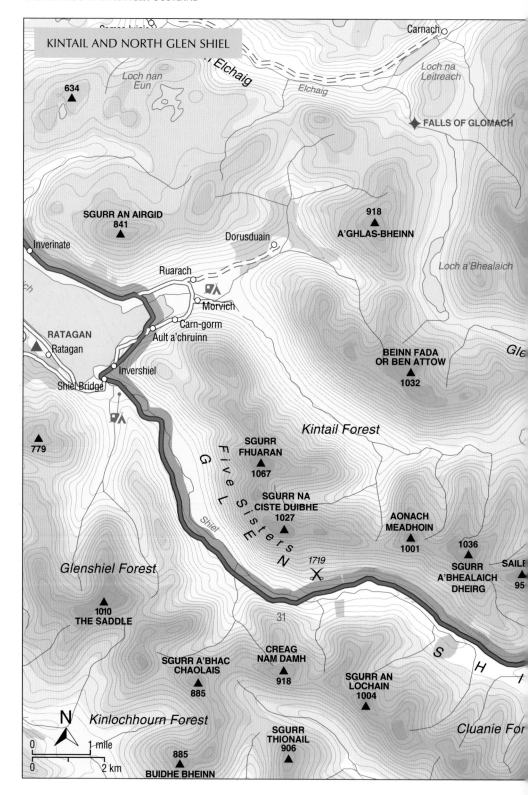

KINTAIL AND NORTH GLEN SHIEL

Carnach

Loch na
Leitreach

Loch nan
Eun

Elchaig

634
▲

◆ FALLS OF GLOMACH

SGURR AN AIRGID
841
▲

Dorusduain

918
▲
A'GHLAS-BHEINN

Loch a'Bhealaich

Inverinate

Ruarach

Morvich

Carn-gorm

Ault a'chruinn

RATAGAN
▲ Ratagan

Invershiel

BEINN FADA
OR BEN ATTOW
▲
1032

Gle

Shiel Bridge

Kintail Forest

▲
779

SGURR
FHUARAN
▲
1067

Five Sisters

SGURR NA
CISTE DUIBHE
1027
▲

AONACH
MEADHOIN
1001
▲

1036
▲

SGURR
A'BHEALAICH
DHEIRG

SAILE

95

G
L
E
N

Shiel

1719
✂

Glenshiel Forest

S

▲
1010
THE SADDLE

31

H

SGURR A'BHAC
CHAOLAIS
▲
885

CREAG
NAM DAMH
▲
918

SGURR AN
LOCHAIN
1004
▲

N

0   1 mile
0   2 km

Kinlochhourn Forest

SGURR
THIONAIL
906
▲

Cluanie For

885
▲
BUIDHE BHEINN

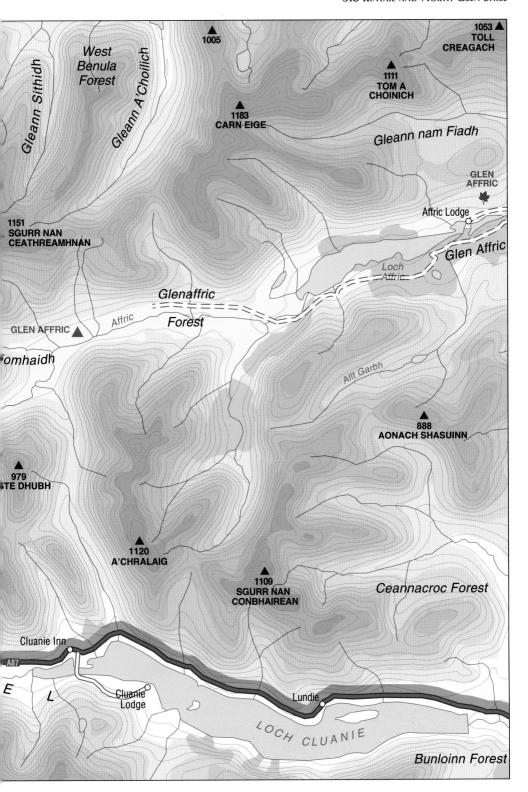

1005 ▲

1053 ▲
TOLL CREAGACH

West Benula Forest

Gleann Sithidh

Gleann A'Choilich

1111 ▲
TOM A CHOINICH

1183 ▲
CARN-EIGE

Gleann nam Fiadh

GLEN AFFRIC

Affric Lodge ○

1151
SGURR NAN CEATHREAMHNAN

Glen Affric

Loch Affric

Glenaffric

Affric

Forest

GLEN AFFRIC ▲

omhaidh

Allt Garbh

888 ▲
AONACH SHASUINN

979 ▲
TE DHUBH

1120 ▲
A'CHRALAIG

1109 ▲
SGURR NAN CONBHAIREAN

Ceannacroc Forest

Cluanie Inn ○

A87

E

L

Cluanie Lodge ○

Lundie ○

LOCH CLUANIE

Bunloinn Forest

⊗ Beinn Fhada and A'Ghlas-bheinn ☆

Beinn Fhada (1032m) is so big that the summit cannot be seen from the road, although the west face rears up above Morvich and the head of Loch Duich. The southern wall of Beinn Fhada is unbroken and extremely steep and any ascent would be unrelentingly hard work. It looks daunting from Gleann Lichd. The north side is a tangle of corries and ridges, with a number of options for interesting ascents. The summit forms a broad plateau, one of the few in the West Highlands and reminiscent of hills like Ben Alder and Creag Meagaidh in the Central Highlands. A'Ghlas-bheinn, by contrast, is a fairly small undistinguished hill with three long ridges leading to its small pointed summit.

Beinn Fhada and A'Ghlas-bheinn are often climbed together, with the latter rather as an afterthought to the bigger hill. The key to a joint ascent is the impressive, narrow and rocky Bealach an Sgairne (508m), reached from Morvich via the Gleann Choinneachain. A stalkers' path runs up into Coire an Sgairne, starting 1km west of the pass and leading onto the spur leading to Meall a'Bhealaich, about 1km from the summit of Beinn Fhada. From the summit a descent can be made over Meall a'Bhealaich and down steep, rocky slopes to the bealach, from where A'Ghlas-bheinn can be climbed by its initially steep southeast ridge. The summit has good views, especially of the long ridge of Beinn Fhada, but it's hard to get excited by A'Ghlas-bheinn. Descent can be made back via the bealach, or down the west ridge to the northern end of Dorusduain Wood and tracks back to Morvich. The walk is 20km long, with 1625m of ascent, and takes 7–9hrs.

Although combining the ascents of these two hills bags two Munros it's not really a satisfactory way of climbing Beinn Fhada, as it misses out the traverse of the whole ridge. This can be begun at Morvich with an ascent of the westernmost top, Beinn Bhuidhe, which gives excellent views over Loch Duich. The route continues over rugged, knobbly terrain to Sgurr a'Choire Ghairbh and then, with some easy scrambling, Meall an Fhuarain Mhoir. Here the ruggedness of the terrain ends and instead there is an almost flat, wide grassy plateau, the Plaide Mhor, that stretches east for almost 2km to the summit. Looking back west from the plateau a wide range of hills is in view, from Sgurr na Ciche and Ladhar Bheinn to The Saddle and Beinn Bhan in Applecross. The most magnificent sight , however, is the North Glen Shiel Ridge, a serrated succession of sharp peaks above deep scalloped corries. From the summit Beinn Fhada narrows, curving round Coire an t-Siosalaich to Sgurr a'Dubh Doire and then running down to its finish at the mouth of the Fionngleann. The return to Morvich can be made up the Fionngleann and then down to Gleann Lichd. The walk is 26km long, with 1700m of ascent, and takes 8–10hrs. Some 6km and 150m of ascent can be saved by descending directly south from Sgurr a'Dubh Doire to the Allt Grannda.

⊗ The Circuit of Beinn Fhada ☆

Paths and tracks encircle Beinn Fhada, and dramatic narrow passes separate it from A'Ghlas-bheinn to the north and the Brothers ridge to the south. The circular walk round the mountain is excellent, taking the walker from the lush woods at Morvich over rocky passes to the head of Glen Affric in the heart of the mountains. The walk is 27km long, with 990m of ascent, and takes a strong walker at least 8hrs. It could be split over two days, with a camp en route, or else an overnight in Camban bothy, in the Fionngleann, or the Glen Affric Youth Hostel, which lies 1km to the east of the route.

Starting at Morvich the route follows the track up Gleann Lichd, with the massive walls of Beinn Fhada to the north and the Five Sisters of Kintail to the south. From Gleann Lichd the path climbs above the Allt Ghrannda to a narrow notch where the stream is squeezed between steep rocks and crashes down in a series of waterfalls. Leaving the Allt Ghrannda the route reaches a high point of 340m below the little knoll of Cnoc Biodaig. Here on this boggy flat stretch of land you are on the watershed of Scotland with streams to the west running to the Irish Sea and those to the east running to the North Sea. The path now descends the Fionngleann past Camban bothy to the head of Glen Affric then turns back west past big and remote Loch a'Bhealaich and climbs up to the narrow pass called the Bealach an Sgairne, at 510m the high point of the walk. From the pass the route runs down Gleann Choinneachain to the conifer plantations of Dorusduain Wood and Morvich

⊗ The Falls of Glomach ☆

Roaring and thundering some 105m down a narrow rock ravine, the Falls of Glomach is perhaps the most tremendous and impressive waterfall in

Scotland (although not the highest, which is Eas a'Chual Aluinn in the Northern Highlands, see 6:6 below). Situated in a narrow side gorge above Glen Elchaig the falls are neither easy to reach or easy to see. You have to approach closely, right to the edge, to really see and feel just how magnificent they are. The falls are not just tall but also very powerful, draining long and wide Gleann Gaorsaic, which contains a chain of three lochs.

The quickest route is along Glen Elchaig from the road end at Camas-luinie, across the Allt a'Ghlomaich (which may be impassable when in spate) and up the path above the gorge to the falls, a distance of 9km, with 480m of ascent, which takes 2½–3½hrs.

The most dramatic and more interesting way to approach the falls is from above, via the 524m Bealach na Sroine. From Morvich follow the maze of forest tracks through the plantations of Dorusduain Wood, taking care not to go astray, to the steep-sided glen of the Allt an Leoid Ghaineamhaich. A narrow path traverses high above the stream then climbs to the Bealach na Sroine. From the pass the path descends into flat, boggy Gleann Gaorsaic just above the falls. The booming noise of the falls grows louder and louder during the descent into the glen. An NTS sign warns 'Danger. Please take great care'. Heed the warning, as the ground around the falls can be slippery.

From the sign all that can be seen is the stream vanishing over the lip of the glen. It's the sound that tells you something dramatic is happening. To see the falls descend the steep narrow path down rock and grass ledges on the left (west) side of the gorge. Sections of the falls come into view until from a small platform you can see it in full, crashing and twisting down the rocks into a small pool far below. The setting is magnificent and wild and the falls spectacular.

The return trip via the Bealach na Sroine is 17km long, with 925m of ascent, and takes some 5–7hrs. The return can be varied by climbing Carnan Cruithneachd, an excellent viewpoint as it sits right on the edge of steep slopes above Glen Elchaig. From the falls to the summit this route is pathless and involves a ford of the Allt na Laoidhre, which is dangerous or impossible when the stream is in spate, so it's one for dry, clear weather. Southwest of the summit a path can be joined that leads back down to Dorusduain Wood. Taking in Carnan Cruithneachd adds 2km and 200m of ascent and an extra hour.

⊕ Sgurr an Airgid

This little hill rises steeply directly above Inverinate village on the northeast shore of Loch Duich. The view along Loch Duich to Skye is excellent, and the ascent makes for a pleasant half day. The easiest route is via a stalkers' path from Lienassie in Strath Croe that leads almost to the col east of the summit. From the col the rocky east ridge can be climbed to the top. Return the same way. From the car park on the A87 at the mouth of Strath Croe the walk is 12km long, with 880m of ascent, taking 4–5hrs.

5:9 GLEN AFFRIC AND NORTH STRATH CLUANIE

Glen Affric is one of the most attractive glens in Scotland, with natural pine and birch woodland and beautiful lochs surrounded by rugged mountains. The forest contains the third largest remnant of natural Scots pine forest in Scotland. This forest is being restored by a combination of planting and fencing to allow regeneration by Trees for Life, in conjunction with the Forestry Commission, which owns much of the land in the lower glen, and the National Trust for Scotland, which owns West Affric, which is above the current forest and consists of open moorland and mountain. Due to the importance of the forest and the beauty of the landscape Glen Affric is designated a Caledonian Forest Reserve, National Scenic Area (NSA) and National Nature Reserve.

Glen Affric is a remote glen, only accessible by vehicle along a 12.5km minor road from the town of Cannich to the east. There is no public transport in the glen, nor any facilities other than Scotland's remotest youth hostel, Alltbeithe, which lies in the heart of the glen, 13km from the end of the public road. A shorter route to the hostel, although with 300m of ascent, runs for 9km from Loch Cluanie up An Caorann Mor and then down the Allt a'Chomhlain glen to Glen Affric.

Although steep-sided the Affric hills are mainly grassy, but a few of the corries are backed with crags.

Five Munros and two Corbetts lie on the south side of Glen Affric. The Munros are known as the Cluanie Horseshoe, and are often climbed from Strath Cluanie, as this provides the nearest access. They really belong to Affric rather than Cluanie, forming the high points on a great horseshoe, with

11 summits in total around the long side glen called Gleann na Ciche, with just one outlier protruding towards Loch Cluanie. Only the outer curve of the horseshoe lies above Strath Cluanie. In a clockwise direction the Munros are Sail Chaorainn ('heel of the rowan tree', 1002m), Sgurr nan Conbhairean ('peak of the keeper of the hounds', 1109m), Carn Ghluasaid ('hill of movement', 957m), A'Chralaig ('the basket, 1120m) and Mullach Fraoch-choire ('summit of the heathery corrie', 1102m). The two Corbetts lie between the eastern arm of the Cluanie Horseshoe and Loch Affric. They are Carn a'Choire Ghairbh ('cairn of the rough corrie', 865m) and Aonach Shasuinn ('ridge of the Saxon', 888m).

On the north side of Glen Affric is another magnificent horseshoe, again with five Munros, one of them an outlier. The horseshoe curves round another side glen, Gleann nam Fiadh, and contains the two highest peaks north of the Great Glen, Mam Sodhail and Carn Eige, which form a pair of huge steep-sided domes that are clearly identifiable from many distant peaks. The most distinctive summit of this group as seen from Glen Affric is Sgurr na Lapaich (1036m), which rises like a sharp spire from the glen. In the first edition of Munro's *Tables* it was give separate mountain status but it's now only classified as a subsidiary top. This demotion can't be blamed on modern revisionists, however: Sir Hugh Munro made it himself in preparation for the second edition of the *Tables*, which he was working on when he died. As Sgurr na Lapaich lies some 3.5km from its 'parent' Munro Mam Sodhail, with 109m of re-ascent it really should be a Munro. The actual Munros are Toll Creagach ('rocky hollow', 1053m), Tom a'Choinich ('hill of the moss', 1112m), Beinn Fhionnlaidh ('Finlay's hill', 1105m), Mam Sodhail ('barn hill', 1181m) and Carn Eighe ('file peak', 1183m). West of these peaks above the head of Glen Affric is a huge complex mountain with many spurs and three Munros – An Socach ('the snout', 921m), Mullach na Dheiragain ('kestrel hill', 982m) and Sgurr nan Ceathreamhnan ('peak of the quarters', 1151m) – plus an outlying Corbett, Sgurr Gaorsaic ('thrusting peak' or 'peak of horror', 839m).

⊗ The Cluanie Horseshoe ☆
Traversing the Cluanie Horseshoe from Strath Cluanie is awkward and means that you have to go out and back along one arm, whereas from Glen Affric only Carn Ghlusaid is out on a limb. The circuit feels more satisfactory from Glen Affric, too. As a return trip from the road it is very long – 47km – as there's a 10km approach walk down Glen

Sgurr na Lapaich and Loch Affric

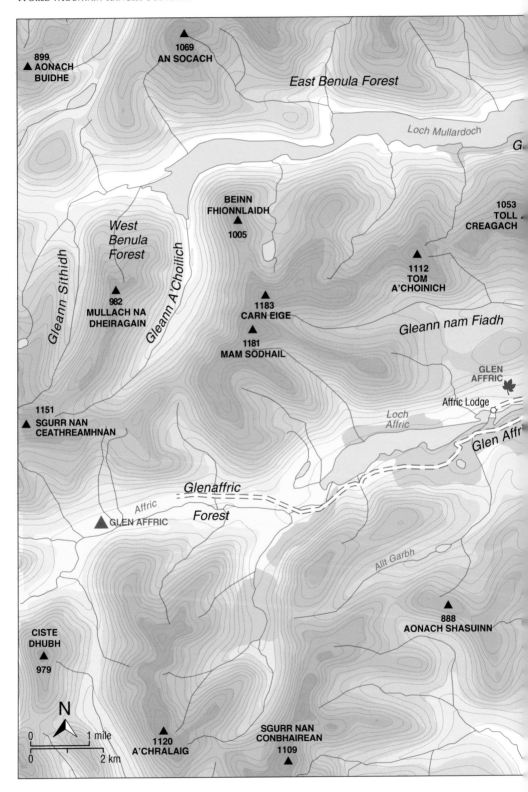

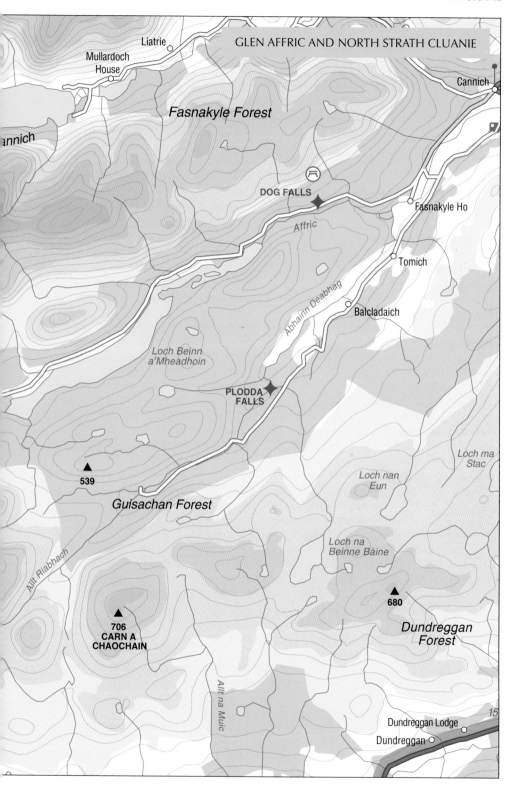

GLEN AFFRIC AND NORTH STRATH CLUANIE

Liatrie

Mullardoch
House

Cannich

Cannich

Fasnakyle Forest

DOG FALLS

Fasnakyle Ho

Affric

Tomich

Abhainn Deabhag

Balcladaich

*Loch Beinn
a'Mheadhoin*

PLODDA
FALLS

*Loch ma
Stac*

▲
539

*Loch nan
Eun*

Guisachan Forest

*Loch na
Beinne Bàine*

Allt Riabhach

▲
680

▲
706
CARN A
CHAOCHAIN

*Dundreggan
Forest*

Allt na Muic

15

Dundreggan Lodge

Dundreggan

Affric. A camp in Glen Affric or a stay at the Youth Hostel makes doing the round in a day much more feasible. Starting and finishing at Athnamulloch at the foot of Gleann na Ciche the walk is 27km long, with 2235m of ascent, and takes 9–11hrs. I think counter-clockwise is most enjoyable, so I'd start the walk by heading west through woodland to the rough, steep northeast ridge of Mullach Fraoch-choire, which leads directly to the summit. The ridge running south from the summit is narrow, with a series of rock pinnacles that can be either scrambled over or bypassed on a narrow path on very steep ground – this section is a serious proposition in winter conditions. Once past the pinnacles the walking is easy, although the ridge remains narrow. In fact, other than this pinnacled section the whole horseshoe is mostly grassy. After A'Chralaig the circuit descends to the low point of the horseshoe, 725m Bealach Coire a'Chait, where if necessary a descent can be made down Gleann na Ciche or south down Coire a'Chait to Loch Cluanie. From the bealach the circuit climbs to the eastern arm of the horseshoe at Sgurr nan Conbhairean. Carn Ghlusaid lies out on a spur to the southeast, and omitting this Munro shortens the route appreciably, as the out and back again route involves 5km of distance and 515m of ascent. From Sgurr nan Conbhairean the walk continues over Sail Chaorainn to the final top on the horseshoe, Tigh Mor a Seilge, from where a descent can be made down to the path in Gleann na Ciche.

For those who don't fancy the long traverse and the walk-in down Glen Affric the two halves of the horseshoe can be climbed in two much shorter trips from Strath Cluanie. For the western arm start at the foot of An Caorann, climb the south ridge of A'Chralaig and continue on to Mullach Fraoch-choire. Return the same way, or else from the 949m col between the latter peak and its subsidiary top, Stob Coire na Cralaig, down into Coire Odhar and the path down An Caorann. This walk is 13.5km long, with 1230m of ascent, and takes 5–7hrs. The eastern half of the horseshoe can be ascended from Lundie in Strath Cluanie by walking west along the old military road and then up an old stalkers' path that climbs to 800m. From the end of the path follow the southwest ridge of Carn Ghluasaid to the summit and then the ridge over Sgurr nan Conbhairean to Sail Chaorainn. Return the same way, or else turn southwest from Sgurr nan Conbhairean to

Drochaid an Tuill Easaich and descend the south ridge of the latter back to the old military road. This walk is 16.5km, long with 1650m of ascent, and takes 6–8hrs.

❷ Ski Touring Traverse of A'Chralaig, Sgurr nan Conbhairean and Carn Ghluasaid

The southern peaks of the Cluanie Horseshoe make for a fine ski tour for experienced ski mountaineers. The recommended route starts on the A87 beside Loch Cluanie and climbs alongside the Allt Coire Lair to Carn Ghluasaid. From A'Chralaig the descent can be made down the south ridge or else by retracing the route to the Bealach Choire a'Chait and skiing easily south into the corrie.

❂ Carn a'Choire Ghairbh and Aonach Shasuinn

Lying in the rolling hill country south of Loch Affric these rather undistinguished Corbetts are quite remote, and the pleasant circuit of their summits is a long excursion. There are good views of Loch Affric and the surrounding higher hills. From the road end in Glen Affric the route takes the track through the forest south of Loch Affric to the Allt Garbh where a footpath leads south to the edge of the forest and a climb up the long east ridge of Carn a'Choire Ghairbh. Drop south to a bealach, then east up the long west ridge of Aonach Shasuinn. The best descent route is from the lower western summit to the path beside the Allt Garbh. This walk is 24km long, with 1370m of ascent, and takes 6–8hrs.

❂ Glen Affric to Loch Duich ☆

One of the classic through-routes in the Highlands runs from Glen Affric to Morvich and Loch Duich via the Bealach an Sgairne (an alternative is via the Fionngleann and Gleann Lichd, but this isn't as fine a route in my opinion). The route is on paths and tracks throughout, and is 27km long, with 675m of ascent, and takes 7–9hrs. Glen Affric Youth Hostel lies halfway along the route, so the walk can easily be split over two days without the need to carry camping equipment.

From the road end in Glen Affric the tracks either side of Loch Affric can be taken. That on the south side is drier. Continue on along the broad glen, with superb views of the mountains either side, to the hostel, and then up Gleann Gniomhaidh to Loch a'Bhealaich. The hills start to close in now as the route climbs to the narrow Bealach an Sgairne, squeezed between Beinn Fhada and A'Ghlas-bheinn. Once through the pass descend Gleann Choinneachain to Dorusduain Wood and Morvich.

🄰 The Circuit of Loch Affric

Loch Affric is one of the most beautiful and unspoilt lochs in Scotland. Lovely woods of pine and birch line its shores with big rolling hills rising behind them. The loch is almost 7km long and encircled by tracks. The 18km circuit of the loch runs through the woods to open country at the western end and gives a good impression of the Glen Affric landscape. The walk starts at the road end in Glen Affric, where there are some magnificent massive Scots pines, some 300 years old. Going clockwise the walk follows the track on the south side of the loch through the woods to the Allt Garbh, where it climbs a little and runs above the trees with some superb views of the North Glen Affric Ridge. The track descends to the head of the loch and then runs west to Athnamulloch and a bridge over the River Affric. A young forest

rises in a big enclosure just west of Athnamulloch. The pines here were planted by Trees for Life in the 1990s: the birches, rowans and willows are natural regeneration. From the bridge the track climbs a little and then is left for a footpath running back east for a traverse above the loch to Affric Lodge and a track back to the start.

🄲 The North Glen Affric Ridge ☆

The traverse of the five Munros lying north of Loch Affric makes for a superb if long expedition, involving some 30km of walking and 2600m of ascent. It will take a strong walker 10–12hrs. If this seems too daunting omitting Beinn Fhionnlaidh, which lies out on a limb to the north from Carn Eighe, cuts out 4.5km and 560m of ascent, while omitting Toll Creagach and descending from the Bealach Toll Easa cuts out a further kilometre and 200m of ascent. The summits can be climbed in two separate walks as well, one to the three western Munros and one to the two eastern ones. But the finest trip is the complete circuit.

The route begins at the car park at the road end in Glen Affric and follows the path above the north

View up Gleann nam Fiadh to Mam Sodhail

shore of Loch Affric. The spire of Sgurr na Lapaich dominates the view. Once below this peak climb steeply to the top and then along the fine ridge running up to Mam Sodhail.

> The huge cairn on the summit of Mam Sodhail is the remains of a stone pile built by the Ordnance Survey who camped here for three days in 1848. Ian R. Mitchell in *Scotland's Mountains Before The Mountaineers* (Luath, 1999) quotes Colonel Winzer of the OS as saying that the stone pile was 23 feet (7m) high and 60 feet (18m) in circumference, a truly massive cairn. The views over the Kintail, Affric and Mullardoch hills are excellent.

A short descent and reascent leads to the summit of Carn Eige, where Colonel Winzer reported discovering a stone pile, showing that the hill had been climbed before 1848. Ian R. Mitchell says that Duncan MacLennan, a former keeper in Glen Affric, suggested to him that this was a watchers' bothy. Beinn Fhionnlaidh now lies just over 2km to the north. The summit is situated above steep slopes dropping down to Loch Mullardoch, and is a superb viewpoint. The climb back up to Carn Eige can seem arduous, however, especially as there is still a long way to go.

From Carn Eige the route is a wonderful ridge walk running west over minor tops to Tom a'Choinich and Toll Creagach. There are extensive views throughout. From Toll Creagach a descent can be made south into Gleann nam Fiadh and a path back to Glen Affric.

An alternative to returning to the start point is to backpack over the hills, descending from Beinn Fhionnlaidh to camp by Loch Mullardoch or in Gleann a'Choilich. This walk omits Sgurr na Lapaich and involves an out and back to Mam Sodhail from Carn Eige. The route starts with an ascent of Toll Creagach by the descent route described above. It's 19km long with 2075m of ascent, and takes 8–10hrs.

❷ Ski Touring on Toll Creagach and Tom a'Choinnich

Both these peaks hold snow well and are excellent for ski touring. They can be approached from Glen Affric via either Coire an t-Sneachda or Coireachan Odhar. The skiing on the wide open slopes of Toll Creagach is delightful and quite easy. Tom a'Choinnich is more serious and some of the ascent up the east ridge will probably have to be done on foot. The descent southeast from the summit is initially very steep and for very good skiers only. Others can return along the ridge and descend from the col between the two peaks at the head of the Allt a'Choire Odhair.

⊗ Sgurr nan Ceathreamhnan, An Socach and Mullach na Dheiragain ☆

Sgurr nan Ceathreamhnan is a vast and spectacular mountain situated in the remote area, between upper Glen Affric in the south and Glen Elchaig in the north. Gleann Gaorsaic separates Sgurr nan Ceathreamhnan from A'Ghlas-bheinn to the west and the Bealach Coire Ghaidheil from Mam Sodhail to the east. Measuring some 9km from south to north, and 7km from east to west, Sgurr nan Ceathreamhnan has a complex structure, with five ridges radiating from the summit above big deep corries. Two of these ridges, the northeast and the east, have Munros of their own – Mullach na Dheiragain and An Socach.

Climbing the three Munros in a day is a long expedition and involves retracing your steps several times. Alltbeithe Youth Hostel or a camp nearby is the best start point. Otherwise there is a 26km round trip from the road end in Glen Affric or an 18km one from Loch Cluanie, as well as the traverse of the Munros, which itself involves 19km with 1530m of ascent. A mountain bike could be used to reach Alltbeithe, although the track is rough in places.

From the hostel a stalkers' path leads up Coire na Cloiche to a 798m bealach on the ridge between Sgurr nan Ceathreamhnan itself and An Socach. The summit of the latter lies just 1km to the east with 140m of ascent and can be quickly climbed. Back at the bealach a rough descent leads northwest down to Loch Coire nan Dearcag then up to 841m Bealach nan Daoine on the northeast ridge of Sgurr nan Ceathreamhnan, which can be followed over Carn na Con Dhu to Mullach na Dheiragain. Turn back along the ridge here and take it all the way to the tiny, pointed, stony summit of Sgurr nan Ceathreamhnan, a great viewpoint for its spreading ridges and corries. Descend by the east ridge to the 798 bealach and down the path in Coire na Cloiche.

Backpacking over the Munros removes all the repeated sections except for the out and back to An Socach and finishes with a descent to Loch Mullardoch from Mullach na Dheiragain. This route is 15km long, with 1415m of ascent, and takes 6–8hrs.

⊗ Sgurr Gaorsaic

Sgurr Gaorsaic is a satellite of Sgurr nan Ceathreamhnan, situated 2.5km southwest of the summit. The two can be climbed together, but because it lies on the far side of Sgurr nan Ceathreamhnan from the other two Munros on the mountain combing the four summits makes for a very long and arduous outing. All approaches to Sgurr Gaorsaic are long. The shortest is from Loch Duich by way of Strath Croe, Gleann Choinneachain, Bealach an Sgairne and Loch a'Bhealaich, followed by an ascent of the southwest slopes. There is an excellent view of massive Sgurr nan Ceathreamhnan from the summit. The round trip from Loch Duich is 19.5km long, with 1215m of ascent, and takes 6–8hrs.

5:10 GLEN CANNICH, GLEN STRATHFARRAR, LOCH MONAR, STRATHCONON AND GLEN CARRON

North of Glen Affric lie the long east–west running valleys of, from south to north, Glen Cannich, Glen Strathfarrar, Strathconon, Strath Bran and Glen Carron. The last two glens have the scenic Inverness to Kyle of Lochalsh railway line, plus the A832 and A890, running through them, and they mark the geological dividing line between the Western and Northwest Highlands. In the east the hills dwindle slowly away to the rich farmlands around the Beauly and Cromarty Firths. On the western seaboard lie Loch Carron and Loch Alsh.

This is big empty country, ideal for long backpacking trips. The hills are mostly big, grassy and rounded – excellent for hillwalking and ski touring, but without much to offer rock climbers. There are 15 Munros and 12 Corbetts in the region. Access is via road and rail in Glen Carron – there are stations at Achanalt, Achnasheen, Achnashellach, Strathcarron and Attadale – and the A831 in Strathglass along the eastern fringe. Minor roads run into the area up Glen Elchaig in the west and Glen Cannich, Glen Strathfarrar and Strathconon in the east.

The most southerly of these glens, Glen Cannich, runs west from the village of Cannich in Strathglass. A minor road runs up the glen for 14km to the dam on Loch Mullardoch. Before the loch was dammed in 1952 Glen Cannich had a reputation as one of the most beautiful glens in Scotland, along with Glen Affric and Glen Strathfarrar, the next glen to the north. W.H. Murray wonderfully describes camping beside the loch, and the beauty of the area, in *Undiscovered Scotland*, published in 1951. Today, although there are still some old pine woods on the south shore of the loch, the upper glen has a desolate air and there is too often a dirty 'bathtub' ring round the shoreline, showing the artificial nature of the loch. In *Scotland's Mountains* (SMT, 1987) Murray says that due to hydroelectric dams and the flooding and felling of woodland Glen Cannich and Glen Strathfarrar are no longer in the category of beautiful glens. The dammed loch is 14km long. There is a rough path on the north shore but it's hard going, often overgrown and muddy, and not one I would recommend.

Beyond the loch Glen Cannich extends for a final 2km. A narrow glen continues 1.5km west past Loch an Droma to a 300m watershed, from where steeper slopes lead down the same distance to Iron Lodge in Srath Duilleach, the northeastern continuation of Glen Elchaig. A track runs down Glen Elchaig for 12km to the end of the public road at Killilan village, not far from the head of Loch Long, a sea loch that runs up from the junction of Loch Alsh and Loch Duich.

Four Munros and four Corbetts lie in an almost straight line on the north side of Glen Elchaig and Glen Cannich. In the west are Sguman Coinntich ('mossy peak', 879m), Faochaig ('the whelk', 868m) and Aonach Buidhe ('yellow ridge', 899m). Above Loch Mullardoch rise An Socach ('the snout', 1069m), An Riabhachan ('the grey one', 1129m), Sgurr na Lapaich ('peak of the bogland', 1150m) and Carn nan Gobhar ('peak of the goats', 992m). Further east Sgorr na Diollaid ('peak of the saddle', 818m) rises between Glen Cannich and Glen Strathfarrar.

North of Glen Cannich is the tautologically named Glen Strathfarrar. The reason for this is unknown but it has been suggested the words 'glen' and 'strath' refer to different parts of the valley. I suspect it is more likely that it is simply a lack of understanding on the part of an English-speaking

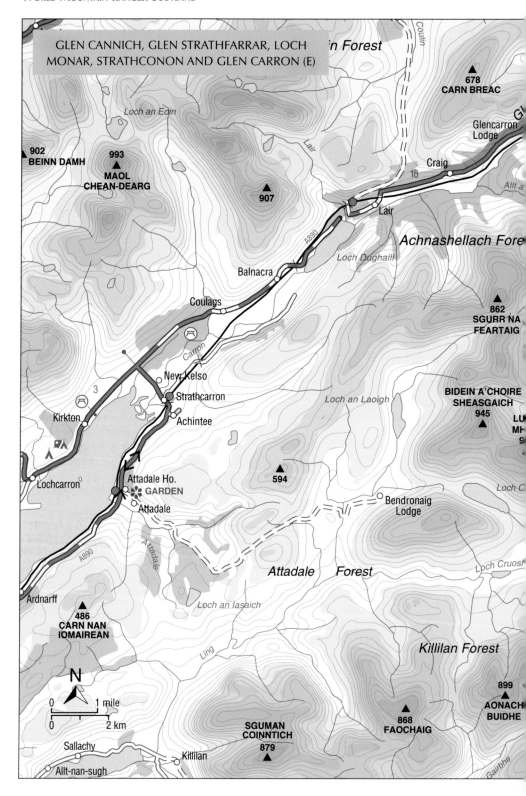

GLEN CANNICH, GLEN STRATHFARRAR, LOCH
MONAR, STRATHCONON AND GLEN CARRON (E)

...n Forest

678
CARN BREAC

Glencarron
Lodge

Loch an Eoin

902
BEINN DAMH

993

MAOL
CHEAN-DEARG

907

Craig

18

Lair

Allt a

Achnashellach Fore

Loch Dùghaill

Balnacra

862
SGURR NA
FEARTAIG

Coulags

Carron

Loch an Laoigh

BIDEIN A'CHOIRE
SHEASGAICH
945

New Kelso

LU
MH
9

Strathcarron

Kirkton

Achintee

3

594

Loch C

Lochcarron

Attadale Ho.
GARDEN

Bendronaig
Lodge

Attadale

Loch Cruosl

Attadale

A890

Attadale   Forest

Ardnarff

486
CARN NAN
IOMAIREAN

Loch an Iasaich

Killilan Forest

Ling

N

0   1 mile

0   2 km

899
AONACH
BUIDHE

868
FAOCHAIG

SGUMAN
COINNTICH
879

Sallachy

Killilan

Allt-nan-sugh

Gairbhe

370

▲
538
CARN MHARTUIN

S T R A T H

Scardroy

Loch Beannacharain

Loch Sgamhain

A890

ron

F O R E

▲
MORUISG
928

Glencarron and
Glenuig Forest

Meig

▲
849
BAC AN EICH

Glen Fhiodhaig

Loch na Caoidhe

▲
1007
MAOILE
LUNNDAIDH

▲
814

▲
1053
SGURR
A'CHAORACHAIN

Vest Monar Forest

East Monar Forest

Loch Monar

Monar Lodge

An Gead Loch

Glenstrathfarrar
Forest

Loch an Tachdaidh

Uisge Misgeach

▲
706
AN CRUACHAN

Glencannich Forest

▲
1150
SGURR NA
LAPAICH

▲
1086
AN RIABHACHAN

▲
1069
AN SOCACH

East Benula Forest

Mullardoch House

Loch Mullardoch

Glen Cannich

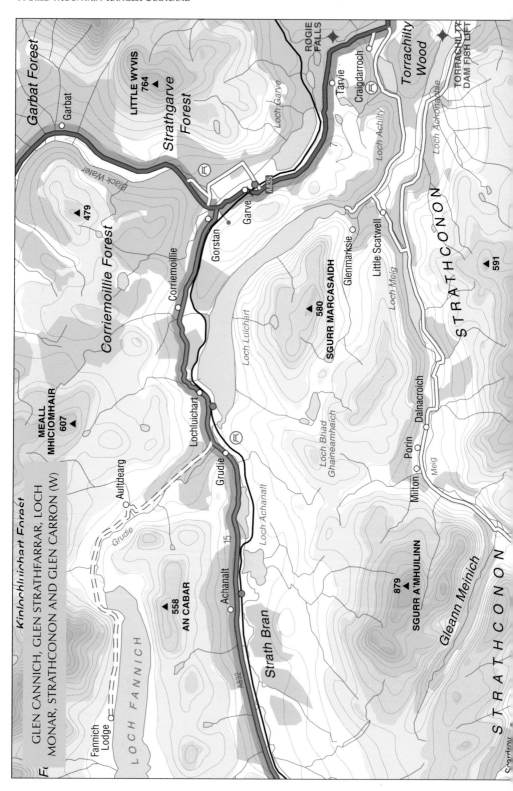

GLEN CANNICH, GLEN STRATHFARRAR, LOCH MONAR, STRATHCONON AND GLEN CARRON (W)

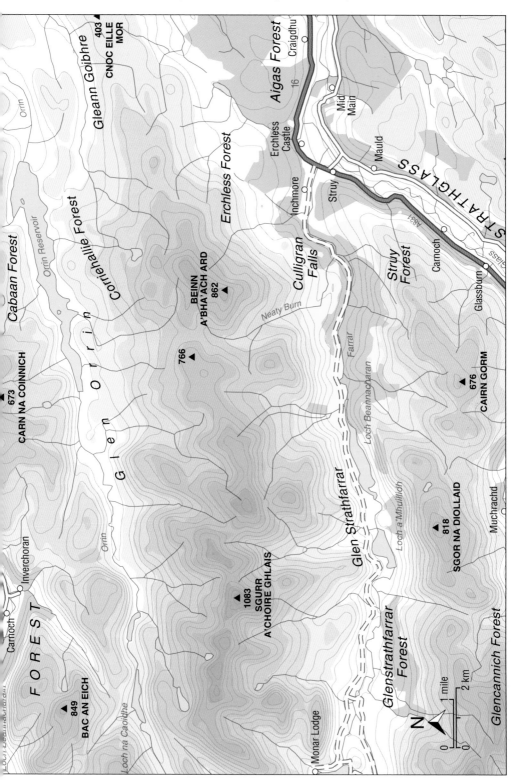

Sgurr na Lapaich from the west

cartographer when asking a Gaelic speaker the name of the glen. The narrow lower glen is wooded, with stands of magnificent Caledonian pines, and makes up the Glen Strathfarrar National Nature Reserve, which is also a Site of Special Scientific Interest. The River Farrar winds through the woods, and this is a lovely and peaceful glen. Beyond Loch Beannacharan the glen is less wooded, as it runs up to the dams at the head of vast Loch Monar, which fills the upper glen for some 12km.

The 22km long road up Glen Strathfarrar is barred by a locked gate at Inchmore, 1km from the junction with the A831 at Struy Bridge. By arrangement with Scottish Natural Heritage in summer the landowners allow a maximum of 25 vehicles per day to use the road between 9am and 6pm in April and October, 9am to 7pm in May and September and 9am to 8pm in June, July and August. The gate is controlled by a gatekeeper who lives nearby. In winter access is via a combination lock on the gate, the number of which (it's changed regularly) can be obtained from the Mountaineering Council of Scotland. Access arrangements for the road may change so consult the MCoS website (www.mcofs. org.uk/strathfarrar-access.asp) for up to date information for planning to take a vehicle along it. There

are of course no restrictions on walking or cycling along the road.

Four Munros and two Corbetts rise to the north of Glen Strathfarrar, while another five Munros and a single Corbett form an impressive horseshoe round the western end of Loch Monar. The easternmost hill is isolated Beinn a'Bha'ach Ard ('hill of the high byre', 862m), which rises above lower Glen Strathfarrar. The high ridge containing the group of Munros known as the Strathfarrar Four or North Glen Strathfarrar Ridge – Sgurr na Ruaidhe ('peak of the redness', 993m), Carn nan Gobhar ('hill of goats', 992m), Sgurr a'Choire Ghlais ('peak of the grey-green corrie', 1083m) and Sgurr Fhuar-thuill ('peak of the cold hollow', 1049m) – lies 7km to the west. Another 5km west An Sidhean ('the fairy hill', 814m) rises from the shore of eastern Loch Monar.

The remote ring of hills around the head of Loch Monar consists of Maoile Lunndaidh ('bare hill of the wet place', 1007m), Sgurr a'Chaorachain ('peak of the rowan-berried place', 1053m), Sgurr Choinnich ('mossy peak', 999m), Beinn Tharsuinn ('transverse hill', 863m), Bidein a'Choire Sheasgaich ('top of the corrie of the fallow cattle', 945m) and Lurg Mhor ('big shank', 986m).

Finally, north of the Strathfarrar and Monar hills lie five Corbetts and a single Munro. The easternmost of these, Meallan nan Uan ('little hill of the lambs', 838m) and Sgurr a'Mhuillin ('peak of the mill', 879m) rise above Strathconon. To their southwest lies Bac an Eich ('hollow of the horse', 849m). The linked pair of Moruisg ('big water', 928m) and Sgurr Coire Ceannaichean ('peak of the merchants' or 'shopkeepers', 914m) lie 12km to the southwest, above Glen Carron. To their west is Sgurr na Feartaig ('peak of the sea-pink', 862m).

The Sgurr na Lapaich Four ☆

The traverse of the fine ridge, containing four Munros, which lies north of Loch Mullardoch is a superb excursion into remote country. It is very long however – 28km in total – and there are 2070m of ascent, so it's best kept for the long days of summer as it will take most walkers at least 10–12hrs. In spring and early summer (April 1 to August 1) it may be possible to arrange a boat trip along the loch, which saves 8km of walking (☎ 01456 415347 for information).

The walk starts by the dam at the east end of Loch Mullardoch. It can be done in either direction, depending on whether you prefer a long walk-in or a long walk-out. Assuming the former, which

is my choice, begin by following the rough and intermittent lochside path as far as the private lodge between Allt Socrach and Allt Coire a'Mhaim. A path beside the latter leads to the grassy southeast ridge of An Socach, one of the most remote Munros, which climbs steeply to the summit. A short descent east is followed by the splendid traverse of 4km long An Riabhachan, which has three distinct tops. The Munro is the easternmost one. The views south, to the north Affric hills, and north, to the Loch Monar, hills are excellent. Descend by the east ridge of An Riabhachan – Creagan Toll an Lochain – which has craggy slopes on the north side, with good views down into deep corries. Next comes the southwest ridge of Sgurr na Lapaich, the highest peak in Scotland north of Carn Eighe. There are stone constructions including a well-made shelter around the summit that probably date from 1846 when an Ordnance Survey party stayed here from July to October. The finest aspect of Sgurr na Lapaich is its complex east face, a tangle of crags and spurs. This is well seen from the descent to the Bealach na Cloiche Duibhe down the excellent path on the east ridge and from the ascent to the last Munro, Carn nan Gobhar. From the latter descend south then southwest to Loch Mullardoch and the path to the start.

Bidein a' Choire Sheasgaich and Lurg Mhor

Sgurr na Lapaich (Mullardoch) from Carn nan Gobhar

⊘ Ski Touring on the Mullardoch Hills ☆

The mostly rounded and smooth broad-sloped hills lying north of Loch Mullardoch are ideal for ski touring, and there are many options with every degree of difficulty. In the east of the area a circuit of Coire an t-Sith, which includes Carn nan Gobhar, is quite easy. The route runs along the lochside path as far as Allt Mullardoch and then follows this burn into the corrie. The slopes to the east can be climbed to the unnamed 815m top, or the col to its northwest, and then the broad ridge over Creag Dubh can be followed to Carn nan Gobhar and then south to the col with Mullach na Maoile, from where a descent can be made back into the corrie. From the end of the public road the route is around 14km, with 950m of ascent, and takes 5–6hrs.

The bigger hills further west give more difficult skiing. A continuation can be made from Sgurr nan Gobhar to Sgurr na Lapaich, but this involves carrying skis up the rocky eastern slopes of the latter. The SMC's *Ski Mountaineering in Scotland* (1987) recommends an approach from Gleann Innis an Loichel to the north, then an ascent of the northeast ridge of Sgurr na Lapaich, followed by skiing the ridge to An Riabhachan, then descending north for a round trip of 14km, with 1290m of ascent, and a time of 6–7hrs.

⊘ Sgumain Coinntich, Faochaig and Aonach Buidhe ☆

The three Corbetts lying west of the Sgurr na Lapaich Munros are more rugged and complex than their higher neighbours, and the traverse of all three is a tougher proposition. It's even longer, at 32km, and involves almost the same amount of ascent at 2010m; 10hrs would be a good time for this round, so it's another walk best kept for the long hours of May and June. Two trips are an easier option, or else an overnight trip.

Aonach Buidhe is the most remote of these hills, lying at the head of Glen Elchaig. There's a 13km approach along the glen from Killilan just to reach its foot. A bicycle can be used for this as there's a good track almost the whole way. The track stops at Iron Lodge, from where a footpath continues up the glen. From Iron Lodge it's a 7km round trip up and down the south ridge of Aonach Buidhe, with 745m of ascent. This can be completed in 3–4hrs. From the summit you can look down into rugged corries on the northern and eastern sides of the hill, a complete contrast to the broad unbroken slopes to the south and west.

A longer and more satisfying route from Iron Lodge is to link Aonach Buidhe with Faochaig. There is a good path from the col between them almost to the summit of Faochaig, from where the southeast ridge can be descended back to Iron Lodge. This circuit is 11km long, with 1260m of ascent, and takes 5–6hrs.

From Faochaig a twisting 6km ridge, with 360m of ascent, leads to Sgumain Coinntich. This is a delightful walk, mostly on grass, over little knolls and bumps and with excellent views all around. From Sgumain Coinntich a descent can be made north to the path beside the Allt a'Choire Mhoir that leads back to Killilan, a distance of 3.5km, or south to the path beside the Allt a'Ghlas-choire, which leads to Glen Elchaig and Killilan, a distance of 6km. If these two routes are used for an ascent of Sgumain Coinntich alone there is an ascent of 945m, which takes 4–5hrs.

Sgorr na Diollaid

Sgorr na Diollaid is the highest of the ragged line of heathery, broken cragged hills that lie between Glen Cannich and Strathfarrar. Being isolated from the bigger hills it's a good viewpoint for the mountains of Glen Affric, Mullardoch and Strathfarrar, which form a sweep from southwest to northwest. The slopes are rough and in places steep, and there's no path, but the hill can still be ascended in a couple of hours from the road in Glen Cannich, starting at the bridge over the river (NH 284 334), from where you can head straight up the southern side of the hill over some knolls to the summit, where there are some rocky tors. Descent can be made by the uphill route or else via the 777m unnamed top 1km to the southwest. (6.5km, 700m ascent, 2½–3½hrs).

The Strathfarrar Four ☆

The traverse of the four Munros rising to the north of Glen Strathfarrar makes for a fine ridge walk with extensive views. None of the peaks is that distinctive by itself but the whole ridge is a tremendous high-level excursion. The walk is long (24.5km) and the logistics are more complex than usual due to the vehicle restrictions on the private road in the glen (see above). If there is only one car then the walk has to be done briskly to ensure enough time to drive back down the glen before the gate is locked for the night. The first or last 6.75km of the walk are along the road. Leaving a car at each end would cut this out, or else a bicycle could be left at one end, which would save much time. Alternatively the traverse could be included in an

overnight or multi-day trip. There are many excellent potential campsites in the glen and on the hills.

The walking on the Strathfarrar Four is quite easy and mostly on grass. However there isn't a distinct path the whole way and the hills are somewhat rounded and shapeless, requiring careful navigation in poor visibility.

The best direction for a traverse is east to west as this gives views of the vast array of hills arcing from the south through west to the north. The walk starts on the track into Coire Mhuillidh that leaves the road in the glen at NH 282 386, just east of Loch a'Mhuillidh. After 2km climb northeast to the first Munro, Sgurr na Ruaidhe. The ridge is now followed westwards over the remaining three Munros to the col before the subsidiary top of Sgurr na Fearstaig (which is worth visiting for the views), where a stalkers' path descends into Toll a'Mhuic and leads back to the road. The route involves 1735m of ascent and takes 8–10hrs.

Skiing the Strathfarrar Four ☆

The round of the Strathfarrar Four gives a ski tour described as magnificent in the SMC's *Ski Mountaineering in Scotland* (1987). The route is the same as for the walking traverse described above, although west to east is recommended for the best downhill runs.

Beinn a' Bha'ach Ard

This little Corbett lies well to the east of the other high hills at the mouth of Glen Strathfarrar and stands out in views across the Beauly Firth from the A9. It's not the most exciting hill to climb, really just the high point of a big area of undulating heather moorland, but its isolation makes it a superb viewpoint, both east over the Beauly Firth to the Black Isle and in a vast sweep to the west over seemingly endless mountains.

The round trip to the summit only takes a few hours and can be made more entertaining by taking in the subsidiary top of Sgurr a'Phollain (855m). The ascent starts at Inchmore, where there is the locked gate on the private road up Glen Strathfarrar. Follow this road for 2km to a power station, where you turn left for a track leading to the Neaty Burn and then up beside this stream. The track can be left anywhere for a climb up the southern or southwestern slopes of Beinn a' Bha'ach Ard. There's no path and there are a few small crags, but these are easily circumvented. After admiring the panorama from the summit continue north and northwest along the broad ridge over a bump to Sgurr a'Phollain and a view north over the Orrin Reservoir. From Sgurr a'Phollain a sketchy path runs east to Carn na Gabhalach then south down to Loch na Beiste, where a clear track runs through woods to Inchmore. The whole circuit is 15km long, with 1000m of ascent, and takes 5–6hrs.

⊛ An Sidhean and Bac an Eich

These two remote Corbetts lie in the heart of the vast area between Glen Strathfarrar, Glen Carron and Strathconon. An Sidhean rises directly from the shore of Loch Monar and fills the space between the Strathfarrar Four and Maoile Lunndaidh and the other Munros to the west. Bac an Eich rises above the head of Strathconon and can be clearly seen in views down the glen. The two hills lie just over 6km apart at either end of a huge broad ridge with a low point of 540m. Neither hill is particularly distinctive in itself but the traverse of the whole ridge is a fine excursion, with a wonderful sense of wildness and remoteness, but it's a long walk if done in a single day. There are fine campsites in the glens and on the hills, so an overnight trip is an excellent idea.

For An Sidhean alone start at the Loch Monar dam and follow the lochside road to Monar Lodge and then the path to Glen Dubh, where the southern shoulder of the hill, called Mullach a' Gharbh-leathaid, can be climbed to the summit. The view west to Maoile Lunnaidh and the hills round the head of Loch Monar is excellent. The return can be varied by descending southeast to Clach a'Chomharraidh on the watershed between Loch Monar and the River Orrin, which runs into Strathconon, then climbing slightly to cross the Druim Dubh ridge, on the far side of which a stalkers' path leads back down to Loch Monar (16km, 1000m ascent, 5–7hrs).

Bac an Eich is most easily climbed from Inverchoran farm in upper Strathconon. The route starts along the track running up Gleann Chorainn, which can be left for an ascent west to the subsidiary top of Sgurr Toll Lochain, which sits above steep broken slopes falling to Loch Toll Lochain, and then northwest to the summit. Return the same way or else descend south to pick up the path at the head of Gleann Chorainn (12.5km, 760m, 4–5hrs).

The traverse of the two hills can be undertaken from the south or the north but the latter is shorter and more scenic. The best start point is the end of the public road along Strathconon, at the west end of Loch Beannacharain, from where a private road leads above the River Meig to Scardroy and then Corrievuic and Corriefeol at the foot of the steep northern slopes of Bac an Eich. Climb these slopes to the subsidiary summit of Creag Coire na Feola, and then follow the broad, easy ridge to Bac an Eich. From the summit descend southwest to Drochaid Coire Mhadaidh, the low point on the traverse. A stalkers' path then leads up steep slopes to the broad, undulating ridge that runs over Stob Coire nan Eun to An Sidhein. Descend northwest from the summit to pick up a stalkers' path that leads down to the Allt an Amise, and then beside that burn northeast to the River Meig on the far side of which lies the path back to the start (23km, 1270m of ascent, 8–10hrs).

⊛ Maoile Lunndaidh, Sgurr a'Chaorachain and Sgurr Choinnich ☆

These three Munros make up the north side of the semicircle of hills round the head of Loch Monar. Maoile Lunndaidh is the easternmost summit, a big, bulky, flat-topped hill with several rugged corries of which the most impressive is the deep, crag-girt slot of Fuar-tholl Mor on the north side. It's a remote hill, separated from Sgurr a'Chaorachain and Sgurr Choinnich by the 450m col of Drochaid Mhuilich. The latter two peaks lie on a 5km long ridge running east–west with craggy slopes to the north and smoother, grassier ones to the south. The three summits can be climbed in one long outing from Craig in Glen Carron to the north. Approaches from any other direction are very long, and would necessitate at least one overnight.

The walk starts along the track through the forestry plantations above the Allt a'Chonais, and then heads into open country, with good views of the steep rocky north faces of Sgurr a'Chaorachain and Sgurr Choinnich. The track curves eastwards below these summits, and Maoile Lunndaidh comes into view. Shortly before Glenuaig Lodge leave the track and head across the hillside towards the mouth of Fuar-tholl Mor. The route crosses the An Crom-allt and passes close to a fine cascade on the burn out of Fuar-tholl Mor. There are good views into this narrow rocky cleft. Continue east to the col between Creag Dhubh Mor and Maoil Lunndaidh, then turn south and climb broad slopes to the summit of the latter. The summit plateau is unusual for the West Highlands, with Beinn Fhada well to the south the only similar hill. Cross the

Bidein a' Choire Sheasgaich rising beyond a sea of mist in Coire Lair and Strath Carron

plateau westwards to the subsidiary top of Carn nam Fiaclan (from where a descent can be made down the western side of Fuar-tholl Mor if Maoile Lunndaidh is being climbed alone), then descend steep slopes to the Drochaid Mhuilich. Above rises the pointed spire of Bidean an Eoin Deirg, which, although a subsidiary top of Sgurr a'Chaorachain, is the most distinctive of the summits in this group (it was classified as a separate mountain in Munro's original *Tables* but demoted to a top in the 1921 revision).

From the col the ascent looks daunting, but there is a wide, steep grassy gully that leads to the ridge just west of the summit. More entertaining is the direct ascent to the summit up very steep craggy slopes (455m of ascent in less than 800m). This is the highlight of the whole walk. It's a Grade 1 or 2 scramble, depending on the exact route, but easier than it appears. Lower down it's a broad buttress, with a mix of little crags and bogs – the latter some of the steepest bogs I've ever seen, at angles between 30 and 45° – which then narrows to a rocky ridge with some easy, not very exposed scrambling. This ridge in turn finishes in a steep face with broken, somewhat loose rocks. Clamber up these and emerge suddenly right at the summit

cairn, a startling and delightful moment as you go from the intricacies of the route and the immediate terrain to a sweeping vista of the hills around Loch Monar. The walking is now easy along the wide ridge over Sgurr a'Chaorachain and Sgurr Choinnich. Descend west from the latter over some little rock steps to the Bealach Crudain and turn right (north) to reach the path descending from the Bealach Bhearnais. The area around the two bealachs can be confusing in mist so care needs to be taken. I was almost caught out here once, and nearly descended south to Loch Monar instead of north to Glen Carron. The path from the Bealach Bhearnais leads back to the outward route above the Allt a'Chonais. The whole route is 31km long, with 1970m of ascent, and takes 10–12hrs. There are many good campsites en route so it could easily be split over two days.

⊗ Beinn Tharsuinn, Bidein a'Choire Sheasgaich and Lurg Mhor ☆

Bidein a'Choire Sheagaich and Lurg Mhor are two of the finest hills in the whole area from Glen Shiel to Glen Carron, yet their remote location makes them less well known and less visited than many more accessible yet less interesting hills. Lurg Mhor is a long wedge of a hill, with a steep-sided summit at the western end and a long ridge stretching out east above Loch Monar. Bidein a'Choire Sheasgaich is a much smaller, more compact hill, with three ridges running up to a fine pointed spire above rocky corries. Beinn Tharsuinn is less distinctive, a long curved hill whose best aspect is the view of the two Munros, especially Bidein a'Choire Sheasgaich, which rises as a distinctive pointed peak across the Bealach an Sgoltaidh.

These three hills make up the western and southern sides of the horseshoe of summits round the head of Loch Monar, and lie in remote and lonely country that requires long approaches. The traverse of all three from Craig in Strathcarron is 29km long, with 2050m of ascent. Although the walk-in is on tracks and paths much of the terrain is rough, steep and pathless so this is a tough walk. Munro baggers might be inclined to skip Beinn Tharsuinn, thinking it will save some time and energy. However doing so involves much extra distance on rough terrain, making it easier to climb than avoid. If this all seems too much for one day then an overnight camp or a stay in Bearnais bothy (NH 021 430) or Bendronaig Lodge bothy (NH 013 388) reduces the effort required. Bearnais bothy is very small, so it would be wise to carry a tent in case it's full. It lies some 4km down the Abhainn Bhearnais from the Bealach Bhearnais, but is most quickly reached via the path from Achnashellach in Glen Carron, which crosses the bealach between Eagan and Sgurr na Feartaig. Bendronaig Lodge lies 4km south of Bearnais bothy, past lonely Loch an Laoigh, and can also be reached by a 12km track from Attadale on Loch Carron that could be cycled.

The round of the hills from Glen Carron starts at Craig and follows the track and path to the Bealach Bhearnais via the Allt a'Chonais and Allt Leathad an Toban. From the bealach climb steep slopes to the grassy ridge of Beinn Tharsuinn. Follow the ridge over the summit and down to a small lochan, where you turn left for a descent to the 541m col with Bidein a'Choire Sheasgaich, the Bealach an Sgoltaidh (the name of which is marked wrongly on the OS 1:50,000 map, being shown down the glen to the east rather than on the pass itself). The steep craggy north buttress of Bidein a'Choire Sheasgaich, which rises directly above the col, looks a daunting prospect but the ascent isn't that difficult and there is only some minor scrambling before the gentler

terrain of the ridge above is reached (although there are some Grade 3 scrambling options) with a final easy walk to the summit. Continue on down to the col with Lurg Mhor and up broad stony slopes to the summit of the latter. If returning to Craig the easiest route is back to the col with Bidein a'Choire Sheasgaich and down northeast to the foot of the southeast ridge of the latter. Curve round this ridge and ascend beside the Allt Bealach Crudain to the Bealach Crudain and then the Bealach Bhearnais, where the outward route is joined.

⊗ Sgurr na Feartaig

Sgurr na Feartaig is a long, curved hill rising above Glen Carron, to which it presents a series of rough, craggy corries. On the south side a wall of steep grassy slopes runs down to the Abhainn Bhearnais. The traverse of Sgurr na Feartaig is a pleasant excursion from Craig in Glen Carron, on tracks and paths the whole way and with excellent views north to the Achnashellach hills and south across the Abhainn Bhearnais to Beinn Tharsuinn. From Craig take the track up the Allt a'Chonais glen. Not far out of the forest leave the track for a path that crosses the burn (NH 069 481), then climbs the broad northeast ridge. The path continues right along the summit ridge, although it bypasses the summit itself by 200m. At the broad lochan-dotted col called Baobh-bhacan Dhuba turn north on a path that descends to the River Carron, from where a forestry track can be followed back east to Craig. The walk is 19km long, with 1180m of ascent, and takes 6–7hrs.

✪ Winter Climbing on Sgurr na Feartaig ☆

The craggy north face of Sgurr na Feartaig is 'a superb venue for waterfall ice in cold weather', according to the SMC Scottish Winter Climbs guidebook (2008). The climbs are conveniently near the road, just 1½hrs walk from Lair in Glen Carron (although this involves a ford of the river, impossible when it's in spate) or a bit longer from Craig, unless a bicycle is used on the forest tracks. The climbs are in the III to V Grades and from 80 to 210m in length. The SMC guidebook gives three stars to The Stonker (Grade IV, 180m) and The Fast Lane (Grade IV, 90m), both first climbed in 1996.

⊗ Beinn Dronaig

Beinn Dronaig is a remote, inaccessible hill lying in the heart of the Attadale Forest area to the east of Loch Carron. Surrounded by higher hills, it's a splendid viewpoint and gives a feeling of being in a vast wilderness. Climbing the hill as part of a multi-day route makes sense, as any day ascent is very long. There is a bothy at its foot at Bendronaig Lodge. The shortest approach route is the 9km path from Achintee in Glen Carron. Slightly longer (11.5km) is the track from Attadale on Loch Carron, which could cycled, although it is quite rough in places.

If walking the Achintee path is the more scenic and enjoyable. This crosses the hills north of the River Attadale to the Uisge Dubh and Bendronaig Lodge. From the latter climb the steep slopes southeast to the summit ridge and follow this east to the summit, where there is a trig point. The only reasonable way back to the start is by the same route. The return trip is 25km long, with 1500m of ascent, and takes 8–10hrs.

⊗ Moruisg and Sgurr nan Ceannaichean

These hills are two of the most accessible in the whole area between Glen Cannich and Glen Carron, as they rise directly from the floor of the latter glen. They are big grassy hills, with crags and corries on the north side. The walking on the summits is easy, and there are wonderful views north to the Torridon hills, Slioch and the distant ragged silhouette of An Teallach and south to Bidein a'Choire Sheasgaich and Lurg Mhor, which appear as pointed spires.

They are usually climbed together, but since Sgurr nan Ceannichean was found to be just below Munro height in 2009 (having only become a Munro in 1981) and thus a Corbett instead some Munro baggers may be inclined to skip it. However it is a fine hill, and the walk between it and Moruisg is most enjoyable, so I would recommend climbing it.

The route starts at the car park in Glen Carron 1km down the glen from Loch Sgamhain (NH 080 520), where a path heads south. After crossing the river on a bridge and going under the railway there are two options. The simplest, but also the toughest as well as the least interesting, is to head straight up the pathless steep grassy slopes above to the summit of Moruisg. More preferable is to follow the path up beside the Alltan na Feola under the cliff of Creag nan Calman, then to turn east up steep slopes to the summit. The walk from Moruisg to Sgurr nan Ceannichean is then easy and a delight. From the summit of the latter descend the north ridge to rejoin the path beside the Alltan na Feola. The walk is just over 12km, long with 1000m of ascent, and takes 4–6hrs.

Moruisg and Sgurr nan Ceannaichean across Strath Carron

⊗ Sgurr a'Mhuillin and Meallan nan Uan

These two Corbetts, the most northerly in the Western Highlands, are well to the east of the other high hills of the area, and are isolated in the midst of an area of much lower undulating moorland. This makes them stand out in views from the east, and from Strath Bhran to the north, where their northern outliers look particularly fine as you travel the glen by train or car. Approaches from the north are long and boggy, however, and the best ascent routes are from Strathconon to the southeast. The Corbetts are the highest points on a complex horseshoe of six peaks around Coire a'Mhuillin. The hills are steep and rugged and the round of the horseshoe is an excellent walk with good views, especially north to the Fannichs.

The walk starts at Strathanmore in Strathconon. Going clockwise, which leaves the highest peak to last, climb steeply west up grassy slopes to the first summit, 734m Creag Ruadh, from where a narrow ridge leads to Meallan nan Uan. Continue on down to the bump of Carnan Fuar. Here the walk can be cut short by heading northeast to Sgurr a'Mhuillin. However if the weather is fine it's worth going north and climbing the two outlying tops of Sgurr a'Ghlas Leathaid (844m) and Sgurr a'Choire Rainich (848m), then returning southeast to Sgurr a'Mhuillin, from where a descent can be made back to Strathanmore. The complete route is 13.5km long, with 1300m of ascent, and takes 5–6hrs.

5:11 THE CAPE WRATH TRAIL: FORT WILLIAM TO ACHNASHELLACH ◔ ☆

Running all the way from Fort William to Cape Wrath, this 324km (203-mile) route is a challenging walk, arguably the toughest long distance trail in Scotland. It's not one for the inexperienced, and it requires camping out, but for the lover of long distance backpacking it is excellent as it pass through some of the wildest and most spectacular scenery in Scotland. As it's not an 'official' route, backed by government money, there are no waymarks or signposts and good navigational skills are required.

Because this isn't an official route it isn't fixed and there are many variations and options. There are two guidebooks to the route and a website where up to date information and some alternative routes can be found – www.capewrathtrail.co.uk.

The main route in the Western Highlands, according to Denis Brook and Phil Hinchliffe's Cicerone guidebook *North to the Cape* (1999), is 133km long and goes in eight stages, from Fort William across Loch Linnhe by ferry and then along Loch Eil to its head. It then heads into the hills, to cut below Gulvain, arriving at Strathan at the head of Loch Arkaig. Entering Knoydart, the trail crosses the Mam na Cloiche Airde to Loch Nevis, then goes on to Barrisdale and Loch Hourn, via the River Carnach and Gleann Unndalain. The south shore of Loch Hourn is followed to Kinloch Hourn then the trail climbs again to cut below The Saddle and descend to Shiel Bridge. Leaving Shiel Bridge the Falls of Glomach are visited en route to Killilan, after which the trail crosses to Strathcarron and Achnashellach via Glen Ling and Attadale.

The section north from Achnashellach is covered in the next chapter.

ACCESS, BASES, MAPS AND GUIDES

Access

Ardgour, Morvern, Sunart and Moidart Corran Ferry across Loch Linnhe, from the A82 between Ballachulish and Fort William, to the A861 to Strontian and Acharacle. A830 from Fort William to Lochailort. A861 south from Lochailort to Acharacle. Railway stations at Glenfinnan and Lochailort.

Glenfinnan and Loch Eil A830 from Fort William. Railway stations at Loch Eil Outward Bound, Locheilside and Glenfinnan.

The Great Glen A82 Fort William to Inverness. B8004 Corpach to Spean Bridge. B8005 Gairlochy to Loch Arkaig. Railway stations at Fort William and Inverness.

Loch Arkaig, Glen Kingie, Glen Pean and Glen Dessary B8004 Spean Bridge to Gairlochy. B8005 Gairlochy to head of Loch Arkaig. Minor road along Loch Arkaig to Strathan.

Knoydart and Loch Quoich Ferry from Mallaig to Inverie. Ferry from Arnisdale to Barrisdale. Railway station at Mallaig. B8004 Spean Bridge to Gairlochy. B8005 Gairlochy to head of Loch Arkaig. Minor road along Loch Arkaig to Strathan. Minor road along Glen Garry from the A87 to Kinloch Hourn.

South Glen Shiel and Glenelg A87 from the A82 at Invergarry in the Great Glen to Shiel Bridge. Minor road from Shiel Bridge to Glenelg. Minor road along Glen Garry and Loch Quoich from the A87 to Kinloch Hourn.

Kintail A87 from the A82 at Invergarry in the Great Glen to Shiel Bridge, Morvich and Dornie. Minor road from Dornie to Killilan.

Strath Cluanie and Glen Affric A831 from Drumnadrochit on the A82 in the Great Glen to Cannich. Minor road from Cannich down Glen Affric. A87 from Invergarry on the A82 in the Great Glen to Loch Cluanie. A887 from Invermoriston on the A82 in the Great Glen down Glen Moriston to the A87.

Glen Cannich and Glen Elchaig A831 from Drumnadrochit on the A82 in the Great Glen to Cannich. Minor road from Cannich down Glen Cannich to Loch Mullardoch. A87 from the A82 at Invergarry in the Great Glen to Dornie. Minor road from Dornie to Killilan.

Glen Strathfarrar, Strathconon and Glen Carron A831 along Strathglass from Cannich or Beauly to Struy. Private road along Glen Strathfarrar (locked gate and restricted access – contact the MCoS for up to date information, and see 5:10 above). Minor road along Strathconon from the A832 at Marybank. A835 from the A9 at Tore north of Inverness to Garve. A832 Garve to Achnasheen. A890 Achnasheen to Strathcarron. Railway stations at Garve, Achanalt, Achnasheen, Achnashellach, Strathcarron.

Bases

Ardgour, Morvern, Sunart and Acharacle Onich, Strontian, Acharacle.

Glenfinnan Glenfinnan, Fort William.

The Great Glen Fort William, Spean Bridge, Invergarry, Fort Augustus, Invermoriston, Drumnadrochit, Inverness.

Loch Arkaig, Glen Kingie, Glen Pean and Glen Dessary Fort William, Spean Bridge, Inverie.

Knoydart and Loch Quoich Inverie, Arnisdale, Glenelg, Invergarry.

South Glen Shiel and Glenelg Shiel Bridge, Glenelg.

Kintail Shiel Bridge.

Glen Moriston and Glen Affric Cannich, Fort Augustus.

Glen Cannich and Glen Elchaig Cannich, Dornie.

Glen Strathfarrar and Strathconon Cannich, Beauly, Inverness, Achnasheen, Strathcarron.

Maps

OS Landranger 1:50,000 25, 26, 33, 34, 40, 41, 49

OS Explorer 1:25,000 383, 391, 392, 398, 399, 400, 413, 414, 415, 428, 429, 430, 431

Harvey's Superwalker 1:25,000 Kintail (Glen Shiel)

Harvey's British Mountain Map 1:40,000 Knoydart, Kintail and Glen Affric

Walking and Scrambling Guides

Guide to Walks in the North-West Highlands by Chris Townsend (Aurum, 2007)

Highland Scrambles North by Iain Thow (SMT, 2006)

Scotland's Far West by Denis Brooke and Phil Hinchcliffe (Cicerone, 2010)

Scrambles in Lochaber by Noel Williams (Cicerone, 1996)

Skye and Kintail (25 Walks) by Hamish Brown (Mercat Press, 2000)

The Cape Wrath Trail: A New 200-mile Walking Route Through the North-west Scottish Highlands by David Paterson (Peak Publishing, 1996)

The Great Glen Way: Two-Way Trail Guide by Paddy Dillon (Cicerone, 2007)

The Great Glen Way by Jacquetta Megarry and Sandra Bardwell (Rucksack Readers, 2005)

The Great Glen Way by Brian Smailes (Challenge, 2003)

The Northwest Highlands by Dave Broadhead, Alec Keith and Ted Maden (SMC, 2004)

North to the Cape: A Trek from Fort William to Cape Wrath by Denis Brook and Phil Hinchcliffe (Cicerone, 1999)

West Highlands by Nick Williams (Pocket Mountains, 2004)

Climbing Guides

Glen Coe by Ken Crockett, Rab Anderson and Dave Cuthbertson (SMC, 2001)

Northern Highlands South: Scottish Mountaineering Club Climbers' Guide edited by Andy Nesbitt (SMT, 2007)

CHAPTER 6: THE NORTHERN HIGHLANDS

The Applecross and Coulin Hills, Torridon, Loch Maree to Loch Broom, the Fannaichs, the Beinn Dearg Hills, Ben Wyvis, Coigach and Assynt and the Far North

THE NORTHERN HIGHLANDS: CHAPTER SUMMARY

Location

Hills north of the Dingwall–Kyle of Lochalsh railway

☆ Highlights

LOW-LEVEL/PASSES WALK

- Through the Coulin Forest from Achnashellach to Torridon (6:1)
- Round the back of Liathach (6:2)
- Poolewe to Corrie Hallie (6:3)
- Knockan Crag (6:6)
- Eas a'Chual Aluinn (6:6)
- Sandwood Bay and Cape Wrath (6:7)

LONG DISTANCE WALK

- The Cape Wrath Trail (6:8)
- The Sutherland Trail (6:9)

SUMMIT WALK

- Beinn Bhan (6:1)
- An Ruadh-stac and Maol Chean-dearg (6:1)
- The Circuit of Coire Lair (6:1)
- Beinn Damh (6:1)
- Beinn Alligin (6:2)
- Beinn Eighe (6:2)
- Beinn Dearg (6:2)
- The Mountain Trail and Meall a'Ghiubhais (6:2)
- Baosbheinn and Beinn an Eoin (6:2)
- Slioch (6:3)
- A'Mhaighdean and Ruadh Stac Mor (6:3)
- The Fisherfield Six (6:3)
- Beinn Dearg Mor and Beinn Dearg Bheag (6:3)
- An Teallach (6:3)
- Meall a'Chrasgaidh, Sgurr nan Clach Geala and Sgurr nan Each (6:4)
- Beinn Liath Mhor Fannaich, Sgurr Mor, Meall Gorm and An Coileachan (6:4)
- The hills around Beinn Dearg (6:5)
- Seana Bhraigh (6:5)
- Cul Mor and Cul Beag (6:6)
- Suilven (6:6)
- Quinag (6:6)
- Conival and Ben More Assynt (6:6)
- The Glas Bheinn–Conival–Breabag Ridge (6:6)
- Ben Stack (6:7)
- Arkle (6:7)
- Foinaven (6:7)
- Ben Hope (6:7)
- Ben Loyal (6:7)

SCRAMBLING

- Beinn Alligin (6:2)
- Liathach (6:2)
- Beinn Eighe (6:2)
- Carnmore Crag and the Fionn Loch Basin (6:3)
- An Teallach (6:3)
- Ben Mor Coigach and Sgurr an Fhidleir (6:6)
- Stac Pollaidh (6:6)
- Cul Mor and Cul Beag (6:6)
- Suilven (6:6)
- Foinaven (6:7)

ROCK CLIMBING

- Beinn Bhan and Sgurr a'Chaorachain (6:1)
- Liathach (6:2)
- Ben Mor Coigach and Sgurr an Fhidleir (6:6)

WINTER CLIMBING

- Beinn Bhan and Sgurr a'Chaorachain (6:1)
- Liathach (6:2)
- An Teallach (6:3)
- Beinn Dearg (6:5)

SKI TOURING

- The Fannaichs (6:4)
- Am Faochagach, Cona 'Mheall and Beinn Dearg (6:5)
- Ben Wyvis (6:5)

OTHER HIGHLIGHTS

- Loch Maree (6:2)
- Corrieshalloch Gorge (6:5)
- The Bone Caves (6:6)
- The Traligill Caves (6:6)

Contents

◂ *Ruadh-stac Mor on Beinn Eighe from Coire Mhic Fhearchair*

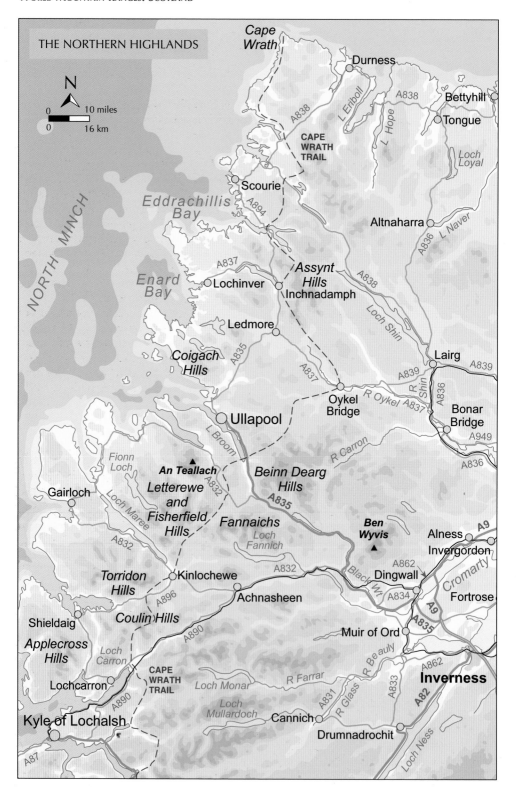

THE NORTHERN HIGHLANDS

N

0   10 miles
0   16 km

NORTH MINCH

Cape Wrath

Durness

A838

Bettyhill

L Eriboll

Tongue

A838

L Hope

Loch Loyal

CAPE WRATH TRAIL

Scourie

Eddrachillis Bay

A894

Altnaharra

A836

L Naver

Loch Loyal

Enard Bay

A837

Lochinver

Assynt Hills

Inchnadamph

A838

Loch Shin

Ledmore

Coigach Hills

A835

A837

Lairg

A839

Oykel Bridge

R Oykel

A837

R Shin

A836

Bonar Bridge

A949

A836

Ullapool

R Carron

An Teallach

Fionn Loch

Letterewe and Fisherfield Hills

A832

Beinn Dearg Hills

A835

Gairloch

Loch Maree

A832

Fannaichs

Loch Fannich

Ben Wyvis

Alness

A9

Invergordon

Torridon Hills

A896

Kinlochewe

A832

Black Wt

Dingwall

A862

Cromarty

Shieldaig

Coulin Hills

Achnasheen

A890

Muir of Ord

A834

Fortrose

Applecross Hills

Loch Carron

CAPE WRATH TRAIL

A835

A9

Lochcarron

A890

Loch Monar

Loch Mullardoch

Cannich

A831

R Farrar

R Glass

R Beauly

A833

A862

Inverness

A82

Kyle of Lochalsh

A87

Drumnadrochit

Loch Ness

388

INTRODUCTION

Nowhere in Britain do mountains so proclaim their individuality
Irvine Butterfield, *The High Mountains of Britain and Ireland*

The Northern Highlands run from Strath Bran and Glen Carron right up to the north coast. The southern boundary marks a geological change in the landscape, and the hills to the north are very different from those to the south. Indeed, the Northern Highlands contain some of the most unusual and distinctive mountains in Scotland. Although there are hills with long ridges and steep grassy slopes, like the Fannaichs, which are reminiscent of hills much further south – and even a Cairngorm Plateau-like hill in Ben Wyvis – many mountains in the Northern Highlands are individual, steep rocky peaks with strange contorted shapes rising above vast areas of low boggy moorland replete with lochs and lochans of all sizes. This is especially so on the western edge of the area, where the hills from Liathach north to Foinaven form a wild array of dramatic shapes. These marvellous summits are not the only attractions of the area; among the hills are beautiful lochs, high waterfalls and remnants of ancient forests, while the coast has great sweeps of sandy beaches, big cliffs and little rocky coves. The hills aren't as packed close together as in the Western Highlands and there is a sense of huge space around them. They are set back a little from the coast, but many big sea lochs cut in below them, and from many summits there is a sense of being close to the sea.

This is a remote area, far from most towns and cities. Ullapool, the biggest town in the area, has a population of 1300. Distances are long, and roads sweep across the landscape with little in the way of fences and buildings alongside them. Everywhere there is a feeling of wildness and the splendour of nature.

Quinag from a camp by Loch Bealach a' Bhuirich

The geological foundations of the landscape, significant throughout Scotland, are here laid bare, stripped of much of the covering that softens and hides them elsewhere. The skeleton of the land is visible. This geology is complex, challenging and scientifically important, hence the creation of the North West Highlands Geopark covering the area from Ullapool to Cape Wrath in 2005 (see Topology and Geography in the Introduction).

The key geological feature is the Moine Thrust, a low-angle fault line that runs from the north coast all the way to the Isle of Skye, mostly lying about 32km inland. The Moine Thrust dates from some 440–410 million years ago, when the massive Caledonian mountain range was being born, and marks the edge of these long-gone ancient mountains. The bulk of the Caledonian mountains consisted of metamorphic Moine schists. Over millions of years tremendous forces pushed the edges of these schists over the sedimentary rocks to the west. The line along which this happened is the Moine Thrust. The complex geology along the Moine Thrust is hard to interpret, and gave rise to a major geological controversy in the late 19th century as older rocks appeared to be lying on top of younger ones, something scientists hadn't encountered before. The solution was that the enormously powerful earth movements of the Moine Thrust had pushed the older rocks over the younger ones. (See Knockan Crag in Section 6:6 for more on this.)

The landscapes east and west of the Moine Thrust are noticeably different to each other. To the east the Moine schists form hills not unlike those in the rest of the Highlands. To the west there is no schist, and the different rocks form very different scenery. The base rock is Lewisian gneiss, at three billion years old one of the oldest rocks on earth. Lewisian gneiss is a colourful rock, often striped, made up of a mix of sedimentary and volcanic rocks that were metamorphosed by extremes of heat and pressure deep in the earth. Intrusions of volcanic rocks like granite were forced through the gneiss in places, forming distinct lines known as dykes that add to the attraction of the landscape. Between 1100 and 900 million years ago the eroded Lewisian gneiss formed a low, undulating landscape. Rivers deposited sands on top of the gneiss, which, over the millennia, were compressed into Torridonian sandstone, a major component of many hills in the Northern Highlands. Another 500 million years later more sand was laid down, this

time to become Cambrian quartzite. These rocks form steep, imposing and spectacular mountains, sculpted by glaciers during the ice ages, which are challenging for walkers and of great interest to rock and ice climbers.

The mountains of the Northern Highlands do not rise as high as those to the south. Sgurr Mor in the Fannaichs is the highest, at 1110m. Only nine other Munros rise above 1000m, but this is the one area in Scotland where height really doesn't matter. There 39 Munros, 42 Corbetts and 41 Grahams in the area, but the designation says nothing about the nature of the hills nor the ease of an ascent. Some of the most spectacular hills, and the toughest to climb, are the lowest. On the western side the hills are mostly steep and rocky. Ridges are narrow, big drops are normal and scrambling is required in places. East of the Moine Thrust the hills are on average higher, but also less steep, with easier walking.

There are no long distance paths with official designation in the area but there are two marvellous unofficial ones, the Cape Wrath Trail, from Achnashellach to Cape Wrath, and the Sutherland Trail, from Lochinver to Tongue, both of which take the backpacker through wild country. There are ample opportunities for constructing your own routes, too.

The effects of the Moine Thrust are seen immediately in the most southern hills of the region, those of the Applecross peninsula and the Coulin Forest between Glen Carron and Glen Torridon. Here is a complex tangle of rock and corrie, pass and peak, lochan and bog that looks very different to the more conventional hills just to the south. The mountains are steep and stony, the routes through them twisted and tortuous. They form a wonderful entry into the magic of the far north. Immediately to the north lies Glen Torridon and three of the most special hills in the Highlands – Beinn Alligin, Liathach and Beinn Eighe – each one a mini-mountain range with steep crags and multiple summits. Beyond the Torridon trio lower but still distinctive peaks make up the Flowerdale Forest. Torridon and Flowerdale are moated on the north by lovely Loch Maree, the last big loch in the Northern Highlands not to be tapped for hydro power.

On the far side of Loch Maree lies one of the biggest unroaded areas in the Northern Highlands, that of Letterewe, Fisherfield and Dundonnell, which contains two of the remotest Munros along

View across the head of Loch Glascarnoch to Beinn Dearg and Cona' Mheall

with one of the most impressive mountains in the Highlands, An Teallach. The hills continue the form of those to the south, with much rock, steep slopes and dramatic shapes. To the east lie the Fannaichs, a big hill group of long ridges, pointed summits and deep corries. Being schist rather than sandstone the Fannaichs look more like the hills much farther south, and, although fine, are less distinctive than their western neighbours. Away to their east, sitting on its own above the Cromarty Firth, is flat-topped Ben Wyvis, which has more in accord with the Cairngorms to its south than the other hills of the Northern Highlands.

North of the Fannaichs lies the Beinn Dearg group, rugged hills crowded round deep corries stretching out to the very remote Munro of Seana Bhraigh. A vast area of low, boggy moorland hills separates these mountains from the next significant ones to the north. These form two lines, one each side of the Moine Thrust. On the west the hills are lower but more individual, a series of curiously shaped rock summits separated by bog and loch. The skyline from Ben Mor Coigach over Cul Beag, Stac Pollaidh, Cul Mor, Suilven and Canisp to Quinag is one of the strangest and most spectacular in Scotland. Not one of those hills reaches Munro

height, however, and some not even Corbett level. To their east lies a higher, unbroken ridge of hills, containing two Munros, and at its base in the tangle of confusion around the Moine Thrust a band of limestone gives rise to a landscape, including caves, which is most unusual in Scotland.

In the west the steep sandstone and quartzite hills continue almost to the north coast. Further east lie the last Munros and lovely Ben Loyal, rising above the north coast.

6:1 APPLECROSS AND COULIN

The southernmost hills in the Northern Highlands form a long wedge of ground trending southwest to northeast between Loch Kishorn, Loch Carron and Glen Carron in the south and Loch Torridon and Glen Torridon in the north. In the west of this region lies the Applecross peninsula, forming a rough triangle between Lochs Kishorn and Torridon. Most of Applecross is relatively low lying moorland, but in the southeast of the peninsula there are two fine Corbetts built from tiers of dark red Torridonian sandstone. These are Beinn Bhan ('white hill', 896m) and Sgurr a'Chaorachain (the

391

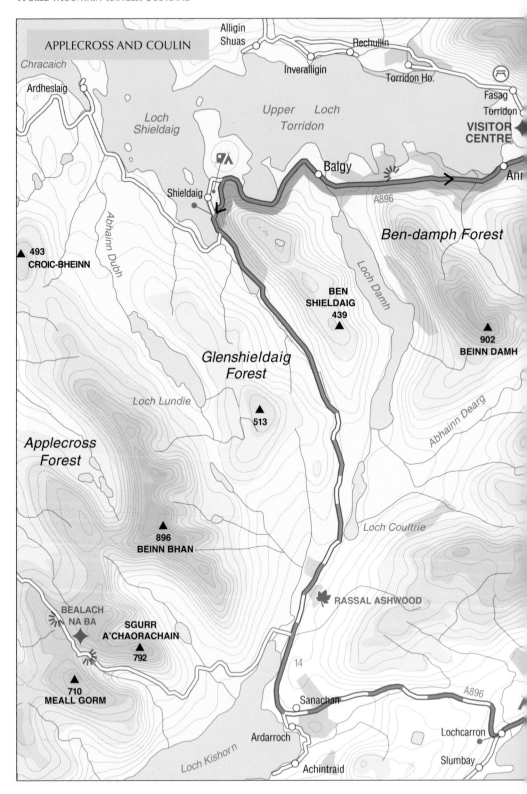

APPLECROSS AND COULIN

Alligin
Shuas

Rechullin

Inveralligin

Torridon Ho.

Chracaich

Ardheslaig

Fasag
Torridon

Loch
Shieldaig

Upper   Loch
Torridon

VISITOR
CENTRE

Balgy

Ann

Shieldaig

A896

Ben-damph Forest

▲ 493
CROIC-BHEINN

Abhainn Dubh

BEN
SHIELDAIG
439
▲

Loch Damh

▲
902
BEINN DAMH

Glenshieldaig
Forest

Loch Lundie

▲
513

Abhainn Dearg

Applecross
Forest

Loch Coultrie

▲
896
BEINN BHAN

RASSAL ASHWOOD

BEALACH
NA BA

SGURR
A'CHAORACHAIN
♦
792
▲

14

▲
710
MEALL GORM

Sanachan

A896

Ardarroch

Lochcarron

Loch Kishorn

Slumbay

Achintraid

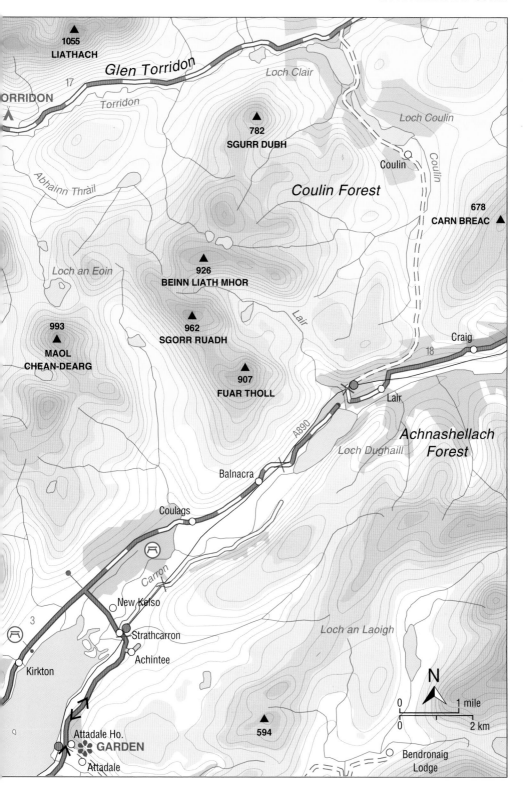

1055
LIATHACH

Glen Torridon

Loch Clair

Torridon

ORRIDON

Abhainn Thràil

782
SGURR DUBH

Loch Coulin

Coulin

Coulin

Coulin Forest

678
CARN BREAC

Loch an Eoin

926
BEINN LIATH MHOR

993
**MAOL
CHEAN-DEARG**

962
SGORR RUADH

Lair

Craig

18

907
FUAR THOLL

Lair

*Achnashellach
Forest*

A890

Loch Dughaill

Balnacra

Coulags

Carron

Loch an Laoigh

New Kelso

3

Strathcarron

Achintee

Kirkton

N

Attadale Ho.
GARDEN

594

Attadale

Bendronaig
Lodge

0   1 mile
0   2 km

name seems obscure – different authors give 'peak of the little sheep', 'peak of the torrent', 'peak of the little field of berries' and 'peak of the rowan-berried place', 792m). Both hills have steep cliff-rimmed corries with many climbing routes. To their south is one of the steepest, highest roads in Scotland, that across the Bealach na Ba at 625m. This narrow, winding road leaves the A896 at Tornapress near the head of Loch Kishorn, climbs steeply up Coire na Ba to the pass, then descends more gently back to sea level at Applecross village on the west coast of the peninsula. The road was originally constructed in 1822 and paved in the 1950s. It was notorious for its hairpin bends: these have been somewhat straightened out, but the road can still be a challenging drive in stormy weather and can be closed by snow in winter.

A long drive round the scenic and interesting coast from Applecross, with some good views over the sea to the islands of Rona and Raasay and across Loch Torridon to the Torridon hills, leads back to the A896 at the head of Loch Shieldaig. The A896 itself separates the Applecross hills from those of the Coulin Forest and connects Glen Carron with Glen Torridon.

East of the A896 lies a tangle of hills in the area known as the Coulin Forest. There are three Munros and five Corbetts here, all of them steep and rocky

– Maol Chean-dearg ('bald red hill', 933m), Sgorr Ruadh ('red peak', 962m), Beinn Liath Mhor ('big grey hill', 926m), An Ruadh-stac ('steep red hill', 892m), Fuar Tholl ('cold hole', 907m), Beinn Damh ('hill of the stag', 902m), Sgorr nan Lochan Uaine ('peak of the little green loch', 871m) and Sgurr Dubh ('black peak', 782m). This is wild, complex country but a network of excellent stalking paths makes the hills surprisingly accessible.

⊗ Beinn Bhan ☆

Beinn Bhan (896m) in Applecross is a magnificent and massive mountain, curving some 12km northwestwards from Loch Kishorn. It forms a long ridge buttressed by terraced sandstone cliffs and bitten into by six corries on the east side and the huge scoop of Coire Attadale on the west. Narrow rock spurs separate the corries, and the whole eastern face looks tremendous when viewed from the A896. Any ascent of the mountain should visit the finest of the eastern corries, Coire na Poite ('corrie of the cauldron'), which lies directly below the summit and has two steep arêtes on either side. These are graded rock climbs – Moderate for A'Chioch ('the breast') on the south side, Severe for A'Phoit ('the cauldron') to the north. A'Chioch is accessible to good scramblers happy with continuous exposure. Most walkers will be content to experience the

The long ridge of Beinn Liath Mhor from the east

wild situation, view the cliffs and then turn away for an easier route. The summit ridge itself is fairly flat and the walking along it is easy.

The best walking route on Beinn Bhan starts on the Bealach na Ba road by the bridge over the River Kishorn, some 400m from the junction with the A896. The route starts on the path heading northwards across the lower slopes of Beinn Bhan. After 2.5km leave the path and head up northwest towards Coire na Poite, with great buttresses and spurs slowly appearing in front of you. In the mouth of the corrie lies its eponymous lochan in a dramatic situation. From here scramblers will head for the imposing rocks of A'Chioch; walkers should continue northwest across the mouth of the next corrie to the north, Coir' an Fhamair ('the giant's corrie'), and then up the Sron Coir' an Fhamair, which is steep and rough but not exposed or difficult. Once on the grassy summit ridge follow the edge of Coir' an Fhamair to the summit of Beinn Bhan, with sensational views down the tiers of cliffs to the boulder-strewn corrie floors.

Beinn Bhan is a superb viewpoint, especially in the direction of the Torridon giants of Beinn Alligin and Liathach to the northeast, and west out over the sea to the jagged crest of the Cuillin on Skye and the distant outline of the hills on Harris in the Outer Hebrides. From the summit a long but easy descent leads down the southeast ridge back to the Kishorn Bridge. The walk is 12km long, with 1100m of ascent, and takes 4½–6hrs.

⊗ Sgurr a'Chaorachain

Although smaller and lower than Beinn Bhan, Sgurr a'Chaorachain (792m) looks more impressive when viewed from Loch Kishorn and the A896, because it lies much closer to the road, from where its dramatic east face is in full view. Long, deep Coire nan Arr ('corrie of the giants') separates Sgurr a'Chaorachain from Beinn Bhan. The cliffs of the east face, tiers of Torridonian sandstone as on Beinn Bhan, are divided by a steep spur on which the summit of the mountain lies. Either side of the summit are Coire a'Chaorachain and Coire na Ba. The road to the Bealach na Ba winds up the latter. The most dramatic feature on the mountain is the narrow turreted ridge forming the north wall of Coire a'Chaorachain, which runs east from a 776m subsidiary top and finishes in a huge cliff. This is known as A'Chioch or Na Ciochan.

The shortest and easiest but also least interesting route up Sgurr a'Chaorachain is from the Bealach na Ba, where a track leads up to a radio mast on a subsidiary top from where it's an easy walk to the main summit. The 6km round trip can be done in under 2hrs and only involves 400m of ascent, but is a poor way to treat the mountain.

A far better route, which is still quite short, is from the Bealach na Ba road just west of the bridge over the Russell Burn from where a track leads to Loch Coire nan Arr. Head upwards across the hillside towards A'Chioch from the loch to the burn running out of Coire a'Chaorachain. Follow the burn into the corrie, with great cliffs rising either side, then cut southwest up steep slopes to the col between the 776m top and the summit and walk up the latter. The easiest descent route is to descend to the Bealach na Ba and walk down the road. The shortest and most exciting is to descend the southeast ridge, which involves some easy scrambling and careful route finding. Using this descent route the round trip is a touch under 6km long, with 700m of ascent, and takes 2½ to 3½hrs.

ⓑ ✵ Climbing on Beinn Bhan and Sgurr a'Chaorachain ☆

The corrie cliffs and rocky buttress of the Applecross Corbetts offer many routes, both to rock and ice climbers, especially the latter. As noted, A'Chioch and A'Phoit on Beinn Bhann are Moderate and Severe rock climbs respectively. In winter A'Chioch is a Grade II snow and ice route described as 'excellent' in the Scottish Mountaineering Club (SMC)'s North-West Highlands guide and 'the best mountaineering route on Beinn Bhan' in Scottish Winter Climbs. It was first climbed by Joe Brown and Tom Patey in 1968. There are many other winter routes, and Scottish Winter Climbs says that the mountain has 'some of the finest winter climbing in the Northern Highlands'. That's when conditions are right, of course, which isn't often on these relatively low west coast cliffs. Scottish Winter Climbs described 20 routes on Beinn Bhan, ranging from Grade I to Grade VII. Four star routes are Silver Tear in Coire na Poite (350m, Grade V – N. Muir, A. Paul, 1977) and Genesis (305m, Grade VII – A. Cave, D. Heselden, February 2000), Die Riesenwand (400m, Grade VII – A. Nisbet, B. Sprunt, January 1980 – a two day climb with a bivouac) and Gully of the Gods (180m, Grade VI – M. Fowler, S. Fenwick, 1983) in Coire an Fhamair.

On Sgurr a'Chaorachain Cioch Nose is a 135m VD graded rock climb up A'Chioch described as a 'the Diff to end all Diffs' by the first ascensionists, Tom Patey and Chris Bonington, in 1960. This traverses into the centre of the cliff then climbs the upper tier. It looks an exciting route in a superb situation.

There are also many middle grade routes on the South Face above the Bealach na Ba road, such as Sword of Gideon (104m, VS, Tom Patey, 1961), described in *North-West Highlands* as Scotland's 'most accessible mountain crag' – that's after you get to Applecross of course. Just across the road is 'Scotland's most accessible winter cliff' on the north face of Meall Gorm, a subsidiary summit of Sgurr a'Chaorachain. The climbs here are just ¼hr walk from the road. Grades range from II to V, and lengths are in the 100–200m range. *Scottish Winter Climbs* doesn't give any routes four stars but Cobalt Buttress (140m, Grade IV – I. Clough, G. Drayton, C. Young, February 1970) gets three.

ⓐ Through the Coulin Forest from Achnashellach to Torridon ☆

The network of stalking paths between Glen Carron and Glen Torridon provides a number of different through-routes between these glens. I think the one going from Achnashellach to Annat on the southeast corner of Upper Loch Torridon is by far the best of these. Indeed it's an ideal approach to the glorious Torridon giants and one of the finest walks through, rather than over, the hills in the whole of the Northern Highlands. Running through the heart of the hills, it's a complex route that crosses three high passes and twists around the three Munros in the area.

The walk starts in Achnashellach, which consists of a few houses half hidden in forest and an unstaffed railway station, and follows a path through dense rhododendron bushes and pine woods and out onto open rocky terrain beside an impressive, pine-clad rocky gorge, down which rushes the River Lair. The fortress-like buttresses of Fuar Tholl to the west dominate the view as the path climbs into long Coire Lair, which curves westwards below the grey quartzite screes of Beinn Liath Mhor. Loch Coire Lair is passed, with the red sandstone cliffs of Sgorr Ruadh towering above it. At the head of the corrie the path climbs steeply to the narrow 650m pass of the Bealach Coire Lair, squeezed between almost touching steep spurs

running down from the two Munros. For the next 3km the path follows a clever and intricate route through very complex, steep, rocky terrain that is a pleasure to walk. To avoid crags on the northern spur of Sgorr Ruadh the path descends 100m north into little Coire Grannda, and then contours 500m west across the rough slopes below the crags to Bealach Ban (550m). Here the steep rocky face of Meall Dearg forces the path southwest across the headwall of Coire Fionnaraich towards the steep rocky dome of Maol Chean-dearg and then west at a path junction to 420m Bealach nan Lice. The complexities are over now, as the path descends to Loch an Eoin, nestling in a wonderful situation below the steep north face of Maol Chean-dearg, and then wanders northwestwards over rough slopes and down to lovely Upper Loch Torridon, with splendid views of Beinn Alligin and Liathach. The walk is 16km long, with 800m of ascent, and takes 5–6hrs.

There are two variants to this route. The first starts some 2.4km from Achnashellach in lower Coire Lair, where a path heads northeast across the southern slopes of Beinn Liath Mhor via 385m Drochaid Coire Lair. It then descends beside the Easan Dorcha to the River Coulin and a track that runs past Lochs Coulin and Clair to the A896 in Glen Torridon, below the eastern end of Liathach. This walk is easier but less dramatic than the one to Annat, and much is on a vehicle track. However the Easan Dorcha and the two lochs are lovely, and well worth a visit. Loch Clair is a classic viewpoint for Liathach too. This route is 13.35km long, with 450m of ascent, and takes 3½–4½hrs.

The other variant starts at Coulags, 6km down Glen Carron from Achnashellach, and follows the path that climbs up beside the Fionn-abhainn into Coire Fionnaraich, to join the route from Achnashellach at the Bealach nan Lice. The Fionn-abhainn glen is lovely and there are good views of An Ruadh-stac, Sgorr Ruadh and Maol Chean-dearg. This route is 12.5km long, with 480m of ascent, and takes 3½–4½hrs. It too has a variant: just over 500m before Loch Coire Fionnaraich a path forks left, climbs over the 588m Bealach a' Choire Ghairbh, sandwiched between An Ruadh-stac and Maol Chean-dearg, then descends to Loch Coire an Ruadh-staic, before curving round the western slopes of Maol Chean-dearg to rejoin the path from the Bealach nan Lice at Loch an Eoin. This variant adds 2km and 200m of ascent to the walk. As an alternative to walking through to Torridon a good day walk would be to ascend the Fionn-abhainn glen to the Bealach nan Lice then go round Maol Chean-dearg by Loch an Eoin and the Bealach a' Choire Ghairbh and back down the glen.

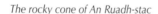 An Ruadh-stac and Maol Chean-dearg ☆

These two great cones of rock can be climbed together from either Glen Carron or Glen Torridon. The easiest route is from the south, taking the path from Coulags beside the Fionn-abhainn and then up to the Bealach a'Choire Ghairbh, as described above. From the bealach head northwest up pale quartzite screes to the final summit cone of Maol Chean-dearg, which is made up of reddish sandstone boulders, hence the name of the mountain: 'bald red head' indeed. The highest point of the little summit plateau is marked by a huge cairn on the northwest side. A few metres further northwest there is a dramatic and vertiginous view down the cliffs of the north face to Loch an Eion. Further north Liathach rises, a magnificent sight.

Return to the bealach, with the massive craggy north face of An Ruadh-stac rearing up before you and looking not a little daunting. The ascent is easier and less exposed than it looks, however, with just some easy scrambling over boulders. An Ruadh-stac is oddly named as it's built of grey quartzite rather than red sandstone. The route climbs the northeast ridge of the mountain, then up the final summit slopes to the top. There are two lochans either side of the ridge, each one at a different height. The easiest descent is to return to the bealach and retrace the outward route back to Coulags. The route is 17.5km long, with 1350m of ascent, and takes 6–8hrs.

The Circuit of Coire Lair ☆

Coire Lair is a magnificent corrie, walled by the dark sandstone blocks of Fuar Tholl and Sgorr Ruadh on the west and the long grey quartzite ridge of Beinn Liath Mhor on the east. The round of these peaks is an excellent and exciting mountain day.

Rising from the floor of Glen Carron the massive rocky bulk of Fuar Tholl stands out in views from the glen, looking especially impressive from Achnashellach. It's arguably the finest hill in the Coulin Forest and one of the finest Corbetts (some would say the best of all). The southern slopes are a mass of heather and boulders, which makes for slow, strenuous walking, so an ascent from this side is not recommended. Better to follow the path into the mouth of Coire Lair and a path junction

The rocky cone of An Ruadh-stac

at 370m. Take the left fork here onto a path that fords the River Lair (dangerous when in spate – a safe alternative is to continue up the corrie and go round Loch Coire Lair), then climbs between Fuar Tholl and Sgorr Ruadh to the broad, lochan dotted Bhealaich Mhoir. Turn south here into little Coire Mainnrichean, below the tremendous rock face of the Mainreachan Buttress, then out of the corrie and up steep grass and scree to the summit and views of the surrounding hills. To descend follow the ridge round over Creag Mainnreachan and back down to the Bhealaich Mhoir. Cross the bealach to Loch a'Bhealaich Mhoir, then climb the slopes above straight to the summit of Sgorr Ruadh. Again the views are extensive and exhilarating. Descend the northwest ridge, then turn off to the Bealach Coire Lair, from where steep slopes with some easy scrambling lead on to the 2km Beinn Liath Mhor ridge. The walk along this ridge on quartzite stones and grass is a joy – easy underfoot with magnificent views all around. Descend the southeast slopes of the mountain to rejoin the path in Coire Lair, and so back to Achnashellach. This circuit is 16.5km long, with 1680m of ascent, and takes 6–8hrs.

✴ Winter Climbs on Fuar Tholl and Sgorr Ruadh

Although there are many rock climbs on these hills it's for the snow and ice climbing that they are particularly prized. There are many routes of every difficulty, most of the hardest being on the steep cliffs of Fuar Tholl, where four star, 170m Tholl Gate, a Grade VI, climbs right up the centre of the northeast facing cliff that lies southeast of the summit. It was first climbed in March 1984 by P. Butler and M. Fowler. Next to it is a three star Grade VII, 190m The Ayatollah, first climbed by I. Dring and M. E. Moran in February 1989. The Mainreachan Buttress has a 180m four star Grade VII route called Snoopy, described as 'very spectacular, with bold pitches on thin ice' in the SMC's *Scottish Winter Climbs*. The first ascent was by C. Dale and A. Nisbett in March 1998. Other Grade VIIs on the buttress, all given three stars by the SMC, are Enigma (230m – S. M. Richardson and C. Cartwright, January 1997), Sleuth (250m – A. Fyffe, H. MacInnes and K. Spence, 1970) and Supersleuth (240m – G. Robertson, P. Benson and J. Currie, February 2002).

The routes on the north and northeast faces of Sgorr Ruadh, overlooking Coire Lair, are a little less

The great east face of Fuar Tholl rising above the Achnashellach forest

severe than those on Fuar Tholl, most of the routes being Grades II, III and IV. There's even a Grade 1 300m snow gully, the Central Couloir, with a three star Grade II nearby, 180m Post Box Gully (A. Fyffe, March 1969). On the north face the somewhat harder 100m Tango In The Night is a Grade VI (S. Aisthorpe, N. Forwood and P. Yardley, 1989).

🔆 Scrambles on the Coulin Forest Hills

The steep buttresses and ridges of these mountains offer some scrambles as alternatives to the walking ascent routes. The lower slopes of An Ruadh-stac can be ascended by a gorge scramble beside the Allt Moin a'Chriathair, reached from the path from Coulags beside the Fionn-abhainn. The route is broken and can be escaped from in many places. It's Grade 2 or 3 depending on the line taken. When the scrambling comes to an end continue uphill to the Eastern Slabs, a Grade 2 scramble given two stars in the SMC's *Highland Scrambles North*.

Maol Chean-dearg offers a Grade 3 scramble on the Ketchil Buttress, which is situated below and to the east of the walking route from the Bealach a'Choire Ghairbh.

Fuar Tholl, unsurprisingly, has a number of scrambling options on its rocky sides. There are a number of lines up the sandstone slabs on the South Flank, graded 1 or 3. On the northwest side the Grade 3 Summit Rib leads up the middle of three buttresses almost to the summit.

Two huge buttresses rise from Coire Lair to the summit slopes of Sgorr Ruadh. These are mainly the province of rock climbers but Highland Scrambles North gives two Grade 3 variants to classic climbs – Academy Ridge, Lower Slabs, which is the lower part of a Very Difficult climb, and Raeburn's Buttress, which avoids the Difficult start of the original route by way of a gully.

The broken quartzite of Beinn Liath Mhor looks less promising for scrambling than the sandstone crags of the other hills, but there is a Grade 3 route on the south side. Southeast Rib climbs a buttress to the west of the path.

🔆 Beinn Damh ☆

Beinn Damh (903m) rises above the southeast corner of Upper Loch Torridon, and is prominent in views across the loch from Torridon village. It forms a long ridge between the Allt Coire Roill and Loch Damh. There are crags on all sides, and the mountain is an impressive sight. The ascent and

traverse of the ridge is a good outing from Torridon. It begins near the Loch Torridon Hotel and takes the path up beside the Allt Coire Roill, which crashes down a splendid tree-lined gorge. Where the path forks leave the river and head southwest into the corrie called Toll Ban ('white hole'). The rough path climbs out of the corrie to reach a wide col that is the low point between Beinn Damh and the subsidiary top of Sgurr na Bana Mhoraire. The short walk to this craggy summit is recommended for the superb view down to Loch Torridon. Turning towards Beinn Damh two minor tops are crossed to a narrow ridge leading to the high point, Spidean Coir'an Laoigh, which is perched dramatically on the edge of steep crags.

There are two options for the descent. Scramblers can descend the northeast ridge, called Stuc Toll nam Biast, to the Drochaid Coire Roill, then go down Coire Roill on an excellent stalkers' path with good views of the cliffs on the east face of Beinn Damh. Walkers should return by the ascent route, a total of 11km, with 1165m of ascent, which takes 4–5hrs.

🔆 Sgorr Dubh and Sgorr nan Lochain Uaine

These two quiet, unfrequented cone-shaped hills rise above Glen Torridon in the northeast corner of the Coulin Forest. Although clearly visible from the road in Glen Torridon these two hills don't draw the eye because of the awe-inspiring view of Liathach just across the glen. In other company they would be much more highly regarded. They are rugged sandstone hills with fine views. The traverse is enjoyable but few walk it. The round starts at the Coire Dubh car park on the A896. A path runs south past Lochan an Iasgair and the SMC's Ling Hut and into Coire a' Cheud-chnoic ('corrie of a hundred hills') which, as the name suggests, is full of hummocky moraines. Continue on round the southern end of Sgorr nan Lochan Uaine almost to Lochain Uaine itself, then climb rough boulder slopes to the summit of the former (873m). The 3km of hill linking Sgorr nan Lochan Uaine with Sgorr Dubh is so broad that it can hardly be called a ridge. It's a mass of knolls, streams and lochans with few clear features and so can be confusing in poor visibility. The walking is rough with much quartzite to cross. The reward for this is the breathtaking view from Sgorr Dubh, with the mighty walls of Beinn Eighe and Liathach soaring into the sky just across Glen Torridon. A rough descent among

Beinn Eighe from the south

boulders and little crags leads west-northwest from the summit to the Ling Hut and the outward path. The route is 12km long, with 1090m of ascent, and takes 5–6hrs.

6:2 TORRIDON

Torridon, one of the magic names of the Scottish mountains, covers the great wedge of magnificent wild hill country lying between Glen Torridon in the south and Loch Maree in the north. Glen Torridon is one of the great glens of Scotland, comparable in splendour with Glen Coe. Three of the finest Scottish mountains rise on the north side of the glen, each with two Munro summits. These are known as the Torridon triptych, and from east to west are: Beinn Eighe ('file mountain'), whose Munros are Ruadh-stac Mor ('big red stack', 1010m) and Spidean Coire nan Clach ('peak of the stony corrie', 993m); Liathach ('the grey one'), whose Munros are Spidean a' Choire Leith ('peak of the grey corrie', 1055m) and Mullach an Rathain ('summit of the pulleys', 1023m); and Beinn Alligin ('mountain of the jewel'), whose Munros are Sgurr Mhor ('big peak', 986m) and Tom na Gruagaich ('hill of the damsel', 922m). These mountains are built of steep tiers of dark Torridonian sandstone, capped in the case of Beinn Eighe and Liathach with pale quartzite.

Glen Torridon is reached by the A896 road from Kinlochewe, which runs below the vast scree slopes of Beinn Eighe and the towering ramparts of Liathach down to the head of Upper Loch Torridon and then along the south shore of the loch – with splendid views across the water to Beinn Alligin – to Shieldaig, where it turns south to Glen Carron. On the north shore of Upper Loch Torridon a minor road runs to Torridon village and on above the loch to terminate at the little settlement of Lower Diabaig. At the foot of Glen Torridon there is a youth hostel, a campsite and a National Trust for Scotland Countryside Centre – the NTS owns much of Torridon including Liathach, Beinn Alligin and the western end of Beinn Eighe. There's a small shop in Torridon village and the Torridon Inn and Loch Torridon Hotel just past the village of Annat on the southeast corner of Upper Loch Torridon. Kinlochewe also has shops, cafés and a hotel and bar.

The Torridon triptych mountains present themselves to the road. These are public mountains, seen by all who travel the roads of the district. To their north lie lower, less well-known but still impressive Torridonian sandstone hills, five of them Corbetts, set farther back from roads. Hidden among the other hills is Beinn Dearg ('red hill', 914m), which lies between Beinn Alligin and Beinn Eighe immediately to the north of Liathach, and is not easily seen from any road. To its north, between Beinn Dearg and the road alongside

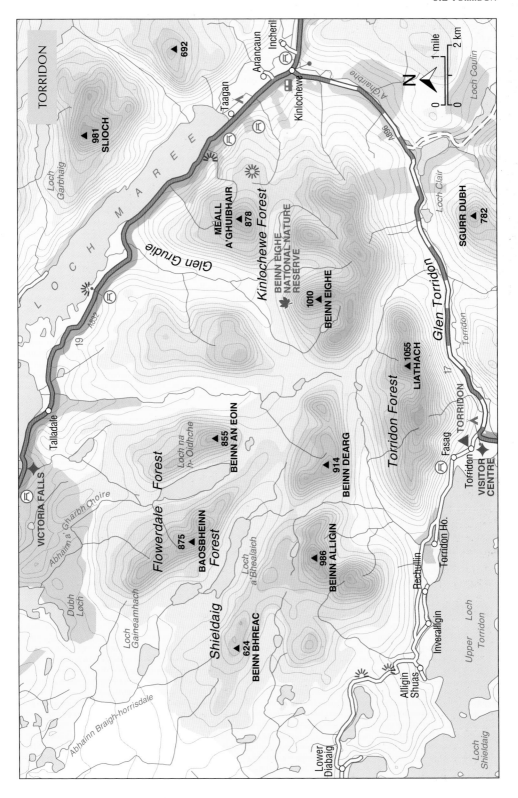

TORRIDON

▲ 692

LOCH MAREE

▲ 981
SLIOCH

Loch Garbhaig

Incheril

Anancaun

Taagan

Kinlochewe

Loch Coulin

A'Chairibhe

A896

Loch Clair

Loch Clair

SGURR DUBH
▲ 782

Glen Grudie

MEALL
A'GHUIBHAIR
▲ 878

Kinlochewe Forest

BEINN EIGHE
NATIONAL NATURE
RESERVE

1010
▲
BEINN EIGHE

Glen Torridon

Torridon

19

R892

Talladale

▲ 1055
LIATHACH

Torridon Forest

17

Loch na
h- Oidhche

▲ 855
BEINN AN EOIN

Fasag

TORRIDON

Torridon

VICTORIA FALLS

Flowerdale Forest

Abhainn a' Gharbh Choire

▲ 875
BAOSBHEINN

▲ 914
BEINN DEARG

Torridon Ho.

VISITOR
CENTRE

Dubh
Loch

Loch
a'Bhealaich

▲ 986
BEINN ALLIGIN

Rechullin

Loch Gaineamhach

Shieldaig
Forest

▲ 624
BEINN BHREAC

Inveralligin

Upper Loch
Torridon

Abhainn Braigh-horrisdale

Alligin
Shuas

Loch
Shieldaig

Lower
Diabaig

N

0 _____ 1 mile
0 _____ 2 km

Loch Maree, lie three mountains running north–south, two of them Corbetts – Baosbheinn ('hill of the forehead' – often given as 'wizard's peak' but Peter Drummond's *Scottish Hill Names: Their Origin and Meaning* (Scottish Mountaineering Trust, 2007) says the more prosaic meaning, describing the shape, is more likely: 875m) and Beinn an Eoin ('hill of the bird', 855m) – and one a Graham – Beinn a'Chearcaill ('hill of the girdle', 725m). This area is known as the Flowerdale Forest. East of these hills two Corbetts face each other across the Allt Toll a' Ghiubhais – Meall a'Ghiubhais ('hill of the pine tree', 887m) and Ruadh-stac Beag ('little red stack', 896m), which is a spur of Beinn Eighe. Beinn Dearg is usually accessed from Glen Torridon, the others from the A832 road alongside Loch Maree. This northern part of Torridon was threatened with hydro-electric developments in the 1980s, 1990s and 2000s, with proposals to dam lochs and rivers. Conservation and outdoor organisations mounted campaigns against these and they were all withdrawn or rejected. It is to be hoped that this wild unspoilt area will be left untouched in the future.

⊗ ⊙ Beinn Alligin ☆

Beinn Alligin (986m) is the westernmost of the Torridon triptych, rising above the shores of Upper Loch Torridon and forming the western side of huge Coire Mhic Nobuil, which curves round the north side of Liathach. Beinn Alligin is crescent-shaped, curving round the deep corrie of Toll a'Mhadaidh Mor ('big hollow of the wolf' or 'fox'), with cliffs and steep scree running down into the corrie. The most prominent feature is a huge chasm splitting the cliffs below Sgurr Mhor from top to bottom. The boulders that crashed down from this crack in the mountainside litter the floor of Toll a'Mhadaidh Mor.

The chasm on Beinn Alligin is called Eag Dhubh na h-Eigheachd, which means 'the black cleft of the crying' or 'wailing'. The legend behind this name is that shepherds used to hear wailing coming from the cleft. Eventually one of them went to investigate and fell down the chasm to his death, whereupon the wailing ceased.

The ascent of Beinn Alligin is rough and steep but not difficult. The traverse of the whole mountain does include some easy scrambling on the Horns of Alligin, three rock towers on the southeast ridge. The climb starts at the car park by the bridge over the Abhainn Coire Mhic Nobuil on the minor road from Torridon to Diabaig. From the road a path climbs up steep, boggy slopes to the mouth of Coir' an Laogh ('corrie of the calf') to the south of Tom na Gruagaich. The path continues up the corrie beside the burn to the ridge and Tom na Gruagaich, whose summit lies right on the edge of cliffs on the rim of Toll a'Mhadaidh Mor. There's a splendid view across the depths of the corrie to the dark slash of the Eag Dhubh and Sgurr Mhor. The rocky ridge round to the latter is narrow for the descent to the low point at 765m, then broader for the ascent, during which you pass above the mouth of the Eag Dhubh. The views throughout are superb, with mountains, sea and islands all in view.

The easiest descent route is to retrace your steps. However more exciting is the traverse of the Horns. From Sgurr Mhor follow the ridge to the 866m subsidiary summit Na Rathanan, then descend southeast over the towers. There's a clear path and the scrambling is easy, but with some exposure. Once below the rocks the path crosses moorland to a bridge over the Abhainn Coire Mhic Nobuil, across which lies the path in the corrie that leads back to the start. The whole circuit is 10km long, with 1200m of ascent, and takes 4–6hrs.

✳ Winter Climbing on Beinn Alligin

Lower and closer to the sea than its Torridon neighbours, Beinn Alligin receives and holds less snow and ice, but in winter conditions it does harbour some highly rated climbs. The Horns of Alligin are rated Grade I, or Grade II if especially icy. There are some climbs on the northeast face of the Horns, of which 250m Deep South Gully (Grade 1) is given three stars in the SMC's *Scottish Winter Climbs*. Two star climbs on the same face are 250m Deep North Gully and 225m Diamond Fire, both Grade II. In Toll a'Mhadaidh Mor the Eag Dhubh is a 400m Grade I snow climb or Grade II if there is some ice. I imagine it must be a stupendous place to be in winter. On the other side of the corrie, on the northeast face of Tom na Gruagaich, is 300m West Coast Boomer, a two star Grade IV.

❂ Liathach ☆

Liathach (1055m) is without doubt one of the most magnificent mountains in Scotland. Some would say it's the finest of all. To Glen Torridon it presents a massive steep wall of terraced sandstone split by narrow gullies that looks unassailable. On the north side there are deep cliff-lined corries. Only at the western end is there a relatively gentle and easy slope. The main ridge has four subsidiary tops as well as the two Munros, and there is another subsidiary top to the north of Mullach an Rathain. The whole mountain stretches some 8km, from Coire Dubh Mor in the west to Coire Mhic Nobuil in the east. It's isolated from other mountains, the highest connecting point being 393m at the head of Coire Dubh.

The traverse of Liathach is one of the classic routes of the Scottish mountains. Mostly it's a rocky walk, albeit very steep in places, but there is a section of Grade 2 scrambling over the Am Fasarinen pinnacles. The terrain is complex and route-finding can be difficult in mist. The best map is Harvey's Torridon Superwalker, as it has a 1:12,500 enlargement of the ridge on the back.

The route is normally done from east to west, probably because Mullach an Rathain was only given Munro status in 1981. Before that starting at the east end meant that Liathach's then single Munro, Spidean a'Choire Leith, could be climbed without having to tackle Am Fasarinen. After 1981 climbing both Munros in one walk meant crossing the pinnacles. However I think west to east is preferable, both for the views and for an easier descent, especially in poor visibility. The southern slopes of Mullach an Rathain can be ascended anywhere between the Allt an Tuill Bhain and the Torridon campsite, with much optional scrambling en route. The edge of Toll Ban above the stream is perhaps the easiest line, although I have made an ascent from behind the campsite that only involved minimal scrambling. If descending this way it's best to head south about 100m west of the summit of Mullach an Rathain and go down the south face and not continue on to the stone-filled gully west of the south face that drops straight down to Torridon village. This once popular route is now badly eroded and very loose.

From Mullach an Rathain fairly broad slopes lead eastwards towards 927m Am Fasarinen. The scrambling over the blocky pinnacles is exciting and exposed, with huge drops into Coire na Caime on the north side. There is a traversing path below

Spidean a' Choire Leith, the highest summit on Liathach

them on the south side, but this is narrow, slippery when wet and eroded at the heads of several gullies, where there are only tufts of grass to cling on to. Once the pinnacles are passed a steep clamber up quartzite boulders leads to Spidean a'Choire Leith, from where there is a wonderful view back over Am Fasarinen to Mullach an Rathain. On the far side of Coire na Caime a pinnacled ridge – the Northern Pinnacles – can be seen. This leads from Mullach an Rathain to the subsidiary top of Meall Dearg ('red hill', 953m), the hardest Munro top on the mainland. The Northern Pinnacles are exposed and a Moderate rock climb, but Meall Dearg can be reached by a steep traverse below them.

From Spidean a'Choire Leith continue on along the rocky ridge over Stob a'Choire Liath Mhor ('peak of the big grey corrie', 983m) and down to a col at 833m. A short distance to the east lies the final summit on the ridge, Stuc a' Choire Dhuibh Bhig ('peak of the little black corrie', 915m), which is worth climbing for the view across Coire Dubh Mor ('big black corrie') to Beinn Eighe. From the 833m col a rough path leads down into Coire Liath Mhor ('big grey corrie') and then Toll a' Meitheach, where it improves and leads down beside the Allt an Doire Ghairbh, to reach Glen Torridon 3.5km from the National Trust for Scotland's Countryside Centre. The traverse is 10.5km long, with 1385m of ascent, and takes 5–7hrs.

For scramblers there are other options on Liathach, apart from Am Fasarinen and the south face of Mullach an Rathain. The East Ridge of Stuc a'Choire Dhuibh Bhig, accessed from the Coire Dubh Mor path, is a Grade 1 or 2, depending on the line taken. The North Ridge of Spidean a'Choire Leith looks a great scramble but requires a long walk-in. Again the grade is 1 or 2 depending on the exact route.

ⓑ Climbing on Liathach ☆

The loose and broken nature of the Liathach cliffs mean it is not well regarded for rock climbing although the East Buttress of Am Fasarinen is a Difficult described as 'quite technical...with a spectacular finish' in *Highlands Scrambles North*, while PC Buttress in Coire na Caime, also Difficult, has 'a good line and good rock'. Both are given one star. The Northern Pinnacles of Mullach an Rathain are a 'serious and exposed' two star Moderate. Although these routes appear in the scramblers' guide, to my mind Difficult and Moderate rock

climbs are not scrambles for walkers, although they may seem so to experienced rock climbers used to much higher grades.

Where Liathach is prized for climbing is in winter conditions, when the rocks freeze, and ice fills the gullies and plasters the cliffs. The main ridge traverse then becomes a Grade II winter route, given three stars in the SMC's *Scottish Winter Climbs*. This guide lists another 61 routes with grades ranging from I to VIII. Of these one is given four stars – 180m Grade V Poachers Falls in Coire Dubh Mor (first climbed by R. McHardy and A. Nisbet in February 1978) – and another six are given three stars: 120m Grade II Northern Pinnacles (first climbed by W. W. Naismith, A. M. Mackay and H. Raeburn in April 1900); 230m Grade V Umbrella Fall (first climbed by M. Fowler and P. Butler in April 1984); 200m Grade VI The Salmon Leap (first climbed by A. Cunningham and A. Nisbet in February 1986); 200m Grade VIII Fubarbundy (first climbed by C. Cartwright and D. Heselden in February 1994); 190m Grade VI Test Department (first climbed by M. Fowler and C. Watts in January 1987, with an ascent of the complete icicle, which did not reach the ground in 1987, by B. Davison, A. Nisbet, S. Anderson and M. Moran in March 1999); and 230m Grade III George (first climbed by I. G. Rowe and M. Kelsey in February 1967, with a variation called Sinister Prong added by J. Grant and J. R. Mackenzie in February 1978), all in Coire Dubh Mor; and 200m Grade II Twisting Gully on the Coire na Caime face of Am Fasarinen (first climbed by R. Urquhart and D. Stevens in March 1955).

ⓚ Round the back of Liathach ☆

Although the south face of Liathach is imposing and dramatic the finest side of the mountain is to the north, where a complex of corries and ridges creates the impression of a whole mountain range rather than one monolithic block. This side of the mountain is well seen from the long corries running below it, and these also give good views of Beinn Dearg and Beinn Alligin. The walk isn't very long and there's a path the whole way but it is rough, rocky and muddy in places. The start and finish of the walk are some 12km apart, too, so transport to or from one end will need to be arranged. Or you could add in a traverse of Liathach! The sense of isolation and remote wild grandeur at the heart of this walk is tremendous. The whole world seems

The magnificent Triple Buttress in Coire Mhic Fhearchair, Beinn Eighe

dominated by rock and water. For the best views I recommend walking east to west, starting at the car park in Glen Torridon near Lochan an Iasgair. A path from here runs up Coire Dubh Mor with the huge walls of Liathach and Beinn Eighe closing in on either side. Emerging into more open country at the head of Coire Mhic Nobuil the path swings west past a chain of small lochs, with superb views into Coire na Caime, with the pinnacles of Am Fasarinen rising at its head. The landscape round these lochs is one of wild and glorious chaos with boulders and rocks scattered everywhere. The path continues down Coire Mhic Nobuil below the unbroken ramparts of Beinn Dearg, and then curves southwards, with Beinn Alligin now in full view, finally descending to the car park on the road beside Upper Loch Torridon in some woods near Torridon House. The walk is 12km long, and takes 3–4hrs.

⊗ ⑤ Beinn Eighe ☆

The third of the Torridon Triptych, Beinn Eighe (1010m), which runs for 7km above upper Glen Torridon, looks less impressive from the glen than Liathach or Beinn Alligin, with monotonous slopes of grey quartzite scree that do not have the dramatic form or grandeur of the terraced sandstone of the other hills. However to the north Beinn Eighe is a very different mountain, with four huge, rocky spurs

split by deep corries, one of which, Coire Mhic Fhearchair, is the finest corrie in Torridon and one of the finest in the Highlands. It has a beautiful lochan and, at its head, the spectacular Triple Buttress. The highest summit on Beinn Eighe, Ruadh-stac Mor, is on the spur that makes up the eastern side of Coire Mhic Fhearchair. Until 1997 this was the only Munro on the mountain, so it was possible to tick Beinn Eighe off in Munro's *Tables* without having ventured onto the main ridge at all. However in the 1997 revision of the Tables Spidean Coire nan Clach on the main ridge was given Munro status.

To appreciate Beinn Eighe fully requires effort. This is very much a hillwalkers' mountain. You have to walk to really see it. A visit to Coire Mhic Fhearchair, as well as an ascent of both Munros, is the minimum needed to gain a feel for Beinn Eighe. Ideally, the whole ridge from Sail Mhor ('big heel') in the west to Sgurr nan Fhir Duibhe ('peak of the black man') in the east should be traversed. It's a long outing, with some easy scrambling, and finishes far from the start point.

Coire Mhic Fhearchair means 'the corrie of Farquar's son', and shares its name with Mullach Coire Mhic Fhearchair not far to the north in the Fisherfield Six hills. Who were Farquar and his son? Ian R. Mitchell reckons Farquar was Farquar MacIntaggart, who was given the Earldom of Ross in the 13th century and the corrie was named for his son William, who was given the lordship of Skye in 1266, as this was a period when Gaelic names were replacing Norse ones, according to *Scotland's Mountains Before the Mountaineers* (Luath, 1999).

The round of Coire Mhic Fhearchair and the two Munros is best walked from west to east, so that Coire Mhic Fhearcair is approached dramatically from below. Start at the car park in Glen Torridon near Lochan an Iasgair and take the path into Coire Dubh Mor. Where the path forks at the head of the corrie take the right hand branch, curving round Sail Mhor. Below Coire Mhic Fhearchair the path runs above the Allt Coire Mhic Fhearchair, which crashes down in cascades and water slides. Ruadh-stac Mor rises to the east, while immediately above tower the buttresses of Sail Mhor. The path climbs beside the stream then suddenly emerges onto the lip of the corrie, with a fantastic view across Loch Coire Mhic Fhearchair to the Triple Buttress, a stupendous cliff consisting of three distinct conical buttresses over 300m high, of which roughly the bottom third is dark Torridonian sandstone and the top two thirds pale Cambrian quartzite. This is one of the most stunning views in the Scottish hills. A rough path leads through the rocks on the eastern shore of the loch to the jumble of boulders and rough ground at its head. Head southeast here, past some little lochans, towards the low point between Ruadh-stac Mor and the main ridge. Reaching this col is the hardest part of the walk, but the effort is mitigated by the wild and mountainous situation. A steep stone and scree choked gully runs down from the col into upper Coire Mhic Fhearchair. This gully is loose and eroded, and better footing can be obtained on its edges or on the rocks to either side, which also offer some easy scrambling. Once the col is attained an easy walk over stony ground leads to Ruadh-stac Mor and excellent views of the corries on each side, with the main ridge of Beinn Eighe stretching out to the east. Return to the col from the summit and continue south, to reach the main ridge at at the east end of Choinneach Mhor ('big moss', 956m), a surprisingly large, flat area of grass and moss. Further easy walking leads eastwards to Spidean Coire nan Clach, with good views throughout. From the summit descend a steep path into little Coire an Laoigh ('corrie of the calves') to the southeast, and on down to the A896 at the head of Glen Torridon, 2km from the start point.

This route is 17km long, with 1180m of ascent, and takes 6–7hrs.

If walking the whole ridge, as either a backpacking trip or with accommodation or transport arranged at the finish, take the previous route into Coire Mhic Fhearchair then either climb Ling and Glover's Route, a Grade 2 scramble that goes up the north face of Sail Mhor to the right of a big gully, or else climb the scree to the southwest of the loch to reach the ridge south of the summit of Sail Mhor and walk along broad slopes to the top of the latter. From Sail Mhor easy walking leads along the ridge to steep rocks abutting the west end of Coinneach Mor. This is the Ceum Grannda, or 'ugly step'. The Grade 2 scramble up this is short but exposed. It can be avoided by a gully to the south. Once over the Ceum Grannda there is a wonderful high-level walk with tremendous views over Spidean Coire nan Clach and Sgurr Ban ('white peak', 970m) to Sgurr nan Fhir Duibhe ('peak of the black man', 963m). Here you can either descend steep, loose slopes into Coire Dhomain to reach a path beside the Allt a' Chuirn that leads down to reach the road 1km outside Kinlochewe, or else turn north and scramble past the shattered pinnacles known as the Bodaich Dubh Beinn Eighe or the Black Carls to the final summit, Creag Dubh ('black crag', 907m). This scramble is only Grade 1 but the rock is very loose. Descend from Creag Dubh by the east ridge to reach the path beside the Allt a'Chuirn. The complete traverse, with an out-and-back to Ruadh-stac Mor, is 22km long, with 1315m of ascent, and takes 8–10hrs.

ⓑ ✳ Climbing in Coire Mhic Fhearchair

The cliffs of Coire Mhic Fhearchair offer many rock climbs in a spectacular setting. They range from the first climb recorded on the Triple Buttress, East Buttress (285m), a Difficult climbed by G. B. Gibbs, E. Backhouse and W. A. Mounsey in 1907, to E3 grade climbs like 90m Cyclonic Westerly on the West Buttress, first climbed by A. Nisbet and G. Ollerhead in 1992, and 95m Turkish Delight on the Eastern Ramparts of the East Buttress, first climbed by A. Cunningham and A. Nisbet in 1987.

In winter conditions the cliffs of Coire Mhic Fhearchair are 'a paradise for mixed climbing', according to the SMC's *Scottish Winter Climbs*. The guide lists 25 routes graded from I to VIII, of which four are given four stars: 95m Grade VIII Sundance, first climbed by G. Robertson and I. Parnell in January 2008; 110m Grade VII Vishnu, first climbed by A. Cunningham and A. Nisbet in February 1988, on the Far East Wall to the left of the Triple Buttress; 270m Grade VI Central Buttress (Piggot's Route), first climbed by K. Spence, J. Rowayne and K. Urquhart in February 1971; and 100m Grade VIII Blood, Sweat and Frozen Tears, first climbed by M. E. Moran and A. Nisbet in March 1993 on the Triple Buttress. For those interested in less technical, lower grade climbs there are several easy snow gully routes – 300m Grade 1 Morrison's Gully and 120m Grade II White's Gully, first climbed by S.White and party in 1910, on Sail Mhor and 400m Grade II Fuselage Gully to the right of the Triple Buttress.

Beinn Dearg ☆

Out of sight behind Liathach and not quite making Munro height (it was resurveyed by the Munro Society in 2007 and found to be definitely below 914.4m), Beinn Dearg is the neglected mountain of Torridon. In almost any other company it would be very highly rated. It's a steep, L-shaped mountain built of terraced sandstone, curving round An Coire Mor ('the big corrie'). The ascent is interesting, the traverse of the almost 4km long summit ridge exciting and the views of the other Torridon peaks excellent. Its situation means that any ascent requires a fairly long walk-in. The shortest is via the Coire Mhic Nobuil path, starting at the car park by the bridge over the Abhainn Coire Mhic Nobuil near Torridon house. After 2km the path crosses the river on a footbridge, shortly beyond which it divides. Take the right fork, which leads up between the Horns of Alligin and the west face of Beinn Dearg to the Bealach a' Chomhla. Just before the bealach turn east and climb the steep, rocky west spur of Stuc Loch na Cabhaig ('peak of the loch of haste', 882m), the northern and westernmost top of Beinn Dearg. A short walk south with some optional easy scrambling leads to Beinn Dearg itself. The summit is almost at the crook of the L, and shortly beyond it the ridge turns eastwards and continues with more optional easy scrambling over several minor tops to the last summit, Carn na Feola ('hill of flesh', 761m), from where a descent can be made south to join the Coire Mhic Nobuil path. The walk is 19km long with 1125m of ascent, and takes 6–8hrs.

Loch Maree ☆

Loch Maree is one of the most beautiful lochs in Scotland and the last big loch in the Northern

Highlands not to be tapped for hydroelectric power. It runs 20km northwestwards, from just outside Kinlochewe to near the sea at Poolewe.

Loch Maree at sunset

Kinlochewe is oddly named – it should logically be Kinlochmaree – suggesting that Loch Maree may once have been called Loch Ewe, perhaps being changed to avoid confusion with Loch Ewe, the arm of the sea at Poolewe. This seems likely, as back in the 17th century map maker Timothy Pont wrote about the 'fresch Loch of Ew' that 'by sum…is called Loch Mulruy' and also 'the salt Lochew'. (See the National Library of Scotland's Pont Maps Website: www.nls.uk/pont/texts/transcripts/ponttext119v-120r.html). As it is, Loch Maree is supposed to be named for St Maelrubha, an Irish missionary who came to Scotland in the 7th century. Maelrubha set up a church on Eilean Ma-Ruibhe (Isle Maree) on Loch Maree. This island was regarded as a sacred place, with a sacred tree and a wishing well, long before Maelrubha's time however, and retained its pagan associations for centuries afterwards. In 1678 members of the local Mackenzie clan sacrificed a bull on the island in the hope of obtaining a cure for a seriously ill clan member, Christine Mackenzie. The local priest criticised them for this non-Christian ritual but Christine Mackenzie did apparently get better.

Loch Maree is mostly less than 1km wide, but near the middle it bulges out to 2.5km wide. In this massive bay there are many islands containing some

The Conservation Cairn on the Mountain Trail with the eastern peaks of Beinn Eighe in the background

THE BEINN EIGHE NATIONAL NATURE RESERVE

Near the head of Loch Maree a remnant of the old forest climbs above the southern shore. This is Coille na Glas-leitir ('the wood of the grey slope'). In 1951 this wood was protected as Britain's first National Nature Reserve, and much work was done on the best ways to restore the forest. Today, under the ownership of Scottish Natural Heritage, the forest is flourishing and expanding, a reminder of what much of the Highlands would once have been like. There's an interesting SNH Visitor Centre at Aultroy on the A832 just outside Kinlochewe, and the story of the reserve can be found in *Beinn Eighe: The Mountain Above The Wood* by J. Laughton Johnston and Dick Balharry (Birlinn, 2001).

of the most ancient and untouched native pine-woods in Scotland. These islands are a National Nature Reserve. The shores of Loch Maree were once heavily wooded too (Pont writes of 'plentie of very fair firr, hollyn oak, elme, ashe, birk and quaking asp, most high, even, thick and great, al alongst this loch'), but these woods were felled to power the many ironworks operating in the area in the 17th and 18th centuries. On either side of the loch rise the splendid hills of the Flowerdale and Letterewe Forests.

⊗ The Mountain Trail and Meall a'Ghiubhais ☆

The Mountain Trail is a waymarked, circular nature trail in the Beinn Eighe National Nature Reserve. It can easily be combined with an ascent of the

Corbett Meall a'Ghiubhais. The walk starts at the SNH car park beside Loch Maree, 4.5km from Kinlochewe, where a Mountain Trail booklet can be obtained. The path is well-made, with regular cairns, although there are some steep and rough sections. It climbs through the forest to the open hillside and a wonderful view back over Loch Maree to the massive block of Slioch. The hillside is rich with low vegetation – heather, juniper, bear-berry, crowberry, mosses and sedges – showing how impoverished many over-grazed hillsides else-where in the Highlands are. The path climbs over quartzite rocks known as Pipe Rock, due to pock-marks from the burrows of worms from over 500 million years ago – some of the oldest evidence for life in Scotland – to reach the massive Conservation

Cairn at 550m and a view of the corries and buttresses of the north side of Beinn Eighe. At the Conservation Cairn the path can be left for a direct route west to Meall a' Ghiubhais and more tremendous views. Return to the Conservation Cairn from the summit and continue along the Mountain Trail as it crosses the rocky ground past little lochs – one of them named Lunar Loch by SNH to commemorate the first moon landing in 1969 – to the An t-Allt, where the path descends beside the deep Allt na h-Airidhe gorge back into the forest. The walk is 10km long, with 955m of ascent, and takes 3–4hrs.

Ruadh-stac Beag

Although a spur of Beinn Eighe, running north from Spidean Coire nan Clach, Ruadh-stac Beag is rarely climbed with the other summits of the mountain. It can be reached via a scramble down the north ridge of Spidean Coire nan Clach, but is more often combined with an ascent of Meall a'Ghiubhais. Ruadh-stac Beag has crags and steep scree on most sides except the south so this is the best ascent route. To reach the southern slopes take either the Mountain Trail from Loch Maree to the Conservation Cairn, and then continue southwest

to the Allt Toll a'Ghiubhais and follow this stream up to Lochan Uaine on the col south of the summit, or take the Pony Track that starts on the A832 1km northwest of Kinlochewe to its highest point, and then on to the Allt Toll a'Ghiubhais. The view from the summit is excellent. The round trip via the Mountain Trail is 13.5km long, with 1150m of ascent; via the Pony Track it's 16.5km, with 995m of ascent. Both routes take around 5–6hrs.

Beinn a'Chearcaill

Beinn a' Chearcaill is a big, bulky hill lying between Strath Lungard and Glen Grudie. It rises gently for several kilometres from Loch Maree but has steep slopes on the east, south and west sides of the summit. It's little visited and gives good views of the higher hills all around, especially Coire Mhic Fhearchair on Beinn Eighe, which lies opposite the summit. Beinn a' Chearcaill can be climbed from Glen Grudie by way of Coire Briste or else from Strath Lungard via the col north of the summit. The round trip via Glen Grudie is 10.5km long, with 700m of ascent, and takes 4–5hrs. Via Strath Lungard it's 15km, with 775m of ascent, and takes 5–6hrs.

Baosbheinn and Beinn an Eoin at dusk from the lip of Coire Mhic Fhearchair on Beinn Eighe

⊗ Baosbheinn and Beinn an Eoin ☆

These two rocky Corbetts form long, almost parallel ridges either side of big Loch na h-Oidhche ('loch of night' or 'darkness'). Formed of steep terraces of Torridonian sandstone, they look striking from the A832 road alongside Loch Maree. Combining the two in one walk makes for a long but exciting expedition with much ascent on steep, rough ground. This can be cut short by way of the track alongside Loch na h-Oidhche. The walk starts at the Am Feur-loch on the A832, between Loch Maree and Loch Bad an Sgalaig, from where a track heads southeast to Loch na h-Oidhche. The first part of the walk goes through the Gairloch Estate Bad an Sgalaig Native Pinewood, a large fenced area in which thousands of young trees have been planted. Soon after the path crosses the Abhainn Loch na h-Oidhche leave it and head to the steep north end of Beinn an Eoin, which is easier to climb than it looks. Once on the main ridge there's a glorious walk with grand views, especially of Baosbheinn, to the final steep summit slopes. The summit itself (855m) is on a narrow ridge and has a stunning view south to the Torridon peaks and north over Loch Maree. From the summit a descent can be made westwards to the head of Loch na h-Oidhche down steep, rough and rocky slopes where careful route-finding is needed to avoid difficulties. There's a locked bothy called Poca Buidhe above the loch. The track from this leads back to the start. If continuing on to Baosbheinn head southwest across big flat sandstone slabs and past little lochans to the southeast ridge, Drochaid a' Ghorm-locha. Climb this to the subsidiary top of Ceann Beag ('little head') and on to the high point, Sgorr Dubh ('black peak', 875m), which lies about half way along Baosbheinn's 5km summit ridge. The views are splendid throughout the traverse of the ridge which is rocky and wild but nowhere difficult or exposed. The ridge ends at Creag an Fhithich ('peak of the raven', 774m). The slopes to the north are craggy and steep, so to descend return along the ridge a short way then descend east. Once on easier ground head northnortheast to a bridge across the Abhainn a'Gharbh Choire and a track north to the outward track. The route is 24km long, with 1880m of ascent, and takes 8–9hrs.

6:3 LETTEREWE, FISHERFIELD AND DUNDONNELL: LOCH MAREE TO LOCH BROOM

North and east of Loch Maree lies one of the largest and remotest wild areas in the Highlands, a vast land of loch and mountain unbroken by roads all the way north to Little Loch Broom, and from the coast east right across the country to Garve. The area is encircled by the A832 – which runs along the south shore of Loch Maree, around the coast and back east along the south shore of Little Loch Broom – and the A835 from Garve to the Braemore Junction. Two very distinct sections divided by the Moine Thrust make up the area. In the west lie the rugged, steep and rocky mountains of Letterewe, Fisherfield and Dundonnell, which are covered in this section, while in the east are the gentler, more grassy Fannaichs, covered in 6:4. The dividing line between the two runs north from Kinlochewe via Loch an Nid to Corrie Hallie. The western area itself can be roughly divided into three sections split by long, loch-filled glens trending southeast to northwest, the glens of Fionn Loch–Dubh Loch–Lochan Fada and Strath na Sealga–Loch na Sealga.

There are nine Munros, seven Corbetts and six Grahams in this region. Between Loch Maree and Fionn Loch–Lochan Fada is the distinctive Munro Slioch ('the spear', 981m) and on a long high ridge stretching northwest the two fine Corbetts of Beinn Lair ('hill of the mare', 859m) and Beinn Airigh Charr ('hill of the bogland shieling', 791m). In the remote heart of the region between Fionn Loch–Lochan Fada is a group of Munros encircling the head of long Gleann na Muice ('valley of the pigs') known as the Fisherfield Six – A'Mhaighdean ('the maiden', 967m), Ruadh Stac Mor ('big red stack', 918m), Beinn Tarsuinn ('transverse hill', 937m), Mullach Coire Mhic Fhearchair ('hill of the corrie of Farquhar's son', 1018m), Sgurr Ban ('white peak', 989m) and Beinn a'Chlaidheimh ('hill of the sword', 916m). To their east across the Abhainn Loch an Nid is the Corbett Creag Rainich ('bracken crag', 807m) while to their west are three more Corbetts – Beinn a' Chasgein Mor ('big forbidding hill', 856m) and the pair of Beinn Dearg Mor ('big red hill', 910m) and Beinn Dearg Bheag ('little red hill', 820m), which tower above Loch na Sealga. North of that loch lies the finest mountain in the region and one of the finest in the Highlands, An Teallach ('the forge'), a spiky, curving ridge of spires and peaks with two Munros, Sgurr Fiona ('white peak', 1060m) and Bidean a' Ghlas Thuill ('peak of the grey-green hollow', 1062m), plus seven named tops or pinnacles. Finally way out to the northwest of An Teallach is the Corbett Sail Mhor ('big heel', 767m).

All these peaks are rough, stony and steep, as are the glens and passes. This is harsh country with a beauty of its own. Approaches are long and often convoluted, and overnight and multi-day trips are the best way to experience the area. There is much rock climbing in the area, especially on the hills around the head of the Fionn Loch and on An Teallach. The latter has winter climbing too.

ⓐ The Heights of Kinlochewe

North of Kinlochewe lies the plateau-like hill of Beinn a' Mhuinidh. Although not that high (692m) Beinn a' Mhuinidh is vast, covering a huge area. A network of paths runs round the hill and its circuit is a fine outing that ventures into wild country. The route starts at Incheril 1km northeast of Kinlochewe, and takes the path running northwest to the Kinlochewe River and Loch Maree, with good views of Beinn Eighe and Meall a' Ghiubhais to the west. The massive bulk of Slioch appears as the path reaches Loch Maree, with to the right the deep gash of Gleann Bianasdail, up which the route climbs. This dramatic glen is wooded lower down, with the stream crashing down in a series of cascades. Higher up the path leaves the edge of the gorge and traverses the eastern slopes of Slioch, with splendid views back down the v-shaped glen to Beinn Eighe, before descending to lonely Lochan Fada and a view of A'Mhaighdean, Ruadh Stac Mor, Beinn Tarsuinn and Mullach Coire Mhic Fhearchair, four of the remotest Munros. The path crosses big stepping stones over the Abhainn an Fhasaigh at its outlet from the loch, before it begins its plunge down Gleann Bianasdail. When in spate this crossing can be difficult and dangerous, with the stepping stones under fast-moving water. Faint paths run round the head of Lochan Fada to a path, also faint at first, which runs southeast past little lochans into Gleann na Muice (not to be confused with its namesake just 6km to the north), where it soon becomes more defined, passing through a large fenced area containing new native forest that was planted in 2004. At the Heights of Kinlochewe, where there is a farm, the path becomes a vehicle track which takes you down the Abhainn Bruachaig glen back to Incheril, with views of long, thin waterfalls tumbling down the crags lining the huge boggy plateau of the Mointeach a'Bhreamanaich to the east. The walk is 22km long, with 655m of ascent, and takes 5–6hrs.

ⓑ Rock Climbing on Beinn a'Mhuinidh

There are many rock climbs on the quartzite cliffs of Beinn a'Mhuinidh that curve round the west corner of the hill overlooking the head of Loch Maree and Gleann Bianasdail. The first route here was a 90m Severe called West Climb, climbed in 1899 by Ling and Inglis Clark. Most routes are much more recent than this, with grades from Difficult to E3. Kevin Howett in *Rock Climbing in Scotland* (Francis Lincoln, 2004) says 'all the routes have a serious feel'. The cliffs are reached from the path from Incheril to Loch Maree.

ⓐ Through-routes

The many excellent paths threading the rocky glens in this region can be linked, with some cross country sections, to make through-routes between roads and settlements, allowing excellent backpacking trips in wild country. This is just a selection of the possibilities.

Incheril to Poolewe

Starting at Incheril just outside Kinlochewe, the 31km path runs northwest to Loch Maree, then along the lochside below Slioch and through some pleasant remnant oak woods to the buildings at Letterewe, where it turns north away from the loch. Where the path divides take the left fork to Srathan Buidhe and descend that glen. Once out of the narrow glen turn northwest at further junctions and follow the path to a wood, where it becomes a track, and then the buildings of Kernsary from where a private road leads to Poolewe.

Poolewe to Corrie Hallie ☆

This 36km route runs through the heart of the mountains and is a superb walk. From Poolewe take the track and path southeast past Kernsary to the foot of Srathan Buidhe. Continue southeast here to the junction with a path running northeast across the exciting Causeway between the Fionn Loch and the Dubh Loch to Carnmore, where there is a bothy. Turn east at Carnmore on the path that leads to the Allt Bruthach an Easgain, then northeast again past Lochan Feith Mhic-illea. Descend Gleann na Muice Beag to Gleann na Muice, which is followed north

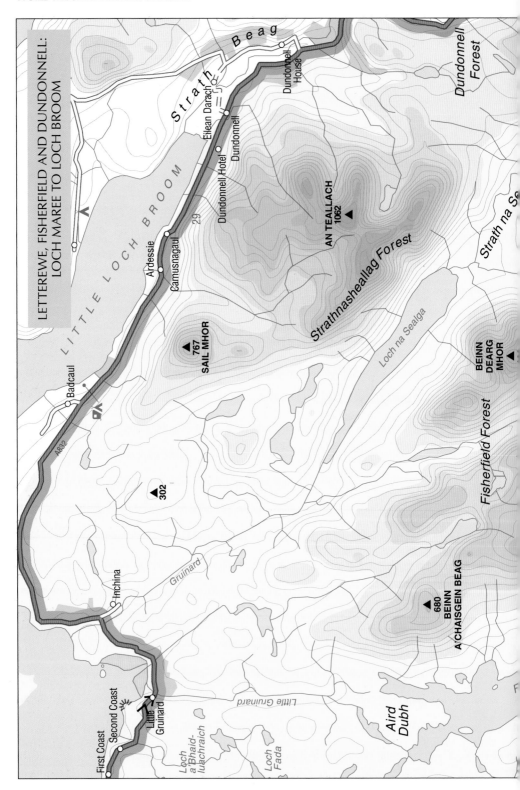

LETTEREWE, FISHERFIELD AND DUNDONNELL: LOCH MAREE TO LOCH BROOM

Dundonnell Forest

Strath Beag

Dundonnell House

Eilean Darach

Dundonnell

Dundonnell Hotel

Strath na Se

LITTLE LOCH BROOM

29

Ardessie

Camusnagaul

A832

AN TEALLACH
1062

Strathnasheallag Forest

Loch na Sealga

Badcaul

SAIL MHOR
767

BEINN
DEARG
MHOR

A832

302

Fisherfield Forest

Inchina

Gruinard

BEINN
A'CHAISGEIN BEAG
680

Little Gruinard

Aird
Dubh

Loch
a'Bhaid-
luachraich

First Coast

Second Coast

Little
Gruinard

Loch
Fada

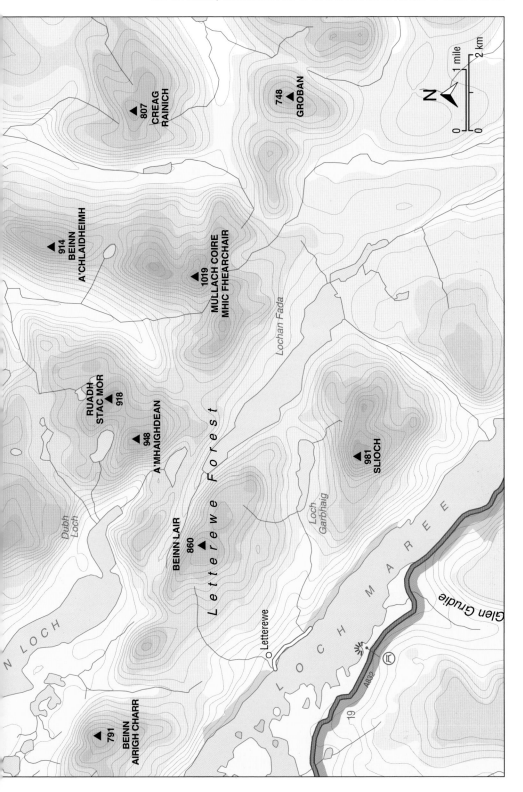

CREAG RAINICH
807

GROBAN
748

BEINN A'CHLAIDHEIMH
914

MULLACH COIRE MHIC FHEARCHAIR
1019

Lochan Fada

RUADH STAC MOR
918

A'MHAIGHDEAN
948

SLIOCH
981

Letterewe Forest

Loch Garbhaig

Dubh Loch

BEINN LAIR
860

N LOCH

Letterewe

BEINN AIRIGH CHARR
791

LOCH MAREE

Glen Grudie

A832

19

1 mile
2 km

N

past Larachantivore to a ford of first the Abhainn Gleann na Muice and then the Abhainn Srath na Sealga. These fords can be dangerous if the rivers are high, and impossible after heavy rain. Popular Shenavall bothy lies on the far side of the rivers. A path leads from the bothy to a track in Gleann Chaorachain that takes you to Corrie Hallie on the A832, 4km south of the Dundonnell Hotel.

Corrie Hallie to Incheril

This 29km route runs down the eastern side of the district and involves a short cross country section. From Corrie Hallie take the track up Gleann Chaorachain and over boggy moorland to the Abhainn Loch an Nid. Continue up this glen past Loch an Nid. Where the main path turns east leave it and continue beside the stream on a sketchy path up to the Bealach na Croise, from where a descent can be made to the head of Lochan Fada and the path down Gleann na Muice to Incheril described in the Heights of Kinlochewe section above.

⊗ Slioch ☆

Slioch is a fortress-like mountain towering above the east end of Loch Maree, and stands out in views across the loch. Built of huge sandstone buttresses it looks impregnable, but on the southeast

side there is a huge corrie running down to Gleann Bianasdail that gives surprisingly easy access to the summit. The dark Torridonian sandstone rests on a base of much older silvery Lewisian Gneiss, and the junction between these rocks can clearly be seen in views across the loch and from the Mountain Trail. Geologically this is known as an unconformity, as there's hundreds of millions of years difference in age between the rocks. Wild goats graze on Slioch and may be seen during the ascent. I once encountered a flock of them looming up out of the mist almost on the summit itself.

Records of first ascents are rare in the Northern Highlands. There are no early ones for Torridon. However Slioch (written as Sleugach) was climbed by an Ordnance Survey team led by Thomas Colby during a marathon 1099 mile (1800km) expedition in the summer of 1819, according to Ian R. Mitchell's *Scotland's Mountains Before the Mountaineers* (Luath, 1999).

The approach to Slioch is on the path from Incheril outside Kinlochewe to Loch Maree and Gleann Bianasdail. The climb starts on the path up Gleann Bianasdail, but in less than 1km this is left for a more sketchy path that leads north to the col between Sgurr Dubh and Meall Each, from where you can cut below the crags of the latter into Coire

View across Loch Maree to Slioch from the Mountain Trail

na Sleaghaich. There's a path up the corrie, or else you can climb on to the southeast ridge and follow this round to the summit. There are two tops, the slightly higher being the northern one, rather than the one with the trig point. The northern one is the best viewpoint too, as it's perched right on the edge of cliffs and gives superb views down Loch Maree, south to the Torridon hills and north to the Fisherfield peaks. To maintain the interest, the views and the height, rather than descending straightaway head east from the summit along a narrow ridge to Sgurr an Tuill Bhan ('peak of the white hollow', 934m) from where you can descend into Coire na Sleaghaich and back to the path in Gleann Bianasdail. The walk is around 22km long, with 1350m of ascent, and takes 7–8hrs.

🔷 A Scramble on Slioch

Surprisingly, given its dramatic cliffs, Slioch does not boast many rock climbs. The steep buttresses don't look good scrambling terrain either. However there is one scrambling route, the Northwest Buttress, which is given two stars in the SMC's *Highland Scrambles North*. It's Grade 2 or 3, depending on the exact route, and is described as 'not particularly exposed'. It leads directly to the summit.

⊗ Beinn Lair, Beinn Airigh Charr and Meall Mheinnidh

Beinn Lair presents long, gentle, grassy slopes to Loch Maree and from the A832 on the far side of the loch hardly looks a distinct hill at all, just a high nondescript ridge. However on the northwest side, hidden from view, is a 5km line of cliffs running above Lochan Fada and Gleann Tulacha. This is a superb mountain wall, one of the longest in the Highlands. Cut off from the nearest road by Loch Maree, Beinn Lair is a remote hill and long approach walks are needed to reach it. The path from Kinlochewe to Poolewe, described in the 'Through-routes' section above, provides the best access. If approaching from Kinlochewe, take the path to the Bealach Mheinnidh from Letterewe, and then climb east to the summit, where there are superb views across Lochan Fada to the Fisherfield hills. Continue along the ridge from the summit on the edge of the cliffs above Gleann Tulacha, and down to another path that leads back to Letterewe. From Poolewe the Bealach Mheinnidh can be reached from the path between Letterewe and

Carnmore. Whichever route is chosen the distance is around 36km, with over 900m of ascent, and is likely to take 11hrs+. A multi-day trip with ascents of other peaks in the area is a good choice.

> Despite its remoteness Beinn Lair is one of the few peaks in the area with an early recorded ascent. Geologist and peak bagger Dr John MacCulloch, who has already been mentioned as making first ascents south of the Great Glen, wrote in his 1824 book *The Highlands and Western Islands of Scotland* that 'Ben Lair will repay the toil of the expedition to its summit'. Of the view north from the mountain MacCulloch writes 'everything is gigantic and terrible; wild and strange and new'. MacCulloch thought Beinn Lair was over 3000 feet high, suggesting, as Ian R. Mitchell says in *Scotland's Mountains Before the Mountaineers* (Luath, 1999), that 'by the early 19th century the figure of 3000 feet already had about it a magical and desirable quality, later merely formalised by Munro in his Tables'.

Beinn Lair can also be combined with Beinn Airigh Charr and Meall Mheinnidh ('grassy or solitary hill'), a 720m Graham that lies between them. Together they form a 14km long mountain wall facing northeastwards over the Fionn Loch and Gleann Tulacha. With steep slopes, subsidiary summits and crags overlooking Loch Maree Beinn Airigh Charr is much more distinctive than Beinn Lair when viewed across the loch. It also stands out in views from the coast around Poolewe. The ascent from Poolewe starts with the walk towards Kernsary and the path to Ardlair on Loch Maree. This last path is left for a stalkers' path that climbs to over 500m and comes to an end not far from the summit, which is then easily reached. There's a wonderful view south over the Flowerdale and Torridon hills. If climbing Beinn Airigh Charr alone return the same way, perhaps taking in the little rocky top of Spidean nan Clach, for a walk of 22km, with 1185m of ascent, which takes 8–9hrs.

For the round of all three hills descend eastwards from Beinn Airigh Charr into Srath Buidhe, climb the northwest ridge of Meall Mheinnidh then descend to the Bealach Mheinnidh and climb

Beinn Lair, returning via the bealach and the path to Poolewe. This long and excellent expedition involves 37km of distance, and 2250m of ascent, and takes 11–13hrs.

⊗ Beinn a'Chaisgein Mor

Beinn a' Chaisgein Mor is a big flat-topped hill with huge, impressive cliffs on its south side. Lying to the east of the Fionn Loch and far from any road it's one of the remotest hills in this region. It can be climbed from Poolewe by the route to Corrie Hallie (see 'Through-routes' above), leaving this at Lochan Feith Mhic'-illean for an easy walk to the summit and extensive views. The distance is 44km, with 1680m of ascent, and the walk takes 11–13hrs. It's hardly likely anyone would do this as a day walk however and Beinn a' Chaisgein Mor is best combined with other hills on a multi-day trip.

⊗ A'Mhaighdean and Ruadh Stac Mor ☆

These two splendid rocky Munros sit right in the wild heart of the region between Loch Maree and Little Loch Broom, far from any roads. A'Mhaighdean is often described as the remotest Munro of all. All approaches are long, that from Poolewe slightly shorter than those from Kinlochewe or Dundonnell. It's still a distance of 16km, with 600m of ascent just to reach Carnmore at the base of the mountains, a walk that takes 4–5hrs. An overnight or multi-day trip is the easiest way to climb the pair, whose summits are just 1km apart. From Poolewe take the route via Kernsary to Carnmore. A'Mhaighdean looks impressive from the path down to the Fionn Loch and over the Causeway. From Carnmore take the path beside the Allt Bruthach an Easain and climb the craggy northwest ridge of A'Mhaighdean. Although steep and rocky any difficulties can be avoided. The summit sits on the edge of cliffs and is a spectacular viewpoint, with one of the finest mountain vistas in Scotland spread out all around, a wild scene of lochs and cliffs. From the summit descend northeast down easy slopes to the col with Ruadh Stac Mor, and then climb the latter by a clever path that twists and turns through the terraces of sandstone crags surrounding the top. Return to the col and down a stalkers' path that runs northwest past Fuar Loch Mor to the Allt Bruthach an Easain path and so back to Carnmore and Poolewe. The round trip from Carnmore is 11km, with 1035m of ascent, and takes 5–7hrs. A round trip from Poolewe would be 43km, with 1800m of ascent, and take 14hrs+.

A'Mhaighdean and Ruadh Stac Mor

Ⓛ Carnmore Crag and the Fionn Loch Basin

Carnmore Crag on the south side of Beinn a' Chaisgein Mor is described as 'home to some of the finest mountain rock climbs in Scotland' (*Highland Scrambles North*) and as having 'some of the finest rock climbing in Britain' (*North-West Highlands*) while Kevin Howett's *Rock Climbing in Scotland* (Frances Lincoln, 2004) says 'its remote setting, sunny aspect and excellent rock combine to give climbing comparable with the best in Britain'. This much praised cliff does look magnificent, a continuous sweep of smooth pale gneiss. There are other rock climbs on the cliffs around Carnmore and the Fionn Loch Basin, and climbers could find much to do for a week or more, justifying the long walk-in.

On Carnmore Crag highly rated climbs include: 240m Fionn Buttress (VS, first climbed by M. J. O'Hara and W. D. Blackwood in 1957) described in *Rock Climbing in Scotland* as 'one of the finest outings in Scotland'; 114m Balaton (E1, first climbed by W. Gorman and C. Higgens in 1966); 102m Dragon (HVS, first climbed by G. J. Fraser and M. J. O'Hara in 1957); 102m Sword (E2, first climbed by R. Isherwood and E. Birch in 1967); 126m Gob (HVS, first climbed by D. Haston and R. Smith in 1960); and 36m The Orange Bow (E5, first climbed by D. Dinwoodie and D. Hawthorn in 1985).

The steep, unbroken rock of Carnmore Crag makes for climbs in the upper grades, but there are easier routes elsewhere in the area. On the northeast cliffs of Beinn Lair, built of hornblende schist, 220m Wisdom Buttress is a classic Very Difficult, first climbed in 1951 by J. Smith, A. Hood and J.S. Orr and described by Kevin Howett as 'a magnificent climb, exposed, sustained and the best of its grade in the area'. A'Mhaighdean has some lower grade climbs on its southwest cliffs, such as 150m Pillar Buttress (Very Difficult, first climbed in 1950), 270m Whitbread' Aiguille (Severe, first climbed in 1957) and 110m Red Slab (Difficult, first climbed in 1957), while on Beinn Airigh Charr there is 330m Face Route (Difficult, first climbed by Ling and Glover in 1910).

Ⓢ Carnmore Crag and the Fionn Loch Basin Scrambles ☆

The rocky hills around Carnmore and the Fionn Loch offer a wealth of scrambles of all types. The SMC's *Highland Scrambles North* describes the area as 'a scrambler's heaven, with several lifetimes' worth of rock' and describes fifteen different routes, although it should be noted that eight of these are actually lower grade rock climbs (the book is subtitled *Scrambles and Easy Climbs*). Of the scrambles four are given two stars – Grey Ridge on the edge of Carnmore Crag on Beinn a'Chaisgein Mor, Kids' Ridge on the West Face of A'Mhaighdean, North Summit Buttress on Beinn Lair and Bell's Route on the northeast face of Beinn Airigh Charr.

⊗ The Gleann na Muice Ridge

A 9km ridge containing four Munros – Beinn Tarsuinn, Mullach Coire Mhic Fhearchair, Sgurr Ban, and Beinn a' Chlaidheimh – makes up the east side of Gleann na Muice. These hills are quite remote, with long walk-ins needed from Kinlochewe in the south or Corrie Hallie in the north. They are not as impressive as the surrounding hills, and some of the walking, over quartzite scree and boulders, is tiresome, but the views are good. If the southern trio are being climbed together then the southern approach is shortest but if Beinn a' Chlaidheimh is included as well, which I recommend, then the northern approach is shorter. Either way an overnight trip is preferable. Starting at Corrie Hallie take the path to Shenavall bothy, ford the Abhainn Srath na Sealga and Abhainn Gleann na Muice (if not in spate), follow the path down Gleann na Muice and then the stream to the wide 525m bealach between A'Mhaighdean and Beinn Tarsuinn. The ascent to the latter up grassy slopes and sandstone slabs to the narrow summit ridge, is enjoyable and easy. To the northwest Ruadh Stac Mor rises as a fine pyramid. The descent to the next col is pleasant enough, but the clamber up the huge mound of quartzite rubble that is Mullach Coire Mhic Fhearchair is tedious. A path leads down scree to the next col, then there is more loose quartzite on Sgurr Ban. A curiosity of this peak is the large area of low angled quartzite slabs on its east face, which can be walked up from Loch an Nid. Once off Sgurr Ban the walking becomes easier and grassier on the lonf southern ridge of Beinn a'Chlaidheimh, a sandstone mountain. From the summit descend northeast to a ford of the Abhainn Loch an Nid, on the far side of which is a path that leads back to the track to Corrie Hallie. The distance is 38km, and there's 2400m of ascent. The walk takes 12hrs+.

⊗ The Fisherfield Six ☆

The round of all six of the Fisherfield Munros is long and challenging, with 44km of distance and 2950m

View over Lochan Fada to Beinn Tarsuinn and Mullach Coire Mhic Fhearchair

of ascent from Corrie Hallie. It will take most walkers 15–20hrs. Staying at Shenavall Bothy or camping nearby in Strath na Sealga cuts the figures to a still long 35km, with 2580m of ascent, which takes 12–15hrs. With either option there are river crossings at each end of the day. The circuit can be done in either direction but I'd go clockwise, to save the finest peaks until last and have a long walk out at the end of the day when tired rather than more hills. Beinn a'Chlaidheimh can be climbed by the descent route described above or by the steeper northwest shoulder from Shenavall. Traverse the four Munros to the col with A'Mhaighdean, then climb the long, grassy southeast slopes of the latter and continue on to Ruadh Stac Mor as described above. From Ruadh Stac Mor descend to Lochan a' Bhraghad, then north to the path in Gleann na Muice Beag which leads back to Gleann na Muice and Shenavall.

⊗ Creag Rainich

Creag Rainich (807m) on the eastern edge of this region is a rather unnoticeable little hill without much of interest except for the good view of the higher hills of the Gleann na Muice Ridge and An Teallach. It's most easily climbed from the east. Take

the track from the A832 alongside Loch a'Bhraoin, then climb easy slopes to the summit from the west end of the loch. The return trip from the A832 is 17km long, with 600m of ascent, and takes 6–7hrs.

⊗ Beinn Dearg Mor and Beinn Dearg Bheag ☆

These two Corbetts are remote, hard to reach and magnificent. They form a long steep ridge above Loch na Sealga with a low point of 593m. Built of Torridonian sandstone, they rise in tiers of rock from the loch and dominate the view from Shenavall. Beinn Dearg Mor (910m) has huge cliff-rimmed Coire nan Clach ('corrie of the stones') at its heart, with massive buttressed ridges enclosing it on either side. Between the two peaks is another big corrie containing Loch Toll an Lochain. On the south side more uniform slopes drop steeply to Srath Beinn Dearg. The ascent of the pair involves a long walk-in from Corrie Hallie, on the A832, to Shenavall, and then a ford of the Abhainn Strath ne Sealga and the Abhainn Gleann na Muice, both potentially dangerous or impossible to cross in wet weather. A little way down Gleann na Muice strike west up the southeast slopes of Beinn Dearg Mor to the summit cairn, which sits right on the rim of the Coire nan Clach cliffs, a dramatic situation. The views of An Teallach to the north and the Fisherfield hills to the south are spectacular. Alternative scrambling routes from this side are the East Buttress, a Grade 3, which rises above Larachantivore in Gleann na Muice, and the Southeast Ridge, a Grade 1/2, which lies at the southeast corner of the peak. From Beinn Dearg Mor the ridge to Beinn Dearg Bheag (820m) is an easy and delightful walk. A descent could be made northwestwards, but this would leave a long, rough walk back along Loch na Sealga. Instead it's better to return to the 593m col and descend – with care – the steep headwall to Loch Toll an Lochain, and then easy slopes to Loch na Sealga and the walk back to Shenavall and Corrie Hallie, which involves a ford of the combined Abhainn Strath na Sealga and Abhainn Gleann na Muice. The route from Corrie Hallie is 32km long, with 1400m of ascent, and takes 10–12hrs.

⚇ ❸ An Teallach ☆

One of the great peaks of the Highlands, An Teallach (1062m) is a magnificent and complex mountain with sandstone spires, deep cliff-girt corries, shapely peaks and huge buttresses. Its distinctive outline is identifiable from many places near and far, but it looks especially grand from the A832 between Braemore Junction and Dundonnell. An Teallach forms a curving ridge running south to north between Strath na Sealga and Dundonnell. The shape is that of a letter 'E', with the spurs of Sail Liath ('grey heel') and Glas Mheall Mor ('big green hill') at either end and the spur of Glas Mheall Liath ('greenish-grey hill') in the middle. Between these spurs lie Glas Toll ('grey-green hollow') and Toll an Lochain ('hollow of the lochain'), the latter one of the finest corries in the Highlands, rivalling Coire Mhic Fhearchair on Beinn Eighe. Another spur projects westwards from Sgurr Fiona but this is a less significant part of the mountain. The finest feature is the pinnacled ridge south of Sgurr Fiona above Loch Toll an Lochain. Most of the mountain is built of Torridonian sandstone but the eastern spurs are capped with quartzite. The two Munros lie less than 1km apart and can be climbed without any scrambling. The best expedition on An Teallach is the traverse of the whole ridge, which does involve some scrambling.

An Teallach first appears by name on a sketch map drawn by map maker Timothy Pont in the 1590s, on which it is called 'Ptalloch'. In John

Thomson's 1832 *County Atlas of Scotland* it's 'Kalloch' with a summit called Kea Cloch. Ian R. Mitchell's *Scotland's Mountains Before the Mountaineers* (Luath, 1999) describes these names as a result of 'a series of cumulative erroneous transliterations, only set right when the first OS men thought to ask a local'. The OS men hadn't arrived when the first recorded ascent was made by Dr John MacCulloch in the early 19th century, as described in his book *The Highlands and Western Islands of Scotland*, published in 1824, and he knew it as Kea Cloch. MacCulloch, who made many first ascents south of the Great Glen as described in earlier chapters, only climbed two mountains north of it – Beinn Lair and An Teallach. Ian R. Mitchell says that the ascent of An Teallach 'was undoubtedly MacCulloch's finest achievement, and also the most significant ascent of a Scottish mountain to that date, especially as it was in the remote northwest, where most tourists still failed to venture'. From MacCulloch's description Mitchell reckons he climbed Sgurr Fiona rather than the slightly higher Bidein a'Ghlas Thuill.

The two Munros of An Teallach can be climbed from Dundonnell without any scrambling being involved by way of the rough path that zigzags up the east shoulder of Meall Garbh ('rough hill') and then divides, one branch continuing up the shoulder, the other up the corrie to its south. Either path leads onto the main ridge and an unnamed 916m top west of Glas Mheall Mor. From here it's a steep climb up the north ridge of Bidein a' Ghlas Thuill. The views from the summit are tremendous. The continuation to Sgurr Fiona is rocky but without difficulty and the views from this peak are even more impressive. If not continuing south, which would mean a long walk back to Dundonnell, the best way back is by the outward route. The round trip is 14km long, with 1430m of ascent, and takes 6–7hrs.

For the traverse of An Teallach a better start point is Corrie Hallie, from where the path to Shenavall can be taken to the foot of Sail Liath, whose broad southeast face can be easily climbed over quartzite rocks and scree. From here on the ascent of Sgurr Fiona becomes rockier and rockier as its pinnacled south ridge is climbed. The direct route is graded a Moderate rock climb and is very exposed in places, but there is a narrow traversing path on the south side that avoids all the scrambling but also the dramatic summits of Corrag Buidhe ('yellow finger') and Lord Berkeley's Seat. The final climb up Sgurr Fiona is back to rough walking as is the continuation over Bidein 'a Ghlas Thuill. To return to Corrie Hallie descend to the col with Ghlas Mheall Liath and drop down steep slopes to Loch Toll an Lochain and one of the most impressive situations in the Highlands. From the corrie follow the burn down into Coir a'Ghiubhsachain and a path to the A832 just less than 1km north of Corrie Hallie. This route is 17km long, with 1480m of ascent, and takes 7–8hrs.

⚙ Winter Climbing on An Teallach ☆

The broken, vegetated sandstone cliffs of An Teallach are not good for rock climbing, but when frozen and under snow and ice there are some highly regarded winter routes. The traverse itself, a Grade II/III depending on whether the crest of the pinnacles is taken direct (the traversing path is 'at least Grade 1'), is given four stars and described as 'arguably the best ridge in Scotland' in the SMC's *Scottish Winter Climbs*. Other highly rated climbs are: 300m Hayfork Gully (four stars, Grade I, first climbed by G. Sang and W. A. Morrison in March 1910); 170m Haystack (three stars, Grade VI, first climbed by D. McGimpsey and A. Nisbet in January 2000) in Glas Toll; 400m Face Route (three stars, Grade IV, first climbed by M. Freeman and N. D. Keir in February 1978); and 400m Lord's Gully (three stars, Grade III, right branch first climbed by J. H. B. Bell and E. E. Roberts at Easter 1923, left branch first climbed by A. Borthwick and F. Fotheringham in February 1973) on the Corrag Buidhe in Toll an Lochain.

⊗ Sail Mhor

Rising some 5km northwest of An Teallach above Little Loch Broom, Sail Mhor is an isolated but easily accessible Corbett. It lies on the 9km ridge that runs west then northwest from Sgurr Fiona, terminating at Sail Bheag (409m). The low point on this ridge is 445m, and Sail Mhor could be climbed in conjunction with An Teallach. Sail Mhor has steep sandstone terraces on three sides but can be easily climbed from the south. It's not a particularly dramatic hill compared with others in the area but the view over the sea to the islands, as well as of the hills to the south, is superb, and it makes a pleasant short day out. The ascent starts at Ardessie on the A832 alongside Little Loch Broom, and takes the path beside the Allt Airdeasaidh past the fine Ardessie Falls. Leave the stream after a couple of

kilometres and climb west into the corrie south of the summit to the col between Sail Mhor and Ruigh Mheallain, then up the southern slopes to the top. Return by the same route, for a walk of 9km, with 750m of ascent, which takes 4–5hrs.

6:4 THE FANNAICHS

The Fannaichs are a small group of mountains, linked by high ridges, lying to the east of the Fisherfield hills. More similar to the hills of Strathfarrar and Mullardoch to the south than those of Torridon or Fisherfield, they are steep-sided but mostly grassy, with few crags or rock outcrops, although there are a couple of cliffs highly rated for winter climbing. The walking is much easier than to the west and the hills are more accessible, rising above the A835 and A832. Instead of rough walking over boulders and scree the Fannaichs provide long easy ridge walks on short grass and flat stones. There are deep, lochan-filled corries among these hills, and many fine campsites. The Fannaichs are named after big Loch Fannich, which lies south of the main part of the range and is now a dammed reservoir, the environs further marred by bulldozed roads along the shores. The meaning of the name is obscure.

There are ten Munros in the Fannaichs, nine of them in a fairly compact group, and one rather distant Corbett out to the east – Beinn Liath Mhor a' Ghiubhais Li ('big grey hill of the coloured pine', 766m). The outlying Munro, the only one south of Loch Fannich, is Fionn Bheinn ('white hill', 933m), which rises just north of Achnasheen. From west to east the other Munros are A'Chailleach ('the old woman', 997m), Sgurr Breac ('speckled peak', 999m), Sgurr nan Each ('peak of the horses', 923m), Sgurr nan Clach Geala ('peak of the white stones', 1093m), Meall a'Chrasgaidh ('hill of the crossing', 934m), Sgurr Mor ('big peak', 1110m), Beinn Liath Mhor Fannaich ('big grey hill of Fannaich', 954m), Meall Gorm ('blue hill', 949m) and An Coileachan ('the little cock', 923m). With high cols between all these hills – the lowest is at 550m between Sgurr Breac and the Sgurr nan Each–Sgurr nan Clach Geala ridge – they lend themselves to a two day trip with a high camp, which I have done a couple of times. As day walks they can be split neatly into three groups, as described below.

Fionn Bheinn

Fionn Bheinn ('white hill', 933m) is an unexciting grassy hump. There are a couple of deep corries to the north and east of the summit that add a touch of character, but basically this is an undistinguished hill. There is however a good view and it is accessible, so there are some plus points. It's also said to make a good ski tour when the snow is deep enough. It can be easily climbed from Achnasheen anywhere up the southern side, the standard route being beside the Allt Achadh na Sine. Descend the same way, or else head east along Sail an Tuim Bhain and pick up the old path that runs south–north across the eastern slopes of the hill. Follow this down to the A832 1km east of Achnasheen. The route is 12km long, with 800m of ascent, and takes 4–5hrs.

A'Chailleach and Sgurr Breac

The two western Fannaichs are the high points on a horseshoe ridge that runs around the U-shaped Nest of Fannich corrie, which runs southeast down to Loch Fannich. To the north of the Munros is the deep corrie of Toll an Lochain, with spurs either side projecting towards Loch a'Bhraoin. The ascent of these hills is a pleasant if undemanding walk.

From the A832 take the track to Loch a'Bhraoin, then the path south to the col east of Sgurr Breac. Climb the steep east ridge of the latter to the summit, then continue east along the fairly broad ridge to A'Chailleach. There are good views west to the Fisherfield hills. Descend via Sron na Goibhre, the spur on the west side of Toll an Lochain. This spur ends in crags which can be avoided by going down right (east) into the mouth of Toll an Lochain, from where a descent can be made down to Loch a'Bnraoin and the outward track. The distance is 19km, with 1020m of ascent, and the walk takes 6–7hrs.

Meall a'Chrasgaidh, Sgurr nan Clach Geala and Sgurr nan Each ☆

These three Munros lie on a long straight ridge running north from Loch Fannich. The central and highest peak, Sgurr nan Clach Geala, is the most distinctive and impressive of all the Fannaichs, a steep mountain with a big rocky hanging corrie on its northeast flanks. Sgurr nan Each to the south also has a craggy east face plus a pointed little summit. Meall a' Chrasgaidh to the north is less distinctive. Just to the east of the ridge between Meall a'Chrasgaidh and Sgurr nan Clach Geala is the minor top of Carn

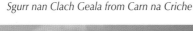

Sgurr nan Clach Geala from Carn na Criche

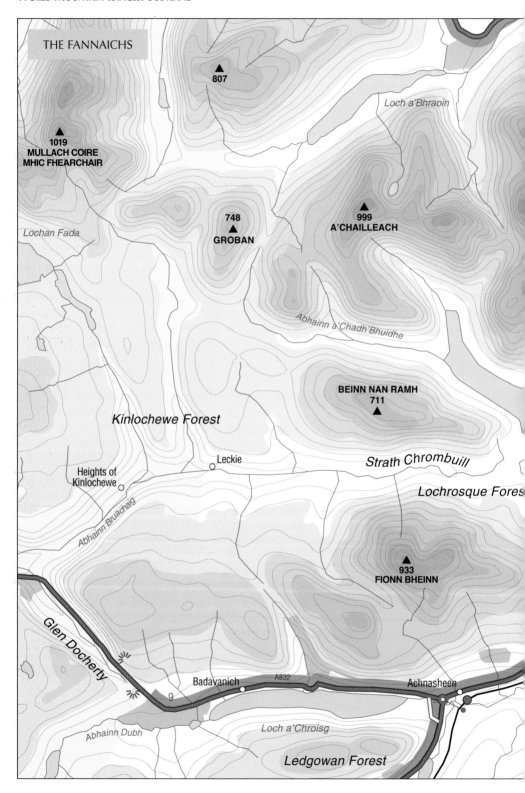

THE FANNAICHS

807

1019
MULLACH COIRE
MHIC FHEARCHAIR

Loch a'Bhraoin

748
GROBAN

999
A'CHAILLEACH

Lochan Fada

Abhainn a'Chadh'Bhuidhe

BEINN NAN RAMH
711

Kinlochewe Forest

Leckie

Strath Chrombuill

Heights of
Kinlochewe

Lochrosque Forest

Abhainn Bruachaig

933
FIONN BHEINN

Glen Docherty

Badavanich   A832

Achnasheen

Abhainn Dubh

Loch a'Chroisg

Ledgowan Forest

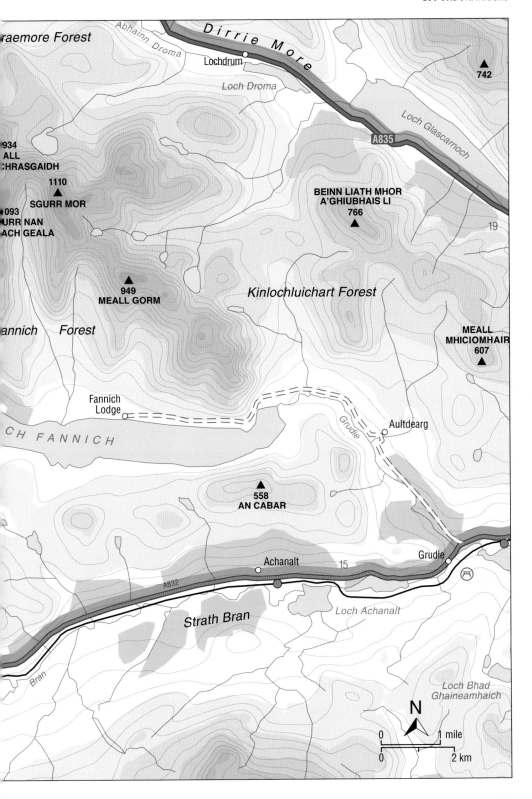

raemore Forest

Abhainn Droma

D i r r i e   M o r e

Lochdrum

Loch Droma

A835

Loch Glascarnoch

742

934
ALL
HRASGAIDH

1110
SGURR MOR

BEINN LIATH MHOR
A'GHIUBHAIS LI
766

093
URR NAN
ACH GEALA

19

949
MEALL GORM

Kinlochluichart Forest

MEALL
MHICIOMHAIR
607

annich   Forest

CH FANNICH

Fannich
Lodge

Grudie

Aultdearg

558
AN CABAR

Grudie

Achanalt

15

Loch Achanalt

A832

Strath Bran

Bran

Loch Bhad
Ghaineamhaich

N

0   1 mile

0   2 km

na Criche, which is the connecting link between these hills, Sgurr Mor and the eastern Fannaichs. The walk along the Sgurr nan Clach Geala ridge is arguably the finest outing in the Fannaichs. It starts on the track from the A832 to Loch a'Bhraoin and the path south of the foot of the loch. After the path crosses the Allt Breabaig head up the northwest ridge of Meall a' Chrasgaidh. There now follows just over 3km of excellent high-level ridge walking over Sgurr nan Clach Geala to Sgurr nan Each. The final ascent to Sgurr nan Clach Geala is the best part of the walk, as it runs along the edge of the cliffs of the east face. From Sgurr nan Each return to the col with Sgurr nan Clach Geala, then descend west to the col at the head of the Allt Breabaig glen and take the path back to the start, for a trip of 19km, with 1080m of ascent, which takes 7–8hrs.

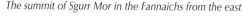 Winter Climbing on Sgurr nan Clach Geala

Being further away from the west coast than most hills in the Northern Highlands, the Fannaichs have a colder climate. Snow comes from both the north and the east so deep cover is more likely here than on An Teallach or the Fisherfield hills. The summer walking routes are excellent mountaineering expeditions when snow covered. There are more serious technical climbs on the cliffs of the east and northeast faces of the highest Fannaichs, Sgurr nan Clach Geala and Sgurr Mor (see below). These cliffs are high on the mountains in superb situations. On Sgurr nan Clach Geala the crag is called Am Biachdaich, and is situated at 750m on the east face. It can be reached from the A832 via the track to Loch a'Bhraoin and the col between Carn na Criche and Sgurr nan Clach Geala, from where a short descent down a sometimes corniced steep slope is needed. In the SMC's *Scottish Winter Climbs* it's described as 'large and impressively steep, one of Scotland's best'. There are climbs in grades from I to VI, of which *Scottish Winter Climbs* gives four stars to 240m Skyscraper Buttress (Grade VI, first ascent by R. J. Archbold, M. Freeman, J. C. Higham and R. A. Smith in February 1978, with a Direct Start added by D. Dinwoodie, C. Jamieson and K. Murphy in February 1986) and three stars to 210m Gamma Gully (Grade V, first ascent P. N. L. Tranter and I. G. Rowe in March 1965).

Beinn Liath Mhor Fannaich, Sgurr Mor, Meall Gorm and An Coileachan ☆

Sgurr Mor, the highest summit in the Northern Highlands as well as the Fannaichs, sits in the

The summit of Sgurr Mor in the Fannaichs from the east

heart of the range, with ridges radiating northwest to Meall a'Chrasgaidh, northeast to Beinn Liath Mhor Fannaich and southeast to Meall Gorm and An Coileachan. Sgurr Mor is a distinctive hill with a fine rocky corrie east of the summit. Beinn Liath Mhor Fannaich, Meall Gorm and An Coileachan are more rounded, although the last two have some rocky corries on their north and east sides. The 10km ridge walk from Beinn Liath Mhor Fannaich to An Coileachan is a superb high-level outing that never drops below 775m, and has wonderful views of An Teallach, the Torridon hills and the Beinn Dearg group to the north. The walk starts just west of Loch Glascarnoch on the A835. Follow the path beside the Abhainn an Torrain Duibh to the confluence with the Allt an Loch Sgeirich, and then walk up the latter for 1km or so, leaving it for the east ridge of Beinn Liath Mhor Fannaich. The walking is rough lower down, with heather, tussocks, boggy ground and boulders, but once high on the ridge it's mostly easy over short grass and stones, and the summits come and go as you stride onwards. From An Coileachan turn back to the last col to the north, the Bealach Ban, then descend northeast to the col with the minor top of Meallan Buidhe and cut above Loch Gorm, before descending rough ground to the Abhainn a' Ghiubhais Li which leads to the Abhainn an Torrain Duibh and the start. The walk is 24km long, with 1300m of ascent, and takes 8–10hrs.

✱ Winter Climbing on Sgurr Mor

The climbing on Sgurr Mor is on the northeast face at 900m, just below the summit. It can be reached from the A832 at the end of Loch Droma by the path to Loch a' Mhadaidh, then an ascent of the broad shoulder south of the loch or Beinn Liath Mhor Fannaich. Described as 'a big serious face', it has long routes in the easier grades, of which 320m The Resurrection (Grade III, first climbed by J. R. Mackenzie and D. Butterfield in March 1980), the central route on the cliff, is given four stars and described as 'a serious route with a great Alpine atmosphere'. The final belay is the summit cairn of Sgurr Mor.

❷ Ski Touring on the Fannaichs ☆

The high ridges of the Fannaichs are excellent ski touring terrain, although approaches are long if there isn't adequate snow low down and skis have to be carried through the heather and peat bogs.

The curving ridge of Meall a'Chrasgaidh, Sgurr Mor and Beinn Liath Fannaich is the most accessible terrain. The SMC's *Ski Mountaineering in Scotland* gives this four stars and a Grade IV rating, saying it is a 'long and serious expedition' with some sections, such as the final ascent of Sgurr Mor, where skis will probably have to be carried and ice axe and crampons used. The route starts at the dam on Loch Droma on the A835 and follows the Allt a'Mhadaidh to Loch a'Mhadaidh, from where Meall a'Chrasgaidh is climbed and the ridge traversed over Sgurr Mor to Beinn Liath Mhor Fannaich and then a descent made northeast from the latter, then north back to the outward track. This route is 17km long, with 1140m of ascent, and takes 7–9hrs.

⛰ Beinn Liath Mhor a'Ghiubhais Li

This hill has an impressive name that belies its nondescript appearance, it being just a rounded bump in the midst of boggy moorland well to the east of the higher Fannaichs. Its isolated position does make it a good viewpoint for the Fannaichs and the Beinn Dearg hills, and it can be climbed in less than 2hrs from the car park on the A835 just before the west end of Loch Glascarnoch. From here follow the eastern edge of the plantations that cover the lower slopes of the north side of the hill, and continue above the trees over Meall Daimh to the summit. Return the same way, or head northwest and descend to a forest track that runs down to the road 1km west of the start. The walk is 7km long, with 500m of ascent, and takes around 3hrs.

6:5 BEINN DEARG AND EASTER ROSS

North of the Fannaichs and the A835 road lies a craggy group of hills collectively named for the highest summit, Beinn Dearg. There are five Munros and one Corbett here – Beinn Dearg ('red hill', 1084m) itself, Cona' Mheall ('adjoining hill', 978m), Am Faochagach ('heathery place', 954m), Meall nan Ceapraichean ('hill of the stubby hillocks', 977m), Eididh nan Clach Geala ('web of the white stones', 927m) and Beinn Enaiglair ('hill of the timid birds', 889m). Farther north but connected to these hills by high ground is one of the remotest Munros, Seana Bhraigh ('old height', 926m) while far to the east (and off the map shown here) is the big plateau hill Ben Wyvis (name obscure but possibly 'awesome

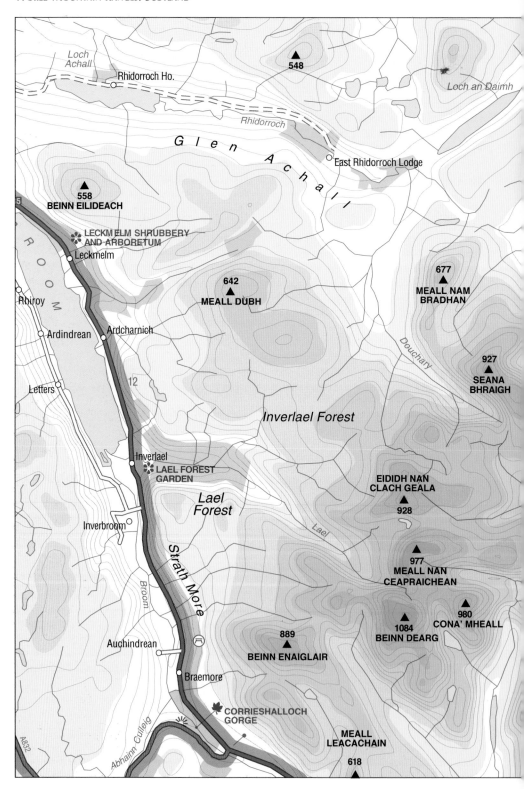

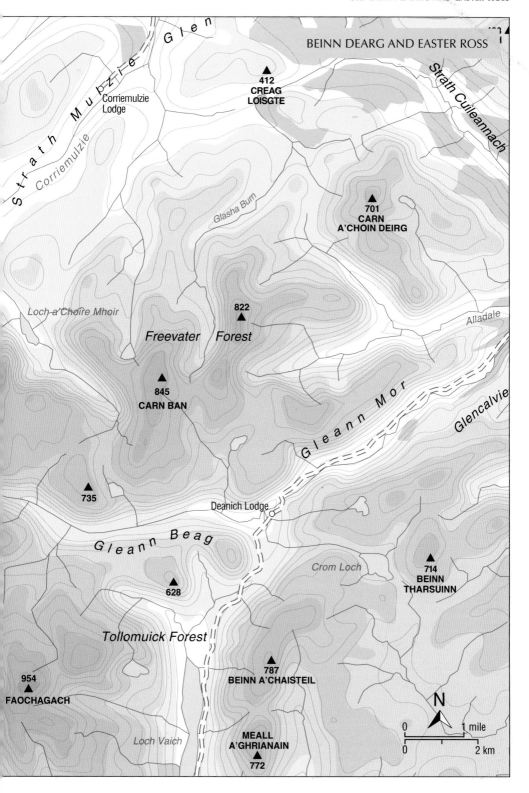

BEINN DEARG AND EASTER ROSS

Strath Mu-zie Glen

Strath Cuileannach

Corriemulzie Lodge

Corriemulzie

▲ 412
CREAG
LOISGTE

Glasha Burn

▲ 701
CARN
A'CHOIN DEIRG

Loch a'Choire Mhoir

Alladale

▲ 822

Freevater Forest

▲ 845
CARN BAN

Gleann Mor

Glencalvie

▲ 735

Deanich Lodge

Gleann Beag

Crom Loch

▲ 714
BEINN
THARSUINN

▲ 628

Tollomuick Forest

954 ▲
FAOCHAGACH

▲ 787
BEINN A'CHAISTEIL

N

Loch Vaich

MEALL
A'GHRIANAIN
772

0   1 mile

0   2 km

427

hill', 1046m). To the southwest of Ben Wyvis lies a Corbett, Little Wyvis ('little awesome hill', 764m). There are three more widely scattered Corbetts between the Beinn Dearg hills and Ben Wyvis, two of them very isolated and remote: Beinn a'Chaisteil ('castle hill', 787m) lies east of Am Faochagach across Loch Vaich, Carn Ban ('white cairn', 845m) lies east of Seana Bhraigh, and Carn Chuinneag ('cairn of the milk pail', 838m) is even further east in the midst of rolling moorland and distant from any other high hills.

Scotland is at its narrowest here – just 43km wide – and these hills stretch almost coast to coast, from Loch Broom to the Cromarty Firth. The western hills of this region are steep and rocky, with cliffs and deep corries. Those to the east are more rounded and rolling. The southern summits are easily accessible from the A835 road but the northern ones are far from public roads in very remote country.

The terrain of these hills is complex and in places featureless, requiring good navigation skills. There is a mix of long moorland walks, steep rocky ascents and grassy ridges. Distances can be long, and multi-day trips for the northern summits are recommended. There is winter climbing on the cliffs of Beinn Dearg, too, and opportunities for ski touring when there is good snow cover.

Although there have been some hydro developments in this area – Loch Vaich and Loch Glascarnoch are both hydro reservoirs – the area is mostly wild and untouched except from overgrazing by deer and bulldozed estate roads. Some attempts at allowing the regeneration of the natural vegetation are taking place and there is a project on the Alladale Estate in the northeast of the region to restore extinct wildlife as well. Unfortunately the estate wishes to do this by enclosing a huge area (the estate includes Carn Ban and runs up to Seana Bhraigh) with a high electrified fence and restricting access, neither of which are acceptable. The aims of the estate are laudable but the proposed methods of achieving them are an attack on access rights and would lead to damage to the landscape with the fence and accompanying bulldozed road. The latter would also be a huge intrusion into the wild feel of the area.

🌐 Corrieshalloch Gorge ☆

Situated close to the Braemore Junction, where the A832 meets the A835 20km southeast of Ullapool, the deep and impressive defile of the Corrieshalloch

Gorge, a National Nature Reserve in the care of the National Trust for Scotland, is easily accessible. From the car park on the A832 a short path leads down to a suspension bridge – built by Sir John Fowler, one of the designers of the Forth Road Bridge, in 1867. From here you can look down the narrow tree-lined gorge to the Falls of Measach, where the Abhainn Droma drops 46m in a great waterfall. There is also a viewing platform extending out over the gorge. The gorge is 60m deep and over 1.5kms long. It was formed by a sudden rush of glacial meltwater some 10,000–13,000 years ago. A rich collection of plants grow on the walls of the gorge and attractive woodland lines the rim.

🌐 Beinn Enaiglair

Beinn Enaiglair rises above the A835 in Strath More and being closer to the road than the other Beinn Dearg hills it stands out in views from both the A835 and the A832 towards Braemore Junction. Beinn Enaiglair is really an outlier of Beinn Dearg, with a col between them at 650m, and the pair can easily be combined. As a hill it's rather nondescript but the views from the summit of the higher hills are good. The ascent starts just east of Braemore Junction on the path beside a forest fence to Home Loch, where a stalkers' path that encircles Beinn Enaiglair is joined. Turn right here, walk up to the col with Meall Doire Faid, then head north to the summit. A descent can be made eastwards down a little corrie to pick up the path again and follow it in either direction back to Home Loch, for a circuit of around 15km, with 840m of ascent, which takes 5–6hrs.

🌐 The hills around Beinn Dearg ☆

Beinn Dearg (1084m) is the highest summit north of the Dingwall to Ullapool road – no other hill this far north breaches 1000m – and a fine rocky mountain. It stands out in views down Loch Broom from Ullapool and the A835. Steep crags run along the northern and eastern slopes, with grassier, less steep slopes to the south and west. The first recorded ascent of Beinn Dearg was by three brothers – William, Charles and Robert Inglis – in either 1863 or 1872. Beinn Dearg is linked to Cona' Mheall by Bealach a' Choire Ghranda (850m), and the two hills are usually climbed together. Cona' Mheall is a stony hill with a long, narrow southern ridge. Coire Ghranda between the two hills is a fine wild corrie with a big lochan, lying below the Beinn Dearg cliffs. Just to the north of Beinn Dearg

The summit of Beinn Dearg from the north

are Meall nan Ceapraichean and Eididh nan Clach Geala, which are less distinctive hills, although in fine wild situations and with some crags on their slopes. They can easily be climbed with the two higher Munros from Inverlael at the head of Loch Broom. The route follows tracks through Lael Forest, then the path up long, narrow Gleann na Sguaib above the waterfalls and deep pools of the River Lael to the Bealach a' Choire Ghranda. From here bouldery slopes lead east to Cona' Mheall and southwest up steep, rocky ground to Beinn Dearg beside a dry stone wall that runs almost to the summit. There is a superb view of the east face of Beinn Dearg from Cona' Mheall. If not going on to the two northerly Munros descent can be made down the long northwest ridge of Beinn Dearg, again with the dry stone wall for company. There are cliffs to the north at first, but where the wall ends these give way and a steep descent can be made into Gleann na Sguaib and the outward path. If including the other two Munros return to Bealach a' Choire Ghranda, then head northwest to Meall nan Ceapraichean and then round the corrie holding Lochan a' Chnapaich to Eididh Clach nan Geala. There are good views west to Loch Broom and Ullapool from the three westerly Munros. The

descent can be made down the west ridge of Eididh Clach nan Geala to the path in Gleann na Sguaib. The round of the four Munros is 26km long, with 1400m of ascent, and takes 8–9hrs.

Beinn Dearg and Cona' Mheall can also be climbed from the south by a rougher, wilder and more strenuous route that starts on the A835 near the east end of Loch Droma and heads north to the boggy western corner of Loch a' Gharbhrain, where the Allt a' Gharbhrain has to be forded, which may not be safe or possible after heavy rain. Continue north past Loch Coire Lair, then climb steeply to the edge of Coire Ghranda and the south ridge of Cona' Mheall. The ascent of this narrow ridge involves a little easy scrambling. From Cona' Mheall cross the Bealach a' Choire Ghranda and follow the wall up Beinn Dearg. From the summit descend southwards along the edge of the cliffs to little Loch nan Eilean and on down to the Allt a' Gharbhrain. The distance is 18km, with 1130m of ascent, and the walk takes 6–7hrs.

✹ Winter Climbing on Beinn Dearg ☆

The cliffs of Beinn Dearg offer much winter climbing. There are routes on the south wall of Gleann na Sguaib and the West Buttress of the summit. On the

Gleann na Sguaib crags 150m Emerald Gully (Grade IV, first climbed by B. Fuller, P. Nunn and A. Riley in March 1970) and 170m Fenian Gully (Grade IV, first climbed by T.W. Patey in March 1968) are both given three stars in *Scottish Winter Climbs*, while on the West Buttress 350m Penguin Gully (Grade III, first climbed by T.W. Patey, W. H. Murray, N.S. Tennent in March 1964 – two of the great climbers of Scottish mountaineering, Patey and Murray, climbing together) gets four stars and 350m The Ice Hose (Grade V, first climbed by I. Dalley, D.M. Nicholls and G.S. Strange in April 1979) three stars.

⊗ Am Faochagach
The easternmost of the Beinn Dearg Munros, Am Faochagach is a big, bulky, rounded hill, the highest point in the large area of rolling hills between Loch Glascarnoch in the south, Gleann Beag in the north, Coire Lair in the west and Loch Vaich in the east. The going on these heathery, boggy hills is rough and often wet. The view west to the more exciting and shapely hills of Beinn Dearg and Cona' Mheall is the reward for climbing Am Faochagach. The quickest ascent route is from the west end of Loch Glascarnoch and up the southwestern slopes. This involves fording the Abhainn a'Garbhrain – which may be impossible when it is in spate – and then crossing the very boggy terrain between Loch a' Gharbhrain and Loch Glascarnoch. From the summit you could continue north to Loch Prille, splendidly situated among steep craggy slopes, with the cascades of the Steall Allt Lair tumbling from it into Coire Lair far below, and up the east ridge of Cona' Mheall and then onto Beinn Dearg for a circuit of Coire Lair. Otherwise retrace your steps, for a walk of 13km, with 750m of ascent, which takes 4–5hrs.

⊙ Ski Touring on Am Faochagach, Cona 'Mheall and Beinn Dearg ☆
The circuit of these three Munros is described as 'a magnificent ski-mountaineering expedition' in the SMC's *Ski Mountaineering in Scotland*, and given four stars. It's a Grade IV route, and so serious and technically demanding. The route starts with the ascent of the south ridge of Am Faochagach, followed by 'a long and easy descent' to Loch Prille and then an ascent of the east ridge of Cona 'Mheall on which crampons may be needed at the top. Steep slopes then lead down from Cona 'Mheall and up Beinn Dearg. The recommended descent, described as 'one of the finest downhill runs in the

district, one to be savoured', goes down the shallow corrie between the south and southwest ridges and then the Allt a' Garbhrain. The potential ski touring north of these hills to Seana Bhraigh should be excellent too, but the remoteness of the terrain would mean at least an overnight trip.

⊗ Beinn a'Chaisteil
Beinn a'Chaisteil lies at the northern end of a long, steep-sided broad ridge on the eastern side of Loch Vaich. The summit is 9km from the A835 at Black Bridge east of Loch Glascarnoch. A private road runs up Strath Vaich and alongside Loch Vaich. At the abandoned buildings of Lubachlaggan the southwest slopes of the hill can be climbed. The lower slopes are covered in deep heather, but there is an old, somewhat sketchy stalkers' path here. Higher up the vegetation is low and sparse and there is much stony ground, making for easier walking. There is a good view of Seana Bhraigh from the summit. To vary the descent head south down the ridge over Meall a'Ghrianain to a track between Strath Vaich and Strath Rannoch, for a total distance of 24km, with 940m of ascent. The walk takes 7–8hrs.

⊗ Seana Bhraigh ☆
Lying some 11km as the crow flies from the nearest public road and far more than that on foot, Seana Bhraigh is one of the contenders for remotest Munro. It's the high point and western end of a huge wedge of high ground that runs 18km from east to west. To the south is long Gleann Beag, to the north Strath Mulzie. Seana Bhraigh connects with the Beinn Dearg hills to the south, with which it is usually grouped, by a narrow 700m strip of land between the head of Gleann Beag and deep Cadha Dearg. Approached from the south Seana Bhraigh is a bulky, grassy hill, with the fine spire of Creag an Duine looking much more imposing than the summit. From the north, however, it is an impressive rock mountain with three huge cliff-rimmed corries, whose crags run for some 5km above Coire Mor. Because approaches are very long an overnight trip to Seana Bhraigh is recommended, perhaps combining its ascent with those of the four Munros to the south.

The most popular route is from Inverlael at the head of Loch Broom, by the path up Gleann a' Mhaidaidh and Coire an Lochain Sgeirich and then northeast over somewhat featureless terrain to the head of Cadha Dearg and the south slopes of

The summit of Seana Bhraigh

the summit. The walk along the edge of the Luchd Coire cliffs to the summit cairn is the highlight of the climb. There are superb views of An Teallach and the Coigach hills from the top. Return by the outward route, for a walk of 26km, with 1425m of ascent, which takes 8–9hrs.

A more spectacular route is that from the north up Strath Mulzie. Cars can be driven along the estate road to a parking area just before Corriemulzie Lodge. From here it is 9km to the foot of Seana Bhraigh and a dramatic view of the northern corries. The northwest ridge leads to the summit. Scramblers may wish to ascend the Creag an Duine ridge on the other side of Luchd Corrie, which leads to the little pointed top of An Sgurr and then Creag an Duine. The scramble is a Grade 1 or 2 depending on the exact route, and is exposed in places. Whichever ascent route is chosen the easiest descent is by the northwest ridge. The return walk from Corriemulzie Lodge is 22km, with 830m of ascent, and takes 7–9hrs.

⊗ Carn Ban
On the same great high plateau, Carn Ban, 6km east of Seana Bhraigh, is one of the remotest Corbetts. It's a big dome-shaped hill with little in the way of distinguishing features, although there are some craggy corries on the north side. The shortest ascent is from Strath Carron to the east via Alladale, a distance of 28km, with 970m of ascent, and a time of 8–9hrs. From the north it can be climbed from the car park near Corriemulzie Lodge in Strath Mulzie via Coire Mor, a round trip of 32km, with 800m of ascent, which takes 9–10hrs. A much longer route is that from Black Bridge to the south via Loch Vaich, Gleann Beag, Loch Sruban Mora and the south ridge. By this route it's 22km, with 650m of ascent one way. These long distances make Carn Ban a hill for multi-day trips, combining it with Seana Bhraigh and the Beinn Dearg hills.

⊗ Ben Wyvis and Little Wyvis
The massive bulk of Ben Wyvis (1046m) is clearly visible from the A9 road as it begins the descent to Inverness from the south. It forms a long, grassy, plateau-like ridge running north then curving northeast. Steep, smooth slopes run down to dense forestry plantations (some clear-felled in the 2000s) on the easily accessible west side. The more interesting but inaccessible and little-visited east side has long spurs and two big craggy corries – Coire na Feola and Choire Mhoir.

431

Ben Wyvis rising above the Garbat Forest

The first recorded ascent of Ben Wyvis was in 1767, by the same James Robertson who made the first recorded ascent of Ben Nevis. Robertson climbed the hill in June and had a snowstorm on the summit. He recorded that lower down the mountain snow 'lay underfoot to a considerable depth'. In his diaries, which are in the National Library of Scotland, Robertson says he navigated in the snowstorm by map and compass, which Ian R. Mitchell in *Scotland's Mountains Before the Mountaineers* (Luath, 1999) says this makes him 'possibly...the first mountaineer with rudimentary mountaineering equipment'. The accessibility of Ben Wyvis made it a popular tourist ascent long before any other mountains north of the Great Glen. In a 'Table of Mountains in Scotland' in *The Scottish Tourist*, edited by W.Rhind and published in 1825, Ben Wyvis is the only mountain beyond the Great Glen listed. By 1850, when most western and northern hills were still unknown, Ian R. Mitchell notes that Ben Wyvis was a standard tourist climb with a big cairn called 'The Monument' on the summit.

Today Ben Wyvis is a very popular climb, with an estimated 8000 ascents a year by the standard route. This begins at Garbat on the A835, where a footpath leads through the forest and up to the little top of An Cabar ('the antler', 950m) where the mossy summit ridge begins. Glas Leathad Mor ('big grey-green slope') is the name of the long, steep, smooth northwest side of the summit ridge and the actual summit itself. The view west to a huge panorama of mountains is inspiring. That east to the wind turbines on Meall an Tuirc is a reminder of the sad encroachment of industrial developments on wild land. The traverse can be continued on from Glas Leathad Mor to Tom a'Choinnich ('mossy hillock') and a descent of the southwest ridge of the latter to a path alongside the Allt a' Gharbh Bhaid and back through the forest to the start. The distance is 14km, with 1020m of ascent, and takes 5–6hrs.

Glas Leathad Beag ('little grey-green slope', 928m), is situated 3km east of Tom a' Choinnich, overlooking Loch Glass. This is listed in the 1997 Munro's *Tables* as a subsidiary top of Ben Wyvis, but its distance from Tom a'Choinnich with an intermediary top in between, and the final rise of 128m, makes it more of a distinct hill than some Munros. It should be listed as a Munro in future editions of the Tables.

Little Wyvis (746m) is a rather nondescript outlier of Ben Wyvis, lying south of the Allt a' Bhealaich Mhoir path to An Cabar, from which it can be easily climbed, for a round trip of 10km, with 620m of ascent, which takes 4–5hrs: or else it can be combined with Ben Wyvis.

☸ Ski Touring on Ben Wyvis ☆

The rounded slopes, smooth grassy terrain and ease of access make Ben Wyvis a good hill for ski touring. Indeed, the SMC's *Ski Mountaineering in Scotland* calls it 'one of the most important ski mountains in the Northern Highlands', and there have been proposals for a downhill ski resort, including the building of a funicular railway, most recently in 1999. Happily, no damaging developments have gone ahead and Ben Wyvis remains a mountain for real skiers. The standard ski tour on the mountain starts at Garbat and goes over Tom a' Choinnich and along the summit ridge over Glas Leathad Mor and then down the bowl of the Allt a' Bhealaich Mor for a long run to the forest and path back to Garbat. This route isn't difficult – Grade II – and is 17km long with 1000m of ascent. It takes 6–7hrs. The smooth slopes of Ben Wyvis can present avalanche danger – Martin Moran was avalanched here during his first continuous winter round of the Munros in 1985 – with the long north-west face between An Cabar and Tom a'Choinnich being particularly dangerous.

☸ Carn Chuinneag

The twin tops of Carn Chuinneag stand out among the rolling heather moorland hills of Easter Ross as it lies well to the east of any hills of comparable height. It can be easily climbed from Strath Carron to the north by way of Glen Calvie, which has some pleasant birch woods, and then stalkers' paths that lead almost to the summit. The round trip is 18km long with 750m of ascent and takes 4–5hrs.

6:6 COIGACH AND ASSYNT

The area from Ullapool north to Kylesku contains some of the most distinctive, unusual and interesting mountains in Scotland, including the iconic peaks of Stac Pollaidh and Suilven. The region is divided by the major geological feature of the Moine Thrust and its associated thrust faults (see Knockan Crag below). The road from Ullapool to Kylesku, which is the main access route for the hills, runs along the edge of the thrust zone. To the west of the road, in the district of Coigach, isolated Torridonian sandstone hills, some capped with silvery quartzite, rise in strange contorted shapes from low undulating boggy moorland known as 'cnoc an lochain' (knolls and pools). The base

rock here is ancient Lewisian gneiss, which drains badly and only forms poor thin soil, hence the watery landscape. These hills are not high – there are no Munros – but they are definitely mountains with steep sides, pointed summits and cliffs. Six of the hills reach Corbett height (between 762 and 914 metres), and five are Grahams (between 610 and 762 metres). From the south they are: Ben Mor Coigach ('big hill of Coigach', 743m); Sgurr an Fhidhleir ('peak of the fiddler', 705m); Beinn an Eoin ('hill of the bird', 619m); Cul Beag ('little back', 769m); Stac Pollaidh ('the stack at the pool', 612m); Cul Mor ('big back', 849m); Suilven ('the pillar', 731m); Canisp ('white hill', 847m); and Quinag ('milk pail'), which has three summits, all Corbetts – Spidean Coinich ('mossy peak', 764m), Sail Gorm ('blue heel', 776m) and Sail Gharbh ('rough heel', 808m). Bounded by sea lochs to the south (Loch Broom) and north (Loch a' Chairn Bhain and Loch Glencoul), Coigach is a wide, blunt peninsula curving round huge Enard Bay with headlands at Rubha Coigeach in the south and the Point of Stoer in the north.

Across the thrust zone to the east, in Assynt, a long ridge of more conventionally shaped higher mountains runs from south to north. Two Munros and two Corbetts lie on or adjacent to this ridge: Breabag ('little height', 815m), Conival ('adjoining hill', 987m); Ben More Assynt ('big hill of Assynt', 998m) and Glas Bheinn ('grey-green hill', 776m). Along the western base of these hills, among the turmoil of the Moine Thrust, is a band of creamy Durness limestone, giving rise to the rich fertile green fields around Elphin and Inchnadamph, plus limestone pavements and caves along the Allt nan Uamh and the River Traligill, a most unusual landscape in the Highlands and the largest area of limestone in the whole of Scotland. At the north end of the Assynt hills is Eas a' Chual Aluinn, the highest waterfall in Britain.

The name Coigach comes from the Gaelic for a fifth, and refers to a land division while Assynt is from the Norse *ass* meaning a rocky ridge.

The steep, rocky terrain of most of the Coigach and Assynt hills means there are plenty of opportunities for scrambling and rock climbing, plus winter climbing when conditions are right. Walkers can climb almost all the hills without any scrambling, but the terrain is often rough and steep and there are many routes for backpackers both over and through the hills.

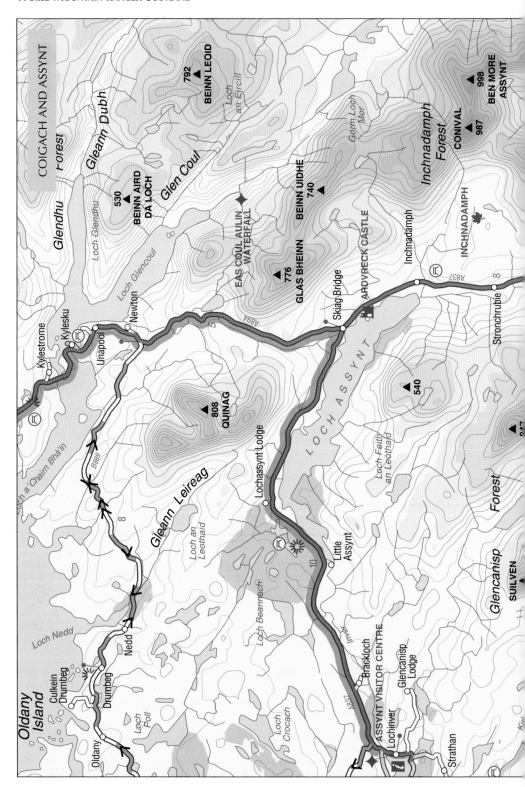

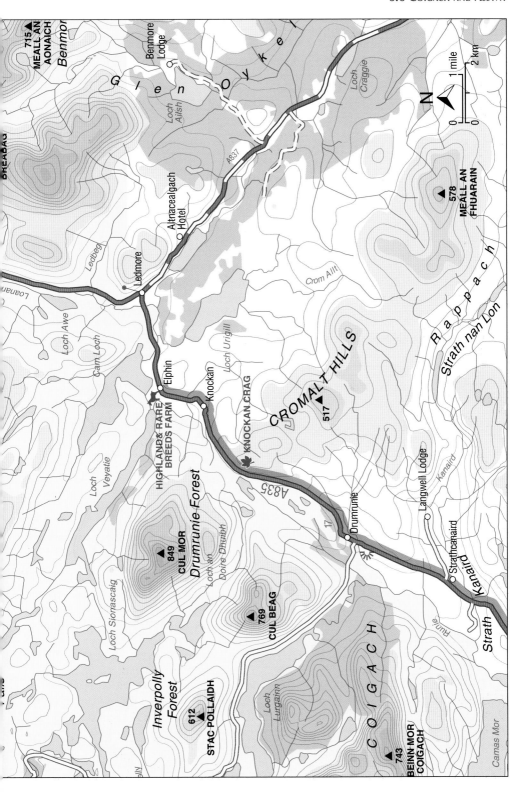

715 ▲
MEALL AN
AONAICH

Benmore

G l e n   O y k e l

Benmore
Lodge

Loch
Ailsh

Loch
Craggie

N

0   1 mile
0   2 km

A837

Altnacealgach
Hotel

Ledbeg

Ledmore

Loch Awe

Loch Veyatie

Cam Loch

Loanan

MEALL AN
FHUARAIN
578 ▲

Crom Allt

R a p p a c h

Strath nan Lon

Elphin

Knockan

Loch Urigill

KNOCKAN CRAG

CROMALT HILLS

517 ▲

HIGHLAND & RARE
BREEDS FARM

Drumrunie Forest

A835

Langwell Lodge

Kanaird

Loch
Veyatie

849 ▲
CUL MOR

Loch an
Doire Dhuibh

Drumrunie

Strathcanaird

Loch Sionascaig

Inverpolly
Forest

769 ▲
CUL BEAG

Loch
Lurgainn

C O I G A C H

Strath Kanaird

Runie

612 ▲
STAC POLLAIDH

BEINN MOR
COIGACH
743 ▲

Camas Mor

As well as the Ullapool–Kylesku road (numbered A835 to Ledmore Junction, A837 to Skiag Bridge and A894 to Kylesku) the area can be accessed by the A837 from Bonar Bridge to the southeast. At Skiag Bridge the A837 turns west and runs to Lochinver from where a minor single track road runs south back to Ullapool.

The main centre for the area is Ullapool, which has all facilities, including a large campsite and an excellent café/restaurant/bookshop called The Ceilidh Place. The town is quite an artistic centre, with many local artists and the Bridge House Art School. Away from Ullapool there is a scattering of hotels, B&Bs and cafés, including the Inchnadamph Hotel on the A837 at the head of Loch Assynt, which has long been popular with walkers and climbers, and the excellent independent hostel at nearby Inchnadamph Lodge. Refreshments can also be had at the excellent tea room at Elphin near Knockan Crag. On the coast the attractive little fishing port of Lochinver gives access to Suilven and Canisp, and has all facilities, including the wonderful Lochinver Larder, which serves truly amazing pies, a real treat after a long day on the hill. South of Lochinver is the village of Inverkirkaig, where you can find the excellent Achins tearoom, craft shop and bookshop. In Kylesku there is the fine Kylesku Hotel plus other facilities. There are also campsites at Ardmair just north of Ullapool, Achnahaird on the coast on the south side of Enard Bay, and Achmelvich, northwest of Achmelvich. In the hills there are many fine wild sites.

Large parts of Coigach are now owned by organisations committed to conservation and restoration. Since 2005 the Assynt Foundation, set up by the local community with the aid of the John Muir Trust, has owned Suilven, Canisp, Cul Mor and the Cam Loch, while the John Muir Trust itself owns Quinag.

❷ ❶ Ben Mor Coigach and Sgurr an Fhidleir ☆

Big, complex, multi-topped hills rise at either end of the Coigach hills – Quinag in the north and Ben Mor Coigach in the south. With two Grahams and five other tops, Ben Mor Coigach is a small mountain range rather than a single mountain. It takes the form of two long ridges, one running southwest, one northwest, each with lines of big cliffs on the outer faces, plus a shorter ridge running southwest from the north end of the massif. Ben Mor Coigach

lies in the middle of the 3km long southwest ridge, which presents a huge wall of rock to the southeast, a vast, gully-riven cliff that looks dramatic from Ardmair on the A835. This high wall gives the impression that Ben Mor Coigach is just this long ridge, as it blocks the view of the other ridges plus the peaks, cliffs and corries of the northern and southern sides. Sgurr an Fhidhleir lies in the middle of the northwest ridge. A splendid view of the mountain in all its glory is that from Loch Broom to the south, either from the Ullapool–Stornoway ferry or the day trip from Ullapool to the Summer Isles (a recommended excursion). Ben Mor Coigach also looks good from the minor road that runs from Drumrunie on the A835 past the north side and then via Achiltibuie to its terminus at Culnacraig below the south side. There is a rough, exciting and dramatic coastal path running from Culnacraig across the steep base of the southwest ridge to Blughasary at the end of a minor road 1km west of the A835 at Strath Canaird.

The traverse of Ben Mor Coigach is one of the finest walks in the Northern Highlands. It can be done from the west, north or south, although the first two involve going out and back along the ridges to include all the tops, so I think the southern ascent from Culnacraig is preferable. The route starts steeply, with a climb onto the blunt end of the southwest ridge, named Garbh Choireachan ('rough corries') on the map, although this must surely apply to the corries either side. Once on the narrow ridge follow it, with some optional easy scrambling, to Ben Mor Coigach, with magnificent views along Loch Broom and over the rest of the mountain. Continue on to the junction with the northwest ridge and follow this to the spectacular, pointed summit of Sgurr an Fhidhleir, with superb views down the steep cliffs to the north to Lochan Tuath. Descend via Beinn nan Caorach to the west, for a round trip of 11km, with 1125m of ascent, which takes 5–6hrs.

The ascent from the north goes via Lochan Tuath and the col south of Sgurr an Fhidhleir, with a descent via the east-northeast ridge over Beinn Tarsuinn. That from the west, which is the quickest to reach by road, follows a track from Blughasary to Loch Eadar dha Bheinn and then up the east shoulder of Speicin Coinnich to the east of Ben Mor Coigach. Descend the same way, or down Garbh Choireachan and along the coastal path from Culnacraig.

Stac Pollaidh from the east

There are some scrambling alternatives for the ascent of Ben Mor Coigach on its south face. Of these the SMC's *Highland Scrambles North* gives the Grade 3 West Ridge Direct two stars.

Climbing on Sgurr an Fhidhleir
The north side of Sgurr an Fhidhleir is a huge and impressive buttress known as the Fiddler's Nose. Many attempts were made to climb this, starting in 1907, before N. Drasdo and C. M. Dixon succeeded in 1962. The route is graded HVS, and is 300m long. Winter conditions are rare this low and this close to the sea, but when these do occur Fiddler's Nose is 'a superb climb of alpine stature graded VII', according to the SMC's *North-West Highlands*.

Stac Pollaidh ☆
Although the lowest of the Coigach hills little Stac Pollaidh is also the most mountainous, a pinnacled crest of shattered sandstone atop steep scree slopes, whose highest point cannot be reached without scrambling. It rises directly above the road to Achiltibuie, and so is very accessible from the south. Its distinctive profile is easily identifiable from near and far. The sandstone of Stac Pollaidh is quite soft and easily eroded by the weather, hence the strange spires and towers of the summit ridge. Feet can erode the mountain too, and the old path directly up the east face became an ugly and potentially dangerous scar, so a new path was built, curving round the mountain to make a complete circuit with a branch running up to the summit ridge from the north. The usual way to reach the path to the summit ridge is round the eastern end of the mountain. The path reaches the ridge towards the eastern end, and there is then a scramble along the crest to the highest point, which lies at the west end. The scramble is spectacular and exciting, but not particularly difficult or exposed, until immediately before the summit where a short tower blocks the way. The few moves up this are graded Difficult. The lower east end of the ridge is much easier to reach. The view from the summit ridge over Loch Sionascaig to Suilven is wonderful. The round trip, encircling the mountain with an ascent to the top, is 5km long, with 550m of ascent, and takes 3–4hrs.

Rock Climbing on Stac Pollaidh
There are many short rock climbs on the Stac Pollaidh cliffs. The Western Buttress Route (90m), the direct route to the summit from the west, was first climbed by Charles Walker, Dr. William Inglis Clark, Mrs Jane Inglis Clark and Miss Mabel Inglis

Clark in 1906 (the last two founded The Ladies' Scottish Climbing Club in 1908). The grade is debateable, as *Highland Scrambles North* says 'it's given Difficult in climbing guides but is severely undergraded'. Other climbs on the mountain are definitely much harder. On the Western Buttress these include 88m November Grooves, a Very Severe first climbed by D. Stewart and G. Cairns in 1954, and on the southeast face 60m Walking On Air, an E4 first climbed by T. Prentice and R. Anderson in 1989, and 40m Expecting to Fly, an E3 first climbed by T. Prentice in 1988.

⊗ ❸ Cul Mor and Cul Beag ☆

These two Corbetts both have broad, relatively gentle slopes on their east sides and crags on the steep north and west faces. Cul Mor is twin-topped, each summit having a small cap of quartzite. Cul Beag is smaller in area, as well as lower, and has one distinct summit. The pair can be climbed together from the A835 at Knockan Crag. Going anticlockwise the ascent starts just north of Lochan an Ais, where a path climbs onto the east shoulder of Cul Mor, which is built of pale quartzite rather than dark sandstone, like most of the mountain. The route curves round the edge of the crags of Coire

Gorm to Cul Mor, the highest peak in Coigach. To the west lies big island-dotted Loch Sionascaig, which has an amazingly convoluted shape, while to the north Suilven and Canisp rise above a vast area of rock and water. If not going on to Cul Beag descent can be made by heading south to the lower top of Creag nan Calman, then east across rough terrain to join the outward route. For the continuation to Cul Beag head east from Creag nan Calman, then head south and round the nose of An Laogh to Lochan Dearg, and a climb to the north ridge not far below the summit. There is a good view of the northern cliffs of Ben Mor Coigach from the top. Descend the east ridge to a path that reaches the A835 1km south of the start. The walk is 17km long, with 1600m of ascent, and takes 7–8hrs.

There are scrambling opportunities on both hills, including Table Rib on the southwest face of Cul Mor and Lurgainn Edge on the east face of Cul Beag, both Grade 3. *Highland Scrambles North* gives Lurgainn Edge three stars and describes it as 'an outstanding route' with 'superb situations'. However it's worth noting that the author also says that it is 'traditionally graded Difficult but really more of a scramble' and that the SMC's *North-West Highlands* gives it as Very Difficult.

Cul Mor and the Cam Loch

Quotation from the geologist James Hutton on the Crag Top Trail at Knockan Crag

Knockan Crag ☆

Knockan Crag is a little cliff rising above the A835 a few kilometres southwest of Elphin, opposite Cul Mor and Cul Beag. In an area of spectacular mountains it doesn't stand out and would be bypassed by everybody but for its international geological importance. It lies on the Moine Thrust and is protected in the Knockan Crag National Nature Reserve, run by Scottish Natural Heritage, which has built an unstaffed visitor centre below the crag with interpretative and interactive displays, plus three circular trails with geological information, rock art and fragments of poetry by Norman MacCaig, whose writing was inspired by this landscape. The Northwest Geo Park (see under 'Topography and Geology' in the introduction'), established in 2004, runs north from Knockan Crag to Cape Wrath. It was in this area that two geologists named Benjamin Peach and John Horne worked in the 1880s and 1890s. At that time the scientific orthodoxy was that rock strata were laid down in chronological order so that newer rocks always overlaid older rocks. But along the line of the Moine Thrust this didn't make sense, as billion year old Moine schists lay on top of 500 million year old Cambrian limestone. Through their fieldwork Peach and Horne showed that over millennia earth movements had forced older rocks sideways over younger rocks, creating a low-angle fault line called a thrust. At Knockan Crag this can be seen clearly, with the dark schists lying over the pale limestone. You can place your hand over the 500 million year gap. Thrusts occur when continents collide and form mountain ranges as they push against each other, squeezing the rocks and forcing them upwards. This happened some 440 to 410 million years ago, when the continent of Laurentia, containing what was to become Scotland, Greenland and North America, collided with continents containing England and Scandinavia. The Caledonian mountain range was formed where they met and along the Moine Thrust Moine schists were pushed westwards over younger sedimentary rocks. There is a memorial to Peach and Horne on the shores of Loch Assynt not far to the north.

Knockan Crag is almost 2km long. The name comes from the Gaelic *creag a' cnocain*, meaning 'crag of the small hill'. The Crag Top Trail runs from the Visitor Centre over the Moine Thrust and along the top of the crag, where there are superb views of Cul Mor. The walk takes about 1hr.

The information provided at Knockan Crag is just a simple introduction to the geology of the area. For those interested in learning more I recommend the British Geological Survey's *Exploring the Landscape of Assynt* (2004), which is a walkers' guidebook and 1:50,000 geological map about the geology and landscape of Assynt and Coigach.

A Circuit of the Cam Loch

There are many beautiful wild lochs in Coigach and Assynt, all worthy of a visit. The circuit of the Cam Loch, which lies north of Elphin and west of Ledmore Junction, is particularly fine and gives exceptional views of Suilven and Cul Mor. Like many lochs in the area the Cam Loch has a convoluted shoreline with many bays and promontories, which probably gave rise to its name, *cam* meaning 'crooked' or 'distorted'. During the ice age the glaciers in this area flowed southeast to northwest, and this is the line lochs take today, following fault lines where weaknesses in the rocks were gouged out by ice and meltwater. The Cam Loch follows this pattern, and also has the Moine Thrust running across the southeast end.

Suilven from the southeast

The walk round the loch starts on the A835 just east of the bridge over the Ledmore River, where a signpost pointing northwest says 'Lochinver 12 Miles'. The path runs up a low knoll from where the loch suddenly comes into view, with the distinctive profile of Suilven rising beyond the far end, a dramatic sight. The path follows the northern shore of the loch, with superb views southwest to twin-topped Cul Mor, while ahead Suilven draws you on. There's a scattering of trees beside the loch, softening the harsh water, rock and bog landscape. Where the Lochinver path turns north stay with the loch and follow it cross country over grass, heather, peat bog, flat rocks and shingle beaches to its head, where there is a lovely sandy beach and a bright green sward of grass, with crags rising above it, a wonderful lunch spot. Returning along the south side of the loch the easiest going is away from the shore on the little knolls above, which give good views over the water. The lush green limestone landscape around Elphin stands out ahead as you tramp back to the A835. The walk is 13km long, and takes 4–5hrs.

⊗ ⬦ Suilven ☆

If one peak symbolises the far northwest of Scotland it is Suilven, an iconic mountain with a distinctive shape and a grandeur that belies its height. Suilven is a long slice of dark Torridonian sandstone, steeply terraced on every side. There are two pointed peaks at the east end – Meall Bheag ('little hill', 610m) and Meall Mheadhonach ('middle hill', 723m) – and a steep-sided dome at the west end, Caisteal Liath ('grey castle', 721m). Seen from the east Suilven looks like a fine spire, from the west a steep bulbous cone. From the south and north the whole ridge can be seen with a low point just off centre, the Bealach Mor ('big pass'), and a pointed peak at the east end and a rounded one at the west. From every direction Suilven looks magnificent. The name is reckoned to be Norse from *sulur*, meaning 'pillar' with *bheinn* (pronounced 'ven') added by Gaelic speakers. It's clearly visible from the sea and was probably a landmark for the Vikings as they sailed down the coast.

Situated in the heart of a vast area of loch, bog and hill, between the Ullapool–Kylesku road and the coast, Suilven is quite remote, with long approaches needed to reach it. There is a path from Elphin to Lochinver that passes by the north side, and this is the usual access route. By this path it's 11km from Elphin to the base of Suilven and 10km from Lochinver. However the finest route starts at Inverkirkaig, crosses Suilven from south to north and finishes at Lochinver. From Inverkirkaig Bridge below the Achins tearoom and bookshop take the path through the lovely woods above the River Kirkaig to the dramatic Falls of Kirkaig, where the river drops 18m down a bowl of tree-lined cliffs in a powerful waterfall. From the falls the path climbs up to long, thin Fionn Loch ('fair loch') and Suilven comes dramatically into view. Head round the loch until below the Bealach Mor, where a path climbs steeply up to the pass. Bizarrely, a seemingly point-less dry stone wall crosses the ridge just above the pass. The ascent to the surprisingly extensive sum-mit of Caisteal Liath from the Bealach is steep and rough, but just a walk. The views are stupendous – west to Lochinver and the island-dotted sea, with the Western Isles a dark line on the horizon, south to Cul Mor and Stac Pollaidh and the distant jag-ged silhouette of An Teallach, north to multi-topped Quinag with the faint lines of Arkle and Foinaven in the distance and east to the nearby whaleback of Canisp with, beyond it, the long dark line of the Ben More Assynt hills. And all around a silvery, watery landscape shining and sparkling, ground out by the ice that scoured away the flanks of Suilven, leaving the mountain we so admire. Caisteal Liath is surrounded by steep crags on three sides, so the only descent route is back to the Bealach Mor. The two eastern summits can be now be climbed, but

this involves sections of Grade 2 or 3 scrambling, exposed in places. From the Bealach Mor descend northeast, down steep loose slopes at first, to the path to Lochinver, which is 6km by road from Inverkirkaig. The walk is 26km long, with 1350m of ascent, and takes 7–8hrs.

⊘ Canisp

Lying some 4km east of Suilven Canisp is a steep-sided ridge without the buttresses and ter-races of its neighbour. In fact it has little in the way of distinguishing features at all, but is easily accessible from the east, and its isolated loca-tion makes it a superb viewpoint. Suilven and Quinag look particularly impressive from the sum-mit. The climb starts on the A837 4km north of Ledmore Junction, at the north end of Loch Awe, and goes up the wide southeast ridge. The round trip is 12km long, with 690m of ascent, and takes 4–5hrs. A more interesting walk is to traverse the mountain, descending the northwest ridge to the Elphin–Lochinver path. Best of all is an overnight trip taking in both Canisp and Suilven.

⊘ Quinag ☆

Quinag is the northernmost of the Coigach hills, and the northernmost of the long line of Torridonian sandstone mountains that runs north

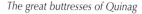

The great buttresses of Quinag

from Applecross. One of the great mountains of the Northern Highlands, it's a small mountain range rather than a single peak, with three summits on three huge buttresses divided by huge rocky corries and deep cols. The shape is that of a curved letter 'Y' some 6km long, with a summit on each arm. The big corries lie on the eastern side. To the west a massive unbroken wall of crags runs the length of the mountain. The two northern peaks, Sail Gorm and Sail Gharbh, are steep-sided, with massive cliffs towering over Kylesku, from where they look particularly impressive. The southern summit, Spidean Coinich, has a long, easy angled east ridge. This ridge is composed of quartzite that has been gently tilted by earth movements, so it slopes towards the east, presenting an easier angle of ascent than if it was horizontal. Between Spidean Coinich and Sail Gharbh is a lovely wild corrie containing Lochan Bealach Cornaidh. At the top of the corrie's headwall is the Bealach Chornaidh at 570m, the lowest point on Quinag.

The traverse of Quinag over all three summits is a very fine walk with interesting terrain throughout and tremendous views. It's also very unusual to be able to climb three Corbetts on one mountain. The route starts at the high point of the A894 from Skiag Bridge to Kylesku, and climbs the east ridge of Spidean Coinich, which mostly consists of bare quartzite, to the quartzite blocks that make up the summit. These loose boulders show that Spidean Coinich protruded out of the ice during the last ice age, as otherwise ice movements would have removed them. There is also a blockfield, as this feature is known, on Sail Gharbh, so it too was ice free during the last ice age. Descend north from Spidean Coinich to the Bealach Chornaidh and leave the pale quartzite for dark sandstone. North of the bealach is a 745m unnamed minor top, the heart of the mountain, which is the point from which the three big ridges radiate. From this top climb north to the summit of Sail Gorm and a grand view southeast over the corrie of Bathaich Cuinneige to the big cliffs on the northwest face of Sail Gharbh and northwest to island-dotted Eddrachillis Bay. Return to the 745m col and head east to Sail Gharbh, the highest summit on Quinag and more dramatic views, this time down to Lochan Bealach Cornaidh with the cliffs of Spidean Coinich rising above the dark waters. Returning over the 745m top for the third time descend from the Bealach a' Chornaidh, steeply at first, to Lochan

Bealach Cornaidh, set in a magnificent situation below the Spidean Coinich cliffs, and a stalkers' path that leads out of the boulder-strewn corrie and back to the start. The walk is 13km long with 1165m of ascent and takes 6–7hrs.

❸ Climbing and Scrambling on Quinag

On the huge cliffs of Sail Gharbh there is a Grade 3 scrambling route up the East Buttress, described in *Highland Scrambles North* as 'technically quite hard in places but without much exposure'. On Barrel Buttress to the west, the biggest and most impressive of Quinag's rock faces, Original Route, a 270m Very Difficult, was first climbed by Raeburn, Mackay and Ling in 1907 and then in winter in 1995 by Simon Richardson and Roger Webb for a Grade VI route described as 'formidable' in the SMC's *North-West Highlands*. On the western cliffs 150m The Water Pipe, a winter Grade II first climbed by Tom Patey in 1965, is described as 'one of the finest deep gullies in Scotland'.

❼ The Bone Caves ☆

High on the side of the lovely limestone glen of the Allt nan Uamh ('burn of the caves'), below the summit of Creag nan Uamh ('crag of the caves'), are four caves where excavations have found the bones of wolves, bears, lynx, arctic foxes and reindeer dating from a time when the climate was much colder. Human artefacts in the caves date back to the Iron Age (700BC to AD500), some may be much earlier. The walk to the Bone Caves is a delightful short excursion through limestone scenery most unusual in the Highlands. The walk starts at a car park on the A837 by a salmon hatchery 6km north of Ledmore Junction. A path runs up the glen to the caves, passing waterfalls, cream-coloured limestone crags and bright green grassland covered with flowers in spring and summer. The river emerges 1km from the road at a mass of rocks at the base of a crag, a spring called Fuaran Allt nan Uamh. Above this spring the river bed is dry except after heavy rain, the water having percolated through the limestone higher up the glen and flowed underground. After another 500m take the right fork at a junction and climb across steep slopes on a narrow path to the Bone Caves. The caves are quite shallow and safe to enter. They don't connect with any other caves or underground passages, but there is an entrance to the longest cave system in Scotland, the Uamh an Claonaite,

Conival and Ben More Assynt from the south ridge of Ben More Assynt

not far away. Return by the same route for a 4km walk, with 200m of ascent, which takes 1–2hrs, or else continue on to Breabag (see below).

The Traligill Caves ☆

Another glen runs through limestone scenery to more caves 4km north of the Bone Caves. This is Traligill – Norse for 'ravine of the trolls' – a place that also has the Gaelic name Gleann Dubh ('black glen'). The short walk starts at Inchnadamph and follows a track to Glenbain, then a path beside the River Traligill. The scenery is typical of that known as karst limestone, with clints and grykes – blocks of limestone divided by clefts, sinkholes, springs, dry valleys and caves. After 2km the river emerges at a spring known as the Traligill Rising. The river bed for the next few hundred metres is dry except after heavy rain. Then the first cave, the Lower Traligill Cave, comes into view, with the river pouring into it. After another 500m three caves can be seen above the river to the south. Head up to these caves to see the Allt a' Bhealaich pouring down Uamh an Uisge ('Cave of the Water'). Uamh an Tartair ('Cave of the Roaring') is dry. These caves give access to a large underground system for experienced cavers. Others should view them from outside, especially those with streams running into them, as these can be very slippery. The round trip to these caves is

6km long, with 150m of ascent, and takes 2hrs. There are good views of Loch Assynt and Quinag during the walk back to Inchnadamph.

Breabag

Breabag is the southernmost of the line of peaks to the west of the Ledmore Junction–Kylesku road. It forms a 7km long, broad whaleback ridge with craggy corries on the east side. The most direct and interesting ascent route is along the Bone Caves path from the A837 described above. Where the path forks either stay beside the stream and follow it up to the ridge just over 1km north of the summit, or climb up to the caves and continue east up to the top. Descend by one of the same routes, for a walk of 10km, with 680m of ascent, which takes 3–4hrs. Alternatively take the ridge north down to the narrow col with Conival, which looks very impressive, and descend beside the Allt a'Bhealaich to the Traligill Caves and Inchnadamph, 4km north of the start point.

Conival and Ben More Assynt ☆

The two highest peaks in Coigach and Assynt, and the only Munros, are steep, rough and rocky, but not distinctive or memorable like Quinag, Suilven or Stac Pollaidh, but despite this the ascent of the pair is a fine walk, with interesting terrain underfoot and splendid views. Despite the distance north the first recorded ascent of Ben More Assynt was in 1863 when it was climbed by the three Inglis brothers, Robert, Charles and William. The Inglis brothers climbed abroad as well as in Scotland and Ian R. Mitchell says in *Scotland's Mountains Before the Mountaineers* (Luath, 1999) that 'these men are as near to crossing that line from mountain lover to mountaineer as we can get', quoting Robert's son, J. G. Inglis, that 'they very early embraced the cult of the 3000ft peak…in jottings of my father's tours, going back to 1846, only peaks over 3000 ft are ever mentioned by name'. I hope having come this far north this doesn't mean that they ignored Quinag, Suilven and the other Coigach peaks, but I suspect that it does.

The standard route for the two peaks starts at Inchnadamph and follows the path beside the River Traligill (see Traligill Caves above), continuing up the glen to a bealach 1km north of Conival, from where the path zigzags up the quartzite screes of the north ridge to the summit and a spectacular view of the Coigach peaks. To the east a long, narrow ridge of broken quartzite connects Conival with Ben More Assynt 1.5km away. This ridge makes for an exciting walk with great views into the rocky corries either side. Ben More Assynt has twin tops – the most northerly is the highest. The easiest way back to Inchnadamph is to retrace your steps. A more interesting if harder alternative is to follow the narrow rocky ridge to the South Top of Ben More Assynt, which involves some very easy scrambling, and then over Carn nan Conbhairean, from where a steep, rough descent can be made to Dubh Loch Mor ('big black loch') in Garbh Corrie ('rough corrie'), an impressive spot with the two Munros rising steeply above. From the loch climb west to the col between Conival and Breabag and descend the Allt a' Bhealaich to Traligill. The walk is 19km long, with 1450m of ascent, and takes 8–9hrs.

Glas Bheinn

Glas Bheinn lies at the northwestern tip of the long ridge that runs south over Conival and Breabag and can be quickly and easily climbed from the high point on the A894 between Skiag Bridge and Kylesku by the northwest ridge. There are screes on the west side of the hill and crags on the north but the summit is flat and extensive. The views are excellent, especially of Quinag just across the A894 to the west. Return the same way

for a walk of 6km, with 550m of ascent, which takes around 3hrs.

The Glas Bheinn–Conival–Breabag Ridge ☆

The traverse of the long ridge from Glas Bheinn over Conival to Breabag is one of the best high-level walks in the Northern Highlands. It's 15km from the summit of Glas Bheinn to the summit of Breabag, nearly all of which is above 700m. The low point is the 500m col between Conival and Breabag. From the summit of Glas Bheinn the ridge runs southeast over long 740m Beinn Uidhe, before turning south at Loch nan Cuaran and crossing Beinn an Fhurain to the north ridge of Conival. Going out and back to Ben More Assynt adds 3km and 250m of ascent to the traverse, but is well worth the effort. From Conival descend to the low point, then climb Breabag and make a final descent down the Allt nan Uamh to the A837. This is some 12km from the start, so transport back will need to be arranged. Throughout the walk the immediate scenery and terrain are interesting and varied, and there are continuous views of the Coigach peaks to the west. The total distance is 22km, with 1750m of ascent (25km and 2000m if Ben More Assynt is included), and the walk takes 10–12hrs.

Eas a'Chual Aluinn ☆

Eas a'Chual Aluinn is the highest waterfall in Britain, with a drop of 200m. It lies in the glen of the Abhainn an Loch Bhig to the south of Loch Glencoul and Loch Beag. The fall isn't on the main stream, but on a side one that crashes down into the glen. It was formed during the ice age when a glacier deepened the glen, cutting through the stream channel and leaving the water to fall down the ice-carved cliffs. Although the highest fall it's nowhere near the most powerful according to Louis Stott's *The Waterfalls of Scotland* (Aberdeen University Press, 1987). Stott says that it discharges around 250 litres of water per second, which is nothing compared to the 1600 litres of the Falls of Glomach (see Chapter 5:8). Much more powerful still are the Falls of Kirkaig (see under Suilven above), which discharge 7000 litres per second. Eas a'Chual Aluinn is still impressive, both for its height and its situation on an open hillside rather than in a ravine like many waterfalls. The surrounding landscape is wild and spectacular too.

Eas a'Chual Aluinn means 'Splendid Falls of Coul'. An alternative local name is the Maiden's

On the ascent of Ben Hope in a late winter storm

Tresses from a legend about a girl who threw herself over the cliff rather than marry a man she didn't love, her long hair spreading out to become the waterfall.

Eas a'Chual Aluinn can be viewed on one of the regular boat trips from Kylesku up Loch Glencoul and Loch Beag. On foot it can be reached from the A894 road at Loch na Gainmhich via Loch a' Bealach a'Bhuirich ('loch of the pass of roaring') and the Bealach a'Bhuirich, a splendid rough and rocky walk through typical cnoc and lochan scenery, with grand views back to Quinag. This route brings you out at the top of the waterfall. Continue along the cliffs a short way southeast, to where most of the falls can be seen from the side with Loch Beag and Loch Glencoul beyond them. Another 500m takes you beyond the cliffs to open slopes leading down to the Abhainn an Loch Bhig. Once down in the narrow glen head northwest to where it widens out, and the long thin line of the falls can be seen tumbling down the cliffs. The easiest route back to the start is to retrace your steps. A more interesting but more arduous alternative is to continue down the glen and along the south shore of Loch Beag to where the loch narrows, before widening again as Loch Glencoul. Cliffs bar the way here, traversed by a narrow, exposed path high above the water. Instead of following this path an ascent can be made southwest up steep, rocky terrain, with many broken crags, to Cnoc na Creige, from where an easy descent can be made back to Loch na Gainmhich. This walk is 13km long, with 1000m of ascent, and takes 5–6hrs.

6:7 THE FAR NORTH

North of Coigach and Assynt the watery cnoc and lochan landscape continues along with a series of impressive mountains, mostly made of glistening, silvery quartzite. The hills are further inland than to the south, many on the watershed between the west and north coasts. There are eight Corbetts and six Grahams here but no Munros, but as with Coigach this does not mean a lack of splendour or ruggedness, and in Foinaven the area has one of the finest hills in Scotland. From the south the hills are: Beinn Leoid ('hill of the slope', 792m); Meall a' Chuail ('hill of the cudgel', 750m); Meall an Fheur Loch ('grassy hill of the loch', 613m); Ben Hee ('fairy hill', 873m); Beinn Direach ('straight hill', 688m); Carn an Tionail ('cairn of the gathering place', 759m); Meallan Liath Coire Mhic Dhughaill ('little grey hill of the corrie of Dougal's son', 801m); Ben Stack ('steep hill', 721m); Sabhal Beag ('little barn', 732m); Meall Horn ('hill of the eagle', 777m); Arkle ('ark hill', 787m); Foinaven ('wart mountain', 911m); Cranstackie ('rocky peak', 800m); and Beinn Spionnaidh ('hill of strength', 772m), the most northerly mountain in Scotland. East of these hills the landscape is one of undulating moorland and large lochs. However towards the north there are three major peaks – the two most northerly Munros, Ben Klibreck ('hill of the cliff slope', 962m) and Ben Hope ('hill of the bay', 927m), and one of the finest Corbetts, Ben Loyal ('law hill', 764m).

As well as the hills the coast of the far north is spectacular and wild, especially the section from Kinlochbervie to Sandwood Bay and on to Cape Wrath, the northwestern point of the Scottish mainland, then east to the Kyle of Durness, one of the big sea lochs that bite inland along the north coast.

This northern part of Sutherland – 'the south land of the Vikings' – is the least populated and remotest area on the mainland of Scotland. Distances are long, roads narrow and facilities few. There are no small towns – Ullapool to the south and Lairg to the southeast being the nearest – and only a few small villages – Kylesku in the southwest, Durness and Tongue on the north coast – with many facilities. The even tinier settlements of Altnaharra in the east and Scorrie, Kinlochbervie

and Rhiconich on the west coast offer accommodation and some facilities and there are isolated hostelries, like the remote Crask Inn on the lonely road from Lairg to Altnaharra that offer sustenance and shelter. There are campsites at Durness and Scourie, and youth hostels in Durness and Tongue, plus an independent hostel in the former.

From the south three long roads give access to the area. From Lairg (where there is a railway station – the nearest to these hills) the A838 runs northwest past long bleak Loch Shin to Laxford Bridge where it turns northeast to the north coast at Durness and then runs east to Tongue. Also from Lairg the A836 runs north to Tongue via Altnaharra. Further west the A835/A837 road from Ullapool runs north to Skiag Bridge, where it becomes the A894 and goes across the Kylesku Bridge and round the coast via Scorrie to join the A838 at Laxford Bridge.

⊗ Beinn Leoid, Meallan a' Chuail and Meall an Fheur Loch

Lying between Glen Coul in the west and Loch Merkland, beside the A838, in the east, these hills share the characteristics of the rough and rocky mountainous west and the softer moorland east. Westward approaches involve crossing much complex rocky terrain, the easiest route being by boat (or

An Caisteal, the summit of Ben Loyal

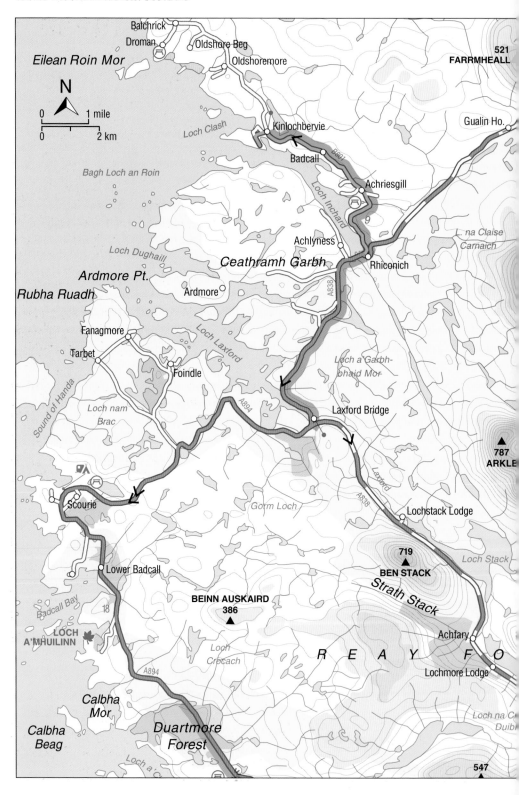

Eilean Roin Mor

Balchrick
Droman
Oldshore Beg
Oldshoremore

521
FARRMHEALL

Loch Clash

Kinlochbervie

Gualin Ho.

Bagh Loch an Roin

Badcall

Achriesgill

Loch Dughaill

Achlyness

L. na Claise
Carnaich

Ceathramh Garbh

Rhiconich

Ardmore Pt.

Rubha Ruadh

Ardmore

Fanagmore

Tarbet

Loch Laxford

Foindle

Loch a 'Garbh-
bhaid Mor

Sound of Handa

Loch nam
Brac

Laxford Bridge

787
ARKLE

Scourie

Gorm Loch

Lochstack Lodge

Loch Stack

Lower Badcall

719
BEN STACK

Badcall Bay

Strath Stack

BEINN AUSKAIRD
386

LOCH
A'MHUILINN

Loch
Crocach

R E A Y   F O

Achfary

Calbha
Mor

Calbha
Beag

Duartmore
Forest

Lochmore Lodge

Loch na C
Duibh

Loch a'

547

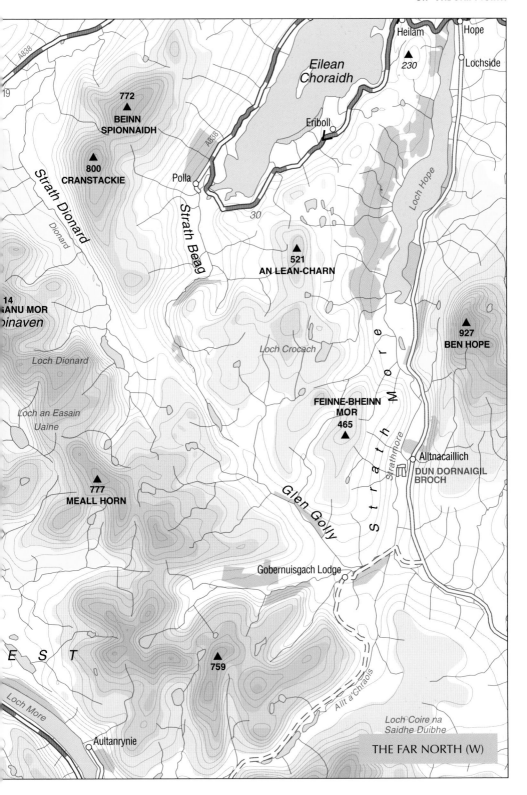

Heilam

Hope

Eilean
Choraidh

▲
230

Lochside

Eriboll

Loch Hope

772
▲
BEINN
SPIONNAIDH

A838

800
▲
CRANSTACKIE

Polla

Strath Dionard

Strath Beag

Dionard

30

521
▲
AN LEAN-CHARN

14
ANU MOR
pinaven

Loch Crocach

927
▲
BEN HOPE

Loch Dionard

Loch an Easain
Uaine

FEINNE-BHEINN
MOR
465
▲

Strath More

Strathmore

Alltnacaillich

DUN DORNAIGIL
BROCH

777
▲
MEALL HORN

Glen Golly

Gobernuisgach Lodge

E   S   T

759
▲

Allt a'Chraois

Loch More

Loch Coire na
Saidhe Duibhe

Aultanrynie

THE FAR NORTH (W)

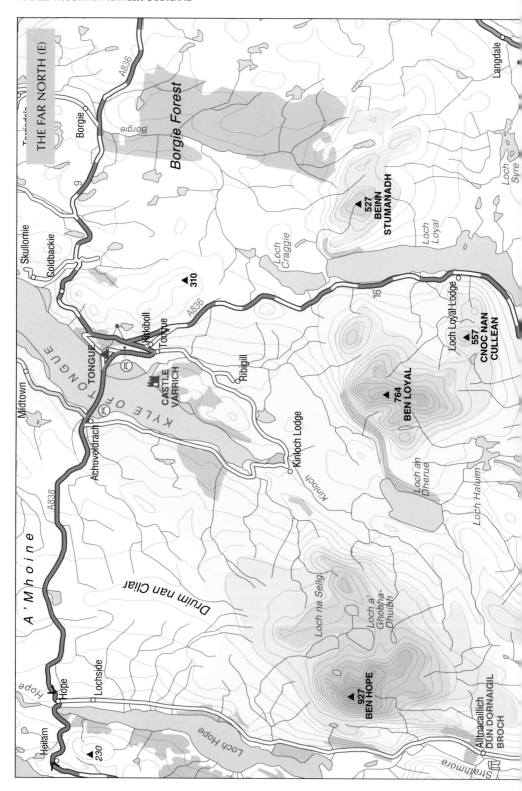

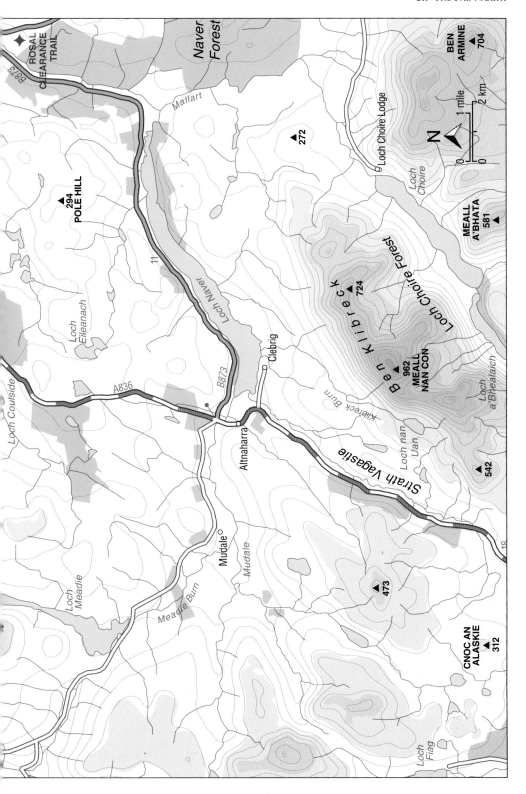

canoe), from Unapool or Kylesku to Glencoul, then up the glen, below the impressive prow of the Stack of Glencoul on the path to Loch an Eircill, from where the southern slopes can be climbed to the summit of Beinn Leoid (792m). The round trip from Glencoul is 14km, with 800m of ascent, and takes 6–7hrs. Adding the lower more eastern peaks would make this a very long trip; these are better climbed from the northeast, starting on the A838 2km south of Loch More, where a stalkers' path heads south towards Meall an Fheur Loch (613m), which can be easily climbed up its northern slopes, and then the broad summit ridge followed to the high point at the eastern end above Loch Merkland. Turn back along the ridge and then south to Meallan a' Chuail (750m) and west to Beinn Leiod. The walking is mostly soft underfoot, with bogs in places, the only rock being a few small crags on the sides of the hills. Return over Meallan a' Chuail, then descend the south ridge to rejoin the stalkers' path for a distance of 16km, with 1260m of ascent, which takes 6–7hrs.

Ben Hee
Ben Hee (873m) is the high point of a huge area of boggy loch-dotted moorland, some of it covered with forestry plantations, which lies northwest of Lairg between the A838 and A836 roads. This is not a very interesting area for walkers, but the easy ascent of Ben Hee is worthwhile for the excellent views, a big sweep of hills from Ben Loyal to the northeast round west over Ben Hope, Foinaven and Quinag to Ben More Assynt. Eastwards bleak moorland stretches into the distance while to the south the long, long line of huge Loch Shin stretches down to Lairg. Ben Hee is a bulky, rounded hill, with some rocky corries on its eastern flanks. It rises above the A838 road and Loch Merkland and the easiest ascent is from West Merkland near the northern end of the loch where a track leads northeastwards towards the Bealach nan Meirleach ('robbers' pass'). After 1.5km a stalkers' path branches off eastwards towards the summit of Ben Hee, which is easily reached from the end of the path. Return the same way or over Meallan Liath Mor to the southwest or Sail Garbh to the northwest, for a walk of around 11km, with 800m of ascent, which takes 4–5hrs.

Meallan Liath Coire Mhic Dhughaill
Meallan Liath Coire Mhic Dhughaill is a complex hill with several twisting ridges and a big rocky corrie on the northeastern side. It rises northeast of

Loch More and the A838 road. For those using OS map sheets it's an awkward hill, as it runs across the edges of three maps. This is where computer mapping has a real advantage. A good circuit is from the south end of Loch More at Kinloch where a track runs up the eastern side of the loch to a stalkers' path that zigzags up the steep slopes above the loch to the wide Meallan Liath Beag ridge which leads to the stony east ridge of the hill and the summit. There's a good view from the top of the surrounding hills. A descent can be made south from the summit to rejoin a stalkers' path above the loch. The distance is 16km, with 1015m of ascent, and the walk takes 6–7hrs.

A longer route from the west runs from the A838 south of Loch Stack past the loch to Lone, then east along a stalkers' path to the Bealach na Feithe on the north side of the hill. Either the Sail Rac or Meall Garbh ridges can be climbed to the summit, the other used for descent. The distance is 25km, with 1240m of ascent, and the walk takes 8–9hrs.

Ben Stack ☆
Ben Stack is the most northerly Graham. It's a steep, craggy and impressive little mountain rising directly above Loch Stack and the A838. Ben Stack stands out in views from the A838 to the south as a rocky pyramid, and is one of the more distinctive and prominent mountains in the district despite its relatively low height. It's a wonderful viewpoint, both for the surrounding mountains and the lochan-filled landscape leading west to the intricate coastline. Ben Stack can be easily climbed up its broad southeast ridge, the Leathad na Stioma, from the A838. There are two rocky tops, of which the most northerly is, just, the highest. Descend the same way or, for a longer walk, down the north ridge to a stalkers' path crossing the western flanks. This path can be followed northeast down to the A838 about 5km from the start, or southwest to a junction with a path down Strath Stack that leads to Achfary on the A838 about 1km from the start. The round trip up and down the southeast ridge is 7km long, with 680m of ascent, and takes 3–4hrs. The traverse of the mountain, with a return down Strath Stack, is 13km long, with 700m of ascent, and takes 5–6hrs.

Meall Horn and Sabhal Beag
Lying to the south and east of the magnificent mountains of Foinaven and Arkle, Meall Horn and Sabhal Beag are easily ignored hills. However they

Foinaven from Arkle

have some nice rocky slopes, especially on the north side of Meall Horn, and their ascent is not without interest. Like their illustrious neighbours the two hills can be climbed from the stalkers' path from Lone up the Allt Horn to the Bealach Horn and could be combined with those mountains on a long day or an overnight trip. The usual ascent route runs from the A838 to Lone, and then up the stalkers' path to 500m below the bealach, where it is left for a climb northeast to Creagan Meall Horn (729m), from where a ridge leads southeast above the craggy northern corries to Meall Horn, and then on over Sabhal Mor to Sabhal Beag and a descent south to the Bealach na Feithe, from where a stalkers' path leads back to Lone. The walk is 25km long, with 1160m of ascent, and takes 7–8hrs.

⊗ Arkle ☆

Arkle is a splendid mountain lying north of Loch Stack and opposite Ben Stack, from where it looks impressive. Built of quartzite, it has steep crags and screes on three sides. Only to the southeast are there less steep slopes. The summit is a narrow, curving ridge running round deep Am Bathaiach. The view north to Foinaven across Loch na Tuadh is superb. The ascent begins on the A838 south of

Loch Stack, with the track to Lone and then the path beside the Allt Horn. Once past the crags running southwest of the summit climb over heather and stones up the long steep southeast slopes to the lower 757m southern summit, and then follow the ridge, which is composed of smooth angular quartzite boulders that are slippery when wet, round to the top. The easiest descent route is back down the southeast ridge, for a walk of 18km, with 760m of ascent, which takes 6–7hrs. More exciting is to descend the slopes of Sail Mhor to the northwest of the summit on steep scree to a stalkers' path that leads south round the base of the mountain to Loch Airigh a'Bhaird and Loch an Nighe Leathaid. Leave the path here and head southeast past the latter loch and below the west face of Arkle to Lone. This route is 20km, with 800m of ascent, and takes 7–8hrs. If planning on the full circuit the route could be started at Lochstack Lodge, at the northwest end of Loch Stack, and the ascent made by Sail Mhor, which reduces the distance by 5km.

⊗ Foinaven ☆

Foinaven is one of the finest mountains in Scotland. With a summit ridge stretching northwards for 5km over five summits, it's really a small mountain range.

On the west side huge, pale quartzite screes form a long unbroken wall that looks forbidding when seen from the A838 (which is forced into a big loop westwards to avoid the mountain and its smaller neighbour Arkle). On the east side, above long Strath Dionard, four long rocky spurs run out above deep craggy corries. The highest summit and the only one with Corbett status is Ganu Mor ('big head', from the Gaelic ceann mor) towards the northern end of the ridge. Ganu Mor is almost Munro height, and for a while it was suspected that it might be a Munro, as the last OS measurement in 1992 gave it as 914m, just 0.4m below Munro height, a measurement made from aerial surveys and only accurate to a metre at best. (This is the measurement currently used on printed maps and on the map in this book.) More precise measurements on the ground, using modern equipment, were carried out by the Munro Society in 2009, and showed that Foinaven is in fact lower than previously thought, at 911m, so it remains a Corbett, a fact that, together with its remoteness, means it will be less climbed than if it was just a few metres higher. However for anyone who loves mountains for their shapes, dramatic features, challenge, beauty and overall magnificence Foinaven is as attractive as any higher mountain.

In some books Foinaven is given as meaning 'white hill' from the Gaelic fionn-bheinn, which seems to make sense given the pale quartzite rocks. However Peter Drummond's Scottish Hill Names: Their Origin and Meaning (Scottish Mountaineering Trust, 2007) says there is little evidence for this meaning and that foinne-bheinn, which is the local pronunciation, is the likely Gaelic. Unfortunately this means that the lovely word Foinaven translates into the unattractive 'wart mountain' in English, probably after the stubby summits. Drummond does say that it may originally be a Norse name, like many in the area, including nearby Arkle, and could come from vind-fjall, meaning 'wind h'ill, or fann-hvitr, meaning 'snow white', again referring to the white rocks. Fann-hvitr would fit with Fannevein, the name recorded by Timothy Pont in the 1590s. One of these Norse names could have been transformed into 'foinne-bheinn' by later Gaelic speakers who did not understand the Norse.

The traverse of the whole mountain from south to north is one of the best high-level walks in the Northern Highlands and, indeed, the whole of Scotland. However the finish is 24km by road from the start, so transport needs to be arranged unless the walk is part of an overnight or multi-day trip, perhaps with a return up Strath Dionard and down the Allt Horn or over Meall Horn and Sabhal Beag. There is a path along the summit ridge, badly eroded in places, which shows that the remote location and lack of Munro height doesn't deter that many walkers.

The traverse starts on the A838 just south of Loch Stack, with the track to Lone and the path beside the Allt Horn to 510m Bealach Horn, from where an easy climb mostly on grass leads up the broad southern slopes of Foinaven to the first summit at 778m, which isn't named on the OS map but is referred to as Craig Dionard or An t-Sail Mor in various guidebooks. As the summit is reached the mass of peaks, corries, cliffs and scree slopes stretching out to the north is revealed, an exciting and inspiring vista. The easy walking continues westwards to another summit not named on the OS map at 808m. Some guidebooks call this Stob Cadha na Beucaich ('peak of the pass of the bellowing'), after the pass just to the north, which is reached by a steep loose stony descent. The climb out of the pass northwards up a narrow ridge, with the big cliffs at the head of Coire na Lurgainn on the right, is also steep and stony. This leads to the stubby crag known as Lord Reay's Seat, which can be easily bypassed on the west, and then A' Ch'eir Ghorm (869m) at the end of a long, thin spur running out to the east. The ridge broadens beyond A' Ch'eir Ghorm and crosses a minor bump before reaching Ganu Mor, which has two cairns, of which the eastern one is the highest. The views throughout the ridge walk are superlative. Ganu Mor is the place to stop and drink them in. The vast wild lochan-spattered landscape all around gives a sense of remoteness and space. Mountains are all around with steep Ben Hope to the east looking dramatic and Ben Klibreck to its south lonely and isolated. In the west the Coigach and Assynt hills stretch southwards with the jagged edge of An Teallach far beyond them. Away to the northwest shines the golden sand of Sandwood Bay. It is a glorious vista. From Ganu Mor continue north along the ridge to the last summit, 902m Ceann Garbh, from where the descent leads down complex craggy terrain to open moorland and a boggy walk to the A838 at Gualin House. This route is 22km long, with 1440m of ascent, and takes 8–9hrs.

The quickest route to Ganu Mor if you just want to bag the Corbett is from the A838 to the north over Ceann Garbh, returning the same way, for a distance of 12km with 990m of ascent and a time of 5–7hrs. This misses much that is best on Foinaven however and involves crossing the boggy moor twice.

⑥ Scrambling on Foinaven ☆

The little-visited east side of Foinaven harbours many, mostly quite difficult, scrambles described in the SMC's *Highland Scrambles North* as 'some of the most atmospheric scrambling in the area'. The easiest access to these is from the estate track down Strath Dionard from the north. Ganu Mor Slabs on the north face of Ganu Mor in Coire Duail, which is given three stars and described as 'quite sustained and serious', ascends slabs made of gneiss to 150m below the summit. Two star routes are the Upper Slabs, Creag Urbhard above Loch Dionard – quartzite this time but again 'sustained and serious' – and Cnoc Duail, North Face on the south side of Coire Duail. All these scrambles are Grade 3, and there is only one scramble easier than this in *Highland Scrambles North*, the Grade 1 Second Dionard Buttress on Creag Urbhard, described as 'easy slabby scrambling in a wild situation' but not given any stars.

⑥ Rock Climbing on Foinaven

The eastern cliffs of Foinaven are remote and rarely visited, so climbing here would be an adventure. Kevin Howett notes in *Rock Climbing in Scotland* (Frances Lincoln, 2004), that 'many of these routes are unrepeated…so let's be cautious out there!'. Howett describes eight routes in grades ranging from Severe to E2. 270m Fingal on Creag Urbhard above Loch Dionard, a Severe first climbed by Tom Patey in 1962, is described as 'a great mountaineering route', while 150m Wrath on the slabs of Cnoc a' Mhadaidh at the north end of the mountain, an E1 first climbed by C. Boulton, T. Lewis and P. Nunn in 1978, has 'a brilliant pitch through the roof'.

⑥ Cranstackie and Beinn Spionnaidh

Rising northeast of Foinaven, these two Corbetts form the most northerly mountain massif in Britain. They take the form of a long, curving, grassy ridge, with Strath Dionard to the west and Loch Eriboll to the east. There is a long line of broken little crags and rocky slopes on the southwest flank of Cranstackie, but overall these are not rocky

mountains. On the east side long boggy moorland stretches down to Loch Eriboll. An ascent of these slopes looks tedious. Much better to start northwest of Beinn Spionnaidh at Carbreck on the A838, from where a track runs south over the River Dionard to the house at Rhigolter. From here the ascent leads steeply up to the 550m col between the two hills, from which can both be easily climbed. A descent can be made down the northwest ridge of either hill. The round trip is 14km long, with 970m of ascent, and takes 5–6hrs. The views from the summits are extensive and impressive. An alternative longer route from the head of Loch Eriboll goes south up Strath Beag to Conamheall and the long southeastern ridge of Cranstackie, from which there are excellent views into the corries of Foinaven. From Beinn Spionnaidh descend southeast back to the start, for a round trip of 17km, with 1100m of ascent, which takes 6–7hrs.

⑥ Sandwood Bay and Cape Wrath ☆

The remote far northwest coast is one of the most impressive in Scotland. Although no high peaks run down to the sea there are low rocky hills not far away, and the feeling of wilderness is similar to that on the mountains. Anyone venturing this far north to climb the hills would do well to spend a day or two exploring the coast, especially that section from Sandwood Bay to Cape Wrath, which is one of the great coastal walks in Britain. Here there are beautiful sandy beaches, huge, dramatic cliffs, towering sea stacks, hidden coves and waterfalls crashing into the sea. Birdwatchers in particular will relish the walk, as there are huge numbers of seabirds, including cormorants, shags, fulmars, guillemots, razorbills, puffins, gannets and kittiwakes.

The walk starts at Blairmore, near the end of a minor road running north from Kinlochbervie, where a track runs north past several lochs to Sandwood Bay. This beautiful 2km curving stretch of sand, with cliffs at either end, is a wild, precious place, owned by the John Muir Trust in order to conserve it's grandeur and magnificence. The tall sea stack visible to the west of the bay is Am Buachaille ('the herdsman'). The sandy beach is backed by sand dunes and a stretch of machair – shell/sand grassland covered in flowers in spring and summer. 'Sandwood' is an Anglicisation of the Gaelic *sandabhat*, which means 'sandy water', the *bhat* (pronounced 'vat') deriving from the Norse *vatn*, which means water. A few hundred metres inland from the sea is big, freshwater Sandwood Loch. The walk crosses the sands to the cliffs to the north, and then runs along the top of these to Cape Wrath, with breathtaking scenery throughout. The highest cliffs rise 90m above the sea, with dramatic views straight down to the crashing waves. The grassy terrain makes for easy walking, although there's no path, just a maze of sheep tracks. There are some streams to be forded that could be difficult or impossible when in spate, but are otherwise no problem.

The walk finishes at Cape Wrath where there is a lighthouse built in 1828 by the grandfather of Robert Louis Stevenson, the author of *Kidnapped*, *Dr Jekyll and Mr Hyde* and *Treasure Island*. 'Wrath' comes from the Norse *hvarf*, which means a headland. It's an important feature for sailors, and would have been significant for the Vikings.

There is a road to Cape Wrath from the Kyle of Durness, but there is no access for private vehicles. In summer a minibus runs along this road from the passenger ferry across the Kyle. This can be booked on ☎ 01971 511343 or 01971 511287. The area around the road is a naval gunnery range. Warning flags are flown when firing is taking place, and information can be obtained from the Tourist Information Centre in Durness. The walk is 19km long and takes 7–8hrs.

⊗ Ben Klibreck

The most northerly Munro but one is a huge, bulky, isolated hill running from southwest to northeast for some 12km, between Loch Choire and Loch Naver. It lies in an area of boggy moorland far from any other high hills. Ben Klibreck (962m) is a grass and heather hill with few rock outcrops other than some crags on the steep slopes west of the summit and no really distinctive features. Other than the remote situation there's nothing to get excited about. The easiest route to the top, which is called Meall nan Con ('hill of the dog'), begins west of the summit on the A836 and climbs to a col south of the summit above Loch nan Uan. Descend the same way for a walk of 10km with 790m of ascent that takes 4–5hrs. A longer, although not necessarily more interesting, route is a traverse from the Crask Inn to Altnaharra, a distance of 15km with 960m of ascent, which takes 6–7hrs. The first recorded ascent of Ben Klibreck was by James Robertson in 1767, who also climbed Ben Hope, meaning that the two most northerly Munros had

first ascents long before much more accessible summits much further south. The name Klibreck, like so many hereabouts, probably comes from the Norse 'klettr brekka', meaning cliff slope.

⊗ Ben Hope ☆

The most northerly Munro (927m) is a fine rocky wedge of a mountain rising in very steep slopes with two sets of cliffs above Strath More, down which runs the minor road from Altnaharra to Hope on the A838. The north and east faces are steep and rocky too, leaving the gently sloping moorland to the south for the easiest ascent route. In Strath More near the end of the long south ridge is Dun Dornaigil, a ruined broch built around 2000 years ago that is well worth a visit. There are two ascent routes from Strath More. The first starts just north of the broch at Alltnacaillich, where a path heads up past a fine waterfall on the Allt na Caillich ('burn of the old woman') to the south ridge, called Leitir Mhuiseil, which rises to the final summit slopes. The second shorter route starts another 2km north and climbs through a break in the cliffs to Leitir Mhuiseil. The view from the top is spacious, with a vast, watery landscape spread out all around. On very clear days Orkney is said to be visible far over the sea to the north. Descend by either of the ascent routes. The round trip from Alltnacaillich is 12km long, with 920m of ascent, and takes 5–6hrs; that from further north 7km, with 920m of ascent, taking 4–5hrs.

Ben Hope is another mountain with a Norse name – from *hop*, meaning bay – and this is a mountain of the sea, lying close to two big sea lochs, Loch Eriboll and the Kyle of Tongue. The first recorded ascent of Ben Hope was in 1767 by James Robertson, who also climbed Ben Klibreck, Ben Wyvis and Ben Nevis. Ian R. Mitchell's *Scotland's Mountains Before the Mountaineers* (Luath, 1999) records a curious story that suggests that 'Ben Hope boasts the first possibly fraudulent claim to have been ascended'. The questionable account is that of one Rev Charles Cordiner, who claimed the ascent in 1776. Mitchell says Cordiner's account contains 'reverential hyperbole' and 'gushing prose' and he clearly doesn't believe that it shows Cordiner reached the summit, although he does allow that he might have been under that impression in the mist, or that by summit he meant a summit ridge. We shall never know.

Ben Hope from the north

⊗ Ben Loyal ☆

The view of the castellated northwest face of Ben Loyal, with its four rugged peaks rising above huge rock buttresses divided by deep corries, is one of the classic mountain scenes in Scotland, dominating views from the A838 causeway across the Kyle of Tongue. Ben Loyal is not so interesting from the south and east, where less dramatic, more uniform slopes rise to the summits. The distinctive appearance of Ben Loyal, unusual in the Northern Highlands, is due to the rock of which it is built, syenite, an igneous rock like granite that weathers to rock tors and buttresses like those of volcanic mountains much further south. In fact Ben Loyal is the only volcanic mountain in the Northern Highlands. The name 'loyal' probably comes from the Gaelic *laghail*, meaning legal, which in turn probably comes from the Norse *laga fiall*, meaning 'law mountain'. So it has nothing to do with loyalty, which meaning is sometimes linked with an oft-used description of the mountain as the 'Queen of the Highlands' that dates back to 1840.

The approach to Ben Loyal starts south of Tongue on the minor road round the Kyle of Tongue, and goes south past the farm of Ribigill and over boggy moorland towards the Bealach Clais nan Ceap, with the towering rock pyramid of

Sgor Chaonasaid, the easternmost top of Ben Loyal, rising ahead. From the mouth of the bealach climb west onto the ridge south of Sgor Chaonasaid for a view of a huge fang of rock to the southwest. This is An Caisteal ('the castle'), the highest summit of Ben Loyal. From Sgor Chaonasaid there is a wonderful ridge walk over Ben Loyal's summits, starting with the twin tors of Sgor a'Bhatain ('boat peak', 708m) and then the rock slabs and ledges of An Caisteal. The view over rolling moorland hills dotted with lochs is spacious. Ben Hope looks rugged to the west, Ben Klibreck rises as a giant whaleback further south. To the north are the turbulent waters of the Pentland Firth. But the best scenery is that of Ben Loyal itself. From An Caisteal continue south to Beinn Bheag ('little hill', 744m) and then curve round the head of big Calbhach Coire to Sgor a' Chleirich ('cleric's peak', 644m) from where there is a great view east across Calbhach Coire to An Caisteal and the other tops. Sgor a' Chleirich being one of the massive cliff-rimmed buttresses of Ben Loyal there is no easy descent directly from the summit. Instead head back to a col south of the summit, from where a descent can be made into wild Calbhach Coire. Steep slopes of peat and grass lead down from the corrie to the beautiful old birch woods of Coille na Cuile that run in a long line

The north face of Ben Loyal

below the northwest face of Ben Loyal. Go through the trees and across the moor beyond to rejoin the path from Ribigill. The walk is 17km long, with 900m of ascent, and takes 6–7hrs.

6:8 ◐ THE CAPE WRATH TRAIL: ACHNASHELLACH TO CAPE WRATH ☆

The Cape Wrath Trail starts in the Western Highlands and runs for 133km from Fort William to Achnashellach. (See 5:11 for information on this section of the route.) In the Northern Highlands the routes runs for 191km in 13 stages from Achnashellach to Cape Wrath as described in Denis Brook and Phil Hinchliffe's Cicerone guidebook *North to the Cape* (1999). The route isn't fixed and variations and updates can be found on the trail website: www.capewrathtrail.co.uk. The trail doesn't climb any hills but there are many opportunities to do so.

In the Northern Highlands the route is wonderful and wild. The guidebook has many variant routes but the main one goes from Achnashellach to Kinlochewe via Loch Clair, up Gleann Bianasdail to Lochan Fada and then over the Bealach na Croise to Loch an Nid, a pathless section. Easier walking then leads north to Corrie Hallie, from where the route crosses low hills to Inverlael via Loch an Tiompain. A rough section follows, pathless in the middle, to Glen Douchary and Loch an Daimh, after which good tracks lead to Oykell Bridge and up Glen Oykel to Loch Ailsh. One of the finest sections of the route follows, along upper Glen Oykel towards Ben More Assynt and Conival, and then over the bealach between the latter and Breabag and down past the Traligill caves to Inchnadamph. Further splendid scenery follows, as the route climbs to the col between Beinn Uidhe and Glas Bheinn then descends via Loch Bealach a'Bhuirich to Loch na Gainmhich and a walk down the A894 to Kylesku. This last stage passes close to Eas a' Chual Aluinn, an essential side trip. From Kylesku the route crosses the Bealach nam Fiann to Achfary, and then to Rhiconich via Strath Stack and Loch a' Garbh-bhaid Mor. A long road section then leads through Kinlochbervie to Blairmore and a superb finish along the coast from Sandwood Bay to Cape Wrath.

6:9 ◖ THE SUTHERLAND TRAIL ☆

The Sutherland Trail is a route from Lochinver to Tongue created by writer and broadcaster – and old friend of the author's – Cameron McNeish in 2008. The route is about 130km and takes about a week to walk. There are options for climbing peaks along the way, especially Suilven, Foinaven and, from the finish, Ben Loyal. In 2009 Cameron made a documentary for the BBC on the walk and the area it goes through called *Sutherland – The Empty Lands?* This is available on DVD from Mountain Media (www.mountain-media.co.uk) which also publishes a book on the trail, *The Sutherland Trail – A journey Through Scotland's North-west*, by Cameron, with photographs by Richard Else, which is packed with interesting information and stories as well as being a guidebook to the trail. The Sutherland Trail looks a great walk for backpackers (although you could stay under a roof every night), especially if summits are climbed along the way.

From Lochinver the trail takes the path to Elphin past Suilven to Lochan Fada, then cuts northeast on a pathless section over the shoulder of Canisp to the River Loanan at Stronchrubie, which is followed north to Inchnadamph. From Inchnadamph the trail takes a stalkers' path that climbs to the bealach between Glas Bheinn and Beinn Uidhe, then descends through complex terrain to the top of the Eas a' Chual Aluinn, from where it crosses the Bealach a' Bhuirich and drops down to Loch na Gaimhich and the A894, which is followed to Kylesku and over the bridge to Kylestrome. The road is left here for a path along the north shore of Loch Glendhu, and then a path past Loch an Leathaid Bhuain to the Bealach nam Fiann and a descent to the A838 at Lochmore Lodge, which is followed through Achfary to the track by Loch Stack to Lone. From Lone Arkle, Meall Horn and Foinaven can be ascended from the path beside the Allt Horn. Back at Lone the Sutherland Trail heads east over the Bealach na Feithe to Gobernuisgach Lodge, and then follows the Strathmore River to reach the minor road in Strath More at Dun Dornaigil. The road is then walked to Loch Hope, where the old Moine Path cuts below the north side of Ben Hope and over to Kinloch Lodge at the foot of the Kyle of Tongue, where the road to Tongue is joined.

ACCESS, BASES, MAPS AND GUIDES

Access

Applecross and Coulin A832 Garve to Kinlochewe. A890 Achnasheen to Achnashellach. A896 Kinlochewe to Lochcarron. Minor road from Tornapress to Applecross. Railway stations at Achnasheen, Achnashellach, Strathcarron.

Torridon A832 Garve to Shieldaig. A896 Kinlochewe to Torridon.

Letterewe, Fisherfield and Dundonnell A832 Garve to Braemore Junction.

The Fannaichs A832 Garve to Achnasheen. A835 Garve to Braemore Junction. Railway station at Achnasheen.

Beinn Dearg and Easter Ross A835 Garve to Ullapool. A837 Invershin to Ledmore.

Coigach, Assynt and the Far North A835 Ullapool to Ledmore. A837 Invershin to Lochinver. A894 Skiag Bridge to Laxford Bridge. A838 Lairg to Tongue via Laxford Bridge. A836 Lairg to Tongue via Altnaharra.

Bases

Applecross and Coulin Achnasheen, Achnashellach, Strathcarron, Lochcarron, Kinlochewe, Torridon, Shieldaig, Applecross.

Torridon Torridon, Kinlochewe.

Letterewe, Fisherfield and Dundonnell Kinlochewe, Poolewe, Dundonnell.

The Fannaichs Achnasheen, Ullapool, Garve.

Beinn Dearg and Easter Ross Ullapool, Garve.

Coigach, Assynt and the Far North Ullapool, Lochinver, Kylesku, Laxford Bridge, Lairg, Altnaharra, Tongue, Durness, Kinlochbervie.

Maps

OS Landranger 1:50,000 9, 10, 15, 16, 19, 20, 21, 24, 25

OS Explorer 1:25,000 428, 429, 433, 435, 434, 436, 437, 439, 440, 442, 443, 445, 446, 447

Harvey's 1:25,000 Superwalker Torridon, Superwalker An Teallach

Walking and Scrambling Guides

Guide to Walks in the North-West Highlands by Chris Townsend (Aurum, 2007)

Highland Scrambles North by Iain Thow (SMT, 2006)

Exploring the Far North West of Scotland by Richard Gilbert (Cordee, 1994)

Exploring the Landscape of Assynt (with 1:50,000 geological map) by Kathryn Goodenough, Elizabeth Pickett, Maarten Krabbendam and Tom Bradwell (British Geological Survey, 2004)

The Cape Wrath Trail: A New 200-mile Walking Route Through the North-west Scottish Highlands by David Paterson (Peak Publishing, 1996)

The Northwest Highlands by Dave Broadhead, Alec Keith and Ted Maden (SMC, 2004)

North to the Cape: A Trek from Fort William to Cape Wrath by Denis Brook and Phil Hinchcliffe (Cicerone, 1999)

Northern Highlands by Nick Williams (Pocket Mountains, 2003)

The Sutherland Trail: A Journey Through North-West Scotland by Cameron McNeish and Richard Else (Mountain Media, 2009)

Skye and the North West Highlands Walks by John Brooks and Neil Wilson (Jarrold, 2003)

Walking in Scotland's Far North by Andy Walmsley (Cicerone, 2003)

Walking in Torridon by Peter Barton, updated by Chris Lowe and Jim Sutherland (Cicerone, 2010)

Climbing Guides

Northern Highlands South edited by Andy Nisbet (SMC, 2007)

Northern Highlands Central edited by Andy Nisbet (SMC, 2006)

Northern Highlands North edited by Andy Nisbet (SMC, 2004)

Other Reading

Beinn Eighe: The Mountain above the Wood by J. Laughton Johnston and Dick Balharry (Birlinn, 2001)

Torridon, the Nature of the Place by Chris Lowe (Wester Ross Net, 2000)

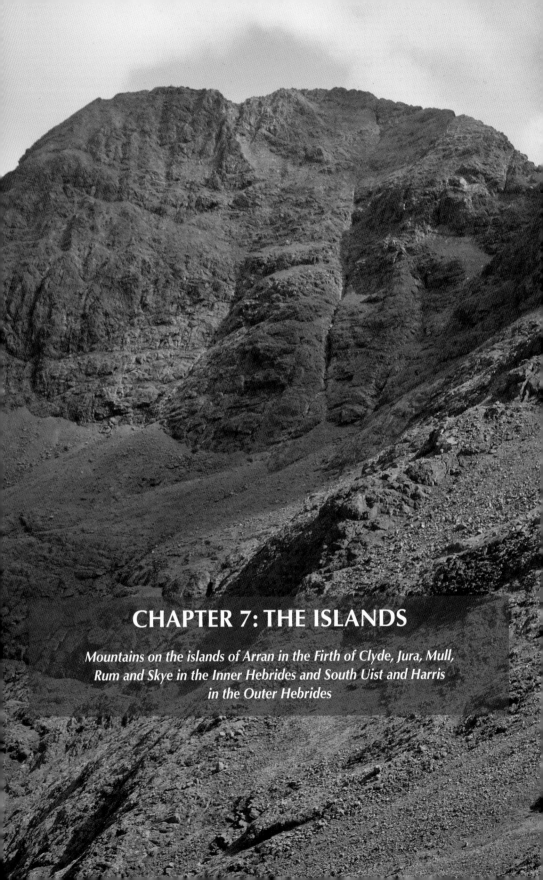

CHAPTER 7: THE ISLANDS

*Mountains on the islands of Arran in the Firth of Clyde, Jura, Mull,
Rum and Skye in the Inner Hebrides and South Uist and Harris
in the Outer Hebrides*

THE ISLANDS: CHAPTER SUMMARY

Location

Hills on the islands off the west coast

☆ Highlights

ⓐ LOW-LEVEL/PASSES WALK
- Brodick to Sannox (7:1)
- Sligachan, Camasunary, Loch Coruisk, Elgol (7:5)

◖ LONG DISTANCE WALK
- The Trotternish Traverse (7:5)

⊗ SUMMIT WALK
- Goatfell (7:1)
- Beinn Tarsuinn, Cir Mhor and Caisteal Abhail (7:1)
- The Paps of Jura (7:2)
- The Western Red Hills (7:5)
- Marsco (7:5)
- Bla Bheinn (7:5)
- Sgurr na Stri (7:5)
- The Cuillin Ridge (7:5)
- The Trotternish Ridge (7:5)
- The Storr and the Sanctuary (7:5)
- The Quiraing (7:5)
- The Clisham Horseshoe (7:6)
- The Oireabhal Ridge and Sron Uladal (7:6)

❸ SCRAMBLING
- Beinn Tarsuinn, Cir Mhor and Caisteal Abhail (7:1)
- Ben More (7:3)
- Askival, Ainshval and the Cuillin Traverse (7:4)
- The Cuillin Ridge (7:5)
- Sgurr Dubh Mor (7:5)

ⓖ ROCK CLIMBING
- A'Chir Ridge and Rosa Pinnacle (7:1)
- Bla Bheinn and the Cuillin Outliers (7:5)
- The Inaccessible Pinnacle and Sgurr Dearg (7:5)
- The Cuillin Traverse (7:5)
- Sron na Ciche (7:5)
- Sron Uladal (7:6)

ⓕ OTHER HIGHLIGHTS
- Loch Coruisk and boat cruises to Loch Coruisk (7:5)

◀ *Sgurr a' Greadaidh from Coir' an Eich, the Cuillin, Isle of Skye*

Beinn Shiantaidh and the Corran River, Paps of Jura ▶

Contents

INTRODUCTION

*Through the gap carved out by the mountain torrent which cleaves the bay you can see
the jagged rocks riding the sky high above the gorge.*
Tom Weir, *Highland Days*

Dozens of wild, beautiful islands lie off the coast of Scotland (Hamish Haswell-Smith lists 165 in his comprehensive book *The Scottish Islands*). Most are rugged, hilly and worth attention from lovers of nature and wild places. However to include many of them would require a book in itself, so in this chapter I have only included the seven islands with summits over 600m, all of them lying off the west coast of the mainland – Arran in the Firth of Clyde, Jura, Mull, Rum and Skye in the Inner Hebrides and South Uist and Harris in the Outer Hebrides. Between them these islands have 13 Munros (12 of them in the Cuillin on Skye), 11 Corbetts and 25 Grahams, plus a wealth of spectacular coastal scenery. Indeed, the mixture of mountainscapes and seascapes gives each of these islands an attractive individuality and character that is subtly different from the others. Each island will be described in more detail below.

The high mountain islands of Scotland form parts of three island groups. Arran, the southernmost of these islands, is the largest of the small group of islands lying in the Firth of Clyde, with the long Kintyre peninsula to the west separating them from the other islands. Jura, Mull, Rum and Skye are all in the Inner Hebrides, which lie just off the west coast. South Uist and Harris are in the Outer Hebrides or Western Isles, a thin strip of islands sometimes known as the Long Isle – from its appearance as one island when viewed from the east – making up the far western edge of Scotland, with nothing beyond them but the Atlantic Ocean. The name Hebrides has two possible derivations: it could be a corruption of the Greek *Haiboudai*, the name used by Ptolemy in

The Cuillin and Camasunary from the coast near Elgol

the 2nd century AD, or it might come from the Norse *havbredey*, meaning 'islands on the edge of the sea', which is both fitting and romantic. Ironically, given that the Hebrides are now the stronghold of Gaelic, the Gaelic name is Innse Gall, which means island of the strangers, a reference to the time when the islands were under Norse rule.

Geologically these islands are diverse, built of rocks ranging from three billion year old Lewisian Gneiss in the Outer Hebrides to igneous basalt and gabbro on Skye, Rum, Mull and Arran, thrown up by volcanic activity that came to an end some 50 million years ago, recent in geological time. All the rocks were sculpted and carved by the ice ages into steep mountains with many cliffs, making the islands great places for rock climbing.

The natural history of the islands is rich and varied too. Trees are less common than on the mainland, partly due to a lack of shelter and exposure to storms coming off the sea but also due to deforestation and over-grazing. A special plant habitat found on the western coasts of the Outer Hebrides is machair – short flower-rich grassland that grows on sand formed from crushed seashells. In spring and summer the display of flowers on machair is beautiful. Bird life is astonishingly rich, with huge colonies of seabirds of many different species. Mountain lovers who are bird watchers will find the islands a paradise. Seals are common round all the islands, and frequently seen. Porpoises, dolphins, whales and whale sharks may be seen too, especially from ferries, while otters are found in harbours and along beaches.

Ferries, mostly run by Caledonian MacBrayne, an island institution, are needed to reach all the islands bar Skye, which is connected to the mainland by a road bridge – although you can still go by ferry if preferred. Ferry travel is relaxing and romantic (except in storms!) and a wonderful way to reach the hills, many of which look superb from out to sea. All the mountain islands have facilities, although on some islands like Jura and Rum these are limited.

7:1 ARRAN

Arran is a small island – 32km long and 18km at the widest point – and the most southerly of the islands with high mountains. It's actually south of Glasgow and roughly equidistant between the Galloway Hills and the Arrochar Alps. The Highland Boundary Fault splits Arran in two. The mountains lie north of this line, so they are in the Highlands despite their southern location. The geology of Arran is complex, making the island popular with geologists. James Hutton, the father of modern geology (see under 'Topography and Geology' in the Introduction), visited Arran in 1787. The mountains are built of granite, remnants of volcanic activity when igneous rock was intruded into the schists and sandstone that underlie the northern half of the island. Sculpted by glaciers into dramatic peaks and spires, Arran's mountains vie with those of Rum as the most impressive island hills outside of Skye. Most of the hills form a huge horseshoe around Glen Rosa on the east side of Arran, with two spurs running out to the north and northeast. There are four Corbetts here, three on the horseshoe, one on the northern spur. These are: Goatfell ('goat hill', 874m); Cir Mhor ('big comb', 799m); Beinn Tarsuinn ('transverse hill', 826m); and, on the spur, Caisteal Abhail (possibly 'castle of the fork', 859m). These are splendid, steep, rocky mountains, among the finest in Scotland, especially Cir Mhor, an uncompromising rock pyramid. To the west of these mountains is a long curving ridge whose highest point, Mullach Buidhe ('yellow hill', 721m), is a Graham.

Arran can be reached from Glasgow in a couple of hours and is a popular holiday destination from the city. It's reached by ferry from Ardrossan to Brodick, the main town on the island. There's a train station in Ardrossan, and Brodick is walking distance from the eastern hills, so a car isn't needed. Brodick has all facilities, and there's a campsite in lower Glen Rosa. Alternatively there's a ferry from Claonaig on the Mull of Kintyre to Lochranza at the north end of the island, which also has a campsite and is within walking distance of the hills. The A841 runs right round the island.

ⓐ Brodick to Sannox ☆

The walk from Brodick to Sannox runs right through the heart of the Arran mountains with splendid views throughout. It starts up Glen Rosa below the great rock horseshoe of Goatfell, Cir Mhor, A'Chir and Beinn Tarsuinn. At the head of the glen the path climbs to The Saddle, the col between Goatfell and Cir Mhor, with the rock faces of the latter towering overhead. The descent north from The Saddle is steep and rocky at first but there is a path. Soon however the angle lessens, and easy walking leads

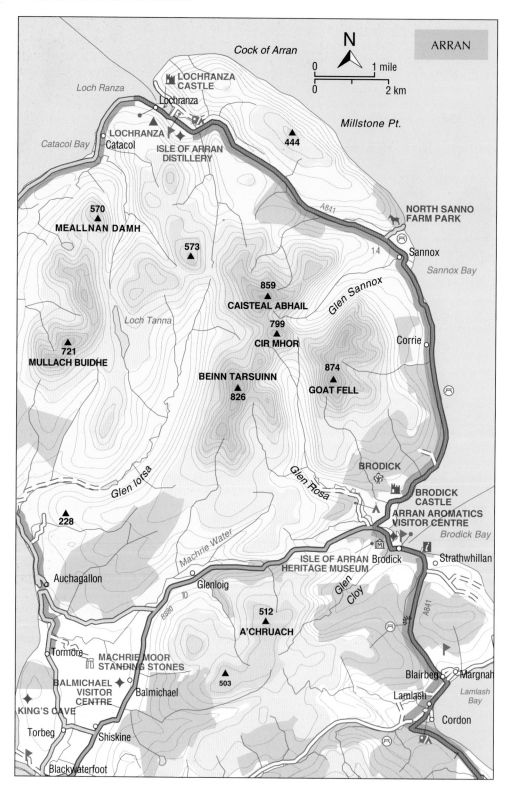

ARRAN

N

Cock of Arran

Millstone Pt.

0 — 1 mile
0 — 2 km

LOCHRANZA
CASTLE
Lochranza
Loch Ranza
LOCHRANZA
Catacol Bay
Catacol
ISLE OF ARRAN
DISTILLERY

444

A841

NORTH SANNO
FARM PARK

570
MEALLNAN DAMH

573

Sannox
14
Sannox Bay

859
CAISTEAL ABHAIL

Glen Sannox

Loch Tanna

799
CIR MHOR

721
MULLACH BUIDHE

BEINN TARSUINN
826

874
GOAT FELL

Corrie

BRODICK

Glen Iorsa

Glen Rosa

BRODICK
CASTLE
ARRAN AROMATICS
VISITOR CENTRE
Brodick Bay

228

Machrie Water

ISLE OF ARRAN
HERITAGE MUSEUM

Brodick
Strathwhillan

Auchagallon

Glenloig

512
A'CHRUACH

Glen
Cloy

A841

B880
10

Tormore

MACHRIE MOOR
STANDING STONES

503

Blairbeg
Margnah

BALMICHAEL
VISITOR
CENTRE
Balmichael

Lamlash
Lamlash
Bay

KING'S CAVE

Torbeg
Shiskine

Cordon

Blackwaterfoot

Arran from the Ardrossan–Brodick ferry

down Glen Sannox. The burns in both glens are attractive, with limpid pools and little waterfalls. The distance is 14km from the centre of Brodick, 12km from the Glen Rosa campsite, with 475m of ascent, and the walk takes 4–5hrs.

⊗ Goatfell ☆

The highest peak on Arran is one of the best-known peaks in Scotland, due to its southern situation and easy access. It forms the eastern side of the Glen Rosa horseshoe and stands out in the view of Arran from the ferry from Ardrossan. It's a rugged, rocky peak with narrow ridges but can be climbed easily by the east ridge. The name is unusual: it sounds English, and is probably an Anglicisation of the likely original Norse name *geitar fjall*, which does indeed mean 'goat fell'. However after the Norse name came a Gaelic one – *Gaoit-bheinn*, 'hill of the wind', which Peter Drummond's *Scottish Hill Names: Their Origin and Meaning* (Scottish Mountaineering Trust, 2007), says was perhaps a Gaelicisation of *geitar* into *gaoit*, with *bheinn* added. In 1772 Thomas Pennant called it 'Goatfield or Gaoit-bheinn', so both names were in use at the same time. The first ascent was by Lugless Willie Lithgow in 1628, making it one of the first hills in

Scotland to have a claimed ascent. Given its prominence in views from the mainland, and its closeness to Glasgow, this isn't too surprising. Lithgow was impressed by the view, noting 'three Kingdoms at one sight', the kingdoms being Ireland, the Isle of Man and England, in the form of the coast of Cumberland. Arran became a popular tourist destination in the 19th century, and the ascent of Goatfell quickly became popular.

The most popular route is from Cladach, 2km from Brodick, and goes through the grounds of Brodick Castle (the castle and adjacent Country Park are owned by the National Trust for Scotland, as is Goatfell, and are well worth visiting) then climbs beside the Cnocan Burn to Coire nam Meann and the narrow, rocky east ridge, which leads to the summit. There is a good path marked with numerous cairns the whole way. There is a viewpoint indicator on the summit showing all the distant points that can be seen. However the most dramatic views are those close to hand, especially down into Glen Rosa far below, across the glen to the other peaks of the horseshoe and north to the great cleft of the Ceum na Caillich – 'the Witch's Step' – on the ridge above Glen Sannox. The easiest descent route is back the same way,

Goatfell and Brodick Bay, Arran

for a walk of 11km, with 900m of ascent, which takes 5–6hrs.

A slightly shorter ascent is from High Corrie 8km by road north of Brodick, where a path climbs west beside the Corrie Burn then cuts south to the east ridge. This route is 8km long, with 885m of ascent, and takes 4–5hrs.

A more adventurous ascent or descent route is via Glen Rosa and the col at its head, called The Saddle, and North Goatfell (818m). The section between The Saddle and North Goatfell is on a narrow rocky ridge and some easy scrambling is required. From Cladach this route is 17km long, with 1045m of ascent, and takes 5–7hrs.

⊗ ⓢ Beinn Tarsuinn, Cir Mhor and Caisteal Abhail ☆

These three Corbetts, lying on the long rocky ridge to the west of Glen Rosa and Glen Sannox, can be climbed in one long, exciting outing. If the long rocky arête of 745m A'Chir ('the comb') between Beinn Tarsuinn (826m) and Cir Mhor (799m) is traversed then rock climbing to Very Difficult standard is required, but A'Chir can easily be bypassed on the western side. The route starts at the end of the road in lower Glen Rosa by the campsite and takes the track up the glen to the Garbh Allt. Take the path west beside this stream through an area fenced for forest regeneration and past some fine waterfalls, and then on up the southeast shoulder of Beinn Nuis (probably 'hill of the fawns', 792m), with the huge cliff on the east face of this subsidiary summit below you. From Beinn Nuis a rock and grass ridge leads easily to Beinn Tarsuinn and a view ahead to the rocky crest of A'Chir and the steep pyramid of Cir Mhor. The descent to the next col winds steeply through boulders. At the col the path divides: the right fork leads on to A'Chir, the left one is the bypass route, a fine narrow path across steep slopes below the granite slabs of A'Chir to the col with Cir Mhor. From here Cir Mhor can be climbed by its southwest ridge, with superb views of the massive buttress of the Rosa Pinnacle on the rocky east face of the hill. The summit is a tiny rock platform with big drops all around and wonderful views of the other Arran peaks. From Cir Mhor the path curves round the edge of Coire na Uaimh to Caisteal Abhail (859m), passing several big rock towers just below the summit, which is itself a block of rock. These towers explain the name of the mountain and its English alternative, The Castles. The view back to the sharp fang of Cir Mhor rising across Coire na Uaimh is tremendous.

From Caisteal Abhail, a complex peak with many spurs, there are several options. If returning to Glen Rosa the easiest route is to descend to the col with Cir Mhor, then take a path across the western slopes of that peak to the col with A'Chir, where a path leads down into Fionn Choire and Glen Rosa. By this route the walk is 20km long, with 1590m of ascent, and takes 7–9hrs. If there is enough time and energy to complete the Glen Rosa Horseshoe, climb back up Cir Mhor and carefully descend the steep, loose east ridge to The Saddle, then continue over North Goatfell and Goatfell. This route is 23km long, with 1115m of ascent, and takes 9–10hrs. If transport can be arranged, or the walk fitted in with bus times, then the ridge running east from Caisteal Abhail above Glen Sannox makes a good descent route for scramblers, as it crosses the deep gash in the ridge called the Witch's Step, which stands out in views of the Arran hills from many places. The scramble on smooth granite slabs across the Witch's Step isn't difficult but it is exposed in places and care is required. Once the difficulties are passed continue along the ridge to 660m Suidhe Fhearghas ('Fergus's Seat'), from where you can drop down into Glen Sannox and walk out to the road at Sannox. The route from Glen Rosa is 16km long, with 1500m of ascent, and takes 7–9hrs.

ⓑ Rock Climbing on Arran

The huge granite cliffs of Arran are ideal for rock climbing, and there are many routes of every grade of difficulty. Early climbers came here in the 1890s, Arran being easily accessible from Glasgow, and climbing has remained popular ever since.

The serrated A'Chir ridge ☆, which is 1.5km long, was first climbed in 1892 by J.A. Gibson and party. By the easiest route it's graded Moderate, though if the crest is taken direct throughout it's a Very Difficult. Dan Bailey describes it as 'one of the most entertaining routes of its kind anywhere' in *Scotland's Mountain Ridges* (Cicerone, 2006), while Kevin Howett in *Rock Climbing in Scotland* (Francis Lincoln, 2004) says it's 'one of the best ridges outside Skye'. Also on A'Chir is 210m Pagoda Ridge, a Severe that climbs Number 4 Buttress on the north face and which is described by Kevin Howett as 'one of the best climbs on the face'. It was first climbed by G.H. Townend and G.C. Curtis in 1943.

Cir Mhor rising out of the mists from Caisteal Abhail

☆ The most impressive rock feature in the Arran hills is the huge Rosa Pinnacle on the south side of Cir Mhor. Of the many routes on the Rosa Pinnacle 162m Sou Wester Slabs, a Very Difficult on the west face first climbed by G. H. Townsend, G. C. Curtis, H. Hare and M. Hawkins in 1944, is described as classic and popular, while 150m Vanishing Point on the same face, an E5 first climbed by C. MacAdam in 1985, is 'a brilliant route, bold and technical', according to Kevin Howett. The long South Ridge of the Rosa Pinnacle, a 318m Very Severe, first climbed by J. F. Hamilton and D. Patterson in 1941, is ranked by Howett as 'one of the best lower-grade outings in Britain'. On 'an azure, sun-drenched day' that is! Across Glen Rosa on the west flank of Goatfell is a vast area of slabs. Of the routes here Howett says that 110m Blankist, graded HVS, is the best. The first ascent was by G .E. Little and K. Howett in 1995.

7:2 JURA

One of the southernmost of the Hebrides, Jura is also one of the wildest, a mass of rocks, scree, peat bogs, thick heather and grassy tussocks. The name is said to come from the Norse *dyr oe*, meaning 'deer island'. There are still thousands of red deer on Jura. The main rock is quartzite and this makes up the small group of hills lying towards the southern end of the island that are known as the Paps of Jura. The name comes from the old Scots word for a breast, and refers to their rounded shapes. There are three paps of which the highest, Beinn an Oir ('hill of gold', 785m) is a Corbett, and Beinn Shiantaidh ('holy hill', 757m) and Beinn a'Chaolais ('hill of the narrows', 733m) are Grahams.

Jura is 50km long and 13km wide, and runs in a northeasterly direction. The population is only 180 and most of the island is uninhabited. The one road is single-track and runs round the coast from the Feolin Ferry on the southwestern side to Lussagiven on the east coast, from where a rougher road leads a little further north. There is no road round the northern tip of Jura or along the long north-western side of the island. The main settlement is Craighouse in the southeast where there is a hotel, Post Office, small shop and the distillery where the Isle of Jura malt whisky is produced. There are no other facilities on the island. However Jura is easily reached from nearby Islay, which lacks high hills but does have all facilities, plus plenty more distilleries to visit during bad weather.

In the summer Jura can be reached by a passenger ferry from Tayvallich on the mainland to Craighouse (see www.jurapassengerferry.com), a

Beinn an Oir and Beinn Shiantaidh, Paps of Jura

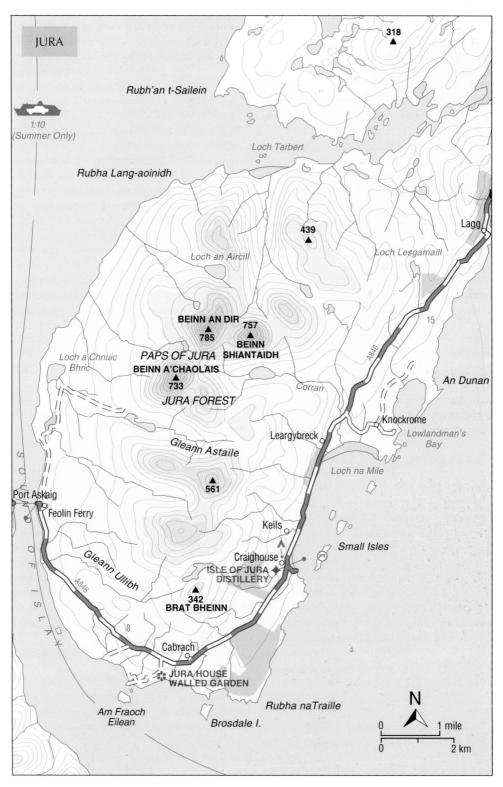

JURA

1:10
(Summer Only)

Rubh'an t-Sailein

Rubha Lang-aoinidh

Loch Tarbert

▲ 318

Loch an Aircill

439 ▲

Loch Lesgamaill

Lagg

15

BEINN AN DIR
▲
785

757
▲
**BEINN
SHIANTAIDH**

PAPS OF JURA

Loch a Chnuic
Bhric

BEINN A'CHAOLAIS
▲
733

JURA FOREST

Corran

An Dunan

Knockrome

*Lowlandman's
Bay*

Gleann Astaile

Leargybreck

Loch na Mile

▲
561

Small Isles

Keils

SOUND

OF

ISLAY

Port Askaig

Feolin Ferry

Gleann Ullibh

A846

Craighouse

**ISLE OF JURA
DISTILLERY**

▲
342
BRAT BHEINN

8

Cabrach

JURA HOUSE
WALLED GARDEN

Am Fraoch
Eilean

Brosdale I.

Rubha naTraille

N

0   1 mile

0   2 km

service that began in 2008. From Islay a car ferry runs from Port Askaig to Feolin year round. Islay itself can be reached by a car ferry from Kennacraig to Port Ellen or Port Askaig.

⊗ The Paps of Jura ☆

The round of the Paps of Jura is a classic walk in fine, wild country. The big dome-shaped hills are steep-sided and covered with quartzite scree and boulders that make for awkward going. This is very rugged country. Most walkers will take at least 7–8hrs for the 14km and 1460m of ascent. Amazingly, fell runners take less than half that time, while covering nearly twice the distance and several more hills, on the annual Isle of Jura Fell Race. This crosses seven summits and is 26km long with 2286m of ascent. It's described as 'one of the toughest challenges in British fell running'. The record times are impressive – 3:06:59 for men, set by Mark Rigby in 1994, and 3:40:33 for women, set by Angela Mudge in 2008. See www.jurafellrace.org.uk for more information.

The circuit of the three Paps starts at the bridge over the Corran River 5km north of Craighouse, where a path leads west across boggy moorland to Loch an t-Siob. From the foot of the loch a rough path leads up steep scree and tongues of grass to Beinn Shiantaidh and a good view of the next two peaks. Rough rocky slopes lead down to the col with Beinn an Oir, whose steep craggy east face rising ahead looks daunting. Rather than attempt this face directly the path goes northwest up more steep scree and grass to the northeast ridge, and then along this to the summit. A distinctive feature on the ascent is a narrow dyke of basalt, the brown rock very visible against the pale quartzite around it. Looking back this dyke can be seen continuing on Beinn Shiantaidh. The path up the northeast ridge of Beinn an Oir passes two walled enclosures and then runs between two crude quartzite walls built of stones cleared from the pathway. This work was probably done by the Ordnance Survey during early surveys. There's a big summit cairn plus a trig point inside a circular windbreak. The views are superb, with hills, sea and wild land all around. The name, 'hill of gold', probably comes from the presence in the rocks of iron pyrites, a mineral known as Fool's Gold due to its metallic yellowish colour. The path to the col with Beinn a'Chaolais goes down open scree slopes at first, then winds an intricate route through small crags on narrow ledges. Another scree ascent follows to the third Pap, then

more scree down to the last col from where boggy slopes lead down to Gleann an t-Siob and Loch an t-Siob and the walk back out to the start.

7:3 MULL

Mull is the second largest of the Inner Hebrides: only the Isle of Skye is bigger. It lies close to the Morvern peninsula, from which it is separated by the Sound of Mull. The island has a roughly triangular shape, broken by the indentations of long sea lochs on the western and southern side. The coast is beautiful with many fine cliffs and beaches. There are many villages on Mull, which has a population of 3000. Tobermory at the north end of the island is the main centre but not the most convenient place for the hills, which lie in the centre of the island. Craignure at the eastern end of the island is closer to the hills and is Mull's main ferry port. There's also a scattering of accommodation around the island plus ample opportunities for wild camping in the hills. Mull is well supplied with roads, the main A848/849 running down the coast from Tobermory to Craignure then west through Glen More and along the south side of Loch Scridain to Fionnphort, on the southwestern tip of the island, where a ferry runs to the island of Iona. The other key road for hillgoers is the B8035 which runs along the north shore of Loch Scridain and then cuts over to Loch na Keal, where it follows the south shore before crossing to Salen on the northeast coast.

Mull is the only island apart from Skye to have a peak of Munro height and it is a magnificent one, Ben More ('big hill', 966m), which lies between Loch Scridain and Loch na Keal. It has a pointed rocky summit from which radiate three long ridges. To the east of Ben More lie Mull's single Corbett, Dun da Ghaoithe ('fort of the two winds', 766m), and Beinn Talaidh ('hill of the cattle', 761m), the highest of the island's seven Grahams.

The geology of Mull is complex, and like Arran and Skye it is a favourite island for geology students. Much of Mull is built of basalt lava flows from volcanic activity on a base of much older schist and gneiss. The mountains, however, are mostly granite, intruded through the basalt by later volcanic activity.

Mull can be easily reached by the regular ferry to Craignure from the town of Oban, where

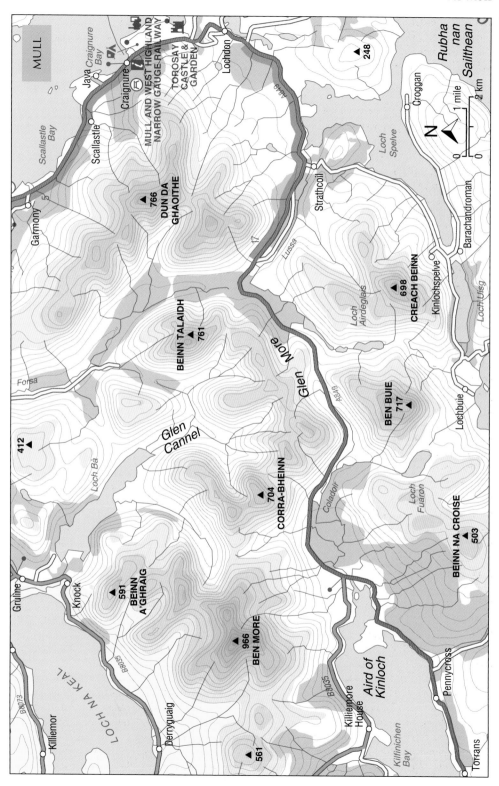

MULL

Java Craignure
Bay
Scallastle Bay
Scallastle Bay

Craignure

MULL AND WEST HIGHLAND NARROW GAUGE RAILWAY

TOROSAY CASTLE & GARDEN

Lochdon

▲ 248

Croggan

Rubha nan Sailthean

N

0   1 mile
0   2 km

Garmony

Scallastle

▲ 766
DUN DA GHAOITHE

17

Loch Spelve

Strathcoil

Lussa

Barachandroman

Forsa

▲ 766
DUN DA GHAOITHE

BEINN TALAIDH
761 ▲

Glen More

Loch Airdeglais

▲ 698
CREACH BEINN

Kinlochspelve

Loch Uisg

▲ 412

Glen Cannel

A849

BEN BUIE
717 ▲

Lochbuie

Loch Bà

Glen More

▲ 704
CORRA-BHEINN

Coladoir

Loch Fuaron

Gruline

Knock

B8035

BEINN A'GHRAIG
591 ▲

BEINN NA CROISE
503 ▲

Killiemor

B8073

Derryguaig

BEN MORE
966 ▲

Aird of Kinloch

B8035

Killiemore House

Pennycross

LOCH NA KEAL

561 ▲

Kilfinichen Bay

Torrans

there is a train station. There are also ferries from Lochaline on the Morvern peninsula across the Sound of Mull to Fishnish and from Kilchoan on the Ardnamurchan peninsula to Tobermory.

❸ Ben More ☆

Ben More rises dramatically above Loch na Keal and is clearly visible on the drive along the B8035 from Salen. It's a stony hill, the remnant of an ancient volcano, with much scree on the upper slopes and small crags in the corries. Some of the rocks are magnetic, which can give inaccurate compass readings. I can vouch for this, having once made an inadvertent traverse of the mountain in thick mist when my compass bearings from the summit were 180° out.

Ben More had an early recorded ascent, the first of an island Munro, in 1784 by William Thornton, an American, and his local guide, named Campbell. However as Ian R. Mitchell points out in *Scotland's Mountains Before the Mountaineers* (Luath, 1999) Campbell would almost certainly have already climbed Ben More, possibly several times.

Ben More can be climbed from the north or south but the former is the most interesting, as the southern slopes are rather undistinguished. From the shore of Loch na Keal a rough path leads up Gleann na Beinne Fada, beside the lovely Abhainn na h-Uamha, which has many pools and cascades, to a bealach at 520m between Beinn Fhada and A'Chioch ('the breast'), a pointed subsidiary peak of Ben More. From the bealach climb south to A'Chioch. The ascent is rocky, with a little easy scrambling. The connecting ridge between A'Chioch and Ben More is narrow and airy, with a superb feeling of being suspended above the world, but it's not difficult, with just a little simple scrambling just before the summit. The view from the summit of the island-strewn sea is spectacular. An easy descent leads down the northwest ridge to a path beside the Abhainn Dhiseig reaching Loch na Keal just over 1.5km west of the start. The round trip is 12km long, with 1070m of ascent, and takes 6–7hrs. The northwest ridge can be used for both ascent and descent if you want to avoid the scrambling. This route is 9km long, with 970m of ascent, and takes 4–5hrs.

⊗ Beinn Talaidh

Beinn Talaidh is a distinctive cone-shaped hill lying between Glen More and Glen Forsa to the east of Ben More. Once it was thought to be 763m and thus

a Corbett, but it is actually two metres lower and so a Graham, not that this changes the nature of this fine little hill in the slightest. Hamish Brown lists it in his 1988 book *Climbing the Corbetts* (Baton Wicks, 1996) and says it first became a Corbett in 1981. In the 1997 Tables it's a Graham. Whatever the exact height it's worth climbing, which can easily be done from the A849 in Glen More via Maol nam Fiadh and the south ridge, for a 5km round trip, with 670m of ascent, which takes around 3hrs.

⊗ Dun da Ghaoithe

Mull's only Corbett rises above Craignure and the Sound of Mull and is prominent in views from the ferry from Oban. The hill forms a long curving horseshoe above Coire Mor ('big corrie'). Unfortunately the slopes above Craignure are covered with plantations, so a direct ascent from the ferry isn't possible. The easiest ascent is from the A849 2km south of Craignure, where a bulldozed track climbs the southern arm of the horseshoe to two telecommunications masts, the second one at almost 550m, but this is not a pleasant or aesthetic route. Better is to head north from Craignure for 2km to Scallastle and climb the east ridge, Maol nan Damh, which leads directly to the summit, from where there are splendid views of the Sound of Mull and Loch Linnhe. Turn north from the summit and descend the northeast ridge, called Beinn Chreagach, leaving this above more plantations to drop back to Scallastle. This walk is 8km long, with 760m of ascent, and takes 3–4hrs.

7:4 RUM

Rum is situated west of Mallaig and the Morar peninsula and south of the Isle of Skye. It's the largest of the group of four islands known as the Small Isles. The high hills of Rum consist of a group of steep, jagged rock peaks in the southern part of the island known as the Rum Cuillin. These mountains look impressive from the south coast of Skye and from the mainland.

Rum has had an unusual history over the last two hundred years. In 1826 most of the population, some 300 people, were cleared from the island by the laird, Alexander Maclean. The people sailed to Canada and the land was turned over to sheep. This was not a success and in 1845 the island became a sporting estate for red deer stalking. In 1887 Rum

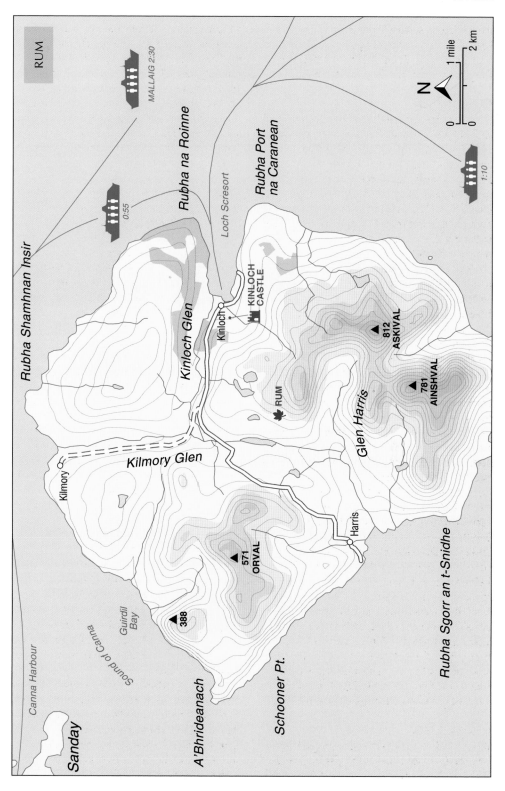

RUM

MALLAIG 2:30

0:55

1:10

Rubha Shamhnan Insir

Rubha na Roinne

Loch Scresort

Rubha Port na Caranean

Kinloch Glen

Kinloch

KINLOCH CASTLE

RUM

ASKIVAL
812

AINSHVAL
781

Glen Harris

Kilmory Glen

Kilmory

ORVAL
571

388

Guirdil Bay

Sound of Canna

Canna Harbour

Sanday

A'Bhrideanach

Schooner Pt.

Harris

Rubha Sgorr an t-Snidhe

N

0   1 mile
0   1   2 km

Askival and Hallival on Rum from the Mallaig to Kinloch ferry

was bought by a Lancashire industrialist called John Bullough. His son George inherited the island and built himself an ornate red sandstone castle in the late 1890s at Kinloch on the east side of the island. George Bullough also built a huge mausoleum in the form of a Greek temple in Glen Harris in the southwest of Rum. The Bullough family remained owners of Rum until 1957, when George Bullough's widow sold the island to the Nature Conservancy Council. Since 1957 Rum has been run as a National Nature Reserve, first by the NCC, then its successor, Scottish Natural Heritage.

Rum is important for its seabirds, especially the vast numbers of Manx shearwaters, a third of the world's population, which nest in burrows in the mountains. Camp high up in the hills and at dusk you'll hear the cries of the birds as they return to their burrows on grassy ledges on the steep hillsides. The first sea eagles to be reintroduced to Scotland – the native eagles were exterminated in the early 1900s – were released on Rum in 1975. The reintroduction was a success, despite some persecution, and there were further releases on Rum and in Eastern Scotland. Rum has also been used for studies of red deer and native woodland restoration. There are also many archaeological

sites – some of the earliest human sites in Scotland have been found on Rum.

The only settlement on Rum is at Kinloch on Loch Scresort, where there are 30 inhabitants, most employed by SNH. In 2008 the Scottish government announced that Kinloch and the surrounding area were to be transferred to the local community and the Isle of Rum Community Trust was established. The rest of the island remains under SNH's ownership.

The name Rum is still sometimes spelled Rhum, a Victorian affectation, although the Ordnance Survey and Scottish Natural Heritage have returned to the original spelling, which probably comes from the Norse *rom oe*, meaning a wide island.

For many years access to Rum was restricted and permission had to be obtained from SNH for hillwalking and camping. This is no longer the case, and the same freedom of access applies in Rum as elsewhere in Scotland. Facilities on Rum are limited and are all at Kinloch, where there is a small general store and Post Office, hostel accommodation in Kinloch Castle and a camping area. There are guided tours of the castle for days when the rain or midges make the hills unattractive.

The mountains of Rum are mostly built of a complex mix of igneous rocks, the remnants of volcanic activity. There are two Corbetts – 812m Askival ('hill of the spear') and 781m Ainshval ('rocky ridge hill'). These are Norse names – the 'val' coming from *fjall*, which means mountain – as is Cuillin, from the Norse *kiolen*, meaning high rocks. The island of Rum and the Cuillin would have been distinctive landmarks for the Vikings as they sailed through the Hebrides so they would certainly have named them.

ⒶAround the Cuillin

The walk round the base of the Rum Cuillin is a fine excursion, with splendid views of the mountains, superb coastal scenery and a visit to the Bullough Mausoleum. At 27km long with 1230m of ascent it can be completed in a day, but also makes a good two-day backpacking trip. The walk is on paths and tracks most of the way but there is one rough cross country section. The circuit starts at Kinloch with the often wet and muddy path that climbs south across the eastern slopes of Hallival and then descends slowly to the Allt na h-Uamha, where it begins a long traverse across the mountainside high above the sea cliffs before descending to the foot of abothies, where there is a grand bothy maintained by the Mountain Bothies Association. This section of the walk crosses rough slopes with many streams and waterfalls and has splendid views over the sea

to the mainland hills on Knoydart and Moidart. The rugged peak of Trollaval ('troll mountain', sometimes spelled Trallval) rises at the head of Glen Dibidil, which runs inland for 2km between the screes and crags of Ainshval and Askival.

From Dibidil the walk continues round the southern tip of Rum to Loch Papadil, with good views across the sea to the Isle of Eigg. The path ends at Papadil, where there is a ruined lodge. The next 5km are rough going, with no path, and the steep shoulder of Ruinsival ('hill of the heap of rocks') has to be crossed before a descent is made to Glen Harris and the bizarre sight of the mausoleum in the wild and remote glen. A wide track leads back north across the hills to the Kinloch Glen and the start. There are good views east to the Cuillin from this track.

ⒷAskival, Ainshval and the Cuillin Traverse ☆

Rum's two Corbetts face each other across Glen Dibidil. Between the two peaks, at the head of the glen, lies Trolleval (702m). Each Corbett can be climbed separately but the best route on Rum links the two as part of the Cuillin Traverse. Dan Bailey in *Scotland's Mountain Ridges* (Cicerone, 2006) describes this as 'quite simply one of the best long scrambling circuits in Scotland, a mountaineering escapade par excellence'. It is indeed excellent

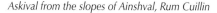

Askival from the slopes of Ainshval, Rum Cuillin

but it should be noted that there is far more rough walking than scrambling and that the most difficult sections can be easily bypassed. The first recorded traverse was made by none other than Sir Hugh Munro himself, which he recorded in the first volume of the *Scottish Mountaineering Club Journal* in 1891.

The traverse starts with the path from Kinloch Castle into Coire Dubh ('black corrie') and up the headwall to the Bealach Bairc-mheall. A short diversion west here leads to the summit of Barkeval ('precipice hill', 591m), where there is an excellent view of the higher summits. From the bealach climb southeast to the rocky summit of Hallival ('ledge hill', 723m). A short rocky section lies below the summit of Hallival, followed by a narrow but grassy ridge down to the col with Askival and up towards the summit of the latter, where rock is again met in the form of the Askival Pinnacle, a steep slab that can be climbed or avoided on the east side. The rock here is gabbro, a very rough volcanic rock that gives excellent grip.

Askival is the highest summit on Rum and has a wonderful all-encompassing view from the Skye hills to the north, along the serrated mountains of the mainland and out west to the Outer Hebrides, a tremendous mix of sea, islands and mountains. The first recorded ascent was in 1764, when it was climbed by the Rev Dr John Walker while on a botanical expedition, according to *Scotland's Mountains Before The Mountaineers* (Luath, 1999). From the little summit descend the west ridge to the Bealach an Oir ('pass of gold'), then either traverse across the grassy eastern slopes of Trollaval to the Bealach an Fhuarain ('pass of the springs') or, preferably, climb Trollaval's east ridge, which involves some easy scrambling. A steep, stony descent leads from Trollaval's twin summits to the Bealach an Fhuarain. The geology changes at this pass, the hills to the south being built of felsite and gneiss on a Torridonian sandstone base rather than gabbro. These smoother rocks are slippery when wet and don't give the grip found on gabbro. The scree path up Ainshval from the bealach avoids the steepest rocks of the ridge on the west lower down and on the east higher up. If the rocky buttress is taken direct it's a Grade 3 scramble. This path is indistinct in places, and can be hard to locate in descent. From the flat summit of Ainshval there are more excellent views. The last of the high peaks of the Rum Cuillin, Sgurr nan Gillean (probably 'peak

of the gullies', 764m), is now a walk, mostly on grass. The east ridge of Sgurr nan Gillean is steep and craggy, so the best descent route is down the south ridge until the cliffs can be turned and a descent made to Dibidil Bothy and the coast path back to Kinloch. This complete traverse is 27km long, with 2025m of ascent, and takes 9–10hrs. It can be shortened by missing out Sgurr nan Gillean and returning from Ainshval to the Bealach an Fhurain, then either descending Glen Dibidil or traversing to the Bealach an Oir and then the Bealach Bairc-mheall and descending Coire Dubh.

Ⓑ Rock Climbing on Rum

The rock climbing on Rum is regarded as some of the best on any island outside Skye. In his guidebook *The Island of Rhum* (Cicerone, 1998) Hamish Brown lists over 100 routes on the cliffs of Barkeval, Hallival, Askival, Trollaval and Ruinsival, many in the lower grades. Among these are Archangel Route, a 120m Very Difficult first climbed by M. Ward and W. H. Murray in 1948, and described by Hamish Brown as 'a route of interest and character', and Central Rib, a 90m Hard Severe first climbed by D. Stewart and D. Bennett in 1950 and described by Brown as 'one of the best routes on Rhum'. Both these climbs are on the big gabbro cliff on the south side of Trollaval called the Harris Buttress, which the Scottish Mountaineering Club (SMC)'s *The Islands of Scotland District Guide* says has 'some of the longest and finest routes on Rhum'.

7:5 SKYE

To many mountaineers Skye is **the** Scottish island because of the Cuillin, that range of steep spiky rock peaks regarded by many as the finest mountains in Britain. Although the Cuillin are spectacular and exciting Skye has much more to offer, with the gentler although still impressive Red Hills and the weird landscape of the Trotternish Ridge, with its pinnacles and landslips, plus some of the wildest and highest coastal cliffs.

Skye is the largest island in the Inner Hebrides and the second largest Scottish island (Lewis and Harris in the Outer Hebrides is the largest). It measures roughly 80km by 50km, covering some 1600km². With over a dozen long sea lochs biting into the land it has a very irregular shape. There are five main peninsulas between the sea lochs – Sleat,

Minginish, Duirinish, Waternish and Trotternish. These peninsulas have been likened to wings, and one of the names of Skye is An t-Eilean Sgiathanach – 'the winged island'. The meaning of Skye itself is obscure, but it could come from the Norse words for 'wing' or 'mist'. Another Gaelic name for Skye is Eilean a'Cheo, the 'misty island'.

The geology of Skye is complicated, and this is another island popular with students of geology. Much of the island is the result of volcanic activity that occurred during the break-up of the Caledonian mountain range and the formation of the Atlantic Ocean some 65 million years ago. Vast amounts of basalt lava spread over the region, covering older sedimentary rocks. The remnants of the largest volcanoes form the Red Hills and the Cuillin. The glaciers of the ice age then carved the landscape into the forms we know today.

The Cuillin is a 14km long, sensational narrow curving rock arête running round the great bowl of Coir' Uisg, which is set in arguably the most impressive mountain landscape in Scotland. The range lies on the Minginish peninsula in the southern half of Skye. The main Cuillin Ridge has many side spurs and a wealth of cliffs, pinnacles, slabs, gullies and towers – a rock wonderland that brings joy to scramblers and climbers and fear to those without a good head for heights. The name Cuillin probably derives from the Norse *kiolen*, meaning 'high rocks'. Standing out from the sea the Cuillin would have been a landmark for the Vikings. Although often called the Cuillins, the Cuillin Hills or the Black Cuillin the correct name is just the Cuillin.

The Red Hills are big, bulky hills with steep sides and rounded summits. They dominate the view between Broadford and Sligachan from the A87, which curls round them along the coast, forming two groups, the Eastern Red Hills between Broadford and Loch Ainort and the Western Red Hills along the south side of Glen Sligachan. The name Red Hills is a translation of the Gaelic *Na Beinnean Dearga*. The pale, pink granite that makes up these hills is the reason for the name. Sometimes they are called the Red Cuillin in contrast to the Black Cuillin to their west, built of dark gabbro. The granite forms vast scree slopes but few crags. Away from the scree the Red Hills are grassy. Much gentler than the Cuillin, the Red Hills are for walkers rather than scramblers and climbers.

There are 12 Munros on Skye, all in the Cuillin, plus two Corbetts and ten Grahams. Of the Munros

Garbh-bheinn, Clach Glas and Bla Bheinn from Marsco

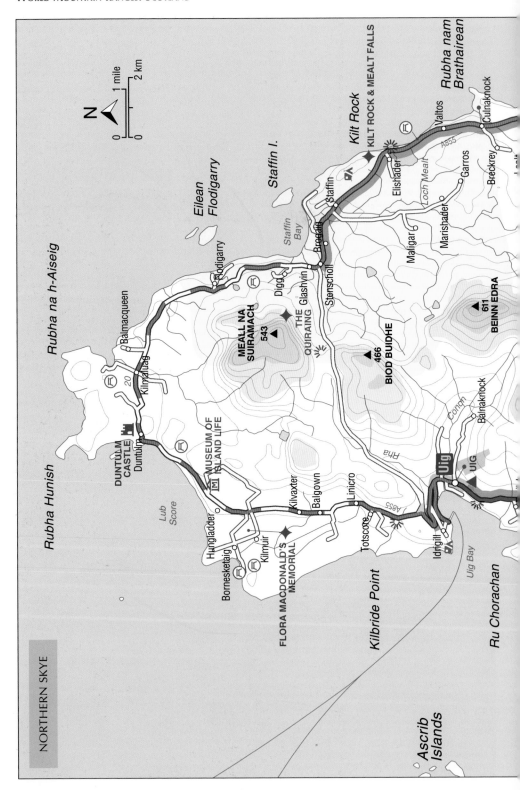

NORTHERN SKYE

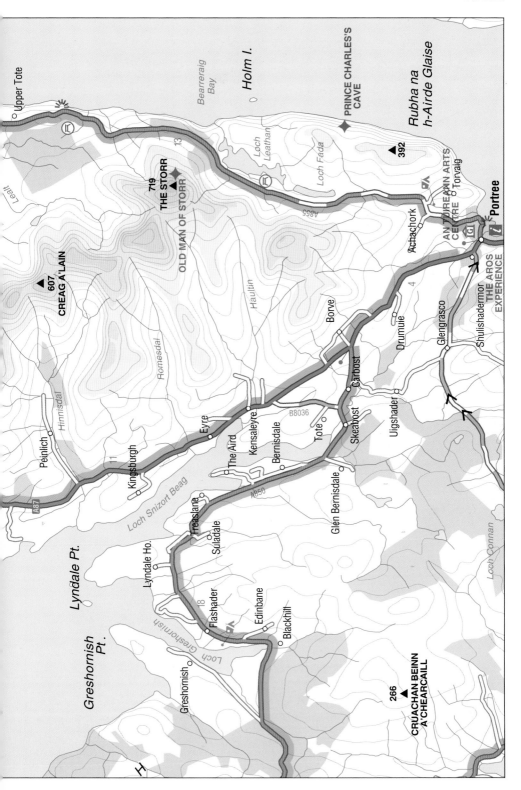

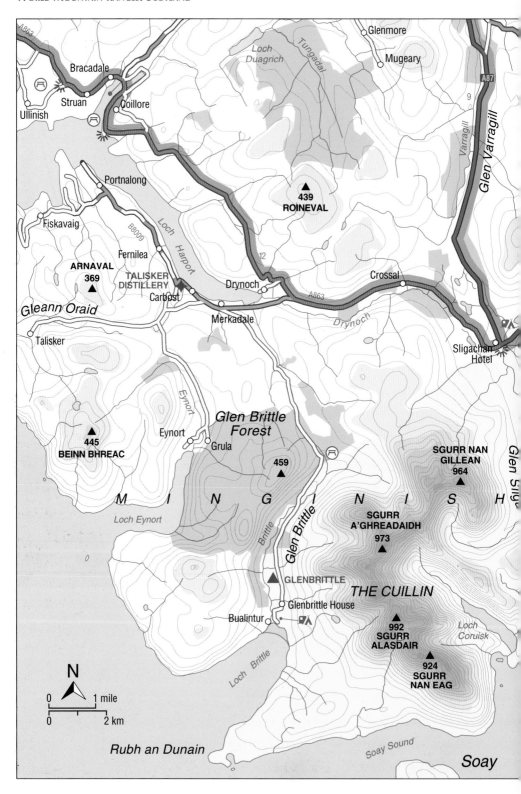

Glenmore

Mugeary

Loch
Duagrich

Bracadale

Struan

Coillore

Ullinish

Portnalong

Fiskavaig

Fernilea

ARNAVAL
369

TALISKER
DISTILLERY

Carbost

Gleann Oraid

Talisker

439
ROINEVAL

Loch Harport

Drynoch

Merkadale

Crossal

Drynoch

Sligachan
Hotel

Glen Varragill

Varragill

Eynort

Glen Brittle
Forest

Eynort

Grula

459

445
BEINN BHREAC

M   I   N   G

Loch Eynort

Brittle

Glen Brittle

G   I   N   I   S   H

SGURR NAN
GILLEAN
964

SGURR
A'GHREADAIDH
973

Glen Sligachan

GLENBRITTLE

Glenbrittle House

Bualintur

THE CUILLIN

992
SGURR
ALASDAIR

924
SGURR
NAN EAG

Loch
Coruisk

N

0   1 mile

0   2 km

Rubh an Dunain

Soay Sound

Soay

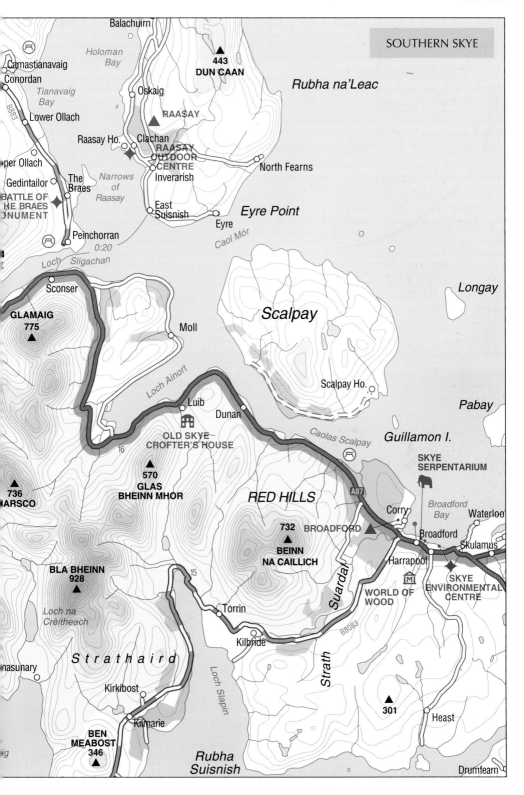

SOUTHERN SKYE

Balachuirn
Holoman Bay
Camastianavaig
Conordan
▲ 443 DUN CAAN
Rubha na'Leac
Oskaig
Tianavaig Bay
Lower Ollach
RAASAY
▲
per Ollach
Raasay Ho.
Clachan
RAASAY OUTDOOR CENTRE
North Fearns
Gedintailor
The Braes
Narrows of Raasay
Inverarish
Eyre Point
BATTLE OF THE BRAES MONUMENT
East Suisnish
Eyre
Caol Mór
Peinchorran
0:20
Longay
Loch Sligachan
Sconser
Scalpay
GLAMAIG 775 ▲
Moll
Loch Ainort
Scalpay Ho.
Pabay
Luib
Dunan
Caolas Scalpay
Guillamon I.
OLD SKYE CROFTER'S HOUSE
16
SKYE SERPENTARIUM
570 GLAS BHEINN MHOR ▲
▲ 736 MARSCO
RED HILLS
A87
Corry
Broadford Bay
Waterloo
732 ▲ BEINN NA CAILLICH
BROADFORD ▲
Broadford
Skulamus
BLA BHEINN 928 ▲
15
Harrapool
SKYE ENVIRONMENTAL CENTRE
Loch na Crèitheach
WORLD OF WOOD
Suardal
Torrin
Strath
S t r a t h a i r d
Kilbride
B8083
nasunary
Loch Slapin
Kirkibost
Kilmarie
▲ 301
Heast
BEN MEABOST 346 ▲
Rubha Suisnish
Drumfearn

Bla Bheinn ('blue hill', 928m) is the odd one out, lying east of the main Cuillin Ridge on the far side of Strath na Creitheach from the others. It's the highest of a group of hills known as the Cuillin Outliers. The other Munros make up the principle peaks on the main Cuillin Ridge. From north to south the Munros are: Sgurr nan Gillean (probably 'peak of the gullies', 964m); Am Basteir (probably 'deep cleft', 934m); Bruach na Frithe ('slope of the wild mountainous land' or 'deer forest', 958m); Sgurr a'Mhadaidh ('peak of the fox', 918m); Sgurr a'Ghreadaidh ('peak of the thrashing', 973m); Sgurr na Banachdich ('milk-maid's peak', 965m); The Inaccessible Pinnacle (986m); Sgurr Mhic Choinnich ('Mackenzie's peak', 948m); Sgurr Alasdair ('Alexander's peak', 992m); Sgurr Dubh Mor ('big black peak', 944m); and Sgurr na Eag ('peak of the notch', 924m). The number of *sgurrs* – 'rocky peaks' – is a strong hint as to the nature of the terrain.

The two Corbetts are very different from each other. Glamaig (probably 'greedy woman', 775m), the highest of the Red Hills, is a huge pile of gran-ite scree rising above Sligachan on the east side of the island. 808m Garbh-bheinn ('rough hill') is a much more rocky hill and one of the Cuillin Outliers, attached to Bla Bheinn by a narrow and difficult ridge.

The Grahams are spread across Skye. Three rise in the east of the island above the narrow channel between Kylerhea and Glenelg on the mainland. These rather undistinguished moorland hills are: Ben Aslak (probably 'breast hill', 610m); Sgurr na Coinnich ('peak of moss', 739m); and Beinn na Caillich ('hill of the old woman', 732m). Further west, rising above Broadford, are the more inter-esting Eastern Red Hills, with another Beinn na Caillich, this one 732m, and Beinn Dearg Mhor ('big red hill', 709m). Belig (probably 'birch bark' or 'thick-lipped', 802m) is the northern summit of the Cuillin Outliers range. In the Western Red Hills there are two Grahams lying south of Glamaig, another Beinn Dearg Mhor (731m) and Marsco (name unclear, often given as 'seagull rock', 736m), one of the most impressive Skye hills out-with the Cuillin. The final two Grahams lie in the far north of Skye on the Trotternish peninsula. These are The Storr (often translated as 'peak' or 'pillar' but it actually just means 'big', 719m) and Hartaval ('rocky hill', 669m).

The main Cuillin Ridge is part of a private estate but Loch Coruisk, Bla Bheinn, Garbh-bheinn,

Marsco and Glamaig are all owned by the John Muir Trust, which has three contiguous Skye estates, Strathaird, Sconser and Torrin.

Skye is easily accessible by the road bridge from Kyle of Lochalsh to Kyleakin. Kyle of Lochalsh can be reached by train from Inverness and by the A87 road from the Great Glen, which then runs across the bridge and along the east side of Skye through Broadford and Portree to Uig on the west side of Trotternish. The more romantic way to reach Skye is by ferry, from either Mallaig to Armadale in the southeast of the island or from Glenelg to Kylerhea, not far from Kyle of Lochalsh. Mallaig is at the end of the West Highland Line from Fort William, a wonderful train journey, and the A830 road. From Armadale the A851 runs north to join the A87 just east of Broadford. The little Glenelg ferry is accessed by a steep, narrow minor road from Shiel Bridge. Another minor road then leads through Glen Arroch to the A87. The northern Cuillin can be reached from Sligachan on the A87, the southern Cuillin from a minor road from the B8009 alongside Loch Harport on the west side of Skye to Glen Brittle. Trotternish is encircled by the A87 and the A855.

Skye is a popular tourist island and has all facil-ities. The small town of Portree is the capital, with a population of around 2,500: the population of the whole island is around 10,000. It's a good base for Trotternish but a little far from the other hills. Broadford on the north coast towards the eastern end of the island also has all facilities and is close to the Eastern Red Hills. For the Cuillin and the Western Red Hills there are two bases, both famous in the history of mountaineering – Sligachan in the north where there is a campsite, bunkhouse, self-catering cottages and the Sligachan Hotel (www.sligachan.co.uk), which was used by many of the early mountaineers and famous climbers; The Seumas Bar at Sligachan is still an excellent place to wile away a stormy day or celebrate a successful Cuillin Ridge traverse, while at the other end of the Cuillin is Glen Brittle, where mountaineers like W. H. Murray and Alastair Borthwick also stayed. Glen Brittle has a campsite with a small shop, a youth hostel and a mountaineering club hut.

⊗ The Eastern Red Hills: Beinn na Caillich and Beinn Dearg Mhor

The bulky pale scree pyramid of Beinn na Caillich rises above the little town of Broadford. It's the high point on a horseshoe of hills surrounding Coire Gorm ('blue corrie'). The circuit of this horseshoe makes for a good short day (4–5hrs). With a distance of 8km it's not a long walk but there are 980m of ascent and the terrain is rough and often steep, with bogs, scree and rock to cross, so it is quite arduous. The round starts at the ruins of Coire-chat-achan ('corrie of the wildcats'), a house where Samuel Johnson and James Boswell stayed during their tour of the Hebrides, at the end of a minor road leading south from the A87. From Coire-chat-achan the route heads up boggy moorland to the stony upper slopes of Beinn na Caillich. The summit itself is grassy and sports a huge cairn and a trig point. There is a splendid view of the mainland hills and Broadford Bay far below, and an even better one west to the serrated Cuillin and the rounded Western Red Hills. The massive summit cairn is said to have been erected over the body of a Norwegian princess so that she could look north to her homeland and winds from Norway would reach her. Beinn na Caillich is the first hill on Skye to have a recorded ascent, by scientist Thomas Pennant in 1772, which isn't surprising given its closeness to Broadford. Of course the Norwegian princess's cairn was already there, so this was hardly a first ascent.

From the summit rough terrain leads down west to the bealach with Beinn Dearg Mhor, which is climbed by its east ridge with fine views into the corries either side. Again there are splendid views from the summit, which also has a large cairn. The ascent south to the next bealach, Bealach Coire Sgreamhach, is on very steep loose scree that requires care. From the bealach a short ascent leads to the third and final summit on the horseshoe, 582m Beinn Dearg Bheag ('little red hill'). Yet again there's a big cairn and a good view. From the summit the descent leads down the east ridge above Coire Odhair and then across boggy moorland back to the start.

The Western Red Hills: Glamaig, Beinn Dearg Mhor and Beinn Dearg Mheadhonach ☆

Three of the Western Red Hills form a long ridge between Loch Ainort and Loch Slapin. Glamaig (775m), Beinn Dearg Mhor ('big red mountain', 731m) and Beinn Dearg Meadhonach ('middle red hill', from its position in the centre of the Western Red Hills, 651m) tower over the A87 road as it climbs over the shoulder of Beinn Dearg Mhor from

Loch Ainort, and descends Gleann Torra-mhichaig. Further north Glamaig rises as a steep pyramid above Sligachan and it's from here that the traverse of the ridge begins, first beside the River Sligachan and then the Allt Daraich which runs through an impressive wooded gorge. Once beyond the gorge climb the long scree-covered northwest ridge of Beinn Dearg Meadhonach, the Druim na Ruaige. The summit is a narrow 250m long ridge with the high point at the southeast end. It's directly above the head of Loch Ainort and there is a great view down the loch. To the west, over Glen Sligachan, Sgurr nan Gillean looks tremendous. The fine views continue throughout the ridge walk down to the Bealach Mosgaraidh and up to the narrow tapered pyramid of Beinn Dearg Mhor. There's a well-built stone cairn on the little summit.

The massive hulk of Glamaig rises to the north of Beinn Dearg Mhor, across the Bealach an Sgairde ('scree pass', 415m). A steep and rocky descent leads down 300m to this bealach, followed by an equally steep climb straight up to the summit of Glamaig, which is called Sgurr Mhairi ('Mary's peak'). The lower summit to the northeast is An Coileach ('little cock'). The summit is actually made of basalt rather than granite, pushed up here by the granite below during volcanic activity. Situated on the coast and north of the other high hills Glamaig is a superb viewpoint, with a dramatic view of the Cuillin and the Trotternish ridge and over the islands of the Inner Sound to the mainland mountains.

There is an annual race up and down Glamaig from Sligachan. This is held in honour of an event in 1899, when a Ghurka called Havildar Harkabir Thapa took 37mins to reach the summit and 18mins to get back down. This amazing exploit was done in bare feet and no one did it any faster for 90 years. Today the record for the ascent and descent stands at an amazing 44mins, 41secs, which was achieved by Mark Rigby in 1997.

To descend from Glamaig just take a direct line towards Sligachan far below. Mostly it's steep scree underfoot, although there are some grassy rakes, until boggy moorland is reached and the angle eases. The walk is 11km long, with 1245m of ascent, and takes 5–6hrs.

Marsco ☆

Marsco rises on the east side of Glen Sligachan, between the Cuillin Outliers and the Western Red

The Western Red Hills from Marsco – from the left Beinn Dearg Mheadhonach, Glamaig and Beinn Dearg Mhor

Hills. Low passes separate it from neighbouring hills and it takes the form of a gently curving steep-sided narrow ridge. From Sligachan it's viewed end on and appears as a distinctive pyramid. There are superb views from the summit, especially of Bla Bheinn, and these combined with its appearance and rugged nature make it the finest of the Red Hills. It's the only one with any rock climbing too, with routes on the crag called Fiaclan Dearg ('red tooth') which bulges out from the western slopes of the hill. The ascent of Marsco is a fine walk even if much of the time is spent on the approach. From Sligachan the walk goes down Glen Sligachan to the Allt na Measarroch, where the path divides, with Marsco rising ahead and pulling you on. A rough muddy path leads beside the Allt na Measarroch to Mam a'Phobuill ('pass of the people', 285m), the high point between Marsco and Beinn Dearg Mheadhonach. There are stories that Bonnie Prince Charlie crossed this pass while on the run from government troops after the Battle of Culloden and the collapse of the 1745 uprising. The pass is an atmospheric place, with steep slopes either side and a view southeast to Garbh-bheinn and Bla Bheinn. To the south is Coire nan Laogh ('corrie of the calves') on the northeast flanks of

Marsco. To reach the top, climb the steep south side of Coire nan Laogh, which reaches the narrow summit ridge southeast of the highest point. The views from Marsco are some of the best from any Scottish summit. The magnificent Cuillin dominates the view, its dark ragged crest curling round deep Harta Corrie. The Western Red Hills look smooth and rounded, in contrast with Beinn Dearg Mhor an almost delicate spire, and Glamaig a bulky dome. Southwards the view is down Strath na Creithach and over the black waters of Loch na Creithach, with dark gully-seamed Bla Bheinn rising above it, to the green meadows and pebble beach at Camasunary and then out over the sea to the distant islands of Rum and Eigg.

Descent can be made down the steep, stony northern side of Coire nan Laogh and back to the Mam a'Phobuill and the path to Sligachan. The walk is 13km long, with 750m of ascent, and takes 4–6hrs.

A shorter if less scenic route up Marsco goes up Coire nam Bruadaran ('corrie of dreams') from the A87 above Loch Ainort to the 325m bealach at its head, and then up the southeast ridge to the summit. The descent can be made down the side of Coire nan Laogh to the Mam a'Phobuill. This route is 8km long, with 730m of ascent, and takes 3–4hrs.

⑥ Rock Climbing on Marsco

What little rock climbing there is in the Red Hills is found on Fiaclan Dearg on Marsco. The first route to be climbed here was in 1943 when Noel Odell, the last man to see Mallory and Irvine on Everest in 1924, made the ascent of his eponymous Odell's Route, a 180m Difficult. There are also Very Difficult, Very Severe and Hard Very Severe routes on the same cliff.

❸ Garbh-bheinn and Belig

Garbh-bheinn (808m) is at the northern end of the Cuillin Outliers and rises above the head of Loch Ainort. On its slopes granite abuts gabbro, the Red Hills meeting the Cuillin. The circuit of Garbh-bheinn and its outlier, Belig (702m), makes for a good short day out. The terrain is boggy lower down and rocky high up, with some steep sections where easy scrambling is required, so this is quite a tough walk despite being only 8km long. There are 1000m of ascent and the round takes 4–5hrs. The walk starts on the A87 at the head of Loch Ainort, where the Allt Coire nam Bruardaran ('burn of the corrie of dreams') thunders down in a big waterfall. From the road the route heads south across boggy moorland to the Druim Eadar Da Choire ('the ridge between the corries'), which is climbed to the 489m summit. A short descent leads to a col where the pale granite of the Red Hills changes to the dark gabbro of the Cuillin, a clear division. Ahead the slopes are rough and rocky, behind smoother and grassier. From the col a stony path climbs the north ridge of Garbh-bheinn over scree and rock, and beside a line of old rusty fence posts, to the summit. This ridge is quite narrow near the top with a little easy scrambling. Throughout the ascent the Cuillin look magnificent. From the top nearby Bla Bheinn looks tempting, but there is no route there for walkers, only for rock climbers and good scramblers (see Rock Climbing on Bla Bheinn and the Cuillin Outliers below).

From the summit descend the stony northeast ridge to 455m Bealach na Beiste ('pass of the beast') and then climb the steep southwest ridge to the narrow summit of Belig, the northernmost of the Cuillin Outliers. The actual summit rocks are basalt rather than gabbro and can be slippery when wet. Looking back Garbh-bheinn rises as a steep pyramid. To the south is the big rocky north face of Sgurr nan Each ('peak of the horses', 720m) with Bla Bheinn rising behind it. To the northeast is Glas Bheinn Mhor ('big grey mountain', 570m), which is geologically one of the Red Hills but is linked to Belig by a 375m col from which it can be easily climbed. If not going over Glas Bheinn Mhor descend by the north ridge of Belig, which is narrow and rocky in places, onto open moorland that leads back to the start.

⊗ Bla Bheinn ☆

The only Skye Munro not on the main Cuillin Ridge, Bla Bheinn (928m) is a tremendous mountain, a massive block of steep gully-seamed gabbro rising between Loch Slapin and Strath na Creitheach, with a long south ridge running down to beautiful Camasunary. Bla Bheinn's shape is that of an arrowhead, with the point to the north. Bla Bheinn looks very impressive across Loch Slapin from the village of Torrin, with the complex rock scenery of the east face rising above the sea. Bla Bheinn is so steep and rocky that there are only two feasible routes for walkers, and one of those involves a short section of easy scrambling.

The first recorded ascent of Bla Bheinn was in 1857 by the very unlikely couple of the poet Algernon Swinburne and English professor John Nicol, who thought it was the highest peak on Skye. Ian R. Mitchell, in *Scotland's Mountains Before the Mountaineers* (Luath, 1999), says that the pair spent most of the summer of 1857 in a drunken stupor, but they did find the time and energy to climb Bla Bheinn.

Bla Bheinn is the Gaelic spelling of the mountain's name. It's sometimes anglicised to Blaven. Peter Drummond, in *Scottish Hill Names: Their Origin and Meaning* (Scottish Mountaineering Trust, 2007), reckons it probably comes from the Norse *bla fjall* – blue mountain, with *bheinn* a Gaelicisation of *fjall*, both words meaning 'mountain'.

The easiest and shortest route begins near the head of Loch Slapin, where the B8083 Broadford to Elgol road crosses the Allt Dunaiche. A path heads towards Bla Bheinn beside the Allt Dunaiche, which runs in a lovely wooded gorge, and then climbs into Coire Uaigneich ('secret corrie'), with the huge cliffs of Bla Bheinn's east face towering overhead. From the corrie the cairned path climbs steep rock and scree slopes to the summit, where

Clach Glas and Bla Bheinn from Marsco

there is a dramatic view across Strath na Creitheach to the main Cuillin Ridge, one of the finest vistas in the Scottish mountains, the Red Hills in contrast looking small and rounded. Southwards Rum and Eigg rise out of the sea, spiky islands in the vast flatness. The descent is by the same route, for a walk of 8km, with 930m of ascent, which takes 5–6hrs.

A longer but more scenic route with splendid views virtually the whole way is via the south ridge. This is mostly a rough walk, but there is a sting in the tail. It starts 400m south of Kilmarie on the Broadford–Elgol road, where it takes an unattractive bulldozed track that runs west over the wide 185m pass called Am Mam ('the breast') and down to Camasunary. The Cuillin Ridge summits can be seen over Am Mam as you climb, but Bla Bheinn is hidden until the top of the pass is reached. The track leads past the foot of Bla Bheinn where it is left for a rough path that climbs the south ridge, on grass initially but then rock the rest of the way, to the south summit (924m). A cleft in the ridge separates this from the higher north summit just 180m away. The descent from the south top into this cleft is steep and involves some easy scrambling. Once in the gap the climb to the north summit is easy. For the descent return to the south summit and either go back down the south ridge or below it to the east, beside the Abhainn nan Leac, back to the Am Mam track. The route is 12km long, with 1200m of ascent, and takes 5–8hrs.

ⓑ Rock Climbing on Bla Bheinn and the Cuillin Outliers ☆

There are rock climbs of all grades on the huge cliffs of Bla Bheinn. The most famous, although barely more than a scramble for experienced rock climbers, is the Clach Glas–Bla Bheinn Traverse. This is graded Moderate, although there are some harder variations. Clach Glas ('grey stone', 786m) is a spectacular fang of rock just to the northeast of Bla Bheinn. Clach Glas was first climbed in 1887 by a party led by Charles Pilkington, who made many climbs in the Cuillin, including the first ascent of the Inaccessible Pinnacle. Pilkington climbed Clach Glas by a gully on the west face. The route is now graded Difficult and called Pilkington's Route.

The traverse of Clach Glas is regarded as one of the best easy climbs on Skye. There is no walker's route to the summit. Clach Glas is reached from the path to Bla Bheinn beside the Allt na Dunaiche, which is left for Choire a' Caise and a clamber up steep rocky slopes to the bealach at the foot of the north ridge. The ascent of the north ridge is steep and exposed in places. In *Skye*

Scrambles (SMT, 2000) Noel Williams says that 'a couple of pitches may justify a rope' on the final tower. From the tiny summit the route goes down the south ridge, starting with an apparent knife-edge arête, actually the edge of a slab, known as the Imposter, to a mossy col known as the Putting Green. From this col a complex route, with several variations, leads up the northeast face of Bla Bheinn to the summit. Noel Williams says this is 'technically the most difficult part of the Clach Glas–Bla Bheinn traverse'.

One of the most impressive rock features on Bla Bheinn is the Great Prow, which overlooks Coire Uaigneich high on the east face. Routes on the Great Prow include 128m Jib (E1, first climbed by M. Boyson and D. Alcock in 1969), 120m Finger In The Dyke (E5, first climbed by P. Thorburn, G. Farquhar and G. Latter in 1997 – described by Kevin Howett in *Rock Climbing in Scotland* as 'serious but atmospheric route up the arête of the Great Prow') and the classic 105m Great Prow itself (VS, first climbed by T. W. Band, P. W. F. Gribbon, N. S. Ross and W. Tauber in 1968).

The east face is split by the Great Scree Gully which leads to the gap between the south and north summits. This was climbed by the Willink brothers in 1873, who then descended part way down a gully on the west face before traversing out.

Although steep the rocks on the west side of Bla Bheinn are broken and riven with gullies, so the climbing here is said to be less interesting than on the east side.

Loch Coruisk ☆

Set in the heart of the Cuillin with the mountains curving round it, Loch Coruisk in Coir' Uisg is the most spectacular, impressive and wildest place in the Scottish mountains. All around the rocky ridges and buttresses of the Cuillin rise to the spires and towers of the summits. The steep rocks start at sea level, and a more mountainous landscape cannot be imagined. The central and southern peaks of the Cuillin Ridge all rise from the corrie floor from Sgurr a'Mhadaidh and Sgurr a'Ghreadaidh at the head of the corrie, round to Gars-bheinn rising above Loch Scavaig. On the east side of the loch runs the less distinctive but still rocky and rugged Druim nan Ramh.

Carved out by ice the loch lies in a glacial hollow called Coir' Uisg. The loch is 2.5km long and 0.5km wide and the bottom is about 30m below sea level. The sea is very close, the River Scavaig

Loch Coruisk and the Cuillin from Sgurr na Stri

☆ BOAT CRUISES TO LOCH CORUISK

A delightful way to reach Coruisk is by boat from Elgol to the south. This is also a traditional way to visit the loch as the first tourists, including J.M.W.Turner, who painted a dramatic picture of the area in 1831 called Loch Coruisk, Skye that can be seen in the National Galleries of Scotland in Edinburgh, and Sir Walter Scott who was here in 1814, came by boat. Two companies run boat trips, Bella Jane (www.bellajane.co.uk) and Misty Isle Boat Trips (www.mistyisleboattrips.co.uk), and you can return an hour or so later on the same boat, arrange to spend the whole day at Coruisk, returning on a later cruise, or take the boat one way and walk out by one of the routes described below

which drains the loch being just 400m long, one of the shortest rivers in the world. This little river runs down gabbro slabs into Loch na Cuilce at the head of Loch Scavaig. On a knoll above the river is a private climbers' hut, the Loch Coruisk Memorial Hut, owned by the Junior Mountaineering Club of Scotland. On the shore of Loch na Cuilce is a landing stage where boats from Elgol (see 'Boat Cruises' below) tie up. There are small islands not far offshore on which seals can usually be seen.

The name Coruisk is an Anglicisation of *Coir' Uisg*, which means 'corrie of water'. As well as the loch there are myriad burns on the hillside that foam white during and after rain, as the steep rocky terrain means water runs off very quickly. Generally the loch is referred to as Coruisk and the corrie in which it lies as Coir' Uisg.

There are a number of paths to Loch Coruisk – see 'Low-level walks' below.

ⓐ Low-level Walks: Sligachan, Camasunary, Loch Coruisk, Elgol ☆

A network of paths on the east side of the Cuillin Ridge makes for some superb low-level walks in rugged, wild country with many options. The paths are rough and often wet and muddy and the remote country which they traverse gives a feeling of adventure and seriousness unusual on glens and passes walks. There are streams to be crossed too, and a short scramble on one path. Even low down this is not terrain for gentle strolls.

Starting in the north at Sligachan a path runs down Glen Sligachan, with the Red Hills and the Cuillin Outliers on one side and the Cuillin Ridge on the other. At the start the view is dominated by the great ragged pyramid of Sgurr nan Gillean, with the scree cone of Glamaig across Glen Sligachan to the east and the slighter pyramid of Marsco down the glen. The path passes below these hills to the Lochan Dubha on the low, gentle

watershed between Loch Sligachan and the north coast and Loch Scavaig and the south coast. Just beyond the lochans the path divides. The left fork heads down Strath na Creitheach below the massive west wall of Bla Bheinn and past dark Loch na Creitheach to Camasunary (from the Gaelic *Camas Fhionnnairigh* – 'bay of the white shieling'), a beautiful bay on Loch Scavaig with a sandy beach backed by a smooth green sward. There's a bothy at the west end of the bay and a locked house at the east end. The right fork climbs to the broad Druim Hain ridge, where there is a stupendous view over Loch Coruisk to the Cuillin. The geology changes at Druim Hain, and the granite of the Red Hills is left for the gabbro of the Cuillin. The path wanders along Druim Hain a short way then forks, with the left branch climbing up Sgurr na Stri (see below) and the right fork descending upper Coire Riabhach and down to Loch Coruisk. The walk from Sligachan to Camasunary is 12km, with 220m of ascent; that from Sligachan to Loch Coruisk 11km, with 410m of ascent. Both walks take 3–4hrs.

The two walks from Sligachan can be linked by the coastal path from Loch Coruisk to Camasunary. This is a very rough and rocky route with a famous scramble called the Bad Step, which may be enjoyable or terrifying, depending on how you view the exposure, which crosses the lower slabs of the south face of Sgurr na Stri as they curve down to the sea. Then at Camasunary the Abhainn Camas Fhionnairigh has to be forded, which can be difficult or impossible when it's in spate. The distance is just 4km, and there's 280m of ascent. It takes 2–3hrs.

If doing the round trip Sligachan–Coruisk–Camasunary–Sligachan (and I recommend this way round for the sudden and magnificent view from Druim Hain) the walk is 28km long, with 900m of ascent, and takes 8–10hrs.

View south from Marsco to Bla Bheinn, Loch Creithach, Camasunary and Sgurr na Stri

Once in the Coruisk basin there is a path round Loch Coruisk that gives superb views of the Cuillin. It's a splendid walk but does involve fording the stream in Coir' Uisg beyond the head of the loch, and the Scavaig River, both of which may be impassable torrents when in spate. There are stepping stones over the Scavaig River but these can be well below the water after heavy rain. The path wanders high up Coir' Uisg beyond the loch, to give a walk of 9km that takes around 3hrs.

Camasunary and Coruisk can also be approached from the south by a path from Elgol, a little village at the end of the B8083 road from Broadford near the tip of the Strathaird peninsula. Elgol lies at the mouth of Loch Scavaig and is a classic viewpoint for the Cuillin. The path to Camasunary is a fine walk along a rugged coastline, with wonderful views of the Cuillin throughout. Steep hillsides run down to the sea and the path cuts across the slopes of Bidein an Fhithich ('peak of the raven') and Ben Cleat ('hill of the rock' or 'cliff'), often high above the waves, before descending to the grassy meadows at the foot of Glen Scaladal. Beyond Glen Scaladal the path runs through strips of attractive deciduous woodland and traverses the lower slopes of Beinn Leacach ('hill of the bare rock') before descending to Camasunary. The walk is just over 5km long and takes 1½–2hrs.

✪ Sgurr na Stri ☆

Sgurr na Stri ('peak of strife', 497m) is a rocky little peak lying between Camasunary and Loch Coruisk and rising steeply from Loch Scavaig. The view of Loch Coruisk and the Cuillin from the top is magnificent, arguably the finest there is, as well as one of the best mountain vistas in Scotland. Sgurr na Stri is steep everywhere except to the north where it is linked to Sgurr Hain. The path from Strath na Creitheach to Coruisk via the Druim Hain gives access to the path to the summit, which runs below Sgurr Hain, past Captain Maryon's Cairn, a pyramid-shaped monument marking where the captain's body was found, and along the north ridge. Several rocky knolls dot the extensive summit area of Sgurr na Stri. The highest pair are at the southern end. The westerly one gives a stunning view over Loch Coruisk to the Cuillin Ridge, which can be seen in its entirety from Gars-bheinn to Sgurr nan Gillean, a magnificent and complex sweep of rock architecture. The easterly summit has good views of Camasunary and Bla Bheinn, but it's the Cuillin that holds the eye.

The easiest route back is to retrace your steps. A pathless alternative is to follow the edge of the steep slopes above Camasunary around the edge of the corrie between Sgurr na Stri and Sgurr Hain, until the angle eases and you can descend into the corrie and down to Camasunary.

Sgurr na Stri is a long way from any roadside starting point. It's only 2km from Druim Hain to the summit but a round trip, whether from Sligachan or Elgol, is around 25km. The long approach can be cancelled out by taking a cruise boat from Elgol (see 'Boat Cruises' above) to Loch Scavaig and back. From the landing stage the round trip is 9km, with 615m of ascent, and takes 3–4hrs.

The Cuillin Ridge ☆

The Cuillin Ridge offers climbers and scramblers a lifetime's worth of exploration. The complexity of this small slice of jagged mountain landscape is astonishing. Every corrie, every ridge, every crag, every gully is different. It's all just rock and water, yet the variety is immense. The gloriousness of the Cuillin leads writers and visitors to extravagant descriptions in an attempt to match the extravagant scenery. In the 1930s Everest mountaineer Frank Smythe thought they were the only real mountain range in Britain. W.H. Murray, in *Mountaineering In Scotland* (Baton Wicks, 1997) said on first visiting the Cuillin 'my wild dreams fell short of the wilder reality', while Ben Humble, author of *The Cuillin of Skye* (a wonderful book, first published in 1952 and sadly long out of print), said 'they have no equal in all the world'. In his book of marvellous photographs and interesting mountain philosophy, *The Cuillin Great Mountain Ridge of Skye* (Constable, 1994), Gordon Stainforth writes 'it is a fantasy, a mountain lover's dream, a vision full of indefinite hopes and climbing possibilities'. This ecstatic adulation is capped by Hamish Brown, who described the Cuillin in *Hamish's Mountain Walk* (Sandstone Press, 2010), the story of the first continuous round of the Munros, as 'Valhalla, Mecca, the Ultimate'.

And this praise is all justified. The Cuillin really are like no other mountains in Scotland: nowhere else does rock form such a myriad shapes; nowhere else is there so much rock at all; nowhere else are so many distinctive peaks crammed together.

This fantastic mountain landscape is actually the last vestige of violent volcanic activity that occurred around sixty million years ago as North America pulled away from Europe and the Atlantic

Ocean widened, forming a chain of volcanoes down the west side of the Highlands. The rocks from which the Cuillin are formed started out as molten magma in a chamber far below the surface of the earth beneath a huge volcano. Slow cooling turned the magma into coarse-grained igneous rock. Dark gabbro is the commonest type, but there are also outcrops of even coarser reddish-brown peridotite. Both rocks have amazing grip, and so are superb for scrambling and climbing. Indeed, so rough is the texture that it can easily remove skin, tear clothing and shred footwear. Intruded into the coarse rocks are dykes of much smoother basalt and dolerite, which cooled more quickly either on or not far below the earth's surface. Basalt is slippery when wet and it's wise to be able to distinguish between it and gabbro. There isn't that much basalt but it does make up the Inaccessible Pinnacle and the summit of the highest peak, Sgurr Alasdair.

Glaciation finished off the process of producing the Cuillin we admire today, scooping out the corries and shaving off the back walls to form the knife-edge arêtes. Weathering continues today and the Cuillin are slowly crumbling and decaying as rocks fall and pinnacles topple. In the 30 years I've been visiting the range there have been significant changes to two standard routes due to rock fall.

Gabbro and peridotite contain iron oxide which is magnetic, and causes compasses to give inaccurate readings. You can place a compass on a slab of gabbro and watch the needle change direction as you move the compass about. To minimise the chance of misleading directions compasses should be held away from rocks and readings taken from different places. Of course if you have a GPS with an electronic compass this won't be a problem.

For walkers the Cuillin is very challenging. For scramblers and climbers the Cuillin is joyous terrain with a myriad opportunities and the pleasure of being able to move over steep, rocky ground for hour after hour. Only three of the Munros – Bruach na Frithe, Sgurr na Banachdich and Sgurr nan Eag – can be climbed without scrambling, and these ascents are rough and rocky. Scrambling, often sustained and exposed, is required to reach the remaining Munros, except for the Inaccessible Pinnacle, the easiest route up which is a Moderate rock climb.

Good route-finding and navigation is essential in the Cuillin. Go wrong and you are likely to find yourself above a sheer drop or on loose, dangerous steep slopes. Most maps are confusing and unhelpful, as they fail to delineate the complex terrain in a clear and useful way. One that does show the terrain well, and the only one I recommend for the Cuillin, is the Harvey's Superwalker The Cuillin, which has an enlargement of the main ridge at 1:12,500 on the back.

In the description below the Cuillin Ridge Munros are described from north to south.

🚩 Sgurr nan Gillean ☆

Sgurr nan Gillean (964m) is one of the best-known and most distinctive peaks in the Cuillin. It's the final summit at the northern end of the range and there is a classic much-photographed and admired view from Sligachan. The summit is tiny and pointed and sends out three long ridges, of which the most notable is Pinnacle Ridge, a Difficult grade rock climb involving an abseil. The easiest ascent route is by the southeast ridge. Although mostly a rough walk this involves a grade 3 exposed scramble just below the summit, making Sgurr nan Gillean one of the hardest of the Cuillin Munros to climb. The southeast ridge is sometimes called the tourist route, but that doesn't mean it's easy. The walk starts by crossing the wet and boggy moorland south of Sligachan on a clear path. This forks twice, both times at bridged stream crossings. Each time cross the bridges, which go over the Allt Dearg Mor and the Allt Dearg Beag ('big' and 'little red burn'). Leaving the moor the path crosses the flat spur of Nead na H-Iolaire ('the eagle's nest') and then Coire Riabhach ('streaked corrie'). From the corrie the path becomes much steeper, threading a way through boulders and scree to the southeast ridge where the scrambling begins. This is easy until the last 100m is reached. Here the ridge is narrow and the scrambling exposed with some hard moves whether the crest of the ridge is taken direct or skirted on the left side. A last few very airy metres lead to the tiny summit. Very steep slopes fall away on all sides and there's a feeling of being suspended in the air.

The views are as grand as you'd expect. The rest of the Cuillin Ridge sweeps round in a huge arc to the southwest. Immediately to the south, almost below your feet, is Lota Corrie, with bigger Harta Corrie beyond it. The Red Hills across Glen Sligachan appear bulky and rounded but to their south Garbhbheinn and Bla Bheinn look rugged and impressive. East lies the sea, reaching out to the island of Scalpay and the mainland, while to the north the Trotternish ridge stretches out into the distance.

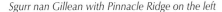

Sgurr nan Gillean with Pinnacle Ridge on the left

The first recorded ascent of Sgurr nan Gillean was in 1836, when the southeast ridge was climbed by local man Duncan MacIntyre, who had made several previous attempts and who discovered this route, and the scientist James David Forbes, who was professor of natural philosophy at Edinburgh University. Interested in the heights of the mountains Forbes returned with a barometer to measure them, which had not been done before, and, with MacIntyre, climbed Sgurr nan Gillean again in 1845 for the second known ascent, this time by the harder west ridge, and also Bruach na Frithe, the first recorded ascent (when Forbes died in 1868 these were still the only known ascents on the Cuillin Ridge). Forbes' measurements with the barometer were surprisingly accurate and he was only about 10m out from the height of Sgurr nan Gillean as measured with modern equipment. Forbes went on to make the first map of the Cuillin, which was fairly accurate and included summit heights. He also made a geological survey that showed that there had been glaciers in the Cuillin.

Returning down the southeast ridge is the easiest descent route. The west ridge involves Moderate or Difficult grade rock climbing, depending on the exact route, and is very exposed in places (older books refer to a prominent pinnacle called the Gendarme on the west ridge – this collapsed in 1987). Only confident climbers should go that way. The return trip via the southeast ridge is 12km long, with 1000m of ascent, and takes 6–7hrs.

➌ Am Basteir, the Basteir Tooth and Sgurr a'Bhasteir ☆

Am Basteir (934m) is a great wedge of rock with very steep slopes above Coire a'Bhasteir to the north and Lota Corrie to the south. The western end is a cliff with a fang of rock known as the Basteir Tooth rising beyond it. The profile of Am Basteir and the Tooth is very distinctive and easily recognised from afar.

The only scrambling route on Am Basteir is from Bealach a'Bhasteir to the east. To reach the bealach take the path from Sligachan over the Allt Dearg Mor to the Allt Dearg Beag, and then alongside the latter to the deep slash of the Bhasteir Gorge (which was first climbed by an Alpine Club party in 1890). A wonderful cairned path leads through slabs high on the west side of the gorge into spectacular Coire a'Bhasteir, from where scree slopes lead to the bealach.

From the bealach the east ridge of Am Basteir leads towards the summit. Although narrow and exposed this would be a relatively easy ascent

Bruach na Frithe (left), Sgurr a'Fionn Choire, Bealach nan Lice and Am Basteir

Am Basteir and the Basteir Tooth

route but for a deep notch just before the summit. The climb down into this notch is graded Severe (older guidebooks give it as just a scramble, but a rockfall in the 1990s made it much harder). There is a Difficult grade option down the ridge on the Lota Corrie side just before the notch, but either way this is a route for climbers. Scramblers should leave the ridge a short distance beyond the Bealach a'Bhasteir and traverse below it on exposed sloping ledges on the Lota Corrie side, on a sketchy path, and then up slabs to the notch from where the summit is easily reached. With sheer drops on three sides Am Basteir is a spectacular perch, with excellent views all around.

The only feasible descent route for scramblers is to retrace the route back to the Bealach a'Bhasteir. From the bealach there are two options – either descend back down Coire a'Bhasteir or take the rough scree path under the north face of Am Basteir and below the Tooth to the Bealach nan Lice ('pass of the flat stones'), where again there are choices. The easiest is to drop down into grassy Fionn Choire ('fair corrie') and traverse round the foot of Meall Odhar to the outward path or, slightly longer, continue north out of the corrie to the path by the Allt Dearg Mor. Much more interesting is to climb 898m

Sgurr a' Bhasteir ('peak of the cleft') on the spur to the north. There is a superb view of Am Basteir, the Basteir Tooth and the Pinnacle Ridge of Sgurr nan Gillean from the summit. Descend from Sgurr a'Bhasteir by the north ridge, which involves a little very easy scrambling, to the bealach with Meall Odhar from where you can descend east to the outward path below the Basteir Gorge. The best option however is to first climb Bruach na Frithe, which is an easy ascent from the Bealach nan Lice, then either descend that peaks' northwest ridge, which involves some easy scrambling, or return to the bealach and descend into Fionn Choire or over Sgurr a'Bhasteir. The route via Sgurr a'Bhasteir is 12km long, with 1200m of ascent, and takes 5–7hrs.

Confident scramblers who want to tackle the Basteir Tooth can do so by the Lota Corrie Route, which climbs across the south side of Am Basteir to the notch between the two peaks. This was the first route up the Tooth, climbed by Cuillin pioneers Norman Collie and John Mackenzie in 1889. Although graded Moderate it's surprisingly easy and without much exposure as it mostly follows a line of sloping ledges and little chimneys. I think it's easier and less challenging than the Inaccessible Pinnacle. From the notch a climb up a fairly gentle slab leads to the stupendous airy perch of the top of the Tooth and a close-up view of the intimidating west face of Am Basteir. Descend by the same route. All other routes on the Tooth are harder. The ascent of Am Basteir from the notch with the Tooth is a Very Difficult Grade rock climb.

☒ Bruach na Frithe ☆

The ascent of Bruach na Frithe via Fionn Choire is probably the easiest way up a Munro in the Cuillin, although careful navigation is needed in poor visibility as some of the terrain is quite featureless. To reach the corrie take the path from Sligachan to Glen Brittle. Leave this path about 1km northeast of the Bealach a'Mhaim ('pass of the breast') and head south across open moorland to the corrie. The spring in the corrie at 820m is one of the highest water sources in the Cuillin. Easy scree slopes lead up the back of the corrie to Bealach nan Lice, from where a path runs below the crags of Sgurr a' Fionn Choire to the east ridge of Bruach na Frithe, which leads easily to the summit.

Bruach na Frithe sports the only triangulation point on the Cuillin Ridge, undoubtedly located here because of the ease of access. On the summit there is a right angle turn in the main ridge, which runs east to west between Sgurr nan Gillean and Bruach na Frithe but here turns south. The first recorded ascent of Bruach na Frithe was by Duncan MacIntyre and James Forbes in 1845, on the same day they made their second ascent of Sgurr nan Gillean. The view is excellent, especially of the savage rock architecture of the Basteir Tooth and Am Basteir just to the east.

Descent can be back down Fionn Choire, over Sgurr a'Bhasteir or down the northwest ridge, which involves a little Grade 2 scrambling. The return trip via Fionn Choire is 14km long, with 950m of ascent, and takes 5–6hrs.

☒ Sgurr a'Mhadaidh and Sgurr a' Ghreadaidh ☆

South of Bruach na Frithe there is a long stretch of ridge lying below 900m. The three peaks in this section are Sgurr na Bhairnich ('limpet peak', 861m), An Caisteal ('the castle', 830m) and Bidein Druim nan Ramh ('peak of the ridge of the oars', 869m). Lying in a relatively remote part of the Cuillin and, more significantly, being below Munro height these summits are rarely visited except by those traversing the whole ridge.

Sgurr a' Ghreadaidh from Sgurr na Banachdich

Sgurr Dearg from Sgurr na Banachdich

The next Munros on the ridge are set right in the heart of the Cuillin in the centre of the ridge and at the head of Coir' Uisg, from where they look superb. Both are long narrow mountains with four summits in the case of Sgurr a'Mhadaidh and two in the case of Sgurr a' Ghreadaidh. The traverse of the four summits of Sgurr a'Mhadaidh is very exposed in places and requires Moderate grade rock climbing. The traverse of Sgurr a'Ghreadaidh's two summits is technically easier, a Grade 3 scramble, but sensationally exposed. However the highest summit of Sgurr a'Mhadaidh lies at the southwest end (none of the other summits reach Munro height) and the highest summit of Sgurr a'Ghreadaidh at the northern end, facing each other across the notch of An Dorus ('the door'), from which both can be climbed by Grade 2/3 scrambles.

An Dorus is reached from the footpath that starts opposite the Youth Hostel in Glen Brittle and runs up big Coire a'Ghreadaidh. The path follows the Allt a'Choire Ghreadaidh, a lovely stream with big pools and waterfalls lower down and waterslides over rock slabs higher up. The short spur of Sgurr Eadar da Choire splits upper Coire a'Ghreadaidh into two smaller corries. The northern one of these is Coire An Dorus (named on the Harvey's map but not the OS ones), situated below the summit of Sgurr a'Mhadaidh and with An Dorus at its head, an obvious pale scree cleft. An Dorus by the way is not an easy pass – the descent on the Coruisk side involves Moderate grade rock climbing.

From An Dorus a short, steep scramble leads to the sloping slabs of the summit of Sgurr a'Mhadaidh. The hardest section is the immediate climb out of An Dorus. After admiring the view with Coruisk far below and Sgurr a'Ghreadaidh big and bulky to the south descend back to An Dorus. The hardest part of the Grade 3 scramble up Sgurr a'Ghreadaidh is again the initial climb out of An Dorus after which there is easier scrambling along the crest of the ridge to the summit.

Sgurr a'Ghreadaidh is one of the finest summits in the Cuillin, with a splendid knife-edge ridge linking the two summits above massive buttresses. The view of the Cuillin Ridge stretching to the north and south is magnificent, as is the view straight down Coir' Uisg. Amazingly the first ascent of Sgurr a'Ghreadaidh was made in 1870 by two teenagers, 15 year old Newton Tribe, who became an experienced alpine mountaineer, and 14 year old John Mackenzie, who became the most famous Cuillin guide and for whom Sgurr Mhic Choinnich is named.

The ridge to the south top of Sgurr a'Ghreadaidh is incredibly airy and exposed, a thrilling scramble for those who like such situations, a terrifying one for those without a very good head for heights. The ridge beyond the south top is narrow too and the scrambling continues over little Sgurr Thormaid ('Norman's peak' – named for Cuillin pioneer Norman Collie, 927m) to Sgurr na Banachdich. There is no easy way off the ridge until Sgurr na Banachdich is reached so continuing south from Sgurr a'Ghreadaidh means committing to more scrambling and a longer day.

Those content with climbing the two Munros from An Dorus and returning down Coire a'Ghreadaidh will have a walk of 9.5km, with 1000m of ascent, which takes 5–7hrs.

⊗ Sgurr na Banachdich ☆

Sgurr na Banachdich lies at the northeast corner of its eponymous corrie, with a long ridge running south to the Bealach Coire na Banachdich, one of the few easy passes across the Cuillin Ridge. Sgurr na Banachdich is often said to be the easiest peak in the Cuillin to climb, although Bruach na Frithe is no harder. This easy ascent isn't via Coire na Banachdich, but via lower Coire a'Ghreadaidh and little Coir' an Eich. Although no scrambling is involved there is scree to be climbed and the walk is strenuous. Navigation can be difficult in poor visibility too, as some of the terrain is surprisingly featureless.

The route starts opposite the Glen Brittle Youth Hostel and follows the path beside the Allt Coire a'Ghreadaidh as far as the Allt Coir' an Eich, which is then taken into little Coir' an Eich ('corrie of the horses'). There are two options for the climb out of the corrie. The first, and best, is to climb north to the 714m An Diollaid ('the saddle') at the end of a spur running northwest from the main ridge. The views from the spur are excellent, especially north to the great west face of Sgurr a'Ghreadaidh. The spur runs into the broad stony western slopes of Sgurr na Banachdich which lead to the summit. Alternatively climb out of Coir' an Eich directly to the western slopes. Both routes are cairned but finding them in descent in mist requires care.

From the west Sgurr na Banachdich is a big rounded scree dome, far less steep and rocky than surrounding peaks. This is not so on the east side, where steep slopes fall abruptly into Coireachan Ruadha ('red corries') far below, a startling sight.

Beyond these corries is dark Loch Coruisk, and beyond that Bla Bheinn looks impressive. The view north is dominated by the huge block of Sgurr a'Ghreadaidh, that south by Sgurr Dearg, with the top of the Inaccessible Pinnacle visible and further away the pointed spires of Sgurr Thearlaich and Sgurr Alasdair. Sgurr na Banachdich is the easternmost Cuillin Munro, which also makes it the easternmost Munro of all. On Sgurr na Banachdich the Cuillin Ridge changes direction from southwest to southeast.

For walkers the easiest descent is to retrace your steps back down Coir' an Eich, for a walk of 7km, with 950m of ascent, which takes 4–5hrs. A slightly harder but more interesting route is along the west ridge to 631m Sgurr nan Gobhar ('peak of the goats'), which involves some Grade 2 scrambling. Sgurr nan Gobhar is the easternmost peak in the Cuillin and a good viewpoint for the main ridge. There are crags round the summit, but these are broken on the southwest side where extensive scree slopes can be descended to the moor below, from where it's an easy walk back to the start. The descent from the summit to the Bealach na Banachdich over three lower tops is also a Grade 2 scramble. From the bealach a descent can be made into Coire na Banachdich, or Sgurr Dearg can be climbed by its northwest ridge.

ⓑ The Inaccessible Pinnacle and Sgurr Dearg ☆

Sgurr Dearg (986m) is one of the easier Cuillin peaks to climb, but protruding above its summit is the famous and extraordinary blade of rock known as the Inaccessible Pinnacle, which is very difficult to climb but which is the highest point of the mountain and the Munro. The ascent of the Inaccessible Pinnacle is a Moderate grade rock climb and so the hardest Munro of all, as no other requires rock climbing. The climbing itself is quite easy but the route is also incredibly exposed, requiring a very good head for heights. Confident rock climbers will stroll up the Inaccessible Pinnacle wondering what the fuss is all about, but walkers and scramblers will find it rather more challenging and will require the security of a rope. As the easiest way down is by abseil a rope is needed anyway.

The Inaccessible Pinnacle is a thin wedge of rock with a short vertical west end and a long sloping east ridge. The sides are sheer and below them very steep rocks fall away a huge distance (some 600m on the northern, Coireachan Ruadha

The Inaccessible Pinnacle from the summit of Sgurr Dearg ▶

side), making it easy to understand the wonderful Victorian description of it as having 'an overhanging and infinite drop on one side and a drop longer and steeper on the other'. The easiest ascent is up the east ridge, which is no more than 30 centimetres wide in places. The summit is a small, boulder-strewn platform. The usual descent is a 20m abseil down the west ridge (which is a Difficult grade rock climb) using a wire hawser fixed round a huge boulder called the Bolster Stone as a belay.

The name Inaccessible Pinnacle was given by the first mountaineers in the mid-19th century. To locals it was simply An Stac, meaning a steep rock or pinnacle. The name An Stac is now given to a lower, less impressive pile of rocks east of the Inaccessible Pinnacle (worth the easy ascent for the good view of the east ridge). The first recorded ascent of Sgurr Dearg (plus Sgurr na Banachdich) was made in 1873 by Sheriff Alexander Nicolson, for whom Sgurr Alasdair was later named, and local shepherd Angus Macrae. They didn't attempt the Inaccessible Pinnacle, however, and Nicolson thought 'the achievement seems hardly worth the trouble'. Seven years later two mountaineers, Lawrence and Charles Pilkington, thought it was worth the trouble and made the first ascent by the east ridge. Thousands have followed since. For Munro baggers this is the most prized summit of all.

Although it is clearly higher Sir Hugh Munro, who never climbed it, only gave the Inaccessible Pinnacle the status of a subsidiary top of Sgurr Dearg in the first edition of his *Tables*. This was changed in the second edition, published in 1921.

The ascent of Sgurr Dearg starts in Glen Brittle at the Glen Brittle Memorial Hut (a mountaineering hut run jointly by the Mountaineering Council of Scotland and the British Mountaineering Council), where a path runs beside the Allt Coire na Banachdich to the Eas Mor ('big waterfall'), a tremendous waterfall in a deep wooded gorge. Here the stream crashes 24m down cliffs into a big pool. It's a very impressive sight, enough for Louis Stott in *The Waterfalls of Scotland* (Aberdeen University Press, 1987) to describe it as 'the grandest mountain fall in Skye'. Above the falls the path divides. Either fork can be taken, and Sgurr Dearg climbed via either Coire na Banachdich or Coire Lagan. I think the most enjoyable route is to ascend via the first and descend via the second, as this gives the best views ahead. To do this take the left fork and stay beside the stream which

climbs below the west ridge of Sgurr Dearg into the mouth of Coire na Banachdich, from where the path goes straight up the corrie towards huge Banachdich Gully, the ascent of which is a Very Difficult grade rock climb. To avoid this the path cuts along the flanks of Sgurr Dearg before heading back on a scree terrace to the bealach. From the bealach it's an easy climb up scree to the long, thin sloping summit ridge of Sgurr Dearg, which provides a good balcony for watching climbers abseiling down from the Inaccessible Pinnacle.

The view from both Sgurr Dearg and the Inaccessible Pinnacle is superb, especially across Coire Lagan to Sgurr Alasdair, with the Great Stone Chute a clear pale scar, and down into Coir' Uisg.

The simplest descent route is back down Coire na Banachdich, but a more interesting round trip can be made by descending Coire Lagan instead. This route is a little more complex, and care needs to be taken to find the correct line when the mist is down. This goes along the south side of the Inaccessible Pinnacle to the base of the east ridge and beneath An Stac on a wide, stony, sloping terrace and then to the Bealach Coire Lagan (despite the name there is no easy way down to Coruisk, so this is not a pass), where steep scree can be descended into Coire Lagan (corrie of the hollow). This corrie is a spectacular place surrounded by tremendous mountains, including the highest in the Cuillin. The floor of the corrie is covered with huge curving slabs, in the midst of which is an attractive lochan. A path leads out of the corrie and onto the moorland below. Where it forks keep right to Loch an Fhir-bhallaich ('lake of the speckled trout') and then down to the Eas Mor and the outward path. The walk is only 8km long, but there are 965m of ascent and 5–7hrs should be allowed.

❸ Sgurr Mhic Choinnich ☆

The great west wall of Sgurr Mhic Choinnich dominates the view up Coire Lagan. The cap-like summit is at the south end of this wall, with a sheer drop beyond it, the ascent of which is a Difficult grade rock climb called King's Chimney. There is no walking route up Sgurr Mhic Choinnich, and the easiest scramble is an exposed Grade 2 scramble along the north ridge. A dramatic feature of the mountain is a sloping ledge that runs across the west face from the Bealach Mhic Choinnich at the south end to the north ridge. From Coire Lagan scramblers can be seen high on the west face on this ledge in what looks like very precarious situations. In fact the traverse of the ledge is not very exposed, as it is quite wide, and there are only a few sections of Grade 2 scrambling, but it is a sensational and exciting experience.

This ledge is generally known as Collie's Ledge, after Norman Collie, who made the second traverse, along with John Mackenzie, in 1888, but Mackenzie had already crossed the ledge a year earlier with the Irish climber Henry Hart. In *Skye Scrambles* (SMT, 2000) Noel Williams calls the ledge Hart's Ledge. Actually, Mackenzie's Ledge would seem more appropriate: John Mackenzie hasn't been forgotten, however, as the whole mountain is named after him, *Mhic Choinnich* being the Gaelic for Mackenzie. John Mackenzie was a mountain guide, the first professional guide in Scotland, who climbed regularly with scientist and mountaineer Norman Collie, the pair being the greatest of all the mountaineering pioneers in the Cuillin. There is a plan for a statue of them to be erected at Sligachan, at the start of the path to Coruisk, on John Muir Trust land (www.skyesculpture.com).

To climb Sgurr Mhic Choinnich take the path from Glen Brittle into Coire Lagan, then clamber up the laborious screes below An Stac to the Bealach Coire Lagan and scramble along the narrow north ridge, which is basalt rather than gabbro, to the airy summit from where there are splendid views. Two-thirds of the way along this ridge Collie's Ledge begins its traverse across the west face.

The easiest descent route is back down the north ridge to Bealach Coire Lagan. More exciting is the traverse of Collie's Ledge to the Bealach Mhic Choinnich and then down a big gully that leads into the Great Stone Chute. There is some easy scrambling near the top of the gully. The route from the Glen Brittle campsite via the north ridge and Collie's Ledge is 9km long, with 980m of ascent, and takes 6–7hrs.

Sgurr Alasdair ☆

The highest peak in the Cuillin is not actually on the main ridge but on a spur running west from Sgurr Thearlaich, forming the southern wall of Coire Lagan. Sgurr Alasdair is a fine pointed peak that stands out in views across Coire Lagan. The

View across Coire Lagan to Sgurr Mhic Choinnich (left), Sgurr Thearlaich, Sgurr Alasdair and Sgurr Sgumain with the Great Stone Chute in the centre.

views from its tiny summit are superb, especially south and west over the island-dotted sea and north across Coire Lagan to Sgurr Dearg and the Inaccessible Pinnacle.

Sgurr Alasdair was first climbed in 1873 by Alexander Nicolson and Angus Macrae on the same day that they made the first recorded ascents of Sgurr na Banachdich and Sgurr Dearg, then considered the highest peak in the Cuillin. Nicolson was a Skye native who had a career on the mainland in academia, newspapers and law, finishing as a sheriff. Macrae, a local shepherd, told Nicolson he didn't know what the mountain was called so Nicolson proposed the name 'Scur a Laghain' to go with Corrie Lagan. However Peter Drummond reports in *Scottish Hill Names: Their Origin and Meaning* (Scottish Mountaineering Trust, 2007) that the guide John Mackenzie said the mountain was called Sgurr Viorach ('pointed peak'). The mountain was named Sgurr Alasdair in honour of Alexander Nicolson (*Alasdair* being the Gaelic for Alexander) by Norman Collie, and that is the name that stuck.

The easiest route up Sgurr Alasdair is from Coire Lagan up the long, tedious screes of the Great Stone Chute to the high col linking Sgurr Alasdair with the main ridge, from where a short Grade 2 scramble along the southeast ridge leads to the summit. The Great Stone Chute sends down its huge fan of scree in the southeast corner of Corrie Lagan. The scree here is very loose, and the ascent is frustrating as you slip back with every step. The larger stones on the edges of the chute make for slightly easier progress. Higher up the chute narrows between rock walls and the scree is very eroded, with packed earth, bedrock and boulders exposed. Care is required here. The easiest routes are next to the side walls. As the chute curves gently you can't see people much higher above, so a watch needs to be kept for any stones that may come bouncing down. It's 400m from the corrie to the top of the stone chute, a laborious ascent.

The narrow col at the top of the Great Stone Chute is not a pass. The scree on the south side ends at the top of a cliff so there is no descent route into Coir' a'Ghrundda. The airy scramble up the southeast ridge comes as a relief after the hard work in the stone chute.

The easiest descent route is back down the Great Stone Chute. The alternative, the southwest

ridge (see below), involves more sustained and harder scrambling. The round trip via the Great Stone Chute is 8km long, with 990m of ascent, and takes 5–6hrs.

From the Great Stone Chute col it's also possible to climb Sgurr Thearlaich (Charles' peak – named for Charles Pilkington who led the first ascent in 1887) by a hard Grade 3 scramble, with the easiest start a short way down the Coir' a'Ghrundda side.

The southwest ridge of Sgurr Alasdair runs over two subsidiary tops, Sgurr Sgumain ('stack peak', once the name of the whole ridge, 947m) and 859m Sron na Ciche ('shoulder of the breast'), that present huge rocky walls to Coire Lagan. In fact, the cliffs on the north face of Sron na Ciche are the biggest in the Cuillin, at 800m long and nearly 300m high. There are many rock climbs on these cliffs (see Rock Climbing in the Cuillin below). The mountain is named after a huge rock protruding from the centre of the face, A'Chioch ('the breast'), which was discovered and named by Norman Collie after he noticed the big shadow it cast. Collie and John Mackenzie made the first ascent in 1906.

Sron na Ciche is divided from Sgurr Sgumain by the Bealach Coir' a'Ghrundda. Sgurr Sgumain, in turn, is divided from Sgurr Alasdair by the Bealach Sgumain. Sgurr Sgumain is a rocky walk from the Bealach Coir' a'Ghrundda, which is reached from Coire Lagan by the 400m of scree and rock of the Sgumain Stone Chute. From the summit the descent to the Bealach Sgumain is a Grade 2/3 scramble. At 921m the Bealach Sgumain is the highest pass in the Cuillin. Very steep scree leads up to it from Coire Lagan. The ascent of Sgurr Alasdair from the Bealach Sgumain is a Grade 3 scramble, with a short climb known as the Bad Step near the start. This can be avoided by a chimney on the Coir' a'Ghrundda side.

❸ Sgurr Dubh Mor ☆

Sgurr Dubh Mor is a steep, pointed peak lying just to the east of the main ridge on a long spur that runs from Sgurr Dubh na Da Bheinn ('black peak of the two hills', 938m) down to Loch Coruisk. The spur is rock all the way and its ascent is a Moderate grade rock climb known as the Dubhs Ridge. This 900m route is regarded as a superb classic: 'There can be few finer ways to the summit of any mountain in the British Isles' (*The Islands of*

Scotland, SMC); 'Arguably the finest outing of its grade in the country' (*Skye Scrambles*). 'A unique climbing experience...it's hard to think of a better one at such a gentle grade...a fabulous maritime setting' (*Scotland's Mountain Ridges*). Much of the route is on sloping gabbro slabs. There is one abseil off Sgurr Dubh Beag ('little black peak', 733m), although this can be avoided. Confident scramblers may not need a rope much of the way but one should be carried.

While the Dubh Ridge may be the most exciting way to reach Sgurr Dubh Mor there is another thoroughly enjoyable route via Coir' a'Ghrundda ('bare corrie') that is mostly walking, although the final ascent to the summit is a Grade 2/3 scramble. There are two routes from Glen Brittle into secluded Coir' a'Ghrundda, which is one of the most magnificent corries in the Cuillin, with a rocky floor mostly filled by Loch Coir' a'Ghrundda, the highest loch in the Cuillin, and huge cliffs, scree slopes and peaks rising all around. The most direct route to Coir' a'Ghrundda is via Coire Lagan and the Bealach Coir' a' Ghrundda, which involves an ascent of the Sgumain Stone Chute and a descent into the corrie. A longer route curves round the base of Sron na Ciche and climbs up lower Coir' a'Ghrundda towards massive, steeply curving slabs that appear to block entry to the upper corrie. The Allt Coir' a'Ghrundda splits the slabs in a big waterfall. The cairned path heads towards, this then cuts up a slanting groove in the rock, an easy scramble not seen until you reach it, to the upper corrie, from where a clamber up steep scree and rock leads to the main ridge at either Bealach Coir' an Lochain ('pass of the corrie of the pool') to the northwest of Sgurr Dubh na Da Bheinn or Bealach a' Garbh-choire ('pass of the rough corrie') to the south of Sgurr Dubh na Da Bheinn. Both bealachs are real passes and can be used to descend to Loch Coruisk, although it should be noted that Garbh-choire lives up to its name and is the roughest corrie in the Cuillin, full of skin-shredding gabbro and peridotite boulders.

Sgurr Dubh na Da Bheinn can be easily climbed from either bealach, cutting below the great rock block of the Caisteal a' Garbh-choire ('castle of the rough corrie') if ascending from the Bealach a' Garbh-choire. From the summit descend east to a col, then scramble up the southwest ridge of Sgurr Dubh Mor. This was the ascent route used

when the peak was first climbed by Alexander Nicolson and Duncan MacIntyre in 1874.

The only easy way back to Glen Brittle is via one of the outward routes. If the ascent is made via lower Coir' a'Ghrundda and the return by the Sgumain Stone Chute the trip is 12km long, with 1325m of ascent, and takes 6–8hrs.

⊗ Sgurr nan Eag and Gars-bheinn ☆

The two southernmost peaks in the Cuillin are tremendous viewpoints and also two of the easiest summits to climb. The section of the main ridge between Bealach a' Garbh-choire and Gars-bheinn only involves very easy scrambling and is barely more than a rough walk.

To reach these mountains from Glen Brittle take one of the routes into Coir' a'Ghrundda described under Sgurr Dubh Mor above and climb up to the Bealach a' Garbh-choire. From the bealach head south along the ridge to the long summit of Sgurr nan Eag. The little scrambling there is on the crest can easily be avoided on the west side where there are paths across the scree.

Although not particularly distinctive, with vast scree slopes either side and few crags, Sgurr nan Eag is a massive mountain forming a huge wall between Coir' a'Ghrundda and Garbh-choire. Ascents can be made up the scree slopes almost anywhere but these are hard work and far less interesting than the route via the Bealach a' Garbh-choire. The view from the summit over the sea to Rum and Eigg and out west to the Outer Hebrides is superb, as is the view north to Sgurr Alasdair and Sgurr Dubh Mor.

The fine ridge walk, with wonderful views throughout, continues southeast over 875m Sgurr a'Choire Bhig (peak of the little corrie) to 895m Gars-bheinn (possibly 'echoing mountain'). From this, the last peak on the Cuillin Ridge, the sea stretches out to the south, a huge island-dotted expanse. Northwards the rock peaks ripple into the distance with most of the Munros visible. On the extensive summit low rock walls mark bivouac sites used by climbers preparing for an early start on the traverse of the whole ridge.

Retracing your steps is the most enjoyable way back but for a circular route a descent can be made down the stony southwest slopes of Gars-bheinn for some 500m to the boggy moorland below. Cross the moorland to a path at around 225m that

The Southern Cuillin rising above Loch Scavaig and Loch Coruisk

leads back to Glen Brittle. The circular route is 15km long with 1400m of ascent and takes 6–8hrs.

Ⓑ The Cuillin Traverse ☆

The greatest expedition in the Cuillin is the traverse of the whole ridge, an expedition that requires rock climbing skills. The first traverse in one day was achieved in 1911 by two pioneering Cuillin climbers, L.G. Shadbolt and A.C. McClaren, who took 12hrs and 18mins. Amazingly the record today is 3hrs, 17mins and 28secs, set by Es Tresidder in May, 2007 (the time is from Gars-bheinn to Sgurr nan Gillean). Times like this require running much of the ridge and soloing all the climbing sections. Most people would be happy to match Shadbolt and McClaren's time from summit to summit and are likely to take 15+hrs from sea level to sea level.

Winter conditions rarely occur in the Cuillin, but when they do the traverse becomes a magnificent alpine expedition. This was first achieved over two days by D. Crabbe, B. Robertson, T. Patey and H. MacInnes in 1965. The current winter record is 9hrs 7mins, set by Steve Ashworth in March 2008.

There is also the Greater Traverse, which continues on from Sgurr nan Gillean over Clach Glas and Bla Bheinn. This was first done in 20hrs in 1939 by I. Charlson and W.E. Forde, followed a few weeks later by W.H. Murray and R.G. Donaldson in 19hrs. The current record time of 11¼hrs was set in 1993 by Mike Lates, who also included Garbhbheinn. An even longer route takes in all the Cuillin Outliers, the Western Red Hills, all the tops on the Cuillin Ridge and other hills such as Sgurr na Stri. In 1999 Rob Woodall ran over all these in 23hrs, 28mins.

There are several possible variations for the traverse, but most climbers take in all the Munros including the two not on the main ridge, Sgurr Dubh Mor and Sgurr Alasdair. South to north is the usual direction, although there doesn't seem to be any particular reason for this. May, June and July provide the most daylight and the first two are the most likely months for dry weather.

From the south the route is mostly walking with a little easy scrambling from Gars-bheinn over Sgurr nan Eag to Bealach a'Garbh-choire. Here the Caisteal a' Garbh-choire can be traversed, by Difficult grade climbing, or bypassed. Next comes Sgurr Dubh na Da Bheinn and an optional diversion out to Sgurr Dubh Mor. Between

Sgurr Dubh na Da Bheinn and Sgurr Thearlaich is one of the major obstacles on the ridge, the deep notch called the Thearlaich-Dubh Gap. An abseil leads into the Gap and a Very Difficult climb out of it. The Gap can be avoided by crossing the screes below it to the Bealach Sgumain, traversing Sgurr Alasdair and regaining the ridge at Sgurr Thearlaich. Moderate climbing leads down to the Bealach Mhic Choinnich from where either Collie's Ledge is taken and the north ridge climbed back to Sgurr Mhic Choinnich or the Difficult grade King's Chimney climbed direct to the summit. After Sgurr Mhic Choinnich comes An Stac, and then the Inaccessible Pinnacle, which can be bypassed, but should really be climbed, which is usually done by the Moderate grade east ridge. Fairly continuous, sometimes exposed and difficult scrambling now leads over Sgurr na Banachdich, Sgurr Thormaid and Sgurr a' Ghreadaidh to the summit of Sgurr a'Mhadaidh, beyond which the going gets harder as the climb over the three lower tops of Sgurr a'Mhaidaidh to the Bealach na Glaic Moire, the lowest point on the ridge, and on over Bidein Druim nan Ramh to the Bealach Harta, involves Difficult grade rock climbing. An Caisteal, which comes next, is a little easier, with some Moderate grade climbing, then the difficulties relent over Sgurr na Bhairnich, Bruach na Frithe and Sgurr a' Fionn Choire, which involve much walking and some Grade 2/3 scrambling. But then comes the Bhasteir Tooth. The direct ascent of this by Naismith's Route is a Very Difficult rock climb. Much easier, but much longer, is the Moderate grade Lota Corrie Route. The direct ascent of Am Basteir from the col with the Bhasteir Tooth is also a Very Difficult rock climb, and again an easier route can be found on the Lota Corrie side. From Am Basteir there's a descent to the Bealach a'Bhasteir. The last Munro now follows, Sgurr nan Gillean, whose west ridge involves Moderate or Difficult rock climbing depending on the exact route. Most climbers will now descend to Sligachan but there are two further peaks, Sgurr Beag and Sgurr na h-Uamha, that could be included if enough energy is left. These involve Moderate grade climbing.

A long traverse of the ridge is a memorable experience, a mountain day never to forget. I've never done the whole ridge in one day but I did a traverse in sunny weather from Sgurr nan Gillean to the Bealach Mhic Choinnich that included Nicolson's Chimney on Sgurr nan Gillean, the Bhasteir Tooth, the Inaccessible Pinnacle and

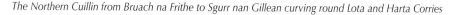

The Northern Cuillin from Bruach na Frithe to Sgurr nan Gillean curving round Lota and Harta Corries

Collie's Ledge. Bidein Druim nan Ramh was skipped by a descent and re-ascent, which was a mistake. Otherwise all the summits were climbed. This was during my continuous walk over all the Munros and Tops and was the highlight of the whole summer-long walk. In my book on the trip I wrote 'It had been a brilliant day – exciting, frightening and inspiring. I would never forget it'. At the Bealach Mhic Choinnich rain started to fall and there was only an hour and half of daylight left so we descended to Glen Brittle. This turned out to be a wise decision as a big storm raged all night and all the next day, which we spent in the Sligachan Hotel bar. The next day I climbed the peaks at the southern end of the ridge in thick mist.

ⓑ Rock Climbing in the Cuillin ☆

The spectacular cliffs, gullies and buttresses of the Cuillin have been popular for rock climbing since the 1870s. The number of climbs is vast, and they cover every grade. Classics already mentioned as part of ascent routes to summits or the traverse of the whole ridge are Nicolson's Chimney on Sgurr nan Gillean (Difficult), Lota Corrie Route (Moderate) and Naismith's Route (Very Difficult) on Am Basteir, the East Ridge of the Inaccessible Pinnacle (Moderate), King's Chimney on Sgurr Mhic Choinnich (Difficult) and the Dubhs Ridge (Moderate).

The vast north face of ☆ Sron na Ciche is the most attractive to rock climbers, and there are many routes here. This cliff towers above Coire Lagan and is easily reached from Glen Brittle. The classic feature is the Cioch, and a number of routes lead to this distinctive block of rock, which is connected to the main cliff by a narrow neck. The easiest way up the Cioch is that used by Collie and Mackenzie on the first ascent in 1906, now known as Collie's Route, and graded Moderate. This takes a mazy route up the Cioch Slab left of the Cioch to a shelf that leads to the neck, from where it's a short climb to the top of the Cioch, a dramatic perch high above Coire Lagan with a real feeling of being suspended in space. The shelf leading to the neck can also be reached by 60m Arrow Route, a Very Difficult climb first ascended by I. Allan in 1944, which goes right up the centre of Cioch Slab. Much, much harder, at E2 is 45m Overhanging Crack, which climbs the Cioch directly (first ascent by M. Hamilton and G. Cohen in 1978), 'a spec-tacular line', according to Kevin Howett's *Rock Climbing in Scotland* (Frances Lincoln, 2004).

Other notable climbs on the Cioch face include: 165m Crack of Doom (Hard Severe – first climbed by D.R. Pye and L.G. Shadbolt in 1918), up the buttress to the right of the Cioch; 90m Bastinado (E1, first climbed by J. Cunningham, J. Allen and W. Smith in 1956) and Cioch Direct (Severe, first climbed by H. Harland and A.P. Abraham in 1907), both up the face to the terrace below the Cioch.

Left of the Cioch face, and separated from it by Eastern Gully, is the Eastern Buttress. Routes here include: 168m Team Machine (E4, first climbed by D. Cuthbertson and G. Latter in 1982 and described as 'scary' by Kevin Howett); 66m Vulcan Wall (HVS, first climbed by H. MacInnes, D.U. Temple and I.S. Clough in 1957); and 70m Uhuru (E3, first climbed by K. Howett and T. Prentice in 1990). Right of the Cioch is the Western Buttress, a huge spread of rock. Routes here include 300m Mallory's Slab and Groove (Very Difficult, first climbed by G.H.L. Mallory, D.R. Pye and L.G. Shadbolt in 1918).

Elsewhere in the Cuillin there are climbs of every standard. Among those regarded as classics or especially worthwhile are: 180m King Cobra (E1, first ascent C.J.S. Bonington and T.W. Patey in 1960) on the east face of Sgurr Mhic Choinnich; 225m Archer Thomson's Route (Severe, first climbed by J.M.A. Thomson, H.O. Jones and L.G. Shadbolt in 1918) on the northwest face of Sgurr a'Mhadaidh; 90m Window Buttress (Difficult, first ascended by J.N. Collie in 1906) on the west spur of Sgurr Dearg (the author once fell off the top pitch due to making a mess of the holds sequence); the West Ridge of the Inaccessible Pinnacle (Difficult – but polished and very slippery when wet as the author discovered – first climbed by A.H. Stocker and A.G. Parker in 1886); 30m South Crack (Hard Very Difficult, first climbed by H. Harland, A.P. Abraham and A.H. Binns in 1906) on the south face of the Inaccessible Pinnacle; Pinnacle Ridge on Sgurr nan Gillean (Difficult, first ascended by C. and L. Pilkington in 1880); King's Cave Chimney (Very Difficult, first climbed by W.W. King, G.B. Gibbs and J. Mackenzie in 1898) between Am Basteir and the Bhasteir Tooth; and Naismith's Route (Difficult, first climbed by W.W. Naismith and A.M. Mackay in 1898) on the Bhasteir Tooth.

The Trotternish Ridge

◈ The Trotternish Ridge ☆

Trotternish is the northernmost peninsula on Skye, lying north of Portree. A wonderful, undulating ridge forms the spine of Trotternish, the traverse of which is a superb walk. The Trotternish Ridge is a scenic delight, full of strange and fantastical rock formations. These were caused by the collapse of the underlying sedimentary rocks on the steeper eastern side under the weight of the basalt lava that had covered them during volcanic activity, giving rise to a series of huge landslides, the biggest in Britain. On the west side gentle green slopes run down to the coast and the ridge looks rather dull: on the east there's a distinctive and dramatic stepped landscape with terraces between the steep crags. This is caused by different layers of basalt eroding at different rates.

◈ The Storr and the Sanctuary ☆

At 719m the Storr is the highest peak on the Trotternish Ridge. It lies near the southern end not far from Portree. More famous and more visited than the summit is the collection of pinnacles and weird rock structures in the area to the east of the summit known as the Sanctuary, of which the most famous is the rock needle called the Old Man of Storr.

The short walk to the Storr starts at the Storr car park on the A855 where a path heads up through a forest. Once out of the trees the massive 200m high cliffs of the east face of the Storr come into view, with the rocks of the Sanctuary in front of it. A short walk takes you into the midst of this bizarre group of eroding towers, turrets and pinnacles. Perhaps the most fantastic formation is a tall, thin wedge of tottering, disintegrating rock with two big holes through it where blocks have fallen out. This is known as both the Needle and the Cathedral. Nearby is the 50m high Old Man of Storr, an undercut obelisk on a bare, eroded platform. The friable rock feels most insecure but the Old Man has been climbed many times, firstly by famous mountaineer Don Whillans in 1955. The grade is Hard Very Severe.

To climb the Storr head north below the east face until the crags become broken and a path climbs through them to Coire Scamadal, which is then followed southwest to the summit. To the north the Trotternish Ridge ripples into the distance in a series of stepped terraces. To the south rises the ragged outline of the Cuillin. The best view, however, is down to the Sanctuary and over the forest to the sea.

The Quiraing and Meall na Suiramach

The shortest and quickest descent is to retrace your steps. A slightly longer route is to head south along the ridge to the Bealach Beag, from where you can descend east to reach the road 800m from the start. The round trip from the Storr car park is 6km long, with 665m of ascent, and takes 3–4hrs.

⊗ The Quiraing ☆

Situated near the northern end of the Trotternish Ridge the Quiraing is the most extraordinary collection of rock formations imaginable. It lies on the eastern slopes of Meall na Suiramach (543m), just 1km from the only road across the Trotternish Ridge, which runs from Staffin to Uig. The Quiraing is only a short stroll from the nearest car park, but a longer walk can be made by climbing Meall na Suiramach and Sron Vourlinn (360m), both good viewpoints.

From the car park where the Staffin–Uig road crosses the Trotternish Ridge a narrow path traverses the hillside below a line of crags towards the weird rocks of the Quiraing. These formations are all packed into a small enclosed space, giving the Quiraing a strange isolated and cut-off feel. Many of the formations have names. The first encountered is the Prison, a narrow slice of jagged rock with steep grass on the seaward side and cliffs on the landward side. Nearby is the Needle, a 36m overhanging pinnacle. Beyond these you enter the heart of the Quiraing with the flat-topped steep-sided knoll called the Table surrounded by contorted shapes. The meaning of Quiraing is probably 'pillared enclosure', from the Gaelic 'cuith raing', according to Peter Drummond's *Scottish Hill Names: Their Origin and Meaning* (Scottish Mountaineering Trust, 2007), which is appropriate.

Behind the Quiraing the cliffs of the east face of Meall na Suiramach block a direct ascent to the summit. A path runs along the base of the cliffs. Follow this for some 800m to where it climbs through a break in the rocks to the ridge. Just to the north is Sron Vourlinn, the northernmost summit on the Trotternish Ridge. From the summit you can see Rubha Hunish, the northern tip of Skye and the sea spreading out to far off islands. Turning south the edge of the cliffs can be followed with excellent views down to the Quiraing. Leave the cliffs for a short ascent to the trig point on the rounded summit of Meall na Suiramach and then head south over Maoladh Mor to the car park. The distance is 8km, with 500m of ascent, and the walk takes 4–5hrs, maybe longer if you linger in the atmospheric Quiraing.

◉ The Trotternish Traverse ☆

The traverse of the Trotternish ridge is one of the finest long distance walks on Skye, a wonderful undulating hike over rolling hills with superb views. Most of the way the walking is easy, with sheep-cropped turf underfoot. However it is 37km long with 2650m of ascent. There are few paths, so good navigation skills are required in poor visibility. Most people are likely to take over 12hrs for the walk. Taking two days, with an overnight camp, is an excellent way to enjoy the whole walk without the pressure of having to complete the distance in a day. The bus that runs from Portree right round the Trotternish Peninsula can take you to the Duntulm Hotel at the north end of the ridge, from where you walk back to Portree.

From the Duntulm Hotel head south on a road, and then a track, to open moorland and the rift of Glen Scamadal, which splits the steep slopes of Sgurr Mor ('big peak', 492m), the first summit on the traverse. Once on Sgurr Mor the route follows the ridge south over summits and bealachs, lovely spacious terrain. The best views are to the east, so hugging the edge of the cliffs that run along the eastern edge of the ridge is the ideal route, although not the most direct. Certainly the edge should be approached at Meall na Suiramach, for views down to the Quiraing and at the Storr for views down to the Sanctuary. The ridge ends with a descent to the A855 near the bridge over the River Chracaig, from where it's a 2.5km walk into Portree.

◉ The Skye Trail

A long walk on Skye linking the mountains of Trotternish, the Red Hills and the Cuillin is a great idea. Anyone can put together such a route of course but there are two versions available in book and DVD form. The latest one comes from Cameron McNeish and runs from Rubha Huinish to Broadford and is called *Skye Trail – A Long Walk Through Eilean a' Cheo*. This walk started life as a BBC TV programme shown at Christmas 2009, to be followed by a book and DVD. The route starts at Rubha Huinish and traverses the Trotternish ridge to Portree. From Portree it follows the coast to the Braes – scene of the last battle on British soil in 1882, when crofters fought police sent to evict them – and then the north shore of Loch Sligachan to the Sligachan Hotel. Passing between the Cuillin and the Red Hills the route continues down Glen Sligachan and over to Coruisk in the heart of the Cuillin. The coast path over the Bad Step is followed to Camasunary, from where Bla Bheinn is climbed by the south ridge. A descent is made to Loch Slapin, the road followed to Torrin, then the path taken round the coast to the cleared villages of Suisinish and Boreraig, with a final walk back north to Broadford. The total distance is around 105km.

Ten years before the Skye Trail came along writer and photographer David Paterson published his gorgeously illustrated book *A Long Walk on the Isle of Skye* (Peak Publishing, 1999) describing a 120km walk from Armadale to Duntulm. Paterson's route crosses the Sleat peninsula from Armadale, then runs along the north coast of Sleat and round the head of Loch Eishort to Boreraig and Suisnish. Loch Slapin is then followed via Torrin to its head, where it is left for the roughest and highest part of the route through the Red Hills and Coulin Outliers via the Bealach na Beiste between Garbh-bheinn and Belig, Druim Eadar Da Choire, and Am Fraoch-choire between Marsco and Ruadh-stac to Glen Sligachan. The route continues up the glen to Sligachan, and then along Loch Sligachan to the road through the Braes to Portree. From Portree the route follows the coastal hills and cliffs west of the Trotternish Ridge to the Storr, and then the ridge to Duntulm. Patterson divides the walk into eight stages.

Both these routes are excellent walks. I have a preference for the Skye Trail, because it goes to Coruisk and over Bla Bheinn. I prefer the finish (or start) at Broadford, too, as I don't find low-lying Sleat very interesting, although I can see that an end to end route is attractive. Walk them both and decide your preference!

7:6 HARRIS

The northern half of the Western Isles consists of by far the largest island in the group, Lewis and Harris. This is where most of the Western Isles' population lives, over 20,000 people. Much of the island is low lying featureless peat moorland and most of the scenic interest is along the coast, which is spectacular and beautiful. Harris makes up the southern half of Lewis and Harris and is divided into two parts by the very narrow neck of land between East Loch Tarbert and West Loch Tarbert ('tarbert' means a narrow isthmus). The only high

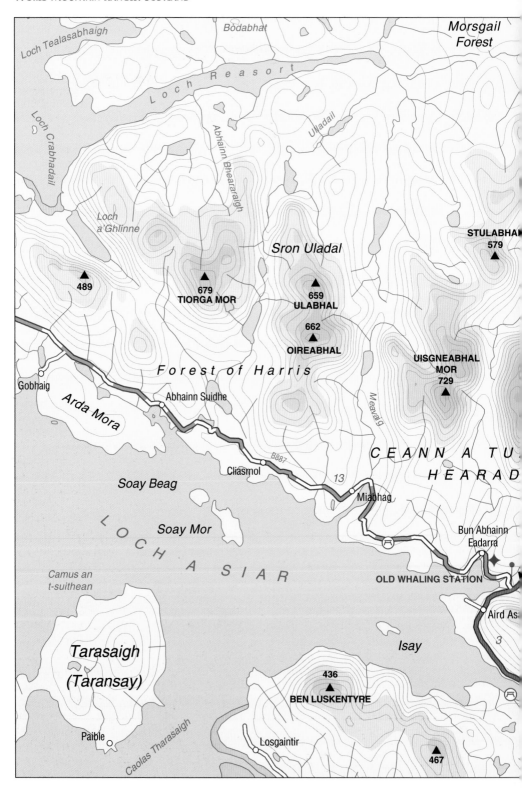

Loch Tealasabhaigh

Bòdabhat

Morsgail Forest

Loch Reasort

Loch Crabhadail

Abhainn Bheararaigh

Ulladail

STULABHA

579

Loch a'Ghlinne

Sron Uladal

489

679
TIORGA MOR

659
ULABHAL

662

OIREABHAL

Forest of Harris

Meavaig

UISGNEABHAL
MOR
729

Gobhaig

Arda Mora

Abhainn Suidhe

B887

CEANN A TU

HEARAD

Cliasmol

13

Soay Beag

Miabhag

LOCH A SIAR

Soay Mor

Bun Abhainn
Eadarra

Camus an
t-suithean

OLD WHALING STATION

Aird As

Tarasaigh
(Taransay)

Isay

3

436

BEN LUSKENTYRE

Paible

Losgaintir

Caolas Tharasaigh

467

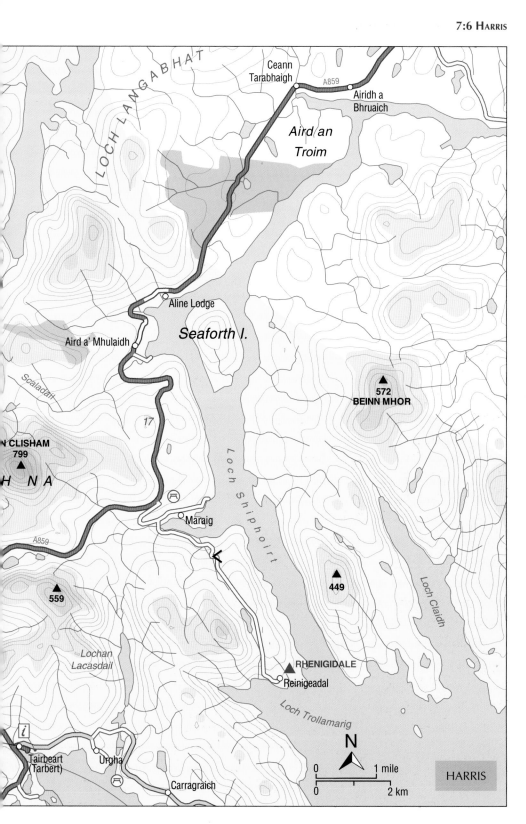

LOCH LANGABHAT

Ceann Tarabhaigh

A859

Airidh a Bhruaich

Aird an Troim

Aline Lodge

Seaforth I.

Aird a' Mhulaidh

Scaladail

▲ 572 BEINN MHOR

17

N CLISHAM 799 ▲

H N A

Loch Shiphoirt

A859

Maraig

▲ 559

▲ 449

Loch Claidh

Lochan Lacasdail

▲ RHENIGIDALE
Reinigeadal

Loch Trollamarig

N

0   1 mile
0   2 km

HARRIS

i

Tairbeart (Tarbert)

Urgha

Carragraich

mountains on Lewis and Harris are found in North Harris. Indeed, this is the only mountainous area in the Western Isles, other than a small area in South Uist, where there are two summits over 600m, and the largest in any of the Hebrides, including Skye. The name Harris reflects this, deriving from either the Norse *hearri*, meaning 'hills', or the Gaelic *na h-airdibh*, meaning the heights, according to Haswell Hamish-Smith's *The Scottish Islands* (Canongate 2004).

Nine of the North Harris hills are over 600m, but none reach Munro height, and there's only one Corbett, An Clisham (possibly 'rocky cliff', 799m), plus three Grahams – Uisgneabhal ('oxen peak', 729m), Tirga Mor (meaning unknown, 679m) and Oireabhal (possibly 'water peak' or 'grouse peak', 662m). The mountains lie north of West Loch Tarbert and form four groups running south–north separated by deep glens. The round of the peaks in each group is an excellent walk. The North Harris hills also harbour one of the most impressive cliffs in Scotland – Sron Uladal ('the nose of Ulli's glen' or 'wolf glen'). The mountains are made of metamorphic Lewisian gneiss, the oldest rocks in Europe, and were heavily glaciated during the last ice age.

North Harris is most easily reached by ferry from Uig on Skye to Tarbert, a journey of 1¾hrs that really makes you aware of how far the Western Isles are from the mainland. There's also a three and a half hour ferry journey from Ullapool to Stornoway but this leaves you much further from the mountains. From Tarbert you can walk to some of the hills and cycle to the others if you don't have a car. There are also bus services along the A859 on the east side of the mountains and the B887 road that runs along the south side (information from www.cne-siar.gov.uk/travel/busservice/current/indexlh.asp). There is no easy access from the north. Tarbert has accommodation and shops and is the best base for the hills.

⊗ The Clisham Horseshoe ☆

Clisham, the highest peak in the Western Isles, lies on a horseshoe of peaks around Loch Mhisteam and the Abhainn Scaladail. These are the easternmost peaks over 600m on North Harris, and easily accessible from the A859. The circuit of the horseshoe is the best expedition in this area. The hills are bulky, steep-sided and quite rocky, with much stone underfoot, although there are few real crags. Clisham can be climbed directly from the A859 on its southern and eastern sides, the shortest

Heading for Mulla-Fo-Dheas from Clisham

route being only a little over 2km. These are not convenient start points for the horseshoe, however. For this the A859 bridge over the Abhainn Scaladail northeast of Clisham is the ideal place. Going clockwise the walk heads southwest on a track marked as the Harris Walkway, then turns west and climbs 552m Tomnabhal, with a good view ahead to Clisham. Descend to the col with Clisham, then climb the steep northeast slopes, a mix of grass and stones, to the summit. The latter is a narrow rocky ridge with a big circular cairn around a trig point stretching right across it. A steep, stony descent west leads to the next col, followed by an equally steep climb to Mulla-Fo-Dheas ('south summit', 743m). Turning north now and on grassier terrain the route crosses Mulla-Fo-Theath ('north summit', 720m) and Mullach na Langa ('summit of the long peak', 614m). A big descent leads northeast to the next col, from where a descent can be made into the Abhainn Scaladail glen and back to the start, but this crosses very wet ground, so it's better to stay on the now rounded and less distinct ridge over Mo Bhiogadall to Creag Mo and then descend round the southern edge of this to the river. There are good views back to Clisham and other hills from this final section. The walk is 14km long, with 1200m of ascent, and takes 7–8hrs.

⊗ The Uisgneabhal Mor Ridge

Uisgneabhal Mor (729m) is the highest in a group of steep, rugged hills lying just to the west of the Clisham hills and separated from them by deep glens and a 250m col. Just 750m northeast of Uisgneabhal is Teileasbhal (697m), and the pair can be combined in a pleasant ridge walk, mostly on grass, although with some stony sections, with a return down the track in long Gleann Mhiabhaig to the west. The views east to the Clisham hills are excellent. The ascent starts where the B887 crosses the Abhainn Mhiabhaig at the head of little Loch Mhiabhaig, climbs to the long southwest ridge of Uisgneabhal Mor and follows this round to the stony summit. A short descent and ascent leads to Teileasbhal. The walk continues along the slowly descending ridge over Creag Stulabhal (513m) to Sron Ard, a craggy nose. Just before the crags a descent can be made west into Gleann Mhiabhaig and the track taken back to the start. The walk is 14km long, with 950m of ascent, and takes 5–6hrs.

⊗ The Oireabhal Ridge and Sron Uladal ☆

Oireabhal is the highest point on the ridge that stretches out north to finish at the great cliff of Sron Uladal. Combining an ascent of the hill with a walk round the base of Sron Uladal is a splendid excursion. The route starts on the B887 beside Loch Leosavay, where a hydro track leads north past Loch Leosaid to the dam at the south end of Loch Chliostar and an ascent east to Oireabhal. From the summit follow the grassy ridge north over 659m Ulabhal (either 'Ulli's peak' or 'wolf peak') and on to the col just before the summit of Sron Uladal. Descend steep slopes in a northeasterly direction from the col, then walk round the base of this awe-inspiring, overhanging cliff. On the west side the cliff runs for 800m at a height of 250m without a break. At its end it overhangs impressively. A path leads below the cliff and then down Gleann Chliostar to the loch and the outward track. The distance is 17km long, with 1200m of ascent, and the walk takes 6–7hrs.

⊗ Tiorga Mor

The westernmost of the Harris peaks over 600m, Tiorga Mor is a rugged, complex hill with good views from the summit. It can be climbed by the southeast ridge, which has some rocky sections, and which is reached from the track from the B887 to Loch Chliostar, and then a descent made southwest down steep slopes into Gleann Leosaid where a path leads back to the outward track at Loch Leosaid. This route is 9.5km long, with 710m of ascent, and takes 4–5hrs. Tiorga Mor could be linked with Oireabhal by descending northeast then east to the north end of Loch Aiseabhat from where an easy ascent leads to the col north of Ulabhal.

ⓑ Sron Uladal ☆

The giant overhanging cliff of Sron Uladal is a remote climbing destination, but the quality of the rock and the routes still attracts climbers, especially those who like hard, committing routes. There are few easy grade climbs on these massive walls. The first climb here was 180m Rush Shelf (Very Difficult) in 1938 by H. J. Irens and F. Solari. Few other climbs were made before the 1960s, when climbs using artificial aids were put up, many of them since free climbed. The first direct ascent of the nose of the cliff was an aid climb, made by J.Porteous and K.Spence in 1969. This was free

The northeast face of Sron Uladal

climbed in 1981 by M. Fowler and A. Meyers, at a grade of E5. The route is 201m long and is called Stone. Kevin Howett, in *Rock Climbing in Scotland* (Francis Lincoln, 2004) describes it as 'splendiferous'. Some routes are so difficult and complex that they take many days. One such is The Scoop, a 170m route on the nose. It was first aid climbed by D. Scott, J. Upton, G. Lee and M. Terry over 6 days in 1969 and then free climbed at a grade of E7 by J. Dawes and P. Pritchard in 1987, again over a 6 day period. Despite the many routes on the cliff its size is so big that it's reckoned there are many new routes to be found.

7:7 SOUTH UIST

Separated from Harris and Lewis by North Uist and Benbecula, South Uist is a remote island. The direct ferry route from Oban to Lochboisdale in the south of the island takes 6hrs. Alternatively the ferry from Uig on Skye to Tarbert on Harris, and then the ferry from Leverburgh on South Harris to Berneray, can be taken, followed by the long road trip through North Uist and Benbecula. Lochboisdale is the centre for the island. The A865 road runs down the west of the island and then east to Lochboisdale.

The glory of South Uist lies in the machair and the shell/sand beaches on the west coast and the line of beautiful inland lochs that stretch the length of the island. Hillwalkers, however, will be drawn here by the remotest 600m summits in Scotland, Hecla ('hooded hill', 606m) and Beinn Mhor ('big hill', 620m), a Graham, which run down the eastern side of the island.

⊗ Beinn Mhor and Hecla

Beinn Mhor can be easily climbed by its southern slopes from the end of the minor road running from the A865 to Loch Aineort. However a circuit of Beinn Mhor, Hecla and Beinn Choradail (527m), which lies between them, is reckoned the best route. This can be started at Loch Dobhrain on the A865, directly west of Hecla, and goes via the northwest ridge of Beinn Mhor, north over Beinn Choradail to Hecla and then down the northwest ridge of the latter. The views east to the Inner Hebrides are said to be superb.

◀ *The west face of Sron Uladal*

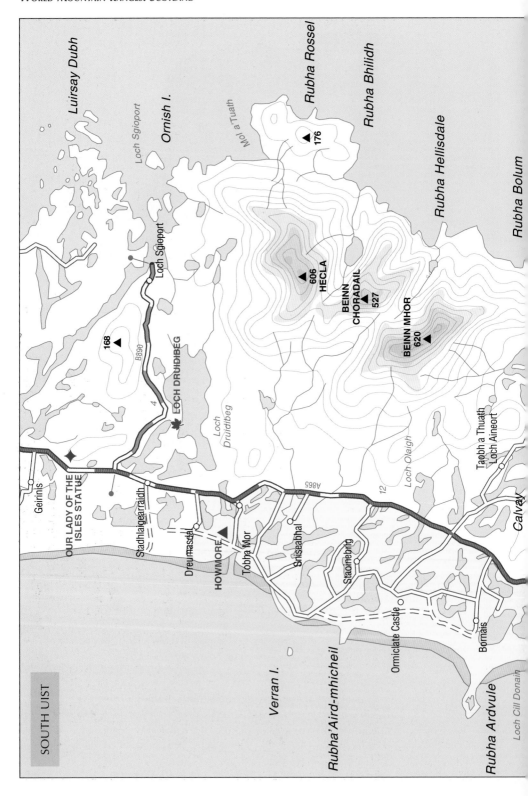

SOUTH UIST

Luirsay Dubh

Loch Sgioport

Ornish I.

Rubha Rossel

Mol a'Tuath

Rubha Bhilidh

▲ 176

Rubha Hellisdale

Rubha Bolum

Loch Sgioport

Loch Sgioport

▲ 606
HECLA

BEINN
CHORADAIL
▲ 527

BEINN MHOR
▲ 620

168 ▲

B890

LOCH DRUIDIBEG

Loch
Druidibeg

Loch Olaigh

Taobh a Thuath
Loch Aineort

4

Geirinis

OUR LADY OF THE
ISLES STATUE

Stadhlaigearraidh

A865

Calvay

12

Dreumasdal

HOWMORE ▲

Tobha Mor

Sniseabhal

Staoinebrig

Ormiclate Castle

Bornais

Verran I.

Rubha'Aird-mhicheil

Rubha Ardvule

Loch Cill Donain

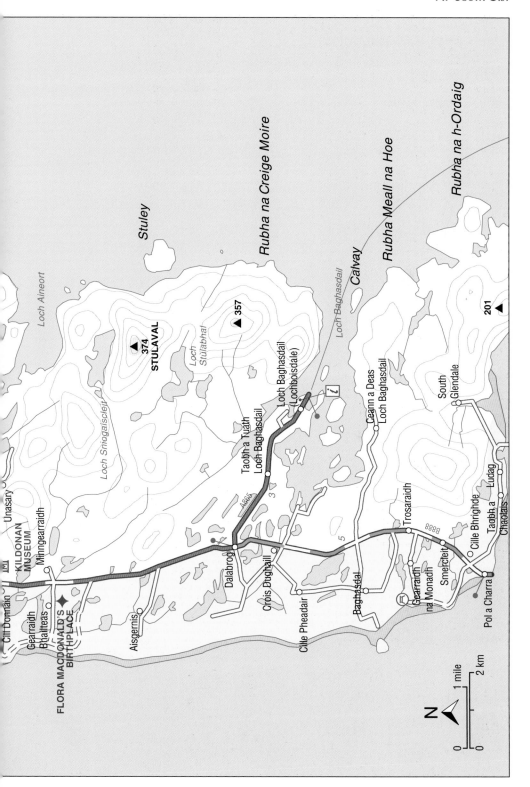

ACCESS, BASES, MAPS AND GUIDES

Access

Arran Ferry from Ardrossan to Brodick (55mins), ferry from Claonaig (Kintyre) to Lochranza (½hr).

Jura Ferry from Kennacraig (Kintyre) to Port Askaig (Islay), 2–5mins; ferry from Port Askaig to Feolin (2mins).

Mull Ferry from Oban to Craignure (40mins), ferry from Lochaline (Morvern) to Fishnish (¼hr), ferry from Kilchoan (Ardnamurchan) to Tobermory (35mins).

Rum Ferry from Mallaig to Kinloch (2–3hrs).

Skye Road bridge from Kyle of Lochalsh to Kyleakin, ferry from Mallaig to Armadale (½hr), ferry from Glenelg to Kylerhea (4mins).

Harris Ferry from Uig (Skye) to Tarbert (1hr 45mins), ferry from Ullapool to Stornoway (3½hrs).

South Uist Ferry from Oban to Lochboisdale (6hrs), ferry from Uig (Skye) to Tarbert (North Harris) (1¾hrs) then ferry from Leverburgh to Berneray and the A865.

Bases

Arran Brodick, Corrie.

Jura Craighouse.

Mull Tobermory, Craignure.

Skye Broadford, Portree, Sligachan, Glen Brittle, Carbost, Dunvegan.

Harris Tarbert.

South Uist Lochboisdale.

Maps

OS Landranger 1:50,000 69, 61, 49, 48, 39, 32, 23, 22, 14, 13

OS Explorer 1:25,000 361, 355, 375, 397, 411, 408, 453, 456

Harvey's 1:25,000 Superwalker Skye The Cuillin, Superwalker Arran

Walking and Scrambling Guides

50 Best Routes on Skye and Raasay by Ralph Storer (David & Charles, 1996)

Guide to Walks in the North-West Highlands (includes four walks on Skye) by Chris Townsend (Aurum, 2007)

The Island of Rhum: A Guide for Walkers, Climbers and Visitors by Hamish Brown (Cicerone, 1988)

The Islands of Scotland including Skye (Scottish Mountaineering Club District Guide) by D.J. Fabian, G.E. Little and D.N. Williams (SMT, 1995)

The Islands: Skye, the Hebrides and Arran by Nick Williams (Pocket Mountains, 2004)

The Isle of Mull by Terry Marsh (Cicerone, 2010)

Isle of Skye by Chris Townsend (Collins, 2010)

The Isle of Skye by Terry Marsh (Cicerone, 2009)

A Long Walk on the Isle of Skye by David Paterson (Peak Publishing, 1999)

The Magic of Skye by W.A. Poucher (Constable, 1949)

Skye Scrambles: Walks, Scrambles and Easy Climbs on the Isle of Skye by Noel Williams (SMT, 2000)

Walking in the Hebrides by Roger Redfern (Cicerone, 1998)

Walking on Jura, Islay and Colonsay by Peter Edwards (Cicerone, 2010)

Walking on Harris and Lewis by Richard Barrett (Cicerone, 2010)

Walking on the Isle of Arran by Paddy Dillon (Cicerone, 1998)

Climbing Guides

Arran, Arrochar and the Southern Highlands by Graham Little, Tom Prentice and Ken Crocket (SMT, 1997)

Skye and the Hebrides: Rock and Ice Climbs (Scottish Mountaineering Club Climbers' Guide) by John MacKenzie (SMT, 1996)

Skye – Rock and Ice Climbs: Scottish Mountaineering Club Climbers' Guide edited by Roger Everett (SMT, 2005)

Other Reading

The Cuillin: Great Mountain Ridge of Skye by Gordon Stainforth (Constable, 1994)

The Heart of Skye by Jim Crumley (Colin Baxter, 1994)

APPENDIX A

Glossary of Common Mountain Words in Gaelic and Scots

GAELIC (SCOTS)	ENGLISH
Aber, abhair	mouth of a river, confluence
Abhainn	river
Achadh (ach, auch)	field, meadow
Airde (ard)	height
Airidh, airigh	mountain pasture, shieling
Allt	stream
Amhainn	river
Aonach	ridge
Ath	ford
Bac	bank
Bad	place
Baile	township
Ban, bhan	white, fair
Beag (beg)	small
Bealach	pass
Beinn	hill or mountain
Beith	birch tree
Ben	hill or mountain, anglicisation of Gaelic *beinn*
Bidean (bidein)	peak
Bin (binn)	hill, Scots adaptation of *beinn*
Binnein	conical top
Biod	pointed top
Bo, ba	cow, cattle
Bod	penis
Bodach	old man
Bothy	hut, shelter
Braigh (brae)	hill, heights
Breac	speckled
Buachaille	herdsman
Buidhe	Yellow
Buiridh (bhuiridh)	roaring (of stags)
Burn	Stream
Cadha	steep slope, pass
Cailleach	old woman
Caisteal	castle, fort
Cam	Crooked
Camas (camus)	Bay
Caol (kyle)	Narrows
Caor	rowan
Carn	hill, pile of stones (cairn)
Cas	steep
Cat	wildcat
Cean (ceann, ken, kin)	head
Choinneach	mossy place, marsh
Cill	church
Cioch (pl. ciche)	breast

GAELIC (SCOTS)	ENGLISH
Cir	comb
Ciste	chest
Clach	stone
Clais	narrow valley, gap
Cleit	cliff
Cnap (cnoc)	hillock
Coille	wood
Coire	corrie, cirque, hollow
Comb (combe)	corrie, cirque, hollow
Craobh	tree
Creachan	rock
Creag	crag, cliff
Croit	croft
Cruach	heap or stack
Cul	back
Da	two
Dail	field
Damh	deer
Darach	oakwood
Dearg	red
Diollaid	saddle, pass
Diridh	divide
Dod (dodd)	bare round hill
Doire	copse, wood
Drochaid	bridge
Drum (druim)	long
Dubh	dark, black
Dun	fort
Each	horse
Eag	notch
Eagach	notched
Eaglais	church
Eas	waterfall
Eighe	file, notched
Eilean	island
Eun (eoin)	bird, birds
Fada (fhada)	long
Fas	level
Fear	man
Fearna	alder
Feith	bog, moss
Fell	hill
Fionn	white, bright
Fraoch	heather
Fuar	cold
Fuaran	spring, well

GAELIC (SCOTS)	ENGLISH
Gabhar	goat
Gaoth	wind
Garbh	rough, stony
Geal	white
Gearr	short
Giuthas	Scots pine
Glac	hollow
Glais	stream
Glas (ghlas)	grey or green
Gleann (glen)	valley
Gorm	blue
Inbhir (inver)	river mouth
Innis (innse)	island or meadow
Iolair	eagle
Knock (nock)	conical hill
Knowe	knoll
Ladhar	hoof, fork
Lag (lagg, lagan)	hollow
Lair	mare
Lairig	pass
Laogh (laoigh)	calf
Law	hill
Lax	salmon
Leac	stone, slab
Learg	slope
Leathad	slope
Leis	lee, leeward
Leitir	steep slope
Liath	grey
Linne	pool
Loch	lake
Lochan	small lake
Lub (luib)	bend
Machair	seaside meadow
Maighdean (mhaighdean)	maiden
Mairg	rust coloured
Mam	rounded hill, pass
Maol	bald head
Meadhon (mheadhoin)	middle
Meall	hill
Moine	moss, bog
Monadh	mountain
Mor (mhor, more)	big
Mounth (mount)	mountain
Muillin (Mhuillin)	mill
Muc (muic)	pig
Mullach	summit
Ness	point or headland
Odhar	dun coloured
Ord	rounded hill

GAELIC (SCOTS)	ENGLISH
Pait	knoll
Pap	breast
Pen	hilltop
Pike	peak
Poite	pot
Poll	pool, pit
Puist	post
Raineach	ferny
Rath	fort
Rig (rigg)	ridge
Righ	king
Ros	headland
Ruadh	red
Rubha (rhu)	coastal headland
Ruigh	shieling
Sail	heel
Saighead	arrow
Saobhaidh	animal's den
Sgiath	wing
Sgurr (sgorr)	rocky peak
Sith	fairy
Sithean	fairy hill
Sloc (slochd)	hollow
Sneachd	snow
Socach	snout
Spidean	peak
Sput (sputan)	spout
Srath (strath)	broad valley
Sron	nose
Stac	steep rock
Steall	waterfall
Stob	peak
Stuc	peak, steep rock
Suidhe	seat
Tairbert (tarbert)	isthmus
Tap (top, tip)	hill top
Tarmachan	ptarmigan
Teallach	forge, hearth
Tigh	house
Toll	hollow
Tom	hill
Torc	bear
Torr	small hill
Traigh	beach
Uaine	green
Uamh	cave
Uig	bay
Uisge	water
Vik	bay, creek

APPENDIX B
Bibliography and Further Reading

Books marked ▶ are especially recommended.

History and Culture

A Cairngorm Chronicle by A.F. Whyte (Millrace, 2007)

▶ *A High and Lonely Place: The Sanctuary and Plight of the Cairngorms* by Jim Crumley (Whittles, 2001)

▶ *Always a Little Further* by Alastair Borthwick (Diadem, 1983)

Autumnal Rambles among the Scottish Mountains by Thomas Grierson (James Hogg, 1851)

Bell's Scottish Climbs by J.H.B. Bell (Gollancz, 1988)

▶ *Ben Nevis: Britain's Highest Mountain* by Ken Crocket and Simon Richardson (SMC, 2007)

Ben Nevis: The Story of Mountain and Glen by Rennie McOwan (Lang Syne, 1990)

The Big Grey Man of Ben Macdhui by Affleck Gray (Birlinn, 2000)

▶ *Burn on the Hill: The Story of the First 'Compleat Munroist'* by Elizabeth Allan (Bidean Books, 1995)

The Cairngorm Gateway by Ann Glen (Scottish Cultural Press, 2008)

▶ *A Century of Scottish Mountaineering: An Anthology from the Scottish Mountaineering Club Journal* edited by W.D. Brooker (SMC, 1988)

▶ *The Cuillin: Great Mountain Ridge of Skye* by Gordon Stainforth (Constable, 1994)

▶ *The First Munroist: The Reverend A.E. Robertson: His Life, Munros and Photographs* by Peter Drummond and Ian Mitchell (The Ernest Press, 1993)

▶ *Glen Feshie: The History and Archaeology of a Highland Glen* by Meryl M. Marshall (North of Scotland Archaeological Society, 2006)

Highlands and Western Islands of Scotland by John MacCulloch (Longman, 1984)

Highways and Byways in the Central Highlands by Seton Gordon (Birlinn, 1995, first published 1935)

Highways and Byways in the West Highlands by Seton Gordon (Birlinn, 1995, first published 1935)

The Life and Times of the Black Pig: A Biography of Ben Macdui by Ronald Turnbull (Millrace, 2007)

Legends of the Cairngorms by Affleck Gray (Mainstream, 1887)

Magic Mountains by Rennie McOwan (Mainstream, 1994)

The Man Who Bought Mountains by Rennie McOwan (National Trust for Scotland, 1978)

▶ *Mountaineering in Scotland* and *Undiscovered Scotland* by W.H. Murray (1947 and 1951, republished in one volume by Baton Wicks, 1997)

▶ *The Munro Phenomenon* by Andrew Dempster (Mainstream, 1995)

▶ *The Munroist's Companion: An Anthology* compiled and edited by Robin N.Campbell (SMT, 1999)

▶ *On the Trail of Queen Victoria in the Highlands* by Ian R. Mitchell (Luath, 2000)

On the Trail of Scotland's Myths and Legends by Stuart McHardy (Luath, 2005)

Recollections of a Tour Made in Scotland by Dorothy Wordsworth (Yale University Press, 1997, written 1803–1805, first published 1874)

▶ *Scotland's Mountains Before the Mountaineers* by Ian R. Mitchell (Luath, 1999)

▶ *Scottish Hill Names: Their Origin and Meaning* by Peter Drummond (Scottish Mountaineering Trust, 2nd revised edition, 2007)

The Scottish Tourist edited by W. Rhind and published in 1825

▶ *Seton Gordon's Scotland* by Seton Gordon (an anthology edited by Hamish Brown, Whittles, 2005)

Skisters: The Story of Scottish Skiing by Myrtle Simpson (Landmark Press, 1982)

The Weathermen of Ben Nevis 1883–1904 by Marjory Roy (The Royal Meteorological Society, 2004)

Recent Walking Accounts

A View from the Ridge by Dave Brown and Ian Mitchell (The Ernest Press, 1991)

▶ Hamish's Mountain Walk: The First Traverse of all the Scottish Munros in One Journey by Hamish Brown (first published 1978, new edition Sandstone Press, 2010)

Hell of a Journey: On Foot through the Scottish Highlands In Winter by Mike Cawthorne (Mercat Press, 2000)

▶ Mountain Days and Bothy Nights by Dave Brown and Ian Mitchell (Luath Press, 1987)

The First Fifty: Munro-Bagging without a Beard by Muriel Gray (Corgi, 1993)

The Last Hundred: Munros, Beards and a Dog by Hamish Brown (Mainstream, 1994)

The Munros and Tops: A Record-Setting Walk in the Scottish Highlands by Chris Townsend (Mainstream, 2nd edition 2003)

▶ The Munros In Winter: 277 Summits in 83 Days by Martin Moran (David & Charles, 1986)

▶ Walking the Watershed: The Border to Cape Wrath along Scotland's Great Divide by Dave Hewitt (TACit Press, 1994)

The Weekend Fix by Craig Weldon (Sandstone Press, 2009)

Wilderness Dreams: The Call of Scotland's Last Wild Places by Mike Cawthorne (The In Pinn, 2007)

Skills

▶ A Chance in a Million? – Scottish Avalanches by Bob Barton and Blyth Wright (SMT, 2nd edition 2000)

Hillwalking by Steve Long (Mountain Leader Training UK, 2003)

Mountaincraft and Leadership edited by Eric Langmuir (Sport Scotland, 1995)

The Backpacker's Handbook by Chris Townsend (Ragged Mountain Press, Third Edition 2005)

▶ The Hillwalker's Guide to Mountaineering by Terry Adby and Stuart Johnston (Cicerone Press, 2003)

The Mountain Skills Training Handbook by Pete Hill and Stuart Johnston (David & Charles, 2000)

Geology, Landscape, Conservation and Natural History Books

Among Mountains by Jim Crumley (Mainstream, 1993)

Beinn Eighe: The Mountain above the Wood by J. Laughton Johnston and Dick Balharry (Birlinn, 2001)

The Cairngorms: Their Natural History and Scenery by Desmond Nethersole-Thompson and Adam Watson (Collins, 1974)

▶ The Carrifran Wildwood Story by Myrtle and Philip Ashmole (Borders Forest Trust, 2009)

Days with the Golden Eagle by Seton Gordon (Whittles, 2002)

The Heart of the Cairngorms by Jim Crumley (Colin Baxter, 1997)

The Heart of Skye by Jim Crumley (Colin Baxter, 1994)

▶ The Highlands and Islands by F. Fraser Darling and Morton Boyd (Collins, 1969)

Flora Celtica: Plants and People in Scotland by William Milliken and Sam Bridgewater (Birlinn, 2004)

Granite and Grit: A Walker's Guide to the Geology of the British Mountains by Ronald Turnbull (Frances Lincoln, 2009)

▶ Hostile Habitats: Scotland's Mountain Environment: a Hillwalkers' Guide to Wildlife and Landscape edited by Nick Kempe and Mark Wrightman (SMT, 2006)

Landscapes and Lives: The Scottish Forest through the Ages by John Fowler (Canongate, 2003)

▶ Land of Mountain and Flood: The Geology and Landforms of Scotland by Alan McKirdy, John Gordon and Roger Crofts (Birlinn, 2007)

The Nature of the Cairngorms: Diversity in a Changing Environment by Philip Shaw and Des Thompson (The Stationery Office, 2006)

Nevis – The Hill, the Glen, the River by Alex Gillespie (Alex Gillespie Photography, 2007)

Revival of the Land: Creag Meagaidh National Nature Reserve by Paul Ramsey (SNH, 1996)

People and Woods in Scotland: A History edited by T.C. Smout (Edinburgh University Press, 2002)

Scotland's Beginnings: Scotland through Time by Michael A. Taylor and Andrew C. Kitchener (NMSE, 2007)

Scotland's Mountains by W.H. Murray (SMT, 1987)

Scottish Birds by Valerie Thom and Norman Arlott (Collins, 2005)

Scottish Wild Flowers by Michael Scott (Collins, 2008)

So Foul and Fair a Day: A History of Scotland's Weather and Climate by Alastair Dawson (Birlinn, 2009)

▶ *The Man Who Found Time: James Hutton and the Discovery of the Earth's Antiquity* by Jack Repcheck (Pocket Books, 2004)

Torridon, the Nature of the Place by Chris Lowe (Wester Ross Net, 2000)

General Hillwalking and Scrambling Guides

▶ *100 Best Routes on Scottish Mountains* by Ralph Storer (Time Warner, 1997)

101 Best Hill Walks in the Scottish Highlands and Islands by Graeme Cornwallis (Fort Publishing, 2009)

50 Classic Routes on Scottish Mountains by Ralph Storer (Luath Press, 2005)

Across Scotland on Foot: A Guide for Walkers and Hill Runners by Ronald Turnbull (Grey Stone Books, 1994)

▶ *Classic Mountain Scrambles in Scotland* by Andrew Dempster (Mainstream, 1992)

Classic Hill Runs and Races in Scotland by Steve Fallon (Pocket Mountains, 2009)

The Corbetts Almanac by Cameron McNeish (The In Pinn, 2nd edition 1999)

▶ *The Corbetts and other Scottish Hills* edited by Rob Milne and Hamish Brown (SMC, 2nd edition 2002)

▶ *The Grahams: A Guide to Scotland's 2000ft Peaks* by Andrew Dempster (Mainstream, 1997)

▶ *The High Mountains of Britain and Ireland: A Guide for Mountain Walkers: Vol 1* by Irvine Butterfield (Baton Wicks, 2nd edition 2004)

The Munro Almanac by Cameron McNeish (The In Pinn, 3rd edition 2005)

▶ *The Munros: Scotland's Highest Mountains* by Cameron McNeish (Lomond Books, 3rd edition 2006)

▶ *The Munros: SMC Hillwalkers Guide Vol 1* edited by Rab Anderson and Donald Bennett (SMC, 3rd edition 2006)

Scotland's Best Small Mountains by Kirstie Shirra (Cicerone, 2010)

▶ *Scotland's Winter Mountains* by Martin Moran (David & Charles, 1998).

▶ *Scottish Hill Tracks* edited by Donald Bennett and Cliff Stone (Scotways/SMT, revised 4th edition 2004)

The Scottish Peaks: A Poucher Guide by W.A. Poucher (Frances Lincoln, 2005)

The Ultimate Guide to the Munros: Vol 1 The Southern Highlands by Ralph Storer (Luath Press, 2008)

The Ultimate Guide to the Munros: Vol 2 Central Highlands South by Ralph Storer (Luath Press, 2009)

Walking the Munros Vol 1: Southern, Central and Western Highlands by Steve Kew (Cicerone, 2004)

Walking the Munros Vol 2: Northern Highlands and the Cairngorms by Steve Kew (Cicerone, 2004)

General Climbing Guides

▶ *Rock Climbing in Scotland* by Kevin Howett (Frances Lincoln, 2004)

▶ *Scotland's Mountain Ridges: Scrambling, Mountaineering and Climbing* by Dan Bailey (Cicerone, 2006)

▶ *Scottish Rock Climbs* edited by Andy Nisbet (SMT, 2005)

▶ *Scottish Winter Climbs: Scottish Mountaineering Club Climbers Guides* by Andy Nisbet, Rab Anderson and Simon Richardson (SMC, 2008)

Ski Touring Guides

▸ *Ski Mountaineering in Scotland* edited by Donald Bennett and Bill Wallace (SMC, 1987)

Ski Touring in Scotland by Angela Oakley (Cicerone, 1991) (Out of print but well worth seeking out)

Guides to Long Distance Routes

The Cape Wrath Trail: A New 200-mile Walking Route through the North-west Scottish Highlands by David Paterson (Peak Publishing, 1996)

The Great Glen Way by Brian Smailes (Challenge, 2003)

▸ *The Great Glen Way: Two-way Trail Guide* by Paddy Dillon (Cicerone, 2007)

▸ *North to the Cape: A Trek from Fort William to Cape Wrath* by Denis Brook and Phil Hinchcliffe (Cicerone Press, 1999)

▸ *The Southern Upland Way* by Alan Castle (Cicerone, 2007)

▸ *The Southern Upland Way: Official Guide* by Roger Smith (Mercat, 2005)

The Southern Upland Way: Recreational Path Guide by Anthony Burton (Auram, 1997)

The Speyside Way by Alan Castle (Cicerone, 2010)

▸ *The Sutherland Trail: A Journey Through North-West Scotland* by Cameron McNeish and Richard Else (Mountain Media, 2009)

▸ *The West Highland Way: Official Guide* edited by Bob Aitken and Roger Smith (Mercat, 8th edition, 2006)

West Highland Way by Charlie Loram (Trailblazer, 2006)

The West Highland Way by Terry Marsh (Cicerone, 2009)

The West Highland Way: Recreational Path Guide by Anthony Burton (Auram, 1996).

The West Highland Way by Jacquetta Megarry (Rucksack Readers, 2003)

CDs and DVDs

The Corbetts – Hillwalker CD-ROM (ISYS)

The Corbetts and other Scottish Hills CD edited by Ken Crocket and Rob Milne (SMC)

Hillwalker Max Scotland (ISYS)

The Munros CD edited by Ken Crocket and Donald Bennett (SMC)

The Munros – Hillwalker CD-ROM (ISYS)

Websites

The Mountaineering Council of Scotland www.mcos.org.uk

MunroMagic.com www.munromagic.com

MunroMap.co.uk www.munromap.co.uk

Scottish Climbing Archive www.scotclimb.org.uk

Scottish Hills www.scottishhills.com

Scottish Mountaineering Club www.smc.org.uk

Sub 3000: The Wee Hill Bashers Site www.sub3000.com

Walk Highlands www.walkhighlands.co.uk

Magazines

The Angry Corrie, quarterly iconoclastic hillwalking fanzine, http://bubl.ac.uk/org/tacit

TGO – The Great Outdoors, monthly hillwalkers' magazine with good Scottish coverage, www.tgomagazine.co.uk

The Scottish Mountaineer, quarterly magazine of the Mountaineering Council of Scotland, www.mcofs.org.uk

Guides to the Southern Uplands

Lowland Outcrops by Graeme Nicoll and Tom Prentice (SMC, 1994)

Southern Uplands by Nick Williams (Pocket Mountains, 2005)

The Border Country: A Walker's Guide by Alan Hall (Cicerone, 3rd edition 2005)

▸ *The Southern Uplands* by Ken Andrew (SMC, 1992)

Walking the Galloway Hills by Paddy Dillon (Cicerone, 1995)

Walking the Lowther Hills by Ronald Turnbull (Cicerone, 1999)

Guides to the Southern Highlands

25 Walks: Loch Lomond and the Trossachs by Roger Smith and John Digney (The Mercat Press, 2004)

▶ *Arran, Arrochar and the Southern Highlands: Rock and Ice Climbs* by Graham Little, Tom Prentice and Ken Crocket (SMC, 1997)

Highland Outcrops by Kevin Howett (SMC, 1998)

Loch Lomond and the Trossachs National Park: East by Tom Prentice (Mica Publishing, 2009)

Loch Lomond and the Trossachs National Park: West by Tom Prentice (Mica Publishing, 2009)

Loch Lomond and the Trossachs National Parks Short Walks edited by Hugh Taylor (Jarrold, 2005)

Loch Lomond, the Trossachs, Stirling and Clackmannan (Pathfinder Guide) by John Brooks, Brian Conduit, Neil Coates, and Ark Creative (Jarrold, 2002)

Southern Highlands by Nick Williams (Pocket Mountains, 2003)

The Rob Roy Way by Jacquetta Megarry and Rennie McOwan (Rucksack Readers, 2006)

▶ *The Southern Highlands* by Donald Bennett (SMC, 1992)

▶ *Walking Loch Lomond and the Trossachs* by Ronald Turnbull (Cicerone, 2009)

Guides to the Central Highlands

▶ *Ben Nevis and Glen Coe* by Ronald Turnbull (Cicerone, 2007)

Ben Nevis and Glen Coe Rambler's Guide by Chris Townsend (Collins, 2000)

Ben Nevis and the Mamores (Classic Munros) by Chris Townsend (Colin Baxter, 2009)

▶ *Ben Nevis Rock and Ice Climbs including Creag Meagaidh, the Aonachs and the Central Highlands* by Simon Richardson (SMT, 2002)

▶ *The Central Highlands (Scottish Mountaineering Club District Guide)* by Peter Hodgkiss (SMT, 1994)

The Central Highlands by Nick Williams (Pocket Mountains, 2004)

Fort William and Glen Coe Walks (Pathfinder Guide) by Hamish Brown (Jarrold/Ordnance Survey, 1992)

Glen Coe (Classic Munros) by Chris Townsend (Colin Baxter, 2008)

Glen Coe by Ken Crocket, Rab Anderson and Dave Cuthbertson (SMT, 2001)

Glen Roy by Scottish National Heritage (Landscape Fashioned by Geology series, SNH, 2004)

Glencoe by Lyndsey Bowditch (National Trust for Scotland, 2005)

Hill Walks Glen Coe and Lochaber by Ruaridh Pringle (The Stationery Office, 1997)

Winter Climbs Ben Nevis and Glencoe by Mike Pescod (Cicerone, 2010)

Guides to the Cairngorms

▶ *The Cairngorms* by Adam Watson (SMC, 6th edition 1992)

The Cairngorms by Nick Williams (Pocket Mountains, 2003)

The Cairngorms: Classic Munros by Chris Townsend (Colin Baxter, 2008)

▶ *The Cairngorms: Scottish Mountaineering Club Climbers' Guide* by Andy Nisbett, Allen Fyffe, Simon Richardson, Wilson Moir and John Lyall (SMC, 2007)

Cairngorms Walks by John Brooks (Jarrold, 1996)

The Glen with More: A Guide to Glenmore Forest Park by Kenny Taylor (FSC, 2003)

▶ *Walking in the Cairngorms* by Ronald Turnbull (Cicerone, 2005)

Winter Climbs in the Cairngorms by Allen Fyffe (Cicerone, 2000)

Guides to the Western Highlands

Glen Coe by Ken Crockett, Rab Anderson and Dave Cuthbertson (SMC, 2001)

Guide to Walks in the North-West Highlands by Chris Townsend (Aurum, 2007)

▸ *Highland Scrambles North* by Iain Thow (SMT, 2006)

▸ *Northern Highlands South: Scottish Mountaineering Club Climbers' Guide* edited by Andy Nesbitt (SMT, 2007)

▸ *The Northwest Highlands* by Dave Broadhead, Alec Keith and Ted Maden (SMC, 2004)

▸ *Scrambles in Lochaber* by Noel Williams (Cicerone, 1996)

Skye and Kintail (25 Walks) by Hamish Brown (Mercat Press, 2000)

West Highlands by Nick Williams (Pocket Mountains, 2004)

Guides to the Northern Highlands

The Cape Wrath Trail: A New 200-mile Walking Route through the North-west Scottish Highlands by David Paterson (Peak Publishing, 1996)

▸ *Exploring the Far North West of Scotland* by Richard Gilbert (Cordee, 1994)

▸ *Exploring the Landscape of Assynt* (with 1:50,000 geological map) by Kathryn Goodenough, Elizabeth Pickett, Maarten Krabbendam and Tom Bradwell (British Geological Survey, 2004)

Guide to Walks in the North-West Highlands by Chris Townsend (Aurum, 2007)

▸ *Highland Scrambles North* by Iain Thow (SMT, 2006)

▸ *North to the Cape: A Trek from Fort William to Cape Wrath* by Denis Brook and Phil Hinchcliffe (Cicerone, 1999)

Northern Highlands by Nick Williams (Pocket Mountains, 2003)

▸ *Northern Highlands Central* edited by Andy Nisbet (SMC, 2006)

▸ *Northern Highlands North* edited by Andy Nisbet (SMC, 2004)

▸ *Northern Highlands South* edited by Andy Nisbet (SMC, 2007)

▸ *The Northwest Highlands* by Dave Broadhead, Alec Keith and Ted Maden (SMC, 2004)

Skye and the North West Highlands Walks by John Brooks and Neil Wilson (Jarrold, 2003)

▸ *The Sutherland Trail: A Journey Through North-West Scotland* by Cameron McNeish and Richard Else (Mountain Media, 2009)

Walking in Scotland's Far North by Andy Walmsley (Cicerone, 2003)

Walking in Torridon by Peter Barton, updated by Chris Lowe and Jim Sutherland (Cicerone, 2010)

Guides to the Islands

50 Best Routes on Skye and Raasay by Ralph Storer (David & Charles, 1996)

▸ *Arran, Arrochar and the Southern Highlands* by Graham Little, Tom Prentice and Ken Crocket (SMT, 1997)

Guide to Walks in the North-West Highlands (includes four walks on Skye) by Chris Townsend (Aurum, 2007)

▸ *The Island of Rhum: A Guide for Walkers, Climbers and Visitors* by Hamish Brown (Cicerone, 1988)

▸ *The Islands of Scotland Including Skye* (Scottish Mountaineering Club District Guide) by D.J. Fabian, G.E. Little and D.N. Williams (SMT, 1995)

The Islands: Skye, the Hebrides and Arran by Nick Williams (Pocket Mountains, 2004)

The Isle of Skye by Terry Marsh (Cicerone, 2009)

Isle of Skye Ramblers' Guide by Chris Townsend (Collins, 2010)

A Long Walk on the Isle of Skye by David Paterson (Peak Publishing, 1999)

▸ *The Magic of Skye* by W.A. Poucher (9th edition, Frances Lincoln, 2005)

The Scottish Islands by Hamish Haswell-Smith (Canongate 2004)

▸ *Skye – Rock and Ice Climbs: Scottish Mountaineering Club Climbers' Guide* edited by Roger Everett (SMT, 2005)

▸ *Skye Scrambles: Walks, Scrambles and Easy Climbs on the Isle of Skye* by Noel Williams (SMT, 2000)

Walking in the Hebrides by Roger Redfern (Cicerone, 1998)

Walking on the Isle of Arran by Paddy Dillon (Cicerone, 1998)

Walking on Jura, Islay and Colonsay by Peter Edwards (Cicerone, 2010)

Walking on Harris and Lewis by Richard Barrett (Cicerone, 2010)

Other Cicerone guides
to Scotland's mountains

Backpacker's Britain: Central and Southern Scottish Highlands by Graham Uney (2008)

Backpacker's Britain: Northern Scotland by Graham Uney (2006)

Ben Nevis and Glen Coe by Ronald Turnbull (2010)

The Border Country by Alan Hall (2005)

The Central Highlands by Peter Koch-Osborne (1998)

The Great Glen Way by Paddy Dillon (2007)

The Isle of Mull by Terry Marsh (2010)

The Isle of Skye by Terry Marsh (2009)

North to the Cape by Denis Brook and Phil Hinchliffe (1999)

Not the West Highland Way by Ronald Turnbull (2010)

The Pentland Hills: A Walker's Guide by Susan Falconer (2008)

Scotland's Best Small Mountains by Kirstie Shirra (2010)

Scotland's Far West by Denis Brook and Phil Hinchliffe (2010)

Scotland's Mountain Ridges by Dan Bailey (2010)

The Scottish Glens 2: The Atholl Glens by Peter Koch-Osborne (1999)

The Scottish Glens 3: The Glens of Rannoch by Peter Koch-Osborne (2004)

The Scottish Glens 4: The Glens of Trossach by Peter Koch-Osborne (2004)

The Scottish Glens 5: The Glens of Argyll by Peter Koch-Osborne (2004)

The Scottish Glens 6: The Great Glen by Peter Koch-Osborne (2004)

Scrambles in Lochaber by Noel Williams (2009)

The Southern Upland Way by Alan Castle (2007)

The Speyside Way by Alan Castle (2010)

The West Highland Way by Terry Marsh (2009)

Walking in Scotland's Far North by Andy Walmsley (2009)

Walking in the Cairngorms by Ronald Turnbull (2008)

Walking in the Hebrides by Roger Redfern (2003)

Walking in the Ochils, Campsie Fells and Lomond Hills by Patrick Baker (2008)

Walking in Torridon by Chris Lowe and Peter Barton (2010)

Walking Loch Lomond and the Trossachs by Ronald Turnbull (2009)

Walking on Harris and Lewis by Richard Barrett (2010)

Walking on Jura, Islay and Colonsay by Peter Edwards (2010)

Walking on the Isle of Arran by Paddy Dillon (2008)

Walking on the Orkney and Shetland Isles by Graham Uney (2009)

Walking the Galloway Hills by Paddy Dillon (2010)

Walking the Lowther Hills by Ronald Turnbull (1999)

Walking the Munros Vol 1: Southern, Central and Western Highlands by Steve Kew (2010)

Walking the Munros Vol 2: Northern Highlands and the Cairngorms by Steve Kew (2008)

Winter Climbs in Ben Nevis and Glen Coe by Mike Pescod (2010)

Winter Climbs in the Cairngorms by Allen Fyffe (2000)

APPENDIX C

Current List of Munros

This is the current list of Munro summits as published in Munro's *Tables* (ranked by height). (The right-hand column gives the number of the OS Landranger map (or maps) on which the summit appears.)

RANK	MUNRO	AREA	HEIGHT (M)	OS MAP
1	Ben Nevis	Central Highlands	1344	41
2	Ben Macdui	Cairngorms	1309	36/43
3	Braeriach	Cairngorms	1296	36/43
4	Cairn Toul	Cairngorms	1291	36/43
5	Sgor an Lochain Uaine	Cairngorms	1258	33
6	Cairn Gorm	Cairngorms	1244	36
7	Aonach Beag (Glen Nevis)	Central Highlands	1234	41
8	Aonach Mor	Central Highlands	1221	41
9	Carn Mor Dearg	Central Highlands	1220	41
10	Ben Lawers	Southern Highlands	1214	51
11	Beinn a' Bhuird – North Top	Cairngorms	1197	36/43
12	Carn Eighe	Western Highlands	1183	25
13	Beinn Mheadhoin	Cairngorms	1182	36
14	Mam Sodhail	Western Highlands	1181	25
15	Stob Choire Claurigh	Central Highlands	1177	41
16	Ben More	Southern Highlands	1174	51
17	Ben Avon – Leabaidh an Daimh Bhuidhe	Cairngorms	1171	36
18	Stob Binnein	Southern Highlands	1165	51
19	Beinn Bhrotain	Cairngorms	1157	43
20	Derry Cairngorm	Cairngorms	1155	36/43
21	Lochnagar – Cac Carn Beag	Cairngorms	1155	44
22	Sgurr nan Ceathreamhnan	Western Highlands	1151	25/33
23	Bidean nam Bian	Central Highlands	1150	41
24	Sgurr na Lapaich (Mullardoch)	Western Highlands	1150	25
25	Ben Alder	Central Highlands	1148	42
26	Geal-Charn (Alder)	Central Highlands	1132	42
27	Binnein Mor	Central Highlands	1130	41
28	Ben Lui	Southern Highlands	1130	50
29	An Riabhachan	Central Highlands	1129	25
30	Creag Meagaidh	Cairngorms	1128	34/42
31	Ben Cruachan	Southern Highlands	1126	50
32	Beinn a'Ghlo – Carn nan Gabhar	Cairngorms	1121	43
33	A'Chralaig	Western Highlands	1120	33
34	An Stuc	Southern Highlands	1118	51
35	Meall Garbh (Ben Lawers)	Southern Highlands	1118	51
36	Sgor Gaoith	Cairngorms	1118	36/43
37	Aonach Beag (Alder)	Central Highlands	1116	42
38	Stob Coire an Laoigh	Central Highlands	1116	41
39	Stob Coire Easain (Loch Treig)	Central Highlands	1115	41
40	Monadh Mor	Cairngorms	1113	43

RANK	MUNRO	AREA	HEIGHT (M)	OS MAP
41	Tom a'Choinich	Western Highlands	1112	25
42	Carn a'Choire Bhoidheach	Cairngorms	1110	44
43	Sgurr Mor (Fannaichs)	Northern Highlands	1110	20
44	Sgurr nan Conbhairean	Western Highlands	1109	34
45	Meall A' Bhuiridh	Central Highlands	1108	41
46	Stob a' Choire Mheadhoin	Central Highlands	1105	41
47	Beinn Ghlas	Southern Highlands	1103	51
48	Beinn Eibhinn	Central Highlands	1102	42
49	Mullach Fraoch-choire	Western Highlands	1102	33
50	Creise	Central Highlands	1100	41
51	Sgurr a'Mhaim	Central Highlands	1099	41
52	Sgurr Choinnich Mor	Central Highlands	1094	41
53	Sgurr nan Clach Geala	Northern Highlands	1093	20
54	Bynack More	Cairngorms	1090	36
55	Stob Gabhar	Central Highlands	1090	50
56	Beinn a'Chlachair	Central Highlands	1087	42
57	Beinn Dearg (Ullapool)	Northern Highlands	1084	20
58	Beinn a'Chaorainn	Cairngorms	1083	36
59	Schiehallion	Southern Highlands	1083	51
60	Sgurr a'Choire Ghlais	Western Highlands	1083	25
61	Beinn a Chreachain	Southern Highlands	1081	50
62	Beinn Heasgarnich	Southern Highlands	1078	51
63	Ben Starav	Central Highlands	1078	50
64	Beinn Dorain	Southern Highlands	1076	50
65	Stob Coire Sgreamhach	Central Highlands	1072	41
66	Braigh Coire Chruinn-bhalgain	Cairngorms	1070	43
67	An Socach (Lapaichs)	Western Highlands	1069	25
68	Meal Corranaich	Southern Highlands	1069	51
69	Glas Maol	Cairngorms	1068	43
70	Sgurr Fhuaran	Western Highlands	1067	33
71	Cairn of Claise	Cairngorms	1064	43
72	An Teallach – Bidein a 'Ghlas Thuill	Northern Highlands	1062	19
73	An Teallach – Sgurr Fiona	Northern Highlands	1060	19
74	Na Gruagaichean	Central Highlands	1056	41
75	Liathach – Spidean a'Choire Leith	Northern Highlands	1055	25
76	Stob Poite Coire Ardair	Central Highlands	1054	34/42
77	Toll Creagach	Western Highlands	1054	25
78	Sgurr a'Chaorachain (Monar)	Western Highlands	1053	25
79	Glas Tulaichean	Cairngorms	1051	43
80	Beinn a'Chaorainn (Laggan)	Central Highlands	1049	34/41
81	Geal Charn – Mullach Coire an Iubhair	Central Highlands	1049	42
82	Sgurr Fhuar-thuill	Western Highlands	1049	25
83	Carn an t-Sagairt Mor	Cairngorms	1047	44
84	Creag Mhor	Southern Highlands	1047	50
85	Ben Wyvis – Glas Leathad Mor	Northern Highlands	1046	20
86	Chno Dearg	Central Highlands	1046	41
87	Cruach Ardrain	Southern Highlands	1046	51/56
88	Beinn Iutharn Mhor	Cairngorms	1045	43
89	Meall nan Tarmachan	Southern Highlands	1044	51

RANK	MUNRO	AREA	HEIGHT (M)	OS MAP
90	Stob Coir'an Albannaich	Central Highlands	1044	50
91	Carn Mairg	Southern Highlands	1041	51
92	Sgurr na Ciche	Western Highlands	1040	33/40
93	Meall Ghaordie	Southern Highlands	1039	51
94	Beinn Achaladair	Southern Highlands	1038	50
95	Carn a'Mhaim	Cairngorms	1037	36/43
96	Sgurr a'Bhealaich Dheirg	Western Highlands	1036	33
97	Gleouraich	Western Highlands	1035	33
98	Carn Dearg (Alder)	Central Highlands	1034	42
99	Am Bodach (Mamores)	Central Highlands	1032	41
100	Beinn Fhada (Kintail)	Western Highlands	1032	33
101	Ben Oss	Southern Highlands	1029	50
102	Carn an Righ	Cairngorms	1029	43
103	Carn Gorm	Southern Highlands	1029	51
104	Sgurr a'Mhaoraich	Western Highlands	1027	33
105	Sgurr na Ciste Duibhe	Western Highlands	1027	33
106	Ben Challum	Southern Highlands	1025	50
107	Sgorr Dhearg (Beinn a'Bheithir)	Central Highlands	1024	41
108	Liathach – Mullach an Rathain	Northern Highlands	1023	25
109	Aonach air Chrith	Western Highlands	1021	33
110	Stob Dearg – Buachaille Etive Mor	Central Highlands	1021	41
111	Ladhar Bheinn	Western Highlands	1020	33
112	Beinn Bheoil	Central Highlands	1019	42
113	Carn an Tuirc	Cairngorms	1019	43
114	Mullach Clach a'Bhlair	Cairngorms	1019	35/36/43
115	Mullach Choire Mhic Fhearchair	Northern Highlands	1018	19
116	Garbh Chioch Mhor	Western Highlands	1013	33/40
117	Cairn Bannoch	Cairngorms	1012	44
118	Beinn Ime	Southern Highlands	1011	56
119	Beinn Udlamain	Central Highlands	1011	42
120	Beinn Eighe – Ruadh-stac Mor	Northern Highlands	1010	25
121	The Saddle	Western Highlands	1010	33
122	Sgurr an Doire Leathain	Western Highlands	1010	33
123	Sgurr Eilde Mor	Central Highlands	1010	41
124	Beinn Dearg (Atholl)	Cairngorms	1008	43
125	Maoile Lunndaidh	Northern Highlands	1007	25
126	An Sgarsoch	Cairngorms	1006	43
127	Carn Liath (Creag Meagaidh)	Central Highlands	1006	34
128	Beinn Fhionnlaidh (Affric)	Western Highlands	1005	25
129	Beinn an Dothaidh	Southern Highlands	1004	50
130	The Devil's Point	Cairngorms	1004	36/43
131	Sgurr an Lochain	Western Highlands	1004	33
132	Sgurr Mor	Western Highlands	1003	33
133	Sail Chaorainn	Western Highlands	1002	34
134	Sgurr na Carnach	Western Highlands	1002	33
135	Aonach Meadhoin	Western Highlands	1001	33
136	Meall Greigh	Southern Highlands	1001	51
137	Sgorr Dhonuill (Beinn a'Bheithir)	Central Highlands	1001	41

RANK	MUNRO	AREA	HEIGHT (M)	OS MAP
138	Sgurr Breac	Northern Highlands	999	20
139	Sgurr Choinnich	Northern Highlands	999	25
140	Stob Ban (Mamores)	Central Highlands	999	41
141	Ben More Assynt	Northern Highlands	998	15
142	Broad Cairn	Cairngorms	998	44
143	Stob Diamh	Southern Highlands	998	50
144	A'Chailleach (Fannaichs)	Northern Highlands	997	19
145	Glas Bheinn Mhor	Southern Highlands	997	50
146	Spidean Mialach	Western Highlands	996	33
147	An Caisteal	Southern Highlands	995	50/56
148	Carn an Fhidhleir (Carn Ealar)	Cairngorms	994	43
149	Sgor na h-Ulaidh	Western Highlands	994	41
150	Beinn Eighe – Spidean Coire nan Clach	Northern Highlands	993	19
151	Sgurr na Ruaidhe	Western Highlands	993	25
152	Carn nan Gobhar (Lapaichs)	Western Highlands	992	25
153	Carn nan Gobhar (Strathfarrar)	Western Highlands	992	25
154	Sgurr Alasdair	Islands – Skye	992	32
155	Sgairneach Mhor	Central Highlands	991	42
156	Beinn Eunaich	Southern Highlands	989	50
157	Sgurr Ban (Letterewe)	Northern Highlands	989	19
158	Conival	Northern Highlands	987	15
159	Creag Leacach	Cairngorms	987	43
160	Druim Shionnach	Western Highlands	987	33
161	Gulvain	Western Highlands	987	41
162	Sgurr Mhor – Beinn Alligin	Northern Highlands	986	19/24
163	Lurg Mhor	Northern Highlands	986	25
164	Sgurr Dearg – Inaccessible Pinnacle	Islands – Skye	986	32
165	Ben Vorlich (Loch Earn)	Southern Highlands	985	57
166	An Gearanach	Central Highlands	982	41
167	Mullach na Dheiragain	Western Highlands	982	25/33
168	Maol Chinn-dearg	Western Highlands	981	33
169	Meall nan Aighean	Central Highlands	981	51
170	Slioch	Northern Highlands	981	19
171	Stob Coire a'Chairn	Central Highlands	981	41
172	Beinn a'Chochuill	Southern Highlands	980	50
173	Ciste Dhubh	Western Highlands	979	33
174	Stob Coire Sgriodain	Central Highlands	979	41
175	Beinn Dubhchraig	Southern Highlands	978	50
176	Cona'Mheall	Northern Highlands	978	20
177	Meall nan Ceapraichean	Northern Highlands	977	20
178	Stob Ban (Grey Corries)	Central Highlands	977	41
179	A'Mharconaich	Central Highlands	975	42
180	Carn a'Gheoidh	Cairngorms	975	43
181	Carn Liath (Beinn a'Ghlo)	Cairngorms	975	43
182	Stuc a 'Chroin	Southern Highlands	975	51/57
183	Beinn Sgritheall	Western Highlands	974	33
184	Ben Lomond	Southern Highlands	974	56
185	Sgurr a' Ghreadaidh	Islands – Skye	973	32
186	Meall Garbh (Carn Mairg)	Southern Highlands	968	51

RANK	MUNRO	AREA	HEIGHT (M)	OS MAP
187	A'Mhaighdean	Northern Highlands	967	19
188	Sgor nam Fiannaidh	Central Highlands	967	41
189	Ben More (Mull)	Islands – Mull	966	48
190	Sgurr na Banachdich	Islands – Skye	965	32
191	Sgurr nan Gillean	Islands – Skye	965	32
192	Carn a'Chlamain	Cairngorms	963	43
193	Sgurr Thuilm	Western Highlands	963	40
194	Ben Klibreck	Northern Highlands	962	16
195	Sgorr Ruadh	Northern Highlands	962	25
196	Beinn nan Aighenan	Central Highlands	960	50
197	Stuchd an Lochain	Southern Highlands	960	51
198	Beinn Fhionnlaidh (Appin)	Central Highlands	959	50
199	Meall Glas	Central Highlands	959	51
200	Bruach na Frithe	Islands – Skye	958	32
201	Stob Dubh (Buachaille Etive Beag)	Central Highlands	958	41
202	Tolmount	Cairngorms	958	44
203	Carn Ghluasaid	Western Highlands	957	34
204	Tom Buidhe	Cairngorms	957	44
205	Saileag	Western Highlands	956	33
206	Sgurr nan Coireachan (Glen Finnan)	Western Highlands	956	40
207	Stob na Broige	Central Highlands	956	41
208	Stob Gaibhre	Central Highlands	955	42
209	Beinn Liath Mhor Fannaich	Northern Highlands	954	20
210	Am Faochagch	Northern Highlands	953	20
211	Beinn Mhanach	Southern Highlands	953	50
212	Meall Dearg (Aonach Eagach)	Central Highlands	953	41
213	Sgurr nan Coireachan (Glen Dessary)	Western Highlands	953	33/40
214	Meal Chuaich	Central Highlands	951	42
215	Meall Gorm	Northern Highlands	949	20
216	Beinn Bhuidhe	Southern Highlands	948	56/50
217	Sgurr Mhic Choinnich	Islands – Skye	948	32
218	Creag a'Mhaim	Western Highlands	947	33
219	Driesh	Cairngorms	947	44
220	Beinn Rulaichean	Southern Highlands	946	56
221	Carn Bhac	Cairngorms	946	43
222	Meall Buidhe (Knoydart)	Western Highlands	946	33/40
223	Sgurr na Sgine	Western Highlands	946	33
224	Bidein a'Choire Sheasgaich	Northern Highlands	945	25
225	Carn Dearg (Monadh Liath)	Central Highlands	945	35
226	Stob A Choire Odhair	Central Highlands	945	50
227	An Socach (Glen Ey)	Cairngorms	944	43
228	Sgurr Dubh Mor	Islands – Skye	944	32
229	Ben Vorlich (Arrochar)	Southern Highlands	943	50/56
230	Binnein Beag	Central Highlands	943	41
231	Carn Dearg (Corrour)	Central Highlands	941	42
232	Carn na Caim	Cairngorms	941	42
233	Beinn a'Chroin	Southern Highlands	940	50/56
234	Luinne Bheinn	Western Highlands	939	33
235	Mount Keen	Cairngorms	939	44

RANK	MUNRO	AREA	HEIGHT (M)	OS MAP
236	Mullach nan Coirean	Central Highlands	939	41
237	Beinn Sgulaird	Central Highlands	937	50
238	Beinn Tarsuinn	Northern Highlands	937	19
239	Sron a'Choire Ghairbh	Western Highlands	937	34
240	A'Bhuidheanach Bheag	Cairngorms	936	42
241	Beinn na Lap	Central Highlands	935	41
242	Am Basteir	Islands – Skye	934	32
243	Meall a'Chrasgidh	Northern Highlands	934	20
244	Beinn Chabhair	Southern Highlands	933	50/56
245	The Cairnwell	Cairngorms	933	43
246	Fionn Bheinn	Northern Highlands	933	20
247	Maol Chean-dearg	Northern Highlands	933	25
248	Meall Buidhe (Glen Lyon)	Southern Highlands	932	51
249	Beinn Bhreac	Cairngorms	931	36/43
250	Ben Chonzie	Southern Highlands	931	51/52
251	A'Chailleach (Monadh Liath)	Central Highlands	930	35
252	Bla Bheinn	Islands – Skye	928	32
253	Mayar	Cairngorms	928	44
254	Meall nan Eun	Central Highlands	928	50
255	Moruisg	Northern Highlands	928	25
256	Ben Hope	Northern Highlands	927	9
257	Eididh nan Clach Geala	Northern Highlands	927	20
258	Beinn Liath Mhor	Northern Highlands	926	25
259	Beinn Narnain	Southern Highlands	926	56
260	Geal Charn (Monadh Liath)	Central Highlands	926	35
261	Meall a'Choire Leith	Southern Highlands	926	51
262	Seana Bhraigh	Northern Highlands	926	20
263	Stob Coire Raineach	Central Highlands	925	41
264	Creag Pitridh	Central Highlands	924	42
265	Sgurr nan Eag	Islands – Skye	924	32
266	An Coileachan	Northern Highlands	923	20
267	Sgurr nan Each	Northern Highlands	923	20
268	Tom na Gruagaich – Beinn Alligin	Northern Highlands	922	19/24
269	An Socach (Affric)	Western Highlands	921	25/33
270	Sgiath Chuil	Central Highlands	921	51
271	Carn Sgulain	Central Highlands	920	35
272	Gairich	Western Highlands	919	33
273	A'Ghlas-bheinn	Western Highlands	918	25/33
274	Creag nan Damh	Western Highlands	918	33
275	Meall na Teanga	Western Highlands	918	34
276	Ruadh Stac Mor	Northern Highlands	918	19
277	Sgurr a'Mhadaidh	Islands – Skye	918	32
278	Carn Aosda	Cairngorms	917	43
279	Geal Charn (Drumochter)	Central Highlands	917	42
280	Beinn a' Chlaidheimh	Northern Highlands	916	19
281	Beinn a' Chleibh	Central Highlands	916	50
282	Beinn Teallach	Central Highlands	915	34/41
283	Ben Vane	Southern Highlands	915	56

APPENDIX D
Current List of Corbetts

The right-hand column gives the number of the OS Landranger map (or maps) on which the summit appears.

RANK	CORBETT	AREA	HEIGHT (M)	OS MAP
1	Beinn Dearg	Northern Highlands	914	24
2	Foinaven	Northern Highlands	914	9
3	Sgurr nan Ceannaichean	Northern Highlands	913	25
4	Sgurr a'Choire-bheithe	Western Highlands	913	33
5	Leathad an Taobhain	Cairngorms	912	43
6	Beinn Bhreac	Cairngorms	912	43
7	The Fara	Central Highlands	911	42
8	Meall Buidhe	Southern Highlands	910	51
9	Beinn Dearg Mor	Northern Highlands	910	19
10	Beinn nan Oighreag	Central Highlands	909	51
11	Streap	Western Highlands	909	40
12	Leum Uilleim	Central Highlands	909	41
13	Beinn Maol Chaluim	Central Highlands	907	41
14	Fuar Tholl	Northern Highlands	907	25
15	Beinn Bhuirich	Central Highlands	903	43
16	Beinn Damh	Northern Highlands	902	24
17	Beinn an Lochain	Southern Highlands	901	56
18	Ben Tee	Western Highlands	901	34
19	Beinn Odhar	Southern Highlands	901	50
20	Beinn Mheadhonach	Cairngorms	901	43
21	Sgurr an Fhuarain	Western Highlands	901	33
22	Culardoch	Cairngorms	900	36/43
22	Aonach Buidhe	Northern Highlands	899	25
24	Sgurr nan Eugallt	Western Highlands	898	33
25	Beinn a'Bhuiridh	Central Highlands	897	50
26	Ben Tirran	Cairngorms	896	44
27	Gairbeinn	Central Highlands	896	34
28	Ruadh-stac Beag	Northern Highlands	896	19
29	Beinn Bhan	Northern Highlands	896	24
30	Creag Mhor	Cairngorms	895	36
31	Beinn a'Chuallaich	Central Highlands	892	42
32	An Ruadh-stac	Northern Highlands	892	25
33	Beinn Enaiglair	Northern Highlands	890	20
34	Aonach Shasuinn	Western Highlands	889	34
35	Creagan na Beinne	Southern Highlands	888	51
36	Sgurr Dhomhnuill	Western Highlands	888	40
37	Ben Aden	Western Highlands	887	33
38	Meall a'Ghiubhais	Northern Highlands	887	19
39	Beinn a'Chaisteil	Southern Highlands	886	50

RANK	CORBETT	AREA	HEIGHT (M)	OS MAP
40	Garbh Bheinn	Western Highlands	885	40
41	Sgurr a'Bhac Chaolais	Western Highlands	885	33
42	The Cobbler	Southern Highlands	884	56
43	Cam Chreag	Southern Highlands	884	50
44	Stob Dubh, Beinn Ceitlein	Central Highlands	883	50
45	Beinn Odhar Bheag	Western Highlands	882	40
46	Rois-Bheinn	Western Highlands	882	40
47	Beinn Chuirn	Southern Highlands	880	50
48	Sgurr Mhurlagain	Western Highlands	880	33
49	Creag Uchdag	Southern Highlands	879	51
50	Ben Ledi	Southern Highlands	879	57
51	Fraochaidh	Central Highlands	879	41
52	Sgurr a'Mhuilinn	Western Highlands	879	25
53	Sguman Coinntich	Western Highlands	879	25
54	Carn an Fhreiceadain	Central Highlands	878	35
55	Creag an Loch	Cairngorms	876	42
56	Baosbheinn	Northern Highlands	875	19
57	Sgurr na Ba Glaise	Western Highlands	874	40
58	Goat Fell	Islands – Arran	874	69
59	Sgorr nan Lochan Uaine	Northern Highlands	873	25
60	Ben Hee	Northern Highlands	873	16
61	Morven	Cairngorms	872	37
62	Stob a'Choin	Southern Highlands	869	56
63	Meall na Meoig, Ben Pharlagain	Central Highlands	868	42
64	Faochaig	Western Highlands	868	25
65	Garbh Bheinn	Central Highlands	867	41
66	Bidein a'Chabair	Western Highlands	867	33
67	Conachcraig	Cairngorms	865	44
68	Carn a'Choire Ghairbh	Western Highlands	865	34
69	Beinn Mhic Chasgaig	Central Highlands	864	41
70	Beinn Tharsuinn	Western Highlands	863	25
71	Cam Chreag	Southern Highlands	862	51
72	Carn Liath	Cairngorms	862	36
73	Meall na h-Aisre	Central Highlands	862	35
74	Beinn a'Bha'ach Ard	Western Highlands	862	26
75	Sgurr na Feartaig	Western Highlands	862	25
76	Beinn Lair	Northern Highlands	860	19
77	Morrone	Cairngorms	859	43
78	Caisteal Abhail	Islands – Arran	859	69
79	Beinn Luibhean	Southern Highlands	858	56
80	Fraoch Bheinn	Western Highlands	858	33
81	Beinn a'Chrulaiste	Central Highlands	857	41
82	Cruach Innse	Central Highlands	857	41
83	Carn Dearg Mor	Cairngorms	857	35
84	Beinn a'Chaisgein Mor	Northern Highlands	857	19
85	Stob an Aonaich Mhoir	Central Highlands	855	42

RANK	CORBETT	AREA	HEIGHT (M)	OS MAP
86	Beinn Bhuidhe	Western Highlands	855	33
87	Beinn an Eoin	Northern Highlands	855	19
88	Creach Bheinn	Western Highlands	853	49
89	Meall an t-Seallaidh	Southern Highlands	852	51
90	Beinn nan Imirean	Southern Highlands	849	51
91	Sgurr Ghiubhsachain	Western Highlands	849	40
92	Bac an Eich	Western Highlands	849	25
93	Cul Mor	Northern Highlands	849	15
94	Ben Donich	Southern Highlands	847	56
95	Canisp	Northern Highlands	847	15
96	Beinn Resipol	Western Highlands	845	40
97	Carn Ban	Northern Highlands	845	20
98	The Merrick	Southern Uplands	843	77
99	Beinn Mholach	Central Highlands	841	42
100	Ben Vrackie	Cairngorms	841	43
101	Sgurr an Airgid	Western Highlands	841	25
102	Broad Law	Southern Uplands	840	72
103	Beinn Trilleachan	Central Highlands	840	50
104	Beinn Udlaidh	Southern Highlands	840	50
105	Ben Rinnes	Cairngorms	840	28
106	Meallan nan Uan	Western Highlands	840	25
107	Sgurr Gaorsaic	Western Highlands	839	25
108	Meall na h-Eilde	Western Highlands	838	34
109	Carn Chuinneag	Northern Highlands	838	20
110	Sron a'Choire Chnapanich	Southern Highlands	837	51
111	Sgurr Cos na Breachd-laoigh	Western Highlands	835	33
112	Creag nan Gabhar	Cairngorms	834	43
113	Carn Dearg	Central Highlands	834	34
114	Beinn Dearg	Southern Highlands	830	51
115	Brown Cow Hill	Cairngorms	829	36
116	Carn Mor	Western Highlands	829	33
117	An Dun	Cairngorms	827	42
118	Beinn Tarsuinn	Islands – Arran	826	69
119	Geal-charn Mor	Central Highlands	824	35
120	White Coomb	Southern Uplands	821	79
121	Benvane	Southern Highlands	821	57
122	Geal Charn	Cairngorms	821	36
123	Beinn Dearg Bheag	Northern Highlands	820	19
124	Beinn Chaorach	Central Highlands	818	50
125	Carn na Drochaide	Cairngorms	818	36
126	Sgorr na Diollaid	Western Highlands	818	25
127	Stob Coire Creagach (Binnein an Fhidhleir)	Southern Highlands	817	56
128	Carn a'Chuilinn	Central Highlands	817	34
129	Carn Dearg	Central Highlands	817	34
130	Breabag	Northern Highlands	815	15
131	Corserine	Southern Uplands	814	77

RANK	CORBETT	AREA	HEIGHT (M)	OS MAP
132	An Stac	Western Highlands	814	40
133	An Sidhean	Western Highlands	814	25
134	Beinn Each	Southern Highlands	813	57
135	Sgor Mor	Cairngorms	813	43
136	Askival	Islands – Rum	812	39
137	Carn na Saobhaidhe	Central Highlands	811	35
138	Creach Bheinn	Central Highlands	810	50
139	Meall a'Bhuachaille	Cairngorms	810	36
140	Meall na Fearna	Southern Highlands	809	57
141	Creag Mac Ranaich	Southern Highlands	809	51
142	Sgurr Innse	Central Highlands	809	41
143	Hart Fell	Southern Uplands	808	78
144	Sail Gharbh, Quinag	Northern Highlands	808	15
145	Garbh-bheinn	Islands – Skye	808	32
146	Monamenach	Cairngorms	807	43
147	Creag Rainich	Northern Highlands	807	19
148	Beinn nam Fuaran	Southern Highlands	806	50
149	Meall nan Subh	Southern Highlands	806	51
150	Ben Gulabin	Cairngorms	806	43
151	Beinn Iaruinn	Central Highlands	805	34
152	Carn Mor	Cairngorms	804	37
153	Beinn na h-Eaglaise	Western Highlands	804	33
154	Geal Charn	Western Highlands	804	34
155	The Sow of Atholl	Central Highlands	803	42
156	Beinn Bhreac-liath	Southern Highlands	802	50
157	Meallan Liath Coire Mhic Dhughaill	Northern Highlands	801	15
158	Cranstackie	Northern Highlands	800	9
159	Cir Mhor	Islands – Arran	799	69
160	Clisham	Islands – Harris	799	13
161	Am Bathach	Western Highlands	798	33
162	Cairnsmore of Carsphairn	Southern Uplands	797	77
163	Beinn Dronaig	Western Highlands	797	25
164	Beinn Mhic-Mhonaidh	Central Highlands	796	50
165	Mam na Gualainn	Central Highlands	796	41
166	Sgurr Coire Choinnichean	Western Highlands	796	33
167	Sgurr an Utha	Western Highlands	796	40
168	Beinn Bhan	Western Highlands	796	34
169	Glas Bheinn	Central Highlands	792	41
170	Carn Ealasaid	Cairngorms	792	36
171	Sgurr a'Chaorachain	Northern Highlands	792	24
172	Beinn Leoid	Northern Highlands	792	15
173	Beinn Airigh Charr	Northern Highlands	791	19
174	Beinn Loinne	Western Highlands	790	34
175	Auchnafree Hill	Southern Highlands	789	52
176	Meall Dubh	Western Highlands	789	34
177	The Brack	Southern Highlands	787	56

RANK	CORBETT	AREA	HEIGHT (M)	OS MAP
178	Meall Tairneachan	Southern Highlands	787	52
179	Beinn a'Chaisteil	Northern Highlands	787	20
180	Arkle	Northern Highlands	787	9
181	Carn na Nathrach	Western Highlands	786	40
182	Beinn na Caillich	Western Highlands	785	33
183	Beinn an Oir	Islands – Jura	785	61
184	Farragon Hill	Southern Highlands	783	52
185	Beinn Mhic Cedidh	Western Highlands	783	40
186	Sgurr Dubh	Northern Highlands	782	25
187	Corryhabbie Hill	Cairngorms	781	37
188	Sgurr Mhic Bharraich	Western Highlands	781	33
189	Ainshval	Islands – Rum	781	39
190	Meall nam Maigheach	Southern Highlands	779	51
191	Beinn Bheula	Southern Highlands	779	56
192	Mount Battock	Cairngorms	778	44
193	Meall Horn	Northern Highlands	777	9
194	Glas Bheinn	Northern Highlands	776	15
195	Sail Gorm, Quinag	Northern Highlands	776	15
196	Shalloch on Minnoch	Southern Uplands	775	77
197	Meall na Leitreach	Central Highlands	775	42
199	Sgorr Craobh a'Chaorainn	Western Highlands	775	40
199	Glamaig	Islands – Skye	775	32
200	Meall a'Phubuill	Western Highlands	774	41
201	Beinn nan Caorach	Western Highlands	773	33
202	Meall Lighiche	Central Highlands	772	41
203	Beinn Spionnaidh	Northern Highlands	772	9
204	Beinn Stacath	Southern Highlands	771	57
205	Stob Coire a'Chearcaill	Western Highlands	771	41
206	Beinn a'Choin	Southern Highlands	770	56
207	Druim Tarsuinn	Western Highlands	770	40
208	Meallach Mhor	Cairngorms	769	35
209	Cul Beag	Northern Highlands	769	15
210	Carn Dearg	Central Highlands	768	34
211	Beinn Liath Mhor a'Ghiubhais Li	Northern Highlands	768	20
212	Sail Mhor	Northern Highlands	767	19
213	Fuar Bheinn	Western Highlands	766	49
214	Dun da Ghaoithe	Islands – Mull	766	49
215	Braigh nan Uamhachan	Western Highlands	765	40
216	Meall an Fhudair	Southern Highlands	764	56
217	Little Wyvis	Northern Highlands	764	20
218	Ben Loyal	Northern Highlands	764	10
219	Spidean Coinich, Quinag	Northern Highlands	764	15
220	Beinn na h-Uamha	Western Highlands	762	40

APPENDIX E
Index of Maps

(Chapter overview maps vary widely in scale according to the area shown and their scales are not given below.)

INDEX

LISTING OF CICERONE GUIDES

For full and up-to-date information on
our ever-expanding list of guides,
visit our website:
www.cicerone.co.uk.

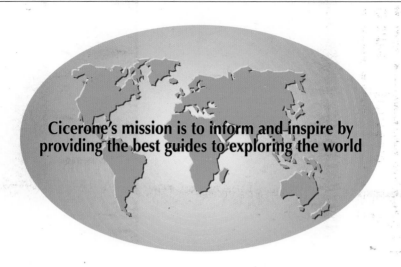

Cicerone's mission is to inform and inspire by providing the best guides to exploring the world

Since its foundation 40 years ago, Cicerone has specialised in publishing guidebooks and has built a reputation for quality and reliability. It now publishes nearly 300 guides to the major destinations for outdoor enthusiasts, including Europe, UK and the rest of the world.

Written by leading and committed specialists, Cicerone guides are recognised as the most authoritative. They are full of information, maps and illustrations so that the user can plan and complete a successful and safe trip or expedition – be it a long face climb, a walk over Lakeland fells, an alpine cycling tour, a Himalayan trek or a ramble in the countryside.

With a thorough introduction to assist planning, clear diagrams, maps and colour photographs to illustrate the terrain and route, and accurate and detailed text, Cicerone guides are designed for ease of use and access to the information.

If the facts on the ground change, or there is any aspect of a guide that you think we can improve, we are always delighted to hear from you.

Cicerone Press
2 Police Square Milnthorpe Cumbria LA7 7PY
Tel: 015395 62069 Fax: 015395 63417
info@cicerone.co.uk www.cicerone.co.uk

Z972807

Community Learning & Libraries
Cymuned Ddysgu a Llyfrgelloedd

This item should be returned or renewed by the
last date stamped below.

Newport
CITY COUNCIL
CYNGOR DINAS
Casnewydd

To renew visit:

www.newport.gov.uk/libraries

'Timothy Snyder is now our most distinguished historian of evil. *Black Earth* casts new light on old darkness. It demonstrates once and for all that the destruction of the Jews was premised on the destruction of states and the institutions of politics. I know of no other historical work on the Holocaust that is so deeply alarmed by its repercussions for the human future. This is a haunted and haunting book—erudite, provocative, and unforgettable'

Leon Wieseltier

'Timothy Snyder argues, eloquently and convincingly, that the world is still susceptible to the inhuman impulses that brought about the Final Solution. This book should be read as admonition by presidents, prime ministers, and in particular by anyone who believes that the past is somehow behind us'

Jeffrey Goldberg

'Always readable, highly sophisticated, and strikingly original'

Bernard Wasserstein, *Jewish Chronicle*

'*Black Earth* is mesmerizing'

Edward Rothstein, *Wall Street Journal*

'Snyder excels in repositioning the Holocaust in a global context'

New Statesman